MySQL Reference Manual

MySQL Reference Manual

Documentation from the Source

Michael "Monty" Widenius,
David Axmark, and MySQL AB

O'REILLY®
COMMUNITY PRESS

Beijing · Cambridge · Farnham · Köln · Paris · Sebastopol · Taipei · Tokyo

MySQL Reference Manual

by Michael "Monty" Widenius, David Axmark, and MySQL AB

Published by O'Reilly & Associates, Inc., 1005 Gravenstein Highway North, Sebastopol, CA 95472.

O'Reilly & Associates books may be purchased for educational, business, or sales promotional use. Online editions are also available for most titles (*safari.oreilly.com*). For more information, contact our corporate/institutional sales department: 800-998-9938 or *corporate@oreilly.com*.

Editor: Andy Oram

Production Editor: Jeffrey Holcomb

Cover Designer: Edie Freedman

Printing History:

> June 2002:   First Edition.

ISBN: 0-596-00265-3

[M]   [8/03]

Table of Contents

Preface

This is the official MySQL™ Reference Manual by the developers of the MySQL software. We are very happy that, together with our publisher O'Reilly & Associates, we can now give you easy access to all the essential information about MySQL, whether you are a user, a developer, or a decision maker.

We are extremely grateful to everyone who has contributed to the widespread deployment of MySQL, which now comprises an estimated three million installations on various Unix, Windows, and Macintosh servers worldwide. MySQL would not be the success that it is today without the help from our users. You have provided MySQL APIs for different programming languages and applications, given us valuable suggestions and constructive criticism, and supplied us with excellent bug reports.

With MySQL now reaching out into new realms, let me take this opportunity to give some background information about MySQL and to address a few common misunderstandings about MySQL.

The MySQL RDBMS is provided by a commercial company, MySQL AB. MySQL AB is a Swedish company formed by my colleague David Axmark and me. Together we have created, developed, and supported MySQL since 1995. It is now March 2002, and MySQL AB has grown to over 40 full-time employees, working from most continents of our planet.

Although numerous people have contributed to the many MySQL APIs, clients, and add-ons, MySQL AB retains the copyright to the server code. This puts us in the unique position of being able to offer our product with dual licensing. With the GPL license, we are at the forefront of promoting open source and free software ideology; with our commercial license, we are a leading commercial database for embedded use in applications.

MySQL AB offers a complete range of support options and services to its users. Open source software is often criticised for not being supported by commercial entities, but we have supported MySQL from the beginning. We are undeniably proud of having created a product that is so stable that customers rarely need to turn to us for help, yet at the same time, we have been providing technical support to customers running MySQL in mission-critical applications for several years.

Lastly, the MySQL server is intended for mission-critical, high-load applications. Yes, we support ACID transactions. Yes, through the InnoDB table handler, we support row-level locking. We feature clustering in the form of MySQL replication. During this year, we will concentrate our development on adding support for subqueries, stored procedures, triggers, and referential integrity. For more details, announcements, and new-version downloads, stay tuned to our web site at http://www.mysql.com/.

In closing, I would like to extend my thanks to all my fellow employees at MySQL AB and also to my wonderful family, who has supported my commitment through the many early years of MySQL. Ett stort tack, Carola, My och Max!

Helsingfors, Finland, March 2002
Michael "Monty" Widenius
CTO and Founder, MySQL AB

1

General Information

The MySQL™ software delivers a very fast, multi-threaded, multi-user, and robust SQL (Structured Query Language) database server. MySQL server is intended for mission-critical, heavy-load production systems as well as for embedding into mass-deployed software. MySQL is a trademark of MySQL AB.

The MySQL software has Dual Licensing, which means you can use the MySQL software free of charge under the GNU General Public License (http://www.gnu.org/licenses/). You can also purchase commercial MySQL licenses from MySQL AB if you do not wish to be bound by the terms of the GPL. See Section 1.4, MySQL Support and Licensing.

The MySQL web site (http://www.mysql.com/) provides the latest information about the MySQL software.

The following list describes some sections of particular interest in this manual:

- For information about the company behind the MySQL Database Server, see Section 1.3, What Is MySQL AB?.

- For a discussion about the capabilities of the MySQL Database Server, see Section 1.2.2, The Main Features of MySQL.

- For installation instructions, see Chapter 2.

- For tips on porting the MySQL Database Software to new architectures or operating systems, see Appendix D.

- For information about upgrading from a Version 3.23 release, see Section 2.5.1, Upgrading from Version 3.23 to Version 4.0.

- For information about upgrading from a Version 3.22 release, see Section 2.5.2, Upgrading from Version 3.22 to Version 3.23.

- For a tutorial introduction to the MySQL Database Server, see Chapter 3.

- For examples of SQL and benchmarking information, see the benchmarking directory (sql-bench in the distribution).

- For a history of new features and bug fixes, see http://www.mysql.com/doc/N/e/News.html.

- For a list of currently known bugs and misfeatures, see Section 1.7.5, Known Errors and Design Deficiencies in MySQL.

- For future plans, see Section 1.8, MySQL and the Future (the TODO).

- For a list of all the contributors to this project, see Appendix C.

Important: Reports of errors (often called bugs), as well as questions and comments, should be sent to the mailing list at *mysql@lists.mysql.com*. See Section 1.6.2.3, How to report bugs or problems. The mysqlbug script should be used to generate bug reports. For source distributions, the mysqlbug script can be found in the scripts directory. For binary distributions, mysqlbug can be found in the bin directory. If you have found a sensitive security bug in MySQL server, you should send an email to *security@mysql.com*.

1.1 About This Manual

This is the MySQL reference manual; it documents MySQL Version 4.0. Being a reference manual, it does not provide general instruction on SQL or relational database concepts.

As the MySQL Database Software is under constant development, the manual is also updated frequently. The most recent version of this manual is available at http://www.mysql.com/documentation/ in many different formats, including Texinfo, plain text, Info, HTML, PostScript, PDF, and Windows HLP versions.

The primary document is the Texinfo file. The HTML version is produced automatically using a modified version of texi2html. The plain text and Info versions are produced with makeinfo. The PostScript version is produced using texi2dvi and dvips. The PDF version is produced with pdftex.

If you have a hard time finding information in the manual, you can try our searchable PHP version at http://www.mysql.com/doc/.

If you have any suggestions concerning additions or corrections to this manual, please send them to the documentation team at *docs@mysql.com*.

This manual is written and maintained by David Axmark, Michael (Monty) Widenius, Jeremy Cole, Arjen Lentz, and Paul DuBois. For other contributors, see Appendix C.

The copyright (2002) to this manual is owned by the Swedish company MySQL AB. See Section 1.4.2, Copyrights and Licenses Used by MySQL.

1.1.1 Conventions Used in This Manual

This manual uses certain typographical conventions:

constant

> Constant-width font is used for command names and options; SQL statements; database, table, and column names; C and Perl code; and environment variables. Example: "To see how mysqladmin works, invoke it with the --help option."

"filename"

> Constant-width font with surrounding quotes is used for filenames and pathnames. Example: "The distribution is installed under the "/usr/local/" directory."

"c"

> Constant-width font with surrounding quotes is also used to indicate character sequences. Example: "To specify a wildcard, use the "%" character."

italic

> Italic font is used for emphasis, *like this*.

boldface

> Boldface font is used for access privilege names (for example, "do not grant the **process** privilege lightly") and occasionally to convey **especially strong emphasis**.

When commands are shown that are meant to be executed by a particular program, the program is indicated by a prompt shown before the command. For example, shell> indicates a command that you execute from your login shell, and mysql> indicates a command that you execute from the mysql client program:

```
shell> type a shell command here
mysql> type a mysql command here
```

Shell commands are shown using Bourne shell syntax. If you are using a csh-style shell, you may need to issue commands slightly differently. For example, the sequence to set an environment variable and run a command looks like this in Bourne shell syntax:

```
shell> VARNAME=value some_command
```

For csh, you would execute the sequence like this:

```
shell> setenv VARNAME value
shell> some_command
```

Often database, table, and column names must be substituted into commands. To indicate that such substitution is necessary, this manual uses db_name, tbl_name and col_name. For example, you might see a statement like this:

```
mysql> SELECT col_name FROM db_name.tbl_name;
```

This means that if you were to enter a similar statement, you would supply your own database, table, and column names, perhaps like this:

```
mysql> SELECT author_name FROM biblio_db.author_list;
```

SQL keywords are not case-sensitive and may be written in uppercase or lowercase. This manual uses uppercase.

In syntax descriptions, square brackets ([and]) are used to indicate optional words or clauses. For example, in the following statement, IF EXISTS is optional:

```
DROP TABLE [IF EXISTS] tbl_name
```

When a syntax element consists of a number of alternatives, the alternatives are separated by vertical bars (|). When one member from a set of choices **may** be chosen, the alternatives are listed within square brackets ([and]):

```
TRIM([[BOTH | LEADING | TRAILING] [remstr] FROM] str)
```

When one member from a set of choices **must** be chosen, the alternatives are listed within braces ({ and }):

```
{DESCRIBE | DESC} tbl_name {col_name | wild}
```

1.2 What Is MySQL?

MySQL, the most popular open source SQL database, is developed and provided by MySQL AB. MySQL AB is a commercial company that builds its business providing services around the MySQL database. See Section 1.3, What Is MySQL AB?.

The MySQL web site (http://www.mysql.com/) provides the latest information about MySQL software and MySQL AB.

MySQL is a database management system.

> A database is a structured collection of data. It may be anything from a simple shopping list to a picture gallery or the vast amounts of information in a corporate network. To add, access, and process data stored in a computer database, you need a database management system such as MySQL Server. Since computers are very good at handling large amounts of data, database management plays a central role in computing, as stand-alone utilities, or as parts of other applications.

MySQL is a relational database management system.

A relational database stores data in separate tables rather than putting all the data in one big storeroom. This adds speed and flexibility. The tables are linked by defined relations making it possible to combine data from several tables on request. The SQL part of "MySQL" stands for "Structured Query Language"—the most common standardised language used to access databases.

MySQL software is open source.

open source means that it is possible for anyone to use and modify. Anybody can download the MySQL software from the Internet and use it without paying anything. Anybody so inclined can study the source code and change it to fit their needs. The MySQL software uses the GPL (GNU General Public License), http://www.gnu.org/licenses/, to define what you may and may not do with the software in different situations. If you feel uncomfortable with the GPL or need to embed MySQL code into a commercial application you can buy a commercially licensed version from us. See Section 1.4.3, MySQL Licenses.

Why use the MySQL Database Server?

The MySQL Database Server is very fast, reliable, and easy to use. If that is what you are looking for, you should give it a try. MySQL server also has a practical set of features developed in close cooperation with our users. You can find a performance comparison of MySQL server to some other database managers on our benchmark page. See Section 5.1.4, The MySQL Benchmark Suite.

MySQL server was originally developed to handle large databases much faster than existing solutions and has been successfully used in highly demanding production environments for several years. Though under constant development, MySQL server today offers a rich and useful set of functions. Its connectivity, speed, and security make MySQL server highly suited for accessing databases on the Internet.

The technical features of MySQL server

For advanced technical information, see Chapter 6. The MySQL Database Software is a client/server system that consists of a multi-threaded SQL server that supports different backends, several different client programs and libraries, administrative tools, and a wide range of programming interfaces (APIs).

We also provide MySQL server as a multi-threaded library which you can link into your application to get a smaller, faster, easier-to-manage product.

There is a large amount of contributed MySQL software available.

It is very likely that you will find that your favorite application or language already supports the MySQL Database Server.

The official way to pronounce MySQL is "My Ess Que Ell" (not "my sequel"), but we don't mind if you pronounce it as "my sequel" or in some other localised way.

1.2.1 History of MySQL

We once started out with the intention of using mSQL to connect to our tables using our own fast low-level (ISAM) routines. However, after some testing we came to the conclusion that mSQL was not fast enough nor flexible enough for our needs. This resulted in a new SQL interface to our database but with almost the same API interface as mSQL. This API was chosen to ease porting of third-party code.

The derivation of the name MySQL is not perfectly clear. Our base directory and a large number of our libraries and tools have had the prefix "my" for well over 10 years. However, Monty's daughter (some years younger) is also named My. Which of the two gave its name to MySQL is still a mystery, even for us.

1.2.2 The Main Features of MySQL

The following list describes some of the important characteristics of the MySQL Database Software. See Section 1.5, MySQL 4.0 in a Nutshell.

Internals and Portability

- Written in C and C++. Tested with a broad range of different compilers.

- No memory leaks. The MySQL code has been tested with Purify, a commercial memory leakage detector.

- Works on many different platforms. See Section 2.2.2, Operating Systems Supported by MySQL.

- Uses GNU Automake (1.4), Autoconf (Version 2.52 or newer), and Libtool for portability.

- APIs for C, C++, Eiffel, Java, Perl, PHP, Python, and Tcl. See Chapter 8.

- Fully multi-threaded using kernel threads. This means it can easily use multiple CPUs if available.

- Very fast B-tree disk tables with index compression.

- A very fast thread-based memory allocation system.

- Very fast joins using an optimised one-sweep multi-join.

- In-memory hash tables which are used as temporary tables.

- SQL functions are implemented through a highly optimised class library and should be as fast as possible! Usually there isn't any memory allocation at all after query initialisation.

Column Types

- Many column types: signed/unsigned integers 1, 2, 3, 4, and 8 bytes long, FLOAT, DOUBLE, CHAR, VARCHAR, TEXT, BLOB, DATE, TIME, DATETIME, TIMES-TAMP, YEAR, SET, and ENUM types. See Section 6.2, Column Types.

- Fixed-length and variable-length records.

- All columns have default values. You can use INSERT to insert a subset of a table's columns; those columns that are not explicitly given values are set to their default values.

Commands and Functions

- Full operator and function support in the SELECT and WHERE parts of queries. For example:

  ```
  mysql> SELECT CONCAT(first_name, " ", last_name)
      -> FROM tbl_name
      -> WHERE income/dependents > 10000 AND age > 30;
  ```

- Full support for SQL GROUP BY and ORDER BY clauses. Support for group functions (COUNT(), COUNT(DISTINCT ...), AVG(), STD(), SUM(), MAX(), and MIN()).

- Support for LEFT OUTER JOIN and RIGHT OUTER JOIN with ANSI SQL and ODBC syntax.

- Aliases on tables and columns are allowed as in the SQL92 standard.

- DELETE, INSERT, REPLACE, and UPDATE return the number of rows that were changed (affected). It is possible to return the number of rows matched instead by setting a flag when connecting to the server.

- The MySQL-specific SHOW command can be used to retrieve information about databases, tables, and indexes. The EXPLAIN command can be used to determine how the optimiser resolves a query.

- Function names do not clash with table or column names. For example, ABS is a valid column name. The only restriction is that for a function call, no spaces are allowed between the function name and the (that follows it. See Section 6.1.6, Is MySQL Picky About Reserved Words?.

- You can mix tables from different databases in the same query (as of Version 3.22).

Security

- A privilege and password system that is very flexible and secure, and allows host-based verification. Passwords are secure because all password traffic is encrypted when you connect to a server.

Scalability and Limits

- Handles large databases. We are using MySQL server with some databases that contain 50 million records and we know of users that use MySQL server with 60,000 tables and about 5,000,000,000 rows.

- Up to 32 indexes per table are allowed. Each index may consist of 1 to 16 columns or parts of columns. The maximum index width is 500 bytes (this may be changed when compiling MySQL server). An index may use a prefix of a CHAR or VARCHAR field.

Connectivity

- Clients may connect to the MySQL server using TCP/IP Sockets, Unix Sockets (Unix), or Named Pipes (NT).

- ODBC (Open-DataBase-Connectivity) support for Win32 (with source). All ODBC 2.5 functions and many others. For example, you can use MS Access to connect to your MySQL server. See Section 8.3, MySQL ODBC Support.

Localisation

- The server can provide error messages to clients in many languages. See Section 4.6.2, Non-English Error Messages.

- Full support for several different character sets, including ISO-8859-1 (Latin1), german, big5, ujis, and more. For example, the Scandinavian characters 'å', 'ä' and 'ö' are allowed in table and column names.

- All data is saved in the chosen character set. All comparisons for normal string columns are case-insensitive.

- Sorting is done according to the chosen character set (the Swedish way by default). It is possible to change this when the MySQL server is started. To see an example of very advanced sorting, look at the Czech sorting code. MySQL server supports many different character sets that can be specified at compile and runtime.

Clients and Tools

- Includes myisamchk, a very fast utility for table checking, optimisation, and repair. All of the functionality of myisamchk is also available through the SQL interface as well. See Chapter 4.

- All MySQL programs can be invoked with the --help or -? options to obtain online assistance.

1.2.3 How Stable Is MySQL?

This section addresses the questions *"How stable is MySQL server?"* and *"Can I depend on MySQL server in this project?"* We will try to clarify these issues and answer some important questions that concern many potential users. The information in this section is based on data gathered from the mailing list, which is very active in identifying problems as well as reporting types of use.

Original code stems back from the early '80s, providing a stable code base, and the ISAM table format remains backward-compatible. At TcX, the predecessor of MySQL AB, MySQL code has worked in projects since mid-1996, without any problems. When the MySQL Database Software was released to a wider public, we noticed that there were some pieces of "untested code" that were quickly found by the new users who made different types of queries from us. Each new release has had fewer portability problems (even though each new release has had many new features).

Each release of the MySQL server has been usable. There have only been problems when users try code from the "gray zones." Naturally, new users don't know what the gray zones are; this section attempts to indicate those that are currently known. The descriptions mostly deal with Version 3.23 of MySQL server. All known and reported bugs are fixed in the latest version, with the exception of those listed in the bugs section, which are things that are design-related. See Section 1.7.5, Known Errors and Design Deficiencies in MySQL.

The MySQL server design is multi-layered with independent modules. Some of the newer modules are listed here with an indication of how well-tested each of them is:

Replication—Gamma
> Large server clusters using replication are in production use, with good results. Work on enhanced replication features is continuing in MySQL 4.0.

InnoDB *tables—Stable (in 3.23 from 3.23.49)*
> The InnoDB transactional table handler has now been declared stable in the MySQL 3.23 tree, starting from version 3.23.49. InnoDB is being used in large, heavy-load production systems.

BDB *tables—Gamma*
> The Berkeley DB code is very stable, but we are still improving the BDB transactional table handler interface in MySQL server, so it will take some time before this is as well tested as the other table types.

FULLTEXT—*Beta*
> Full-text search works but is not yet widely used. Important enhancements are being implemented for MySQL 4.0.

MyODBC 2.50 *(uses ODBC SDK 2.5)—Gamma*

Increasingly in wide use. Some issues brought up appear to be application-related and independent of the ODBC driver or underlying database server.

Automatic recovery of MyISAM *tables—Gamma*

This status only regards the new code in the MyISAM table handler that checks if the table was closed properly on open and executes an automatic check/repair of the table if it wasn't.

Bulk-insert—Alpha

New feature in MyISAM tables in MySQL 4.0 for faster insert of many rows.

Locking—Gamma

This is very system-dependent. On some systems there are big problems using standard OS locking (fcntl()). In these cases, you should run mysqld with the --skip-locking flag. Problems are known to occur on some Linux systems, and on SunOS when using NFS-mounted filesystems.

MySQL AB provides high-quality support for paying customers, but the MySQL mailing list usually provides answers to common questions. Bugs are usually fixed right away with a patch; for serious bugs, there is almost always a new release.

1.2.4 How Big Can MySQL Tables Be?

MySQL Version 3.22 has a 4G limit on table size. With the new MyISAM table type in MySQL Version 3.23, the maximum table size is pushed up to 8 million terabytes (2 ^ 63 bytes).

Note, however, that operating systems have their own file-size limits. Here are some examples:

Operating System	File-Size Limit
Linux-Intel 32 bit	2G, 4G or more, depends on Linux version
Linux-Alpha	8T (?)
Solaris 2.5.1	2G (possible 4G with patch)
Solaris 2.6	4G
Solaris 2.7 Intel	4G
Solaris 2.7 UltraSPARC	512G

On Linux 2.2 you can get bigger tables than 2G by using the LFS patch for the ext2 filesystem. On Linux 2.4 patches also exist for ReiserFS to get support for big files.

This means that the table size for MySQL databases is normally limited by the operating system.

By default, MySQL tables have a maximum size of about 4G. You can check the maximum table size for a table with the SHOW TABLE STATUS command or with the myisamchk -dv table_name. See Section 4.5.6, SHOW Syntax.

If you need bigger tables than 4G (and your operating system supports this), you should set the AVG_ROW_LENGTH and MAX_ROWS parameter when you create your table. See Section 6.5.3, CREATE TABLE Syntax. You can also set these later with ALTER TABLE. See Section 6.5.4, ALTER TABLE Syntax.

If your big table is going to be read-only, you could use myisampack to merge and compress many tables to one. myisampack usually compresses a table by at least 50%, so you can have, in effect, much bigger tables. See Section 4.7.4, myisampack, the MySQL Compressed Read-Only Table Generator.

You can go around the operating system file limit for MyISAM data files by using the RAID option. See Section 6.5.3, CREATE TABLE Syntax.

Another solution can be the included MERGE library, which allows you to handle a collection of identical tables as one. See Section 7.2, MERGE Tables.

1.2.5 Year 2000 Compliance

The MySQL server itself has no problems with Year 2000 (Y2K) compliance:

*   MySQL server uses Unix time functions and has no problems with dates until 2069; all 2-digit years are regarded to be in the range 1970 to 2069, which means that if you store 01 in a year column, MySQL server treats it as 2001.

*   All MySQL date functions are stored in one file, sql/time.cc, and are coded very carefully to be year 2000-safe.

*   In MySQL Version 3.22 and later, the new YEAR column type can store years 0 and 1901 to 2155 in 1 byte and display them using 2 or 4 digits.

You may run into problems with applications that use MySQL server in a way that is not Y2K-safe. For example, many old applications store or manipulate years using 2-digit values (which are ambiguous) rather than 4-digit values. This problem may be compounded by applications that use values such as 00 or 99 as "missing" value indicators.

Unfortunately, these problems may be difficult to fix because different applications may be written by different programmers, each of whom may use a different set of conventions and date-handling functions.

Here is a simple demonstration illustrating that MySQL server doesn't have any problems with dates until the year 2030:

```
mysql> DROP TABLE IF EXISTS y2k;
Query OK, 0 rows affected (0.01 sec)

mysql> CREATE TABLE y2k (date DATE,
    ->                   date_time DATETIME,
    ->                   time_stamp TIMESTAMP);
Query OK, 0 rows affected (0.00 sec)

mysql> INSERT INTO y2k VALUES
    -> ("1998-12-31","1998-12-31 23:59:59",19981231235959),
    -> ("1999-01-01","1999-01-01 00:00:00",19990101000000),
    -> ("1999-09-09","1999-09-09 23:59:59",19990909235959),
    -> ("2000-01-01","2000-01-01 00:00:00",20000101000000),
    -> ("2000-02-28","2000-02-28 00:00:00",20000228000000),
    -> ("2000-02-29","2000-02-29 00:00:00",20000229000000),
    -> ("2000-03-01","2000-03-01 00:00:00",20000301000000),
    -> ("2000-12-31","2000-12-31 23:59:59",20001231235959),
    -> ("2001-01-01","2001-01-01 00:00:00",20010101000000),
    -> ("2004-12-31","2004-12-31 23:59:59",20041231235959),
    -> ("2005-01-01","2005-01-01 00:00:00",20050101000000),
    -> ("2030-01-01","2030-01-01 00:00:00",20300101000000),
    -> ("2050-01-01","2050-01-01 00:00:00",20500101000000);
Query OK, 13 rows affected (0.01 sec)
Records: 13  Duplicates: 0  Warnings: 0

mysql> SELECT * FROM y2k;
+------------+---------------------+----------------+
| date       | date_time           | time_stamp     |
+------------+---------------------+----------------+
| 1998-12-31 | 1998-12-31 23:59:59 | 19981231235959 |
| 1999-01-01 | 1999-01-01 00:00:00 | 19990101000000 |
| 1999-09-09 | 1999-09-09 23:59:59 | 19990909235959 |
| 2000-01-01 | 2000-01-01 00:00:00 | 20000101000000 |
| 2000-02-28 | 2000-02-28 00:00:00 | 20000228000000 |
| 2000-02-29 | 2000-02-29 00:00:00 | 20000229000000 |
| 2000-03-01 | 2000-03-01 00:00:00 | 20000301000000 |
| 2000-12-31 | 2000-12-31 23:59:59 | 20001231235959 |
| 2001-01-01 | 2001-01-01 00:00:00 | 20010101000000 |
| 2004-12-31 | 2004-12-31 23:59:59 | 20041231235959 |
| 2005-01-01 | 2005-01-01 00:00:00 | 20050101000000 |
| 2030-01-01 | 2030-01-01 00:00:00 | 20300101000000 |
| 2050-01-01 | 2050-01-01 00:00:00 | 00000000000000 |
+------------+---------------------+----------------+
13 rows in set (0.00 sec)
```

This shows that the DATE and DATETIME types will not give any problems with future dates (they handle dates until the year 9999).

The TIMESTAMP type, which is used to store the current time, has a range up to only 2030-01-01. TIMESTAMP has a range of 1970 to 2030 on 32-bit machines (signed value). On 64-bit machines it handles times up to 2106 (unsigned value).

Even though MySQL server is Y2K-compliant, it is your responsibility to provide unambiguous input. See Section 6.2.2.1, Y2K issues and datetypes for MySQL server's rules for dealing with ambiguous date input data (data containing 2-digit year values).

1.3 What Is MySQL AB?

MySQL AB is the company of the MySQL founders and main developers. MySQL AB was originally established in Sweden by David Axmark, Allan Larsson, and Michael Monty Widenius.

All the developers of the MySQL server are employed by the company. We are a virtual organisation with people in a dozen countries around the world. We communicate extensively over the Net every day with each other and with our users, supporters and partners.

We are dedicated to developing the MySQL software and spreading our database to new users. MySQL AB owns the copyright to the MySQL source code, the MySQL logo and trademark, and this manual. See Section 1.2, What Is MySQL?.

The MySQL core values show our dedication to MySQL and open source.

We want the MySQL Database Software to be:

- The best and the most widely used database in the world.

- Available and affordable for all.

- Easy to use.

- Continuously improving while remaining fast and safe.

- Fun to use and improve.

- Free from bugs.

MySQL AB and the people at MySQL AB:

- Promote open source philosophy and support the open source community.

- Aim to be good citizens.

- Prefer partners that share our values and mind-set.

- Answer email and provide support.

- Are a virtual company, networking with others.

- Work against software patents.

The MySQL web site (http://www.mysql.com/) provides the latest information about MySQL and MySQL AB.

1.3.1 The Business Model and Services of MySQL AB

One of the most common questions we encounter is: *"How can you make a living from something you give away for free?"* This is how.

MySQL AB makes money on support, services, commercial licenses, and royalties, and we use these revenues to fund product development and to expand the MySQL business.

The company has been profitable since its inception. In October 2001, we accepted venture financing from leading Scandinavian investors and a handful of business angels. This investment is used to solidify our business model and build a basis for sustainable growth.

1.3.1.1 Support

MySQL AB is run and owned by the founders and main developers of the MySQL database. The developers are committed to giving support to customers and other users in order to stay in touch with their needs and problems. All our support is given by qualified developers. Really tricky questions are answered by Michael Monty Widenius, principal author of the MySQL server. See Section 1.4.1, Support Offered by MySQL AB.

To order support at various levels, visit the order section at https://order.mysql.com/ or contact our sales staff at *sales@mysql.com*.

1.3.1.2 Training and certification

MySQL AB delivers MySQL and related training worldwide. We offer both open courses and in-house courses tailored to the specific needs of your company. MySQL Training is also available through our partners, the Authorised MySQL Training Centers.

Our training material uses the same example databases as our documentation and our sample applications, and it is always updated to reflect the latest MySQL version. Our trainers are backed by the development team to guarantee the quality of the training and the continuous development of the course material. This also ensures that no questions raised during the courses remain unanswered.

Attending our training courses will enable you to achieve your goals related to your MySQL applications. You will also:

- Save time.
- Improve the performance of your application(s).
- Reduce or eliminate the need for additional hardware, decreasing cost.
- Enhance security.

- Increase customers' and co-workers' satisfaction.

- Prepare yourself for MySQL Certification.

If you are interested in our training as a potential participant or as a training partner, please visit the training section at http://www.mysql.com/training/ or contact us at: *training@mysql.com*.

We plan to release the MySQL Certification Program in 2002. For details see http://www.mysql.com/training/certification.html. If you would like to be kept informed about the MySQL Certification Program, please email *certification@mysql.com*.

1.3.1.3 Consulting

MySQL AB and its Authorised Partners offer consulting services to users of MySQL server and to those who embed MySQL server in their own software, all over the world.

Our consultants can help you design and tune your databases, construct efficient queries, tune your platform for optimal performance, resolve migration issues, set up replication, build robust transactional applications, and more. We also help customers embed MySQL server in their products and applications for large-scale deployment.

Our consultants work in close collaboration with our development team, which ensures the technical quality of our professional services. Consulting assignments range from 2-day power-start sessions to projects that span weeks and months. Our expertise not only covers MySQL server, but also extends into programming and scripting languages such as PHP, Perl, and more.

If you are interested in our consulting services or want to become a consulting partner, please visit the consulting section of our web site at http://www.mysql.com/consulting/ or contact our consulting staff at *consulting@mysql.com*.

1.3.1.4 Commercial licenses

The MySQL database is released under the GNU General Public License (GPL). This means that the MySQL software can be used free of charge under the GPL. If you do not want to be bound by the GPL terms (like the requirement that your own application becomes GPL as well), you may purchase a commercial license for the same product from MySQL AB at https://order.mysql.com/. Since MySQL AB owns the copyright to the MySQL source code, we are able to employ Dual Licensing which means that the same product is available under GPL and under a commercial license. This does not in any way affect the open source commitment of MySQL AB. For details about when a commercial license is required, please see Section 1.4.3, MySQL Licenses.

We also sell commercial licenses of third-party open source GPL software that adds value to MySQL server. A good example is the InnoDB transactional table handler that offers ACID support, row-level locking, crash recovery, multi-versioning, foreign key support, and more. See Section 7.5, InnoDB Tables.

1.3.1.5 Partnering

MySQL AB has a worldwide partner programme that covers training courses, consulting & support, publications plus reselling and distributing MySQL and related products. MySQL AB Partners get visibility on the http://www.mysql.com/ web site and the right to use special versions of the MySQL trademarks to identify their products and promote their business.

If you are interested in becoming a MySQL AB Partner, please email *partner@mysql.com*.

The word MySQL and the MySQL dolphin logo are trademarks of MySQL AB. See Section 1.4.4, MySQL AB Logos and Trademarks. These trademarks represent a significant value that the MySQL founders have built over the years.

1.3.1.6 Advertising

The MySQL web site (http://www.mysql.com/) is popular among developers and users. In October 2001, we served 10 million page views. Our visitors represent a group that makes purchase decisions and recommendations for both software and hardware. Twelve percent of our visitors authorise purchase decisions, and only nine percent are not involved in purchase decisions at all. More than 65% have made one or more online business purchase within the last half-year, and 70% plan to make one in the next months.

If you are interested in placing banner ads on our web site, http://www.mysql.com/, please send an email message to *advertising@mysql.com*.

1.3.2 Contact Information

The MySQL web site (http://www.mysql.com/) provides the latest information about MySQL and MySQL AB.

For press service and inquiries not covered in our News releases (http://www.mysql.com/news/), please send email to *press@mysql.com*.

If you have a valid support contract with MySQL AB, you will get timely, precise answers to your technical questions about the MySQL software. For more information, see Section 1.4.1, Support Offered by MySQL AB. You can order your support contract at https://order.mysql.com/, or send an email message to *sales@mysql.com*.

For information about MySQL training, please visit the training section at http://www.mysql.com/training/. If you have restricted access to the Internet, please contact the MySQL AB training staff at *training@mysql.com*. See Section 1.3.1.2, Training and certification.

For information on the MySQL Certification Program, please see http://www.mysql.com/training/certification.html. If you would like to be kept informed about the MySQL Certification Program, please email *certification@mysql.com*. See Section 1.3.1.2, Training and certification.

If you're interested in consulting, please visit the consulting section at http://www.mysql.com/consulting/. If you have restricted access to the Internet, please contact the MySQL AB consulting staff at *consulting@mysql.com*. See Section 1.3.1.3, Consulting.

Commercial licenses may be purchased online at https://order.mysql.com/. There you will also find information on how to fax your purchase order to MySQL AB. If you have questions regarding licensing or you want a quote for a high-volume license deal, please fill in the contact form on our web site (http://www.mysql.com/) or send an email message to *licensing@mysql.com* (for licensing questions) or to *sales@mysql.com* (for sales inquiries). See Section 1.4.3, MySQL Licenses.

If you represent a business that is interested in partnering with MySQL AB, please send email to *partner@mysql.com*. See Section 1.3.1.5, Partnering.

If you are interested in placing a banner advertisement on the MySQL web site (http://www.mysql.com/), please send email to *advertising@mysql.com*. See Section 1.3.1.6, Advertising.

For more information on the MySQL trademark policy, refer to http://www.mysql.com/company/trademark.html or send email to *trademark@mysql.com*. See Section 1.4.4, MySQL AB Logos and Trademarks.

If you are interested in any of the MySQL AB jobs listed in our jobs section (http://www.mysql.com/development/jobs/), please send an email message to *jobs@mysql.com*. Please do not send your CV as an attachment, but rather as plain text at the end of your email message.

For general discussion among our many users, please direct your attention to the appropriate mailing list. See Section 1.6.2, MySQL Mailing Lists.

Reports of errors (often called bugs), as well as questions and comments, should be sent to the mailing list at *mysql@lists.mysql.com*. If you have found a sensitive security bug in the MySQL server, please send an email to *security@mysql.com*. See Section 1.6.2.3, How to report bugs or problems.

If you have benchmark results that we can publish, please contact us at *benchmarks@mysql.com*.

If you have any suggestions concerning additions or corrections to this manual, please send them to the manual team at *docs@mysql.com*.

For questions or comments about the workings or content of the MySQL web site (http://www.mysql.com/), please send email to *webmaster@mysql.com*.

Questions about the MySQL Portals (http://www.mysql.com/portal/) may be sent to *portals@mysql.com*.

MySQL AB has a privacy policy, which can be read at http://www.mysql.com/company/ privacy.html. For any queries regarding this policy, please email *privacy@mysql.com*.

For all other inquires, please send email to *info@mysql.com*.

1.4 MySQL Support and Licensing

This section describes MySQL support and licensing arrangements.

1.4.1 Support Offered by MySQL AB

Technical support from MySQL AB means individualised answers to your unique problems direct from the software engineers who code the MySQL database engine.

We try to take a broad and inclusive view of technical support. Almost any problem involving MySQL software is important to us if it's important to you. Typically customers seek help on how to get different commands and utilities to work, remove performance bottlenecks, restore crashed systems, understand operating system or networking impacts on MySQL, set up best practices for backup and recovery, utilise APIs, etc. Our support covers only the MySQL server and our own utilities, not third-party products that access the MySQL server, though we try to help with these where we can.

Detailed information about our various support options is given at https://order.mysql.com/, where support contracts can also be ordered online. If you have restricted access to the Internet, contact our sales staff at *sales@mysql.com*.

Technical support is like life insurance. You can live happily without it for years, but when your hour arrives it becomes critically important, yet it's too late to buy it! If you use MySQL Server for important applications and encounter sudden troubles, it might take too long to figure out all the answers yourself. You may need immediate access to the most experienced MySQL troubleshooters available, those employed by MySQL AB.

1.4.2 Copyrights and Licenses Used by MySQL

MySQL AB owns the copyright to the MySQL source code, the MySQL logos and trademarks and this manual. See Section 1.3, What Is MySQL AB?. Several different licenses are relevant to the MySQL distribution:

1. All the MySQL-specific source in the server, the mysqlclient library and the client, as well as the GNU readline library is covered by the GNU General Public License. See http://www.mysql.com/doc/G/P/GPL-license.html. The text of this license can also be found as the file COPYING in the distributions.

2. The GNU getopt library is covered by the GNU Lesser General Public License. See http://www.mysql.com/doc/L/G/LGPL-license.html.

3. Some parts of the source (the regexp library) are covered by a Berkeley-style copyright.

4. Older versions of MySQL (3.22 and earlier) are subject to a more strict license (http://www.mysql.com/support/arrangements/mypl.html). See the documentation of the specific version for information.

5. The manual is currently **not** distributed under a GPL-style license. Use of the manual is subject to the following terms:

   - Conversion to other formats is allowed, but the actual content may not be altered or edited in any way.

   - You may create a printed copy for your own personal use.

   - For all other uses, such as selling printed copies or using (parts of) the manual in another publication, prior written agreement from MySQL AB is required.

   Please email *docs@mysql.com* for more information or if you are interested in doing a translation.

For information about how the MySQL licenses work in practice, please refer to Section 1.4.3, MySQL Licenses. Also see Section 1.4.4, MySQL AB Logos and Trademarks.

1.4.3 MySQL Licenses

The MySQL software is released under the GNU General Public License (GPL), which probably is the best known open source license. The formal terms of the GPL license can be found at http://www.gnu.org/licenses/. See also http://www.gnu.org/licenses/gpl-faq.html and http://www.gnu.org/philosophy/enforcing-gpl.html.

Since the MySQL software is released under the GPL, it may often be used for free, but for certain uses you may want or need to buy commercial licenses from MySQL AB at https://order.mysql.com/.

Older versions of MySQL (3.22 and earlier) are subject to a more strict license (http://www.mysql.com/support/arrangements/mypl.html). See the documentation of the specific version for information.

Please note that the use of the MySQL software under commercial license, GPL, or the old MySQL license does not automatically give you the right to use MySQL AB trademarks. See Section 1.4.4, MySQL AB Logos and Trademarks.

1.4.3.1 Using the MySQL software under a commercial license

The GPL license is contagious in the sense that when a program is linked to a GPL program the resulting product must also be released under GPL lest you break the license terms and forfeit your right to use the GPL program altogether.

You need a commercial license:

- When you link a program with code from the MySQL software or from GPL released clients and don't want the resulting product to be GPL, maybe because you want to build a commercial product or keep the added non-GPL code closed source for other reasons. When purchasing commercial licenses, you are not using the MySQL software under GPL even though it's the same code.

- When you distribute a non-GPL application that **only** works with the MySQL software and ship it with the MySQL software. This type of solution is actually considered to be linking even if it's done over a network.

- When you distribute copies of the MySQL software without providing the source code as required under the GPL license.

- When you want to support the further development of the MySQL database even if you don't formally need a commercial license. Purchasing support directly from MySQL AB is another good way of contributing to the development of the MySQL software, with immediate advantages for you. See Section 1.4.1, Support Offered by MySQL AB.

If you require a license, you will need one for each installation of the MySQL software. This covers any number of CPUs on a machine, and there is no artificial limit on the number of clients that connect to the server in any way.

To purchase commercial licenses and support, please visit the order section of our web site at https://order.mysql.com/. If you have special licensing needs or you have restricted access to the Internet, please contact our sales staff at *sales@mysql.com*.

1.4.3.2 Using the MySQL software for free under GPL

You can use the MySQL software for free under the GPL:

- When you link a program with code from the MySQL software and release the resulting product under GPL.

- When you distribute the MySQL source code bundled with other programs that are not linked to or dependent on MySQL server for their functionality even if you sell the distribution commercially.

- When using the MySQL software internally in your company.

- When you are an Internet Service Provider (ISPs) offering web hosting with MySQL servers for your customers. On the other hand, we do encourage people to use ISPs that have MySQL support, as this will give them the confidence that if they have some problem with the MySQL installation, their ISP will in fact have the resources to solve the problem for them.

  All ISPs that want to keep themselves up-to-date should subscribe to our announce mailing list so that they can be aware of critical issues that may be relevant for their MySQL installations.

  Note that even if an ISP does not have a commercial license for MySQL server, they should at least give their customers read access to the source of the MySQL installation so that the customers can verify that it is patched correctly.

- When you use the MySQL Database Software in conjunction with a web server, you do not need a commercial license. This is true even if you run a commercial web server that uses MySQL server, because you are not selling an embedded MySQL version yourself. However, in this case we would like you to purchase MySQL support because the MySQL software is helping your enterprise.

If your use of MySQL database software does not require a commercial license, we encourage you to purchase support from MySQL AB anyway. This way you contribute toward MySQL development and also gain immediate advantages for yourself. See Section 1.4.1, Support Offered by MySQL AB.

If you use the MySQL database software in a commercial context such that you profit by its use, we ask that you further the development of the MySQL software by purchasing some level of support. We feel that if the MySQL database helps your business, it is reasonable to ask that you help MySQL AB. (Otherwise, if you ask us support questions, you are not only using for free something into which we've put a lot a work, you're asking us to provide free support, too.)

1.4.4 MySQL AB Logos and Trademarks

Many users of the MySQL database want to display the MySQL AB dolphin logo on their web sites, books, or boxed products. We welcome and encourage this, although it should be noted that the word MySQL and the MySQL dolphin logo are trademarks of MySQL AB and may only be used as stated in our trademark policy at http://www.mysql.com/company/trademark.html.

1.4.4.1 The original MySQL logo

The MySQL dolphin logo was designed by the Finnish advertising agency Priority in 2001. The dolphin was chosen as a suitable symbol for the MySQL database since it is a smart, fast, and lean animal, effortlessly navigating oceans of data. We also happen to like dolphins.

The original MySQL logo may only be used by representatives of MySQL AB and by those having a written agreement allowing them to do so.

1.4.4.2 MySQL logos that may be used without written permission

We have designed a set of special *Conditional Use* logos that may be downloaded from our web site at http://www.mysql.com/downloads/logos.html and used on third-party web sites without written permission from MySQL AB. The use of these logos is not entirely unrestricted but, as the name implies, subject to our trademark policy that is also available on our web site. You should read through the trademark policy if you plan to use them. The requirements are basically:

- Use the logo you need as displayed on the http://www.mysql.com/ site. You may scale it to fit your needs, but not change colours or design, or alter the graphics in any way.

- Make it evident that you, and not MySQL AB, are the creator and owner of the site that displays the MySQL trademark.

- Don't use the trademark in a way that is detrimental to MySQL AB or to the value of MySQL AB trademarks. We reserve the right to revoke the right to use the MySQL AB trademark.

- If you use the trademark on a web site, make it clickable, leading directly to http://www.mysql.com/.

- If you are using the MySQL database under GPL in an application, your application must be open source and be able to connect to a MySQL server.

Contact us at *trademark@mysql.com* to inquire about special arrangements to fit your needs.

1.4.4.3 When do you need a written permission
to use MySQL logos?

In the following cases you need a written permission from MySQL AB before using MySQL logos:

- When displaying any MySQL AB logo anywhere except on your web site.

- When displaying any MySQL AB logo except the *Conditional Use* logos mentioned previously on web sites or elsewhere.

Out of legal and commercial reasons we have to monitor the use of MySQL trademarks on products, books, etc. We will usually require a fee for displaying MySQL AB logos on commercial products, since we think it is reasonable that some of the revenue is returned to fund further development of the MySQL database.

1.4.4.4 MySQL AB partnership logos

MySQL partnership logos may only be used by companies and persons having a written partnership agreement with MySQL AB. Partnerships include certification as a MySQL trainer or consultant. Please see Section 1.3.1.5, Partnering.

1.4.4.5 Using the word MySQL in printed text or presentations

MySQL AB welcomes references to the MySQL database, but note that the word MySQL is a trademark of MySQL AB. Because of this, you should append the trademark symbol (^{TM}) to the first or most prominent use of the word MySQL in a text and where appropriate, state that MySQL is a trademark of MySQL AB. Please refer to our trademark policy at http://www.mysql.com/company/trademark.html for details.

1.4.4.6 Using the word MySQL in company and product names

Use of the word MySQL in product or company names or in Internet domain names is not allowed without written permission from MySQL AB.

1.5 MySQL 4.0 in a Nutshell

Dateline: 16 October 2001, Uppsala, Sweden

Long promised by MySQL AB and long awaited by our users, MySQL server 4.0 is now available in alpha version for download from http://www.mysql.com/ and our mirrors.

Main new features of MySQL server 4.0 are geared toward our existing business and community users, enhancing the MySQL database software as the solution for mission-critical, heavy-load database systems. Other new features target the users of embedded databases.

1.5.1 Stepwise Rollout

The rollout of MySQL server 4.0 will come in several steps, with the first version labelled 4.0.0 already containing most of the new features. Additional features will be incorporated into MySQL 4.0.1, 4.0.2, and onward; very probably within a couple of months, MySQL 4.0 will be labelled beta. Further new features will then be added in MySQL 4.1, which was targeted for alpha release in third quarter 2002.

1.5.2 Ready for Immediate Development Use

Users are not recommended to switch their production systems to MySQL server 4.0 until it is released in beta version. However, even the initial release has passed our extensive test suite without any errors on any of the platforms we test on. Due to the large number of new features, we thus recommend MySQL server 4.0 even in alpha form for development use, with the release schedule of MySQL server 4.0 being such that it will reach stable state before the deployment of user applications now under development.

1.5.3 Embedded MySQL

libmysqld makes MySQL server suitable for a vastly expanded realm of applications. Using the embedded MySQL server library, one can embed MySQL server into various applications and electronics devices, where the end user has no knowledge of there actually being an underlying database. Embedded MySQL server is ideal for use behind the scenes in Internet appliances, public kiosks, turnkey hardware/software combination units, high performance Internet servers, self-contained databases distributed on CD-ROM, etc.

Many users of libmysqld will benefit from the MySQL *Dual Licensing*. For those not wishing to be bound by the GPL, the software is also made available under a commercial license. The embedded MySQL library uses the same interface as the normal client library, so it is convenient and easy to use. See Section 8.4.9, libmysqld, the Embedded MySQL Server Library.

1.5.4 Other Features Available
from MySQL 4.0.0

- Version 4.0 further increases *the speed of MySQL server* in a number of areas, such as bulk INSERTs, searching on packed indexes, creation of FULLTEXT indexes, as well as COUNT(DISTINCT).

- The table handler InnoDB is now offered as a feature of the standard MySQL server, including full support for transactions and row-level locking.

- MySQL server 4.0 will support secure traffic between the client and the server, greatly increasing security against malicious intrusion and unauthorised access. Web applications being a cornerstone of MySQL use, web developers have been able to use Secure Socket Layer (SSL) to secure the traffic between the the end user browser and the web application, be it written in PHP, Perl, ASP or using any other web development tool. However, the traffic between the development tool and the mysqld server process has been protected only by virtue of them being processes residing on computers within the same firewall. In MySQL server 4.0, the mysqld server daemon process can itself use SSL, thus enabling secure traffic to MySQL databases from, say, a Windows application residing outside the firewall.

- Our German, Austrian, and Swiss users will note that we have a new character set, latin_de, which corrects the *German sorting order*, placing German umlauts in the same order as German telephone books.

- Features to simplify migration from other database systems to MySQL Server include TRUNCATE TABLE (like in Oracle) and IDENTITY as a synonym for automatically incremented keys (like in Sybase). Many users will also be happy to learn that

MySQL server now supports the UNION statement, a long-awaited standard SQL feature.

- In the process of building features for new users, we have not forgotten requests by the community of loyal users. We have multi-table DELETE statements. By adding support for symbolic linking to MyISAM on the table level (and not just the database level as before), as well as by enabling symlink handling by default on Windows, we hope to show that we take enhancement requests seriously. Functions like SQL_CALC_FOUND_ROWS and FOUND_ROWS() make it possible to know how many rows a query would have returned without a LIMIT clause.

1.5.5 Future MySQL 4.0 Features

For the upcoming MySQL server 4.0 releases (4.0.1, 4.0.2, and onward), expect the following features now still under development:

- Mission-critical, heavy-load users of MySQL server will appreciate the additions to our replication system and our online hot backup. Later versions of 4.0 will include fail-safe replication; already existing in 4.0.0, the LOAD DATA FROM MASTER command will soon automate slave setup. The online backup will make it easy to add a new replication slave without taking down the master, and have a very low performance penalty on update-heavy systems.

- A convenience feature for Database Administrators is that mysqld parameters (startup options) can soon be set without taking down the servers.

- The new FULLTEXT search properties of MySQL server 4.0 enable the use of FULLTEXT indexing of large text masses with both binary and natural-language searching logic. Users can customise minimal word length and define their own stop word lists in any human language, enabling a new set of applications to be built on MySQL server.

- Many read-heavy applications will benefit from further increased speed through the rewritten key cache.

- Many developers will also be happy to see the MySQL command help in the client.

1.5.6 MySQL 4.1, The Following
Development Release

Internally, through a new .frm file format for table definitions, MySQL server 4.0 lays the foundation for the new features of MySQL server 4.1 and onward, such as nested subqueries, stored procedures, and foreign key integrity rules, which form the top of the wish list for many of our customers. Along with those, we will also include simpler additions, such as multi-table UPDATE statements.

After those additions, critics of the MySQL Database Server have to be more imaginative than ever in pointing out deficiencies in the MySQL Database Management System. For long already known for its stability, speed, and ease of use, MySQL server will then match the requirement checklist of very demanding buyers.

1.6 MySQL Information Sources

1.6.1 MySQL Portals

The MySQL Portals (http://www.mysql.com/portal/) represent the ultimate resource to find MySQL AB Partners, as well as books, or other MySQL-related solutions that you may be looking for. Items are categorised and rated in order to make it easy for you to locate information.

By registering as a user, you will have the ability to comment on and rate items presented in portals. You will also receive relevant newsletters according to your user profile that you may update at any time.

Some of the current MySQL Portal categories include:

Partners
  Find MySQL AB partners worldwide.

Books
  Comment on, vote for, and buy books related to MySQL.

Development
  Various links to different sites that are using MySQL server for different purposes, with a description of each site. This information can give you an idea of who uses the MySQL database software and how MySQL server can fulfill requirements.

  Let us know about *your* site or success story, too! Visit http://www.mysql.com/feedback/testimonial.php.

Software
  Find, buy, and download several applications and wrappers that make use of the MySQL server.

Distributions
  From here you can find the various Linux distributions and other software packages that contain the MySQL software.

Service Providers
  Companies providing MySQL-related services.

1.6.2 MySQL Mailing Lists

This section introduces you to the MySQL mailing lists, and gives some guidelines as to how to use them. By subscribing to a mailing list, you will receive as email messages all other postings on the list, and you will be able to send in your own questions and answers.

1.6.2.1 The MySQL Mailing Lists

To subscribe to the main MySQL mailing list, send a message to the electronic mail address *mysql-subscribe@lists.mysql.com*.

To unsubscribe from the main MySQL mailing list, send a message to the electronic mail address *mysql-unsubscribe@lists.mysql.com*.

Only the address to which you send your messages is significant. The subject line and the body of the message are ignored.

If your reply address is not valid, you can specify your address explicitly, by adding a hyphen to the subscribe or unsubscribe command word, followed by your address with the @ character in your address replaced by a =. For example, to subscribe `your_name@host.domain`, send a message to `mysql-subscribe-your_name=host.domain@lists.mysql.com`.

Mail to *mysql-subscribe@lists.mysql.com* or *mysql-unsubscribe@lists.mysql.com* is handled automatically by the ezmlm mailing list processor. Information about ezmlm is available at the ezmlm web site (http://www.ezmlm.org/).

To post a message to the list itself, send your message to `mysql@lists.mysql.com`. However, please **do not** send mail about subscribing or unsubscribing to *mysql@lists.mysql.com* because any mail sent to that address is distributed automatically to thousands of other users.

Your local site may have many subscribers to *mysql@lists.mysql.com*. If so, it may have a local mailing list, so messages sent from `lists.mysql.com` to your site are propagated to the local list. In such cases, please contact your system administrator to be added to or dropped from the local MySQL list.

If you wish to have traffic for a mailing list go to a separate mailbox in your mail program, set up a filter based on the message headers. You can use either the `List-ID:` or `Delivered-To:` headers to identify list messages.

The following MySQL mailing lists exist:

announce-subscribe@lists.mysql.com announce
> This is for announcement of new versions of MySQL and related programs. This is a low-volume list all MySQL users should subscribe to.

mysql-subscribe@lists.mysql.com `mysql`
> The main list for general MySQL discussion. Please note that some topics are better discussed on the more-specialised lists. If you post to the wrong list, you may not get an answer!

mysql-digest-subscribe@lists.mysql.com `mysql-digest`
> The `mysql` list in digest form. That means you get all individual messages, sent as one large mail message once a day.

bugs-subscribe@lists.mysql.com `bugs`
> On this list you should only post a full, repeatable bug report using the `mysqlbug` script (if you are running on Windows, you should include a description of the operating system and the MySQL version). Preferably, you should test the problem using the latest stable or development version of MySQL server before posting! Anyone should be able to repeat the bug by just using `mysql test < script` on the included test case. All bugs posted on this list will be corrected or documented in the next MySQL release! If only small code changes are needed, we will also post a patch that fixes the problem.

bugs-digest-subscribe@lists.mysql.com `bugs-digest`
> The `bugs` list in digest form.

internals-subscribe@lists.mysql.com `internals`
> A list for people who work on the MySQL code. On this list one can also discuss MySQL development and post patches.

internals-digest-subscribe@lists.mysql.com `internals-digest`
> A digest version of the `internals` list.

java-subscribe@lists.mysql.com `java`
> Discussion about the MySQL server and Java. Mostly about the JDBC drivers.

java-digest-subscribe@lists.mysql.com `java-digest`
> A digest version of the `java` list.

win32-subscribe@lists.mysql.com `win32`
> All things concerning the MySQL software on Microsoft operating systems such as Windows 9x/Me/NT/2000/XP.

win32-digest-subscribe@lists.mysql.com `win32-digest`
> A digest version of the `win32` list.

myodbc-subscribe@lists.mysql.com `myodbc`
> All things about connecting to the MySQL server with ODBC.

myodbc-digest-subscribe@lists.mysql.com `myodbc-digest`
> A digest version of the `myodbc` list.

mycc-subscribe@lists.mysql.com `mycc`
> All things about the MySQL `MyCC` graphical client.

mycc-digest-subscribe@lists.mysql.com `mycc-digest`
> A digest version of the `mycc` list.

plusplus-subscribe@lists.mysql.com `plusplus`
> All things concerning programming with the C++ API to MySQL.

plusplus-digest-subscribe@lists.mysql.com `plusplus-digest`
> A digest version of the `plusplus` list.

msql-mysql-modules-subscribe@lists.mysql.com `msql-mysql-modules`
> A list about the Perl support for MySQL with msql-mysql-modules.

msql-mysql-modules-digest-subscribe@lists.mysql.com `msql-mysql-modules-digest`
> A digest version of the `msql-mysql-modules` list.

You subscribe or unsubscribe to all lists in the same way as described previously. In your subscribe or unsubscribe message, just put the appropriate mailing list name rather than `mysql`. For example, to subscribe to or unsubscribe from the `myodbc` list, send a message to *myodbc-subscribe@lists.mysql.com* or *myodbc-unsubscribe@lists.mysql.com*.

If you can't get an answer for your questions from the mailing list, one option is to pay for support from MySQL AB, which will put you in direct contact with MySQL developers. See Section 1.4.1, Support Offered by MySQL AB.

The following table shows some MySQL mailing in languages other than English. Note that these are not operated by MySQL AB, so we can't guarantee the quality on these.

mysql-france-subscribe@yahoogroups.com
> A French mailing list

list@tinc.net
> A Korean mailing list. Email `subscribe mysql your@email.address` to this list.

mysql-de-request@lists.4t2.com
> A German mailing list. Email `subscribe mysql-de your@email.address` to this list. You can find information about this mailing list at http://www.4t2.com/mysql/.

mysql-br-request@listas.linkway.com.br
> A Portugese mailing list. Email `subscribe mysql-br your@email.address` to this list.

mysql-alta@elistas.net
> A Spanish mailing list. Email `subscribe mysql your@email.address` to this list.

1.6.2.2 Asking questions or reporting bugs

Before posting a bug report or question, please do the following:

- Start by searching the MySQL online manual at:

  http://www.mysql.com/doc/

  We try to keep the manual up to date by updating it frequently with solutions to newly found problems!

- Search the MySQL mailing list archives:

  http://lists.mysql.com/

- You can also use http://www.mysql.com/search.html to search all the web pages (including the manual) that are located at http://www.mysql.com/.

If you can't find an answer in the manual or the archives, check with your local MySQL expert. If you still can't find an answer to your question, go ahead and read the next section about how to send mail to *mysql@lists.mysql.com*.

1.6.2.3 How to report bugs or problems

Writing a good bug report takes patience, but doing it right the first time saves time for us and for you. A good bug report containing a full test case for the bug will make it very likely that we will fix it in the next release. This section will help you write your report correctly so that you don't waste your time doing things that may not help us much or at all.

We encourage everyone to use the `mysqlbug` script to generate a bug report (or a report about any problem), if possible. `mysqlbug` can be found in the `scripts` directory in the source distribution, or for a binary distribution, in the `bin` directory under your MySQL installation directory. If you are unable to use `mysqlbug`, you should still include all the necessary information listed in this section.

The `mysqlbug` script helps you generate a report by determining much of the following information automatically, but if something important is missing, please include it with your message! Please read this section carefully and make sure that all the information described here is included in your report.

The normal place to report bugs and problems is *mysql@lists.mysql.com*. If you can make a test case that clearly demonstrates the bug, you should post it to the *bugs@lists.mysql.com* list. Note that on this list you should only post a full, repeatable bug report using the `mysqlbug` script. If you are running on Windows, you should include a description of the operating system and the MySQL version. Preferably, you should test the problem using the latest stable or development version of MySQL server before posting! Anyone should be able to repeat the bug by just using "`mysql test < script`" on the included test case or run the shell or Perl script that is included in the bug report. All bugs posted on the bugs list will be corrected or documented in the next MySQL release! If only small code changes are needed to correct this problem, we will also post a patch that fixes the problem.

If you have found a sensitive security bug in MySQL, you should send an email to *security@mysql.com*.

Remember that it is possible to respond to a message containing too much information, but not to one containing too little. Often people omit facts because they think they know the cause of a problem and assume that some details don't matter. A good principle is: if you are in doubt about stating something, state it! It is a thousand times faster and less troublesome to write a couple of lines more in your report than to be forced to ask again and wait for the answer because you didn't include enough information the first time.

The most common errors are that people don't indicate the version number of the MySQL distribution they are using, or don't indicate what platform they have the MySQL server installed on (including the platform version number). This is highly relevant information, and in 99 cases out of 100 the bug report is useless without it! Very often we get questions like, "Why doesn't this work for me?" Then we find that the feature requested wasn't implemented in that MySQL version, or that a bug described in a report has been fixed already in newer MySQL versions. Sometimes the error is platform-dependent; in such cases, it is next to impossible to fix anything without knowing the operating system and the version number of the platform.

Remember also to provide information about your compiler, if it is related to the problem. Often people find bugs in compilers and think the problem is MySQL-related. Most compilers are under development all the time and become better version by version. To determine whether your problem depends on your compiler, we need to know what compiler is used. Note that every compiling problem should be regarded as a bug report and reported accordingly.

It is most helpful when a good description of the problem is included in the bug report. That is, a good example of all the things you did that led to the problem and the problem itself exactly described. The best reports are those that include a full example showing how to reproduce the bug or problem. See Section D.1.6, Making a Test Case When You Experience Table Corruption.

If a program produces an error message, it is very important to include the message in your report! If we try to search for something from the archives using programs, it is better that the error message reported exactly matches the one that the program produces. (Even the case should be observed!) You should never try to remember what the error message was; instead, copy and paste the entire message into your report!

If you have a problem with MyODBC, you should try to generate a MyODBC trace file. See Section 8.3.7, Reporting Problems with MyODBC.

Please remember that many of the people who will read your report will do so using an 80-column display. When generating reports or examples using the `mysql` command line tool, you should therefore use the `--vertical` option (or the `\G` statement terminator) for output that would exceed the available width for such a display (for example, with the `EXPLAIN SELECT` statement; see the example later in this section).

Please include the following information in your report:

- The version number of the MySQL distribution you are using (for example, MySQL Version 3.22.22). You can find out which version you are running by executing `mysqladmin version`. `mysqladmin` can be found in the `bin` directory under your MySQL installation directory.

- The manufacturer and model of the machine you are working on.

- The operating system name and version. For most operating systems, you can get this information by executing the Unix command `uname -a`.

- Sometimes the amount of memory (real and virtual) is relevant. If in doubt, include these values.

- If you are using a source distribution of the MySQL software, the name and version number of the compiler used is needed. If you have a binary distribution, the distribution name is needed.

- If the problem occurs during compilation, include the exact error message(s) and also a few lines of context around the offending code in the file where the error occurred.

- If `mysqld` died, you should also report the query that crashed `mysqld`. You can usually find this out by running `mysqld` with logging enabled. See Section D.1.5, Using Log Files to Find Cause of Errors in mysqld.

- If any database table is related to the problem, include the output from `mysqldump --no-data db_name tbl_name1 tbl_name2` .... This is very easy to do and is a powerful way to get information about any table in a database that will help us create a situation matching the one you have.

- For speed-related bugs or problems with `SELECT` statements, you should always include the output of `EXPLAIN SELECT` ..., and at least the number of rows that the `SELECT` statement produces. The more information you give about your situation, the more likely it is that someone can help you! For example, the following is an example of a very good bug report (it should of course be posted with the `mysqlbug` script):

  Example run using the `mysql` command line tool (note the use of the `\G` statement terminator for statements whose output width would otherwise exceed that of an 80-column display device):

```
mysql> SHOW VARIABLES;
mysql> SHOW COLUMNS FROM ...\G
       <output from SHOW COLUMNS>
mysql> EXPLAIN SELECT ...\G
       <output from EXPLAIN>
mysql> FLUSH STATUS;
mysql> SELECT ...;
       <A short version of the output from SELECT,
       including the time taken to run the query>
mysql> SHOW STATUS;
       <output from SHOW STATUS>
```

- If a bug or problem occurs while running mysqld, try to provide an input script that will reproduce the anomaly. This script should include any necessary source files. The more closely the script can reproduce your situation, the better. If you can make a reproduceable test case, you should post this to *bugs@lists.mysql.com* for a high-priority treatment!

  If you can't provide a script, you should at least include the output from mysqladmin variables extended-status processlist in your mail to provide some information of how your system is performing!

- If you can't produce a test case in a few rows, or if the test table is too big to be mailed to the mailing list (more than 10 rows), you should dump your tables using mysqldump and create a README file that describes your problem.

  Create a compressed archive of your files using tar and gzip or zip, and use ftp to transfer the archive to ftp://support.mysql.com/pub/mysql/secret/. Then send a short description of the problem to *bugs@lists.mysql.com*.

- If you think that the MySQL server produces a strange result from a query, include not only the result, but also your opinion of what the result should be, and an account describing the basis for your opinion.

- When giving an example of the problem, it's better to use the variable names, table names, etc., that exist in your actual situation than to come up with new names. The problem could be related to the name of a variable or table! These cases are rare, perhaps, but it is better to be safe than sorry. After all, it should be easier for you to provide an example that uses your actual situation, and it is by all means better for us. In case you have data you don't want to show to others, you can use ftp to transfer it to ftp://support.mysql.com/pub/mysql/secret/. If the data is really top secret and you don't want to show it even to us, then go ahead and provide an example using other names, but please regard this as the last choice.

- Include all the options given to the relevant programs, if possible. For example, indicate the options that you use when you start the mysqld daemon and that you use to run any MySQL client programs. The options to programs like mysqld and mysql, and to the configure script, are often keys to answers and are very relevant! It is never a bad idea to include them anyway! If you use any modules, such as Perl or

PHP, please include the version number(s) of those as well.

- If your question is related to the privilege system, please include the output of mysqlaccess, the output of mysqladmin reload, and all the error messages you get when trying to connect! When you test your privileges, you should first run mysqlaccess. After this, execute mysqladmin reload version and try to connect with the program that gives you trouble. mysqlaccess can be found in the bin directory under your MySQL installation directory.

- If you have a patch for a bug, that is good. But don't assume the patch is all we need, or that we will use it, if you don't provide some necessary information such as test cases showing the bug that your patch fixes. We might find problems with your patch or we might not understand it at all; if so, we can't use it.

  If we can't verify exactly what the patch is meant for, we won't use it. Test cases will help us here. Show that the patch will handle all the situations that may occur. If we find a borderline case (even a rare one) where the patch won't work, it may be useless.

- Guesses about what the bug is, why it occurs, or what it depends on are usually wrong. Even the MySQL team can't guess such things without first using a debugger to determine the real cause of a bug.

- Indicate in your mail message that you have checked the reference manual and mail archive so that others know you have tried to solve the problem yourself.

- If you get a parse error, please check your syntax closely! If you can't find something wrong with it, it's extremely likely that your current version of MySQL server doesn't support the query you are using. If you are using the current version and the manual at http://www.mysql.com/doc/ doesn't cover the syntax you are using, MySQL server doesn't support your query. In this case, your only options are to implement the syntax yourself or email *licensing@mysql.com* and ask for an offer to implement it!

  If the manual covers the syntax you are using, but you have an older version of MySQL server, you should check the MySQL change history to see when the syntax was implemented. In this case, you have the option of upgrading to a newer version of MySQL server. See http://www.mysql.com/doc/N/e/News.html.

- If you have a problem such that your data appears corrupt or you get errors when you access some particular table, you should first check and then try repairing your tables with myisamchk or CHECK TABLE and REPAIR TABLE. See Chapter 4.

- If you often get corrupted tables you should try to find out when and why this happens. In this case, the mysql-data-directory/'hostname'.err file may contain some information about what happened. See Section 4.9.1, The Error Log. Please include any relevant information from this file in your bug report. Normally mysqld should **never** crash a table if nothing killed it in the middle of an update! If you can find the cause of mysqld dying, it's much easier for us to provide you with a fix for the problem. See Section A.1, How to Determine What Is Causing Problems.

* If possible, download and install the most recent version of MySQL server and check whether it solves your problem. All versions of the MySQL software are thoroughly tested and should work without problems. We believe in making everything as backward-compatible as possible, and you should be able to switch MySQL versions without any hassle. See Section 2.2.3, Which MySQL Version to Use.

If you are a support customer, please cross-post the bug report to *mysql-support@mysql.com* for higher-priority treatment, as well as to the appropriate mailing list to see if someone else has experienced (and perhaps solved) the problem.

For information on reporting bugs in MyODBC, see Section 8.3.4, How to Report Problems with MyODBC.

For solutions to some common problems, see Appendix A.

When answers are sent to you individually and not to the mailing list, it is considered good etiquette to summarise the answers and send the summary to the mailing list so that others may have the benefit of responses you received that helped you solve your problem!

1.6.2.4 Guidelines for answering questions on the mailing list

If you consider your answer to have broad interest, you may want to post it to the mailing list instead of replying directly to the individual who asked. Try to make your answer general enough that people other than the original poster may benefit from it. When you post to the list, please make sure that your answer is not a duplication of a previous answer.

Try to summarise the essential part of the question in your reply; don't feel obliged to quote the entire original message.

Please don't post mail messages from your browser with HTML mode turned on! Many users don't read mail with a browser!

1.7 How Standards-Compatible Is MySQL?

This section describes how MySQL relates to the ANSI SQL standards. MySQL server has many extensions to the ANSI SQL standards, and here you will find out what they are and how to use them. You will also find information about functionality missing from MySQL server, and how to work around some differences.

Our goal is to not, without a very good reason, restrict MySQL server usability for any usage. Even if we don't have the resources to do development for every possible use, we are always willing to help and offer suggestions to people who are trying to use MySQL server in new territories.

One of our main goals with the product is to continue to work toward ANSI 99 compliancy, but without sacrificing speed or reliability. We are not afraid to add extensions to SQL or support for non-SQL features if this greatly increases the usability of MySQL server for a big part of our users. (The new HANDLER interface in MySQL server 4.0 is an example of this strategy. See Section 6.4.2, HANDLER Syntax.)

We will continue to support transactional and non-transactional databases to satisfy both heavy web/logging usage and mission-critical 24/7 usage.

MySQL server was designed from the start to work with medium size databases (10-100 million rows, or about 100M per table) on small computer systems. We will continue to extend MySQL server to work even better with terabyte-size databases, as well as to make it possible to compile a reduced MySQL version that is more suitable for hand-held devices and embedded usage. The compact design of the MySQL server makes both of these directions possible without any conflicts in the source tree.

We are currently not targeting realtime support or clustered databases (even if you can already do a lot of things with our replication services).

We don't believe that one should have native XML support in the database, but will instead add the XML support our users request from us on the client side. We think it's better to keep the main server code as "lean and clean" as possible and instead develop libraries to deal with the complexity on the client side. This is part of the strategy mentioned previously of not sacrificing speed or reliability in the server.

1.7.1 What Standards Does MySQL Follow?

Entry-level SQL92. ODBC levels 0-3.51.

We are aiming toward supporting the full ANSI SQL99 standard, but without concessions to speed and quality of the code.

1.7.2 Running MySQL in ANSI Mode

If you start mysqld with the --ansi option, the following behavior of MySQL server changes:

- || is string concatenation instead of OR.
- You can have any number of spaces between a function name and the (. This forces all function names to be treated as reserved words.
- " will be an identifier quote character (like the MySQL server ` quote character) and not a string quote character.

- REAL will be a synonym for FLOAT instead of a synonym for DOUBLE.

- The default transaction isolation level is SERIALIZABLE. See Section 6.7.3, SET TRANSACTION Syntax.

This is the same as using --sql-mode=REAL_AS_FLOAT,PIPES_AS_CON-CAT,ANSI_QUOTES, IGNORE_SPACE,SERIALIZE,ONLY_FULL_GROUP_BY.

1.7.3 MySQL Extensions to ANSI SQL92

MySQL server includes some extensions that you probably will not find in other SQL databases. Be warned that if you use them, your code will not be portable to other SQL servers. In some cases, you can write code that includes MySQL extensions, but is still portable, by using comments of the form /*! . . . */. In this case, MySQL server will parse and execute the code within the comment as it would any other MySQL statement, but other SQL servers will ignore the extensions. For example:

```
SELECT /*! STRAIGHT_JOIN */ col_name FROM table1,table2 WHERE ...
```

If you add a version number after the '!', the syntax will be executed only if the MySQL version is equal to or newer than the used version number:

```
CREATE /*!32302 TEMPORARY */ TABLE (a int);
```

This means that if you have Version 3.23.02 or newer, MySQL Server will use the TEMPORARY keyword.

The following is a list of MySQL extensions:

- The field types MEDIUMINT, SET, ENUM, and the different BLOB and TEXT types.

- The field attributes AUTO_INCREMENT, BINARY, NULL, UNSIGNED, and ZEROFILL.

- All string comparisons are case-insensitive by default, with sort ordering determined by the current character set (ISO-8859-1 Latin1 by default). If you don't like this, you should declare your columns with the BINARY attribute or use the BINARY cast, which causes comparisons to be done according to the ASCII order used on the MySQL server host.

- MySQL server maps each database to a directory under the MySQL data directory, and tables within a database to filenames in the database directory.

  This has a few implications:

  — Database names and table names are case-sensitive in MySQL server on operating systems that have case-sensitive filenames (like most Unix systems). See Section 6.1.3, Case Sensitivity in Names.

  — Database, table, index, column, or alias names may begin with a digit (but may not consist solely of digits).

— You can use standard system commands to back up, rename, move, delete, and copy tables. For example, to rename a table, rename the `.MYD`, `.MYI`, and `.frm` files to which the table corresponds.

- In SQL statements, you can access tables from different databases with the `db_name.tbl_name` syntax. Some SQL servers provide the same functionality but call this `User space`. MySQL server doesn't support tablespaces as in: `create table ralph.my_table . . . IN my_tablespace`.

- `LIKE` is allowed on numeric columns.

- Use of `INTO OUTFILE` and `STRAIGHT_JOIN` in a `SELECT` statement. See Section 6.4.1, `SELECT` Syntax.

- The `SQL_SMALL_RESULT` option in a `SELECT` statement.

- `EXPLAIN SELECT` to get a description on how tables are joined.

- Use of index names, indexes on a prefix of a field, and use of `INDEX` or `KEY` in a `CREATE TABLE` statement. See Section 6.5.3, `CREATE TABLE` Syntax.

- Use of `TEMPORARY` or `IF NOT EXISTS` with `CREATE TABLE`.

- Use of `COUNT(DISTINCT list)` where `list` is more than one element.

- Use of `CHANGE col_name`, `DROP col_name`, or `DROP INDEX`, `IGNORE` or `RENAME` in an `ALTER TABLE` statement. See Section 6.5.4, `ALTER TABLE` Syntax.

- Use of `RENAME TABLE`. See Section 6.5.5, `RENAME TABLE` Syntax.

- Use of multiple `ADD`, `ALTER`, `DROP`, or `CHANGE` clauses in an `ALTER TABLE` statement.

- Use of `DROP TABLE` with the keywords `IF EXISTS`.

- You can drop multiple tables with a single `DROP TABLE` statement.

- The `LIMIT` clause of the `DELETE` statement.

- The `DELAYED` clause of the `INSERT` and `REPLACE` statements.

- The `LOW_PRIORITY` clause of the `INSERT`, `REPLACE`, `DELETE`, and `UPDATE` statements.

- Use of `LOAD DATA INFILE`. In many cases, this syntax is compatible with Oracle's `LOAD DATA INFILE`. See Section 6.4.9, `LOAD DATA INFILE` Syntax.

- The `ANALYZE TABLE`, `CHECK TABLE`, `OPTIMIZE TABLE`, and `REPAIR TABLE` statements.

- The `SHOW` statement. See Section 4.5.6, `SHOW` Syntax.

- Strings may be enclosed by either `"` or `'`, not just by `'`.

- Use of the escape \ character.

- The SET OPTION statement. See Section 5.5.6, SET Syntax.

- You don't need to name all selected columns in the GROUP BY part. This gives better performance for some very specific, but quite normal queries. See Section 6.3.7, Functions for Use with GROUP BY Clauses.

- One can specify ASC and DESC with GROUP BY.

- To make it easier for users who come from other SQL environments, MySQL server supports aliases for many functions. For example, all string functions support both ANSI SQL syntax and ODBC syntax.

- MySQL server understands the || and && operators to mean logical OR and AND, as in the C programming language. In MySQL server, || and OR are synonyms, as are && and AND. Because of this nice syntax, MySQL server doesn't support the ANSI SQL || operator for string concatenation; use CONCAT() instead. Because CONCAT() takes any number of arguments, it's easy to convert use of the || operator to MySQL server.

- CREATE DATABASE or DROP DATABASE. See Section 6.5.1, CREATE DATABASE Syntax.

- The % operator is a synonym for MOD(). That is, N % M is equivalent to MOD(N,M). % is supported for C programmers and for compatibility with PostgreSQL.

- The =, <>, <= ,<, >=,>, <<, >>, <=>, AND, OR, or LIKE operators may be used in column comparisons to the left of the FROM in SELECT statements. For example:

  ```
  mysql> SELECT col1=1 AND col2=2 FROM tbl_name;
  ```

- The LAST_INSERT_ID() function. See Section 8.4.3.126, mysql_insert_id().

- The REGEXP and NOT REGEXP extended regular expression operators.

- CONCAT() or CHAR() with one argument or more than two arguments. (In MySQL server, these functions can take any number of arguments.)

- The BIT_COUNT(), CASE, ELT(), FROM_DAYS(), FORMAT(), IF(), PASSWORD(), ENCRYPT(), MD5(), ENCODE(), DECODE(), PERIOD_ADD(), PERIOD_DIFF(), TO_DAYS(), or WEEKDAY() functions.

- Use of TRIM() to trim substrings. ANSI SQL only supports removal of single characters.

- The GROUP BY functions STD(), BIT_OR(), and BIT_AND().

- Use of REPLACE instead of DELETE + INSERT. See Section 6.4.8, REPLACE Syntax.

- The FLUSH, RESET and DO statements.

- The ability to set variables in a statement with :=:

```
SELECT @a:=SUM(total),@b=COUNT(*),@a/@b AS avg FROM test_table;
SELECT @t1:=(@t2:=1)+@t3:=4,@t1,@t2,@t3;
```

1.7.4 MySQL Differences Compared to ANSI SQL92

We try to make MySQL server follow the ANSI SQL standard and the ODBC SQL standard, but in some cases MySQL server does things differently:

- For VARCHAR columns, trailing spaces are removed when the value is stored. See Section 1.7.5, Known Errors and Design Deficiencies in MySQL.

- In some cases, CHAR columns are silently changed to VARCHAR columns. See Section 6.5.3.1, Silent column specification changes.

- Privileges for a table are not automatically revoked when you delete a table. You must explicitly issue a REVOKE to revoke privileges for a table. See Section 4.3.1, GRANT and REVOKE Syntax.

- NULL AND FALSE will evaluate to NULL and not to FALSE. This is because we don't think it's good to have to evaluate a lot of extra conditions in this case.

For a prioritised list indicating when new extensions will be added to MySQL server, you should consult the online MySQL TODO list at http://www.mysql.com/documentation/manual.php?section=TODO. That is the latest version of the TODO list in this manual. See Section 1.8, MySQL and the Future (the TODO).

1.7.4.1 Sub-SELECTs

MySQL server currently only supports nested queries of the form INSERT ... SELECT ... and REPLACE ... SELECT .... You can, however, use the function IN() in other contexts. Sub-selects are scheduled for implementation in Version 4.x.

Meanwhile, you can often rewrite the query without a sub-select:

```
SELECT * FROM table1 WHERE id IN (SELECT id FROM table2);
```

This can be rewritten as:

```
SELECT table1.* FROM table1,table2 WHERE table1.id=table2.id;
```

The queries:

```
SELECT * FROM table1 WHERE id NOT IN (SELECT id FROM table2);
SELECT * FROM table1 WHERE NOT EXISTS (SELECT id FROM table2
                                       WHERE table1.id=table2.id);
```

Can be rewritten as:

```
SELECT table1.* FROM table1 LEFT JOIN table2 ON table1.id=table2.id
                                       WHERE table2.id IS NULL;
```

For more complicated subqueries you can often create temporary tables to hold the sub-query. In some cases, however, this option will not work. The most frequently encountered of these cases arises with DELETE statements, for which standard SQL does not support joins (except in sub-selects). For this situation there are two options available until subqueries are supported by MySQL server.

The first option is to use a procedural programming language (such as Perl or PHP) to submit a SELECT query to obtain the primary keys for the records to be deleted, and then use these values to construct the DELETE statement (DELETE FROM . . . WHERE . . . IN (key1, key2, . . .)).

The second option is to use interactive SQL to construct a set of DELETE statements automatically, using the MySQL extension CONCAT() (in lieu of the standard || operator). For example:

```
SELECT CONCAT('DELETE FROM tab1 WHERE pkid = ', tab1.pkid, ';')
  FROM tab1, tab2
  WHERE tab1.col1 = tab2.col2;
```

You can place this query in a script file and redirect input from it to the mysql command-line interpreter, piping its output back to a second instance of the interpreter:

```
shell> mysql --skip-column-names mydb < myscript.sql | mysql mydb
```

MySQL server 4.0 supports multi-table deletes that can be used to efficiently delete rows based on information from one table or even from many tables at the same time.

1.7.4.2 SELECT INTO TABLE

MySQL server doesn't yet support the Oracle SQL extension: SELECT . . . INTO TABLE . . . . MySQL server supports instead the ANSI SQL syntax INSERT INTO . . . SELECT . . . , which is basically the same thing. See Section 6.4.3.1, INSERT . . . SELECT syntax.

```
INSERT INTO tblTemp2 (fldID) SELECT tblTemp1.fldOrder_ID
    FROM tblTemp1 WHERE tblTemp1.fldOrder_ID > 100;
```

Alternatively, you can use SELECT INTO OUTFILE . . . or CREATE TABLE . . . SELECT.

1.7.4.3 Transactions and atomic operations

MySQL server supports transactions with the InnoDB and BDB Transactional table handlers. See Chapter 7. InnoDB provides ACID compliancy.

However, the non-transactional table types in MySQL server such as MyISAM follow another paradigm for data integrity called "Atomic Operations." Atomic operations often offer equal or even better integrity with much better performance. With MySQL server supporting both paradigms, the user is able to decide if he needs the speed of atomic operations or if he need to use transactional features in his applications. This choice can be made on a per-table basis.

How does one use the features of MySQL server to maintain rigorous integrity and how do these features compare with the transactional paradigm?

1. In the transactional paradigm, if your applications are written in a way that is dependent on the calling of ROLLBACK instead of COMMIT in critical situations, transactions are more convenient. Transactions also ensure that unfinished updates or corrupting activities are not committed to the database; the server is given the opportunity to do an automatic rollback and your database is saved.

    MySQL server, in almost all cases, allows you to resolve potential problems by including simple checks before updates and by running simple scripts that check the databases for inconsistencies and automatically repair or warn if such an inconsistency occurs. Note that just by using the MySQL log or even adding one extra log, one can normally fix tables perfectly with no data integrity loss.

2. More often than not, fatal transactional updates can be rewritten to be atomic. Generally speaking, all integrity problems that transactions solve can be done with LOCK TABLES or atomic updates, ensuring that you never will get an automatic abort from the database, which is a common problem with transactional databases.

3. Even a transactional system can lose data if the server goes down. The difference between different systems lies in just how small the time-lap is where they could lose data. No system is 100% secure, only "secure enough." Even Oracle, reputed to be the safest of transactional databases, is reported to sometimes lose data in such situations.

    To be safe with MySQL server, whether using transactional tables or not, you only need to have backups and have the update logging turned on. With this you can recover from any situation that you could with any other transactional database. It is, of course, always good to have backups, independent of which database you use.

The transactional paradigm has its benefits and its drawbacks. Many users and application developers depend on the ease with which they can code around problems where an abort appears to be, or is necessary. However, even if you are new to the atomic operations paradigm, or more familiar with transactions, do consider the speed benefit that nontransactional tables can offer on the order of three to five times the speed of the fastest and most optimally tuned transactional tables.

In situations where integrity is of highest importance, MySQL server offers transactionlevel or better reliability and integrity even for non-transactional tables. If you lock tables with LOCK TABLES, all updates will stall until any integrity checks are made. If you only obtain a read lock (as opposed to a write lock), reads and inserts are still allowed to happen. The new inserted records will not be seen by any of the clients that have a read lock until they release their read locks. With INSERT DELAYED you can queue inserts into a local queue, until the locks are released, without having the client wait for the insert to complete. See Section 6.4.4, INSERT DELAYED Syntax.

"Atomic," in the sense that we mean it, is nothing magical. It only means that you can be sure that while each specific update is running, no other user can interfere with it, and there will never be an automatic rollback (which can happen with transactional tables if you are not very careful). MySQL server also guarantees that there will not be any dirty reads.

Following are some techniques for working with non-transactional tables:

- Loops that need transactions normally can be coded with the help of LOCK TABLES, and you don't need cursors when you can update records on the fly.

- To avoid using ROLLBACK, you can use the following strategy:

  1. Use LOCK TABLES . . . to lock all the tables you want to access.

  2. Test conditions.

  3. Update if everything is okay.

  4. Use UNLOCK TABLES to release your locks.

  This is usually a much faster method than using transactions with possible ROLL-BACKs, although not always. The only situation this solution doesn't handle is when someone kills the threads in the middle of an update. In this case, all locks will be released but some of the updates may not have been executed.

- You can also use functions to update records in a single operation. You can get a very efficient application by using the following techniques:

  — Modify fields relative to their current value.

  — Update only those fields that actually have changed.

For example, when we are doing updates to some customer information, we update only the customer data that has changed and test only that none of the changed data, or data that depends on the changed data, has changed compared to the original row. The test for changed data is done with the WHERE clause in the UPDATE statement. If the record wasn't updated, we give the client a message: "Some of the data you have changed has been changed by another user." Then we show the old row versus the new row in a window, so the user can decide which version of the customer record he should use.

This gives us something that is similar to column locking but is actually even better because we only update some of the columns, using values that are relative to their current values. This means that typical UPDATE statements look something like these:

```
UPDATE tablename SET pay_back=pay_back+'relative change';

UPDATE customer
  SET
    customer_date='current_date',
    address='new address',
    phone='new phone',
    money_he_owes_us=money_he_owes_us+'new_money'
  WHERE
    customer_id=id AND address='old address' AND phone='old phone';
```

As you can see, this is very efficient and works even if another client has changed the
values in the pay_back or money_he_owes_us columns.

- In many cases, users have wanted ROLLBACK and/or LOCK TABLES for the purpose of
  managing unique identifiers for some tables. This can be handled much more efficiently by using an AUTO_INCREMENT column and either the SQL function
  LAST_INSERT_ID() or the C API function mysql_insert_id(). See Section
  8.4.3.126, mysql_insert_id().

You can generally code around row-level locking. Some situations really need it, but
they are very few. InnoDB tables support row-level locking. With MyISAM, you can
use a flag column in the table and do something like the following:

```
UPDATE tbl_name SET row_flag=1 WHERE id=ID;
```

MySQL returns 1 for the number of affected rows if the row was found and
row_flag wasn't already 1 in the original row.

You can think of it as though MySQL server changed the preceding query to:

```
UPDATE tbl_name SET row_flag=1 WHERE id=ID AND row_flag <> 1;
```

1.7.4.4 Stored procedures and triggers

A stored procedure is a set of SQL commands that can be compiled and stored in the
server. Once this has been done, clients don't need to keep re-issuing the entire query but
can refer to the stored procedure. This provides better performance because the query has
to be parsed only once, and less information needs to be sent between the server and the
client. You can also raise the conceptual level by having libraries of functions in the
server.

A trigger is a stored procedure that is invoked when a particular event occurs. For example, you can install a stored procedure that is triggered each time a record is deleted from
a transaction table and that automatically deletes the corresponding customer from a customer table when all his transactions are deleted.

The planned update language will be able to handle stored procedures. Our aim is to have
stored procedures implemented in MySQL server around version 4.1. We are also looking
at triggers.

1.7.4.5 Foreign keys

Note that foreign keys in SQL are not used to join tables, but are used mostly for checking referential integrity (foreign key constraints). If you want to get results from multiple tables from a SELECT statement, you do this by joining tables:

```
SELECT * FROM table1,table2 WHERE table1.id = table2.id;
```

Section 6.4.1.1, JOIN syntax. See Section 3.5.6, Using Foreign Keys.

In MySQL server 3.23.44 and up, InnoDB tables support checking of foreign key constraints. See Section 7.5, InnoDB Tables. For other table types, MySQL server does parse the FOREIGN KEY syntax in CREATE TABLE commands, but without further action being taken.

The FOREIGN KEY syntax without ON DELETE . . . is mostly used for documentation purposes. Some ODBC applications may use this to produce automatic WHERE clauses, but this is usually easy to override. FOREIGN KEY is sometimes used as a constraint check, but this check is unnecessary in practice if rows are inserted into the tables in the right order.

In MySQL server, you can work around the problem of ON DELETE . . . not being implemented by adding the appropriate DELETE statement to an application when you delete records from a table that has a foreign key. In practice this is as quick (in some cases quicker) and much more portable than using foreign keys.

In MySQL server 4.0 you can use multi-table delete to delete rows from many tables with one command. See Section 6.4.6, DELETE Syntax.

In the near future we will extend the FOREIGN KEY implementation so that the information will be saved in the table specification file and may be retrieved by mysqldump and ODBC. At a later stage we will implement the foreign key constraints for applications that can't easily be coded to avoid them.

Do keep in mind that foreign keys are often misused, which can cause severe problems. Even when used properly, it is not a magic solution for the referential integrity problem, although it does make things easier in some cases.

Some advantages of foreign key enforcement:

- Assuming proper design of the relations, foreign key constraints will make it more difficult for a programmer to introduce an inconsistency into the database.
- Using cascading updates and deletes can simplify the client code.
- Properly designed foreign key rules aid in documenting relations between tables.

Disadvantages:

- Mistakes, which are easy to make in designing key relations, can cause severe problems—for example, circular rules, or the wrong combination of cascading deletes.

- A properly written application will make sure internally that it is not violating referential integrity constraints before proceding with a query. Thus, additional checks on the database level will only slow down performance for such an application.

- It is not uncommon for a DBA to make such a complex topology of relations that it becomes very difficult, and in some cases impossible, to back up or restore individual tables.

1.7.4.6 Views

It is planned to implement views in MySQL server around version 4.1.

Views are mostly useful for letting users access a set of relations as one table (in read-only mode). Many SQL databases don't allow one to update any rows in a view, but you have to do the updates in the separate tables.

As MySQL server is mostly used in applications and on web systems where the application writer has full control on the database usage, most of our users haven't regarded views to be very important. (At least no one has been interested enough in this to be prepared to finance the implementation of views.)

One doesn't need views in MySQL server to restrict access to columns, as MySQL server has a very sophisticated privilege system. See Section 4.2, General Security Issues and the MySQL Access Privilege System.

1.7.4.7 – as the start of a comment

Some other SQL databases use – to start comments. MySQL server has # as the start comment character. You can also use the C comment style /* this is a comment */ with MySQL server. See Section 6.1.5, Comment Syntax.

MySQL server Version 3.23.3 and above support the – comment style, provided the comment is followed by a space. This is because this comment style has caused many problems with automatically generated SQL queries that have used something like the following code, where we automatically insert the value of the payment for !payment!:

```
UPDATE tbl_name SET credit=credit-!payment!
```

Think about what happens if the value of payment is negative. Because 1--1 is legal in SQL, the consequences of allowing comments to start with – are terrible.

Using our implementation of this method of commenting in MySQL server Version 3.23.3 and up, 1-- This is a comment is actually safe.

Another safe feature is that the mysql command-line client removes all lines that start with –.

The following information is relevant only if you are running a MySQL version earlier than 3.23.3:

If you have a SQL program in a text file that contains – comments you should use:

```
shell> replace " --" " #" < text-file-with-funny-comments.sql \
       | mysql database
```

instead of the usual:

```
shell> mysql database < text-file-with-funny-comments.sql
```

You can also edit the command file "in place" to change the – comments to # comments:

```
shell> replace " --" " #"-text-file-with-funny-comments.sql
```

Change them back with this command:

```
shell> replace " #" " --"-text-file-with-funny-comments.sql
```

1.7.5 Known Errors and Design Deficiencies in MySQL

The following problems are known and have a very high priority to get fixed:

- ANALYZE TABLE on a BDB table may in some case make the table unusable until one has restarted mysqld. When this happens you will see errors like the following in the MySQL error file:

  ```
  001207 22:07:56  bdb:  log_flush: LSN past current end-of-log
  ```

- Don't execute ALTER TABLE on a BDB table on which you are running multi-statement transactions until all those transactions complete. (The transaction will probably be ignored.)

- ANALYZE TABLE, OPTIMIZE TABLE, and REPAIR TABLE may cause problems on tables for which you are using INSERT DELAYED.

- Doing a LOCK TABLE . . . and FLUSH TABLES . . . doesn't guarantee that there isn't a half-finished transaction in progress on the table.

- BDB tables are a bit slow to open. If you have many BDB tables in a database, it will take a long time to use the mysql client on the database if you are not using the –A option or if you are using rehash. This is especially notable when you have a big table cache.

- The current replication protocol cannot deal with LOAD DATA INFILE and line terminator characters of more than 1 character.

The following problems are known and will be fixed in due time:

- When using SET CHARACTER SET, one can't use translated characters in database, table, and column names.

- DELETE FROM merge_table used without a WHERE will only clear the mapping for the table, not delete everything in the mapped tables.

- You cannot build the server in another directory when using MIT-pthreads. Because this requires changes to MIT-pthreads, we are not likely to fix this. See Section 2.3.6, MIT-pthreads Notes.

- BLOB values can't "reliably" be used in GROUP BY or ORDER BY or DISTINCT. Only the first max_sort_length bytes (default 1024) are used when comparing BLOBs in these cases. This can be changed with the -O max_sort_length option to mysqld. A workaround for most cases is to use a substring: SELECT DISTINCT LEFT(blob,2048) FROM tbl_name.

- Calculation is done with BIGINT or DOUBLE (both are normally 64 bits long). It depends on the function which precision one gets. The general rule is that bit functions are done with BIGINT precision, IF, and ELT() with BIGINT or DOUBLE precision and the rest with DOUBLE precision. One should try to avoid using unsigned long long values if they resolve to be bigger than 63 bits (9223372036854775807) for anything else than bit fields! MySQL server 4.0 has better BIGINT handling than 3.23.

- All string columns, except BLOB and TEXT columns, automatically have all trailing spaces removed when retrieved. For CHAR types this is okay, and may be regarded as a feature according to ANSI SQL92. The bug is that in MySQL server, VARCHAR columns are treated the same way.

- You can only have up to 255 ENUM and SET columns in one table.

- safe_mysqld redirects all messages from mysqld to the mysqld log. One problem with this is that if you execute mysqladmin refresh to close and reopen the log, stdout and stderr are still redirected to the old log. If you use --log extensively, you should edit safe_mysqld to log to 'hostname'.err instead of 'hostname'.log so you can easily reclaim the space for the old log by deleting the old one and executing mysqladmin refresh.

- In the UPDATE statement, columns are updated from left to right. If you refer to an updated column, you will get the updated value instead of the original value. For example:

    ```
    mysql> UPDATE tbl_name SET KEY=KEY+1,KEY=KEY+1;
    ```

    This will update KEY with 2 instead of with 1.

- You can't use temporary tables more than once in the same query. For example, the following doesn't work:

  ```
  mysql> SELECT * FROM temporary_table, temporary_table AS t2;
  ```

- RENAME doesn't work with TEMPORARY tables or tables used in a MERGE table.

- The optimiser may handle DISTINCT differently if you are using 'hidden' columns in a join or not. In a join, hidden columns are counted as part of the result (even if they are not shown) while in normal queries hidden columns don't participate in the DIS-TINCT comparison. We will probably change this in the future to never compare the hidden columns when executing DISTINCT.

  An example of this is:

  ```
  SELECT DISTINCT mp3id FROM band_downloads
         WHERE userid = 9 ORDER BY id DESC;
  ```

  and

  ```
  SELECT DISTINCT band_downloads.mp3id
         FROM band_downloads,band_mp3
         WHERE band_downloads.userid = 9
         AND band_mp3.id = band_downloads.mp3id
         ORDER BY band_downloads.id DESC;
  ```

  In the second case you may in MySQL server 3.23.x get two identical rows in the result set (because the hidden id column may differ).

  Note that this happens only for queries where you don't have the ORDER BY columns in the result, something that you are not allowed to do in ANSI SQL.

- Because MySQL server allows you to work with table types that don't support trans-actions, and thus can't rollback data, some things behave a little differently in MySQL server than in other SQL servers. This is just to ensure that MySQL server never needs to do a rollback for a SQL command. This may be a little awkward at times as column values must be checked in the application, but this will actually give you a nice speed increase as it allows MySQL server to do some optimisations that otherwise would be very hard to do.

  If you set a column to an incorrect value, MySQL server will, instead of doing a roll-back, store the best possible value in the column:

  — If you try to store a value outside the range in a numerical column, MySQL server will instead store the smallest or biggest possible value in the column.

  — If you try to store a string that doesn't start with a number into a numerical col-umn, MySQL server will store 0 into it.

  — If you try to store NULL into a column that doesn't take NULL values, MySQL server will store 0 or " (empty string) in it instead. (This behavior can, however, be changed with the -DDONT_USE_DEFAULT_FIELDS compile option.)

— MySQL allows you to store some wrong date values into DATE and DATETIME columns (like 2000-02-31 or 2000-02-00). If the date is totally wrong, MySQL server will store the special 0000-00-00 date value in the column.

— If you set an ENUM column to an unsupported value, it will be set to the error value empty string, with numeric value 0.

— If you set a SET column to an unsupported value, the value will be ignored.

• If you execute a PROCEDURE on a query that returns an empty set, in some cases the PROCEDURE will not transform the columns.

• Creation of a table of type MERGE doesn't check if the underlying tables are of compatible types.

• MySQL server can't yet handle NaN, -Inf, and Inf values in double. Using these will cause problems when trying to export and import data. We should as an intermediate solution change NaN to NULL (if possible) and -Inf and Inf to the minimum respective maximum possible double value.

• LIMIT on negative numbers are treated as big positive numbers.

• If you use ALTER TABLE to first add a UNIQUE index to a table used in a MERGE table and then use ALTER TABLE to add a normal index on the MERGE table, the key order will be different for the tables if there was an old key that was not unique in the table. This is because ALTER TABLE puts UNIQUE keys before normal keys to be able to detect duplicate keys as early as possible.

The following are known bugs in earlier versions of MySQL:

• You can get a hung thread if you do a DROP TABLE on a table that is one among many tables that is locked with LOCK TABLES.

• In the following case you can get a core dump:

— Delayed insert handler has pending inserts to a table.

— LOCK table with WRITE.

— FLUSH TABLES.

• Before MySQL server Version 3.23.2 an UPDATE that updated a key with a WHERE on the same key may have failed because the key was used to search for records and the same row may have been found multiple times:

```
UPDATE tbl_name SET KEY=KEY+1 WHERE KEY > 100;
```

A workaround is to use:

```
mysql> UPDATE tbl_name SET KEY=KEY+1 WHERE KEY+0 > 100;
```

This will work because MySQL server will not use an index on expressions in the WHERE clause.

- Before MySQL server Version 3.23, all numeric types where treated as fixed-point fields. That means you had to specify how many decimals a floating-point field shall have. All results were returned with the correct number of decimals.

For platform-specific bugs, see the sections about compiling and porting.

1.8 MySQL and the Future (the TODO)

This appendix lists the features that we plan to implement in MySQL server.

Everything in this list is approximately in the order it will be done. If you want to affect the priority order, please register a license or support us and tell us what you want to have done more quickly. See Section 1.4, MySQL Support and Licensing.

The plan is that we in the future will support the full ANSI SQL99 standard, but with a lot of useful extensions. The challenge is to do this without sacrifying the speed or compromising the code.

1.8.1 Things That Should Be in 4.0

We are now in the final stages of the development of the MySQL server 4.0. server. The target is to quickly implement the rest of the following features and then shift development to MySQL server 4.1. See Section 1.5, MySQL 4.0 in a Nutshell.

The news section for 4.0 includes a list of the features we have already implemented in the 4.0 tree. See http://www.mysql.com/doc/N/e/News-4.0.x.html.

This section lists features not yet implemented in the current version of MySQL server 4.0, which will, however, be implemented in later versions of MySQL 4.0. This being very volatile information, please consider this list valid only if you are reading it from the MySQL web site (http://www.mysql.com/).

- Allow users to change startup options without taking down the server.
- Better command-line argument handling.
- New key cache, which will give better performance when using many threads.
- New table definition file format (.frm files). This will enable us to not run out of bits when adding more table options. One will still be able to use the old .frm file format with 4.0. All newly created tables will, however, use the new format.

  The new file format will enable us to add new column types, more options for keys, and possibly to store and retrieve FOREIGN KEY definitions.

- SHOW COLUMNS FROM table_name (used by mysql client to allow expansions of column names) should not open the table, only the definition file. This will require less memory and be much faster.

- SET SQL_DEFAULT_TABLE_TYPE=[MyISAM | INNODB | BDB | HEAP].

1.8.2 Things That Should Be in 4.1

The following features are planned for inclusion into MySQL 4.1. Note that because we have many developers that are working on different projects, there will also be many additional features. There is also a small chance that some of these features will be added to MySQL 4.0. Some of the work on MySQL 4.1 is already in progress.

- Subqueries. SELECT id FROM t WHERE grp IN (SELECT grp FROM g WHERE u > 100)

- Foreign keys, including cascading delete.

- Fail-safe replication.

- Replication should work with RAND() and user variables @var.

- Online backup with very low performance penalty. The online backup will make it easy to add a new replication slave without taking down the master.

- Derived tables:

```
SELECT a.col1, b.col2
    FROM (SELECT MAX(col1) AS col1 FROM root_table) a,
    other_table b
    WHERE a.col1=b.col1;
```

This could be done by automatically creating temporary tables for the derived tables for the duration of the query.

- Allow DELETE on MyISAM tables to use the record cache. To do this, we need to update the threads record cache when we update the .MYD file.

- When using SET CHARACTER SET we should translate the whole query at once and not only strings. This will enable users to use the translated characters in database, table, and column names.

- Add record_in_range() method to MERGE tables to be able to choose the right index when there are many to choose from. We should also extend the info interface to get the key distribution for each index, if analyze is run on all subtables.

- RENAME TABLE on a table used in an active MERGE table may corrupt the table.

- A faster, smaller embedded MySQL library. (Compatible with the old one.)

- Stable openssl support. (MySQL 4.0 supports rudimentary, not 100% tested, support for openssl).

- Add support for sorting on UNICODE.

- Character set casts and syntax for handling multiple character sets.

- Help for all commands from the client.

- New faster client/server protocol which will support prepared statements, bound parameters, and bound result columns, binary transfer of data, warnings . . .

- Add database and real table name (in case of alias) to the MYSQL_FIELD structure.

- Add options to the client/server protocol to get progress notes for long running commands.

- Implement RENAME DATABASE. To make this safe for all table handlers, it should work as follows:

  — Create the new database.

  — For every table do a rename of the table to another database, as we do with the RENAME command.

  — Drop the old database.

- Add true VARCHAR support (there is already support for this in MyISAM).

- Optimise BIT type to take 1 bit (now BIT takes 1 char).

- New internal file interface change. This will make all file handling much more general and make it easier to add extensions like RAID. (the current implementation is a hack.)

- Better in-memory (HEAP) tables:

  — Support for B-tree indexes

  — Dynamic size rows

  — Faster row handling (less copying)

1.8.3 Things That Must Be Done in the Real Near Future

- Atomic   multi-table   updates—e.g.,   update   items,month   set items.price=month.price where items.id=month.id;;

- Don't allow more than a defined number of threads to run MyISAM recover at the same time.

- Change INSERT . . . SELECT to optionally use concurrent inserts.

- Return the original field types() when doing SELECT MIN(column) . . . GROUP BY.

- Multiple result sets.

- Make it possible to specify `long_query_time` with a granularity in microseconds.

- Add a configurable prompt to the `mysql` command-line client, with options like database in use, time and date . . .

- Link the `myisampack` code into the server.

- Port of the MySQL code to QNX.

- Port of the MySQL code to BeOS.

- Port of the MySQL clients to LynxOS.

- Add a temporary key buffer cache during `INSERT/DELETE/UPDATE` so that we can gracefully recover if the index file gets full.

- If you perform an `ALTER TABLE` on a table that is symlinked to another disk, create temporary tables on this disk.

- Implement a `DATE/DATETIME` type that handles time zone information properly so that dealing with dates in different time zones is easier.

- FreeBSD and MIT-pthreads; do sleeping threads take CPU time?

- Check if locked threads take any CPU time.

- Fix configure so that one can compile all libraries (like `MyISAM`) without threads.

- Add an option to periodically flush key pages for tables with delayed keys if they haven't been used in a while.

- Allow join on key parts (optimisation issue).

- `INSERT SQL_CONCURRENT` and `mysqld --concurrent-insert` to do a concurrent insert at the end of the file if the file is read-locked.

- Server-side cursors.

- Check if `lockd` works with modern Linux kernels; if not, we have to fix `lockd`! To test this, start `mysqld` with `--enable-locking` and run the different fork* test suits. They shouldn't give any errors if `lockd` works.

- Allow SQL variables in `LIMIT`, like in `LIMIT @a, @b`.

- Allow update of variables in `UPDATE` statements. For example: `UPDATE TABLE foo SET @a=a+b,a=@a, b=@a+c`.

- Change when user variables are updated so that one can use them with `GROUP BY`, as in the following example: `SELECT id, @a:=COUNT(*), SUM(sum_col)/@a FROM table_name GROUP BY id`.

- Don't add automatic `DEFAULT` values to columns. Give an error when using an `INSERT` that doesn't contain a column that doesn't have a `DEFAULT`.

- Fix `libmysql.c` to allow two `mysql_query()` commands in a row without reading results or give a nice error message when one does this.

- Check why MIT-pthreads `ctime()` doesn't work on some FreeBSD systems.

- Add an `IMAGE` option to `LOAD DATA INFILE` to not update `TIMESTAMP` and `AUTO_INCREMENT` fields.

- Added `LOAD DATE INFILE ... UPDATE` syntax.

  — For tables with primary keys, if the data contains the primary key, entries matching that primary key are updated from the remainder of the columns. However, columns **missing** from the incoming data feed are not touched.

  — For tables with primary keys that are missing some part of the key in the incoming data stream, or that have no primary key, the feed is treated as a `LOAD DATA INFILE ... REPLACE INTO` now.

- Make `LOAD DATA INFILE` understand syntax like:

```
LOAD DATA INFILE 'file_name.txt' INTO TABLE tbl_name
    TEXT_FIELDS (text_field1, text_field2, text_field3)
    SET table_field1=CONCAT(text_field1, text_field2),
        table_field3=23
    IGNORE text_field3
```

This can be used to skip over extra columns in the text file, or update columns based on expressions of the read data.

- `LOAD DATA INFILE 'file_name' INTO TABLE 'table_name' ERRORS TO err_table_name`. This would cause any errors and warnings to be logged into the `err_table_name` table. That table would have a structure like:

```
line_number     - line number in data file
error_message   - the error/warning message
and maybe
data_line       - the line from the data file
```

- Automatic output from `mysql` to Netscape.

- `LOCK DATABASES` (with various options.)

- `DECIMAL` and `NUMERIC` types can't read exponential numbers; `Field_decimal::store(const char *from,uint len)` must be recoded to fix this.

- Functions: ADD_TO_SET(value,set) and REMOVE_FROM_SET(value,set).

- Add use of `t1 JOIN t2 ON ...` and `t1 JOIN t2 USING ...` Currently, you can only use this syntax with `LEFT JOIN`.

- Many more variables for `show status`. Records reads and updates. Selects on 1 table and selects with joins. Mean number of tables in select. Number of `ORDER BY` and `GROUP BY` queries.

- If you abort mysql in the middle of a query, you should open another connection and kill the old running query. Alternatively, an attempt should be made to detect this in the server.

- Add a handler interface for table information so that you can use it as a system table. This would be a bit slow if you requested information about all tables, but very flexible. SHOW INFO FROM tbl_name for basic table information should be implemented.

- NATURAL JOIN.

- Allow SELECT a FROM crash_me LEFT JOIN crash_me2 USING (a); in this case a is assumed to come from the crash_me table.

- Fix so that ON and USING works with the JOIN join type.

- Oracle-like CONNECT BY PRIOR . . . to search hierarchy structures.

- mysqladmin copy database new-database; requires COPY command to be added to mysqld.

- Processlist should show number of queries/threads.

- SHOW HOSTS for printing information about the hostname cache.

- DELETE and REPLACE options to the UPDATE statement (this will delete rows when one gets a duplicate key error while updating).

- Change the format of DATETIME to store fractions of seconds.

- Add all missing ANSI92 and ODBC 3.0 types.

- Change table names from empty strings to NULL for calculated columns.

- Don't use Item_copy_string on numerical values to avoid number->string->number conversion in case of: SELECT COUNT(*)*(id+0) FROM table_name GROUP BY id

- Make it possible to use the new GNU regexp library instead of the current one (the GNU library should be much faster than the old one).

- Change so that ALTER TABLE doesn't abort clients that execute INSERT DELAYED.

- Fix so that when columns are referenced in an UPDATE clause, they contain the old values from before the update started.

- Add simulation of pread()/pwrite() on Windows to enable concurrent inserts.

- A logfile analyser that could parse out information about which tables are hit most often, how often multi-table joins are executed, etc. It should help users identify areas or table design that could be optimised to execute much more efficient queries.

- Add SUM(DISTINCT).

- Add ANY(), EVERY(), and SOME() group functions. In ANSI SQL these work only on boolean columns, but we can extend these to work on any columns/expressions by applying: value == 0 -> FALSE and value <> 0 -> TRUE.

- Fix that the type for MAX(column) is the same as the column type:

```
mysql> CREATE TABLE t1 (a DATE);
mysql> INSERT INTO t1 VALUES (NOW());
mysql> CREATE TABLE t2 SELECT MAX(a) FROM t1;
mysql> SHOW COLUMNS FROM t2;
```

- Come up with a nice syntax for a statement that will UPDATE the row if it exists and INSERT a new row if the row didn't exist (like REPLACE works with INSERT / DELETE).

1.8.4 Things That Have to Be Done Sometime

- Implement function: get_changed_tables(timeout,table1,table2,...).

- Change reading through tables to use memmap when possible. Now only compressed tables use memmap.

- Add a new privilege Show_priv for SHOW commands.

- Make the automatic timestamp code nicer. Add timestamps to the update log with SET TIMESTAMP=#;.

- Use read/write mutex in some places to get more speed.

- Full foreign key support. One probably wants to implement a procedural language first.

- Simple views (first on one table, later on any expression).

- Automatically close some tables if a table, temporary table, or temporary files gets error 23 (not enough open files).

- When one finds a field=#, change all occurrences of field to #. Now this is only done for some simple cases.

- Change all const expressions with calculated expressions if possible.

- Optimise key = expression. At the moment only key = field or key = constant are optimised.

- Join some of the copy functions for nicer code.

- Change sql_yacc.yy to an inline parser to reduce its size and get better error messages (5 days).

- Change the parser to use only one rule per different number of arguments in function.

- Use of full calculation names in the order part (for ACCESS97).

- MINUS, INTERSECT, and FULL OUTER JOIN. (Currently UNION [in 4.0] and LEFT OUTER JOIN are supported.)

- SQL_OPTION MAX_SELECT_TIME=# to put a time limit on a query.

- Make the update log to a database.

- Negative LIMIT to retrieve data from the end.

- Alarm around client connect/read/write functions.

- Please note the changes to safe_mysqld: according to FSSTND (which Debian tries to follow) PID files should go into /var/run/<progname>.pid and log files into /var/log. It would be nice if you could put the "DATADIR" in the first declaration of "pidfile" and "log", so the placement of these files can be changed with a single statement.

- Allow a client to request logging.

- Add use of zlib() for gzip-ed files to LOAD DATA INFILE.

- Fix sorting and grouping of BLOB columns (partly solved now).

- Stored procedures. Triggers are also being looked at.

- A simple (atomic) update language that can be used to write loops and such in the MySQL server.

- Change to use semaphores when counting threads. One should first implement a semaphore library to MIT-pthreads.

- Don't assign a new AUTO_INCREMENT value when one sets a column to 0. Use NULL instead.

- Add full support for JOIN with parentheses.

- As an alternative for one thread/connection manage a pool of threads to handle the queries.

- Allow one to get more than one lock with GET_LOCK. When doing this, one must also handle the possible deadlocks this change will introduce.

Time is given according to amount of work, not real time.

1.8.5 Things We Have No Plans to Do

- Nothing; we aim toward full ANSI 92/ANSI 99 compliancy.

1.9 How MySQL Compares to Other Databases

Our users have successfully run their own benchmarks against a number of open source and traditional database servers. We are aware of tests against Oracle server, DB/2 server, Microsoft SQL server, and other commercial products. Due to legal reasons we are restricted from publishing some of those benchmarks in our reference manual.

This section includes a comparison with mSQL for historical reasons and with PostgreSQL as it is also an open source database. If you have benchmark results that we can publish, please contact us at *benchmarks@mysql.com.*

For comparative lists of all supported functions and types as well as measured operational limits of many different database systems, see the crash-me web page at http://www.mysql.com/information/crash-me.php.

1.9.1 How MySQL Compares to mSQL

Performance

For a true comparison of speed, consult the growing MySQL benchmark suite. See Section 5.1.4, The MySQL Benchmark Suite.

Because there is no thread creation overhead, a small parser, few features, and simple security, mSQL should be quicker at:

- Tests that perform repeated connects and disconnects, running a very simple query during each connection.

- INSERT operations into very simple tables with few columns and keys.

- CREATE TABLE and DROP TABLE.

- SELECT on something that isn't an index. (A table scan is very easy.)

Because these operations are so simple, it is hard to be better at them when you have a higher startup overhead. After the connection is established, MySQL server should perform much better.

On the other hand, MySQL server is much faster than mSQL (and most other SQL implementations) on the following:

- Complex SELECT operations.

- Retrieving large results (MySQL server has a better, faster, and safer protocol).

- Tables with variable-length strings because MySQL server has more efficient handling and can have indexes on VARCHAR columns.

- Handling tables with many columns.

- Handling tables with large record lengths.

- SELECT with many expressions.

- SELECT on large tables.

- Handling many connections at the same time. MySQL server is fully multi-threaded. Each connection has its own thread, which means that no thread has to wait for another (unless a thread is modifying a table another thread wants to access). In mSQL, once one connection is established, all others must wait until the first has finished, regardless of whether the connection is running a query that is short or long. When the first connection terminates, the next can be served, while all the others wait again, etc.

- Joins. mSQL can become pathologically slow if you change the order of tables in a SELECT. In the benchmark suite, a time more than 15,000 times slower than MySQL server was seen. This is due to mSQL's lack of a join optimiser to order tables in the optimal order. However, if you put the tables in exactly the right order in mSQL2 and the WHERE is simple and uses index columns, the join will be relatively fast! See Section 5.1.4, The MySQL Benchmark Suite.

- ORDER BY and GROUP BY.

- DISTINCT.

- Using TEXT or BLOB columns.

SQL Features

- GROUP BY and HAVING. mSQL does not support GROUP BY at all. MySQL server supports a full GROUP BY with both HAVING and the following functions: COUNT(), AVG(), MIN(), MAX(), SUM(), and STD(). COUNT(*) is optimised to return very quickly if the SELECT retrieves from one table, no other columns are retrieved, and there is no WHERE clause. MIN() and MAX() may take string arguments.

- INSERT and UPDATE with calculations. MySQL server can do calculations in an INSERT or UPDATE. For example:

```
mysql> UPDATE SET x=x*10+y WHERE x<20;
```

- Aliasing. MySQL server has column aliasing.

- Qualifying column names. In MySQL server, if a column name is unique among the tables used in a query, you do not have to use the full qualifier.

- SELECT with functions. MySQL server has many functions (too many to list here; see Section 6.3, Functions for Use in SELECT and WHERE Clauses).

Disk Space Efficiency

That is, how small can you make your tables?

MySQL server has very precise types, so you can create tables that take very little space. An example of a useful MySQL datatype is the `MEDIUMINT` that is 3 bytes long. If you have 100 million records, saving even 1 byte per record is very important.

`mSQL2` has a more limited set of column types, so it is more difficult to get small tables.

Stability

This is harder to judge objectively. For a discussion of MySQL server stability, see Section 1.2.3, How Stable Is MySQL?.

We have no experience with `mSQL` stability, so we cannot say anything about that.

Price

Another important issue is the license. MySQL server has a more flexible license than `mSQL`, and is also less expensive than `mSQL`. Whichever product you choose to use, remember to at least consider paying for a license or email support.

Perl Interfaces

MySQL server has basically the same interfaces to Perl as `mSQL` with some added features.

JDBC (Java)

MySQL server currently has a lot of different JDBC drivers:

- The mm driver: a type 4 JDBC driver by Mark Matthews *mmatthew@ecn.pur-due.edu*. This is released under the LGPL.

- The Resin driver: this is a commercial JDBC driver released under open source. http://www.caucho.com/projects/jdbc-mysql/index.xtp

- The gwe driver: a Java interface by GWE technologies (not supported anymore).

- The jms driver: an improved gwe driver by Xiaokun Kelvin ZHU *X.Zhu@brad.ac.uk* (not supported anymore).

- The twz driver: a type 4 JDBC driver by Terrence W. Zellers *zellert@voicenet.com*. This is commercial but is free for private and educational use (not supported anymore).

The recommended driver is the mm driver. The Resin driver may also be good (at least the benchmarks look good), but we haven't received that much information about this yet.

We know that `mSQL` has a JDBC driver, but we have too little experience with it to compare.

Rate of Development

MySQL server has a small core team of developers, but we are quite used to coding C and C++ very rapidly. Because threads, functions, GROUP BY, and so on are still not implemented in mSQL, it has a lot of catching up to do. To get some perspective on this, you can view the mSQL HISTORY file for the last year and compare it with the News section of the MySQL Reference Manual (see http://www.mysql.com/doc/N/e/News.html). It should be pretty obvious which one has developed most rapidly.

Utility Programs

Both mSQL and MySQL server have many interesting third-party tools. Because it is very easy to port upward (from mSQL to MySQL server), almost all the interesting applications that are available for mSQL are also available for MySQL server.

MySQL server comes with a simple msql2mysql program that fixes differences in spelling between mSQL and MySQL server for the most-used C API functions. For example, it changes instances of msqlConnect() to mysql_connect(). Converting a client program from mSQL to MySQL server usually requires only minor effort.

1.9.1.1 How to convert mSQL tools for MySQL

According to our experience, it doesn't take long to convert tools such as msql-tcl and msqljava that use the mSQL C API so that they work with the MySQL C API.

The conversion procedure is:

1. Run the shell script msql2mysql on the source. This requires the replace program, which is distributed with MySQL server.

2. Compile.

3. Fix all compiler errors.

Differences between the mSQL C API and the MySQL C API are:

*   MySQL server uses a MYSQL structure as a connection type (mSQL uses an int).

*   mysql_connect() takes a pointer to a MYSQL structure as a parameter. It is easy to define one globally or to use malloc() to get one. mysql_connect() also takes two parameters for specifying the user and password. You may set these to NULL, NULL for default use.

*   mysql_error() takes the MYSQL structure as a parameter. Just add the parameter to your old msql_error() code if you are porting old code.

*   MySQL server returns an error number and a text error message for all errors. mSQL returns only a text error message.

*   Some incompatibilities exist as a result of MySQL server supporting multiple connections to the server from the same process.

1.9.1.2 How mSQL and MySQL client/server communications protocols differ

There are enough differences that it is impossible (or at least not easy) to support both.

The most significant ways in which the MySQL protocol differs from the mSQL protocol are listed here:

- A message buffer may contain many result rows.

- The message buffers are dynamically enlarged if the query or the result is bigger than the current buffer, up to a configurable server and client limit.

- All packets are numbered to catch duplicated or missing packets.

- All column values are sent in ASCII. The lengths of columns and rows are sent in packed binary coding (1, 2, or 3 bytes).

- MySQL can read in the result unbuffered (without having to store the full set in the client).

- If a single read/write takes more than 30 seconds, the server closes the connection.

- If a connection is idle for 8 hours, the server closes the connection.

1.9.1.3 How mSQL 2.0 SQL syntax differs from MySQL

Column types.

MySQL server
: Has the following additional types (among others; see Section 6.5.3, CREATE TABLE Syntax):

- ENUM type for one of a set of strings.

- SET type for many of a set of strings.

- BIGINT type for 64-bit integers.

MySQL server also supports the following additional type attributes:

- UNSIGNED option for integer and floating-point columns.

- ZEROFILL option for integer columns.

- AUTO_INCREMENT option for integer columns that are a PRIMARY KEY. See Section 8.4.3.126, mysql_insert_id().

- DEFAULT value for all columns.

mSQL2
: mSQL column types correspond to the MySQL types shown in the following table:

mSQL type	Corresponding MySQL type
CHAR(len)	CHAR(len)
TEXT(len)	TEXT(len). len is the maximal length. And LIKE works.
INT	INT. With many more options!
REAL	REAL. Or FLOAT. Both 4- and 8-byte versions are available.
UINT	INT UNSIGNED
DATE	DATE. Uses ANSI SQL format rather than mSQL's own format.
TIME	TIME
MONEY	DECIMAL(12,2). A fixed-point value with two decimals.

Index creation.

MySQL server

> Indexes may be specified at table creation time with the CREATE TABLE statement.

mSQL

> Indexes must be created after the table has been created, with separate CREATE INDEX statements.

To insert a unique identifier into a table.

MySQL server

> Use AUTO_INCREMENT as a column type specifier. See Section 8.4.3.126, mysql_insert_id().

mSQL

> Create a SEQUENCE on a table and select the _seq column.

To obtain a unique identifier for a row.

MySQL server

> Add a PRIMARY KEY or UNIQUE key to the table and use this. New in Version 3.23.11: If the PRIMARY or UNIQUE key consists of only one column and this is of type integer, one can also refer to it as _rowid.

mSQL

> Use the _rowid column. Observe that _rowid may change over time depending on many factors.

To get the time a column was last modified.

MySQL server

> Add a TIMESTAMP column to the table. This column is automatically set to the current date and time for INSERT or UPDATE statements if you don't give the column a value or if you give it a NULL value.

mSQL

Use the _timestamp column.

NULL **value comparisons.**

MySQL server

MySQL server follows ANSI SQL, and a comparison with NULL is always NULL.

mSQL

In mSQL, NULL = NULL is TRUE. You must change =NULL to IS NULL and <>NULL to IS NOT NULL when porting old code from mSQL to MySQL server.

String comparisons.

MySQL server

Normally, string comparisons are performed in case-independent fashion with the sort order determined by the current character set (ISO-8859-1 Latin1 by default). If you don't like this, declare your columns with the BINARY attribute, which causes comparisons to be done according to the ASCII order used on the MySQL server host.

mSQL

All string comparisons are performed in case-sensitive fashion with sorting in ASCII order.

Case-insensitive searching.

MySQL server

LIKE is a case-insensitive or case-sensitive operator, depending on the columns involved. If possible, MySQL uses indexes if the LIKE argument doesn't start with a wildcard character.

mSQL

Use CLIKE.

Handling of trailing spaces.

MySQL server

Strips all spaces at the end of CHAR and VARCHAR columns. Use a TEXT column if this behavior is not desired.

mSQL

Retains trailing space.

WHERE **clauses.**

MySQL server

MySQL correctly prioritises everything (AND is evaluated before OR). To get mSQL behavior in MySQL server, use parentheses (as shown in an example later in this section).

mSQL

> Evaluates everything from left to right. This means that some logical calculations
> with more than three arguments cannot be expressed in any way. It also means you
> must change some queries when you upgrade to MySQL server. You do this easily
> by adding parentheses. Suppose you have the following mSQL query:

```
mysql> SELECT * FROM table WHERE a=1 AND b=2 OR a=3 AND b=4;
```

> To make MySQL server evaluate this the way that mSQL would, you must add paren-
> theses:

```
mysql> SELECT * FROM table WHERE (a=1 AND (b=2 OR (a=3 AND (b=4))));
```

Access control.

MySQL server

> Has tables to store grant (permission) options per user, host, and database. See Sec-
> tion 4.2.6, How the Privilege System Works.

mSQL

> Has a file mSQL.acl in which you can grant read/write privileges for users.

1.9.2 How MySQL Compares to PostgreSQL

When reading the following, please note that both products are continually evolving. We
at MySQL AB and the PostgreSQL developers are both working on making our respective databases as good as possible, so we are both a serious alternative to any commercial
database.

The following comparison is made by us at MySQL AB. We have tried to be as accurate
and fair as possible, but although we know MySQL server thoroughly, we don't have a
full knowledge of all PostgreSQL features, so we may have got some things wrong. We
will, however, correct these when they come to our attention.

We would first like to note that PostgreSQL and MySQL server are both widely used
products, but with different design goals, even if we are both striving toward ANSI SQL
compliancy. This means that for some applications MySQL server is more suited, while
for others PostgreSQL is more suited. When choosing which database to use, you should
first check if the database's feature set satisfies your application. If you need raw speed,
MySQL server is probably your best choice. If you need some of the extra features that
only PostgreSQL can offer, you should use PostgreSQL.

1.9.2.1 MySQL and PostgreSQL development strategies

When adding things to MySQL server we take pride to do an optimal, definite solution.
The code should be so good that we shouldn't have any need to change it in the foresee-
able future. We also do not like to sacrifice speed for features but instead will do our

utmost to find a solution that will give maximal throughput. This means that development will take a little longer, but the end result will be well worth this. This kind of development is only possible because all server code are checked by one of a few (currently two) persons before it's included in the MySQL server.

We at MySQL AB believe in frequent releases to be able to push out new features quickly to our users. Because of this we do a new small release about every three weeks, and a major branch every year. All releases are thoroughly tested with our testing tools on a lot of different platforms.

PostgreSQL is based on a kernel with lots of contributors. In this setup it makes sense to prioritise adding a lot of new features, instead of implementing them optimally, because one can always optimise things later if there arises a need for this.

Another big difference between MySQL server and PostgreSQL is that nearly all of the code in the MySQL server is coded by developers that are employed by MySQL AB and are still working on the server code. The exceptions are the transaction engines and the regexp library.

This is in sharp contrast to the PostgreSQL code, the majority of which is coded by a big group of people with different backgrounds. It was only recently that the PostgreSQL developers announced that their current developer group had finally had time to take a look at all the code in the current PostgreSQL release.

Both of the aforementioned development methods have their own merits and drawbacks. We here at MySQL AB think, of course, that our model is better because our model gives better code consistency, more optimal and reusable code, and in our opinion, fewer bugs. Because we are the authors of the MySQL server code, we are better able to coordinate new features and releases.

1.9.2.2 Featurewise comparison of MySQL and PostgreSQL

On the crash-me page (http://www.mysql.com/information/crash-me.php) you can find a list of those database constructs and limits that one can detect automatically with a program. Note, however, that a lot of the numerical limits may be changed with startup options for their respective databases. This web page is, however, extremely useful when you want to ensure that your applications work with many different databases or when you want to convert your application from one database to another.

MySQL server offers the following advantages over PostgreSQL:

- MySQL Server is generally much faster than PostgreSQL. MySQL 4.0.1 also has a query cache that can boost up the query speed for mostly-read-only sites many times.

- MySQL has a much larger user base than PostgreSQL. Therefore, the code is tested more and has historically proven more stable than PostgreSQL. MySQL server is used more in production environments than PostgreSQL, mostly thanks to the fact that MySQL AB, formerly TCX DataKonsult AB, has provided top-quality commercial support for MySQL server from the day it was released, whereas until recently PostgreSQL was unsupported.

- MySQL server works better on Windows than PostgreSQL does. MySQL server runs as a native Windows application (a service on NT/2000/XP), while PostgreSQL is run under the Cygwin emulation. We have heard that PostgreSQL is not yet that stable on Windows but we haven't been able to verify this ourselves.

- MySQL has more APIs to other languages and is supported by more existing programs than PostgreSQL. See Appendix B.

- MySQL server works on 24/7 heavy-duty systems. In most circumstances you never have to run any cleanups on MySQL server. PostgreSQL doesn't yet support 24/7 systems because you have to run VACUUM once in a while to reclaim space from UPDATE and DELETE commands and to perform statistics analyses that are critical to get good performance with PostgreSQL. VACUUM is also needed after adding a lot of new rows to a table. On a busy system with lots of changes, VACUUM must be run very frequently, in the worst cases even many times a day. During the VACUUM run, which may take hours if the database is big, the database is, from a production standpoint, practically dead. Please note: in PostgreSQL version 7.2, basic vacuuming no longer locks tables, thus allowing normal user access during the vacuum. A new VACUUM FULL command does old-style vacuum by locking the table and shrinking the on-disk copy of the table.

- MySQL replication has been thoroughly tested, and is used by sites like:

  — Yahoo Finance (http://finance.yahoo.com/)

  — Mobile.de (http://www.mobile.de/)

  — Slashdot (http://www.slashdot.org/)

- Included in the MySQL distribution are two different testing suites, mysql-test-run and crash-me (http://www.mysql.com/information/crash-me.php), as well as a benchmark suite. The test system is actively updated with code to test each new feature and almost all reproduceable bugs that have come to our attention. We test MySQL server with these on a lot of platforms before every release. These tests are more sophisticated than anything we have seen from PostgreSQL, and they ensure that the MySQL server is kept to a high standard.

- There are far more books in print about MySQL server than about PostgreSQL. O'Reilly, SAMS, Que, and New Riders are all major publishers with books about MySQL. All MySQL features are also documented in the MySQL online manual because when a new feature is implemented, the MySQL developers are required to document it before it's included in the source.

- MySQL server supports more of the standard ODBC functions than PostgreSQL.

- MySQL server has a much more sophisticated ALTER TABLE.

- MySQL server has support for tables without transactions for applications that need all the speed they can get. The tables may be memory-based, HEAP tables or disk based MyISAM. See Chapter 7.

- MySQL server has support for two different table handlers that support transactions, InnoDB, and BerkeleyDB. Because every transaction engine performs differently under different conditions, this gives the application writer more options to find an optimal solution for his or her setup, if need be per individual table. See Chapter 7.

- MERGE tables gives you a unique way to instantly make a view over a set of identical tables and use these as one. This is perfect for systems where you have log files that you order, for example, by month. See Section 7.2, MERGE Tables.

- The option to compress read-only tables, but still have direct access to the rows in the table, gives you better performance by minimising disk reads. This is very useful when you are archiving things. See Section 4.7.4, myisampack, the MySQL Compressed Read-Only Table Generator.

- MySQL server has internal support for full-text search. See Section 6.8, MySQL Full-Text Search.

- You can access many databases from the same connection (depending, of course, on your privileges).

- MySQL server is coded from the start to be multi-threaded, while PostgreSQL uses processes. Context switching and access to common storage areas is much faster between threads than between separate processes. This gives MySQL server a big speed advantage in multi-user applications and also makes it easier for MySQL server to take full advantage of symmetric multiprocessor (SMP) systems.

- MySQL server has a much more sophisticated privilege system than PostgreSQL. While PostgreSQL only supports INSERT, SELECT, and UPDATE/DELETE grants per user on a database or a table, MySQL server allows you to define a full set of different privileges on the database, table, and column level. MySQL server also allows you to specify the privilege on host and user combinations. See Section 4.3.1, GRANT and REVOKE Syntax.

- MySQL server supports a compressed client/server protocol which improves performance over slow links.

- MySQL server employs a "table handler" concept, and is the only relational database we know of built around this concept. This allows different low-level table types to be called from the SQL engine, and each table type can be optimised for different performance characteristics.

- All MySQL table types (except InnoDB) are implemented as files (one table per file), which makes it really easy to back up, move, delete, and even symlink databases and tables, even when the server is down.

- Tools to repair and optimise MyISAM tables (the most common MySQL table type). A repair tool is only needed when a physical corruption of a data file happens, usually from a hardware failure. It allows a majority of the data to be recovered.

- Upgrading MySQL server is painless. When you are upgrading MySQL Server, you don't need to dump/restore your data, as you have to do with most PostgreSQL upgrades.

Drawbacks with MySQL server compared to PostgreSQL:

- The transaction support in MySQL server is not yet as well tested as PostgreSQL's system.

- Because MySQL server uses threads, which are not yet flawless on many OSes, one must either use binaries from http://www.mysql.com/downloads/, or carefully follow our instructions on http://www.mysql.com/doc/I/n/Installing_source.html to get an optimal binary that works in all cases.

- Table locking, as used by the non-transactional MyISAM tables, is in many cases faster than page locks, row locks, or versioning. The drawback, however, is that if one doesn't take into account how table locks work, a single long-running query can block a table for updates for a long time. This can usually be avoided when designing the application. If not, one can always switch the trouble table to use one of the transactional table types. See Section 5.3.2, Table Locking Issues.

- With UDF (user-defined functions) one can extend MySQL server with both normal SQL functions and aggregates, but this is not yet as easy or as flexible as in PostgreSQL. See Section 9.2, Adding New Functions to MySQL.

- Updates that run over multiple tables are harder to do in MySQL server. This will, however, be fixed in MySQL server 4.0.2 with multi-table UPDATE and in MySQL server 4.1 with subselects. In MySQL server 4.0 one can use multi-table deletes to delete from many tables at the same time. See Section 6.4.6, DELETE Syntax.

PostgreSQL currently offers the following advantages over MySQL server:

Note that because we know the MySQL road map, we have included in the following table the version when MySQL server should support this feature. Unfortunately we couldn't do this for previous comparisons, because we don't know the PostgreSQL roadmap.

Feature	MySQL version
Subselects	4.1
Foreign keys	4.1
Views	5.0
Stored procedures	5.0
Triggers	5.0
Unions	4.0
Full join	4.1
Constraints	4.1 or 5.0
Cursors	4.1 or 5.0
R-trees	4.1 (for MyISAM tables)
Inherited tables	Not planned
Extensible type system	Not planned

Other reasons someone may consider using PostgreSQL:

- Standard usage in PostgreSQL is closer to ANSI SQL in some cases.

- One can speed up PostgreSQL by coding things as stored procedures.

- For geographical data, R-trees make PostgreSQL better than MySQL server. (note: MySQL version 4.1 will have R-trees for MyISAM tables).

- The PostgreSQL optimiser can do some optimisation that the current MySQL optimiser can't do. Most notable is doing joins when you don't have the proper keys in place and doing a join where you are using different keys combined with OR. The MySQL benchmark suite at http://www.mysql.com/information/benchmarks.html shows you what kind of constructs you should watch out for when using different databases.

- PostgreSQL has a bigger team of developers that contribute to the server.

Drawbacks with PostgreSQL compared to MySQL server:

- VACUUM makes PostgreSQL hard to use in a 24/7 environment.

- Only transactional tables.

- Much slower INSERT, DELETE, and UPDATE.

For a complete list of drawbacks, you should also examine the first table in this section.

1.9.2.3 Benchmarking MySQL and PostgreSQL

The only open source benchmark that we know of that can be used to benchmark MySQL server and PostgreSQL (and other databases) is our own. It can be found at http://www.mysql.com/information/benchmarks.html.

We have many times asked the PostgreSQL developers and some PostgreSQL users to help us extend this benchmark to make it the definitive benchmark for databases, but unfortunately we haven't gotten any feedback for this.

We, the MySQL developers, have, because of this, spent a lot of hours to get maximum performance from PostgreSQL for the benchmarks, but because we don't know PostgreSQL intimately, we are sure that there are things that we have missed. We have on the benchmark page documented exactly how we did run the benchmark so that it should be easy for anyone to repeat and verify our results.

The benchmarks are usually run with and without the `--fast` option. When run with `--fast` we are trying to use every trick the server can do to get the code to execute as fast as possible. The idea is that the normal run should show how the server would work in a default setup and the `--fast` run shows how the server would do if the application developer would use extensions in the server to make his application run faster.

When running with PostgreSQL and `--fast` we do a `VACUUM` after every major table `UPDATE` and `DROP TABLE` to make the database in perfect shape for the following `SELECT`s. The time for `VACUUM` is measured separately.

When running with PostgreSQL 7.1.1 we could, however, not run with `--fast` because during the `INSERT` test, the postmaster (the PostgreSQL deamon) died and the database was so corrupted that it was impossible to restart postmaster. After this happened twice, we decided to postpone the `--fast` test until the next PostgreSQL release. The details about the machine we run the benchmark on can be found on the benchmark page.

Before going to the other benchmarks we know of, we would like to give some background on benchmarks.

It's very easy to write a test that shows **any** database to be the best database in the world, by just restricting the test to something the database is very good at and not testing anything that the database is not good at. If one, after doing this, summarises the result as a single figure, things are even easier.

This would be like us measuring the speed of MySQL server compared to PostgreSQL by looking at the summary time of the MySQL benchmarks on our web page. Based on this MySQL server would be more than 40 times faster than PostgreSQL, something that is, of course, not true. We could make things even worse by just taking the test where PostgreSQL performs worst and claim that MySQL server is more than 2000 times faster than PostgreSQL.

The case is that MySQL does a lot of optimisations that PostgreSQL doesn't do. This is, of course, also true the other way around. An SQL optimiser is a very complex thing, and a company could spend years just making the optimiser faster and faster.

When looking at the benchmark results you should look for things that you do in your application and just use these results to decide which database would be best suited for your application. The benchmark results also show things a particular database is not good at and should give you a notion about things to avoid and what you may have to do in other ways.

We know of two benchmark tests that claim that PostgreSQL performs better than MySQL server. These both where multi-user tests, a test that we here at MySQL AB haven't had time to write and include in the benchmark suite, mainly because it's a big task to do this in a manner that is fair to all databases.

One is the benchmark paid for by Great Bridge, the company that for 16 months attempted to build a business based on PostgreSQL but now has ceased operations. This is probably the worst benchmark we have ever seen anyone conduct. This was not only tuned to only test what PostgreSQL is absolutely best at, but it was also totally unfair to every other database involved in the test.

Note: We know that even some of the main PostgreSQL developers did not like the way Great Bridge conducted the benchmark, so we don't blame the PostgreSQL team for the way the benchmark was done.

This benchmark has been condemned in a lot of postings and newsgroups, so here we will just briefly repeat some things that were wrong with it.

- The tests were run with an expensive commercial tool that makes it impossible for an open source company like us to verify the benchmarks, or even check how the benchmarks were really done. The tool is not even a true benchmark tool, but an application/setup testing tool. To refer to this as a "standard" benchmark tool is to stretch the truth a long way.

- Great Bridge admitted that they had optimised the PostgreSQL database (with VAC-UUM before the test) and tuned the startup for the tests, something they hadn't done for any of the other databases involved. They say "This process optimises indexes and frees up disk space a bit. The optimised indexes boost performance by some margin." Our benchmarks clearly indicate that the difference in running a lot of selects on a database with and without VACUUM can easily differ by a factor of 10.

- The test results were also strange. The AS3AP test documentation mentions that the test does "selections, simple joins, projections, aggregates, one-tuple updates, and bulk updates."

  PostgreSQL is good at doing SELECTs and JOINs (especially after a VACUUM), but doesn't perform as well on INSERTs or UPDATEs. The benchmarks seem to indicate that only SELECTs were done (or very few updates). This could easily explain the good results for PostgreSQL in this test. The bad results for MySQL will be obvious a bit down in this document.

- They did run the so-called benchmark from a Windows machine against a Linux machine over ODBC, a setup that no normal database user would ever do when running a heavy multi-user application. This tested more the ODBC driver and the Windows protocol used between the clients than the database itself.

- When running the database against Oracle and MS-SQL (Great Bridge has indirectly indicated the databases they used in the test), they didn't use the native protocol but instead ODBC. Anyone that has ever used Oracle knows that all real applications use the native interface instead of ODBC. Doing a test through ODBC and claiming that the results had anything to do with using the database in a real-world situation can't be regarded as fair. They should have done two tests with and without ODBC to provide the right facts (after having gotten experts to tune all involved databases, of course).

- They refer to the TPC-C tests, but they don't mention anywhere that the test they did was not a true TPC-C test and they were not even allowed to call it a TPC-C test. A TPC-C test can only be conducted by the rules approved by the TPC Council (http://www.tpc.org/). Great Bridge didn't do that. By doing this they have both violated the TPC trademark and miscredited their own benchmarks. The rules set by the TPC Council are very strict to ensure that no one can produce false results or make unprovable statements. Apparently Great Bridge wasn't interested in doing this.

- After the first test, we contacted Great Bridge and mentioned to them some of the obvious mistakes they had done with MySQL server:

  — Running with a debug version of our ODBC driver

  — Running on a Linux system that wasn't optimised for threads

  — Using an old MySQL version when there was a recommended newer one available

  — Not starting MySQL server with the right options for heavy multi-user use (the default installation of MySQL server is tuned for minimal resource use)

  Great Bridge did run a new test, with our optimised ODBC driver and with better startup options for MySQL server, but refused to either use our updated glibc library or our standard binary (used by 80% of our users), which was statically linked with a fixed glibc library.

  According to what we know, Great Bridge did nothing to ensure that the other databases were set up correctly to run well in their test environment. We are sure, however, that they didn't contact Oracle or Microsoft to ask for their advice in this matter. ;)

- The benchmark was paid for by Great Bridge, and they decided to publish only partial, chosen results (instead of publishing it all).

Tim Perdue, a long-time PostgreSQL fan and a reluctant MySQL user, published a comparison on PHPbuilder (http://www.phpbuilder.com/columns/tim20001112.php3).

When we became aware of the comparison, we phoned Tim Perdue about this because there were a lot of strange things in his results. For example, he claimed that MySQL server had a problem with five users in his tests, when we know that there are users with similar machines as his that are using MySQL server with 2000 simultaneous connections doing 400 queries per second. (In this case the limit was the web bandwidth, not the database.)

It sounded like he was using a Linux kernel that either had some problems with many threads, such as kernels before 2.4, which had a problem with many threads on multi-CPU machines. We have documented in this manual how to fix this and Tim should be aware of this problem.

The other possible problem could have been an old glibc library and that Tim didn't use a MySQL binary from our site, which is linked with a corrected glibc library, but had compiled a version of his own. In any of these cases, the symptom would have been exactly what Tim had measured.

We asked Tim if we could get access to his data so that we could repeat the benchmark and if he could check the MySQL version on the machine to find out what was wrong and he promised to come back to us about this. He has not done that yet.

Because of this we can't put any trust in this benchmark either. :(

Over time things also change and the preceding benchmarks are not that relevant anymore. MySQL server now has a couple of different table handlers with different speed/concurrency tradeoffs. See Chapter 7. It would be interesting to see how the above tests would run with the different transactional table types in MySQL server. PostgreSQL has, of course, also got new features since the test was made. As these tests are not publicly available there is no way for us to know how the database would perform in the same tests today.

Conclusion:

The only benchmarks that exist today that anyone can download and run against MySQL server and PostgreSQL are the MySQL benchmarks. We here at MySQL AB believe that open source databases should be tested with open source tools! This is the only way to ensure that no one does tests that nobody can reproduce and use this to claim that one database is better than another. Without knowing all the facts it's impossible to answer the claims of the tester.

The thing we find strange is that every test we have seen about PostgreSQL, that is impossible to reproduce, claims that PostgreSQL is better in most cases while our tests, which anyone can reproduce, clearly show otherwise. With this we don't want to say that PostgreSQL isn't good at many things (it is!) or that it isn't faster than MySQL server under certain conditions. We would just like to see a fair test where PostgreSQL performs very well, so that we could get some friendly competition going!

For more information about our benchmark suite, see Section 5.1.4, The MySQL Benchmark Suite.

We are working on an even better benchmark suite, including multi-user tests, and a better documentation of what the individual tests really do and how to add more tests to the suite.

2

MySQL Installation

This chapter describes how to obtain and install MySQL:

- For a list of sites from which you can obtain MySQL, see Section 2.2.1, How to Get MySQL.

- To see which platforms are supported, see Section 2.2.2, Operating Systems Supported by MySQL. Please note that not all supported systems are equally good for running MySQL on them. On some it is much more robust and efficient than others—see Section 2.2.2, Operating Systems Supported by MySQL for details.

- Several versions of MySQL are available in both binary and source distributions. We also provide public access to our current source tree for those who want to see our most recent developments and help us test new code. To determine which version and type of distribution you should use, see Section 2.2.3, Which MySQL Version to Use. When in doubt, use the binary distribution.

- Installation instructions for binary and source distributions are described in Section 2.2.7, Installing a MySQL Binary Distribution, and Section 2.3, Installing a MySQL Source Distribution. Each set of instructions includes a section on system-specific problems you may run into.

- For post-installation procedures, see Section 2.4, Post-Installation Setup and Testing. These procedures apply whether you install MySQL using a binary or source distribution.

2.1 Quick Standard Installation of MySQL

2.1.1 Installing MySQL on Linux

The recommended way to install MySQL on Linux is by using an RPM file. The MySQL RPMs are currently being built on a RedHat Version 6.2 system but should work on other versions of Linux that support rpm and use glibc.

If you have problems with an RPM file, for example, if you receive the error "Sorry, the host 'xxxx' could not be looked up"—see Section 2.6.1.1, Linux notes for binary distributions.

The RPM files you may want to use are:

- MySQL-VERSION.i386.rpm

  The MySQL server. You will need this unless you only want to connect to a MySQL server running on another machine.

- MySQL-client-VERSION.i386.rpm

  The standard MySQL client programs. You probably always want to install this package.

- MySQL-bench-VERSION.i386.rpm

  Tests and benchmarks. Requires Perl and msql-mysql-modules RPMs.

- MySQL-devel-VERSION.i386.rpm

  Libraries and include files needed if you want to compile other MySQL clients, such as the Perl modules.

- MySQL-VERSION.src.rpm

  This contains the source code for all of the previous packages. It can also be used to try to build RPMs for other architectures (for example, Alpha or SPARC).

To see all files in an RPM package, run:

```
shell> rpm -qpl MySQL-VERSION.i386.rpm
```

To perform a standard minimal installation, run:

```
shell> rpm -i MySQL-VERSION.i386.rpm MySQL-client-VERSION.i386.rpm
```

To install just the client package, run:

```
shell> rpm -i MySQL-client-VERSION.i386.rpm
```

The RPM places data in /var/lib/mysql. The RPM also creates the appropriate entries in /etc/rc.d/ to start the server automatically at boot time. (This means that if you have performed a previous installation, you may want to make a copy of your previously installed MySQL startup file if you made any changes to it, so you don't lose your changes.)

After installing the RPM file(s), the `mysqld` daemon should be running and you should now be able to start using MySQL. See Section 2.4, Post-Installation Setup and Testing.

If something goes wrong, you can find more information in the binary installation chapter. See Section 2.2.7, Installing a MySQL Binary Distribution.

2.1.2 Installing MySQL on Windows

The MySQL server for Windows is available in two distribution types:

1. The binary distribution contains a setup program which installs everything you need so that you can start the server immediately.

2. The source distribution contains all the code and support files for building the executables using the VC++ 6.0 compiler. See Section 2.3.7, Windows Source Distribution.

Generally speaking, you should use the binary distribution.

You will need the following:

*   A 32-bit Windows Operating System such as 9x, Me, NT, 2000, or XP. The NT family (NT, Windows 2000 and XP) permits running the MySQL server as a service. See Section 2.6.2.2, Starting MySQL on Windows NT, 2000, or XP.

    If you want to use tables bigger than 4G, you should install MySQL on an NTFS or newer filesystem. Don't forget to use `MAX_ROWS` and `AVG_ROW_LENGTH` when you create the table. See Section 6.5.3, `CREATE TABLE` Syntax.

*   TCP/IP protocol support.

*   A copy of the MySQL binary or distribution for Windows, which can be downloaded from http://www.mysql.com/downloads/.

    Note: The distribution files are supplied with a zipped format and we recommend the use of an adequate FTP client with resume feature to avoid corruption of files during the download process.

*   A `ZIP` program to unpack the distribution file.

*   Enough space on the hard drive to unpack, install, and create the databases in accorandance with your requirements.

*   If you plan to connect to the MySQL server via `ODBC`, you will also need the `MyODBC` driver. See Section 8.3, MySQL ODBC Support.

2.1.2.1 Installing the binaries

1. If you are working on an NT/2000/XP server, logon as a user with with administrator privileges.

2. If you are doing an upgrade of an earlier MySQL installation, it is necessary to stop the server. If you are running the server as a service, use:

    ```
    C:\> NET STOP MySQL
    ```

    Otherwise, use:

    ```
    C:\mysql\bin> mysqladmin -u root shutdown
    ```

3. On NT/2000/XP machines, if you want to change the server executable (e.g., -max or -nt), it is also necessary to remove the service:

    ```
    C:\mysql\bin> mysqld-max-nt --remove
    ```

4. Unzip the distribution file to a temporary directory.

5. Run the setup.exe file to begin the installation process. If you want to install into another directory than the default c:\mysql, use the Browse button to specify your preferred directory.

6. Finish the install process.

2.1.2.2 Preparing the windows MySQL environment

Starting with MySQL 3.23.38, the Windows distribution includes both the normal and the **MySQL-Max** server binaries. Here is a list of the different MySQL servers you can use:

Binary	Description
mysqld	Compiled with full debugging and automatic memory allocation checking, symbolic links, InnoDB, and BDB tables.
mysqld-opt	Optimised binary with no support for transactional tables.
mysqld-nt	Optimised binary for NT/2000/XP with support for named pipes. You can run this version on Windows 9x/Me, but in this case no named pipes are created and you must have TCP/IP installed.
mysqld-max	Optimised binary with support for symbolic links, InnoDB and BDB tables.
mysqld-max-nt	Like mysqld-max, but compiled with support for named pipes.

Starting from 3.23.50, named pipes are only enabled if one starts mysqld with --enable-named-pipe.

All of the preceding binaries are optimised for the Pentium Pro processor but should work on any Intel processor >= i386.

You will need to use an option file to specify your MySQL configuration under the following circumstances:

- The installation or data directories are different from the default locations (c:\mysql and c:\mysql\data).

- You want to use one of these servers:

   — mysqld.exe

   — mysqld-max.exe

   — mysqld-max-nt.exe

- You need to tune the server settings.

Normally you can use the WinMySQLAdmin tool to edit the option file my.ini. In this case you don't have to worry about the following section.

There are two option files with the same function: my.cnf and my.ini. However, to avoid confusion, it's best if you use only of one them. Both files are plain text. The my.cnf file, if used, should be created in the root directory of the C drive. The my.ini file, if used, should be created in the Windows system directory. (This directory is typically something like C:\WINDOWS or C:\WINNT. You can determine its exact location from the value of the windir environment variable.) MySQL looks first for the my.ini file, then for the my.cnf file.

If your PC uses a boot loader where the C drive isn't the boot drive, your only option is to use the my.ini file. Also note that if you use the WinMySQLAdmin tool, it uses only the my.ini file. The \mysql\bin directory contains a help file with instructions for using this tool.

Using notepad.exe, create the option file and edit the [mysqld] section to specify values for the basedir and datadir parameters:

```
[mysqld]
# set basedir to installation path, e.g., c:/mysql
basedir=the_install_path
# set datadir to location of data directory,
# e.g., c:/mysql/data or d:/mydata/data
datadir=the_data_path
```

Note that Windows pathnames should be specified in option files using forward slashes rather than backslashes. If you do use backslashes, you must double them.

If you would like to use a data directory different from the default of c:\mysql\data, you must copy the entire contents of the c:\mysql\data directory to the new location.

If you want to use the InnoDB transactional tables, you need to manually create two new directories to hold the InnoDB data and log files—e.g., c:\ibdata and c:\iblogs. You will also need to add some extra lines to the option file. See Section 7.5.2, InnoDB Startup Options.

If you don't want to use InnoDB tables, add the skip-innodb option to the option file.

Now you are ready to test starting the server.

2.1.2.3 Starting the server for the first time

Testing from a DOS command prompt is the best thing to do because the server displays status messages that appear in the DOS window. If something is wrong with your configuration, these messages will make it easier for you to identify and fix any problems.

Make sure you are in the directory where the server is located, then enter this command:

```
C:\mysql\bin> mysqld-max --standalone
```

You should see the following messages as the server starts up:

```
InnoDB: The first specified data file c:\ibdata\ibdata1 did not exist:
InnoDB: a new database to be created!
InnoDB: Setting file c:\ibdata\ibdata1 size to 209715200
InnoDB: Database physically writes the file full: wait...
InnoDB: Log file c:\iblogs\ib_logfile0 did not exist: new to be created
InnoDB: Setting log file c:\iblogs\ib_logfile0 size to 31457280
InnoDB: Log file c:\iblogs\ib_logfile1 did not exist: new to be created
InnoDB: Setting log file c:\iblogs\ib_logfile1 size to 31457280
InnoDB: Log file c:\iblogs\ib_logfile2 did not exist: new to be created
InnoDB: Setting log file c:\iblogs\ib_logfile2 size to 31457280
InnoDB: Doublewrite buffer not found: creating new
InnoDB: Doublewrite buffer created
InnoDB: creating foreign key constraint system tables
InnoDB: foreign key constraint system tables created
011024 10:58:25  InnoDB: Started
```

For further information about running MySQL on Windows, see Section 2.6.2, Windows Notes.

2.2 General Installation Issues

2.2.1 How to Get MySQL

Check the MySQL homepage (http://www.mysql.com/) for information about the current version and for downloading instructions.

Our main download mirror is located at:

http://mirrors.sunsite.dk/mysql/

If you are interested in becoming a MySQL mirror site, you may anonymously rsync with: rsync://sunsite.dk/ftp/mirrors/mysql/. Please send email to *webmaster@mysql.com* notifying us of your mirror to be added to the following list.

If you have problems downloading from our main site, try using one of the following mirrors.

Please report bad or out-of-date mirrors to *webmaster@mysql.com*.

Europe:

- Armenia [AbideWeb Technologies] @ WWW (http://mysql.abideweb.com/) FTP (ftp://mysql.abideweb.com/mirrors/MySQL/)

- Austria [Univ. of Technology/Vienna] @ WWW (http://gd.tuwien.ac.at/db/mysql/) FTP (ftp://gd.tuwien.ac.at/db/mysql/)

- Belgium [BELNET] @ WWW (http://mysql.belnet.be/) FTP (ftp://ftp.belnet.be/mirror/ftp.mysql.com/pub/mysql/)

- Bulgaria [online.bg/Sofia] @ WWW (http://mysql.online.bg/) FTP (ftp://mysql.online.bg/)

- Czech Republic [Masaryk University in Brno] @ WWW (http://mysql.linux.cz/) FTP (ftp://ftp.fi.muni.cz/pub/mysql/)

- Czech Republic [www.gin.cz] @ WWW (http://mysql.gin.cz/) FTP (ftp://ftp.gin.cz/pub/MIRRORS/www.mysql.com/)

- Czech Republic [www.sopik.cz] @ WWW (http://www.mysql.cz/)

- Denmark [Borsen] @ WWW (http://mysql.borsen.dk/)

- Denmark [SunSITE] @ WWW (http://mirrors.sunsite.dk/mysql/) FTP (ftp://sunsite.dk/mirrors/mysql/)

- Estonia [OK Interactive] @ WWW (http://mysql.mirror.ok.ee/)

- Finland [KPNQwest] @ WWW (http://mysql.kpnqwest.fi/)

- Finland [tonnikala.net] @ WWW (http://mysql.tonnikala.org/)

- France [free.fr] @ WWW (http://mysql-mirror.free.fr/) FTP (ftp://ftp.free.fr/pub/MySQL/)

- France [Netsample] @ WWW (http://www.mysql.netsample.com/)

- France [Omegatomic] @ WWW (http://mysql.omegatomic.com/)

- Germany [GWDG] @ WWW (http://ftp.gwdg.de/pub/misc/mysql/) FTP (ftp://ftp.gwdg.de/pub/misc/mysql/)

- Germany [SunSITE Central Europe] @ WWW (http://sunsite.informatik.rwth-aachen.de/mysql/) FTP (ftp://sunsite.informatik.rwth-aachen.de/pub/mirror/www.mysql.com/)

- Germany [Tiscali] @ WWW (http://filepile.tiscali.de/mirror/mysql/) FTP (ftp://filepile.tiscali.de/mirror/mysql/)

- Germany [Wolfenbuettel] @ WWW (http://www.fh-wolfenbuettel.de/ftp/pub/database/mysql/) FTP (ftp://ftp.fh-wolfenbuettel.de/pub/database/mysql/)

- Greece [NTUA, Athens] @ WWW (http://www.ntua.gr/mysql/) FTP (ftp://ftp.ntua.gr/pub/databases/mysql/)

- Hungary [stop.hu] @ WWW (http://mysql.mirror.stop.hu/)

- Hungary [TiszaneT] @ WWW (http://mysql.tiszanet.hu/) FTP (ftp://mysql.tiszanet.hu/pub/mirrors/mysql/)

- Hungary [Xenia] @ WWW (http://mysql.sote.hu/) FTP (ftp://xenia.sote.hu/pub/mirrors/www.mysql.com/)

- Iceland [GM] @ WWW (http://mysql.gm.is/) FTP (ftp://ftp.gm.is/pub/mysql/)

- Ireland [Esat Net] @ WWW (http://ftp.esat.net/mirrors/download.sourceforge.net/pub/mirrors/mysql/) FTP (ftp://ftp.esat.net/mirrors/download.sourceforge.net/pub/mirrors/mysql/)

- Ireland [MD NMTB Media] @ WWW (http://mirrors.nmtbmedia.com/mysql/)

- Italy [feelinglinux.com] @ WWW (http://mysql.feelinglinux.com/)

- Italy [Teta Srl] @ WWW (http://www.teta.it/mysql/)

- Italy [tzone.it] @ WWW (http://mysql.tzone.it/)

- Latvia [linux.lv] @ FTP (ftp://ftp.linux.lv/pub/software/mysql/)

- Netherlands [OMS-Net] @ WWW (http://mysql.oms-net.nl/)

- Netherlands [ProServe] @ WWW (http://mysql.proserve.nl/)

- Netherlands [WideXS BV] @ WWW (http://mysql.mirror.widexs.nl/) FTP (ftp://mirror.widexs.nl/pub/mysql/)

- Norway [Brainpeddlers AS] @ WWW (http://mysql.brainpeddlers.com/)

- Poland [ncservice.com/Gdansk] @ WWW (http://mysql.service.net.pl/)

- Poland [SunSITE] @ WWW (http://sunsite.icm.edu.pl/mysql/) FTP (ftp://sunsite.icm.edu.pl/pub/unix/mysql/)

- Portugal [Instituto Supertior Técnico] @ WWW (http://darkstar.ist.utl.pt/mysql/) FTP (ftp://darkstar.ist.utl.pt/pub/mysql/)

- Portugal [Netc] @ WWW (http://ftp.netc.pt/pub/mysql/) FTP (ftp://ftp.netc.pt/pub/mysql/)

- Portugal [Netvisão] @ WWW (http://mysql.netvisao.pt/) FTP (ftp://mirrors2.netvisao.pt/pub/mysql/)

- Romania [roedu.net/Bucharest] @ FTP (ftp://ftp.roedu.net/pub/mirrors/ftp.mysql.com/)

- Russia [DirectNet] @ WWW (http://mysql.directnet.ru/) FTP (ftp://ftp.dn.ru/pub/MySQL/)

- Russia [Scientific Center/Chernogolovka] @ FTP (ftp://ftp.chg.ru/pub/databases/mysql/)

- Slovenia [ARNES] @ WWW (http://ftp.arnes.si/mysql/) FTP (ftp://ftp.arnes.si/packages/mysql/)

- Spain [GMC Control Systems] @ WWW (http://mysql.neptuno2000.com/) FTP (ftp://ftp.neptuno2000.com/pub/mysql/)

- Sweden [Sunet] @ WWW (http://ftp.sunet.se/pub/unix/databases/relational/mysql/) FTP (ftp://ftp.sunet.se/pub/unix/databases/relational/mysql/)

- Switzerland [SunSITE] @ WWW (http://sunsite.cnlab-switch.ch/ftp/mirror/mysql/) FTP (ftp://sunsite.cnlab-switch.ch/mirror/mysql/)

- Turkey [proGEN] @ WWW (http://mysql.progen.com.tr/)

- UK [PLiG/UK] @ WWW (http://ftp.plig.org/pub/mysql/) FTP (ftp://ftp.plig.org/pub/mysql/)

- Ukraine [ISP Alkar Teleport/Dnepropetrovsk] @ WWW (http://mysql.dp.ua/) FTP (ftp://ftp.tlk-l.net/pub/mirrors/mysql.com/)

- Ukraine [PACO] @ WWW (http://mysql.paco.net.ua/) FTP (ftp://mysql.paco.net.ua/)

- Yugoslavia [open source Network of Yugoslavia] @ WWW (http://mysql.boa.org.yu/) FTP (ftp://ftp.linux.org.yu/pub/MySQL/)

North America:

- Canada [Tryc] @ WWW (http://web.tryc.on.ca/mysql/)

- Mexico [UAM] @ WWW (http://mysql.azc.uam.mx/) FTP (ftp://mysql.azc.uam.mx/mirrors/mysql/)

- Mexico [UNAM] @ WWW (http://mysql.unam.mx/) FTP (ftp://mysql.unam.mx/pub/mysql/)

- USA [adgrafix.com / Boston, MA] @ WWW (http://mysql.adgrafix.com/)

- USA [Fast Mirror / Englewood, CO] @ WWW (http://mysql.fastmirror.com/)

- USA [Hurricane Electric / San Jose, CA] @ WWW (http://mysql.he.net/)

- USA [netNumina / Cambridge, MA] @ WWW (http://mysql.mirrors.netnumina.com/)

- USA [NIXC / Vienna, VA] @ WWW (http://mysql.nixc.net/) FTP (ftp://mysql.nixc.net/pub/mysql/)

- USA [Oregon State University / Corvallis, OR] @ WWW (http://mysql.orst.edu/) FTP (ftp://ftp.orst.edu/pub/mysql/)

- USA [University of Wisconsin / Wisconsin] @ WWW (http://mirror.sit.wisc.edu/ mysql/) FTP (ftp://mirror.sit.wisc.edu/mirrors/mysql/)

- USA [UUNet] @ WWW (http://mysql.secsup.org/) FTP (ftp://mysql.secsup.org/pub/ software/mysql/)

- USA [ValueClick / Los Angeles, CA] @ WWW (http://mysql.valueclick.com/) FTP (ftp://mysql.valueclick.com/pub/mysql/)

South America:

- Argentina [bannerlandia.com] @ WWW (http://mysql.bannerlandia.com.ar/) FTP (ftp://mysql.bannerlandia.com.ar/mirrors/mysql/)

- Chile [PSINet] @ WWW (http://mysql.psinet.cl/) FTP (ftp://ftp.psinet.cl/pub/ database/mysql/)

- Chile [Tecnoera] @ WWW (http://mysql.tecnoera.com/)

- Chile [Vision] @ WWW (http://mysql.vision.cl/)

- Costa Rica [Ogmios Communications] @ WWW (http://mysql.ogmios.co.cr/) FTP (ftp://mysql.ogmios.co.cr/pub/mysql/)

Asia:

- China [Gremlins/Hong Kong] @ WWW (http://mysql.gremlins.com.hk/) FTP (ftp://ftp.mirrors.gremlins.com.hk/mysql/)

- China [HKLPG/Hong Kong] @ WWW (http://mysql.hklpg.org/)

- China [linuxforum.net] @ FTP (http://www2.linuxforum.net/mirror/mysql/)

- China [shellhung.org/Hong Kong] @ WWW (http://mysql.shellhung.org/) FTP (ftp://ftp.shellhung.org/pub/Mirror/mysql/)

- Indonesia [CBN] @ WWW (http://mysql.cbn.net.id/)

- Indonesia [incaf.net] @ WWW (http://mysql.incaf.net/) FTP (ftp://mysql.incaf.net/)

- Indonesia [M-Web] @ WWW (http://mysql.mweb.net.id/)

- Indonesia [web.id] @ WWW (http://mysql.itb.web.id/) FTP (ftp://mysql.itb.web.id/ pub/MySQL/)

- Japan [Soft Agency] @ WWW (http://www.softagency.co.jp/MySQL/)

- Japan [u-aizu.ac.jp/Aizu] @ FTP (ftp://ftp.u-aizu.ac.jp/ftp/pub/dbms/mysql/ mysql.com/)

- Philippines [Ateneo de Zamboanga University] @ WWW (http://mysql.adzu.edu.ph/)

- Singapore [HJC] @ WWW (http://mysql.hjc.edu.sg/) FTP (ftp://ftp.hjc.edu.sg/ mysql/)

- South Korea [HolyNet] @ WWW (http://mysql.holywar.net/)

- South Korea [Webiiz] @ WWW (http://mysql.webiiz.com/)

- Taiwan [nctu.edu/HsinChu] @ WWW (http://mysql.nctu.edu.tw/)

- Taiwan [TTN] @ WWW (http://mysql.ttn.net/)

Australia:

- Australia [planetmirror.com] @ WWW (http://mysql.planetmirror.com/) FTP (ftp://planetmirror.com/pub/mysql/)

Africa:

- South African Republic [Mweb] @ WWW (http://www.mysql.mweb.co.za/)

- South African Republic [The Internet Solution/Johannesburg] @ FTP (ftp://ftp.is.co.za/linux/mysql/)

2.2.2 Operating Systems Supported by MySQL

We use GNU Autoconf, so it is possible to port MySQL to all modern systems with working Posix threads and a C++ compiler. (To compile only the client code, a C++ compiler is required but not threads.) We use and develop the software ourselves primarily on Sun Solaris (Versions 2.5 - 2.7) and SuSE Linux Version 7.x.

Note that for many operating systems, the native thread support works only in the latest versions. MySQL has been reported to compile successfully on the following operating system/thread package combinations:

- AIX 4.x with native threads. See Section 2.6.6.4, IBM-AIX notes.

- Amiga.

- BSDI 2.x with the included MIT-pthreads package. See Section 2.6.4.5, BSD/OS Version 2.x notes.

- BSDI 3.0, 3.1 and 4.x with native threads. See Section 2.6.4.5, BSD/OS Version 2.x notes.

- DEC Unix 4.x with native threads. See Section 2.6.6.6, Alpha-DEC-Unix notes (Tru64).

- FreeBSD 2.x with the included MIT-pthreads package. See Section 2.6.4.1, FreeBSD notes.

- FreeBSD 3.x and 4.x with native threads. See Section 2.6.4.1, FreeBSD notes.

- HP-UX 10.20 with the included MIT-pthreads package. See Section 2.6.6.2, HP-UX Version 10.20 notes.

- HP-UX 11.x with the native threads. See Section 2.6.6.3, HP-UX Version 11.x notes.

- Linux 2.0+ with LinuxThreads 0.7.1+ or `glibc` 2.0.7+. See Section 2.6.1, Linux Notes (All Linux Versions).

- Mac OS X Server. See Section 2.6.5, Mac OS X Notes.

- NetBSD 1.3/1.4 Intel and NetBSD 1.3 Alpha (Requires GNU make). See Section 2.6.4.2, NetBSD notes.

- OpenBSD > 2.5 with native threads. OpenBSD < 2.5 with the included MIT-pthreads package. See Section 2.6.4.3, OpenBSD 2.5 notes.

- OS/2 Warp 3, FixPack 29 and OS/2 Warp 4, FixPack 4. See Section 2.6.7, OS/2 Notes.

- SGI Irix 6.x with native threads. See Section 2.6.6.8, SGI Irix notes.

- Solaris 2.5 and above with native threads on SPARC and x86. See Section 2.6.3, Solaris Notes.

- SunOS 4.x with the included MIT-pthreads package. See Section 2.6.3, Solaris Notes.

- Caldera (SCO) OpenServer with a recent port of the FSU Pthreads package. See Section 2.6.6.9, Caldera (SCO) notes.

- Caldera (SCO) UnixWare 7.0.1. See Section 2.6.6.10, Caldera (SCO) Unixware Version 7.0 notes.

- Tru64 Unix

- Windows 9x, Me, NT, 2000 and XP. See Section 2.6.2, Windows Notes.

Note that not all platforms are suited equally well for running MySQL. How well a certain platform is suited for a high-load mission-critical MySQL server is determined by the following factors:

- General stability of the thread library. A platform may have excellent reputation otherwise, but if the thread library is unstable in the code that is called by MySQL, even if everything else is perfect, MySQL will be only as stable as the thread library.

- The ability of the kernel and/or thread library to take advantage of **SMP** on multiprocessor systems. In other words, when a process creates a thread, it should be possible for that thread to run on a different CPU than the original process.

- The ability of the kernel and/or the thread library to run many threads which acquire/ release a mutex over a short critical region frequently without excessive context switches. In other words, if the implementation of `pthread_mutex_lock()` is too anxious to yield CPU time, this will hurt MySQL tremendously. If this issue is not taken care of, adding extra CPUs will actually make MySQL slower.

- General filesystem stability/performance.

- Ability of the filesystem to deal with large files at all and deal with them efficiently, if your tables are big.

- Our level of expertise here at MySQL AB with the platform. If we know a platform well, we introduce platform-specific optimisations/fixes enabled at compile time. We can also provide advice on configuring your system optimally for MySQL.

- The amount of testing of similar configurations we have done internally.

- The number of users that have successfully run MySQL on that platform in similar configurations. If this number is high, the chances of hitting some platform-specific surprises are much smaller.

Based on the preceding criteria, the best platforms for running MySQL at this point are x86 with SuSE Linux 7.1, 2.4 kernel, and ReiserFS (or any similar Linux distribution) and SPARC with Solaris 2.7 or 2.8. FreeBSD comes third, but we really hope it will join the top club once the thread library is improved. We also hope that at some point we will be able to include all other platforms on which MySQL compiles, runs okay, but not quite with the same level of stability and performance, into the top category. This will require some effort on our part in cooperation with the developers of the OS/library components MySQL depends upon. If you are interested in making one of those components better, are in a position to influence their development, and need more detailed instructions on what MySQL needs to run better, send an email to *internals@lists.mysql.com*.

Please note that the preceding comparison is not to say that one OS is better or worse than the other in general. We are talking about choosing a particular OS for a dedicated purpose—running MySQL, and compare platforms in that regard only. With this in mind, the result of this comparison would be different if we included more issues into it. And in some cases, the reason one OS is better than the other could simply be that we have put forth more effort into testing on and optimising for that particular platform. We are just stating our observations to help you decide on which platform to use MySQL on in your setup.

2.2.3 Which MySQL Version to Use

The first decision to make is whether you want to use the latest development release or the last stable release:

- Normally, if you are beginning to use MySQL for the first time or trying to port it to some system for which there is no binary distribution, we recommend going with the stable release (currently version 3.23). Note that all MySQL releases are checked with the MySQL benchmarks and an extensive test suite before each release (even the development releases).

- Otherwise, if you are running an old system and want to upgrade, but don't want to take chances with a non-seamless upgrade, you should upgrade to the latest in the same branch you are using (where only the last version number is newer than yours). We have tried to fix only fatal bugs and make small, relatively safe changes to that version.

The second decision to make is whether you want to use a source distribution or a binary distribution. In most cases you should probably use a binary distribution, if one exists for your platform, as this generally will be easier to install than a source distribution.

In the following cases you probably will be better off with a source installation:

- If you want to install MySQL at some explicit location. (The standard binary distributions are "ready to run" at any place, but you may want to get even more flexibility).

- To be able to satisfy different user requirements, we are providing two different binary versions: one compiled with the non-transactional table handlers (a small, fast binary), and one configured with the most important extended options like transaction-safe tables. Both versions are compiled from the same source distribution. All native MySQL clients can connect to both MySQL versions.

    The extended MySQL binary distribution is marked with the –max suffix and is configured with the same options as mysqld-max. See Section 4.7.5, mysqld-max, an Extended mysqld Server.

    If you want to use the MySQL-Max RPM, you must first install the standard MySQL RPM.

- If you want to configure mysqld with some extra features that are not in the standard binary distributions. Here is a list of the most common extra options that you may want to use:

    — --with-innodb
    — --with-berkeley-db
    — --with-raid
    — --with-libwrap
    — --with-named-z-lib   (This is done for some of the binaries)
    — --with-debug[=full]

- The default binary distribution is normally compiled with support for all character sets and should work on a variety of processors from the same processor family.

    If you want a faster MySQL server you may want to recompile it with support for only the character sets you need, use a better compiler (like pgcc), or use compiler options that are better optimised for your processor.

- If you have found a bug and reported it to the MySQL development team you will probably receive a patch that you need to apply to the source distribution to get the bug fixed.

- If you want to read (and/or modify) the C and C++ code that makes up MySQL, you should get a source distribution. The source code is always the ultimate manual. Source distributions also contain more tests and examples than binary distributions.

The MySQL naming scheme uses release numbers that consist of three numbers and a suffix. For example, a release name like `mysql-3.21.17-beta` is interpreted like this:

- The first number (3) describes the file format. All Version 3 releases have the same file format.

- The second number (21) is the release level. Normally there are two to choose from. One is the release/stable branch (currently 23) and the other is the development branch (currently 4.0). Normally both are stable, but the development version may have quirks, may be missing documentation on new features, or may fail to compile on some systems.

- The third number (17) is the version number within the release level. This is incremented for each new distribution. Usually you want the latest version for the release level you have chosen.

- The suffix (`beta`) indicates the stability level of the release. The possible suffixes are:

  — `alpha` indicates that the release contains some large section of new code that hasn't been 100% tested. Known bugs (usually there are none) should be documented in the News section. See http://www.mysql.com/doc/N/e/News.html. There are also new commands and extensions in most alpha releases. Active development that may involve major code changes can occur on an alpha release, but everything will be tested before doing a release. There should be no known bugs in any MySQL release.

  — `beta` means that all new code has been tested. No major new features that could cause corruption on old code are added. There should be no known bugs. A version changes from alpha to beta when there haven't been any reported fatal bugs within an alpha version for at least a month and we don't plan to add any features that could make any old command more unreliable.

  — `gamma` is a beta that has been around a while and seems to work fine. Only minor fixes are added. This is what many other companies call a release.

  — If there is no suffix, it means that the version has been run for a while at many different sites with no reports of bugs other than platform-specific bugs. Only critical bug fixes are applied to the release. This is what we call a stable release.

All versions of MySQL are run through our standard tests and benchmarks to ensure that they are relatively safe to use. Because the standard tests are extended over time to check for all previously found bugs, the test suite keeps getting better.

Note that all releases have been tested at least with:

An internal test suite
> This is part of a production system for a customer. It has many tables with hundreds of megabytes of data.

The MySQL benchmark suite
> This runs a range of common queries. It is also a test to see whether the latest batch of optimisations actually made the code faster. See Section 5.1.4, The MySQL Benchmark Suite.

The crash-me *test*
> This tries to determine what features the database supports and what its capabilities and limitations are. See Section 5.1.4, The MySQL Benchmark Suite.

Another test is that we use the newest MySQL version in our internal production environment, on at least one machine. We have more than 100 gigabytes of data to work with.

2.2.4 Installation Layouts

This section describes the default layout of the directories created by installing binary and source distributions.

A binary distribution is installed by unpacking it at the installation location you choose (typically /usr/local/mysql) and creates the following directories in that location:

Directory	Contents of directory
bin	Client programs and the mysqld server
data	Log files, databases
include	Include (header) files
lib	Libraries
scripts	mysql_install_db
share/ mysql	Error message files
sql-bench	Benchmarks

A source distribution is installed after you configure and compile it. By default, the installation step installs files under /usr/local, in the following subdirectories:

Directory	Contents of directory
bin	Client programs and scripts
include/mysql	Include (header) files
info	Documentation in Info format
lib/mysql	Libraries
libexec	The mysqld server
share/mysql	Error message files
sql-bench	Benchmarks and crash-me test
var	Databases and log files

Within an installation directory, the layout of a source installation differs from that of a binary installation in the following ways:

- The mysqld server is installed in the libexec directory rather than in the bin directory.

- The data directory is var rather than data.

- mysql_install_db is installed in the /usr/local/bin directory rather than in /usr/local/mysql/scripts.

- The header file and library directories are include/mysql and lib/mysql rather than include and lib.

You can create your own binary installation from a compiled source distribution by executing the script scripts/make_binary_distribution.

2.2.5 How and When Updates Are Released

MySQL is evolving quite rapidly here at MySQL AB and we want to share this with other MySQL users. We try to make a release when we have very useful features that others seem to have a need for.

We also try to help out users who request features that are easy to implement. We take note of what our licensed users want to have, and we especially take note of what our extended email supported customers want and try to help them out.

No one has to download a new release. The News section will tell you if the new release has something you really want. See http://www.mysql.com/doc/N/e/News.html.

We use the following policy when updating MySQL:

- For each minor update, the last number in the version string is incremented. When there are major new features or minor incompatibilities with previous versions, the second number in the version string is incremented. When the file format changes, the first number is increased.

- Stable-tested releases are meant to appear about 1-2 times a year, but if small bugs are found, a release with only bug fixes will be released.

- Working releases/bug fixes to old releases are meant to appear about every 1-8 weeks.

- Binary distributions for some platforms will be made by us for major releases. Other people may make binary distributions for other systems but probably less frequently.

- We usually make patches available as soon as we have located and fixed small bugs. They are posted to *bugs@lists.mysql.com* and will be added to the next release.

- For non-critical but annoying bugs, we will add them the MySQL source repository and they will be fixed in the next release.

- If there is, by any chance, a fatal bug in a release we will make a new release as soon as possible. We would like other companies to do this, too.

The current stable release is Version 3.23; we have already moved active development to Version 4.0. Bugs will still be fixed in the stable version. We don't believe in a complete freeze, as this also leaves out bug fixes and things that "must be done." "Somewhat frozen" means that we may add small things that "almost surely will not affect anything that's already working."

MySQL uses a slightly different naming scheme from most other products. In general it's relatively safe to use any version that has been out for a couple of weeks without being replaced with a new version. See Section 2.2.3, Which MySQL Version to Use.

2.2.6 MySQL Binaries Compiled by MySQL AB

As a service, we at MySQL AB provide a set of binary distributions of MySQL that are compiled at our site or at sites where customers kindly have given us access to their machines.

These distributions are generated with `scripts/make_binary_distribution` and are configured with the following compilers and options:

SunOS 4.1.4 2 sun4c with gcc 2.7.2.1

```
CC=gcc CXX=gcc CXXFLAGS="-O3 -felide-constructors" ./configure
--prefix=/usr/local/mysql      --disable-shared      --with-extra-
charsets=complex --enable-assembler
```

SunOS 5.5.1 (and above) sun4u with egcs 1.0.3a or 2.90.27 or gcc 2.95.2 and newer

```
CC=gcc CFLAGS="-O3" CXX=gcc CXXFLAGS="-O3 -felide-constructors
-fno-exceptions -fno-rtti" ./configure --prefix=/usr/local/mysql
--with-low-memory --with-extra-charsets=complex --enable-assem-
bler
```

SunOS 5.6 i86pc with gcc 2.8.1

```
CC=gcc CXX=gcc CXXFLAGS=-O3 ./configure --prefix=/usr/local/
mysql --with-low-memory --with-extra-charsets=complex
```

Solaris 2.8 sparc with gcc 2.95.3

```
CC=gcc    CFLAGS="-O3    -fno-omit-frame-pointer"    CXX=gcc
CXXFLAGS="-O3 -fno-omit-frame-pointer -felide-constructors -fno-
exceptions  -fno-rtti"  ./configure  --prefix=/usr/local/mysql
"--with-comment=Official    MySQL    binary"    --with-extra-
charsets=complex  "--with-server-suffix="  --enable-thread-safe-
client --enable-local-infile --enable-assembler --disable-shared
```

Linux 2.0.33 i386 with pgcc 2.90.29 (egcs 1.0.3a)

```
CFLAGS="-O3    -mpentium    -mstack-align-double"    CXX=gcc
CXXFLAGS="-O3 -mpentium -mstack-align-double -felide-construc-
tors -fno-exceptions -fno-rtti" ./configure --prefix=/usr/local/
mysql    --enable-assembler    --with-mysqld-ldflags=-all-static
--with-extra-charsets=complex
```

Linux 2.2.x with x686 with gcc 2.95.2

```
CFLAGS="-O3 -mpentiumpro" CXX=gcc CXXFLAGS="-O3 -mpentiumpro
-felide-constructors  -fno-exceptions  -fno-rtti"  ./configure
--prefix=/usr/local/mysql    --enable-assembler    --with-mysqld-
ldflags=-all-static  --disable-shared  --with-extra-charset=com-
plex
```

SCO 3.2v5.0.4 i386 with gcc 2.7-95q4

```
CC=gcc CXX=gcc CXXFLAGS=-O3 ./configure --prefix=/usr/local/
mysql --with-extra-charsets=complex
```

AIX 2 4 with gcc 2.7.2.2

```
CC=gcc CXX=gcc CXXFLAGS=-O3 ./configure --prefix=/usr/local/
mysql --with-extra-charsets=complex
```

OSF/1 V4.0 564 alpha with gcc 2.8.1

```
CC=gcc CFLAGS=-O CXX=gcc CXXFLAGS=-O3 ./configure --prefix=/usr/
local/mysql --with-low-memory --with-extra-charsets=complex
```

Irix 6.3 IP32 with gcc 2.8.0

```
CC=gcc CXX=gcc CXXFLAGS=-O3 ./configure --prefix=/usr/local/
mysql --with-extra-charsets=complex
```

BSDI BSD/OS 3.1 i386 with gcc 2.7.2.1

```
CC=gcc CXX=gcc CXXFLAGS=-O ./configure --prefix=/usr/local/mysql
--with-extra-charsets=complex
```

BSDI BSD/OS 2.1 i386 with gcc *2.7.2*

```
CC=gcc  CXX=gcc  CXXFLAGS=-O3  ./configure  --prefix=/usr/local/
mysql --with-extra-charsets=complex
```

Anyone who has more optimal options for any of the preceding configurations listed can always mail them to the developer's mailing list at *internals@lists.mysql.com*.

RPM distributions prior to MySQL Version 3.22 are user-contributed. Beginning with Version 3.22, the RPMs are generated by us at MySQL AB.

If you want to compile a debug version of MySQL, you should add --with-debug or --with-debug=full to the preceding configure lines and remove any -fomit-frame-pointer options.

For the Windows distribution, please see Section 2.1.2, Installing MySQL on Windows.

2.2.7 Installing a MySQL Binary Distribution

See also Section 2.1.2.1, Installing the binaries, see Section 2.1.1, Installing MySQL on Linux, and Section 8.4.7, Building Client Programs.

You need the following tools to install a MySQL binary distribution:

* GNU gunzip to uncompress the distribution.

* A reasonable tar to unpack the distribution. GNU tar is known to work. Sun tar is known to have problems.

An alternative installation method under Linux is to use RPM (RedHat Package Manager) distributions. See Section 2.1.1, Installing MySQL on Linux.

If you run into problems, **please always use** mysqlbug *when posting questions to mysql@lists.mysql.com*. Even if the problem isn't a bug, mysqlbug gathers system information that will help others solve your problem. By not using mysqlbug, you lessen the likelihood of getting a solution to your problem! You will find mysqlbug in the bin directory after you unpack the distribution. See Section 1.6.2.3, How to report bugs or problems.

The basic commands you must execute to install and use a MySQL binary distribution are:

```
shell> groupadd mysql
shell> useradd -g mysql mysql
shell> cd /usr/local
shell> gunzip < /path/to/mysql-VERSION-OS.tar.gz | tar xvf -
shell> ln -s full-path-to-mysql-VERSION-OS mysql
shell> cd mysql
shell> scripts/mysql_install_db
shell> chown -R root  .
shell> chown -R mysql data
```

```
shell> chgrp -R mysql .
shell> bin/safe_mysqld --user=mysql &
or
shell> bin/mysqld_safe --user=mysql &
if you are running MySQL 4.x
```

You can add new users using the bin/mysql_setpermission script if you install the DBI and Msql-Mysql-modules Perl modules.

A more detailed description follows.

To install a binary distribution, follow these steps, then proceed to Section 2.4, Post-Installation Setup and Testing, for post-installation setup and testing:

1. Pick the directory under which you want to unpack the distribution, and move into it. In the following example, we unpack the distribution under /usr/local and create a directory /usr/local/mysql into which MySQL is installed. (The following instructions, therefore, assume you have permission to create files in /usr/local. If that directory is protected, you will need to perform the installation as root.)

2. Obtain a distribution file from one of the sites listed in Section 2.2.1, How to Get MySQL.

    MySQL binary distributions are provided as compressed tar archives and have names like mysql-VERSION-OS.tar.gz, where VERSION is a number (for example, 3.21.15), and OS indicates the type of operating system for which the distribution is intended (for example, pc-linux-gnu-i586).

3. If you see a binary distribution marked with the -max prefix, this means that the binary has support for transaction-safe tables and other features. See Section 4.7.5, mysqld-max, an Extended mysqld Server. Note that all binaries are built from the same MySQL source distribution.

4. Add a user and group for mysqld to run as:

    ```
    shell> groupadd mysql
    shell> useradd -g mysql mysql
    ```

    These commands add the mysql group and the mysql user. The syntax for useradd and groupadd may differ slightly on different versions of Unix. They may also be called adduser and addgroup. You may wish to call the user and group something else instead of mysql.

5. Change into the intended installation directory:

    ```
    shell> cd /usr/local
    ```

6. Unpack the distribution and create the installation directory:

    ```
    shell> gunzip < /path/to/mysql-VERSION-OS.tar.gz | tar xvf -
    shell> ln -s full-path-to-mysql-VERSION-OS mysql
    ```

The first command creates a directory named mysql-VERSION-OS. The second command makes a symbolic link to that directory. This lets you refer more easily to the installation directory as /usr/local/mysql.

7. Change into the installation directory:

    ```
    shell> cd mysql
    ```

    You will find several files and subdirectories in the mysql directory. The most important for installation purposes are the bin and scripts subdirectories.

    bin

    > This directory contains client programs and the server You should add the full pathname of this directory to your PATH environment variable so that your shell finds the MySQL programs properly. See Appendix E.

    scripts

    > This directory contains the mysql_install_db script used to initialise the mysql database containing the grant tables that store the server access permissions.

8. If you would like to use mysqlaccess and have the MySQL distribution in some non-standard place, you must change the location where mysqlaccess expects to find the mysql client. Edit the bin/mysqlaccess script at approximately line 18. Search for a line that looks like this:

    ```
    $MYSQL     = '/usr/local/bin/mysql';    # path to mysql executable
    ```

    Change the path to reflect the location where mysql actually is stored on your system. If you do not do this, you will get a Broken pipe error when you run mysqlaccess.

9. Create the MySQL grant tables (necessary only if you haven't installed MySQL before):

    ```
    shell> scripts/mysql_install_db
    ```

    Note that MySQL versions older than Version 3.22.10 started the MySQL server when you run mysql_install_db. This is no longer true!

10. Change ownership of binaries to root and ownership of the data directory to the user that you will run mysqld as:

    ```
    shell> chown -R root  /usr/local/mysql/.
    shell> chown -R mysql /usr/local/mysql/data
    shell> chgrp -R mysql /usr/local/mysql/.
    ```

    The first command changes the owner attribute of the files to the root user, the second one changes the owner attribute of the data directory to the mysql user, and the third one changes the group attribute to the mysql group.

11. If you want to install support for the Perl DBI/DBD interface, see Section 2.7, Perl Installation Comments.

12. If you would like MySQL to start automatically when you boot your machine, you can copy support-files/mysql.server to the location where your system has its startup files. More information can be found in the support-files/mysql.server script itself and in Section 2.4.3, Starting and Stopping MySQL Automatically.

After everything has been unpacked and installed, you should initialise and test your distribution.

You can start the MySQL server with the following command:

```
shell> bin/safe_mysqld --user=mysql &
```

Now proceed to Section 4.7.2, safe_mysqld, the Wrapper Around mysqld, and Section 2.4, Post-Installation Setup and Testing.

2.3 Installing a MySQL Source Distribution

Before you proceed with the source installation, check first to see if our binary is available for your platform and if it will work for you. We put a lot of effort into making sure that our binaries are built with the best possible options.

You need the following tools to build and install MySQL from source:

- GNU gunzip to uncompress the distribution.

- A reasonable tar to unpack the distribution. GNU tar is known to work. Sun tar is known to have problems.

- A working ANSI C++ compiler. gcc >= 2.95.2, egcs >= 1.0.2 or egcs 2.91.66, SGI C++, and SunPro C++ are some of the compilers that are known to work. libg++ is not needed when using gcc. gcc 2.7.x has a bug that makes it impossible to compile some perfectly legal C++ files, such as sql/sql_base.cc. If you only have gcc 2.7.x, you must upgrade your gcc to be able to compile MySQL. gcc 2.8.1 is also known to have problems on some platforms, so it should be avoided if a new compiler exists for the platform.

  gcc >= 2.95.2 is recommended when compiling MySQL Version 3.23.x.

- A good make program. GNU make is always recommended and is sometimes required. If you have problems, we recommend trying GNU make 3.75 or newer.

If you are using a recent version of gcc, recent enough to understand the -fno-exceptions option, it is **very important** that you use it. Otherwise, you may compile a binary that crashes randomly. We also recommend that you use -felide-constructors and -fno-rtti along with -fno-exceptions. When in doubt, do the following:

```
CFLAGS="-O3" CXX=gcc CXXFLAGS="-O3 -felide-constructors -fno-exceptions \
      -fno-rtti" ./configure --prefix=/usr/local/mysql --enable-assembler \
      --with-mysqld-ldflags=-all-static
```

On most systems this will give you a fast and stable binary.

If you run into problems, **please always use** mysqlbug *when posting questions to mysql@lists.mysql.com*. Even if the problem isn't a bug, mysqlbug gathers system information that will help others solve your problem. By not using mysqlbug, you lessen the likelihood of getting a solution to your problem! You will find mysqlbug in the scripts directory after you unpack the distribution. See Section 1.6.2.3, How to report bugs or problems.

2.3.1 Quick Installation Overview

The basic commands you must execute to install a MySQL source distribution are:

```
shell> groupadd mysql
shell> useradd -g mysql mysql
shell> gunzip < mysql-VERSION.tar.gz | tar -xvf -
shell> cd mysql-VERSION
shell> ./configure --prefix=/usr/local/mysql
shell> make
shell> make install
shell> scripts/mysql_install_db
shell> chown -R root  /usr/local/mysql
shell> chown -R mysql /usr/local/mysql/var
shell> chgrp -R mysql /usr/local/mysql
shell> cp support-files/my-medium.cnf /etc/my.cnf
shell> /usr/local/mysql/bin/safe_mysqld --user=mysql &
or
shell> /usr/local/mysql/bin/mysqld_safe --user=mysql &
if you are running MySQL 4.x.
```

If you want to have support for InnoDB tables, you should edit the /etc/my.cnf file and remove the # character before the parameter that starts with innodb_ . . . . See Section 4.1.2, my.cnf Option Files, and Section 7.5.2, InnoDB Startup Options.

If you start from a source RPM, do the following:

```
shell> rpm --rebuild MySQL-VERSION.src.rpm
```

This will make a binary RPM that you can install.

You can add new users using the bin/mysql_setpermission script if you install the DBI and Msql-Mysql-modules Perl modules.

A more detailed description follows.

To install a source distribution, follow these steps, then proceed to Section 2.4, Post-Installation Setup and Testing, for post-installation initialisation and testing:

1. Pick the directory under which you want to unpack the distribution, and move into it.

2. Obtain a distribution file from one of the sites listed in Section 2.2.1, How to Get MySQL.

3. If you are interested in using Berkeley DB tables with MySQL, you will need to obtain a patched version of the Berkeley DB source code. Please read the chapter on Berkeley DB tables before proceeding. See Section 7.6, BDB or Berkeley_DB Tables.

   MySQL source distributions are provided as compressed `tar` archives and have names like `mysql-VERSION.tar.gz`, where `VERSION` is a number like 4.0.

4. Add a user and group for `mysqld` to run as:

   ```
   shell> groupadd mysql
   shell> useradd -g mysql mysql
   ```

   These commands add the `mysql` group and the `mysql` user. The syntax for `useradd` and `groupadd` may differ slightly on different versions of Unix. They may also be called `adduser` and `addgroup`. You may wish to call the user and group something else instead of `mysql`.

5. Unpack the distribution into the current directory:

   ```
   shell> gunzip < /path/to/mysql-VERSION.tar.gz | tar xvf -
   ```

   This command creates a directory named `mysql-VERSION`.

6. Change into the top-level directory of the unpacked distribution:

   ```
   shell> cd mysql-VERSION
   ```

   Note that currently you must configure and build MySQL from this top-level directory. You cannot build it in a different directory.

7. Configure the release and compile everything:

   ```
   shell> ./configure --prefix=/usr/local/mysql
   shell> make
   ```

   When you run `configure`, you might want to specify some options. Run `./configure --help` for a list of options. See Section 2.3.3, Typical `configure` Options, discusses some of the more useful options.

   If `configure` fails, and you are going to send mail to *mysql@lists.mysql.com* to ask for assistance, please include any lines from `config.log` that you think can help solve the problem. Also include the last couple of lines of output from `configure` if `configure` aborts. Post the bug report using the `mysqlbug` script. See Section 1.6.2.3, How to report bugs or problems.

   If the compile fails, see Section 2.3.5, Problems Compiling?, for help with a number of common problems.

8. Install everything:

   ```
   shell> make install
   ```

   You might need to run this command as root.

9. Create the MySQL grant tables (necessary only if you haven't installed MySQL before):

   ```
   shell> scripts/mysql_install_db
   ```

   Note that MySQL versions older than Version 3.22.10 started the MySQL server when you run mysql_install_db. This is no longer true!

10. Change ownership of binaries to root and ownership of the data directory to the user that you will run mysqld as:

    ```
    shell> chown -R root  /usr/local/mysql
    shell> chown -R mysql /usr/local/mysql/var
    shell> chgrp -R mysql /usr/local/mysql
    ```

    The first command changes the owner attribute of the files to the root user, the second one changes the owner attribute of the data directory to the mysql user, and the third one changes the group attribute to the mysql group.

11. If you want to install support for the Perl DBI/DBD interface, see Section 2.7, Perl Installation Comments.

12. If you would like MySQL to start automatically when you boot your machine, you can copy support-files/mysql.server to the location where your system has its startup files. More information can be found in the support-files/mysql.server script itself and in Section 2.4.3, Starting and Stopping MySQL Automatically.

After everything has been installed, you should initialise and test your distribution:

```
shell> /usr/local/mysql/bin/safe_mysqld --user=mysql &
```

If that command fails immediately with mysqld daemon ended, you can find some information in the file mysql-data-directory/'hostname'.err. The likely reason is that you already have another mysqld server running. See Section 4.1.4, Running Multiple MySQL Servers on the Same Machine.

Now proceed to Section 2.4, Post-Installation Setup and Testing.

2.3.2 Applying Patches

Sometimes patches appear on the mailing list or are placed in the patches area of the MySQL web site (http://www.mysql.com/Downloads/Patches/).

To apply a patch from the mailing list, save the message in which the patch appears in a file, change into the top-level directory of your MySQL source tree, and run these commands:

```
shell> patch -p1 < patch-file-name
shell> rm config.cache
shell> make clean
```

Patches from the FTP site are distributed as plain text files or as files compressed with gzip. Apply a plain patch as shown previously for mailing list patches. To apply a compressed patch, change into the top-level directory of your MySQL source tree and run these commands:

```
shell> gunzip < patch-file-name.gz | patch -p1
shell> rm config.cache
shell> make clean
```

After applying a patch, follow the instructions for a normal source install, beginning with the ./configure step. After running the make install step, restart your MySQL server.

You may need to bring down any currently running server before you run make install. (Use mysqladmin shutdown to do this.) Some systems do not allow you to install a new version of a program if it replaces the version that is currently executing.

2.3.3 Typical configure Options

The configure script gives you a great deal of control over how you configure your MySQL distribution. Typically you do this using options on the configure command-line. You can also affect configure using certain environment variables. See Appendix E. For a list of options supported by configure, run this command:

```
shell> ./configure --help
```

Some of the more commonly-used configure options are described here:

- To compile just the MySQL client libraries and client programs and not the server, use the --without-server option:

  ```
  shell> ./configure --without-server
  ```

  If you don't have a C++ compiler, mysql will not compile (it is the one client program that requires C++). In this case, you can remove the code in configure that tests for the C++ compiler and then run ./configure with the --without-server option. The compile step will still try to build mysql, but you can ignore any warnings about mysql.cc. (If make stops, try make -k to tell it to continue with the rest of the build even if errors occur.)

- If you want to get an embedded MySQL library (libmysqld.a) you should use the --with-embedded-server option.

- If you don't want your log files and database directories located under /usr/local/ var, use a configure command, something like one of these:

```
shell> ./configure --prefix=/usr/local/mysql
shell> ./configure --prefix=/usr/local \
        --localstatedir=/usr/local/mysql/data
```

The first command changes the installation prefix so that everything is installed under /usr/local/mysql rather than the default of /usr/local. The second command preserves the default installation prefix, but overrides the default location for database directories (normally /usr/local/var) and changes it to /usr/local/mysql/data. After you have compiled MySQL, you can change these options with option files. See Section 4.1.2, my.cnf Option Files.

- If you are using Unix and you want the MySQL socket located somewhere other than the default location (normally in the directory /tmp or /var/run) use a configure command like this:

```
shell> ./configure --with-unix-socket-path=/usr/local/mysql/tmp/mysql.sock
```

Note that the given file must be an absolute pathname! You can also later change the location mysql.sock by using the MySQL option files. See Section A.4.5, How to Protect or Change the MySQL Socket File /tmp/mysql.sock.

- If you want to compile statically linked programs (for example, to make a binary distribution, to get more speed, or to work around problems with some RedHat Linux distributions), run configure like this:

```
shell> ./configure --with-client-ldflags=-all-static \
        --with-mysqld-ldflags=-all-static
```

- If you are using gcc and don't have libg++ or libstdc++ installed, you can tell configure to use gcc as your C++ compiler:

```
shell> CC=gcc CXX=gcc ./configure
```

When you use gcc as your C++ compiler, it will not attempt to link in libg++ or libstdc++.

Here are some common environment variables to set depending on the compiler you are using:

Compiler	Recommended options
gcc 2.7.2.1	CC=gcc CXX=gcc CXXFLAGS="-O3 -felide-constructors"
egcs 1.0.3a	CC=gcc CXX=gcc CXXFLAGS="-O3 -felide-constructors -fno-exceptions -fno-rtti"
gcc 2.95.2	CFLAGS="-O3 -mpentiumpro" CXX=gcc CXXFLAGS="-O3 -mpentiumpro \ -felide-constructors -fno-exceptions -fno-rtti"
pgcc 2.90.29 or newer	CFLAGS="-O3 -mpentiumpro -mstack-align-double" CXX=gcc \ CXXFLAGS="-O3 -mpentiumpro -mstack-align-double -felide-constructors \ -fno-exceptions -fno-rtti"

In most cases you can get a reasonably optimal MySQL binary by using the options from the preceding table and adding the following options to the configure line:

```
--prefix=/usr/local/mysql --enable-assembler \
--with-mysqld-ldflags=-all-static
```

The full configure line would, in other words, be something like the following for all recent gcc versions:

```
CFLAGS="-O3 -mpentiumpro" CXX=gcc CXXFLAGS="-O3 -mpentiumpro \
-felide-constructors -fno-exceptions -fno-rtti" ./configure \
--prefix=/usr/local/mysql --enable-assembler \
--with-mysqld-ldflags=-all-static
```

The binaries we provide on the MySQL web site at http://www.mysql.com/ are all compiled with full optimisation and should be perfect for most users. See Section 2.2.6, MySQL Binaries Compiled by MySQL AB. There are some things you can tweak to make an even faster binary, but this is only for advanced users. See Section 5.5.3, How Compiling and Linking Affects the Speed of MySQL.

If the build fails and produces errors about your compiler or linker not being able to create the shared library libmysqlclient.so.# (# is a version number), you can work around this problem by giving the --disable-shared option to configure. In this case, configure will not build a shared libmysqlclient.so.# library.

- You can configure MySQL not to use DEFAULT column values for non-NULL columns (that is, columns that are not allowed to be NULL). This causes INSERT statements to generate an error unless you explicitly specify values for all columns that require a non-NULL value. To suppress use of default values, run configure like this:

```
shell> CXXFLAGS=-DDONT_USE_DEFAULT_FIELDS ./configure
```

- By default, MySQL uses the ISO-8859-1 (Latin1) character set. To change the default set, use the --with-charset option:

```
shell> ./configure --with-charset=CHARSET
```

CHARSET may be one of big5, cp1251, cp1257, czech, danish, dec8, dos, euc_kr, gb2312, gbk, german1, hebrew, hp8, hungarian, koi8_ru, koi8_ukr, latin1, latin2, sjis, swe7, tis620, ujis, usa7, or win1251ukr. See Section 4.6.1, The Character Set Used for Data and Sorting.

If you want to convert characters between the server and the client, you should take a look at the SET OPTION CHARACTER SET command. See Section 5.5.6, SET Syntax.

Warning: If you change character sets after having created any tables, you will have to run myisamchk -r -q on every table. Your indexes may be sorted incorrectly otherwise. (This can happen if you install MySQL, create some tables, then reconfigure MySQL to use a different character set and reinstall it.)

With the option `--with-extra-charset=LIST` you can define which additional character sets should be incompiled in the server.

Here `LIST` is either a list of character sets separated with spaces, `complex` to include all characters that can't be dynamically loaded, or `all` to include all character sets into the binaries.

- To configure MySQL with debugging code, use the `--with-debug` option:

    ```
    shell> ./configure --with-debug
    ```

    This causes a safe memory allocator to be included that can find some errors and that provides output about what is happening. See Section D.1, Debugging a MySQL Server.

- If your client programs are using threads, you need to also compile a thread-safe version of the MySQL client library with the `--enable-thread-safe-client` configure options. This will create a `libmysqlclient_r` library with which you should link your threaded applications. See Section 8.4.8, How to Make a Threaded Client.

- Options that pertain to particular systems can be found in the system-specific section of this manual. See Section 2.6, Operating System–Specific Notes.

2.3.4 Installing from the Development Source Tree

Caution: You should read this section only if you are interested in helping us test our new code. If you just want to get MySQL up and running on your system, you should use a standard release distribution (either a source or binary distribution will do).

To obtain our most recent development source tree, use these instructions:

1. Download `BitKeeper` from http://www.bitmover.com/cgi-bin/download.cgi. You will need `Bitkeeper` 2.0 or newer to access our repository.

2. Follow the instructions to install it.

3. After `BitKeeper` is installed, first go to the directory you want to work from, and then use this command if you want to clone the MySQL 3.23 branch:

    ```
    shell> bk clone bk://work.mysql.com:7000 mysql
    ```

    To clone the 4.0 branch, use this command instead:

    ```
    shell> bk clone bk://work.mysql.com:7001 mysql-4.0
    ```

In the preceding examples the source tree will be set up in the `mysql/` or `mysql-4.0/` subdirectory of your current directory.

The initial download of the source tree may take a while, depending on the speed of your connection; be patient.

4. You will need GNU autoconf 2.52, automake 1.4, libtool, and m4 to run the next set of commands.

    automake (1.5) doesn't yet work.

    If you get some strange error during this stage, check that you really have libtool installed!

    ```
    shell> cd mysql
    shell> bk -r edit
    shell> aclocal; autoheader; autoconf;  automake;
    shell> ./configure  # Add your favorite options here
    shell> make
    ```

    A collection of our standard configure scripts is located in the BUILD/ subdirectory. If you are lazy, you can use BUILD/compile-pentium-debug. To compile on a different architecture, modify the script by removing flags that are Pentium-specific.

5. When the build is done, run make install. Be careful with this on a production machine; the command may overwrite your live release installation. If you have another installation of MySQL, we recommand that you run ./configure with different values for the prefix, tcp-port, and unix-socket-path options than those used for your production server.

6. Play hard with your new installation and try to make the new features crash. Start by running make test. See Section 9.1.2, MySQL Test Suite.

7. If you have gotten to the make stage and the distribution does not compile, please report it to *bugs@lists.mysql.com*. If you have installed the latest versions of the required GNU tools, and they crash trying to process our configuration files, please report that also. However, if you execute aclocal and get a command not found error or a similar problem, do not report it. Instead, make sure all the necessary tools are installed and that your PATH variable is set correctly so that your shell can find them.

8. After the initial bk clone operation to get the source tree, you should run bk pull periodically to get the updates.

9. You can examine the change history for the tree with all the diffs by using bk scc-stool. If you see some funny diffs or code that you have a question about, do not hesitate to send email to *internals@lists.mysql.com*. Also, if you think you have a better idea on how to do something, send an email to the same address with a patch. bk diffs will produce a patch for you after you have made changes to the source. If you do not have the time to code your idea, just send a description.

10. BitKeeper has a nice help utility that you can access via bk helptool.

2.3.5 Problems Compiling?

All MySQL programs compile cleanly for us with no warnings on Solaris using gcc. On other systems, warnings may occur due to differences in system include files. See Section 2.3.6, MIT-pthreads Notes for warnings that may occur when using MIT-pthreads. For other problems, check the following list.

The solution to many problems involves reconfiguring. If you do need to reconfigure, take note of the following:

- If configure is run after it already has been run, it may use information that was gathered during its previous invocation. This information is stored in config.cache. When configure starts up, it looks for that file and reads its contents if it exists, on the assumption that the information is still correct. That assumption is invalid when you reconfigure.

- Each time you run configure, you must run make again to recompile. However, you may want to remove old object files from previous builds first because they were compiled using different configuration options.

To prevent old configuration information or object files from being used, run these commands before rerunning configure:

```
shell> rm config.cache
shell> make clean
```

Alternatively, you can run make distclean.

The following list describes some of the problems when compiling MySQL that have been found to occur most often:

- If you get errors when compiling sql_yacc.cc, such as the ones shown here, you have probably run out of memory or swap space:

  ```
  Internal compiler error: program cclplus got fatal signal 11
    or
  Out of virtual memory
    or
  Virtual memory exhausted
  ```

  The problem is that gcc requires huge amounts of memory to compile sql_yacc.cc with inline functions. Try running configure with the --with-low-memory option:

  ```
  shell> ./configure --with-low-memory
  ```

  This option causes -fno-inline to be added to the compile line if you are using gcc and -O0 if you are using something else. You should try the --with-low-memory option even if you have so much memory and swap space that you think you can't possibly have run out. This problem has been observed to occur even on systems with generous hardware configurations, and the --with-low-memory option usually fixes it.

- By default, configure picks c++ as the compiler name and GNU c++ links with -lg++. If you are using gcc, that behavior can cause problems during configuration such as this:

```
configure: error: installation or configuration problem:
C++ compiler cannot create executables.
```

You might also observe problems during compilation related to g++, libg++, or libstdc++.

One cause of these problems is that you may not have g++, or you may have g++ but not libg++, or libstdc++. Take a look at the config.log file. It should contain the exact reason why your c++ compiler didn't work! To work around these problems, you can use gcc as your C++ compiler. Try setting the environment variable CXX to "gcc -O3". For example:

```
shell> CXX="gcc -O3" ./configure
```

This works because gcc compiles C++ sources as well as g++ does, but does not link in libg++ or libstdc++ by default.

Another way to fix these problems, of course, is to install g++, libg++, and libstdc++.

- If your compile fails with errors, such as any of the following, you must upgrade your version of make to GNU make:

```
making all in mit-pthreads
make: Fatal error in reader: Makefile, line 18:
Badly formed macro assignment
  or
make: file 'Makefile' line 18: Must be a separator (:
  or
pthread.h: No such file or directory
```

Solaris and FreeBSD are known to have troublesome make programs.

GNU make Version 3.75 is known to work.

- If you want to define flags to be used by your C or C++ compilers, do so by adding the flags to the CFLAGS and CXXFLAGS environment variables. You can also specify the compiler names this way using CC and CXX. For example:

```
shell> CC=gcc
shell> CFLAGS=-O3
shell> CXX=gcc
shell> CXXFLAGS=-O3
shell> export CC CFLAGS CXX CXXFLAGS
```

See Section 2.2.6, MySQL Binaries Compiled by MySQL AB, for a list of flag definitions that have been found to be useful on various systems.

- If you get an error message like this, you need to upgrade your gcc compiler:

  ```
  client/libmysql.c:273: parse error before '__attribute__'
  ```

  gcc 2.8.1 is known to work, but we recommend using gcc 2.95.2 or egcs 1.0.3a instead.

- If you get errors such as those shown here when compiling mysqld, configure didn't correctly detect the type of the last argument to accept(), getsockname(), or getpeername():

  ```
  cxx: Error: mysqld.cc, line 645: In this statement, the referenced
       type of the pointer value "&length" is "unsigned long", which
       is not compatible with "int".
  new_sock = accept(sock, (struct sockaddr *)&cAddr, &length);
  ```

  To fix this, edit the config.h file (which is generated by configure). Look for these lines:

  ```
  /* Define as the base type of the last arg to accept */
  #define SOCKET_SIZE_TYPE XXX
  ```

  Change XXX to size_t or int, depending on your operating system. (Note that you will have to do this each time you run configure because configure regenerates config.h.)

- The sql_yacc.cc file is generated from sql_yacc.yy. Normally the build process doesn't need to create sql_yacc.cc, because MySQL comes with an already generated copy. However, if you do need to re-create it, you might encounter this error:

  ```
  "sql_yacc.yy", line xxx fatal: default action causes potential...
  ```

  This is a sign that your version of yacc is deficient. You probably need to install bison (the GNU version of yacc) and use that instead.

- If you need to debug mysqld or a MySQL client, run configure with the --with-debug option, then recompile and link your clients with the new client library. See Section D.2, Debugging a MySQL Client.

2.3.6 MIT-pthreads Notes

This section describes some of the issues involved in using MIT-pthreads.

Note that on Linux you should **not** use MIT-pthreads but install LinuxThreads! See Section 2.6.1, Linux Notes (All Linux Versions).

If your system does not provide native thread support, you will need to build MySQL using the MIT-pthreads package. This includes older FreeBSD systems, SunOS 4.x, Solaris 2.4 and earlier, and some others. See Section 2.2.2, Operating Systems Supported by MySQL.

- On most systems, you can force MIT-pthreads to be used by running `configure` with the `--with-mit-threads` option:

      shell> ./configure --with-mit-threads

  Building in a non-source directory is not supported when using MIT-pthreads because we want to minimise our changes to this code.

- The checks that determine whether to use MIT-pthreads occur only during the part of the configuration process that deals with the server code. If you have configured the distribution using `--without-server` to build only the client code, clients will not know whether MIT-pthreads is being used and will use Unix socket connections by default. Because Unix sockets do not work under MIT-pthreads, this means you will need to use `-h` or `--host` when you run client programs.

- When MySQL is compiled using MIT-pthreads, system locking is disabled by default for performance reasons. You can tell the server to use system locking with the `--use-locking` option.

- Sometimes the pthread `bind()` command fails to bind to a socket without any error message (at least on Solaris). The result is that all connections to the server fail. For example:

      shell> mysqladmin version
      mysqladmin: connect to server at '' failed;
      error: 'Can't connect to mysql server on localhost (146)'

  The solution to this is to kill the `mysqld` server and restart it. This has only happened to us when we have forced the server down and done a restart immediately.

- With MIT-pthreads, the `sleep()` system call isn't interruptible with `SIGINT` (break). This is only noticeable when you run `mysqladmin --sleep`. You must wait for the `sleep()` call to terminate before the interrupt is served and the process stops.

- When linking, you may receive warning messages like these (at least on Solaris); they can be ignored:

      ld: warning: symbol '_iob' has differing sizes:
          (file /my/local/pthreads/lib/libpthread.a(findfp.o) value=0x4;
      file /usr/lib/libc.so value=0x140);
          /my/local/pthreads/lib/libpthread.a(findfp.o) definition taken
      ld: warning: symbol '__iob' has differing sizes:
          (file /my/local/pthreads/lib/libpthread.a(findfp.o) value=0x4;
      file /usr/lib/libc.so value=0x140);
          /my/local/pthreads/lib/libpthread.a(findfp.o) definition taken

- Some other warnings also can be ignored:

      implicit declaration of function 'int strtoll(...)'
      implicit declaration of function 'int strtoul(...)'

- We haven't gotten `readline` to work with MIT-pthreads. (This isn't needed, but may be interesting for someone.)

2.3.7 Windows Source Distribution

You will need the following:

- VC++ 6.0 compiler (updated with 4 or 5 SP and Pre-processor package) The Pre-processor package is necessary for the macro assembler. More details at: http://msdn.microsoft.com/vstudio/sp/vs6sp5/faq.asp.

- The MySQL source distribution for Windows, which can be downloaded from http://www.mysql.com/downloads/.

Building MySQL

1. Create a work directory (e.g., workdir).

2. Unpack the source distribution in the aforementioned directory.

3. Start the VC++ 6.0 compiler.

4. In the `File` menu, select `Open Workspace`.

5. Open the `mysql.dsw` workspace you find on the work directory.

6. From the `Build` menu, select the `Set Active Configuration` menu.

7. Click over the screen selecting `mysqld - Win32 Debug` and click OK.

8. Press F7 to begin the build of the debug server, libs, and some client applications.

9. When the compilation finishes, copy the libs and the executables to a separate directory.

10. Compile the release versions that you want, in the same way.

11. Create the directory for the MySQL stuff: e.g., `c:\mysql`

12. From the workdir directory copy for the c:\mysql directory the following directories:

    - Data
    - Docs
    - Share

13. Create the directory `c:\mysql\bin` and copy all the servers and clients that you compiled previously.

14. If you want, also create the `lib` directory and copy the libs that you compiled previously.

15. Do a clean using Visual Studio.

Set up and start the server in the same way as for the binary Windows distribution. See Section 2.1.2.2, Preparing the windows MySQL environment.

2.4 Post-Installation Setup and Testing

Once you've installed MySQL (from either a binary or source distribution), you need to initialise the grant tables, start the server, and make sure that the server works okay. You may also wish to arrange for the server to be started and stopped automatically when your system starts up and shuts down.

Normally you install the grant tables and start the server like this for installation from a source distribution:

```
shell> ./scripts/mysql_install_db
shell> cd mysql_installation_directory
shell> ./bin/safe_mysqld --user=mysql &
```

For a binary distribution (not RPM or pkg packages), do this:

```
shell> cd mysql_installation_directory
shell> ./bin/mysql_install_db
shell> ./bin/safe_mysqld --user=mysql &
```

This creates the mysql database which will hold all database privileges, the test database which you can use to test MySQL, and also privilege entries for the user that run mysql_install_db and a root user (without any passwords). This also starts the mysqld server.

mysql_install_db will not overwrite any old privilege tables, so it should be safe to run in any circumstances. If you don't want to have the test database you can remove it with mysqladmin -u root drop test.

Testing is most easily done from the top-level directory of the MySQL distribution. For a binary distribution, this is your installation directory (typically something like /usr/local/mysql). For a source distribution, this is the main directory of your MySQL source tree. In the commands shown in this section and in the following subsections, BINDIR is the path to the location in which programs like mysqladmin and safe_mysqld are installed. For a binary distribution, this is the bin directory within the distribution. For a source distribution, BINDIR is probably /usr/local/bin, unless you specified an installation directory other than /usr/local when you ran configure. EXECDIR is the location in which the mysqld server is installed. For a binary distribution, this is the same as BINDIR. For a source distribution, EXECDIR is probably /usr/local/libexec.

Testing is described in detail:

1. If necessary, start the mysqld server and set up the initial MySQL grant tables containing the privileges that determine how users are allowed to connect to the server. This is normally done with the mysql_install_db script:

```
shell> scripts/mysql_install_db
```

Typically, `mysql_install_db` needs to be run only the first time you install MySQL. Therefore, if you are upgrading an existing installation, you can skip this step. (However, `mysql_install_db` is quite safe to use and will not update any tables that already exist, so if you are unsure of what to do, you can always run `mysql_install_db`.)

`mysql_install_db` creates six tables (`user`, `db`, `host`, `tables_priv`, `columns_priv`, and `func`) in the `mysql` database. A description of the initial privileges is given in Section 4.3.4, Setting Up the Initial MySQL Privileges. Briefly, these privileges allow the MySQL `root` user to do anything, and allow anybody to create or use databases with a name of `test` or starting with `test_`.

If you don't set up the grant tables, the following error will appear in the log file when you start the server:

```
mysqld: Can't find file: 'host.frm'
```

This may also happen with a binary MySQL distribution if you don't start MySQL by executing exactly `./bin/safe_mysqld`! See Section 4.7.2, `safe_mysqld`, the Wrapper Around `mysqld`.

You might need to run `mysql_install_db` as `root`. However, if you prefer, you can run the MySQL server as an unprivileged (non-`root`) user, provided that the user can read and write files in the database directory. Instructions for running MySQL as an unprivileged user are given in Section A.3.2, How to Run MySQL as a Normal User.

If you have problems with `mysql_install_db`, see Section 2.4.1, Problems Running `mysql_install_db`.

There are some alternatives to running the `mysql_install_db` script as it is provided in the MySQL distribution:

- You may want to edit `mysql_install_db` before running it, to change the initial privileges that are installed into the grant tables. This is useful if you want to install MySQL on a lot of machines with the same privileges. In this case you probably should need only to add a few extra INSERT statements to the `mysql.user` and `mysql.db` tables!

- If you want to change things in the grant tables after installing them, you can run `mysql_install_db`, then use `mysql -u root mysql` to connect to the grant tables as the MySQL `root` user and issue SQL statements to modify the grant tables directly.

- It is possible to re-create the grant tables completely after they have already been created. You might want to do this if you've already installed the tables but then want to re-create them after editing `mysql_install_db`.

For more information about these alternatives, see Section 4.3.4, Setting Up the Initial MySQL Privileges.

2.   Start the MySQL server like this:

```
shell> cd mysql_installation_directory
shell> bin/safe_mysqld &
```

If you have problems starting the server, see Section 2.4.2, Problems Starting the MySQL server.

3.   Use mysqladmin to verify that the server is running. The following commands provide a simple test to check that the server is up and responding to connections:

```
shell> BINDIR/mysqladmin version
shell> BINDIR/mysqladmin variables
```

The output from mysqladmin version varies slightly depending on your platform and version of MySQL, but should be similar to that shown here:

```
shell> BINDIR/mysqladmin version
mysqladmin  Ver 8.14 Distrib 3.23.32, for linux on i586
Copyright (C) 2000 MySQL AB & MySQL Finland AB & TCX DataKonsult AB
This software comes with ABSOLUTELY NO WARRANTY. This is free software,
and you are welcome to modify and redistribute it under the GPL license.

Server version          3.23.32-debug
Protocol version        10
Connection              Localhost via Unix socket
TCP port                3306
UNIX socket             /tmp/mysql.sock
Uptime:                 16 sec

Threads: 1  Questions: 9  Slow queries: 0
Opens: 7  Flush tables: 2  Open tables: 0
Queries per second avg: 0.000
Memory in use: 132K  Max memory used: 16773K
```

To get a feeling for what else you can do with BINDIR/mysqladmin, invoke it with the --help option.

4.   Verify that you can shut down the server:

```
shell> BINDIR/mysqladmin -u root shutdown
```

5.   Verify that you can restart the server. Do this using safe_mysqld or by invoking mysqld directly. For example:

```
shell> BINDIR/safe_mysqld --log &
```

If safe_mysqld fails, try running it from the MySQL installation directory (if you are not already there). If that doesn't work, see Section 2.4.2, Problems Starting the MySQL server.

6. Run some simple tests to verify that the server is working. The output should be
   similar to what is shown here:

```
shell> BINDIR/mysqlshow
+-----------+
| Databases |
+-----------+
| mysql     |
+-----------+

shell> BINDIR/mysqlshow mysql
Database: mysql
+--------------+
|    Tables    |
+--------------+
| columns_priv |
| db           |
| func         |
| host         |
| tables_priv  |
| user         |
+--------------+

shell> BINDIR/mysql -e "SELECT host,db,user FROM db" mysql
+------+--------+------+
| host | db     | user |
+------+--------+------+
| %    | test   |      |
| %    | test_% |      |
+------+--------+------+
```

There is also a benchmark suite in the sql-bench directory (under the MySQL
installation directory) that you can use to compare how MySQL performs on different platforms. The sql-bench/Results directory contains the results from many
runs against different databases and platforms. To run all tests, execute these commands:

```
shell> cd sql-bench
shell> run-all-tests
```

If you don't have the sql-bench directory, you are probably using an RPM for a
binary distribution. (Source distribution RPMs include the benchmark directory.) In
this case, you must first install the benchmark suite before you can use it. Beginning
with MySQL Version 3.22, there are benchmark RPM files named mysql-bench-
VERSION-i386.rpm that contain benchmark code and data.

If you have a source distribution, you can also run the tests in the tests subdirectory. For example, to run auto_increment.tst, do this:

```
shell> BINDIR/mysql -vvf test < ./tests/auto_increment.tst
```

The expected results are shown in the ./tests/auto_increment.res file.

2.4.1 **Problems Running** `mysql_install_db`

The purpose of the `mysql_install_db` script is to generate new MySQL privilege tables. It will not affect any other data! It will also not do anything if you already have MySQL privilege tables installed!

If you want to re-create your privilege tables, you should take down the `mysqld` server, if it's running, and then do something like:

```
mv mysql-data-directory/mysql mysql-data-directory/mysql-old
mysql_install_db
```

This section lists problems you might encounter when you run `mysql_install_db`:

`mysql_install_db` *doesn't install the grant tables*

> You may find that `mysql_install_db` fails to install the grant tables and terminates after displaying the following messages:

```
starting mysqld daemon with databases from XXXXXX
mysql daemon ended
```

> In this case, you should examine the log file very carefully! The log should be located in the directory XXXXXX named by the error message, and should indicate why `mysqld` didn't start. If you don't understand what happened, include the log when you post a bug report using `mysqlbug`! See Section 1.6.2.3, How to report bugs or problems.

There is already a `mysqld` *daemon running*

> In this case, you probably don't have to run `mysql_install_db` at all. You have to run `mysql_install_db` only once, when you install MySQL the first time.

Installing a second `mysqld` *daemon doesn't work when one daemon is running*

> This can happen when you already have an existing MySQL installation, but want to put a new installation in a different place (for example, for testing, or perhaps you simply want to run two installations at the same time). Generally the problem that occurs when you try to run the second server is that it tries to use the same socket and port as the old one. In this case you will get the error message: `Can't start server: Bind on TCP/IP port: Address already in use` or `Can't start server: Bind on unix socket` .... See Section 4.1.3, Installing Many Servers on the Same Machine.

You don't have write access to `/tmp`

> If you don't have write access to create a socket file at the default place (in `/tmp`) or permission to create temporary files in `/tmp`, you will get an error when running `mysql_install_db` or when starting or using `mysqld`.

> You can specify a different socket and temporary directory as follows:

```
shell> TMPDIR=/some_tmp_dir/
shell> MYSQL_UNIX_PORT=/some_tmp_dir/mysqld.sock
shell> export TMPDIR MYSQL_UNIX_PORT
```

See Section A.4.5, How to Protect or Change the MySQL Socket File /tmp/
mysql.sock.

some_tmp_dir should be the path to some directory for which you have write permission. See Appendix E.

After this you should be able to run mysql_install_db and start the server with
these commands:

```
shell> scripts/mysql_install_db
shell> BINDIR/safe_mysqld &
```

mysqld *crashes immediately*

If you are running RedHat Version 5.0 with a version of glibc older than 2.0.7-5,
you should make sure you have installed all glibc patches! There is a lot of information about this in the MySQL mail archives. Links to the mail archives are available online at http://lists.mysql.com/. Also, see Section 2.6.1, Linux Notes (All
Linux Versions).

You can also start mysqld manually using the --skip-grant-tables option and
add the privilege information yourself using mysql:

```
shell> BINDIR/safe_mysqld --skip-grant-tables &
shell> BINDIR/mysql -u root mysql
```

From mysql, manually execute the SQL commands in mysql_install_db. Make
sure you run mysqladmin flush-privileges or mysqladmin reload afterward
to tell the server to reload the grant tables.

2.4.2 Problems Starting the MySQL server

If you are going to use tables that support transactions (InnoDB, BDB), you should first
create a my.cnf file and set startup options for the table types you plan to use. See Chapter
7.

Generally, you start the mysqld server in one of these ways:

- By invoking mysql.server. This script is used primarily at system startup and shutdown, and is described more fully in Section 2.4.3, Starting and Stopping MySQL
  Automatically.

- By invoking safe_mysqld, which tries to determine the proper options for mysqld
  and then runs it with those options. See Section 4.7.2, safe_mysqld, the Wrapper
  Around mysqld.

- For Windows NT/2000/XP, please see Section 2.6.2.2, Starting MySQL on Windows NT, 2000, or XP.

- By invoking mysqld directly.

When the mysqld daemon starts up, it changes the directory to the data directory. This is where it expects to write log files and the pid (process ID) file, and where it expects to find databases.

The data directory location is hardwired in when the distribution is compiled. However, if mysqld expects to find the data directory somewhere other than where it really is on your system, it will not work properly. If you have problems with incorrect paths, you can find out what options mysqld allows and what the default path settings are by invoking mysqld with the --help option. You can override the defaults by specifying the correct pathnames as command-line arguments to mysqld. (These options can be used with safe_mysqld as well.)

Normally you should need to tell mysqld only the base directory under which MySQL is installed. You can do this with the --basedir option. You can also use --help to check the effect of changing path options (note that --help **must** be the final option of the mysqld command). For example:

```
shell> EXECDIR/mysqld --basedir=/usr/local --help
```

Once you determine the path settings you want, start the server without the --help option.

Whichever method you use to start the server, if it fails to start up correctly, check the log file to see if you can find out why. Log files are located in the data directory (typically /usr/local/mysql/data for a binary distribution, /usr/local/var for a source distribution, and \mysql\data\mysql.err on Windows). Look in the data directory for files with names of the form host_name.err and host_name.log where host_name is the name of your server host. Then check the last few lines of these files:

```
shell> tail host_name.err
shell> tail host_name.log
```

Look for something like the following in the log file:

```
000729 14:50:10  bdb:  Recovery function for LSN 1 27595 failed
000729 14:50:10  bdb:  warning: ./test/t1.db: No such file or directory
000729 14:50:10  Can't init databases
```

This means that you didn't start mysqld with --bdb-no-recover and Berkeley DB found something wrong with its log files when it tried to recover your databases. To be able to continue, you should move away the old Berkeley DB log file from the database directory to some other place, where you can later examine it. The log files are named log.0000000001, where the number will increase over time.

If you are running `mysqld` with BDB table support and `mysqld` core dumps at start this could be because of some problems with the BDB recover log. In this case you can try starting `mysqld` with `--bdb-no-recover`. If this helps, then you should remove all `log.*` files from the data directory and try starting `mysqld` again.

If you get the following error, it means that some other program (or another `mysqld` server) is already using the TCP/IP port or socket `mysqld` is trying to use:

```
Can't start server: Bind on TCP/IP port: Address already in use
  or
Can't start server : Bind on unix socket...
```

Use `ps` to make sure that you don't have another `mysqld` server running. If you can't find another server running, you can try to execute the command `telnet your-host-name tcp-ip-port-number` and press Enter a couple of times. If you don't get an error message like `telnet: Unable to connect to remote host: Connection refused`, something is using the TCP/IP port `mysqld` is trying to use. See Section 2.4.1, Problems Running `mysql_install_db` and Section 4.1.4, Running Multiple MySQL Servers on the Same Machine.

If `mysqld` is currently running, you can find out what path settings it is using by executing this command:

```
shell> mysqladmin variables
```

or

```
shell> mysqladmin -h 'your-host-name' variables
```

If you get `Errcode 13`, which means `Permission denied`, when starting `mysqld` this means that you didn't have the right to read/create files in the MySQL database or log directory. In this case you should either start `mysqld` as the root user or change the permissions for the involved files and directories so that you have the right to use them.

If `safe_mysqld` starts the server but you can't connect to it, you should make sure you have an entry in `/etc/hosts` that looks like this:

```
127.0.0.1       localhost
```

This problem occurs only on systems that don't have a working thread library and for which MySQL must be configured to use MIT-pthreads.

If you can't get `mysqld` to start you can try to make a trace file to find the problem. See Section D.1.2, Creating Trace Files.

If you are using InnoDB tables, refer to the InnoDB-specific startup options. See Section 7.5.2, InnoDB Startup Options.

If you are using BDB (Berkeley DB) tables, you should familiarise yourself with the different BDB specific startup options. See Section 7.6.3, BDB Startup Options.

2.4.3 Starting and Stopping MySQL Automatically

The `mysql.server` and `safe_mysqld` scripts can be used to start the server automatically at system startup time. `mysql.server` can also be used to stop the server.

The `mysql.server` script can be used to start or stop the server by invoking it with `start` or `stop` arguments:

```
shell> mysql.server start
shell> mysql.server stop
```

`mysql.server` can be found in the `share/mysql` directory under the MySQL installation directory or in the `support-files` directory of the MySQL source tree.

Before `mysql.server` starts the server, it changes the directory to the MySQL installation directory, then invokes `safe_mysqld`. You might need to edit `mysql.server` if you have a binary distribution that you've installed in a non-standard location. Modify it to `cd` into the proper directory before it runs `safe_mysqld`. If you want the server to run as some specific user, add an appropriate `user` line to the `/etc/my.cnf` file, as shown later in this section.

`mysql.server stop` brings down the server by sending a signal to it. You can take down the server manually by executing `mysqladmin shutdown`.

You might want to add these start and stop commands to the appropriate places in your `/etc/rc*` files when you start using MySQL for production applications. Note that if you modify `mysql.server`, and then upgrade MySQL sometime, your modified version will be overwritten, so you should make a copy of your edited version that you can reinstall.

If your system uses `/etc/rc.local` to start external scripts, you should append the following to it:

```
/bin/sh -c 'cd /usr/local/mysql ; ./bin/safe_mysqld --user=mysql &'
```

You can also add options for `mysql.server` in a global `/etc/my.cnf` file. A typical `/etc/my.cnf` file might look like this:

```
[mysqld]
datadir=/usr/local/mysql/var
socket=/var/tmp/mysql.sock
port=3306
user=mysql

[mysql.server]
basedir=/usr/local/mysql
```

The `mysql.server` script understands the following options: `datadir`, `basedir`, and `pid-file`.

The following table shows which option groups each of the startup scripts read from option files:

Script	Option groups
`mysqld`	`mysqld` and `server`
`mysql.server`	`mysql.server`, `mysqld`, and `server`
`safe_mysqld`	`mysql.server`, `mysqld`, and `server`

See Section 4.1.2, `my.cnf` Option Files.

2.5 Upgrading/Downgrading MySQL

You can always move the MySQL form and data files between different versions on the same architecture as long as you have the same base version of MySQL. The current base version is 3. If you change the character set when running MySQL (which may also change the sort order), you must run `myisamchk -r -q` on all tables. Otherwise, your indexes may not be ordered correctly.

If you are afraid of new versions, you can always rename your old `mysqld` to something like `mysqld-old-version-number`. If your new `mysqld` then does something unexpected, you can simply shut it down and restart with your old `mysqld`!

When you do an upgrade you should also back up your old databases, of course.

If after an upgrade, you experience problems with recompiled client programs, like `Commands out of sync` or unexpected core dumps, you probably have used an old header or library file when compiling your programs. In this case you should check the date for your `mysql.h` file and `libmysqlclient.a` library to verify that they are from the new MySQL distribution. If not, please recompile your programs!

If you get some problems that the new `mysqld` server doesn't want to start or that you can't connect without a password, check that you don't have some old `my.cnf` file from your old installation! You can check this with: `program-name --print-defaults`. If this outputs anything other than the program name, you have an active `my.cnf` file that will affect things!

It is a good idea to rebuild and reinstall the `Msql-Mysql-modules` distribution whenever you install a new release of MySQL, particularly if you notice symptoms such as all your `DBI` scripts dumping core after you upgrade MySQL.

2.5.1 Upgrading from Version 3.23 to Version 4.0

You can use your old data files without any modification with Version 4.0. If you want to move your data from a MySQL 4.0 server to an older server, you have to use mysqldump.

Old clients should work with a Version 4.0 server without any problems.

The following lists tell what you have to watch out for when upgrading to version 4.0;

- DOUBLE and FLOAT columns are now honoring the UNSIGNED flag on storage (before, UNSIGNED was ignored for these columns).

- Use ORDER BY column DESC now always sorts NULL values first; in 3.23 this was not always consistent.

- SHOW INDEX has 2 columns more (Null and Index_type) than it had in 3.23.

- SIGNED is a reserved word.

- The result of all bitwise operators |, &, <<, >>, and ~ is now unsigned. This may cause problems if you are using them in a context where you want a signed result. See Section 6.3.5, Cast Functions.

- **Note**: when you use subtraction between integer values where one is of type UNSIGNED, the result will be unsigned! In other words, before upgrading to MySQL 4.0, you should check your application for cases where you are subtracting a value from an unsigned entity and want a negative answer or subtracting an unsigned value from an integer column. You can disable this behaviour by using the --sql-mode=NO_UNSIGNED_SUBTRACTION option when starting mysqld. See Section 6.3.5, Cast Functions.

- To use MATCH ... AGAINST (... IN BOOLEAN MODE) with your tables, you need to rebuild them with ALTER TABLE table_name TYPE=MyISAM, **even** if they are of MyISAM type.

- LOCATE() and INSTR() are case-sensitive if one of the arguments is a binary string.

- STRCMP() now uses the current character set when doing comparisons, which means that the default comparison behavior now is case-insensitive.

- HEX(string) now returns the characters in string converted to hexadecimal. If you want to convert a number to hexadecimal, you should ensure that you call HEX() with a numeric argument.

- In 3.23, INSERT INTO ... SELECT always had IGNORE enabled. In 4.0.1, MySQL will stop (and possibly roll back) in case of an error if you don't specify IGNORE.

- `safe_mysqld` is renamed to `mysqld_safe`.

- The old C API functions `mysql_drop_db`, `mysql_create_db`, and `mysql_con-nect` are not supported anymore, unless you compile MySQL with `CFLAGS=-DUSE_OLD_FUNCTIONS`. Instead of doing this, it is preferable to change the client to use the new 4.0 API.

- In the `MYSQL_FIELD` structure, `length` and `max_length` have changed from `unsigned int` to `unsigned long`. This should not cause any other problems than some warnings if you use these to `printf()` type function.

- You should use `TRUNCATE TABLE` when you want to delete all rows from a table and you don't care how many rows were deleted. (Because `TRUNCATE TABLE` is faster than `DELETE FROM table_name`).

- You will get an error if you have an active `LOCK TABLES` or transaction when trying to execute `TRUNCATE TABLE` or `DROP DATABASE`.

- You should use integers to store values in BIGINT columns (instead of using strings, as you did in MySQL 3.23). Using strings will still work, but using integers is more efficient.

- Format of `SHOW OPEN TABLE` has changed.

- Multi-threaded clients should use `mysql_thread_init()` and `mysql_thread_end()`. See Section 8.4.8, How to Make a Threaded Client.

- If you want to recompile the Perl DBD::mysql module, you must get Msql-Mysql-modules version 1.2218 or newer because the older DBD modules used the deprecated `drop_db()` call.

- `RAND(seed)` returns a different random number series in 4.0 than in 3.23; this was done to further differentiate `RAND(seed)` and `RAND(seed+1)`.

2.5.2 Upgrading from Version 3.22 to Version 3.23

MySQL Version 3.23 supports tables of the new `MyISAM` type and the old `ISAM` type. You don't have to convert your old tables to use these with Version 3.23. By default, all new tables will be created with type `MyISAM` (unless you start `mysqld` with the `--default-table-type=isam` option). You can change an `ISAM` table to a `MyISAM` table with `ALTER TABLE table_name TYPE=MyISAM` or the Perl script `mysql_convert_table_format`.

Version 3.22 and 3.21 clients will work without any problems with a Version 3.23 server.

The following list tells what you have to watch out for when upgrading to Version 3.23:

- All tables that use the `tis620` character set must be fixed with `myisamchk -r` or `REPAIR TABLE`.

- If you do a DROP DATABASE on a symbolic linked database, both the link and the original database are deleted. (This didn't happen in 3.22 because configure didn't detect the readlink system call.)

- OPTIMIZE TABLE now only works for MyISAM tables. For other table types, you can use ALTER TABLE to optimise the table. During OPTIMIZE TABLE the table is now locked from other threads.

- The MySQL client mysql is now by default started with the option --no-named-commands (-g). This option can be disabled with --enable-named-commands (-G). This may cause incompatibility problems in some cases—for example, in SQL scripts that use named commands without a semicolon! Long format commands still work from the first line.

- Date functions that work on parts of dates (like MONTH()) will now return 0 for 0000-00-00 dates. (MySQL 3.22 returned NULL.)

- If you are using the german character sort order, you must repair all your tables with isamchk -r, as we have made some changes in the sort order!

- The default return type of IF will now depend on both arguments and not only the first argument.

- AUTO_INCREMENT will not work with negative numbers. The reason for this is that negative numbers caused problems when wrapping from -1 to 0. AUTO_INCREMENT for MyISAM tables is no handled at a lower level and is much faster than before. For MyISAM tables old numbers are also not reused anymore, even if you delete some rows from the table.

- CASE, DELAYED, ELSE, END, FULLTEXT, INNER, RIGHT, THEN, and WHEN are now reserved words.

- FLOAT(X) is now a true floating-point type and not a value with a fixed number of decimals.

- When declaring DECIMAL(length,dec) the length argument no longer includes a place for the sign or the decimal point.

- A TIME string must now be of one of the following formats: [[[DAYS] [H]H:]MM:]SS[.fraction] or [[[[[H]H]H]H]MM]SS[.fraction].

- LIKE now compares strings using the same character comparison rules as =. If you require the old behavior, you can compile MySQL with the CXXFLAGS=-DLIKE_CMP_TOUPPER flag.

- REGEXP is now case-insensitive for normal (not binary) strings.

- When you check/repair tables you should use CHECK TABLE or myisamchk for MyISAM tables (.MYI) and isamchk for ISAM (.ISM) tables.

- If you want your mysqldump files to be compatible between MySQL Version 3.22 and Version 3.23, you should not use the --opt or --full option to mysqldump.

- Check all your calls to DATE_FORMAT() to make sure there is a % before each format character. (MySQL Version 3.22 did allow this syntax.)

- mysql_fetch_fields_direct is now a function (it was a macro) and it returns a pointer to a MYSQL_FIELD instead of a MYSQL_FIELD.

- mysql_num_fields() can no longer be used on a MYSQL* object (it's now a function that takes MYSQL_RES* as an argument, so you should use mysql_field_count() instead).

- In MySQL Version 3.22, the output of SELECT DISTINCT . . . was almost always sorted. In Version 3.23, you must use GROUP BY or ORDER BY to obtain sorted output.

- SUM() now returns NULL, instead of 0, if there are no matching rows. This is according to ANSI SQL.

- An AND or OR with NULL values will now return NULL instead of 0. This mostly affects queries that use *not* on an AND/OR expression as NOT NULL = NULL. LPAD() and RPAD() will shorten the result string if it's longer than the length argument.

2.5.3 Upgrading from Version 3.21 to Version 3.22

Nothing that affects compatibility has changed between versions 3.21 and 3.22. The only pitfall is that new tables that are created with DATE type columns will use the new way to store the date. You can't access these new fields from an old version of mysqld.

After installing MySQL Version 3.22, you should start the new server and then run the mysql_fix_privilege_tables script. This will add the new privileges that you need to use the GRANT command. If you forget this, you will get Access denied when you try to use ALTER TABLE, CREATE INDEX, or DROP INDEX. If your MySQL root user requires a password, you should give this as an argument to mysql_fix_privilege_tables.

The C API interface to mysql_real_connect() has changed. If you have an old client program that calls this function, you must place a 0 for the new db argument (or recode the client to send the db element for faster connections). You must also call mysql_init() before calling mysql_real_connect()! This change was done to allow the new mysql_options() function to save options in the MYSQL handler structure.

The mysqld variable key_buffer has changed names to key_buffer_size, but you can still use the old name in your startup files.

2.5.4 Upgrading from Version 3.20 to Version 3.21

If you are running a version older than Version 3.20.28 and want to switch to Version 3.21, you need to do the following:

You can start the `mysqld` Version 3.21 server with `safe_mysqld —old-protocol` to use it with clients from a Version 3.20 distribution. In this case, the new client function `mysql_errno()` will not return any server error, only `CR_UNKNOWN_ERROR` (but it works for client errors), and the server uses the old `password()` checking rather than the new one.

If you are **not** using the `--old-protocol` option to `mysqld`, you will need to make the following changes:

- All client code must be recompiled. If you are using ODBC, you must get the new `MyODBC` 2.x driver.

- The script `scripts/add_long_password` must be run to convert the `Password` field in the `mysql.user` table to `CHAR(16)`.

- All passwords must be reassigned in the `mysql.user` table (to get 62-bit rather than 31-bit passwords).

- The table format hasn't changed, so you don't have to convert any tables.

MySQL Version 3.20.28 and above can handle the new `user` table format without affecting clients. If you have a MySQL version earlier than Version 3.20.28, passwords will no longer work with it if you convert the `user` table. So to be safe, you should first upgrade to at least Version 3.20.28 and then upgrade to Version 3.21.

The new client code works with a 3.20.x `mysqld` server, so if you experience problems with 3.21.x, you can use the old 3.20.x server without having to recompile the clients again.

If you are not using the `--old-protocol` option to `mysqld`, old clients will issue the error message:

```
ERROR: Protocol mismatch. Server Version = 10 Client Version = 9
```

The new Perl `DBI/DBD` interface also supports the old `mysqlperl` interface. The only change you have to make if you use `mysqlperl` is to change the arguments to the `connect()` function. The new arguments are: `host`, `database`, `user`, and `password` (the `user` and `password` arguments have changed places). See Section 8.2.2, The `DBI` Interface.

The following changes may affect queries in old applications:

- HAVING must now be specified before any ORDER BY clause.

- The parameters to LOCATE() have been swapped.

- There are some new reserved words. The most notable are DATE, TIME, and TIMES-TAMP.

2.5.5 Upgrading to Another Architecture

If you are using MySQL Version 3.23, you can copy the .frm, .MYI, and .MYD files between different architectures that support the same floating-point format. (MySQL takes care of any byte-swapping issues.)

The MySQL ISAM data and index files (.ISD and *.ISM, respectively) are architecture-dependent and in some cases OS-dependent. If you want to move your applications to another machine that has a different architecture or OS than your current machine, you should not try to move a database by simply copying the files to the other machine. Use mysqldump instead.

By default, mysqldump will create a file full of SQL statements. You can then transfer the file to the other machine and feed it as input to the mysql client.

Try mysqldump --help to see what options are available. If you are moving the data to a newer version of MySQL, you should use mysqldump --opt with the newer version to get a fast, compact dump.

The easiest (although not the fastest) way to move a database between two machines is to run the following commands on the machine on which the database is located:

```
shell> mysqladmin -h 'other hostname' create db_name
shell> mysqldump --opt db_name \
       | mysql -h 'other hostname' db_name
```

If you want to copy a database from a remote machine over a slow network, you can use:

```
shell> mysqladmin create db_name
shell> mysqldump -h 'other hostname' --opt --compress db_name \
       | mysql db_name
```

You can also store the result in a file, then transfer the file to the target machine and load the file into the database there. For example, you can dump a database to a file on the source machine like this:

```
shell> mysqldump --quick db_name | gzip > db_name.contents.gz
```

(The file created in this example is compressed.) Transfer the file containing the database contents to the target machine and run these commands there:

```
shell> mysqladmin create db_name
shell> gunzip < db_name.contents.gz | mysql db_name
```

You can also use mysqldump and mysqlimport to accomplish the database transfer. For big tables, this is much faster than simply using mysqldump. In the following commands, DUMPDIR represents the full pathname of the directory you use to store the output from mysqldump.

First, create the directory for the output files and dump the database:

```
shell> mkdir DUMPDIR
shell> mysqldump --tab=DUMPDIR db_name
```

Then transfer the files in the DUMPDIR directory to some corresponding directory on the target machine and load the files into MySQL there:

```
shell> mysqladmin create db_name              # create database
shell> cat DUMPDIR/*.sql | mysql db_name      # create tables in database
shell> mysqlimport db_name DUMPDIR/*.txt      # load data into tables
```

Also, don't forget to copy the mysql database because that's where the grant tables (user, db, host) are stored. You may have to run commands as the MySQL root user on the new machine until you have the mysql database in place.

After you import the mysql database on the new machine, execute mysqladmin flush-privileges so that the server reloads the grant table information.

2.6 Operating System–Specific Notes

2.6.1 Linux Notes (All Linux Versions)

The following notes regarding glibc apply only to the situation when you build MySQL yourself. If you are running Linux on an x86 machine, in most cases it is much better for you to just use our binary. We link our binaries against the best patched version of glibc we can come up with and with the best compiler options, in an attempt to make it suitable for a high-load server. So if you read the following text, and are in doubt about what you should do, try our binary first to see if it meets your needs, and worry about your own build only after you have discovered that our binary is not good enough. In that case, we would appreciate a note about it, so we can build a better binary next time. For a typical user, even for setups with a lot of concurrent connections and/or tables exceeding 2GB limit, our binary in most cases is the best choice.

MySQL uses LinuxThreads on Linux. If you are using an old Linux version that doesn't have glibc2, you must install LinuxThreads before trying to compile MySQL. You can get LinuxThreads at http://www.mysql.com/Downloads/Linux/.

Note: We have seen some strange problems with Linux 2.2.14 and MySQL on SMP systems. If you have a SMP system, we recommend you upgrade to Linux 2.4 as soon as possible! Your system will be faster and more stable by doing this!

Note that `glibc` versions before and including Version 2.1.1 have a fatal bug in `pthread_mutex_timedwait` handling, which is used when you do INSERT DELAYED. We recommend that you not use INSERT DELAYED before upgrading glibc.

If you plan to have 1000+ concurrent connections, you will need to make some changes to LinuxThreads, recompile it, and relink MySQL against the new `libpthread.a`. Increase `PTHREAD_THREADS_MAX` in `sysdeps/unix/sysv/linux/bits/local_lim.h` to 4096 and decrease `STACK_SIZE` in `linuxthreads/internals.h` to 256 KB. The paths are relative to the root of `glibc` Note that MySQL will not be stable with around 600-1000 connections if `STACK_SIZE` is the default of 2 M.

If MySQL can't open enough files, or connections, it may be that you haven't configured Linux to handle enough files.

In Linux 2.2 and onward, you can check the number of allocated file handlers by doing:

```
cat /proc/sys/fs/file-max
cat /proc/sys/fs/dquot-max
cat /proc/sys/fs/super-max
```

If you have more than 16M of memory, you should add something like the following in your boot script (`/etc/rc/boot.local` on SuSE):

```
echo 65536 > /proc/sys/fs/file-max
echo 8192 > /proc/sys/fs/dquot-max
echo 1024 > /proc/sys/fs/super-max
```

You can also run the preceding commands from the command-line as root, but in this case your old limits will be used the next time your computer reboots.

You should also add /etc/my.cnf:

```
[safe_mysqld]
open-files-limit=8192
```

This should allow MySQL to create up to 8192 connections + files.

The `STACK_SIZE` constant in LinuxThreads controls the spacing of thread stacks in the address space. It needs to be large enough so that there will be plenty of room for the stack of each individual thread, but small enough to keep the stack of some threads from running into the global `mysqld` data. Unfortunately, the Linux implementation of `mmap()`, as we have experimentally discovered, will successfully unmap an already mapped region if you ask it to map out an address already in use, zeroing out the data on the entire page, instead of returning an error. So, the safety of `mysqld` or any other threaded application depends on the "gentleman" behavior of the code that creates threads. The user must take measures to make sure the number of running threads at any time is sufficiently low for thread stacks to stay away from the global heap. With mysqld, you should enforce this "gentleman" behavior by setting a reasonable value for the max_connections variable.

If you build MySQL yourself and do not want to mess with patching LinuxThreads, you should set max_connections to a value no higher than 500. It should be even less if you have a large key buffer, large heap tables, or some other things that make mysqld allocate a lot of memory, or if you are running a 2.2 kernel with a 2GB patch. If you are using our binary or RPM version 3.23.25 or later, you can safely set max_connections at 1500, assuming no large key buffer or heap tables with lots of data. The more you reduce STACK_SIZE in LinuxThreads the more threads you can safely create. We recommend the values between 128K and 256K.

If you use a lot of concurrent connections, you may suffer from a "feature" in the 2.2 kernel that penalises a process for forking or cloning a child in an attempt to prevent a fork bomb attack. This will cause MySQL not to scale well as you increase the number of concurrent clients. On single-CPU systems, we have seen this manifested in a very slow thread creation, which means it may take a long time to connect to MySQL (as long as 1 minute), and it may take just as long to shut it down. On multiple-CPU systems, we have observed a gradual drop in query speed as the number of clients increases. In the process of trying to find a solution, we have received a kernel patch from one of our users, who claimed it made a lot of difference for his site. The patch is available at http://www.mysql.com/Downloads/Patches/linux-fork.patch. We have now done rather extensive testing of this patch on both development and production systems. It has significantly improved MySQL performance without causing any problems and we now recommend it to our users who are still running high-load servers on 2.2 kernels. This issue has been fixed in the 2.4 kernel, so if you are not satisfied with the current performance of your system, rather than patching your 2.2 kernel, it might be easier to just upgrade to 2.4, which will also give you a nice SMP boost in addition to fixing this fairness bug.

We have tested MySQL on the 2.4 kernel on a 2-CPU machine and found MySQL scales **much** better—there was virtually no slowdown on queries throughput all the way up to 1000 clients, and the MySQL scaling factor (computed as the ratio of maximum throughput to the throughput with one client) was 180%. We have observed similar results on a 4-CPU system—virtually no slowdown as the number of clients was increased up to 1000, and 300% scaling factor. So for a high-load SMP server we would definitely recommend the 2.4 kernel at this point. We have discovered that it is essential to run the mysqld process with the highest possible priority on the 2.4 kernel to achieve maximum performance. This can be done by adding the renice -20 $$ command to safe_mysqld. In our testing on a 4-CPU machine, increasing the priority gave a 60% increase in throughput with 400 clients.

We are currently also trying to collect more info on how well MySQL performs on the 2.4 kernel on 4-way and 8-way systems. If you have access to such a system and have done some benchmarks, please send an email to *docs@mysql.com* with the results. We will include them in the manual.

There is another issue that greatly hurts MySQL performance, especially on SMP systems. The implementation of mutex in LinuxThreads in glibc-2.1 is very bad for programs with many threads that only hold the mutex for a short time. On an SMP system, ironic as it is, if you link MySQL against unmodified LinuxThreads, removing processors from the machine improves MySQL performance in many cases. We have made a patch available for glibc 2.1.3 to correct this behavior (http://www.mysql.com/Downloads/Linux/linuxthreads-2.1-patch).

With glibc-2.2.2 MySQL version 3.23.36 will use the adaptive mutex, which is much better than even the patched one in glibc-2.1.3. Be warned, however, that under some conditions, the current mutex code in glibc-2.2.2 overspins, which hurts MySQL performance. The chance of this condition can be reduced by renicing the mysqld process to the highest priority. We have also been able to correct the overspin behavior with a patch, available at http://www.mysql.com/Downloads/Linux/linuxthreads-2.2.2.patch. It combines the correction of overspin, maximum number of threads, and stack spacing all in one. You will need to apply it in the linuxthreads directory with the patch -p0 </tmp/linuxthreads-2.2.2.patch. We hope it will be included in some form in future releases of glibc-2.2. In any case, if you link against glibc-2.2.2 you still need to correct STACK_SIZE and PTHREAD_THREADS_MAX. We hope that the defaults will be corrected to some more acceptable values for high-load MySQL setup in the future so that your own build can be reduced to ./configure; make; make install.

We recommend that you use the preceding patches to build a special static version of libpthread.a and use it only for statically linking against MySQL. We know that the patches are safe for MySQL and significantly improve its performance, but we cannot say anything about other applications. If you link other applications against the patched version of the library, or build a patched shared version and install it on your system, you are doing it at your own risk with regard to other applications that depend on LinuxThreads.

If you experience any strange problems during the installation of MySQL, or with some common utilities hanging, it is very likely that they are either library- or compiler-related. If this is the case, using our binary will resolve them.

One known problem with the binary distribution is that with older Linux systems that use libc (like RedHat 4.x or Slackware), you will get some non-fatal problems with hostname resolution. See Section 2.6.1.1, Linux notes for binary distributions.

When using LinuxThreads you will see a minimum of three processes running. These are in fact threads. There will be one thread for the LinuxThreads manager, one thread to handle connections, and one thread to handle alarms and signals.

Note that the Linux kernel and the LinuxThread library can by default only have 1024 threads. This means that you can only have up to 1021 connections to MySQL on an unpatched system. The page http://www.volano.com/linuxnotes.html contains information on how to go around this limit.

If you see a dead mysqld daemon process with ps, this usually means that you have found a bug in MySQL or you have a corrupted table. See Section A.4.1, What to Do if MySQL Keeps Crashing.

To get a core dump on Linux if mysqld dies with a SIGSEGV signal, you can start mysqld with the --core-file option. Note that you also probably need to raise the core file size by adding ulimit -c 1000000 to safe_mysqld or starting safe_mysqld with --core-file-sizes=1000000. See Section 4.7.2, safe_mysqld, the Wrapper Around mysqld.

If you are linking your own MySQL client and get the error:

```
ld.so.1: ./my: fatal: libmysqlclient.so.4:
open failed: No such file or directory
```

when executing them, the problem can be avoided by one of the following methods:

- Link the client with the following flag (instead of -Lpath): -Wl,r/path-lib-mysqlclient.so.

- Copy libmysqclient.so to /usr/lib.

- Add the pathname of the directory where libmysqlclient.so is located to the LD_RUN_PATH environment variable before running your client.

If you are using the Fujitsu compiler (fcc / FCC) you will have some problems compiling MySQL because the Linux header files are very gcc-oriented.

The following configure line should work with fcc/FCC:

```
CC=fcc CFLAGS="-O -K fast -K lib -K omitfp -Kpreex -D_GNU_SOURCE \
-DCONST=const -DNO_STRTOLL_PROTO" CXX=FCC CXXFLAGS="-O -K fast -K lib \
-K omitfp -K preex --no_exceptions --no_rtti -D_GNU_SOURCE -DCONST=const \
-Dalloca=__builtin_alloca -DNO_STRTOLL_PROTO \
'-D_EXTERN_INLINE=static __inline'" ./configure --prefix=/usr/local/mysql \
--enable-assembler --with-mysqld-ldflags=-all-static --disable-shared \
--with-low-memory
```

2.6.1.1 Linux notes for binary distributions

MySQL needs at least Linux Version 2.0.

Warning: We have reports from some MySQL users that they have experienced serious stability problems with MySQL with Linux kernel 2.2.14. If you are using this kernel you should upgrade to 2.2.19 (or newer) or to a 2.4 kernel. If you have a multi-CPU box, then you should seriously consider using 2.4, as this will give you a significant speed boost.

The binary release is linked with -static, which means you do not normally need to worry about which version of the system libraries you have. You need not install Linux-Threads, either. A program linked with -static is slightly bigger than a dynamically linked program but also slightly faster (3-5%). One problem, however, is that you can't use user-definable functions (UDFs) with a statically linked program. If you are going to write or use UDF functions (this is something only for C or C++ programmers), you must compile MySQL yourself, using dynamic linking.

If you are using a libc-based system (instead of a glibc2 system), you will probably get some problems with hostname resolving and getpwnam() with the binary release. (This is because glibc unfortunately depends on some external libraries to resolve host-names and getpwent(), even when compiled with -static.) In this case you probably get the following error message when you run mysql_install_db:

```
Sorry, the host 'xxxx' could not be looked up
```

or the following error when you try to run mysqld with the --user option:

```
getpwnam: No such file or directory
```

You can solve this problem in one of the following ways:

- Get a MySQL source distribution (an RPM or the tar.gz distribution) and install this instead.

- Execute mysql_install_db --force. This will not execute the resolveip test in mysql_install_db. The downside is that you can't use hostnames in the grant tables; you must use IP numbers instead (except for localhost). If you are using an old MySQL release that doesn't support --force, you have to remove the resolveip test in mysql_install with an editor.

- Start mysqld with su instead of using --user.

The Linux-Intel binary and RPM releases of MySQL are configured for the highest possible speed. We are always trying to use the fastest stable compiler available.

MySQL Perl support requires Version Perl 5.004_03 or newer.

On some Linux 2.2 versions, you may get the error Resource temporarily unavailable when you do a lot of new connections to a mysqld server over TCP/IP.

The problem is that Linux has a delay between when you close a TCP/IP socket and until this is actually freed by the system. As there is only room for a finite number of TCP/IP slots, you will get the preceding error if you try to do too many new TCP/IP connections during a small time, like when you run the MySQL test-connect benchmark over TCP/IP.

We have mailed about this problem a couple of times to different Linux mailing lists but have never been able to resolve this properly.

The only known 'fix' to this problem is to use persistent connections in your clients or to use sockets, if you are running the database server and clients on the same machine. We hope that the Linux 2.4 kernel will fix this problem in the future.

2.6.1.2 Linux x86 notes

MySQL requires libc Version 5.4.12 or newer. It's known to work with libc 5.4.46. glibc Version 2.0.6 and later should also work. There have been some problems with the glibc RPMs from RedHat, so if you have problems, check whether there are any updates! The glibc 2.0.7-19 and 2.0.7-29 RPMs are known to work.

If you are using gcc 3.0 and above to compile MySQL, you must install the libstdc++v3 library before compiling MySQL; if you don't do this you will get an error about a missing __cxa_pure_virtual symbol during linking!

On some older Linux distributions, configure may produce an error like this:

```
Syntax error in sched.h. Change _P to __P in the /usr/include/sched.h file.
See the Installation chapter in the Reference Manual.
```

Just do what the error message says and add an extra underscore to the _P macro that has only one underscore, then try again.

You may get some warnings when compiling; the following can be ignored:

```
mysqld.cc -o objs-thread/mysqld.o
mysqld.cc: In function 'void init_signals()':
mysqld.cc:315: warning: assignment of negative value '-1' to
'long unsigned int'
mysqld.cc: In function 'void * signal_hand(void *)':
mysqld.cc:346: warning: assignment of negative value '-1' to
'long unsigned int'
```

In Debian GNU/Linux, if you want MySQL to start automatically when the system boots, do the following:

```
shell> cp support-files/mysql.server /etc/init.d/mysql.server
shell> /usr/sbin/update-rc.d mysql.server defaults 99
```

mysql.server can be found in the share/mysql directory under the MySQL installation directory or in the support-files directory of the MySQL source tree.

If mysqld always core dumps when it starts up, the problem may be that you have an old /lib/libc.a. Try renaming it, then remove sql/mysqld and do a new make install and try again. This problem has been reported on some Slackware installations.

If you get the following error when linking mysqld, it means that your libg++.a is not installed correctly:

```
/usr/lib/libc.a(putc.o): In function '_IO_putc':
putc.o(.text+0x0): multiple definition of '_IO_putc'
```

You can avoid using `libg++.a` by running `configure` like this:

```
shell> CXX=gcc ./configure
```

If you are running gcc 3.0 and above, you can't use the preceding trick with a setting to CXX=gcc.

2.6.1.3 Linux SPARC notes

In some implementations, `readdir_r()` is broken. The symptom is that SHOW DATABASES always returns an empty set. This can be fixed by removing HAVE_READDIR_R from `config.h` after configuring and before compiling.

Some problems will require patching your Linux installation. The patch can be found at http://www.mysql.com/Downloads/patches/Linux-sparc-2.0.30.diff. This patch is against the Linux distribution `sparclinux-2.0.30.tar.gz` that is available at `vger.rutgers.edu` (a version of Linux that was never merged with the official 2.0.30). You must also install LinuxThreads Version 0.6 or newer.

2.6.1.4 Linux-Alpha notes

MySQL Version 3.23.12 is the first MySQL version that is tested on Linux-Alpha. If you plan to use MySQL on Linux-Alpha, you should ensure that you have this version or newer.

We have tested MySQL on Alpha with our benchmarks and test suite, and it appears to work nicely. The main thing we haven't yet had time to test is how things works with many concurrent users.

When we compiled the standard MySQL binary, we were using SuSE 6.4, kernel 2.2.13-SMP, Compaq C compiler (V6.2-504), and Compaq C++ compiler (V6.3-005) on a Comaq DS20 machine with an Alpha EV6 processor.

You can find the above compilers at http://www.support.compaq.com/alpha-tools/). By using these compilers, instead of gcc, we get about 9-14% better performance with MySQL.

Note that the configure line optimised the binary for the current CPU; this means you can only use our binary if you have an Alpha EV6 processor. We also compile statically to avoid library problems.

```
CC=ccc CFLAGS="-fast" CXX=cxx CXXFLAGS="-fast -noexceptions -nortti" \
./configure --prefix=/usr/local/mysql --disable-shared \
--with-extra-charsets=complex --enable-thread-safe-client \
--with-mysqld-ldflags=-non_shared --with-client-ldflags=-non_shared
```

If you want to use egcs, the following configure line worked for us:

```
CFLAGS="-O3 -fomit-frame-pointer" CXX=gcc \
CXXFLAGS="-O3 -fomit-frame-pointer -felide-constructors \
-fno-exceptions -fno-rtti" ./configure --prefix=/usr/local/mysql \
--disable-shared
```

Some known problems when running MySQL on Linux-Alpha:

- Debugging threaded applications like MySQL will not work with gdb 4.18. You should download and use gdb 5.1 instead!

- If you try linking mysqld statically when using gcc, the resulting image will core dump at startup. In other words, **don't** use --with-mysqld-ldflags=-all-static with gcc.

2.6.1.5 Linux PowerPC notes

MySQL should work on MkLinux with the newest glibc package (tested with glibc 2.0.7).

2.6.1.6 Linux MIPS notes

To get MySQL to work on Qube2, (Linux Mips), you need the newest glibc libraries (glibc-2.0.7-29C2 is known to work). You must also use the egcs C++ compiler (egcs-1.0.2-9, gcc 2.95.2 or newer).

2.6.1.7 Linux IA64 notes

To get MySQL to compile on Linux IA64, we use the following compile line, using gcc-2.96:

```
CC=gcc CFLAGS="-O3 -fno-omit-frame-pointer" CXX=gcc \
CXXFLAGS="-O3 -fno-omit-frame-pointer -felide-constructors \
-fno-exceptions -fno-rtti" ./configure --prefix=/usr/local/mysql \
"--with-comment=Official MySQL binary" --with-extra-charsets=complex
```

On IA64 the MySQL client binaries are using shared libraries. This means that if you install our binary distribution in some other place than /usr/local/mysql you need to either modify /etc/ld.so.conf or add the path to the directory where you have libmysqlclient.so to the LD_LIBRARY_PATH environment variable.

See Section A.3.1, Problems When Linking with the MySQL Client Library.

2.6.2 Windows Notes

This section describes using MySQL on Windows. This information is also provided in the README file that comes with the MySQL Windows distribution. See Section 2.1.2, Installing MySQL on Windows.

2.6.2.1 Starting MySQL on Windows 95, 98, or Me

MySQL uses TCP/IP to connect a client to a server. (This will allow any machine on your network to connect to your MySQL server.) Because of this, you must install TCP/IP on your machine before starting MySQL. You can find TCP/IP on your Windows CD-ROM.

Note that if you are using an old Windows 95 release (for example, OSR2), it's likely that you have an old Winsock package; MySQL requires Winsock 2! You can get the newest Winsock from http://www.microsoft.com/. Windows 98 has the new Winsock 2 library.

To start the mysqld server, you should start an MS-DOS window and type:

```
C:\> C:\mysql\bin\mysqld
```

This will start mysqld in the background without a window.

You can kill the MySQL server by executing:

```
C:\> C:\mysql\bin\mysqladmin -u root shutdown
```

This calls the MySQL administration utility as user 'root', which is the default Administrator in the MySQL grant system. Please note that the MySQL grant system is wholly independent from any login users under Windows.

Note that Windows 95/98/Me don't support creation of named pipes. So on those platforms, you can only use named pipes to connect to a remote MySQL server running on a Windows NT/2000/XP server host. (The MySQL server must also support named pipes, of course. For example, using mysqld-opt under NT/2000/XP will not allow named pipe connections. You should use either mysqld-nt or mysqld-max-nt.)

If mysqld doesn't start, please check the \mysql\data\mysql.err file to see if the server wrote any message there to indicate the cause of the problem. You can also try to start the server with mysqld --standalone; in this case, you may get some useful information on the screen that may help solve the problem.

The last option is to start mysqld with --standalone --debug. In this case mysqld will write a log file C:\mysqld.trace that should contain the reason why mysqld doesn't start. See Section D.1.2, Creating Trace Files.

Use mysqld --help to display all the options that mysqld understands!

2.6.2.2 Starting MySQL on Windows NT, 2000, or XP

To get MySQL to work with TCP/IP on Windows NT 4, you must install service pack 3 (or newer)!

Normally you should install MySQL as a service on Windows NT/2000/XP. In case the server was already running, first stop it using the following command:

```
C:\mysql\bin> mysqladmin -u root shutdown
```

This calls the MySQL administration utility as user 'root', which is the default Administrator in the MySQL grant system. Please note that the MySQL grant system is wholly independent from any login users under Windows.

Now install the server service:

```
C:\mysql\bin> mysqld-max-nt --install
```

If any options are required, they must be specified as "Start parameters" in the Windows Services utility before you start the MySQL service.

The Services utility (Windows Service Control Manager) can be found in the Windows Control Panel (under Administrative Tools on Windows 2000). It is advisable to close the Services utility while performing the --install or --remove operations prevent some odd errors.

For information about which server binary to run, see Section 2.1.2.2, Preparing the windows MySQL environment.

Please note that from MySQL Version 3.23.44, you have the choice of setting up the service as Manual instead (if you don't wish the service to be started automatically during the boot process):

```
C:\mysql\bin> mysqld-max-nt --install-manual
```

The service is installed with the name MySQL. Once installed, it can be immediately started from the Services utility, or by using the command NET START MySQL.

Once running, mysqld-max-nt can be stopped using mysqladmin from the Services utility, or by using the command NET STOP MySQL.

When running as a service, the operating system will automatically stop the MySQL service on computer shutdown. In MySQL versions < 3.23.47, Windows only waited for a few seconds for the shutdown to complete, and killed the database server process if the time limit was exceeded (potentially causing problems). For instance, at the next startup the InnoDB table handler had to do crash recovery. Starting from MySQL Version 3.23.48, Windows will wait longer for the MySQL server shutdown to complete. If you notice this is not enough for your installation, it is safest to run the MySQL server not as a service, but from the Command prompt, and shut it down with mysqladmin shutdown.

There is a problem that Windows NT (but not Windows 2000/XP) by default only waits 20 seconds for a service to shut down, and after that kills the service process. You can increase this default by opening the Registry Editor \winnt\system32\regedt32.exe and editing the value of WaitToKillServiceTimeout at HKEY_LOCAL_MACHINE\SYSTEM\CurrentControlSet\Control in the Registry tree. Specify the new larger value in milliseconds—for example, 120000, to have Windows NT wait up to 120 seconds.

Please note that when run as a service, `mysqld-max-nt` has no access to a console and so no messages can be seen. Errors can be checked in `c:\mysql\data\mysql.err`.

If you have problems installing `mysqld-max-nt` as a service, try starting it with the full path:

```
C:\> C:\mysql\bin\mysqld-max-nt --install
```

If this doesn't work, you can get `mysqld-max-nt` to start properly by fixing the path in the registry!

If you don't want to start `mysqld-max-nt` as a service, you can start it as follows:

```
C:\> C:\mysql\bin\mysqld-max-nt --standalone
```

or

```
C:\> C:\mysql\bin\mysqld --standalone --debug
```

The last method gives you a debug trace in `C:\mysqld.trace`. See Section D.1.2, Creating Trace Files.

2.6.2.3 Running MySQL on Windows

MySQL supports TCP/IP on all Windows platforms and named pipes on NT/2000/XP. The default is to use named pipes for local connections on NT/2000/XP and TCP/IP for all other cases if the client has TCP/IP installed. The hostname specifies which protocol is used:

Hostname	Protocol
NULL (none)	On NT/2000/XP, try named pipes first; if that doesn't work, use TCP/IP. On 9x/Me, TCP/IP is used.
.	Named pipes.
localhost	TCP/IP to current host.
hostname	TCP/IP.

You can force a MySQL client to use named pipes by specifying the `--pipe` option or by specifying `.` as the hostname. Use the `--socket` option to specify the name of the pipe.

Note that starting from 3.23.50, named pipes are only enabled if mysqld is started with `--enable-named-pipe`. This is because some users have experienced problems shutting down the MySQL server when one uses named pipes.

You can test whether MySQL is working by executing the following commands:

```
C:\> C:\mysql\bin\mysqlshow
C:\> C:\mysql\bin\mysqlshow -u root mysql
C:\> C:\mysql\bin\mysqladmin version status proc
C:\> C:\mysql\bin\mysql test
```

If `mysqld` is slow to answer to connections on Windows 9x/Me, there is probably a problem with your DNS. In this case, start `mysqld` with `--skip-name-resolve` and use only `localhost` and IP numbers in the MySQL grant tables. You can also avoid DNS when connecting to a `mysqld-nt` MySQL server running on NT/2000/XP by using the `--pipe` argument to specify use of named pipes. This works for most MySQL clients.

There are two versions of the MySQL command-line tool:

Binary	Description
mysql	Compiled on native Windows, which offers very limited text-editing capabilities.
mysqlc	Compiled with the Cygnus GNU compiler and libraries, which offers `readline` editing.

If you want to use `mysqlc.exe`, you must copy `C:\mysql\lib\cygwinb19.dll` to your Windows system directory (`\windows\system` or similar place).

The default privileges on Windows give all local users full privileges to all databases without specifying a password. To make MySQL more secure, you should set a password for all users and remove the row in the `mysql.user` table that has `Host='localhost'` and `User="`.

You should also add a password for the `root` user. The following example starts by removing the anonymous user that can be used by anyone to access the `test` database, then sets a `root` user password:

```
C:\> C:\mysql\bin\mysql mysql
mysql> DELETE FROM user WHERE Host='localhost' AND User='';
mysql> QUIT
C:\> C:\mysql\bin\mysqladmin reload
C:\> C:\mysql\bin\mysqladmin -u root password your_password
```

After you've set the password, if you want to take down the `mysqld` server, you can do so using this command:

```
C:\> mysqladmin --user=root --password=your_password shutdown
```

If you are using the old shareware version of MySQL Version 3.21 under Windows, the preceding command will fail with an error: `parse error near 'SET OPTION password'`. The fix is to upgrade to the current MySQL version, which is freely available.

With the current MySQL versions you can easily add new users and change privileges with `GRANT` and `REVOKE` commands. See Section 4.3.1, `GRANT` and `REVOKE` Syntax.

2.6.2.4 Connecting to a remote MySQL from Windows with SSH

Here is a note about how to connect to get a secure connection to remote MySQL server with SSH (by David Carlson, *dcarlson@mplcomm.com*):

- Install an SSH client on your Windows machine. As a user, the best non-free one I've found is from SecureCRT from http://www.vandyke.com/. Another option is f-secure from http://www.f-secure.com/. You can also find some free ones on Google at http://directory.google.com/Top/Computers/Security/Products_and_Tools/Cryptography/SSH/Clients/Windows/.

- Start your Windows SSH client. Set Host_Name = yourmysqlserver_URL_or_IP. Set userid=your_userid to log in to your server (probably not the same as your MySQL login/password.

- Set up port forwarding. Either do a remote forward (set local_port: 3306, remote_host: yourmysqlservername_or_ip, remote_port: 3306) or a local forward (set port: 3306, host: localhost, remote port: 3306).

- Save everything, otherwise you'll have to redo it the next time.

- Log in to your server with the SSH session you just created.

- On your Windows machine, start some ODBC application (such as Access).

- Create a new file in Windows and link to MySQL using the ODBC driver the same way you normally do, except type in localhost for the MySQL host server, not yourmysqlservername.

You should now have an ODBC connection to MySQL, encrypted using SSH.

2.6.2.5 Splitting data across different disks on windows

Beginning with MySQL Version 3.23.16, the mysqld-max and mysql-max-nt servers in the MySQL distribution are compiled with the -DUSE_SYMDIR option. This allows you to put a database on different disks by adding a symbolic link to it (in a manner similar to the way that symbolic links work on Unix).

On Windows, you make a symbolic link to a database by creating a file that contains the path to the destination directory and saving this in the mysql_data directory under the filename database.sym. Note that the symbolic link will be used only if the directory mysql_data_dir\database doesn't exist.

For example, if the MySQL data directory is C:\mysql\data and you want to have database foo located at D:\data\foo, you should create the file C:\mysql\data\foo.sym that contains the text D:\data\foo\. After that, all tables created in the database foo will be created in D:\data\foo.

Note that because of the speed penalty you get when opening every table, we have not enabled this by default even if you have compiled MySQL with support for this. To enable symlinks you should put the following entry into your my.cnf or my.ini file:

```
[mysqld]
use-symbolic-links
```

In MySQL 4.0 we will enable symlinks by default. Then you should instead use the `skip-symlink` option if you want to disable this.

2.6.2.6 Compiling MySQL clients on Windows

In your source files, you should include `windows.h` before you include `mysql.h`:

```
#if defined(_WIN32) || defined(_WIN64)
#include <windows.h>
#endif
#include <mysql.h>
```

You can either link your code with the dynamic `libmysql.lib` library, which is just a wrapper to load in `libmysql.dll` on demand, or link with the static `mysqlclient.lib` library.

Note that as the mysqlclient libraries are compiled as threaded libraries, you should also compile your code to be multi-threaded!

2.6.2.7 MySQL-Windows compared to Unix MySQL

MySQL-Windows has by now proven itself to be very stable. This version of MySQL has the same features as the corresponding Unix version with the following exceptions:

Windows 95 and threads

Windows 95 leaks about 200 bytes of main memory for each thread creation. Each connection in MySQL creates a new thread, so you shouldn't run `mysqld` for an extended time on Windows 95 if your server handles many connections! Other versions of Windows don't suffer from this bug.

Concurrent reads

MySQL depends on the `pread()` and `pwrite()` calls to be able to mix INSERT and SELECT. Currently we use mutexes to emulate `pread()`/`pwrite()`. We will, in the long run, replace the file level interface with a virtual interface so that we can use the `readfile()`/`writefile()` interface on NT/2000/XP to get more speed. The current implementation limits the number of open files MySQL can use to 1024, which means that you will not be able to run as many concurrent threads on NT/2000/XP as on Unix.

Blocking read

MySQL uses a blocking read for each connection. This means that:

• A connection will not be disconnected automatically after 8 hours, as happens with the Unix version of MySQL.

- If a connection hangs, it's impossible to break it without killing MySQL.

- `mysqladmin kill` will not work on a sleeping connection.

- `mysqladmin shutdown` can't abort as long as there are sleeping connections.

We plan to fix this problem when our Windows developers have figured out a nice workaround.

DROP DATABASE

You can't drop a database that is in use by some thread.

Killing MySQL from the task manager

You can't kill MySQL from the task manager or with the shutdown utility in Windows 95. You must take it down with `mysqladmin shutdown`.

Case-insensitive names

Filenames are case-insensitive on Windows, so database and table names are also case-insensitive in MySQL for Windows. The only restriction is that database and table names must be specified using the same case throughout a given statement. See Section 6.1.3, Case Sensitivity in Names.

The \ directory character

Pathname components in Windows 95 are separated by the \ character, which is also the escape character in MySQL. If you are using LOAD DATA INFILE or SELECT . . . INTO OUTFILE, you must double the \ character:

```
mysql> LOAD DATA INFILE "C:\\tmp\\skr.txt" INTO TABLE skr;
mysql> SELECT * INTO OUTFILE 'C:\\tmp\\skr.txt' FROM skr;
```

Alternatively, use Unix-style filenames with / characters:

```
mysql> LOAD DATA INFILE "C:/tmp/skr.txt" INTO TABLE skr;
mysql> SELECT * INTO OUTFILE 'C:/tmp/skr.txt' FROM skr;
```

Can't open named pipe *error*

If you use a MySQL 3.22 version on NT with the newest mysql-clients you will get the following error:

```
error 2017: can't open named pipe to host: . pipe...
```

This is because the release version of MySQL uses named pipes on NT by default. You can avoid this error by using the --host=localhost option to the new MySQL clients or create an option file C:\my.cnf that contains the following information:

```
[client]
host = localhost
```

Starting from 3.23.50, named pipes are only enabled if mysqld is started with --enable-named-pipe.

Access denied for user *error*

If you get the error Access denied for user: 'some-user@unknown' to database 'mysql' when accessing a MySQL server on the same machine, this means that MySQL can't resolve your hostname properly.

To fix this, you should create a file \windows\hosts with the following information:

```
127.0.0.1        localhost
```

ALTER TABLE

While you are executing an ALTER TABLE statement, the table is locked from usage by other threads. This has to do with the fact that on Windows, you can't delete a file that is in use by another threads. (In the future, we may find some way to work around this problem.)

DROP TABLE on a table that is in use by a MERGE table will not work on Windows because MERGE handler does the table mapping hidden from the upper layer of MySQL. Because Windows doesn't allow you to drop files that are open, you first must flush all MERGE tables (with FLUSH TABLES) or drop the MERGE table before dropping the table. We will fix this at the same time we introduce VIEWs.

DATA DIRECTORY and INDEX DIRECTORY directives in CREATE TABLE are ignored on Windows because Windows doesn't support symbolic links.

Here are some open issues for anyone who might want to help us with the Windows release:

* Make a single-user MYSQL.DLL server. This should include everything in a standard MySQL server, except thread creation. This will make MySQL much easier to use in applications that don't need a true client/server and don't need to access the server from other hosts.

* Add some nice start and shutdown icons to the MySQL installation.

* When registering mysqld as a service with --install (on NT) it would be nice if you could also add default options on the command-line. For the moment, the workaround is to list the parameters in the C:\my.cnf file instead.

* It would be real nice to be able to kill mysqld from the task manager. For the moment, you must use mysqladmin shutdown.

* Port readline to Windows for use in the mysql command-line tool.

* GUI versions of the standard MySQL clients (mysql, mysqlshow, mysqladmin, and mysqldump) would be nice.

* It would be nice if the socket read and write functions in net.c were interruptible. This would make it possible to kill open threads with mysqladmin kill on Windows.

- mysqld always starts in the "C" locale and not in the default locale. We would like to have mysqld use the current locale for the sort order.

- Add macros to use the faster thread-safe increment/decrement methods provided by Windows.

Other Windows-specific issues are described in the README file that comes with the MySQL-Windows distribution.

2.6.3 Solaris Notes

On Solaris, you may run into trouble even before you get the MySQL distribution unpacked! Solaris tar can't handle long filenames, so you may see an error like this when you unpack MySQL:

```
x mysql-3.22.12-beta/bench/Results/ATIS-mysql_odbc-NT_4.0-cmp-db2,\
informix,ms-sql,mysql,oracle,solid,sybase, 0 bytes, 0 tape blocks
tar: directory checksum error
```

In this case, you must use GNU tar (gtar) to unpack the distribution. You can find a precompiled copy for Solaris at http://www.mysql.com/Downloads/.

Sun-native threads work only on Solaris 2.5 and higher. For Version 2.4 and earlier, MySQL will automatically use MIT-pthreads. See Section 2.3.6, MIT-pthreads Notes.

If you get the following error from configure:

```
checking for restartable system calls... configure: error can not run test
programs while cross compiling
```

this means that you have something wrong with your compiler installation! In this case you should upgrade your compiler to a newer version. You may also be able to solve this problem by inserting the following row into the config.cache file:

```
ac_cv_sys_restartable_syscalls=${ac_cv_sys_restartable_syscalls='no'}
```

If you are using Solaris on a SPARC, the recommended compiler is gcc 2.95.2. You can find this at http://gcc.gnu.org/. Note that egcs 1.1.1 and gcc 2.8.1 don't work reliably on SPARC!

The recommended configure line when using gcc 2.95.2 is:

```
CC=gcc CFLAGS="-O3" \
CXX=gcc CXXFLAGS="-O3 -felide-constructors -fno-exceptions -fno-rtti" \
./configure --prefix=/usr/local/mysql --with-low-memory --enable-assembler
```

If you have an UltraSPARC, you can get 4% more performance by adding "-mcpu=v8 -Wa,-xarch=v8plusa" to CFLAGS and CXXFLAGS.

If you have a Sun Workshop (Fortre) 5.3 (or newer) compiler, you can run configure like this:

```
CC=cc CFLAGS="-Xa -fast -xO4 -native -xstrconst -mt" \
CXX=CC CXXFLAGS="-noex -xO4 -mt" \
./configure --prefix=/usr/local/mysql --enable-assembler
```

In the MySQL benchmarks, we got a 6% speedup on an UltraSPARC when using Sun Workshop 5.3 compared to using gcc with -mcpu flags.

If you get a problem with fdatasync or sched_yield, you can fix this by adding LIBS=-lrt to the configure line.

The following paragraph is relevant only for compilers older than WorkShop 5.3:

You may also have to edit the configure script to change this line:

```
#if !defined(__STDC__) || __STDC__ != 1
```

to this:

```
#if !defined(__STDC__)
```

If you turn on __STDC__ with the -Xc option, the Sun compiler can't compile with the Solaris pthread.h header file. This is a Sun bug (broken compiler or broken include file).

If mysqld issues the following error message when you run it, you have tried to compile MySQL with the Sun compiler without enabling the multi-thread option (-mt):

```
libc internal error: _rmutex_unlock: rmutex not held
```

Add -mt to CFLAGS and CXXFLAGS and try again.

If you are using the SFW version of gcc (which comes with Solaris 8), you must add /opt/sfw/lib to the environment variable LD_LIBRARY_PATH before running configure.

If you are using the gcc available from sunfreeware.com, you may have many problems. You should recompile gcc and GNU binutils on the machine you will be running them from to avoid any problems.

If you get the following error when compiling MySQL with gcc, it means that your gcc is not configured for your version of Solaris:

```
shell> gcc -O3 -g -O2 -DDBUG_OFF  -o thr_alarm ...
./thr_alarm.c: In function 'signal_hand':
./thr_alarm.c:556: too many arguments to function 'sigwait'
```

The proper thing to do in this case is to get the newest version of gcc and compile it with your current gcc compiler! At least for Solaris 2.5, almost all binary versions of gcc have old, unusable include files that will break all programs that use threads (and possibly other programs)!

Solaris doesn't provide static versions of all system libraries (libpthreads and libdl), so you can't compile MySQL with --static. If you try to do so, you will get the error:

```
ld: fatal: library -ldl: not found

or

undefined reference to 'dlopen'

or

cannot find -lrt
```

If too many processes try to connect very rapidly to mysqld, you will see this error in the MySQL log:

```
Error in accept: Protocol error
```

You might try starting the server with the --set-variable back_log=50 option as a workaround for this. See Section 4.1.1, mysqld Command-Line Options.

If you are linking your own MySQL client, you might get the following error when you try to execute it:

```
ld.so.1: ./my: fatal: libmysqlclient.so.#:
open failed: No such file or directory
```

The problem can be avoided by one of the following methods:

- Link the client with the following flag (instead of –Lpath): -Wl,r/full-path-to-libmysqlclient.so.

- Copy libmysqclient.so to /usr/lib.

- Add the pathname of the directory where libmysqlclient.so is located to the LD_RUN_PATH environment variable before running your client.

If you have problems with configure trying to link with -lz and you don't have zlib installed, you have two options:

- If you want to be able to use the compressed communication protocol, you need to get and install zlib from ftp.gnu.org.

- Configure with --with-named-z-libs=no.

If you are using gcc and have problems with loading UDF functions into MySQL, try adding -lgcc to the link line for the UDF function.

If you would like MySQL to start automatically, you can copy support-files/mysql.server to /etc/init.d and create a symbolic link to it named /etc/rc3.d/S99mysql.server.

As Solaris doesn't support core files for `setuid()` applications, you can't get a core file from `mysqld` if you are using the `--user` option.

2.6.3.1 Solaris 2.7/2.8 notes

You can normally use a Solaris 2.6 binary on Solaris 2.7 and 2.8. Most of the Solaris 2.6 issues also apply for Solaris 2.7 and 2.8.

Note that MySQL Versions 3.23.4 and above should be able to autodetect new versions of Solaris and enable workarounds for the following problems!

Solaris 2.7 / 2.8 has some bugs in the include files. You may see the following error when you use `gcc`:

```
/usr/include/widec.h:42: warning: 'getwc' redefined
/usr/include/wchar.h:326: warning: this is the location of the previous
definition
```

If this occurs, you can do the following to fix the problem:

Copy `/usr/include/widec.h` to `.../lib/gcc-lib/os/gcc-version/include` and change line 41 from:

```
#if     !defined(lint) && !defined(__lint)
```

to

```
#if     !defined(lint) && !defined(__lint) && !defined(getwc)
```

Alternatively, you can edit `/usr/include/widec.h` directly. Either way, after you make the fix, you should remove `config.cache` and run `configure` again!

If you get errors like this when you run `make`, it's because `configure` didn't detect the `curses.h` file (probably because of the error in `/usr/include/widec.h`):

```
In file included from mysql.cc:50:
/usr/include/term.h:1060: syntax error before ','
/usr/include/term.h:1081: syntax error before ';'
```

The solution to this is to do one of the following:

*   Configure with `CFLAGS=-DHAVE_CURSES_H CXXFLAGS=-DHAVE_CURSES_H ./configure`.
*   Edit `/usr/include/widec.h` as indicated previously and rerun configure.
*   Remove the `#define HAVE_TERM` line from `config.h` file and run `make` again.

If you get a problem that your linker can't find `-lz` when linking your client program, the problem is probably that your `libz.so` file is installed in `/usr/local/lib`. You can fix this by one of the following methods:

- Add /usr/local/lib to LD_LIBRARY_PATH.

- Add a link to libz.so from /lib.

- If you are using Solaris 8, you can install the optional zlib from your Solaris 8 CD distribution.

- Configure MySQL with the --with-named-z-libs=no option.

2.6.3.2 Solaris x86 notes

On Solaris 2.8 on x86, mysqld will core dump if you run 'strip'.

If you are using gcc or egcs on Solaris x86 and you experience problems with core dumps under load, you should use the following configure command:

```
CC=gcc CFLAGS="-O3 -fomit-frame-pointer -DHAVE_CURSES_H" \
CXX=gcc \
CXXFLAGS="-O3 -fomit-frame-pointer -felide-constructors -fno-exceptions \
-fno-rtti -DHAVE_CURSES_H" \
./configure --prefix=/usr/local/mysql
```

This will avoid problems with the libstdc++ library and with C++ exceptions.

If this doesn't help, you should compile a debug version and run it with a trace file or under gdb. See Section D.1.3, Debugging mysqld under gdb.

2.6.4 BSD Notes

This section provides information for the various BSD flavours, as well as specific versions within those.

2.6.4.1 FreeBSD notes

FreeBSD 3.x is recommended for running MySQL since the thread package is much more integrated.

The easiest and therefore the preferred way to install is to use the mysql-server and mysql-client ports available on http://www.freebsd.org/.

Using these gives you:

- A working MySQL with all optimisations known to work on your version of FreeBSD enabled.

- Automatic configuration and build.

- Startup scripts installed in /usr/local/etc/rc.d.

- Ability to see which files that are installed with pkg_info -L, and to remove them all with pkg_delete if you no longer want MySQL on that machine.

It is recommended you use MIT-pthreads on FreeBSD 2.x and native threads on Versions 3 and up. It is possible to run with native threads on some late 2.2.x versions but you may encounter problems shutting down mysqld.

The MySQL Makefiles require GNU make (gmake) to work. If you want to compile MySQL you need to install GNU make first.

Be sure to have your name resolver set up correct. Otherwise, you may experience resolver delays or failures when connecting to mysqld.

Make sure that the localhost entry in the /etc/hosts file is correct (otherwise, you will have problems connecting to the database). The /etc/hosts file should start with a line:

```
127.0.0.1       localhost localhost.your.domain
```

The recommended way to compile and install MySQL on FreeBSD with gcc (2.95.2 and up) is:

```
CC=gcc CFLAGS="-O2 -fno-strength-reduce" \
CXX=gcc CXXFLAGS="-O2 -fno-rtti -fno-exceptions -felide-constructors \
-fno-strength-reduce" \
./configure --prefix=/usr/local/mysql --enable-assembler
gmake
gmake install
./scripts/mysql_install_db
cd /usr/local/mysql
./bin/mysqld_safe &
```

If you notice that configure will use MIT-pthreads, you should read the MIT-pthreads notes. See Section 2.3.6, MIT-pthreads Notes.

If you get an error from make install that it can't find /usr/include/pthreads, configure didn't detect that you need MIT-pthreads. This is fixed by executing these commands:

```
shell> rm config.cache
shell> ./configure --with-mit-threads
```

FreeBSD is also known to have a very low default file handle limit. See Section A.2.16, File Not Found. Uncomment the ulimit -n section in safe_mysqld or raise the limits for the mysqld user in /etc/login.conf (and rebuild it with cap_mkdb /etc/login.conf). Also be sure you set the appropriate class for this user in the password file if you are not using the default (use: chpass mysqld-user-name). See Section 4.7.2, safe_mysqld, the Wrapper Around mysqld.

If you have a lot of memory you should consider rebuilding the kernel to allow MySQL to take more than 512M of RAM. Take a look at option MAXDSIZ in the LINT config file for more info.

If you get problems with the current date in MySQL, setting the TZ variable will probably help. See Appendix E.

To get a secure and stable system you should only use FreeBSD kernels that are marked –RELEASE.

2.6.4.2 NetBSD notes

To compile on NetBSD you need GNU make. Otherwise, the compile will crash when make tries to run lint on C++ files.

2.6.4.3 OpenBSD 2.5 notes

On OpenBSD Version 2.5, you can compile MySQL with native threads with the following options:

```
CFLAGS=-pthread CXXFLAGS=-pthread ./configure --with-mit-threads=no
```

2.6.4.4 OpenBSD 2.8 notes

Our users have reported that OpenBSD 2.8 has a threading bug which causes problems with MySQL. The OpenBSD developers have fixed the problem, but as of January 25th, 2001, it's only available in the "-current" branch. The symptoms of this threading bug are: slow response, high load, high CPU usage, and crashes.

If you get an error like Error in accept:: Bad file descriptor or error 9 when trying to open tables or directories, the problem is probably that you haven't allocated enough file descriptors for MySQL.

In this case try starting safe_mysqld as root with the following options:

```
--user=mysql --open-files-limit=2048
```

2.6.4.5 BSD/OS Version 2.x notes

If you get the following error when compiling MySQL, your ulimit value for virtual memory is too low:

```
item_func.h: In method 'Item_func_ge::Item_func_ge(const Item_func_ge &)':
item_func.h:28: virtual memory exhausted
make[2]: *** [item_func.o] Error 1
```

Try using ulimit -v 80000 and run make again. If this doesn't work and you are using bash, try switching to csh or sh; some BSDI users have reported problems with bash and ulimit.

If you are using gcc, you may also have to use the --with-low-memory flag for configure to be able to compile sql_yacc.cc.

If you get problems with the current date in MySQL, setting the TZ variable will probably help. See Appendix E.

2.6.4.6   BSD/OS Version 3.x notes

Upgrade to BSD/OS Version 3.1. If that is not possible, install BSDIpatch M300-038.

Use the following command when configuring MySQL:

```
shell> env CXX=shlicc++ CC=shlicc2 \
        ./configure \
            --prefix=/usr/local/mysql \
            --localstatedir=/var/mysql \
            --without-perl \
            --with-unix-socket-path=/var/mysql/mysql.sock
```

The following is also known to work:

```
shell> env CC=gcc CXX=gcc CXXFLAGS=-O3 \
        ./configure \
            --prefix=/usr/local/mysql \
            --with-unix-socket-path=/var/mysql/mysql.sock
```

You can change the directory locations if you wish, or just use the defaults by not specifying any locations.

If you have problems with performance under heavy load, try using the --skip-thread-priority option to mysqld! This will run all threads with the same priority; on BSDI Version 3.1, this gives better performance (at least until BSDI fixes their thread scheduler).

If you get the error virtual memory exhausted while compiling, you should try using ulimit -v 80000 and run make again. If this doesn't work and you are using bash, try switching to csh or sh; some BSDI users have reported problems with bash and ulimit.

2.6.4.7   BSD/OS Version 4.x notes

BSDI Version 4.x has some thread-related bugs. If you want to use MySQL on this, you should install all thread-related patches. At least M400-023 should be installed.

On some BSDI Version 4.x systems, you may get problems with shared libraries. The symptom is that you can't execute any client programs—for example, mysqladmin. In this case you need to reconfigure not to use shared libraries with the --disable-shared option to configure.

Some customers have had problems on BSDI 4.0.1 that the mysqld binary after a while can't open tables. This is because some library/system-related bug causes mysqld to change the current directory without asking for this!

The fix is to either upgrade to 3.23.34 or, after running `configure`, remove the line `#define HAVE_REALPATH` from `config.h` before running make.

Note that this means that you can't symbolic link a database directory to another database directory or symbolic link a table to another database on BSDI! (Making a symbolic link to another disk is okay.)

2.6.5 Mac OS X Notes

2.6.5.1 Mac OS X public beta

MySQL should work without any problems on Mac OS X public beta (Darwin). You don't need the pthread patches for this OS!

2.6.5.2 Mac OS X server

Before trying to configure MySQL on Mac OS X server you must first install the pthread package from http://www.prnet.de/RegEx/mysql.html.

Our binary for Mac OS X is compiled on Rhapsody 5.5 with the following configure line:

```
CC=gcc CFLAGS="-O2 -fomit-frame-pointer" CXX=gcc CXXFLAGS="-O2 \
-fomit-frame-pointer" ./configure --prefix=/usr/local/mysql \
"--with-comment=Official MySQL binary" --with-extra-charsets=complex \
--disable-shared
```

You might want to also add aliases to your shell's resource file to access `mysql` and `mysqladmin` from the command-line:

```
alias mysql '/usr/local/mysql/bin/mysql'
alias mysqladmin '/usr/local/mysql/bin/mysqladmin'
```

2.6.6 Other Unix Notes

2.6.6.1 HP-UX notes for binary distributions

Some of the binary distributions of MySQL for HP-UX are distributed as an HP depot file and as a tar file. To use the depot file you must be running at least HP-UX 10.x to have access to HP's software depot tools.

The HP version of MySQL was compiled on an HP 9000/8xx server under HP-UX 10.20, and uses MIT-pthreads. It is known to work well under this configuration. MySQL Versions 3.22.26 and newer can also be built with HP's native thread package.

Other configurations that may work:

* HP 9000/7xx running HP-UX 10.20+

* HP 9000/8xx running HP-UX 10.30

The following configurations almost definitely won't work:

- HP 9000/7xx or 8xx running HP-UX 10.x where x < 2

- HP 9000/7xx or 8xx running HP-UX 9.x

To install the distribution, use one of the following commands, where /path/to/depot is the full pathname of the depot file:

- To install everything, including the server, clients, and development tools:

      shell> /usr/sbin/swinstall -s /path/to/depot mysql.full

- To install only the server:

      shell> /usr/sbin/swinstall -s /path/to/depot mysql.server

- To install only the client package:

      shell> /usr/sbin/swinstall -s /path/to/depot mysql.client

- To install only the development tools:

      shell> /usr/sbin/swinstall -s /path/to/depot mysql.developer

The depot places binaries and libraries in /opt/mysql and data in /var/opt/mysql. The depot also creates the appropriate entries in /etc/init.d and /etc/rc2.d to start the server automatically at boot time. Obviously, this entails being root to install.

To install the HP-UX tar.gz distribution, you must have a copy of GNU tar.

2.6.6.2 HP-UX Version 10.20 notes

There are a couple of small problems when compiling MySQL on HP-UX. We recommend that you use gcc instead of the HP-UX native compiler because gcc produces better code!

We recommend using gcc 2.95 on HP-UX. Don't use high optimisation flags (like -O6), as this may not be safe on HP-UX.

Note that MIT-pthreads can't be compiled with the HP-UX compiler because it can't compile .S (assembler) files.

The following configure line should work:

```
CFLAGS="-DHPUX -I/opt/dce/include -fpic" \
CXXFLAGS="-DHPUX -I/opt/dce/include -felide-constructors -fno-exceptions \
-fno-rtti" CXX=gcc ./configure --with-pthread \
--with-named-thread-libs='-ldce' --prefix=/usr/local/mysql --disable-shared
```

If you are compiling gcc 2.95 yourself, you should NOT link it with the DCE libraries (libdce.a or libcma.a) if you want to compile MySQL with MIT-pthreads. If you mix the DCE and MIT-pthreads packages you will get a mysqld to which you cannot connect. Remove the DCE libraries while you compile gcc 2.95!

2.6.6.3 HP-UX Version 11.x notes

For HP-UX Version 11.x we recommend MySQL Version 3.23.15 or later.

Because of some critical bugs in the standard HP-UX libraries, you should install the following patches before trying to run MySQL on HP-UX 11.0:

```
PHKL_22840 Streams cumulative
PHNE_22397 ARPA cumulative
```

This will solve the problem of getting EWOULDBLOCK from recv() and EBADF from accept() in threaded applications.

If you are using gcc 2.95.1 on an unpatched HP-UX 11.x system, you will get the error:

```
In file included from /usr/include/unistd.h:11,
                 from ../include/global.h:125,
                 from mysql_priv.h:15,
                 from item.cc:19:
/usr/include/sys/unistd.h:184: declaration of C function ...
/usr/include/sys/pthread.h:440: previous declaration ...
In file included from item.h:306,
                 from mysql_priv.h:158,
                 from item.cc:19:
```

The problem is that HP-UX doesn't define pthreads_atfork() consistently. It has conflicting prototypes in /usr/include/sys/unistd.h:184 and /usr/include/sys/pthread.h:440 (the details follow).

One solution is to copy /usr/include/sys/unistd.h into mysql/include and edit unistd.h and change it to match the definition in pthread.h. Here's the diff:

```
183,184c183,184
<       extern int pthread_atfork(void (*prepare)(), void (*parent)(),
<                                           void (*child)());
---
>       extern int pthread_atfork(void (*prepare)(void), void (*parent)(void),
>                                           void (*child)(void));
```

After this, the following configure line should work:

```
CFLAGS="-fomit-frame-pointer -O3 -fpic" CXX=gcc \
CXXFLAGS="-felide-constructors -fno-exceptions -fno-rtti -O3" \
./configure --prefix=/usr/local/mysql --disable-shared
```

Here is some information that a HP-UX Version 11.x user sent us about compiling MySQL with HP-UX:x compiler:

```
Environment:
     proper compilers.
         setenv CC cc
         setenv CXX aCC
     flags
         setenv CFLAGS -D_REENTRANT
```

```
            setenv CXXFLAGS -D_REENTRANT
            setenv CPPFLAGS -D_REENTRANT
    % aCC -V
    aCC: HP ANSI C++ B3910B X.03.14.06
    % cc -V /tmp/empty.c
    cpp.ansi: HP92453-01 A.11.02.00 HP C Preprocessor (ANSI)
    ccom: HP92453-01 A.11.01.00 HP C Compiler
    cc: "/tmp/empty.c", line 1: warning 501: Empty source file.


configuration:
    ./configure  --with-pthread         \
    --prefix=/source-control/mysql      \
    --with-named-thread-libs=-lpthread \
    --with-low-memory

    added '#define _CTYPE_INCLUDED' to include/m_ctype.h. This
    symbol is the one defined in HP's /usr/include/ctype.h:

    /* Don't include std ctype.h when this is included */
    #define _CTYPE_H
    #define __CTYPE_INCLUDED
    #define _CTYPE_INCLUDED
    #define _CTYPE_USING   /* Don't put names in global namespace. */
```

- I had to use the compile-time flag –D_REENTRANT to get the compiler to recognise the prototype for `localtime_r`. Alternatively I could have supplied the prototype for `localtime_r`. But I wanted to catch other bugs without needing to run into them. I wasn't sure where I needed it, so I added it to all flags.

- The optimisation flags used by MySQL (-O3) are not recognised by HP's compilers. I did not change the flags.

If you get the following error from `configure`:

```
checking for cc option to accept ANSI C... no
configure: error: MySQL requires a ANSI C compiler (and a C++ compiler).
Try gcc. See the Installation chapter in the Reference Manual.
```

check that you don't have the path to the K&R compiler before the path to the HP-UX C and C++ compiler.

2.6.6.4 IBM-AIX notes

Automatic detection of xlC is missing from Autoconf, so a `configure` command something like this is needed when compiling MySQL (this example uses the IBM compiler):

```
export CC="xlc_r -ma -O3 -qstrict -qoptimize=3 -qmaxmem=8192 "
export CXX="xlC_r -ma -O3 -qstrict -qoptimize=3 -qmaxmem=8192"
export CFLAGS="-I /usr/local/include"
export LDLFAGS="-L /usr/local/lib"
export CPPFLAGS=$CFLAGS
export CXXFLAGS=$CFLAGS
```

```
./configure --prefix=/usr/local \
                --localstatedir=/var/mysql \
                --sysconfdir=/etc/mysql \
                --sbindir='/usr/local/bin' \
                --libexecdir='/usr/local/bin' \
                --enable-thread-safe-client \
                --enable-large-files
```

The preceding options were used to compile the MySQL distribution that can be found at
http://www-frec.bull.com/.

If you change the –O3 to –O2 in the preceding configure line, you must also remove the
-qstrict option (this is a limitation in the IBM C compiler).

If you are using gcc or egcs to compile MySQL, you **must** use the -fno-exceptions
flag, as the exception handling in gcc/egcs is not thread-safe! (This is tested with egcs
1.1.) There are also some known problems with IBM's assembler, which may cause it to
generate bad code when used with gcc.

We recommend the following configure line with egcs and gcc 2.95 on AIX:

```
CC="gcc -pipe -mcpu=power -Wa,-many" \
CXX="gcc -pipe -mcpu=power -Wa,-many" \
CXXFLAGS="-felide-constructors -fno-exceptions -fno-rtti" \
./configure --prefix=/usr/local/mysql --with-low-memory
```

The -Wa,-many is necessary for the compile to be successful. IBM is aware of this problem but is in no hurry to fix it because of the workaround available. We don't know if the
-fno-exceptions is required with gcc 2.95, but as MySQL doesn't use exceptions
and the preceding option generates faster code, we recommend that you should always
use this option with egcs / gcc.

If you get a problem with assembler code try changing the -mcpu=xxx to match your
CPU. Typically power2, power, or powerpc may need to be used. Alternatively you might
need to use 604 or 604e. I'm not positive but I would think using "power" would likely be
safe most of the time, even on a power2 machine.

If you don't know what your CPU is, do a "uname -m". This will give you back a string
that looks like "000514676700", with a format of xxyyyyyymmss where xx and ss are
always 0's, yyyyyy is a unique system id, and mm is the id of the CPU Planar. A chart of
these values can be found at http://publib.boulder.ibm.com/doc_link/en_US/a_doc_lib/
cmds/aixcmds5/uname.htm. This will give you a machine type and a machine model you
can use to determine what type of CPU you have.

If you have problems with signals (MySQL dies unexpectedly under high load) you may
have found an OS bug with threads and signals. In this case you can tell MySQL not to
use signals by configuring with:

```
shell> CFLAGS=-DDONT_USE_THR_ALARM CXX=gcc \
       CXXFLAGS="-felide-constructors -fno-exceptions -fno-rtti \
       -DDONT_USE_THR_ALARM" \
       ./configure --prefix=/usr/local/mysql --with-debug --with-low-memory
```

This doesn't affect the performance of MySQL, but has the side effect that you can't kill clients that are "sleeping" on a connection with mysqladmin kill or mysqladmin shutdown. Instead, the client will die when it issues its next command.

On some versions of AIX, linking with libbind.a makes getservbyname core dump. This is an AIX bug and should be reported to IBM.

For AIX 4.2.1 and gcc you have to make the following changes.

After configuring, edit config.h and include/my_config.h and change the line that says:

```
#define HAVE_SNPRINTF 1
```

to:

```
#undef HAVE_SNPRINTF
```

And finally, in mysqld.cc you need to add a prototype for initgoups:

```
#ifdef _AIX41
extern "C" int initgroups(const char *,int);
#endif
```

2.6.6.5 SunOS 4 notes

On SunOS 4, MIT-pthreads is needed to compile MySQL, which in turn means you will need GNU make.

Some SunOS 4 systems have problems with dynamic libraries and libtool. You can use the following configure line to avoid this problem:

```
shell> ./configure --disable-shared --with-mysqld-ldflags=-all-static
```

When compiling readline, you may get warnings about duplicate defines. These may be ignored.

When compiling mysqld, there will be some implicit declaration of function warnings. These may be ignored.

2.6.6.6 Alpha-DEC-Unix notes (Tru64)

If you are using egcs 1.1.2 on Digital Unix, you should upgrade to gcc 2.95.2, as egcs on DEC has some serious bugs!

When compiling threaded programs under Digital Unix, the documentation recommends using the -pthread option for cc and cxx and the libraries -lmach -lexc (in addition to –lpthread). You should run `configure` something like this:

```
CC="cc -pthread" CXX="cxx -pthread -O" \
./configure --with-named-thread-libs="-lpthread -lmach -lexc -lc"
```

When compiling `mysqld`, you may see a couple of warnings like this:

```
mysqld.cc: In function void handle_connections()':
mysqld.cc:626: passing long unsigned int *' as argument 3 of
accept(int,sockadddr *, int *)'
```

You can safely ignore these warnings. They occur because `configure` can detect only errors, not warnings.

If you start the server directly from the command-line, you may have problems with it dying when you log out. (When you log out, your outstanding processes receive a SIGHUP signal.) If so, try starting the server like this:

```
shell> nohup mysqld [options] &
```

`nohup` causes the command following it to ignore any SIGHUP signal sent from the terminal. Alternatively, start the server by running `safe_mysqld`, which invokes `mysqld` using `nohup` for you. See Section 4.7.2, `safe_mysqld`, the Wrapper Around `mysqld`.

If you get a problem when compiling mysys/get_opt.c, just remove the line #define _NO_PROTO from the start of that file!

If you are using Compaq's CC compiler, the following configure line should work:

```
CC="cc -pthread"
CFLAGS="-O4 -ansi_alias -ansi_args -fast -inline speed all -arch host"
CXX="cxx -pthread"
CXXFLAGS="-O4 -ansi_alias -ansi_args -fast -inline speed all -arch host \
-noexceptions -nortti"
export CC CFLAGS CXX CXXFLAGS
./configure \
--prefix=/usr/local/mysql \
--with-low-memory \
--enable-large-files \
--enable-shared=yes \
--with-named-thread-libs="-lpthread -lmach -lexc -lc"
gnumake
```

If you get a problem with libtool, when compiling with shared libraries as mentioned previously, when linking `mysql`, you should be able to get around this by issuing:

```
cd mysql
/bin/sh ../libtool --mode=link cxx -pthread  -O3 -DDBUG_OFF \
-O4 -ansi_alias -ansi_args -fast -inline speed \
-speculate all \ -arch host  -DUNDEF_HAVE_GETHOSTBYNAME_R \
-o mysql  mysql.o readline.o sql_string.o completion_hash.o \
../readline/libreadline.a -lcurses \
../libmysql/.libs/libmysqlclient.so  -lm
```

```
cd ..
gnumake
gnumake install
scripts/mysql_install_db
```

2.6.6.7 Alpha-DEC-OSF/1 notes

If you have problems compiling and have DEC CC and gcc installed, try running configure like this:

```
CC=cc CFLAGS=-O CXX=gcc CXXFLAGS=-O3 \
./configure --prefix=/usr/local/mysql
```

If you get problems with the c_asm.h file, you can create and use a 'dummy' c_asm.h file with:

```
touch include/c_asm.h
CC=gcc CFLAGS=-I./include \
CXX=gcc CXXFLAGS=-O3 \
./configure --prefix=/usr/local/mysql
```

Note that the following problems with the ld program can be fixed by downloading the latest DEC (Compaq) patch kit from: http://ftp.support.compaq.com/public/unix/.

On OSF/1 V4.0D and compiler "DEC C V5.6-071 on Digital Unix V4.0 (Rev. 878)" the compiler had some strange behavior (undefined asm symbols). /bin/ld also appears to be broken (problems with _exit undefined errors occuring while linking mysqld). On this system, we have managed to compile MySQL with the following configure line, after replacing /bin/ld with the version from OSF 4.0C:

```
CC=gcc CXX=gcc CXXFLAGS=-O3 ./configure --prefix=/usr/local/mysql
```

With the Digital compiler "C++ V6.1-029", the following should work:

```
CC=cc -pthread
CFLAGS=-O4 -ansi_alias -ansi_args -fast -inline speed -speculate all \
       -arch host
CXX=cxx -pthread
CXXFLAGS=-O4 -ansi_alias -ansi_args -fast -inline speed -speculate all \
        -arch host -noexceptions -nortti
export CC CFLAGS CXX CXXFLAGS
./configure --prefix=/usr/mysql/mysql --with-mysqld-ldflags=-all-static \
            --disable-shared --with-named-thread-libs="-lmach -lexc -lc"
```

In some versions of OSF/1, the alloca() function is broken. Fix this by removing the line in config.h that defines 'HAVE_ALLOCA'.

The alloca() function also may have an incorrect prototype in /usr/include/alloca.h. The warning resulting from this can be ignored.

configure will use the following thread libraries automatically: --with-named-thread-libs="-lpthread -lmach -lexc -lc".

When using gcc, you can also try running `configure` like this:

```
shell> CFLAGS=-D_PTHREAD_USE_D4 CXX=gcc CXXFLAGS=-O3 ./configure ...
```

If you have problems with signals (MySQL dies unexpectedly under high load), you may have found an OS bug with threads and signals. In this case you can tell MySQL not to use signals by configuring with:

```
shell> CFLAGS=-DDONT_USE_THR_ALARM \
       CXXFLAGS=-DDONT_USE_THR_ALARM \
       ./configure ...
```

This doesn't affect the performance of MySQL, but has the side effect that you can't kill clients that are "sleeping" on a connection with `mysqladmin kill` or `mysqladmin shutdown`. Instead, the client will die when it issues its next command.

With gcc 2.95.2, you will probably run into the following compile error:

```
sql_acl.cc:1456: Internal compiler error in 'scan_region', at except.c:2566
Please submit a full bug report.
```

To fix this you should change to the `sql` directory and do a "cut and paste" of the last gcc line, but change -O3 to -O0 (or add -O0 immediately after gcc if you don't have any -O option on your compile line). After this is done you can just change back to the top-level directly and run make again.

2.6.6.8 SGI Irix notes

If you are using Irix Version 6.5.3 or newer, `mysqld` will only be able to create threads if you run it as a user with `CAP_SCHED_MGT` privileges (like `root`) or give the `mysqld` server this privilege with the following shell command:

```
shell> chcap "CAP_SCHED_MGT+epi" /opt/mysql/libexec/mysqld
```

You may have to undefine some things in `config.h` after running `configure` and before compiling.

In some Irix implementations, the `alloca()` function is broken. If the `mysqld` server dies on some `SELECT` statements, remove the lines from `config.h` that define `HAVE_ALLOC` and `HAVE_ALLOCA_H`. If `mysqladmin create` doesn't work, remove the line from `config.h` that defines `HAVE_READDIR_R`. You may have to remove the `HAVE_TERM_H` line as well.

SGI recommends that you install all of the patches on this page as a set: http://support.sgi.com/surfzone/patches/patchset/6.2_indigo.rps.html.

At the very minimum, you should install the latest kernel rollup, the latest `rld` rollup, and the latest `libc` rollup.

You definitely need all the POSIX patches on this page, for pthreads support: http://support.sgi.com/surfzone/patches/patchset/6.2_posix.rps.html

If you get something like the following error when compiling mysql.cc:

```
"/usr/include/curses.h", line 82: error(1084): invalid combination of type
```

type the following in the top-level directory of your MySQL source tree:

```
shell> extra/replace bool curses_bool < /usr/include/curses.h \
> include/curses.h
shell> make
```

There have also been reports of scheduling problems. If only one thread is running, things go slow. Avoid this by starting another client. This may lead to a two- to ten-fold increase in execution speed thereafter for the other thread. This is a poorly understood problem with Irix threads; you may have to improvise to find solutions until this can be fixed.

If you are compiling with gcc, you can use the following configure command:

```
CC=gcc CXX=gcc CXXFLAGS=-O3 \
./configure --prefix=/usr/local/mysql --enable-thread-safe-client \
--with-named-thread-libs=-lpthread
```

On Irix 6.5.11 with native Irix C and C++ compilers Version 7.3.1.2, the following is reported to work:

```
CC=cc CXX=CC CFLAGS='-O3 -n32 -TARG:platform=IP22 -I/usr/local/include \
-L/usr/local/lib' CXXFLAGS='-O3 -n32 -TARG:platform=IP22 \
-I/usr/local/include -L/usr/local/lib' ./configure \
--prefix=/usr/local/mysql --with-innodb --with-berkeley-db \
--with-libwrap=/usr/local \
--with-named-curses-libs=/usr/local/lib/libncurses.a
```

2.6.6.9 Caldera (SCO) notes

The current port is tested only on a "sco3.2v5.0.4" and "sco3.2v5.0.5" system. There has also been a lot of progress on a port to "sco 3.2v4.2".

For the moment the recommended compiler on OpenServer is gcc 2.95.2. With this you should be able to compile MySQL with just:

```
CC=gcc CXX=gcc ./configure ... (options)
```

1. For OpenServer 5.0.X you need to use gcc-2.95.2p1 or newer from the Skunkware (http://www.caldera.com/skunkware/) and choose browser OpenServer packages or by ftp to ftp2.caldera.com in the pub/skunkware/osr5/devtools/gcc directory.

2. You need the port of GCC 2.5.x for this product and the Development system. They are required on this version of Caldera (SCO) Unix. You cannot just use the GCC Dev system.

3. You should get the FSU Pthreads package and install it first. This can be found at http://www.cs.wustl.edu/˜schmidt/ACE_wrappers/FSU-threads.tar.gz. You can also get a precompiled package from http://www.mysql.com/Downloads/SCO/FSU-threads-3.5c.tar.gz.

4. FSU Pthreads can be compiled with Caldera (SCO) Unix 4.2 with tcpip. With OpenServer 3.0 or Open Desktop 3.0 (OS 3.0 ODT 3.0), with the Caldera (SCO) Development System installed using a good port of GCC 2.5.x ODT, or with OS 3.0, you will need a good port of GCC 2.5.x There are a lot of problems without a good port. The port for this product requires the SCO Unix Development system. Without it, you are missing the libraries and the linker that are needed.

5. To build FSU Pthreads on your system, do the following:

    a. Run ./configure in the threads/src directory and select the SCO OpenServer option. This command copies Makefile.SCO5 to Makefile.

    b. Run make.

    c. To install in the default /usr/include directory, login as root, then cd to the thread/src directory and run make install.

6. Remember to use GNU make when making MySQL.

7. If you don't start safe_mysqld as root, you probably will get only the default 110 open files per process. mysqld will write a note about this in the log file.

8. With SCO 3.2V5.0.5, you should use FSU Pthreads version 3.5c or newer. You should also use gcc 2.95.2 or newer!

    The following configure command should work:

    ```
    shell> ./configure --prefix=/usr/local/mysql --disable-shared
    ```

9. With SCO 3.2V4.2, you should use FSU Pthreads version 3.5c or newer. The following configure command should work:

    ```
    shell> CFLAGS="-D_XOPEN_XPG4" CXX=gcc CXXFLAGS="-D_XOPEN_XPG4" \
           ./configure \
               --prefix=/usr/local/mysql \
               --with-named-thread-libs="-lgthreads -lsocket -lgen -lgthreads" \
               --with-named-curses-libs="-lcurses"
    ```

    You may get some problems with some include files. You'll find new SCO-specific include files at http://www.mysql.com/Downloads/SCO/SCO-3.2v4.2-includes.tar.gz. You should unpack this file in the include directory of your MySQL source tree.

Caldera (SCO) development notes:

•   MySQL should automatically detect FSU Pthreads and link mysqld with -lgthreads -lsocket -lgthreads.

- The Caldera (SCO) development libraries are re-entrant in FSU Pthreads. Caldera claims that its libraries' functions are re-entrant, so they must be re-entrant with FSU Pthreads. FSU Pthreads on OpenServer tries to use the SCO scheme to make re-entrant libraries.

- FSU Pthreads (at least the version at http://www.mysql.com/) comes linked with GNU `malloc`. If you encounter problems with memory usage, make sure that `gmalloc.o` is included in `libgthreads.a` and `libgthreads.so`.

- In FSU Pthreads, the following system calls are pthreads-aware: `read()`, `write()`, `getmsg()`, `connect()`, `accept()`, `select()`, and `wait()`.

- The CSSA-2001-SCO.35.2 (the patch is listed in custom as erg711905-dscr_remap security patch (version 2.0.0) breaks FSU threads and makes mysqld unstable. You have to remove this one if you want to run mysqld on an OpenServer 5.0.6 machine.

If you want to install DBI on Caldera (SCO), you have to edit the `Makefile` in DBI-xxx and each subdirectory.

Note that the following assumes gcc 2.95.2 or newer:

```
OLD:                                    NEW:
CC = cc                                 CC = gcc
CCCDLFLAGS = -KPIC -Wl,-Bexport         CCCDLFLAGS = -fpic
CCDLFLAGS = -wl,-Bexport                CCDLFLAGS =

LD = ld                                 LD = gcc -G -fpic
LDDLFLAGS = -G -L/usr/local/lib         LDDLFLAGS = -L/usr/local/lib
LDFLAGS = -belf -L/usr/local/lib        LDFLAGS = -L/usr/local/lib

LD = ld                                 LD = gcc -G -fpic
OPTIMISE = -Od                          OPTIMISE = -O1

OLD:
CCCFLAGS = -belf -dy -w0 -U M_XENIX -DPERL_SCO5 -I/usr/local/include

NEW:
CCFLAGS = -U M_XENIX -DPERL_SCO5 -I/usr/local/include
```

This is because the Perl dynaloader will not load the `DBI` modules if they were compiled with `icc` or `cc`.

Perl works best when compiled with `cc`.

2.6.6.10 Caldera (SCO) Unixware Version 7.0 notes

You must use a version of MySQL at least as recent as Version 3.22.13 because that version fixes some portability problems under Unixware.

We have been able to compile MySQL with the following `configure` command on Unixware Version 7.0.1:

```
CC=cc CXX=CC ./configure --prefix=/usr/local/mysql
```

If you want to use gcc, you must use gcc 2.95.2 or newer.

Caldera provides libsocket.so.2 at ftp://stage.caldera.com/pub/security/tools for pre-OSR506 security fixes. Also, the telnetd fix at *ftp://stage.caldera.com/pub/security/openserver/CSSA-2001-SCO.10/* as both libsocket.so.2 and libresolv.so.1 with instructions for installing on pre-OSR506 systems.

It's probably a good idea to install the above patches before trying to compile/use MySQL.

2.6.7 OS/2 Notes

MySQL uses quite a few open files. Because of this, you should add something like the following to your CONFIG.SYS file:

```
SET EMXOPT=-c -n -h1024
```

If you don't do this, you will probably run into the following error:

```
File 'xxxx' not found (Errcode: 24)
```

When using MySQL with OS/2 Warp 3, FixPack 29 or above is required. With OS/2 Warp 4, FixPack 4 or above is required. This is a requirement of the Pthreads library. MySQL must be installed in a partition that supports long filenames such as HPFS, FAT32, etc.

The INSTALL.CMD script must be run from OS/2's own CMD.EXE and may not work with replacement shells such as 4OS2.EXE.

The scripts/mysql-install-db script has been renamed. It is now called install.cmd and is a REXX script, which will set up the default MySQL security settings and create the WorkPlace Shell icons for MySQL.

Dynamic module support is compiled in but not fully tested. Dynamic modules should be compiled using the Pthreads runtime library.

```
gcc -Zdll -Zmt -Zcrtdll=pthrdrtl -I../include -I../regex -I.. \
    -o example udf_example.cc -L../lib -lmysqlclient udf_example.def
mv example.dll example.udf
```

Note: Due to limitations in OS/2, UDF module name stems must not exceed 8 characters. Modules are stored in the /mysql2/udf directory; the safe-mysqld.cmd script will put this directory in the BEGINLIBPATH environment variable. When using UDF modules, specified extensions are ignored—the extenions is assumed to be .udf. For example, in Unix, the shared module might be named example.so and you would load a function from it like this:

```
mysql> CREATE FUNCTION metaphon RETURNS STRING SONAME "example.so";
```

In OS/2, the module would be named `example.udf`, but you would not specify the module extension:

```
mysql> CREATE FUNCTION metaphon RETURNS STRING SONAME "example";
```

2.6.8 BeOS Notes

We are really interested in getting MySQL to work on BeOS, but unfortunately we don't have any person who knows BeOS or has time to do a port.

We are interested in finding someone to do a port, and we will help them with any technical questions they may have while doing the port.

We have previously talked with some BeOS developers that have said that MySQL is 80% ported to BeOS, but we haven't heard from them in a while.

2.6.9 Novell Netware Notes

We are really interested in getting MySQL to work on Netware, but unfortunately we don't have any person who knows Netware or has time to do a port.

We are interested in finding someone to do a port, and we will help them with any technical questions they may have while doing the port.

2.7 Perl Installation Comments
2.7.1 Installing Perl on Unix

Perl support for MySQL is provided by means of the DBI/DBD client interface. See Section 8.2, MySQL Perl API. The Perl DBD/DBI client code requires Perl Version 5.004 or later. The interface **will not work** if you have an older version of Perl.

MySQL Perl support also requires that you've installed MySQL client programming support. If you installed MySQL from RPM files, client programs are in the client RPM, but client programming support is in the developer RPM. Make sure you've installed the latter RPM.

As of Version 3.22.8, Perl support is distributed separately from the main MySQL distribution. If you want to install Perl support, the files you will need can be obtained from http://www.mysql.com/Downloads/Contrib/.

The Perl distributions are provided as compressed `tar` archives and have names like `MODULE-VERSION.tar.gz`, where `MODULE` is the module name and `VERSION` is the version number. You should get the `Data-Dumper`, `DBI`, and `Msql-Mysql-modules` distributions and install them in that order. The installation procedure is shown next. The example shown is for the `Data-Dumper` module, but the procedure is the same for all three distributions:

1. Unpack the distribution into the current directory:

   ```
   shell> gunzip < Data-Dumper-VERSION.tar.gz | tar xvf -
   ```

   This command creates a directory named Data-Dumper-VERSION.

2. Change into the top-level directory of the unpacked distribution:

   ```
   shell> cd Data-Dumper-VERSION
   ```

3. Build the distribution and compile everything:

   ```
   shell> perl Makefile.PL
   shell> make
   shell> make test
   shell> make install
   ```

The make test command is important because it verifies that the module is working. Note that when you run that command during the Msql-Mysql-modules installation to exercise the interface code, the MySQL server must be running or the test will fail.

It is a good idea to rebuild and reinstall the Msql-Mysql-modules distribution whenever you install a new release of MySQL, particularly if you notice symptoms such as all your DBI scripts dumping core after you upgrade MySQL.

If you don't have the right to install Perl modules in the system directory or if you do install local Perl modules, the following reference may help you:

   http://www.iserver.com/support/contrib/perl5/modules.html

Look under the heading Installing New Modules that Require Locally Installed Modules.

2.7.2 Installing ActiveState Perl on Windows

To install the MySQL DBD module with ActiveState Perl on Windows, you should do the following:

- Get ActiveState Perl from http://www.activestate.com/Products/ActivePerl/ and install it.

- Open a DOS shell.

- If required, set the HTTP_proxy variable. For example, you might try:

   ```
   set HTTP_proxy=my.proxy.com:3128
   ```

- Start the PPM program:

```
C:\> c:\perl\bin\ppm.pl
```

- If you have not already done so, install DBI:

```
ppm> install DBI
```

- If this succeeds, run the following command:

```
install \
ftp://ftp.de.uu.net/pub/CPAN/authors/id/JWIED/DBD-mysql-1.2212.x86.ppd
```

This should work at least with ActiveState Perl Version 5.6.

If you can't get this to work, you should instead install the MyODBC driver and connect to MySQL server through ODBC:

```
use DBI;
$dbh= DBI->connect("DBI:ODBC:$dsn","$user","$password") ||
   die "Got error $DBI::errstr when connecting to $dsn\n";
```

2.7.3 Installing the MySQL Perl Distribution on Windows

The MySQL Perl distribution contains DBI, DBD:MySQL, and DBD:ODBC.

- Get the Perl distribution for Windows from http://www.mysql.com/download.html.

- Unzip the distribution in C: so that you get a C:\PERL directory.

- Add the directory C:\PERL\BIN to your path.

- Add the C:\PERL\BIN\MSWIN32-x86-thread or C:\PERL\BIN\MSWIN32-x86 directory to your path.

- Test that perl works by executing perl -v in a DOS shell.

2.7.4 Problems Using the Perl DBI/DBD Interface

If Perl reports that it can't find the ../mysql/mysql.so module, the problem is probably that Perl can't locate the shared library libmysqlclient.so.

You can fix this by any of the following methods:

- Compile the Msql-Mysql-modules distribution with perl Makefile.PL -static -config rather than perl Makefile.PL.

- Copy libmysqlclient.so to the directory where your other shared libraries are located (probably /usr/lib or /lib).

- On Linux you can add the pathname of the directory where libmysqlclient.so is located to the /etc/ld.so.conf file.

- Add the pathname of the directory where `libmysqlclient.so` is located to the `LD_RUN_PATH` environment variable.

If you get the following errors from `DBD-mysql`, you are probably using gcc (or using an old binary compiled with gcc):

```
/usr/bin/perl: can't resolve symbol '__moddi3'
/usr/bin/perl: can't resolve symbol '__divdi3'
```

Add `-L/usr/lib/gcc-lib/ . . .  -lgcc` to the link command when the `mysql.so` library gets built (check the output from `make` for `mysql.so` when you compile the Perl client). The `-L` option should specify the pathname of the directory where `libgcc.a` is located on your system.

Another cause of this problem may be that Perl and MySQL aren't both compiled with gcc. In this case, you can solve the mismatch by compiling both with gcc.

If you get the following error from `Msql-Mysql-modules` when you run the tests:

```
t/00base...........install_driver(mysql) failed:
Can't load '../blib/arch/auto/DBD/mysql/mysql.so' for module DBD::mysql:
../blib/arch/auto/DBD/mysql/mysql.so: undefined symbol:
uncompress at /usr/lib/perl5/5.00503/i586-linux/DynaLoader.pm line 169.
```

it means that you need to include the compression library, -lz, to the link line. To do this, make the following change in the file `lib/DBD/mysql/Install.pm`:

```
$sysliblist .= " -lm";
```

to

```
$sysliblist .= " -lm -lz";
```

After this, you **must** run 'make realclean' and then proceed with the installation from the beginning.

If you want to use the Perl module on a system that doesn't support dynamic linking (like Caldera/SCO) you can generate a static version of Perl that includes `DBI` and `DBD-mysql`. The way this works is that you generate a version of Perl with the `DBI` code linked in and install it on top of your current Perl. Then you use that to build a version of Perl that additionally has the `DBD` code linked in, and install that.

On Caldera (SCO), you must have the following environment variables set:

```
shell> LD_LIBRARY_PATH=/lib:/usr/lib:/usr/local/lib:/usr/progressive/lib
or
shell> LD_LIBRARY_PATH=/usr/lib:/lib:/usr/local/lib:/usr/ccs/lib:\
/usr/progressive/lib:/usr/skunk/lib
shell> LIBPATH=/usr/lib:/lib:/usr/local/lib:/usr/ccs/lib:\
/usr/progressive/lib:/usr/skunk/lib
shell> MANPATH=scohelp:/usr/man:/usr/local1/man:/usr/local/man:\
/usr/skunk/man:
```

First, create a Perl that includes a statically linked DBI by running these commands in the directory where your DBI distribution is located:

```
shell> perl Makefile.PL -static -config
shell> make
shell> make install
shell> make perl
```

Then you must install the new Perl. The output of make perl will indicate the exact make command you will need to execute to perform the installation. On Caldera (SCO), this is make -f Makefile.aperl inst_perl MAP_TARGET=perl.

Next, use the just-created Perl to create another Perl that also includes a statically linked DBD::mysql by running these commands in the directory where your Msql-Mysql-modules distribution is located:

```
shell> perl Makefile.PL -static -config
shell> make
shell> make install
shell> make perl
```

Finally, you should install this new Perl. Again, the output of make perl indicates the command to use.

3

Tutorial Introduction

This chapter provides a tutorial introduction to MySQL by showing how to use the `mysql` client program to create and use a simple database. `mysql` (sometimes referred to as the "terminal monitor" or just "monitor") is an interactive program that allows you to connect to a MySQL server, run queries, and view the results. `mysql` may also be used in batch mode: you place your queries in a file beforehand, then tell `mysql` to execute the contents of the file. Both ways of using `mysql` are covered here.

To see a list of options provided by `mysql`, invoke it with the `--help` option:

```
shell> mysql --help
```

This chapter assumes that `mysql` is installed on your machine and that a MySQL server is available to which you can connect. If this is not true, contact your MySQL administrator. (If **you** are the administrator, you will need to consult other sections of this manual.)

This chapter describes the entire process of setting up and using a database. If you are interested only in accessing an already-existing database, you may want to skip over the sections that describe how to create the database and the tables it contains.

Because this chapter is tutorial in nature, many details are necessarily left out. Consult the relevant sections of the manual for more information on the topics covered here.

3.1 Connecting to and Disconnecting from the Server

To connect to the server, you'll usually need to provide a MySQL username when you invoke mysql and, most likely, a password. If the server runs on a machine other than the one where you log in, you'll also need to specify a hostname. Contact your administrator to find out what connection parameters you should use to connect (that is, what host, username, and password to use). Once you know the proper parameters, you should be able to connect like this:

```
shell> mysql -h host -u user -p
Enter password: ********
```

The ******** represents your password; enter it when mysql displays the Enter password: prompt.

If that works, you should see some introductory information followed by a mysql> prompt:

```
shell> mysql -h host -u user -p
Enter password: ********
Welcome to the MySQL monitor.  Commands end with ; or \g.
Your MySQL connection id is 459 to server version: 3.22.20a-log

Type 'help' for help.

mysql>
```

The prompt tells you that mysql is ready for you to enter commands.

Some MySQL installations allow users to connect as the anonymous (unnamed) user to the server running on the local host. If this is the case on your machine, you should be able to connect to that server by invoking mysql without any options:

```
shell> mysql
```

After you have connected successfully, you can disconnect any time by typing QUIT at the mysql> prompt:

```
mysql> QUIT
Bye
```

You can also disconnect by pressing Control-D.

Most examples in the following sections assume you are connected to the server. They indicate this by the mysql> prompt.

3.2 Entering Queries

Make sure you are connected to the server, as discussed in the previous section. Doing so will not in itself select any database to work with, but that's okay. At this point, it's more important to find out a little about how to issue queries than to jump right in creating tables, loading data into them, and retrieving data from them. This section describes the basic principles of entering commands, using several queries you can try out to familiarise yourself with how mysql works.

Here's a simple command that asks the server to tell you its version number and the current date. Type it in as shown here following the mysql> prompt and press Enter:

```
mysql> SELECT VERSION(), CURRENT_DATE;
+--------------+--------------+
| VERSION()    | CURRENT_DATE |
+--------------+--------------+
| 3.22.20a-log | 1999-03-19   |
+--------------+--------------+
1 row in set (0.01 sec)
mysql>
```

This query illustrates several things about mysql:

- A command normally consists of a SQL statement followed by a semicolon. (There are some exceptions where a semicolon is not needed. QUIT, mentioned earlier, is one of them. We'll get to others later.)

- When you issue a command, mysql sends it to the server for execution and displays the results, then prints another mysql> to indicate that it is ready for another command.

- mysql displays query output as a table (rows and columns). The first row contains labels for the columns. The rows following are the query results. Normally, column labels are the names of the columns you fetch from database tables. If you're retrieving the value of an expression rather than a table column (as in the example just shown), mysql labels the column using the expression itself.

- mysql shows how many rows were returned and how long the query took to execute, which gives you a rough idea of server performance. These values are imprecise because they represent wall clock time (not CPU or machine time), and because they are affected by factors such as server load and network latency. (For brevity, the "rows in set" line is not shown in the remaining examples in this chapter.)

Keywords may be entered in any lettercase. The following queries are equivalent:

```
mysql> SELECT VERSION(), CURRENT_DATE;
mysql> select version(), current_date;
mysql> SeLeCt vErSiOn(), current_DATE;
```

Here's another query. It demonstrates that you can use mysql as a simple calculator:

```
mysql> SELECT SIN(PI()/4), (4+1)*5;
+-------------+---------+
| SIN(PI()/4) | (4+1)*5 |
+-------------+---------+
|    0.707107 |      25 |
+-------------+---------+
```

The commands shown thus far have been relatively short, single-line statements. You can even enter multiple statements on a single line. Just end each one with a semicolon:

```
mysql> SELECT VERSION(); SELECT NOW();
+--------------+
| VERSION()    |
+--------------+
| 3.22.20a-log |
+--------------+

+---------------------+
| NOW()               |
+---------------------+
| 1999-03-19 00:15:33 |
+---------------------+
```

A command need not be given all on a single line, so lengthy commands that require several lines are not a problem. mysql determines where your statement ends by looking for the terminating semicolon, not by looking for the end of the input line. (In other words, mysql accepts free-format input: it collects input lines but does not execute them until it sees the semicolon.)

Here's a simple multiple-line statement:

```
mysql> SELECT
    -> USER()
    -> ,
    -> CURRENT_DATE;
+--------------------+--------------+
| USER()             | CURRENT_DATE |
+--------------------+--------------+
| joesmith@localhost | 1999-03-18   |
+--------------------+--------------+
```

In this example, notice how the prompt changes from mysql> to -> after you enter the first line of a multiple-line query. This is how mysql indicates that it hasn't seen a complete statement and is waiting for the rest. The prompt is your friend because it provides valuable feedback. If you use that feedback, you will always be aware of what mysql is waiting for.

If you decide you don't want to execute a command that you are in the process of entering, cancel it by typing \c:

```
mysql> SELECT
    -> USER()
    -> \c
mysql>
```

Here, too, notice the prompt. It switches back to mysql> after you type \c, providing feedback to indicate that mysql is ready for a new command.

The following table shows each of the prompts you may see and summarises what they mean about the state that mysql is in:

Prompt	Meaning
mysql>	Ready for new command.
->	Waiting for next line of multiple-line command.
'>	Waiting for next line, collecting a string that begins with a single quote (').
">	Waiting for next line, collecting a string that begins with a double quote (").

Multiple-line statements commonly occur by accident when you intend to issue a command on a single line, but forget the terminating semicolon. In this case, mysql waits for more input:

```
mysql> SELECT USER()
    ->
```

If this happens to you (you think you've entered a statement but the only response is a -> prompt), most likely mysql is waiting for the semicolon. If you don't notice what the prompt is telling you, you might sit there for a while before realising what you need to do. Enter a semicolon to complete the statement, and mysql will execute it:

```
mysql> SELECT USER()
    -> ;
+--------------------+
| USER()             |
+--------------------+
| joesmith@localhost |
+--------------------+
```

The '> and "> prompts occur during string collection. In MySQL, you can write strings surrounded by either ' or " characters (for example, 'hello' or "goodbye"), and mysql lets you enter strings that span multiple lines. When you see a '> or "> prompt, it means that you've entered a line containing a string that begins with a ' or " quote character, but have not yet entered the matching quote that terminates the string. That's fine if you really are entering a multiple-line string, but how likely is that? Not very. More often, the '> and "> prompts indicate that you've inadvertently left out a quote character. For example:

```
mysql> SELECT * FROM my_table WHERE name = "Smith AND age < 30;
    ">
```

If you enter this SELECT statement, then press Enter and wait for the result, nothing will happen. Instead of wondering why this query takes so long, notice the clue provided by the "> prompt. It tells you that mysql expects to see the rest of an unterminated string. (Do you see the error in the statement? The string "Smith is missing the second quote.)

At this point, what do you do? The simplest thing is to cancel the command. However, you cannot just type \c in this case because mysql interprets it as part of the string that it is collecting! Instead, enter the closing quote character (so mysql knows you've finished the string), then type \c:

```
mysql> SELECT * FROM my_table WHERE name = "Smith AND age < 30;
    "> "\c
mysql>
```

The prompt changes back to mysql>, indicating that mysql is ready for a new command.

It's important to know what the '> and "> prompts signify because if you mistakenly enter an unterminated string, any further lines you type will appear to be ignored by mysql—including a line containing QUIT! This can be quite confusing, especially if you don't know that you need to supply the terminating quote before you can cancel the current command.

3.3 Creating and Using a Database

Now that you know how to enter commands, it's time to access a database.

Suppose you have several pets in your home (your menagerie) and you'd like to keep track of various types of information about them. You can do so by creating tables to hold your data and loading them with the desired information. Then you can answer different sorts of questions about your animals by retrieving data from the tables. This section shows you how to:

- Create a database
- Create a table
- Load data into the table
- Retrieve data from the table in various ways
- Use multiple tables

The menagerie database will be simple (deliberately), but it is not difficult to think of real-world situations in which a similar type of database might be used. For example, a database like this could be used by a farmer to keep track of livestock, or by a veterinarian to keep track of patient records. A menagerie distribution containing some of the queries and sample data used in the following sections can be obtained from the MySQL web site. It's available in either compressed `tar` format (http://www.mysql.com/Downloads/Contrib/Examples/menagerie.tar.gz) or Zip format (http://www.mysql.com/Downloads/Contrib/Examples/menagerie.zip).

Use the `SHOW` statement to find out what databases currently exist on the server:

```
mysql> SHOW DATABASES;
+----------+
| Database |
+----------+
| mysql    |
| test     |
| tmp      |
+----------+
```

The list of databases is probably different on your machine, but the `mysql` and `test` databases are likely to be among them. The `mysql` database is required because it describes user access privileges. The `test` database is often provided as a workspace for users to try things out.

If the `test` database exists, try to access it:

```
mysql> USE test
Database changed
```

Note that `USE`, like `QUIT`, does not require a semicolon. (You can terminate such statements with a semicolon if you like; it does no harm.) The `USE` statement is special in another way, too: it must be given on a single line.

You can use the `test` database (if you have access to it) for the examples that follow, but anything you create in that database can be removed by anyone else with access to it. For this reason, you should probably ask your MySQL administrator for permission to use a database of your own. Suppose you want to call yours `menagerie`. The administrator needs to execute a command like this:

```
mysql> GRANT ALL ON menagerie.* TO your_mysql_name;
```

where `your_mysql_name` is the MySQL username assigned to you.

3.3.1 Creating and Selecting a Database

If the administrator creates your database for you when setting up your permissions, you can begin using it. Otherwise, you need to create it yourself:

```
mysql> CREATE DATABASE menagerie;
```

Under Unix, database names are case-sensitive (unlike SQL keywords), so you must always refer to your database as `menagerie`, not as `Menagerie` or `MENAGERIE`. This is also true for table names. (Under Windows, this restriction does not apply, although you must refer to databases and tables using the same lettercase throughout a given query.)

Creating a database does not select it for use; you must do that explicitly. To make menagerie the current database, use this command:

```
mysql> USE menagerie
Database changed
```

Your database needs to be created only once, but you must select it for use each time you begin a mysql session. You can do this by issuing a USE statement as shown perviously. Alternatively, you can select the database on the command-line when you invoke mysql. Just specify its name after any connection parameters that you might need to provide. For example:

```
shell> mysql -h host -u user -p menagerie
Enter password: ********
```

Note that menagerie is not your password on the command just shown. If you want to supply your password on the command-line after the -p option, you must do so with no intervening space (for example, as -pmypassword, not as -p mypassword). However, putting your password on the command-line is not recommended because doing so exposes it to snooping by other users logged in on your machine.

3.3.2 Creating a Table

Creating the database is the easy part, but at this point it's empty, as SHOW TABLES will tell you:

```
mysql> SHOW TABLES;
Empty set (0.00 sec)
```

The harder part is deciding what the structure of your database should be: what tables you will need and what columns will be in each of them.

You'll want a table that contains a record for each of your pets. This can be called the pet table, and it should contain, as a bare minimum, each animal's name. Because the name by itself is not very interesting, the table should contain other information. For example, if more than one person in your family keeps pets, you might want to list each animal's owner. You might also want to record some basic descriptive information such as species and sex.

How about age? That might be of interest, but it's not a good thing to store in a database. Age changes as time passes, which means you'd have to update your records often. Instead, it's better to store a fixed value such as date of birth. Then, whenever you need age, you can calculate it as the difference between the current date and the birth date. MySQL provides functions for doing date arithmetic, so this is not difficult. Storing birth date rather than age has other advantages, too:

- You can use the database for tasks such as generating reminders for upcoming pet birthdays. (If you think this type of query is somewhat silly, note that it is the same question you might ask in the context of a business database to identify clients to whom you'll soon need to send out birthday greetings, for that computer-assisted personal touch.)

- You can calculate age in relation to dates other than the current date. For example, if you store death date in the database, you can easily calculate how old a pet was when it died.

Other types of information would probably be useful in the pet table, but the ones identified so far are sufficient for now: name, owner, species, sex, birth, and death.

Use a CREATE TABLE statement to specify the layout of your table:

```
mysql> CREATE TABLE pet (name VARCHAR(20), owner VARCHAR(20),
    -> species VARCHAR(20), sex CHAR(1), birth DATE, death DATE);
```

VARCHAR is a good choice for the name, owner, and species columns because the column values will vary in length. The lengths of those columns need not all be the same, and need not be 20. You can pick any length from 1 to 255, whatever seems most reasonable to you. (If you make a poor choice and it turns out later that you need a longer field, MySQL provides an ALTER TABLE statement.)

Animal sex can be represented in a variety of ways—for example, "m" and "f", or perhaps "male" and "female". It's simplest to use the single characters "m" and "f".

Using the DATE datatype for the birth and death columns is a fairly obvious choice.

Now that you have created a table, SHOW TABLES should produce some output:

```
mysql> SHOW TABLES;
+---------------------+
| Tables in menagerie |
+---------------------+
| pet                 |
+---------------------+
```

To verify that your table was created the way you expected, use a DESCRIBE statement:

```
mysql> DESCRIBE pet;
+---------+-------------+------+-----+---------+-------+
| Field   | Type        | Null | Key | Default | Extra |
+---------+-------------+------+-----+---------+-------+
| name    | varchar(20) | YES  |     | NULL    |       |
| owner   | varchar(20) | YES  |     | NULL    |       |
| species | varchar(20) | YES  |     | NULL    |       |
| sex     | char(1)     | YES  |     | NULL    |       |
| birth   | date        | YES  |     | NULL    |       |
| death   | date        | YES  |     | NULL    |       |
+---------+-------------+------+-----+---------+-------+
```

You can use DESCRIBE any time—for example, if you forget the names of the columns in your table or what types they are.

3.3.3 Loading Data into a Table

After creating your table, you need to populate it. The LOAD DATA and INSERT statements are useful for this.

Suppose your pet records can be described as shown here. (Observe that MySQL expects dates in YYYY-MM-DD format; this may be different than what you are used to.)

Name	Owner	Species	Sex	Birth	Death
Fluffy	Harold	cat	f	1993-02-04	
Claws	Gwen	cat	m	1994-03-17	
Buffy	Harold	dog	f	1989-05-13	
Fang	Benny	dog	m	1990-08-27	
Bowser	Diane	dog	m	1998-08-31	1995-07-29
Chirpy	Gwen	bird	f	1998-09-11	
Whistler	Gwen	bird		1997-12-09	
Slim	Benny	snake	m	1996-04-29	

Because you are beginning with an empty table, an easy way to populate it is to create a text file containing a row for each of your animals, then load the contents of the file into the table with a single statement.

You could create a text file pet.txt containing one record per line, with values separated by tabs, and given in the order in which the columns were listed in the CREATE TABLE statement. For missing values (such as unknown sexes or death dates for animals that are still living), you can use NULL values. To represent these in your text file, use \N. For example, the record for Whistler the bird would look like this (where the whitespace between values is a single tab character):

Name	Owner	Species	Sex	Birth	Death
Whistler	Gwen	bird	\N	1997-12-09	\N

To load the text file pet.txt into the pet table, use this command:

```
mysql> LOAD DATA LOCAL INFILE "pet.txt" INTO TABLE pet;
```

You can specify the column value separator and end of line marker explicitly in the LOAD DATA statement if you wish, but the defaults are tab and linefeed. These are sufficient for the statement to read the file pet.txt properly.

When you want to add new records one at a time, the INSERT statement is useful. In its simplest form, you supply values for each column, in the order in which the columns were listed in the CREATE TABLE statement. Suppose Diane gets a new hamster named Puffball. You could add a new record using an INSERT statement like this:

```
mysql> INSERT INTO pet
    -> VALUES ('Puffball','Diane','hamster','f','1999-03-30',NULL);
```

Note that string and date values are specified as quoted strings here. Also, with INSERT, you can insert NULL directly to represent a missing value. You do not use \N like you do with LOAD DATA.

From this example, you should be able to see that there would be a lot more typing involved to load your records initially using several INSERT statements rather than a single LOAD DATA statement.

3.3.4 Retrieving Information from a Table

The SELECT statement is used to pull information from a table. The general form of the statement is:

```
SELECT what_to_select
FROM which_table
WHERE conditions_to_satisfy
```

what_to_select indicates what you want to see. This can be a list of columns, or * to indicate "all columns." which_table indicates the table from which you want to retrieve data. The WHERE clause is optional. If it's present, conditions_to_satisfy specifies conditions that rows must satisfy to qualify for retrieval.

3.3.4.1 Selecting all data

The simplest form of SELECT retrieves everything from a table:

```
mysql> SELECT * FROM pet;
+----------+--------+---------+------+------------+------------+
| name     | owner  | species | sex  | birth      | death      |
+----------+--------+---------+------+------------+------------+
| Fluffy   | Harold | cat     | f    | 1993-02-04 | NULL       |
| Claws    | Gwen   | cat     | m    | 1994-03-17 | NULL       |
| Buffy    | Harold | dog     | f    | 1989-05-13 | NULL       |
| Fang     | Benny  | dog     | m    | 1990-08-27 | NULL       |
| Bowser   | Diane  | dog     | m    | 1998-08-31 | 1995-07-29 |
| Chirpy   | Gwen   | bird    | f    | 1998-09-11 | NULL       |
| Whistler | Gwen   | bird    | NULL | 1997-12-09 | NULL       |
| Slim     | Benny  | snake   | m    | 1996-04-29 | NULL       |
| Puffball | Diane  | hamster | f    | 1999-03-30 | NULL       |
+----------+--------+---------+------+------------+------------+
```

This form of SELECT is useful if you want to review your entire table—for instance, after you've just loaded it with your initial dataset. As it happens, the output just shown reveals an error in your data file: Bowser appears to have been born after he died! Consulting your original pedigree papers, you find that the correct birth year is 1989, not 1998.

There are are least a couple of ways to fix this:

- Edit the file `pet.txt` to correct the error, then empty the table and reload it using DELETE and LOAD DATA:

```
mysql> SET AUTOCOMMIT=1;  # Used for quick re-create of the table
mysql> DELETE FROM pet;
mysql> LOAD DATA LOCAL INFILE "pet.txt" INTO TABLE pet;
```

However, if you do this, you must also re-enter the record for Puffball.

- Fix only the erroneous record with an UPDATE statement:

```
mysql> UPDATE pet SET birth = "1989-08-31" WHERE name = "Bowser";
```

As shown here, it is easy to retrieve an entire table. But typically you don't want to do that, particularly when the table becomes large. Instead, you're usually more interested in answering a particular question, in which case you specify some constraints on the information you want. Let's look at some selection queries in terms of questions about your pets that they answer.

3.3.4.2 Selecting particular rows

You can select only particular rows from your table. For example, if you want to verify the change that you made to Bowser's birth date, select Bowser's record like this:

```
mysql> SELECT * FROM pet WHERE name = "Bowser";
+--------+-------+---------+------+------------+------------+
| name   | owner | species | sex  | birth      | death      |
+--------+-------+---------+------+------------+------------+
| Bowser | Diane | dog     | m    | 1989-08-31 | 1995-07-29 |
+--------+-------+---------+------+------------+------------+
```

The output confirms that the year is correctly recorded now as 1989, not 1998.

String comparisons are normally case-insensitive, so you can specify the name as "bowser", "BOWSER", etc. The query result will be the same.

You can specify conditions on any column, not just name. For example, if you want to know which animals were born after 1998, test the birth column:

```
mysql> SELECT * FROM pet WHERE birth >= "1998-1-1";
+----------+-------+---------+------+------------+-------+
| name     | owner | species | sex  | birth      | death |
+----------+-------+---------+------+------------+-------+
| Chirpy   | Gwen  | bird    | f    | 1998-09-11 | NULL  |
| Puffball | Diane | hamster | f    | 1999-03-30 | NULL  |
+----------+-------+---------+------+------------+-------+
```

You can combine conditions, for example, to locate female dogs:

```
mysql> SELECT * FROM pet WHERE species = "dog" AND sex = "f";
+-------+--------+---------+------+------------+-------+
| name  | owner  | species | sex  | birth      | death |
+-------+--------+---------+------+------------+-------+
| Buffy | Harold | dog     | f    | 1989-05-13 | NULL  |
+-------+--------+---------+------+------------+-------+
```

The preceding query uses the AND logical operator. There is also an OR operator:

```
mysql> SELECT * FROM pet WHERE species = "snake" OR species = "bird";
+----------+-------+---------+------+------------+-------+
| name     | owner | species | sex  | birth      | death |
+----------+-------+---------+------+------------+-------+
| Chirpy   | Gwen  | bird    | f    | 1998-09-11 | NULL  |
| Whistler | Gwen  | bird    | NULL | 1997-12-09 | NULL  |
| Slim     | Benny | snake   | m    | 1996-04-29 | NULL  |
+----------+-------+---------+------+------------+-------+
```

AND and OR may be intermixed. If you do that, it's a good idea to use parentheses to indicate how conditions should be grouped:

```
mysql> SELECT * FROM pet WHERE (species = "cat" AND sex = "m")
    -> OR (species = "dog" AND sex = "f");
+-------+--------+---------+------+------------+-------+
| name  | owner  | species | sex  | birth      | death |
+-------+--------+---------+------+------------+-------+
| Claws | Gwen   | cat     | m    | 1994-03-17 | NULL  |
| Buffy | Harold | dog     | f    | 1989-05-13 | NULL  |
+-------+--------+---------+------+------------+-------+
```

3.3.4.3 Selecting particular columns

If you don't want to see entire rows from your table, just name the columns in which you're interested, separated by commas. For example, if you want to know when your animals were born, select the name and birth columns:

```
mysql> SELECT name, birth FROM pet;
+----------+------------+
| name     | birth      |
+----------+------------+
| Fluffy   | 1993-02-04 |
| Claws    | 1994-03-17 |
| Buffy    | 1989-05-13 |
| Fang     | 1990-08-27 |
| Bowser   | 1989-08-31 |
| Chirpy   | 1998-09-11 |
| Whistler | 1997-12-09 |
| Slim     | 1996-04-29 |
| Puffball | 1999-03-30 |
+----------+------------+
```

To find out who owns pets, use this query:

```
mysql> SELECT owner FROM pet;
+--------+
| owner  |
+--------+
| Harold |
| Gwen   |
| Harold |
| Benny  |
| Diane  |
| Gwen   |
| Gwen   |
| Benny  |
| Diane  |
+--------+
```

However, notice that the query simply retrieves the owner field from each record, and some of them appear more than once. To minimise the output, retrieve each unique output record just once by adding the keyword DISTINCT:

```
mysql> SELECT DISTINCT owner FROM pet;
+--------+
| owner  |
+--------+
| Benny  |
| Diane  |
| Gwen   |
| Harold |
+--------+
```

You can use a WHERE clause to combine row selection with column selection. For example, to get birth dates for dogs and cats only, use this query:

```
mysql> SELECT name, species, birth FROM pet
    -> WHERE species = "dog" OR species = "cat";
+--------+---------+------------+
| name   | species | birth      |
+--------+---------+------------+
| Fluffy | cat     | 1993-02-04 |
| Claws  | cat     | 1994-03-17 |
| Buffy  | dog     | 1989-05-13 |
| Fang   | dog     | 1990-08-27 |
| Bowser | dog     | 1989-08-31 |
+--------+---------+------------+
```

3.3.4.4 Sorting rows

You may have noticed in the preceding examples that the result rows are displayed in no particular order. However, it's often easier to examine query output when the rows are sorted in some meaningful way. To sort a result, use an ORDER BY clause.

Here are animal birthdays, sorted by date:

```
mysql> SELECT name, birth FROM pet ORDER BY birth;
+----------+------------+
| name     | birth      |
+----------+------------+
| Buffy    | 1989-05-13 |
| Bowser   | 1989-08-31 |
| Fang     | 1990-08-27 |
| Fluffy   | 1993-02-04 |
| Claws    | 1994-03-17 |
| Slim     | 1996-04-29 |
| Whistler | 1997-12-09 |
| Chirpy   | 1998-09-11 |
| Puffball | 1999-03-30 |
+----------+------------+
```

To sort in reverse order, add the DESC (descending) keyword to the name of the column
you are sorting by:

```
mysql> SELECT name, birth FROM pet ORDER BY birth DESC;
+----------+------------+
| name     | birth      |
+----------+------------+
| Puffball | 1999-03-30 |
| Chirpy   | 1998-09-11 |
| Whistler | 1997-12-09 |
| Slim     | 1996-04-29 |
| Claws    | 1994-03-17 |
| Fluffy   | 1993-02-04 |
| Fang     | 1990-08-27 |
| Bowser   | 1989-08-31 |
| Buffy    | 1989-05-13 |
+----------+------------+
```

You can sort on multiple columns. For example, to sort by type of animal, then by birth
date within animal type with youngest animals first, use the following query:

```
mysql> SELECT name, species, birth FROM pet ORDER BY species, birth DESC;
+----------+---------+------------+
| name     | species | birth      |
+----------+---------+------------+
| Chirpy   | bird    | 1998-09-11 |
| Whistler | bird    | 1997-12-09 |
| Claws    | cat     | 1994-03-17 |
| Fluffy   | cat     | 1993-02-04 |
| Fang     | dog     | 1990-08-27 |
| Bowser   | dog     | 1989-08-31 |
| Buffy    | dog     | 1989-05-13 |
| Puffball | hamster | 1999-03-30 |
| Slim     | snake   | 1996-04-29 |
+----------+---------+------------+
```

Note that the DESC keyword applies only to the column name immediately preceding it (birth); species values are still sorted in ascending order.

3.3.4.5 Date calculations

MySQL provides several functions that you can use to perform calculations on dates—for example, to calculate ages or extract parts of dates.

To determine how many years old each of your pets is, compute the difference in the year part of the current date and the birth date, then subtract one if the current date occurs earlier in the calendar year than the birth date. The following query shows, for each pet, the birth date, the current date, and the age in years.

```
mysql> SELECT name, birth, CURRENT_DATE,
    ->  (YEAR(CURRENT_DATE)-YEAR(birth))
    ->  - (RIGHT(CURRENT_DATE,5)<RIGHT(birth,5))
    ->  AS age
    ->  FROM pet;
+----------+------------+--------------+------+
| name     | birth      | CURRENT_DATE | age  |
+----------+------------+--------------+------+
| Fluffy   | 1993-02-04 | 2001-08-29   |    8 |
| Claws    | 1994-03-17 | 2001-08-29   |    7 |
| Buffy    | 1989-05-13 | 2001-08-29   |   12 |
| Fang     | 1990-08-27 | 2001-08-29   |   11 |
| Bowser   | 1989-08-31 | 2001-08-29   |   11 |
| Chirpy   | 1998-09-11 | 2001-08-29   |    2 |
| Whistler | 1997-12-09 | 2001-08-29   |    3 |
| Slim     | 1996-04-29 | 2001-08-29   |    5 |
| Puffball | 1999-03-30 | 2001-08-29   |    2 |
+----------+------------+--------------+------+
```

Here, YEAR() pulls out the year part of a date and RIGHT() pulls off the rightmost five characters that represent the MM-DD (calendar year) part of the date. The part of the expression that compares the MM-DD values evaluates to 1 or 0, which adjusts the year difference down a year if CURRENT_DATE occurs earlier in the year than birth. The full expression is somewhat ungainly, so an alias (age) is used to make the output column label more meaningful.

The query works, but the result could be scanned more easily if the rows were presented in some order. This can be done by adding an ORDER BY name clause to sort the output by name:

```
mysql> SELECT name, birth, CURRENT_DATE,
    ->  (YEAR(CURRENT_DATE)-YEAR(birth))
    ->  - (RIGHT(CURRENT_DATE,5)<RIGHT(birth,5))
    ->  AS age
    ->  FROM pet ORDER BY name;
```

```
+-----------+------------+--------------+------+
| name      | birth      | CURRENT_DATE | age  |
+-----------+------------+--------------+------+
| Bowser    | 1989-08-31 | 2001-08-29   |   11 |
| Buffy     | 1989-05-13 | 2001-08-29   |   12 |
| Chirpy    | 1998-09-11 | 2001-08-29   |    2 |
| Claws     | 1994-03-17 | 2001-08-29   |    7 |
| Fang      | 1990-08-27 | 2001-08-29   |   11 |
| Fluffy    | 1993-02-04 | 2001-08-29   |    8 |
| Puffball  | 1999-03-30 | 2001-08-29   |    2 |
| Slim      | 1996-04-29 | 2001-08-29   |    5 |
| Whistler  | 1997-12-09 | 2001-08-29   |    3 |
+-----------+------------+--------------+------+
```

To sort the output by age rather than name, just use a different ORDER BY clause:

```
mysql> SELECT name, birth, CURRENT_DATE,
    -> (YEAR(CURRENT_DATE)-YEAR(birth))
    -> - (RIGHT(CURRENT_DATE,5)<RIGHT(birth,5))
    -> AS age
    -> FROM pet ORDER BY age;
+-----------+------------+--------------+------+
| name      | birth      | CURRENT_DATE | age  |
+-----------+------------+--------------+------+
| Chirpy    | 1998-09-11 | 2001-08-29   |    2 |
| Puffball  | 1999-03-30 | 2001-08-29   |    2 |
| Whistler  | 1997-12-09 | 2001-08-29   |    3 |
| Slim      | 1996-04-29 | 2001-08-29   |    5 |
| Claws     | 1994-03-17 | 2001-08-29   |    7 |
| Fluffy    | 1993-02-04 | 2001-08-29   |    8 |
| Fang      | 1990-08-27 | 2001-08-29   |   11 |
| Bowser    | 1989-08-31 | 2001-08-29   |   11 |
| Buffy     | 1989-05-13 | 2001-08-29   |   12 |
+-----------+------------+--------------+------+
```

A similar query can be used to determine age at death for animals that have died. You determine which animals these are by checking whether the death value is NULL. Then, for those with non-NULL values, compute the difference between the death and birth values:

```
mysql> SELECT name, birth, death,
    -> (YEAR(death)-YEAR(birth)) - (RIGHT(death,5)<RIGHT(birth,5))
    -> AS age
    -> FROM pet WHERE death IS NOT NULL ORDER BY age;
+--------+------------+------------+------+
| name   | birth      | death      | age  |
+--------+------------+------------+------+
| Bowser | 1989-08-31 | 1995-07-29 |    5 |
+--------+------------+------------+------+
```

The query uses death IS NOT NULL rather than death <> NULL because NULL is a special value. This is explained later. See Section 3.3.4.6, Working with NULL values.

What if you want to know which animals have birthdays next month? For this type of calculation, year and day are irrelevant; you simply want to extract the month part of the birth column. MySQL provides several date-part extraction functions, such as YEAR(), MONTH(), and DAYOFMONTH(). MONTH() is the appropriate function here. To see how it works, run a simple query that displays the value of both birth and MONTH(birth):

```
mysql> SELECT name, birth, MONTH(birth) FROM pet;
+----------+------------+--------------+
| name     | birth      | MONTH(birth) |
+----------+------------+--------------+
| Fluffy   | 1993-02-04 |            2 |
| Claws    | 1994-03-17 |            3 |
| Buffy    | 1989-05-13 |            5 |
| Fang     | 1990-08-27 |            8 |
| Bowser   | 1989-08-31 |            8 |
| Chirpy   | 1998-09-11 |            9 |
| Whistler | 1997-12-09 |           12 |
| Slim     | 1996-04-29 |            4 |
| Puffball | 1999-03-30 |            3 |
+----------+------------+--------------+
```

Finding animals with birthdays in the upcoming month is easy, too. Suppose the current month is April. Then the month value is 4 and you look for animals born in May (month 5) like this:

```
mysql> SELECT name, birth FROM pet WHERE MONTH(birth) = 5;
+-------+------------+
| name  | birth      |
+-------+------------+
| Buffy | 1989-05-13 |
+-------+------------+
```

There is a small complication if the current month is December, of course. You don't just add one to the month number (12) and look for animals born in month 13 because there is no such month. Instead, you look for animals born in January (month 1).

You can even write the query so that it works no matter what the current month is. That way you don't have to use a particular month number in the query. DATE_ADD() allows you to add a time interval to a given date. If you add a month to the value of NOW(), then extract the month part with MONTH(), the result produces the month in which to look for birthdays:

```
mysql> SELECT name, birth FROM pet
    -> WHERE MONTH(birth) = MONTH(DATE_ADD(NOW(), INTERVAL 1 MONTH));
```

A different way to accomplish the same task is to add 1 to get the next month after the current one (after using the modulo function (MOD) to wrap around the month value to 0 if it is currently 12):

```
mysql> SELECT name, birth FROM pet
    -> WHERE MONTH(birth) = MOD(MONTH(NOW()), 12) + 1;
```

Note that MONTH returns a number between 1 and 12. And MOD(something,12) returns a number between 0 and 11. So the addition has to be after the MOD(), otherwise we would go from November (11) to January (1).

3.3.4.6 Working with NULL values

The NULL value can be surprising until you get used to it. Conceptually, NULL means missing value or unknown value and it is treated somewhat differently than other values. To test for NULL, you cannot use the arithmetic comparison operators such as =, <, or <>. To demonstrate this for yourself, try the following query:

```
mysql> SELECT 1 = NULL, 1 <> NULL, 1 < NULL, 1 > NULL;
+----------+-----------+----------+----------+
| 1 = NULL | 1 <> NULL | 1 < NULL | 1 > NULL |
+----------+-----------+----------+----------+
|     NULL |      NULL |     NULL |     NULL |
+----------+-----------+----------+----------+
```

Clearly you get no meaningful results from these comparisons. Use the IS NULL and IS NOT NULL operators instead:

```
mysql> SELECT 1 IS NULL, 1 IS NOT NULL;
+-----------+---------------+
| 1 IS NULL | 1 IS NOT NULL |
+-----------+---------------+
|         0 |             1 |
+-----------+---------------+
```

Note that two NULL are compared as equal when you do a GROUP BY.

In MySQL, 0 or NULL means false and anything else means true. The default truth value from a boolean operation is 1.

When doing an ORDER BY, NULL values are always sorted first, even if you are using DESC.

This special treatment of NULL is why, in the previous section, it was necessary to determine which animals are no longer alive using death IS NOT NULL instead of death <> NULL.

3.3.4.7 Pattern matching

MySQL provides standard SQL pattern matching as well as a form of pattern matching based on extended regular expressions similar to those used by Unix utilities such as vi, grep, and sed.

SQL pattern matching allows you to use _ to match any single character and % to match an arbitrary number of characters (including zero characters). In MySQL, SQL patterns

are case-insensitive by default. Some examples are shown next. You don't use = or <>
with SQL patterns; use the LIKE or NOT LIKE comparison operators instead.

To find names beginning with b:

```
mysql> SELECT * FROM pet WHERE name LIKE "b%";
+--------+--------+---------+------+------------+------------+
| name   | owner  | species | sex  | birth      | death      |
+--------+--------+---------+------+------------+------------+
| Buffy  | Harold | dog     | f    | 1989-05-13 | NULL       |
| Bowser | Diane  | dog     | m    | 1989-08-31 | 1995-07-29 |
+--------+--------+---------+------+------------+------------+
```

To find names ending with fy:

```
mysql> SELECT * FROM pet WHERE name LIKE "%fy";
+--------+--------+---------+------+------------+-------+
| name   | owner  | species | sex  | birth      | death |
+--------+--------+---------+------+------------+-------+
| Fluffy | Harold | cat     | f    | 1993-02-04 | NULL  |
| Buffy  | Harold | dog     | f    | 1989-05-13 | NULL  |
+--------+--------+---------+------+------------+-------+
```

To find names containing a w:

```
mysql> SELECT * FROM pet WHERE name LIKE "%w%";
+----------+--------+---------+------+------------+------------+
| name     | owner  | species | sex  | birth      | death      |
+----------+--------+---------+------+------------+------------+
| Claws    | Gwen   | cat     | m    | 1994-03-17 | NULL       |
| Bowser   | Diane  | dog     | m    | 1989-08-31 | 1995-07-29 |
| Whistler | Gwen   | bird    | NULL | 1997-12-09 | NULL       |
+----------+--------+---------+------+------------+------------+
```

To find names containing exactly five characters, use the _ pattern character:

```
mysql> SELECT * FROM pet WHERE name LIKE "_____";
+-------+--------+---------+------+------------+-------+
| name  | owner  | species | sex  | birth      | death |
+-------+--------+---------+------+------------+-------+
| Claws | Gwen   | cat     | m    | 1994-03-17 | NULL  |
| Buffy | Harold | dog     | f    | 1989-05-13 | NULL  |
+-------+--------+---------+------+------------+-------+
```

The other type of pattern matching provided by MySQL uses extended regular expressions. When you test for a match for this type of pattern, use the REGEXP and NOT REG-
EXP operators (or RLIKE and NOT RLIKE, which are synonyms).

Some characteristics of extended regular expressions are:

• . matches any single character.

- A character class [. . .] matches any character within the brackets. For example, [abc] matches a, b, or c. To name a range of characters, use a dash. [a-z] matches any lowercase letter, whereas [0-9] matches any digit.

- * matches zero or more instances of the thing preceding it. For example, x* matches any number of x characters, [0-9]* matches any number of digits, and .* matches any number of anything.

- The pattern matches if it occurs anywhere in the value being tested. (SQL patterns match only if they match the entire value.)

- To anchor a pattern so that it must match the beginning or end of the value being tested, use ^ at the beginning or $ at the end of the pattern.

To demonstrate how extended regular expressions work, the LIKE queries shown previously are rewritten here to use REGEXP.

To find names beginning with b, use ^ to match the beginning of the name:

```
mysql> SELECT * FROM pet WHERE name REGEXP "^b";
+--------+--------+---------+------+------------+------------+
| name   | owner  | species | sex  | birth      | death      |
+--------+--------+---------+------+------------+------------+
| Buffy  | Harold | dog     | f    | 1989-05-13 | NULL       |
| Bowser | Diane  | dog     | m    | 1989-08-31 | 1995-07-29 |
+--------+--------+---------+------+------------+------------+
```

Prior to MySQL Version 3.23.4, REGEXP is case-sensitive, and the previous query will return no rows. To match either lowercase or uppercase b, use this query instead:

```
mysql> SELECT * FROM pet WHERE name REGEXP "^[bB]";
```

From MySQL 3.23.4 on, to force a REGEXP comparison to be case-sensitive, use the BINARY keyword to make one of the strings a binary string. This query will match only lowercase b at the beginning of a name:

```
mysql> SELECT * FROM pet WHERE name REGEXP BINARY "^b";
```

To find names ending with fy, use $ to match the end of the name:

```
mysql> SELECT * FROM pet WHERE name REGEXP "fy$";
+--------+--------+---------+------+------------+--------+
| name   | owner  | species | sex  | birth      | death  |
+--------+--------+---------+------+------------+--------+
| Fluffy | Harold | cat     | f    | 1993-02-04 | NULL   |
| Buffy  | Harold | dog     | f    | 1989-05-13 | NULL   |
+--------+--------+---------+------+------------+--------+
```

To find names containing a lowercase or uppercase w, use this query:

```
mysql> SELECT * FROM pet WHERE name REGEXP "w";
+----------+-------+---------+------+------------+------------+
| name     | owner | species | sex  | birth      | death      |
+----------+-------+---------+------+------------+------------+
| Claws    | Gwen  | cat     | m    | 1994-03-17 | NULL       |
| Bowser   | Diane | dog     | m    | 1989-08-31 | 1995-07-29 |
| Whistler | Gwen  | bird    | NULL | 1997-12-09 | NULL       |
+----------+-------+---------+------+------------+------------+
```

Because a regular expression pattern matches if it occurs anywhere in the value, it is not necessary in the previous query to put a wildcard on either side of the pattern to get it to match the entire value like it would be if you used a SQL pattern.

To find names containing exactly five characters, use ^ and $ to match the beginning and end of the name, and five instances of . in between:

```
mysql> SELECT * FROM pet WHERE name REGEXP "^.....$";
+-------+--------+---------+------+------------+-------+
| name  | owner  | species | sex  | birth      | death |
+-------+--------+---------+------+------------+-------+
| Claws | Gwen   | cat     | m    | 1994-03-17 | NULL  |
| Buffy | Harold | dog     | f    | 1989-05-13 | NULL  |
+-------+--------+---------+------+------------+-------+
```

You could also write the previous query using the {n} "repeat-n-times" operator:

```
mysql> SELECT * FROM pet WHERE name REGEXP "^.{5}$";
+-------+--------+---------+------+------------+-------+
| name  | owner  | species | sex  | birth      | death |
+-------+--------+---------+------+------------+-------+
| Claws | Gwen   | cat     | m    | 1994-03-17 | NULL  |
| Buffy | Harold | dog     | f    | 1989-05-13 | NULL  |
+-------+--------+---------+------+------------+-------+
```

3.3.4.8 Counting rows

Databases are often used to answer the question, "How often does a certain type of data occur in a table?" For example, you might want to know how many pets you have, or how many pets each owner has, or you might want to perform various kinds of censuses on your animals.

Counting the total number of animals you have is the same question as "How many rows are in the pet table?" because there is one record per pet. The COUNT() function counts the number of non-NULL results, so the query to count your animals looks like this:

```
mysql> SELECT COUNT(*) FROM pet;
+----------+
| COUNT(*) |
+----------+
|        9 |
+----------+
```

Earlier, you retrieved the names of the people who owned pets. You can use COUNT() if you want to find out how many pets each owner has:

```
mysql> SELECT owner, COUNT(*) FROM pet GROUP BY owner;
+--------+----------+
| owner  | COUNT(*) |
+--------+----------+
| Benny  |        2 |
| Diane  |        2 |
| Gwen   |        3 |
| Harold |        2 |
+--------+----------+
```

Note the use of GROUP BY to group together all records for each owner. Without it, all you get is an error message:

```
mysql> SELECT owner, COUNT(owner) FROM pet;
ERROR 1140 at line 1: Mixing of GROUP columns (MIN(),MAX(),COUNT()...)
with no GROUP columns is illegal if there is no GROUP BY clause
```

COUNT() and GROUP BY are useful for characterising your data in various ways. The following examples show different ways to perform animal census operations.

Number of animals per species:

```
mysql> SELECT species, COUNT(*) FROM pet GROUP BY species;
+---------+----------+
| species | COUNT(*) |
+---------+----------+
| bird    |        2 |
| cat     |        2 |
| dog     |        3 |
| hamster |        1 |
| snake   |        1 |
+---------+----------+
```

Number of animals per sex:

```
mysql> SELECT sex, COUNT(*) FROM pet GROUP BY sex;
+------+----------+
| sex  | COUNT(*) |
+------+----------+
| NULL |        1 |
| f    |        4 |
| m    |        4 |
+------+----------+
```

(In this output, NULL indicates sex unknown.)

Number of animals per combination of species and sex:

```
mysql> SELECT species, sex, COUNT(*) FROM pet GROUP BY species, sex;
+---------+------+----------+
| species | sex  | COUNT(*) |
+---------+------+----------+
| bird    | NULL |        1 |
| bird    | f    |        1 |
| cat     | f    |        1 |
| cat     | m    |        1 |
| dog     | f    |        1 |
| dog     | m    |        2 |
| hamster | f    |        1 |
| snake   | m    |        1 |
+---------+------+----------+
```

You need not retrieve an entire table when you use COUNT(). For example, the previous query, when performed just on dogs and cats, looks like this:

```
mysql> SELECT species, sex, COUNT(*) FROM pet
    -> WHERE species = "dog" OR species = "cat"
    -> GROUP BY species, sex;
+---------+------+----------+
| species | sex  | COUNT(*) |
+---------+------+----------+
| cat     | f    |        1 |
| cat     | m    |        1 |
| dog     | f    |        1 |
| dog     | m    |        2 |
+---------+------+----------+
```

Or, if you wanted the number of animals per sex only for known-sex animals:

```
mysql> SELECT species, sex, COUNT(*) FROM pet
    -> WHERE sex IS NOT NULL
    -> GROUP BY species, sex;
+---------+------+----------+
| species | sex  | COUNT(*) |
+---------+------+----------+
| bird    | f    |        1 |
| cat     | f    |        1 |
| cat     | m    |        1 |
| dog     | f    |        1 |
| dog     | m    |        2 |
| hamster | f    |        1 |
| snake   | m    |        1 |
+---------+------+----------+
```

3.3.4.9 Using more than one table

The pet table keeps track of which pets you have. If you want to record other information about them, such as events in their lives like visits to the vet or when litters are born, you need another table. What should this table look like? It needs:

- To contain the pet name so that you know which animal each event pertains to.

- A date so that you know when the event occurred.

- A field to describe the event.

- An event type field, if you want to be able to categorise events.

Given these considerations, the CREATE TABLE statement for the event table might look like this:

```
mysql> CREATE TABLE event (name VARCHAR(20), date DATE,
    -> type VARCHAR(15), remark VARCHAR(255));
```

As with the pet table, it's easiest to load the initial records by creating a tab-delimited text file containing the information:

Name	Date	Type	Remark
Fluffy	1995-05-15	litter	4 kittens, 3 female, 1 male
Buffy	1993-06-23	litter	5 puppies, 2 female, 3 male
Buffy	1994-06-19	litter	3 puppies, 3 female
Chirpy	1999-03-21	vet	needed beak straightened
Slim	1997-08-03	vet	broken rib
Bowser	1991-10-12	kennel	
Fang	1991-10-12	kennel	
Fang	1998-08-28	birthday	Gave him a new chew toy
Claws	1998-03-17	birthday	Gave him a new flea collar
Whistler	1998-12-09	birthday	First birthday

Load the records like this:

```
mysql> LOAD DATA LOCAL INFILE "event.txt" INTO TABLE event;
```

Based on what you've learned from the queries you've run on the pet table, you should be able to perform retrievals on the records in the event table; the principles are the same. But when is the event table by itself insufficient to answer questions you might ask?

Suppose you want to find out the ages of each pet when they had their litters. The event table indicates when this occurred, but to calculate the age of the mother, you need her birth date. Because that is stored in the pet table, you need both tables for the query:

```
mysql> SELECT pet.name,
    -> (TO_DAYS(date) - TO_DAYS(birth))/365 AS age,
    -> remark
    -> FROM pet, event
    -> WHERE pet.name = event.name AND type = "litter";
```

```
+---------+------+-----------------------------+
| name    | age  | remark                      |
+---------+------+-----------------------------+
| Fluffy  | 2.27 | 4 kittens, 3 female, 1 male |
| Buffy   | 4.12 | 5 puppies, 2 female, 3 male |
| Buffy   | 5.10 | 3 puppies, 3 female         |
+---------+------+-----------------------------+
```

There are several things to note about this query:

- The FROM clause lists two tables because the query needs to pull information from both of them.

- When combining (joining) information from multiple tables, you need to specify how records in one table can be matched to records in the other. This is easy because they both have a name column. The query uses the WHERE clause to match up records in the two tables based on the name values.

- Because the name column occurs in both tables, you must be specific about which table you mean when referring to the column. This is done by prepending the table name to the column name.

You need not have two different tables to perform a join. Sometimes it is useful to join a table to itself, if you want to compare records in a table to other records in that same table. For example, to find breeding pairs among your pets, you can join the pet table with itself to pair up males and females of like species:

```
mysql> SELECT p1.name, p1.sex, p2.name, p2.sex, p1.species
    -> FROM pet AS p1, pet AS p2
    -> WHERE p1.species = p2.species AND p1.sex = "f" AND p2.sex = "m";
+---------+------+--------+------+---------+
| name    | sex  | name   | sex  | species |
+---------+------+--------+------+---------+
| Fluffy  | f    | Claws  | m    | cat     |
| Buffy   | f    | Fang   | m    | dog     |
| Buffy   | f    | Bowser | m    | dog     |
+---------+------+--------+------+---------+
```

In this query, we specify aliases for the table name in order to refer to the columns and keep straight which instance of the table each column reference is associated with.

3.4 Getting Information About Databases and Tables

What if you forget the name of a database or table, or what the structure of a given table is (for example, what its columns are called)? MySQL addresses this problem through several statements that provide information about the databases and tables it supports.

You have already seen SHOW DATABASES, which lists the databases managed by the server. To find out which database is currently selected, use the DATABASE() function:

```
mysql> SELECT DATABASE();
+-------------+
| DATABASE() |
+-------------+
| menagerie   |
+-------------+
```

If you haven't selected any database yet, the result is blank.

To find out what tables the current database contains (for example, when you're not sure about the name of a table), use this command:

```
mysql> SHOW TABLES;
+----------------------+
| Tables in menagerie  |
+----------------------+
| event                |
| pet                  |
+----------------------+
```

If you want to find out about the structure of a table, the DESCRIBE command is useful; it displays information about each of a table's columns:

```
mysql> DESCRIBE pet;
+---------+-------------+------+-----+---------+-------+
| Field   | Type        | Null | Key | Default | Extra |
+---------+-------------+------+-----+---------+-------+
| name    | varchar(20) | YES  |     | NULL    |       |
| owner   | varchar(20) | YES  |     | NULL    |       |
| species | varchar(20) | YES  |     | NULL    |       |
| sex     | char(1)     | YES  |     | NULL    |       |
| birth   | date        | YES  |     | NULL    |       |
| death   | date        | YES  |     | NULL    |       |
+---------+-------------+------+-----+---------+-------+
```

Field indicates the column name, Type is the datatype for the column, NULL indicates whether the column can contain NULL values, Key indicates whether the column is indexed, and Default specifies the column's default value.

If you have indexes on a table, SHOW INDEX FROM tbl_name produces information about them.

3.5 Examples of Common Queries

Here are examples of how to solve some common problems with MySQL.

Some of the examples use the table shop to hold the price of each article (item number) for certain traders (dealers). Supposing that each trader has a single fixed price per article, then (article, dealer) is a primary key for the records.

Start the command-line tool mysql and select a database:

```
mysql your-database-name
```

(In most MySQL installations, you can use the database-name 'test').

You can create the example table as:

```
CREATE TABLE shop (
  article  INT(4) UNSIGNED ZEROFILL  DEFAULT '0000'  NOT NULL,
  dealer   CHAR(20)                  DEFAULT ''       NOT NULL,
  price    DOUBLE(16,2)              DEFAULT '0.00'   NOT NULL,
  PRIMARY KEY(article, dealer));

INSERT INTO shop VALUES
(1,'A',3.45),(1,'B',3.99),(2,'A',10.99),(3,'B',1.45),(3,'C',1.69),
(3,'D',1.25),(4,'D',19.95);
```

Okay, so the example data is:

```
mysql> SELECT * FROM shop;
```

article	dealer	price
0001	A	3.45
0001	B	3.99
0002	A	10.99
0003	B	1.45
0003	C	1.69
0003	D	1.25
0004	D	19.95

3.5.1 The Maximum Value for a Column

"What's the highest item number?"

```
SELECT MAX(article) AS article FROM shop
```

article
4

3.5.2 The Row Holding the Maximum of a Certain Column

"Find number, dealer, and price of the most expensive article."

In ANSI SQL this is easily done with a sub-query:

```
SELECT article, dealer, price
FROM   shop
WHERE  price=(SELECT MAX(price) FROM shop)
```

In MySQL (which does not yet have sub-selects), just do it in two steps:

1. Get the maximum price value from the table with a SELECT statement.

2. Using this value compile the actual query:

```
SELECT article, dealer, price
FROM   shop
WHERE  price=19.95
```

Another solution is to sort all rows descending by price and only get the first row using the MySQL-specific LIMIT clause:

```
SELECT article, dealer, price
FROM   shop
ORDER BY price DESC
LIMIT 1
```

NOTE: If there are several most expensive articles (for example, each $19.95) the LIMIT solution shows only one of them!

3.5.3 Maximum of Column per Group

"What's the highest price per article?"

```
SELECT article, MAX(price) AS price
FROM   shop
GROUP BY article
```

```
+---------+-------+
| article | price |
+---------+-------+
|    0001 |  3.99 |
|    0002 | 10.99 |
|    0003 |  1.69 |
|    0004 | 19.95 |
+---------+-------+
```

3.5.4 The Rows Holding the Group-Wise Maximum of a Certain Field

"For each article, find the dealer(s) with the most expensive price."

In ANSI SQL, I'd do it with a sub-query like this:

```
SELECT article, dealer, price
FROM   shop s1
WHERE  price=(SELECT MAX(s2.price)
             FROM shop s2
```

```
                    WHERE s1.article = s2.article);
```

In MySQL it's best to do it in several steps:

1.   Get the list of (article,maxprice).

2.   For each article get the corresponding rows that have the stored maximum price.

This can easily be done with a temporary table:

```
CREATE TEMPORARY TABLE tmp (
        article INT(4) UNSIGNED ZEROFILL DEFAULT '0000' NOT NULL,
        price   DOUBLE(16,2)             DEFAULT '0.00' NOT NULL);

LOCK TABLES shop read;

INSERT INTO tmp SELECT article, MAX(price) FROM shop GROUP BY article;

SELECT shop.article, dealer, shop.price FROM shop, tmp
WHERE shop.article=tmp.article AND shop.price=tmp.price;

UNLOCK TABLES;

DROP TABLE tmp;
```

If you don't use a TEMPORARY table, you must also lock the 'tmp' table. "Can it be done with a single query?" Yes, but only by using a quite inefficient trick that I call the "MAX-CONCAT trick":

```
SELECT article,
       SUBSTRING( MAX( CONCAT(LPAD(price,6,'0'),dealer) ), 7) AS dealer,
   0.00+LEFT(      MAX( CONCAT(LPAD(price,6,'0'),dealer) ), 6) AS price
FROM    shop
GROUP BY article;
```

```
+---------+--------+-------+
| article | dealer | price |
+---------+--------+-------+
|    0001 | B      |  3.99 |
|    0002 | A      | 10.99 |
|    0003 | C      |  1.69 |
|    0004 | D      | 19.95 |
+---------+--------+-------+
```

The last example can, of course, be made a bit more efficient by doing the splitting of the concatenated column in the client.

3.5.5 Using User Variables

You can use MySQL user variables to remember results without having to store them in temporary variables in the client. See Section 6.1.4, User Variables.

For example, to find the articles with the highest and lowest price you can do:

```
mysql> SELECT @min_price:=MIN(price),@max_price:=MAX(price) FROM shop;
mysql> SELECT * FROM shop WHERE price=@min_price OR price=@max_price;
+---------+--------+-------+
| article | dealer | price |
+---------+--------+-------+
|    0003 | D      |  1.25 |
|    0004 | D      | 19.95 |
+---------+--------+-------+
```

3.5.6 Using Foreign Keys

In MySQL 3.23.44 and up, InnoDB tables support checking of foreign key constraints.
See Section 7.5, InnoDB Tables. See also Section 1.7.4.5, Foreign keys.

You don't actually need foreign keys to join 2 tables. The only things MySQL currently
doesn't do (in types other than InnoDB), are CHECK to make sure that the keys you use
really exist in the table(s) you're referencing and automatically delete rows from a table
with a foreign key definition. If you use your keys like normal, it'll work just fine:

```
CREATE TABLE person (
    id SMALLINT UNSIGNED NOT NULL AUTO_INCREMENT,
    name CHAR(60) NOT NULL,
    PRIMARY KEY (id)
);

CREATE TABLE shirt (
    id SMALLINT UNSIGNED NOT NULL AUTO_INCREMENT,
    style ENUM('t-shirt', 'polo', 'dress') NOT NULL,
    color ENUM('red', 'blue', 'orange', 'white', 'black') NOT NULL,
    owner SMALLINT UNSIGNED NOT NULL REFERENCES persons,
    PRIMARY KEY (id)
);


INSERT INTO person VALUES (NULL, 'Antonio Paz');

INSERT INTO shirt VALUES
(NULL, 'polo', 'blue', LAST_INSERT_ID()),
(NULL, 'dress', 'white', LAST_INSERT_ID()),
(NULL, 't-shirt', 'blue', LAST_INSERT_ID());


INSERT INTO person VALUES (NULL, 'Lilliana Angelovska');

INSERT INTO shirt VALUES
(NULL, 'dress', 'orange', LAST_INSERT_ID()),
(NULL, 'polo', 'red', LAST_INSERT_ID()),
(NULL, 'dress', 'blue', LAST_INSERT_ID()),
(NULL, 't-shirt', 'white', LAST_INSERT_ID());
```

```
SELECT * FROM person;
+----+---------------------+
| id | name                |
+----+---------------------+
|  1 | Antonio Paz         |
|  2 | Lilliana Angelovska |
+----+---------------------+

SELECT * FROM shirt;
+----+---------+--------+-------+
| id | style   | color  | owner |
+----+---------+--------+-------+
|  1 | polo    | blue   |     1 |
|  2 | dress   | white  |     1 |
|  3 | t-shirt | blue   |     1 |
|  4 | dress   | orange |     2 |
|  5 | polo    | red    |     2 |
|  6 | dress   | blue   |     2 |
|  7 | t-shirt | white  |     2 |
+----+---------+--------+-------+

SELECT s.* FROM person p, shirt s
  WHERE p.name LIKE 'Lilliana%'
    AND s.owner = p.id
    AND s.color <> 'white';

+----+-------+--------+-------+
| id | style | color  | owner |
+----+-------+--------+-------+
|  4 | dress | orange |     2 |
|  5 | polo  | red    |     2 |
|  6 | dress | blue   |     2 |
+----+-------+--------+-------+
```

3.5.7 Searching on Two Keys

MySQL doesn't yet optimise when you search on two different keys combined with OR (searching on one key with different OR parts is optimised quite well):

```
SELECT field1_index, field2_index FROM test_table WHERE field1_index = '1'
OR    field2_index = '1'
```

The reason is that we haven't yet had time to come up with an efficient way to handle this in the general case. (The AND handling is, in comparison, now completely general and works very well.)

For the moment you can solve this very efficiently by using a TEMPORARY table. This type of optimisation is also very good if you are using very complicated queries where the SQL server does the optimisations in the wrong order.

```
CREATE TEMPORARY TABLE tmp
SELECT field1_index, field2_index FROM test_table WHERE field1_index = '1';
INSERT INTO tmp
SELECT field1_index, field2_index FROM test_table WHERE field2_index = '1';
SELECT * from tmp;
DROP TABLE tmp;
```

The way to solve the query shown here is, in effect, a UNION of two queries. See Section 6.4.1.2, UNION syntax.

3.5.8 Calculating Visits per Day

The following shows an idea of how you can use the bit group functions to calculate the number of days per month a user has visited a web page:

```
CREATE TABLE t1 (year YEAR(4), month INT(2) UNSIGNED ZEROFILL,
                 day INT(2) UNSIGNED ZEROFILL);
INSERT INTO t1 VALUES(2000,1,1),(2000,1,20),(2000,1,30),(2000,2,2),
                 (2000,2,23),(2000,2,23);
SELECT year,month,BIT_COUNT(BIT_OR(1<<day)) AS days FROM t1
       GROUP BY year,month;
```

Which returns:

```
+------+-------+------+
| year | month | days |
+------+-------+------+
| 2000 |    01 |    3 |
| 2000 |    02 |    2 |
+------+-------+------+
```

The above calculates how many different days was used for a given year/month combination, with automatic removal of duplicate entries.

3.5.9 Using AUTO_INCREMENT

The AUTO_INCREMENT attribute can be used to generate a unique identity for new rows:

```
CREATE TABLE animals (id MEDIUMINT NOT NULL AUTO_INCREMENT,
name CHAR(30) NOT NULL, PRIMARY KEY (id));
INSERT INTO animals (name) VALUES ("dog"),("cat"),("penguin"),
("lax"),("whale");
SELECT * FROM animals;
```

Which returns:

```
+----+---------+
| id | name    |
+----+---------+
|  1 | dog     |
|  2 | cat     |
|  3 | penguin |
```

```
| 4 | lax   |
| 5 | whale |
+---+-------+
```

For MyISAM and BDB tables you can specify AUTO_INCREMENT on secondary column in a multi-column key. In this case the generated value for the auto-increment column is calculated as MAX(auto_increment_column)+1) WHERE prefix=given-prefix. This is useful when you want to put data into ordered groups.

```
CREATE TABLE animals (grp ENUM('fish','mammal','bird') NOT NULL,
          id MEDIUMINT NOT NULL AUTO_INCREMENT
          PRIMARY KEY (grp,id));
INSERT INTO animals (grp,name) VALUES("mammal","dog"),("mammal","cat"),
          ("bird","penguin"),("fish","lax"),("mammal","whale");
SELECT * FROM animals ORDER BY grp,id;
```

Which returns:

```
+--------+----+---------+
| grp    | id | name    |
+--------+----+---------+
| fish   | 1  | lax     |
| mammal | 1  | dog     |
| mammal | 2  | cat     |
| mammal | 3  | whale   |
| bird   | 1  | penguin |
+--------+----+---------+
```

Note that in this case, the AUTO_INCREMENT value will be reused if you delete the row with the biggest AUTO_INCREMENT value in any group.

You can get the used AUTO_INCREMENT key with the LAST_INSERT_ID() SQL function or the mysql_insert_id() API function.

3.6 Using mysql in Batch Mode

In the previous sections, you used mysql interactively to enter queries and view the results. You can also run mysql in batch mode. To do this, put the commands you want to run in a file, then tell mysql to read its input from the file:

```
shell> mysql < batch-file
```

If you are running mysql under windows and have some special characters in the file that cause problems, you can do:

```
dos> mysql -e "source batch-file"
```

If you need to specify connection parameters on the command-line, the command might look like this:

```
shell> mysql -h host -u user -p < batch-file
Enter password: ********
```

When you use mysql this way, you are creating a script file, then executing the script.

If you want the script to continue even if you have errors, you should use the --force command-line option.

Why use a script? Here are a few reasons:

- If you run a query repeatedly (say, every day or every week), making it a script allows you to avoid retyping it each time you execute it.

- You can generate new queries from existing ones that are similar by copying and editing script files.

- Batch mode can also be useful while you're developing a query, particularly for multiple-line commands or multiple-statement sequences of commands. If you make a mistake, you don't have to retype everything. Just edit your script to correct the error, then tell mysql to execute it again.

- If you have a query that produces a lot of output, you can run the output through a pager rather than watching it scroll off the top of your screen:

  ```
  shell> mysql < batch-file | more
  ```

- You can catch the output in a file for further processing:

  ```
  shell> mysql < batch-file > mysql.out
  ```

- You can distribute your script to other people so that they can run the commands, too.

- Some situations do not allow for interactive use—for example, when you run a query from a cron job. In this case, you must use batch mode.

The default output format is different (more concise) when you run mysql in batch mode than when you use it interactively. For example, the output of SELECT DISTINCT species FROM pet looks like this when run interactively:

```
+----------+
| species  |
+----------+
| bird     |
| cat      |
| dog      |
| hamster  |
| snake    |
+----------+
```

But it looks like this when run in batch mode:

```
species
bird
cat
dog
hamster
snake
```

If you want to get the interactive output format in batch mode, use `mysql -t`. To echo to the output the commands that are executed, use `mysql -vvv`.

You can also use scripts in the `mysql` command-line prompt by using the `source` command:

```
mysql> source filename;
```

3.7 Queries from Twin Project

At Analytikerna and Lentus, we have been doing the systems and field work for a big research project. This project is a collaboration between the Institute of Environmental Medicine at Karolinska Institutet Stockholm and the Section on Clinical Research in Aging and Psychology at the University of Southern California.

The project involves a screening part where all twins in Sweden older than 65 years are interviewed by telephone. Twins who meet certain criteria are passed on to the next stage. In this latter stage, twins who want to participate are visited by a doctor/nurse team. Some of the examinations include physical and neuropsychological examination, laboratory testing, neuroimaging, psychological status assessment, and family history collection. In addition, data is collected on medical and environmental risk factors.

More information about the Twin studies can be found at: http://www.imm.ki.se/TWIN/TWINUKW.HTM.

The latter part of the project is administered with a web interface written using Perl and MySQL.

Each night all data from the interviews is moved into a MySQL database.

3.7.1 Find All Non-Distributed Twins

The following query is used to determine who goes into the second part of the project:

```
SELECT
        CONCAT(p1.id, p1.tvab) + 0 AS tvid,
        CONCAT(p1.christian_name, " ", p1.surname) AS Name,
        p1.postal_code AS Code,
        p1.city AS City,
        pg.abrev AS Area,
        IF(td.participation = "Aborted", "A", " ") AS A,
        p1.dead AS dead1,
        l.event AS event1,
```

```
        td.suspect AS tsuspect1,
        id.suspect AS isuspect1,
        td.severe AS tsevere1,
        id.severe AS isevere1,
        p2.dead AS dead2,
        l2.event AS event2,
        h2.nurse AS nurse2,
        h2.doctor AS doctor2,
        td2.suspect AS tsuspect2,
        id2.suspect AS isuspect2,
        td2.severe AS tsevere2,
        id2.severe AS isevere2,
        l.finish_date
FROM
        twin_project AS tp
        /* For Twin 1 */
        LEFT JOIN twin_data AS td ON tp.id = td.id
                AND tp.tvab = td.tvab
        LEFT JOIN informant_data AS id ON tp.id = id.id
                AND tp.tvab = id.tvab
        LEFT JOIN harmony AS h ON tp.id = h.id
                AND tp.tvab = h.tvab
        LEFT JOIN lentus AS l ON tp.id = l.id
                AND tp.tvab = l.tvab
        /* For Twin 2 */
        LEFT JOIN twin_data AS td2 ON p2.id = td2.id
                AND p2.tvab = td2.tvab
        LEFT JOIN informant_data AS id2 ON p2.id = id2.id
                AND p2.tvab = id2.tvab
        LEFT JOIN harmony AS h2 ON p2.id = h2.id
                AND p2.tvab = h2.tvab
        LEFT JOIN lentus AS l2 ON p2.id = l2.id
                AND p2.tvab = l2.tvab,
        person_data AS p1,
        person_data AS p2,
        postal_groups AS pg
WHERE
        /* p1 gets main twin and p2 gets his/her twin. */
        /* ptvab is a field inverted from tvab */
        p1.id = tp.id AND p1.tvab = tp.tvab AND
        p2.id = p1.id AND p2.ptvab = p1.tvab AND
        /* Just the sceening survey */
        tp.survey_no = 5 AND
        /* Skip if partner died before 65 but allow emigration (dead=9) */
        (p2.dead = 0 OR p2.dead = 9 OR
         (p2.dead = 1 AND
          (p2.death_date = 0 OR
           (((TO_DAYS(p2.death_date) - TO_DAYS(p2.birthday)) / 365)
            >= 65))))
        AND
        (
        /* Twin is suspect */
        (td.future_contact = 'Yes' AND td.suspect = 2) OR
        /* Twin is suspect - Informant is Blessed */
```

```
              (td.future_contact = 'Yes' AND td.suspect = 1
                                          AND id.suspect = 1) OR
              /* No twin - Informant is Blessed */
              (ISNULL(td.suspect) AND id.suspect = 1
                                  AND id.future_contact = 'Yes') OR
              /* Twin broken off - Informant is Blessed */
              (td.participation = 'Aborted'
               AND id.suspect = 1 AND id.future_contact = 'Yes') OR
              /* Twin broken off - No inform - Have partner */
              (td.participation = 'Aborted' AND ISNULL(id.suspect)
                                          AND p2.dead = 0))
              AND
              l.event = 'Finished'
              /* Get at area code */
              AND SUBSTRING(p1.postal_code, 1, 2) = pg.code
              /* Not already distributed */
              AND (h.nurse IS NULL OR h.nurse=00 OR h.doctor=00)
              /* Has not refused or been aborted */
              AND NOT (h.status = 'Refused' OR h.status = 'Aborted'
              OR h.status = 'Died' OR h.status = 'Other')
      ORDER BY
              tvid;
```

Some explanations:

`CONCAT(p1.id, p1.tvab) + 0 AS tvid`

> We want to sort on the concatenated `id` and `tvab` in numerical order. Adding 0 to the result causes MySQL to treat the result as a number.

column `id`

> This identifies a pair of twins. It is a key in all tables.

column `tvab`

> This identifies a twin in a pair. It has a value of 1 or 2.

column `ptvab`

> This is an inverse of `tvab`. When `tvab` is 1 this is 2, and vice versa. It exists to save typing and to make it easier for MySQL to optimise the query.

This query demonstrates, among other things, how to do lookups on a table from the same table with a join (p1 and p2). In the example, this is used to check whether a twin's partner died before the age of 65. If so, the row is not returned.

All of the preceding information exists in all tables with twin-related information. We have a key on both `id`, `tvab` (all tables) and `id`, `ptvab` (`person_data`) to make queries faster.

On our production machine (a 200MHz UltraSPARC), this query returns about 150-200 rows and takes less than 1 second.

The current number of records in the tables used in this example:

Table	Rows
person_data	71074
lentus	5291
twin_project	5286
twin_data	2012
informant_data	663
harmony	381
postal_groups	100

3.7.2 Show a Table on Twin Pair Status

Each interview ends with a status code called event. The following query is used to display a table over all twin pairs combined by event. This indicates in how many pairs both twins are finished, in how many pairs one twin is finished and the other refused, and so on.

```
SELECT
        t1.event,
        t2.event,
        COUNT(*)
FROM
        lentus AS t1,
        lentus AS t2,
        twin_project AS tp
WHERE
        /* We are looking at one pair at a time */
        t1.id = tp.id
        AND t1.tvab=tp.tvab
        AND t1.id = t2.id
        /* Just the sceening survey */
        AND tp.survey_no = 5
        /* This makes each pair only appear once */
        AND t1.tvab='1' AND t2.tvab='2'
GROUP BY
        t1.event, t2.event;
```

3.8 Using MySQL with Apache

There are programs that let you authenticate your users from a MySQL database and also let you log your log files into a MySQL table. See Section 1.6.1, MySQL Portals.

You can change the Apache logging format to be easily readable by MySQL by putting the following into the Apache configuration file:

```
LogFormat \
        "\"%h\",%{%Y%m%d%H%M%S}t,%>s,\"%b\",\"%{Content-Type}o\",   \
        \"%U\",\"%{Referer}i\",\"%{User-Agent}i\""
```

In MySQL you can do something like this:

```
LOAD DATA INFILE '/local/access_log' INTO TABLE table_name
FIELDS TERMINATED BY ',' OPTIONALLY ENCLOSED BY '"' ESCAPED BY '\\'
```

4

Database Administration

4.1 Configuring MySQL

4.1.1 `mysqld` Command-Line Options

In most cases you should manage mysqld options through option files. See Section 4.1.2, `my.cnf` Option Files.

`mysqld` and `mysqld.server` read options from the `mysqld` and `server` groups. `mysqld_safe` read options from the `mysqld`, `server`, `mysqld_safe`, and `safe_mysqld` groups. An embedded MySQL server usually reads options from the `server`, `embedded`, and `xxxxx_SERVER`, where `xxxxx` is the name of the application.

`mysqld` accepts the following command-line options:

`--ansi`

    Use ANSI SQL syntax instead of MySQL syntax. See Section 1.7.2, Running MySQL in ANSI Mode.

`-b, --basedir=path`

Path to installation directory. All paths are usually resolved relative to this.

`--big-tables`

Allow big result sets by saving all temporary sets on file. It solves most 'table full' errors, but also slows down the queries where in-memory tables would suffice. Since Version 3.23.2, MySQL is able to solve it automatically by using memory for small temporary tables and switching to disk tables where necessary.

`--bind-address=IP`

IP address to bind to.

`--character-sets-dir=path`

Directory where character sets are. See Section 4.6.1, The Character Set Used for Data and Sorting.

`--chroot=path`

Chroot `mysqld` daemon during startup. Recommended security measure. It will somewhat limit LOAD DATA INFILE and SELECT . . . INTO OUTFILE though.

`--core-file`

Write a core file if `mysqld` dies. For some systems you must also specify `--core-file-size` to `safe_mysqld`. See Section 4.7.2, `safe_mysqld`, the Wrapper Around `mysqld`. Note that on some systems like Solaris, you will not get a core file if you are also using the `--user` option.

`-h, --datadir=path`

Path to the database root.

`--debug[ . . . ]=`

If MySQL is configured with `--with-debug`, you can use this option to get a trace file of what `mysqld` is doing. See Section D.1.2, Creating Trace Files.

`--default-character-set=charset`

Set the default character set. See Section 4.6.1, The Character Set Used for Data and Sorting.

`--default-table-type=type`

Set the default table type for tables. See Chapter 7.

`--delay-key-write-for-all-tables`

Don't flush key buffers between writes for any MyISAM table. See Section 5.5.2, Tuning Server Parameters.

`--des-key-file=filename`

Read the default keys used by DES_ENCRYPT() and DES_DECRYPT() from this file.

`--enable-locking`

> Enable system locking. Note that if you use this option on a system on which `lockd` does not fully work (as on Linux), you will easily get mysqld to deadlock.

`--enable-named-pipe`

> Enable support for named pipes (only on NT/Win2000/XP).

`-T, --exit-info`

> This is a bit mask of different flags one can use for debugging the mysqld server; one should not use this option if one doesn't know exactly what it does!

`--flush`

> Flush all changes to disk after each SQL command. Normally MySQL only does a write of all changes to disk after each SQL command and lets the operating system handle the syncing to disk. See Section A.4.1, What to Do if MySQL Keeps Crashing.

`-?, --help`

> Display short help and exit.

`--init-file=file`

> Read SQL commands from this file at startup.

`-L, --language=...`

> Client error messages in given language. May be given as a full path. See Section 4.6.2, Non-English Error Messages.

`-l, --log[=file]`

> Log connections and queries to file. See Section 4.9.2, The General Query Log.

`--log-isam[=file]`

> Log all ISAM/MyISAM changes to file (only used when debugging ISAM/MyISAM).

`--log-slow-queries[=file]`

> Log all queries that have taken more than `long_query_time` seconds to execute to file. See Section 4.9.5, The Slow Query Log.

`--log-update[=file]`

> Log updates to file.# where # is a unique number if not given. See Section 4.9.3, The Update Log.

`--log-long-format`

> Log some extra information to update log. If you are using `--log-slow-queries`, then queries that are not using indexes are logged to the slow query log.

`--low-priority-updates`

> Table-modifying operations (INSERT/DELETE/UPDATE) will have lower priority than selects. It can also be done via {INSERT | REPLACE | UPDATE | DELETE} LOW_PRIORITY ... to lower the priority of only one query, or by SET OPTION

SQL_LOW_PRIORITY_UPDATES=1 to change the priority in one thread. See Section 5.3.2, Table Locking Issues.

`--memlock`

Lock the mysqld process in memory. This works only if your system supports the mlockall() system call (like Solaris). This may help if you have a problem where the operating system is causing mysqld to swap on disk.

`--myisam-recover [=option[,option...]]]`

Option is any combination of DEFAULT, BACKUP, FORCE or QUICK. You can also set this explicitly to " " if you want to disable this option. If this option is used, mysqld will, on open, check if the table is marked as crashed or if the table wasn't closed properly. (The last option only works if you are running with --skip-locking.) If this is the case, mysqld will run check on the table. If the table was corrupted, mysqld will attempt to repair it.

The following options affect how the repair works.

Option	Description
DEFAULT	The same as not giving any option to --myisam-recover.
BACKUP	If the data table was changed during recover, save a backup of the table_name.MYD data file as table_name-datetime.BAK.
FORCE	Run recover even if we will lose more than one row from the .MYD file.
QUICK	Don't check the rows in the table if there aren't any delete blocks.

Before a table is automatically repaired, MySQL will add a note about this in the error log. If you want to be able to recover from most things without user intervention, you should use the options BACKUP, FORCE. This will force a repair of a table even if some rows would be deleted, but it will keep the old data file as a backup so that you can later examine what happened.

`--pid-file=path`

Path to pid file used by safe_mysqld.

`-P, --port=...`

Port number to listen for TCP/IP connections.

`-o, --old-protocol`

Use the 3.20 protocol for compatibility with some very old clients. See Section 2.5.4, Upgrading from Version 3.20 to Version 3.21.

`--one-thread`

Only use one thread (for debugging under Linux). See Section D.1, Debugging a MySQL Server.

-O, --set-variable var=option

> Give a variable a value. --help lists variables. You can find a full description for all variables in the SHOW VARIABLES section in this manual. See Section 4.5.6.4, SHOW VARIABLES. The tuning server parameters section includes information on how to optimise these. See Section 5.5.2, Tuning Server Parameters.

--safe-mode

> Skip some optimisation stages. Implies --skip-delay-key-write.

--safe-show-database

> Don't show databases for which the user doesn't have any privileges.

--safe-user-create

> If this is enabled, a user can't create new users with the GRANT command, if the user doesn't have **insert** privileges to the mysql.user table or any column in this table.

--skip-concurrent-insert

> Turn off the ability to select and insert at the same time on MyISAM tables. (This is only to be used if you think you have found a bug in this feature.)

--skip-delay-key-write

> Ignore the delay_key_write option for all tables. See Section 5.5.2, Tuning Server Parameters.

--skip-grant-tables

> This option causes the server not to use the privilege system at all. This gives everyone **full access** to all databases! (You can tell a running server to start using the grant tables again by executing mysqladmin flush-privileges or mysqladmin reload.)

--skip-host-cache

> Never use hostname cache for faster name-ip resolution, but query the DNS server on every connect instead. See Section 5.5.5, How MySQL Uses DNS.

--skip-locking

> Don't use system locking. To use isamchk or myisamchk you must shut down the server. See Section 1.2.3, How Stable Is MySQL?. Note that in MySQL Version 3.23 you can use REPAIR and CHECK to repair/check MyISAM tables.

--skip-name-resolve

> Hostnames are not resolved. All Host column values in the grant tables must be IP numbers or localhost. See Section 5.5.5, How MySQL Uses DNS.

--skip-networking

> Don't listen for TCP/IP connections at all. All interaction with mysqld must be made via Unix sockets. This option is highly recommended for systems where only local requests are allowed. See Section 5.5.5, How MySQL Uses DNS.

`--skip-new`

Don't use new, possibly wrong routines. Implies `--skip-delay-key-write`. This will also set the default table type to ISAM. See Section 7.3, ISAM Tables.

`--skip-symlink`

Don't delete or rename files that a symlinked file in the data directory points to.

`--skip-safemalloc`

If MySQL is configured with `--with-debug=full`, all programs will check the memory for overruns for every memory allocation and memory freeing. As this checking is very slow, you can avoid this, when you don't need memory checking, by using this option.

`--skip-show-database`

Don't allow 'SHOW DATABASE' commands, unless the user has **process** privilege.

`--skip-stack-trace`

Don't write stack traces. This option is useful when you are running mysqld under a debugger. See Section D.1, Debugging a MySQL Server.

`--skip-thread-priority`

Disable using thread priorities for faster response time.

`--socket=path`

Socket file to use for local connections instead of default `/tmp/mysql.sock`.

`--sql-mode=option[,option[,option . . . ]]`

Option can be any combination of REAL_AS_FLOAT, PIPES_AS_CONCAT, ANSI_QUOTES, IGNORE_SPACE, SERIALIZE, and ONLY_FULL_GROUP_BY. It can also be empty (`""`) if you want to reset this.

Specifying all of these options is the same as using —ansi. With this option one can turn on only needed SQL modes. See Section 1.7.2, Running MySQL in ANSI Mode.

`--transaction-isolation= { READ-UNCOMMITTED | READ-COMMITTED | REPEATABLE-READ | SERIALIZABLE }`

Sets the default transaction isolation level. See Section 6.7.3, SET TRANSACTION Syntax.

`-t, --tmpdir=path`

Path for temporary files. It may be useful if your default `/tmp` directory resides on a partition too small to hold temporary tables.

`-u, --user= [user_name | userid]`

Run mysqld daemon as user user_name or userid (numeric). This option is **mandatory** when starting mysqld as root.

`-V, --version`
> Output version information and exit.

`-W, --warnings`
> Print out warnings like `Aborted connection...` to the `.err` file. See Section A.2.9, Communication Error/ Aborted Connection.

4.1.2 `my.cnf` Option Files

MySQL can, since Version 3.22, read default startup options for the server and for clients from option files.

MySQL reads default options from the following files on Unix:

Filename	Purpose
`/etc/my.cnf`	Global options
`DATADIR/my.cnf`	Server-specific options
`defaults-extra-file`	The file specified with —defaults-extra-file=#
`~/.my.cnf`	User-specific options

`DATADIR` is the MySQL data directory (typically `/usr/local/mysql/data` for a binary installation or `/usr/local/var` for a source installation). Note that this is the directory that was specified at configuration time, not the one specified with `--datadir` when `mysqld` starts up! (`--datadir` has no effect on where the server looks for option files because it looks for them before it processes any command-line arguments).

MySQL reads default options from the following files on Windows:

Filename	Purpose
`windows-system-direc-tory\my.ini`	Global options
`C:\my.cnf`	Global options

Note that on Windows, you should specify all paths with / instead of \. If you use \, you need to specify this twice, as \ is the escape character in MySQL.

MySQL tries to read option files in the order listed previously. If multiple option files exist, an option specified in a file read later takes precedence over the same option specified in a file read earlier. Options specified on the command-line take precedence over options specified in any option file. Some options can be specified using environment variables. Options specified on the command-line or in option files take precedence over environment variable values. See Appendix E.

The following programs support option files: `mysql`, `mysqladmin`, `mysqld`, `mysqld_safe`, `mysql.server`, `mysqldump`, `mysqlimport`, `mysqlshow`, `mysqlcheck`, myisamchk, and myisampack.

Any long option that may be given on the command-line when running a MySQL program can be given in an option file as well (without the leading double dash). Run the program with --help to get a list of available options.

An option file can contain lines of the following forms:

#comment
> Comment lines start with # or ;. Empty lines are ignored.

[group]
> group is the name of the program or group for which you want to set options. After a group line, any option or set-variable lines apply to the named group until the end of the option file or another group line is given.

option
> This is equivalent to --option on the command-line.

option=value
> This is equivalent to --option=value on the command-line.

set-variable = variable=value
> This is equivalent to --set-variable variable=value on the command-line. This syntax must be used to set a mysqld variable.

The client group allows you to specify options that apply to all MySQL clients (not mysqld). This is the perfect group to use to specify the password you use to connect to the server. (But make sure the option file is readable and writable only by yourself.)

Note that for options and values, all leading and trailing blanks are automatically deleted. You may use the escape sequences \b, \t, \n, \r, \\, and \s in your value string (\s == blank).

Here is a typical global option file:

```
[client]
port=3306
socket=/tmp/mysql.sock

[mysqld]
port=3306
socket=/tmp/mysql.sock
set-variable = key_buffer_size=16M
set-variable = max_allowed_packet=1M

[mysqldump]
quick
```

Here is typical user option file:

```
[client]
# The following password will be sent to all standard MySQL clients
password=my_password

[mysql]
no-auto-rehash
set-variable = connect_timeout=2

[mysqlhotcopy]
interactive-timeout
```

If you have a source distribution, you will find sample configuration files named my-xxxx.cnf in the support-files directory. If you have a binary distribution, look in the DIR/support-files directory, where DIR is the pathname to the MySQL installation directory (typically /usr/local/mysql). Currently there are sample configuration files for small, medium, large, and very large systems. You can copy my-xxxx.cnf to your home directory (rename the copy to .my.cnf) to experiment with this.

All MySQL clients that support option files support the following options:

Option	Description
—no-defaults	Don't read any option files.
—print-defaults	Print the program name and all options that it will get.
—defaults-file=full-path-to-default-file	Only use the given configuration file.
—defaults-extra-file=full-path-to-default-file	Read this configuration file after the global configuration file but before the user configuration file.

Note that the preceding options must be first on the command-line to work! --print-defaults may, however, be used directly after the --defaults-xxx-file commands.

Note for developers: option file handling is implemented simply by processing all matching options (that is, options in the appropriate group) before any command-line arguments. This works nicely for programs that use the last instance of an option that is specified multiple times. If you have an old program that handles multiple-specified options this way but doesn't read option files, you need add only two lines to give it that capability. Check the source code of any of the standard MySQL clients to see how to do this.

In shell scripts you can use the my_print_defaults command to parse the config files:

```
shell> my_print_defaults client mysql
--port=3306
--socket=/tmp/mysql.sock
--no-auto-rehash
```

The preceding output contains all options for the groups 'client' and 'mysql'.

4.1.3 Installing Many Servers on the Same Machine

In some cases you may want to have many different mysqld daemons (servers) running on the same machine. You may, for example, want to run a new version of MySQL for testing together with an old version that is in production. Another case is when you want to give different users access to different mysqld servers that they manage themselves.

One way to get a new server running is by starting it with a different socket and port as follows:

```
shell> MYSQL_UNIX_PORT=/tmp/mysqld-new.sock
shell> MYSQL_TCP_PORT=3307
shell> export MYSQL_UNIX_PORT MYSQL_TCP_PORT
shell> scripts/mysql_install_db
shell> bin/safe_mysqld &
```

The environment variables appendix includes a list of other environment variables you can use to affect mysqld. See Appendix E.

This is the quick and dirty way that one commonly uses for testing. The nice thing with this is that all connections you do in the preceding shell will automatically be directed to the new running server!

If you need to do this more permanently, you should create an option file for each server. See Section 4.1.2, my.cnf Option Files. In your startup script that is executed at boot time you should specify for both servers:

```
safe_mysqld --default-file=path-to-option-file
```

At least the following options should be different per server:

*   port=#
*   socket=path
*   pid-file=path

The following options should be different, if they are used:

*   log=path
*   log-bin=path
*   log-update=path
*   log-isam=path
*   bdb-logdir=path

If you want more performance, you can also specify the following differently:

- tmpdir=path

- bdb-tmpdir=path

Section 4.1.1, `mysqld` Command-Line Options.

If you are installing binary MySQL versions (.tar files) and start them with `./bin/safe_mysqld`, in most cases the only option you need to add/change is the `socket` and `port` argument to `safe_mysqld`.

Section 4.1.4, Running Multiple MySQL Servers on the Same Machine.

4.1.4 Running Multiple MySQL Servers on the Same Machine

There are circumstances when you might want to run multiple servers on the same machine. For example, you might want to test a new MySQL release while leaving your existing production setup undisturbed. Or you might be an Internet service provider that wants to provide independent MySQL installations for different customers.

If you want to run multiple servers, the easiest way is to compile the servers with different TCP/IP ports and socket files so they are not both listening to the same TCP/IP port or socket file. See Section 4.7.3, `mysqld_multi`, Program for Managing Multiple MySQL servers.

Assume an existing server is configured for the default port number and socket file. Then configure the new server with a `configure` command something like this:

```
shell> ./configure  --with-tcp-port=port_number \
           --with-unix-socket-path=file_name \
           --prefix=/usr/local/mysql-3.22.9
```

Here `port_number` and `file_name` should be different from the default port number and socket file pathname, and the `--prefix` value should specify an installation directory different from the one under which the existing MySQL installation is located.

You can check the socket used by any currently executing MySQL server with this command:

```
shell> mysqladmin -h hostname --port=port_number variables
```

Note that if you specify "`localhost`" as a hostname, `mysqladmin` will default to using Unix sockets instead of TCP/IP.

If you have a MySQL server running on the port you used, you will get a list of some of the most important configurable variables in MySQL, including the socket name.

You don't have to recompile a new MySQL server just to start with a different port and socket. You can change the port and socket to be used by specifying them at runtime as options to `safe_mysqld`:

```
shell> /path/to/safe_mysqld --socket=file_name --port=port_number
```

mysqld_multi can also take safe_mysqld (or mysqld) as an argument and pass the options from a configuration file to safe_mysqld and further to mysqld.

If you run the new server on the same database directory as another server with logging enabled, you should also specify the name of the log files to safe_mysqld with --log, --log-update, or --log-slow-queries. Otherwise, both servers may be trying to write to the same log file.

Warning: normally you should never have two servers that update data in the same database! If your OS doesn't support fault-free system locking, this may lead to unpleasant surprises!

If you want to use another database directory for the second server, you can use the --datadir=path option to safe_mysqld.

Note also that starting several MySQL servers (mysqlds) in different machines and letting them access one data directory over NFS is generally a **bad idea**! The problem is that the NFS will become the bottleneck with the speed. It is not meant for such use. And last but not least, you would still have to come up with a solution for ensuring that two or more mysqlds are not interfering with each other. At the moment there is no platform that would 100% reliably do the file locking (lockd daemon usually) in every situation. Yet there would be one more possible risk with NFS; it would make the work even more complicated for lockd daemon to handle. So make it easy for yourself and forget about the idea. The working solution is to have one computer with an operating system that efficiently handles threads and have several CPUs in it.

When you want to connect to a MySQL server that is running with a different port than the port that is compiled into your client, you can use one of the following methods:

- Start the client with --host 'hostname' --port=port_number to connect with TCP/IP, or [--host localhost] --socket=file_name to connect via a Unix socket.

- In your C or Perl programs, you can give the port or socket arguments when connecting to the MySQL server.

- If you are using the Perl DBD::mysql module you can read the options from the MySQL option files. See Section 4.1.2, my.cnf Option Files.

```
$dsn = "DBI:mysql:test;mysql_read_default_group=client;
        mysql_read_default_file=/usr/local/mysql/data/my.cnf"
$dbh = DBI->connect($dsn, $user, $password);
```

- Set the MYSQL_UNIX_PORT and MYSQL_TCP_PORT environment variables to point to the Unix socket and TCP/IP port before you start your clients. If you normally use a specific socket or port, you should place commands to set these environment variables in your .login file. See Appendix E.

- Specify the default socket and TCP/IP port in the `.my.cnf` file in your home directory. See Section 4.1.2, `my.cnf` Option Files.

4.2 General Security Issues and the MySQL Access Privilege System

MySQL has an advanced but non-standard security/privilege system. This section describes how it works.

4.2.1 General Security Guidelines

Anyone using MySQL on a computer connected to the Internet should read this section to avoid the most common security mistakes.

In discussing security, we emphasize the necessity of fully protecting the entire server host (not simply the MySQL server) against all types of applicable attacks: eavesdropping, altering, playback, and denial of service. We do not cover all aspects of availability and fault tolerance here.

MySQL uses security based on Access Control Lists (ACLs) for all connections, queries, and other operations that a user may attempt to perform. There is also some support for SSL-encrypted connections between MySQL clients and servers. Many of the concepts discussed here are not specific to MySQL at all; the same general ideas apply to almost all applications.

When running MySQL, follow these guidelines whenever possible:

- **Do not ever** give anyone (except the mysql root user) access to the `user` table in the `mysql` database! This is critical. **The encrypted password is the real password in MySQL.** Anyone who knows the password which is listed in the `user` table and has access to the host listed for the account **can easily log in as that user**.

- Learn the MySQL access privilege system. The GRANT and REVOKE commands are used for controlling access to MySQL. Do not grant any more privileges than necessary. Never grant privileges to all hosts.

  Checklist:

  — Try `mysql -u root`. If you are able to connect successfully to the server without being asked for a password, you have problems. Anyone can connect to your MySQL server as the MySQL `root` user with full privileges! Review the MySQL installation instructions, paying particular attention to the item about setting a `root` password.

— Use the command SHOW GRANTS and check to see who has access to what. Remove those privileges that are not necessary using the REVOKE command.

- Do not keep any plain-text passwords in your database. When your computer becomes compromised, the intruder can take the full list of passwords and use them. Instead use MD5() or another one-way hashing function.

- Do not choose passwords from dictionaries. There are special programs to break them. Even passwords like "xfish98" are very bad. Much better is "duag98" which contains the same word "fish" but typed one key to the left on a standard QWERTY keyboard. Another method is to use "Mhall" which is taken from the first characters of each word in the sentence "Mary had a little lamb." This is easy to remember and type, but difficult to guess for someone who does not know it.

- Invest in a firewall. This protects you from at least 50% of all types of exploits in any software. Put MySQL behind the firewall or in a demilitarised zone (DMZ).

Checklist:

— Try to scan your ports from the Internet using a tool such as nmap. MySQL uses port 3306 by default. This port should be inaccessible from untrusted hosts. Another simple way to check whether your MySQL port is open is to try the following command from some remote machine, where server_host is the hostname of your MySQL server:

```
shell> telnet server_host 3306
```

If you get a connection and some garbage characters, the port is open, and should be closed on your firewall or router, unless you really have a good reason to keep it open. If telnet just hangs or the connection is refused, everything is OK; the port is blocked.

- Do not trust any data entered by your users. They can try to trick your code by entering special or escaped character sequences in web forms, URLs, or whatever application you have built. Be sure that your application remains secure if a user enters something like "; DROP DATABASE mysql;". This is an extreme example, but large security leaks and data loss may occur as a result of hackers using similar techniques, if you do not prepare for them.

Also remember to check numeric data. A common mistake is to protect only strings. Sometimes people think that if a database contains only publicly available data that it need not be protected. This is incorrect. At least denial-of-service type attacks can be performed on such databases. The simplest way to protect from this type of attack is to use apostrophes around the numeric constants: SELECT * FROM table WHERE ID='234' rather than SELECT * FROM table WHERE ID=234. MySQL automatically converts this string to a number and strips all non-numeric symbols from it.

Checklist:

— All web applications:

    — Try to enter ' and " in all your web forms. If you get any kind of MySQL error, investigate the problem right away.

    — Try to modify any dynamic URLs by adding %22 ("), %23 (#), and %27 (') in the URL.

    — Try to modify datatypes in dynamic URLs from numeric ones to character ones containing characters from previous examples. Your application should be safe against this and similar attacks.

    — Try to enter characters, spaces, and special symbols instead of numbers in numeric fields. Your application should remove them before passing them to MySQL or your application should generate an error. Passing unchecked values to MySQL is very dangerous!

    — Check data sizes before passing them to MySQL.

    — Consider having your application connect to the database using a different username than the one you use for administrative purposes. Do not give your applications any more access privileges than they need.

— Users of PHP:

    — Check out the `addslashes()` function. As of PHP 4.0.3, a `mysql_escape_string()` function is available that is based on the function of the same name in the MySQL C API.

— Users of MySQL C API:

    — Check out the `mysql_real_escape_string()` API call.

— Users of MySQL++:

    — Check out the `escape` and `quote` modifiers for query streams.

— Users of Perl DBI:

    — Check out the `quote()` method or use placeholders.

— Users of Java JDBC:

    — Use a `PreparedStatement` object and placeholders.

- Do not transmit plain (unencrypted) data over the Internet. Such data is accessible to everyone who has the time and ability to intercept it and use it for their own purposes. Instead, use an encrypted protocol such as SSL or SSH. MySQL supports internal SSL connections as of Version 4.0.0. SSH port-forwarding can be used to create an encrypted (and compressed) tunnel for the communication.

- Learn to use the `tcpdump` and `strings` utilities. For most cases, you can check whether MySQL data streams are unencrypted by issuing a command like the following:

```
shell> tcpdump -l -i eth0 -w - src or dst port 3306 | strings
```

(This works under Linux and should work with small modifications under other systems.) Warning: If you do not see data this doesn't always actually mean that it is encrypted. If you need high security, you should consult with a security expert.

4.2.2 How to Make MySQL Secure Against Crackers

When you connect to a MySQL server, you normally should use a password. The password is not transmitted in clear text over the connection, however the encryption algorithm is not very strong, and with some effort a clever attacker can crack the password if he is able to sniff the traffic between the client and the server. If the connection between the client and the server goes through an untrusted network, you should use an SSH tunnel to encrypt the communication.

All other information is transferred as text that can be read by anyone who is able to watch the connection. If you are concerned about this, you can use the compressed protocol (in MySQL Version 3.22 and above) to make things much harder. To make things even more secure you should use ssh. You can find an open source ssh client at http://www.openssh.org/, and a commercial ssh client at http://www.ssh.com/. With this, you can get an encrypted TCP/IP connection between a MySQL server and a MySQL client.

If you are using MySQL 4.0, you can also use internal openssl support. See Section 4.3.8, Using Secure Connections.

To make a MySQL system secure, you should strongly consider the following suggestions:

- Use passwords for all MySQL users. Remember that anyone can log in as any other person as simply as `mysql -u other_user db_name` if other_user has no password. It is common behavior with client/server applications that the client may specify any username. You can change the password of all users by editing the `mysql_install_db` script before you run it, or only the password for the MySQL root user like this:

```
shell> mysql -u root mysql
mysql> UPDATE user SET Password=PASSWORD('new_password')
    ->             WHERE user='root';
mysql> FLUSH PRIVILEGES;
```

- Don't run the MySQL daemon as the Unix `root` user. This is very dangerous because any user with the **file** privilege will be able to create files as `root` (for example, `~root/.bashrc`). To prevent this, `mysqld` will refuse to run as `root` unless it is specified directly using a `--user=root` option.

  `mysqld` can be run as an ordinary unprivileged user instead. You can also create a new Unix user `mysql` to make everything even more secure. If you run `mysqld` as another Unix user, you don't need to change the `root` username in the `user` table, because MySQL usernames have nothing to do with Unix usernames. To start `mysqld` as another Unix user, add a `user` line that specifies the username to the `[mysqld]` group of the `/etc/my.cnf` option file or the `my.cnf` option file in the server's data directory. For example:

  ```
  [mysqld]
  user=mysql
  ```

  This will cause the server to start as the designated user whether you start it manually or by using `safe_mysqld` or `mysql.server`. For more details, see Section A.3.2, How to Run MySQL as a Normal User.

- Don't support symlinks to tables (this can be disabled with the `--skip-symlink` option). This is especially important if you run `mysqld` as root, as anyone who has write access to the mysqld data directories could then delete any file in the system! See Section 5.6.1.2, Using symbolic links for tables.

- Check that the Unix user that `mysqld` runs as is the only user with read/write privileges in the database directories.

- Don't give the **process** privilege to all users. The output of `mysqladmin pro- cesslist` shows the text of the currently executing queries, so any user who is allowed to execute that command might be able to see if another user issues an `UPDATE user SET password=PASSWORD('not_secure')` query.

  `mysqld` reserves an extra connection for users who have the **process** privilege so that a MySQL `root` user can log in and check things even if all normal connections are in use.

- Don't give the **file** privilege to all users. Any user who has this privilege can write a file anywhere in the filesystem with the privileges of the `mysqld` daemon! To make this a bit safer, all files generated with `SELECT ... INTO OUTFILE` are readable to everyone, and you cannot overwrite existing files.

  The **file** privilege may also be used to read any file accessible to the Unix user that the server runs as. This could be abused, for example, by using `LOAD DATA` to load `/etc/passwd` into a table, which can then be read with `SELECT`.

- If you don't trust your DNS, you should use IP numbers instead of hostnames in the grant tables. In any case, you should be very careful about creating grant table entries using hostname values that contain wildcards!

- If you want to restrict the number of connections for a single user, you can do this by setting the max_user_connections variable in mysqld.

4.2.3   Startup Options for mysqld Concerning Security

The following mysqld options affect security:

--local-infile[=(0|1)]

If one uses --local-infile=0, one can't use LOAD DATA LOCAL INFILE.

--safe-show-database

With this option, SHOW DATABASES returns only those databases for which the user has some kind of privilege.

--safe-user-create

If this is enabled, a user can't create new users with the GRANT command, if the user doesn't have the **insert** privilege for the mysql.user table. If you want to give a user access to just create new users with those privileges that the user has a right to grant, you should give the user the following privilege:

```
mysql> GRANT INSERT(user) ON mysql.user TO 'user'@'hostname';
```

This will ensure that the user can't change any privilege columns directly, but has to use the GRANT command to give privileges to other users.

--skip-grant-tables

This option causes the server not to use the privilege system at all. This gives everyone **full access** to all databases! (You can tell a running server to start using the grant tables again by executing mysqladmin flush-privileges or mysqladmin reload.)

--skip-name-resolve

Hostnames are not resolved. All Host column values in the grant tables must be IP numbers or localhost.

--skip-networking

Don't allow TCP/IP connections over the network. All connections to mysqld must be made via Unix sockets. This option is unsuitable for systems that use MIT-pthreads because the MIT-pthreads package doesn't support Unix sockets.

--skip-show-database

With this option, the SHOW DATABASES statement doesn't return anything.

4.2.4 Security Issues with LOAD DATA LOCAL

In MySQL 3.23.49 and MySQL 4.0.2, we added some new options to deal with possible security issues when it comes to LOAD DATA LOCAL.

There are two possible problems with supporting this command:

As the reading of the file is initiated from the server, one could theoretically create a patched MySQL server that could read any file on the client machine that the current user has read access to, when the client issues a query against the table.

In a web environment where the clients are connecting from a web server, a user could use LOAD DATA LOCAL to read any files that the web server process has read access to (assuming a user could run any command against the SQL server).

There are two separate fixes for this:

If you don't configure MySQL with --enable-local-infile, LOAD DATA LOCAL will be disabled by all clients, unless mysql_options(. . . MYSQL_OPT_LOCAL_INFILE, 0) is called in the client. See Section 8.4.3.159, mysql_options().

For the mysql command-line client, LOAD DATA LOCAL can be enabled by specifying the option --local-infile[=1], or disabled with --local-infile=0.

By default, all MySQL clients and libraries are compiled with --enable-local-infile, to be compatible with MySQL 3.23.48 and before.

One can disable all LOAD DATA LOCAL commands in the MySQL server by starting mysqld with --local-infile=0.

In the case that LOAD DATA INFILE is disabled in the server or the client, you will get the error message (1148):

```
The used command is not allowed with this MySQL version
```

4.2.5 What the Privilege System Does

The primary function of the MySQL privilege system is to authenticate a user connecting from a given host, and to associate that user with privileges on a database such as **select**, **insert**, **update**, and **delete**.

Additional functionality includes the ability to have an anonymous user and to grant privileges for MySQL-specific functions such as LOAD DATA INFILE and administrative operations.

4.2.6 How the Privilege System Works

The MySQL privilege system ensures that all users may do exactly the things that they are supposed to be allowed to do. When you connect to a MySQL server, your identity is determined by **the host from which you connect** and **the username you specify**. The system grants privileges according to your identity and **what you want to do**.

MySQL considers both your hostname and username in identifying you because there is little reason to assume that a given username belongs to the same person everywhere on the Internet. For example, the user joe who connects from office.com need not be the same person as the user joe who connects from elsewhere.com. MySQL handles this by allowing you to distinguish users on different hosts that happen to have the same name: you can grant joe one set of privileges for connections from office.com, and a different set of privileges for connections from elsewhere.com.

MySQL access control involves two stages:

- Stage 1: The server checks whether you are even allowed to connect.

- Stage 2: Assuming you can connect, the server checks each request you issue to see whether you have sufficient privileges to perform it. For example, if you try to select rows from a table in a database or drop a table from the database, the server makes sure you have the **select** privilege for the table or the **drop** privilege for the database.

The server uses the user, db, and host tables in the mysql database at both stages of access control. The fields in these grant tables are shown here:

Table name	user	db	host
Scope fields	Host	Host	Host
	User	Db	Db
	Password	User	
Privilege fields	Select_priv	Select_priv	Select_priv
	Insert_priv	Insert_priv	Insert_priv
	Update_priv	Update_priv	Update_priv
	Delete_priv	Delete_priv	Delete_priv
	Index_priv	Index_priv	Index_priv
	Alter_priv	Alter_priv	Alter_priv
	Create_priv	Create_priv	Create_priv
	Drop_priv	Drop_priv	Drop_priv
	Grant_priv	Grant_priv	Grant_priv
	Refer-ences_priv		
	Reload_priv		
	Shutdown_priv		
	Process_priv		
	File_priv		

For the second stage of access control (request verification), the server may, if the request involves tables, additionally consult the `tables_priv` and `columns_priv` tables. The fields in these tables are shown here:

Table name	tables_priv	columns_priv
Scope fields	Host	Host
	Db	Db
	User	User
	Table_name	Table_name
		Column_name
Privilege fields	Table_priv	Column_priv
	Column_priv	
Other fields	Timestamp	Timestamp
	Grantor	

Each grant table contains scope fields and privilege fields.

Scope fields determine the scope of each entry in the tables—that is, the context in which the entry applies. For example, a `user` table entry with `Host` and `User` values of `'thomas.loc.gov'` and `'bob'` would be used for authenticating connections made to the server by `bob` from the host `thomas.loc.gov`. Similarly, a `db` table entry with `Host`, `User`, and `Db` fields of `'thomas.loc.gov'`, `'bob'`, and `'reports'` would be used when `bob` connects from the host `thomas.loc.gov` to access the `reports` database. The `tables_priv` and `columns_priv` tables contain scope fields indicating tables or table/column combinations to which each entry applies.

For access-checking purposes, comparisons of `Host` values are case-insensitive. `User`, `Password`, `Db`, and `Table_name` values are case-sensitive. `Column_name` values are case-insensitive in MySQL Versions 3.22.12 or later.

Privilege fields indicate the privileges granted by a table entry, that is, what operations can be performed. The server combines the information in the various grant tables to form a complete description of a user's privileges. The rules used to do this are described in Section 4.2.10, Access Control, Stage 2: Request Verification.

Scope fields are strings, declared as shown here; the default value for each is the empty string:

Field name	Type	Notes
Host	CHAR(60)	
User	CHAR(16)	
Password	CHAR(16)	
Db	CHAR(64)	(CHAR(60) for the tables_priv and columns_priv tables)
Table_name	CHAR(60)	
Column_name	CHAR(60)	

In the user, db, and host tables, all privilege fields are declared as ENUM('N','Y') —each can have a value of 'N' or 'Y', and the default value is 'N'.

In the tables_priv and columns_priv tables, the privilege fields are declared as SET fields:

Table name	Field name	Possible set elements
tables_priv	Table_priv	'Select', 'Insert', 'Update', 'Delete', 'Create', 'Drop', 'Grant', 'References', 'Index', 'Alter'
tables_priv	Column_priv	'Select', 'Insert', 'Update', 'References'
columns_priv	Column_priv	'Select', 'Insert', 'Update', 'References'

Briefly, the server uses the grant tables like this:

- The user table scope fields determine whether to allow or reject incoming connections. For allowed connections, any privileges granted in the user table indicate the user's global (superuser) privileges. These privileges apply to **all** databases on the server.

- The db and host tables are used together:

  — The db table scope fields determine which users can access which databases from which hosts. The privilege fields determine which operations are allowed.

  — The host table is used as an extension of the db table when you want a given db table entry to apply to several hosts. For example, if you want a user to be able to use a database from several hosts in your network, leave the Host value empty in the user's db table entry, then populate the host table with an entry for each of those hosts. This mechanism is described more detail in Section 4.2.10, Access Control, Stage 2: Request Verification.

- The tables_priv and columns_priv tables are similar to the db table, but are more fine-grained: they apply at the table and column levels rather than at the database level.

Note that administrative privileges (**reload, shutdown,** etc.) are specified only in the user table. This is because administrative operations are operations on the server itself and are not database-specific, so there is no reason to list such privileges in the other grant tables. In fact, only the user table need be consulted to determine whether you can perform an administrative operation.

The **file** privilege is specified only in the user table, too. It is not an administrative privilege as such, but your ability to read or write files on the server host is independent of the database you are accessing.

The mysqld server reads the contents of the grant tables once, when it starts up. Changes to the grant tables take effect as indicated in Section 4.3.3, When Privilege Changes Take Effect.

When you modify the contents of the grant tables, it is a good idea to make sure that your changes set up privileges the way you want. For help in diagnosing problems, see Section 4.2.11, Causes of Access denied Errors. For advice on security issues, see Section 4.2.2, How to Make MySQL Secure Against Crackers.

A useful diagnostic tool is the mysqlaccess script, which Yves Carlier has provided for the MySQL distribution. Invoke mysqlaccess with the --help option to find out how it works. Note that mysqlaccess checks access using only the user, db, and host tables. It does not check table- or column-level privileges.

4.2.7 Privileges Provided by MySQL

Information about user privileges is stored in the user, db, host, tables_priv, and columns_priv tables in the mysql database (that is, in the database named mysql). The MySQL server reads the contents of these tables when it starts up and under the circumstances indicated in Section 4.3.3, When Privilege Changes Take Effect.

The names used in this manual to refer to the privileges provided by MySQL are shown here, along with the table column name associated with each privilege in the grant tables and the context in which the privilege applies:

Privilege	Column	Context
select	Select_priv	tables
insert	Insert_priv	tables
update	Update_priv	tables
delete	Delete_priv	tables
index	Index_priv	tables
alter	Alter_priv	tables
create	Create_priv	databases, tables, or indexes
drop	Drop_priv	databases or tables
grant	Grant_priv	databases or tables

Privilege	Column	Context
references	Refer- ences_priv	databases or tables
reload	Reload_priv	server administration
shutdown	Shutdown_priv	server administration
process	Process_priv	server administration
file	File_priv	file access on server

The **select, insert, update**, and **delete** privileges allow you to perform operations on rows in existing tables in a database.

SELECT statements require the **select** privilege only if they actually retrieve rows from a table. You can execute certain SELECT statements even without permission to access any of the databases on the server. For example, you could use the mysql client as a simple calculator:

```
mysql> SELECT 1+1;
mysql> SELECT PI()*2;
```

The **index** privilege allows you to create or drop (remove) indexes.

The **alter** privilege allows you to use ALTER TABLE.

The **create** and **drop** privileges allow you to create new databases and tables, or to drop (remove) existing databases and tables.

Note that if you grant the **drop** privilege for the mysql database to a user, that user can drop the database in which the MySQL access privileges are stored!

The **grant** privilege allows you to give to other users those privileges you possess.

The **file** privilege gives you permission to read and write files on the server using the LOAD DATA INFILE and SELECT . . . INTO OUTFILE statements. Any user to whom this privilege is granted can read or write any file that the MySQL server can read or write.

The remaining privileges are used for administrative operations, which are performed using the mysqladmin program. The following table shows which mysqladmin commands each administrative privilege allows you to execute:

Privilege	Commands permitted to privilege holders
reload	reload, refresh, flush-privileges, flush-hosts, flush-logs, and flush-tables
shutdown	shutdown
process	processlist, kill

The reload command tells the server to re-read the grant tables. The refresh command flushes all tables and opens and closes the log files. flush-privileges is a synonym for reload. The other flush-* commands perform functions similar to refresh but are more limited in scope, and may be preferable in some instances. For example, if you want to flush just the log files, flush-logs is a better choice than refresh.

The shutdown command shuts down the server.

The processlist command displays information about the threads executing within the server. The kill command kills server threads. You can always display or kill your own threads, but you need the **process** privilege to display or kill threads initiated by other users. See Section 4.5.5, KILL Syntax.

It is a good idea in general to grant privileges only to those users who need them, but you should exercise particular caution in granting certain privileges:

- The **grant** privilege allows users to give away their privileges to other users. Two users with different privileges and with the **grant** privilege are able to combine privileges.

- The **alter** privilege may be used to subvert the privilege system by renaming tables.

- The **file** privilege can be abused to read any world-readable file on the server into a database table, the contents of which can then be accessed using SELECT. This includes the contents of all databases hosted by the server!

- The **shutdown** privilege can be abused to deny service to other users entirely, by terminating the server.

- The **process** privilege can be used to view the plain text of currently executing queries, including queries that set or change passwords.

- Privileges on the mysql database can be used to change passwords and other access privilege information. (Passwords are stored encrypted, so a malicious user cannot simply read them to know the plain text password.) If they can access the mysql.user password column, they can use it to log into the MySQL server for the given user. (With sufficient privileges, the same user can replace a password with a different one.)

There are some things that you cannot do with the MySQL privilege system:

- You cannot explicitly specify that a given user should be denied access. That is, you cannot explicitly match a user and then refuse the connection.

- You cannot specify that a user has privileges to create or drop tables in a database but not to create or drop the database itself.

4.2.8 Connecting to the MySQL server

MySQL client programs generally require that you specify connection parameters when you want to access a MySQL server: the host you want to connect to, your username, and your password. For example, the mysql client can be started like this (optional arguments are enclosed between [and]):

```
shell> mysql [-h host_name] [-u user_name] [-pyour_pass]
```

Alternate forms of the -h, -u, and -p options are --host=host_name, --user=user_name, and --password=your_pass. Note that there is *no space* between -p or --password= and the password following it.

Note: Specifying a password on the command-line is not secure! Any user on your system may then find out your password by typing a command like: ps auxww. See Section 4.1.2, my.cnf Option Files.

mysql uses default values for connection parameters that are missing from the command-line:

- The default hostname is localhost.
- The default username is your Unix login name.
- No password is supplied if -p is missing.

Thus, for a Unix user joe, the following commands are equivalent:

```
shell> mysql -h localhost -u joe
shell> mysql -h localhost
shell> mysql -u joe
shell> mysql
```

Other MySQL clients behave similarly.

On Unix systems, you can specify different default values to be used when you make a connection so that you need not enter them on the command-line each time you invoke a client program. This can be done in a couple of ways:

- You can specify connection parameters in the [client] section of the .my.cnf configuration file in your home directory. The relevant section of the file might look like this:

```
[client]
host=host_name
user=user_name
password=your_pass
```

See Section 4.1.2, my.cnf Option Files.

- You can specify connection parameters using environment variables. The host can be specified for mysql using MYSQL_HOST. The MySQL username can be specified using USER (this is for Windows only). The password can be specified using MYSQL_PWD (but this is insecure; see the next section). See Appendix E.

4.2.9 Access Control, Stage 1: Connection Verification

When you attempt to connect to a MySQL server, the server accepts or rejects the connection based on your identity and whether you can verify your identity by supplying the correct password. If not, the server denies access to you completely. Otherwise, the server accepts the connection, then enters Stage 2 and waits for requests.

Your identity is based on two pieces of information:

- The host from which you connect
- Your MySQL username

Identity checking is performed using the three user table scope fields (Host, User, and Password). The server accepts the connection only if a user table entry matches your hostname and user name, and you supply the correct password.

Values in the user table scope fields may be specified as follows:

- A Host value may be a hostname or an IP number, or 'localhost' to indicate the local host.

- You can use the wildcard characters % and _ in the Host field.

- A Host value of '%' matches any hostname.

- A blank Host value means that the privilege should be anded with the entry in the host table that matches the given hostname. You can find more information about this in the next chapter.

- As of MySQL Version 3.23, for Host values specified as IP numbers, you can specify a netmask indicating how many address bits to use for the network number. For example:

```
mysql> GRANT ALL PRIVILEGES ON db.*
    -> TO david@'192.58.197.0/255.255.255.0';
```

This will allow everyone to connect from an IP where the following is true:

```
user_ip & netmask = host_ip.
```

In the preceding example all IP:s in the interval 192.58.197.0 - 192.58.197.255 can connect to the MySQL server.

- Wildcard characters are not allowed in the User field, but you can specify a blank value, which matches any name. If the user table entry that matches an incoming connection has a blank username, the user is considered to be the anonymous user (the user with no name), rather than the name that the client actually specified. This means that a blank username is used for all further access checking for the duration of the connection (that is, during Stage 2).

- The Password field can be blank. This does not mean that any password matches. It means the user must connect without specifying a password.

Non-blank Password values represent encrypted passwords. MySQL does not store passwords in plaintext form for anyone to see. Rather, the password supplied by a user who is attempting to connect is encrypted (using the PASSWORD() function). The encrypted password is then used when the client/server is checking if the password is correct. (This is done without the encrypted password ever traveling over the connection.) Note that from MySQL's point of view the encrypted password is the REAL password, so you should not give anyone access to it! In particular, don't give normal users read access to the tables in the mysql database!

The following examples show how various combinations of Host and User values in user table entries apply to incoming connections:

Host value	User value	Connections matched by entry
'thomas.loc.gov'	'fred'	fred, connecting from thomas.loc.gov
'thomas.loc.gov'	"	Any user, connecting from thomas.loc.gov
'%'	'fred'	fred, connecting from any host
'%'	"	Any user, connecting from any host
'%.loc.gov'	'fred'	fred, connecting from any host in the loc.gov domain
'x.y.%'	'fred'	fred, connecting from x.y.net, x.y.com, x.y.edu, etc. (this is probably not useful)
'144.155.166.177'	'fred'	fred, connecting from the host with IP address 144.155.166.177
'144.155.166.%'	'fred'	fred, connecting from any host in the 144.155.166 class C subnet
'144.155.166.0/ 255.255.255.0'	'fred'	Same as previous example

Because you can use IP wildcard values in the Host field (for example, '144.155.166.%' to match every host on a subnet), there is the possibility that someone might try to exploit this capability by naming a host 144.155.166.somewhere.com. To foil such attempts, MySQL disallows matching on hostnames that start with digits and a dot. Thus, if you have a hostnamed something like 1.2.foo.com, its name will never match the Host column of the grant tables. Only an IP number can match an IP wildcard value.

An incoming connection may be matched by more than one entry in the user table. For example, a connection from thomas.loc.gov by fred would be matched by several of the entries shown in the preceding table. How does the server choose which entry to use if more than one matches? The server resolves this question by sorting the user table after reading it at startup time, then looking through the entries in sorted order when a user attempts to connect. The first matching entry is the one that is used.

user table sorting works as follows. Suppose the user table looks like this:

```
+-----------+----------+-
| Host      | User     | ...
+-----------+----------+-
| %         | root     | ...
| %         | jeffrey  | ...
| localhost | root     | ...
| localhost |          | ...
+-----------+----------+-
```

When the server reads in the table, it orders the entries with the most-specific Host values first ('%' in the Host column means "any host" and is least specific). Entries with the same Host value are ordered with the most-specific User values first (a blank User value means "any user" and is least specific). The resulting sorted user table looks like this:

```
+-----------+----------+-
| Host      | User     | ...
+-----------+----------+-
| localhost | root     | ...
| localhost |          | ...
| %         | jeffrey  | ...
| %         | root     | ...
+-----------+----------+-
```

When a connection is attempted, the server looks through the sorted entries and uses the first match found. For a connection from localhost by jeffrey, the entries with 'localhost' in the Host column match first. Of those, the entry with the blank username matches both the connecting hostname and username. (The '%'/'jeffrey' entry would have matched, too, but it is not the first match in the table.)

Here is another example. Suppose the user table looks like this:

```
+-----------------+----------+-
| Host            | User     | ...
+-----------------+----------+-
| %               | jeffrey  | ...
| thomas.loc.gov  |          | ...
+-----------------+----------+-
```

The sorted table looks like this:

```
+-----------------+----------+-
| Host            | User     | ...
+-----------------+----------+-
| thomas.loc.gov  |          | ...
| %               | jeffrey  | ...
+-----------------+----------+-
```

A connection from thomas.loc.gov by jeffrey is matched by the first entry, whereas a connection from whitehouse.gov by jeffrey is matched by the second.

A common misconception is to think that for a given username, all entries that explicitly name that user will be used first when the server attempts to find a match for the connection. This is simply not true. The previous example illustrates this, where a connection from thomas.loc.gov by jeffrey is first matched not by the entry containing 'jeffrey' as the User field value, but by the entry with no username!

If you have problems connecting to the server, print out the user table and sort it by hand to see where the first match is being made.

4.2.10 Access Control, Stage 2: Request Verification

Once you establish a connection, the server enters Stage 2. For each request that comes in on the connection, the server checks whether you have sufficient privileges to perform it, based on the type of operation you wish to perform. This is where the privilege fields in the grant tables come into play. These privileges can come from any of the user, db, host, tables_priv, or columns_priv tables. The grant tables are manipulated with GRANT and REVOKE commands. See Section 4.3.1, GRANT and REVOKE Syntax. (You may find it helpful to refer to Section 4.2.6, How the Privilege System Works, which lists the fields present in each of the grant tables.)

The user table grants privileges that are assigned to you on a global basis and that apply no matter what the current database is. For example, if the user table grants you the **delete** privilege, you can delete rows from any database on the server host! In other words, user table privileges are superuser privileges. It is wise to grant privileges in the user table only to superusers such as server or database administrators. For other users, you should leave the privileges in the user table set to 'N' and grant privileges on a database-specific basis only, using the db and host tables.

The db and host tables grant database-specific privileges. Values in the scope fields may be specified as follows:

- The wildcard characters % and _ can be used in the Host and Db fields of either table.

- A '%' Host value in the db table means "any host." A blank Host value in the db table means "consult the host table for further information."

- A '%' or blank Host value in the host table means "any host."

- A '%' or blank Db value in either table means "any database."

- A blank User value in either table matches the anonymous user.

The db and host tables are read in and sorted when the server starts up (at the same time that it reads the user table). The db table is sorted on the Host, Db, and User scope fields, and the host table is sorted on the Host and Db scope fields. As with the user table, sorting puts the most-specific values first and least-specific values last, and when the server looks for matching entries, it uses the first match that it finds.

The tables_priv and columns_priv tables grant table- and column-specific privileges. Values in the scope fields may be specified as follows:

- The wildcard characters % and _ can be used in the Host field of either table.

- A '%' or blank Host value in either table means "any host."

- The Db, Table_name, and Column_name fields cannot contain wildcards or be blank in either table.

The tables_priv and columns_priv tables are sorted on the Host, Db, and User fields. This is similar to db table sorting, although the sorting is simpler because only the Host field may contain wildcards.

The request verification process is described next. (If you are familiar with the access-checking source code, you will notice that the description here differs slightly from the algorithm used in the code. The description is equivalent to what the code actually does; it differs only to make the explanation simpler.)

For administrative requests (**shutdown, reload,** etc.), the server checks only the user table entry because that is the only table that specifies administrative privileges. Access is granted if the entry allows the requested operation and denied otherwise. For example, if you want to execute mysqladmin shutdown but your user table entry doesn't grant the **shutdown** privilege to you, access is denied without even checking the db or host tables. (They contain no Shutdown_priv column, so there is no need to do so.)

For database-related requests (**insert, update,** etc.), the server first checks the user's global (superuser) privileges by looking in the user table entry. If the entry allows the requested operation, access is granted. If the global privileges in the user table are insufficient, the server determines the user's database-specific privileges by checking the db and host tables:

1. The server looks in the db table for a match on the Host, Db, and User fields. The Host and User fields are matched to the connecting user's hostname and MySQL username. The Db field is matched to the database the user wants to access. If there is no entry for the Host and User, access is denied.

2. If there is a matching db table entry and its Host field is not blank, that entry defines the user's database-specific privileges.

3. If the matching db table entry's Host field is blank, it signifies that the host table enumerates which hosts should be allowed access to the database. In this case, a further lookup is done in the host table to find a match on the Host and Db fields. If no host table entry matches, access is denied. If there is a match, the user's database-specific privileges are computed as the intersection (**not** the union!) of the privileges in the db and host table entries—that is, the privileges that are 'Y' in both entries. (This way you can grant general privileges in the db table entry and then selectively restrict them on a host-by-host basis using the host table entries.)

After determining the database-specific privileges granted by the db and host table entries, the server adds them to the global privileges granted by the user table. If the result allows the requested operation, access is granted. Otherwise, the server checks the user's table and column privileges in the tables_priv and columns_priv tables and adds those to the user's privileges. Access is allowed or denied based on the result.

Expressed in boolean terms, the preceding description of how a user's privileges are calculated may be summarised like this:

```
global privileges
OR (database privileges AND host privileges)
OR table privileges
OR column privileges
```

It may not be apparent why, if the global user entry privileges are initially found to be insufficient for the requested operation, the server adds those privileges to the database-, table-, and column-specific privileges later. The reason is that a request might require more than one type of privilege. For example, if you execute an INSERT . . . SELECT statement, you need both **insert** and **select** privileges. Your privileges might be such that the user table entry grants one privilege and the db table entry grants the other. In this case, you have the necessary privileges to perform the request, but the server cannot tell that from either table by itself; the privileges granted by the entries in both tables must be combined.

The host table can be used to maintain a list of secure servers.

At TcX, the host table contains a list of all machines on the local network. These are granted all privileges.

You can also use the host table to indicate hosts that are **not** secure. Suppose you have a machine public.your.domain that is located in a public area that you do not consider secure. You can allow access to all hosts on your network except that machine by using host table entries like this:

```
+----------------------+----+-
| Host                 | Db |  ...
+----------------------+----+-
| public.your.domain   | %  |  ... (all privileges set to 'N')
| %.your.domain        | %  |  ... (all privileges set to 'Y')
+----------------------+----+-
```

Naturally, you should always test your entries in the grant tables (for example, using mysqlaccess) to make sure your access privileges are actually set up the way you think they are.

4.2.11 Causes of Access denied Errors

If you encounter Access denied errors when you try to connect to the MySQL server, the following list indicates some courses of action you can take to correct the problem:

- After installing MySQL, did you run the mysql_install_db script to set up the initial grant table contents? If not, do so. See Section 4.3.4, Setting Up the Initial MySQL Privileges. Test the initial privileges by executing this command:

  ```
  shell> mysql -u root test
  ```

  The server should let you connect without error. You should also make sure you have a file user.MYD in the MySQL database directory. Ordinarily, this is PATH/var/mysql/user.MYD, where PATH is the pathname to the MySQL installation root.

- After a fresh installation, you should connect to the server and set up your users and their access permissions:

  ```
  shell> mysql -u root mysql
  ```

  The server should let you connect because the MySQL root user has no password initially. That is also a security risk, so setting the root password is something you should do while you're setting up your other MySQL users.

  If you try to connect as root and get this error:

  ```
  Access denied for user: '@unknown' to database mysql
  ```

  this means that you don't have an entry in the user table with a User column value of 'root' and that mysqld cannot resolve the hostname for your client. In this case, you must restart the server with the --skip-grant-tables option and edit your /etc/hosts or \windows\hosts file to add an entry for your host.

- If you get an error like the following:

  ```
  shell> mysqladmin -u root -pxxxxx ver
  Access denied for user: 'root@localhost' (Using password: YES)
  ```

  it means that you are using a wrong password. See Section 4.3.6, Setting Up Passwords.

If you have forgotten the root password, you can restart `mysqld` with `--skip-grant-tables` to change the password. You can find more about this option later on in this section.

If you get the preceding error even if you haven't specified a password, you entered a wrong password in some `my.ini` file. See Section 4.1.2, `my.cnf` Option Files. You can avoid using option files with the `--no-defaults` option, as follows:

```
shell> mysqladmin --no-defaults -u root ver
```

- If you updated an existing MySQL installation from a version earlier than Version 3.22.11 to Version 3.22.11 or later, did you run the `mysql_fix_privilege_tables` script? If not, do so. The structure of the grant tables changed with MySQL Version 3.22.11 when the GRANT statement became functional.

- If your privileges seem to have changed in the middle of a session, it may be that a superuser has changed them. Reloading the grant tables affects new client connections, but it also affects existing connections as indicated in Section 4.3.3, When Privilege Changes Take Effect.

- If you can't get your password to work, remember that you must use the PASSWORD() function if you set the password with the INSERT, UPDATE, or SET PASSWORD statements. The PASSWORD() function is unnecessary if you specify the password using the GRANT ... INDENTIFIED BY statement or the `mysqladmin password` command. See Section 4.3.6, Setting Up Passwords.

- `localhost` is a synonym for your local hostname, and is also the default host to which clients try to connect if you specify no host explicitly. However, connections to `localhost` do not work if you are running on a system that uses MIT-pthreads (`localhost` connections are made using Unix sockets, which are not supported by MIT-pthreads). To avoid this problem on such systems, you should use the `--host` option to name the server host explicitly. This will make a TCP/IP connection to the `mysqld` server. In this case, you must have your real hostname in `user` table entries on the server host. (This is true even if you are running a client program on the same host as the server.)

- If you get an Access denied error when trying to connect to the database with `mysql -u user_name db_name`, you may have a problem with the `user` table. Check this by executing `mysql -u root mysql` and issuing this SQL statement:

```
mysql> SELECT * FROM user;
```

The result should include an entry with the Host and User columns matching your computer's hostname and your MySQL username.

- The Access denied error message will tell you who you are trying to log in as, the host from which you are trying to connect, and whether you were using a password. Normally, you should have one entry in the `user` table that exactly matches the hostname and username that were given in the error message. For example if you get an error message that contains `Using password: NO`, this means that you tried to login without a password.

- If you get the following error connecting from a different host than the one on which the MySQL server is running, there is no row in the `user` table matching that host:

  ```
  Host ... is not allowed to connect to this MySQL server
  ```

  You can fix this by using the command-line tool `mysql` (on the server host!) to add a row to the `user`, `db`, or `host` table for the user/hostname combination from which you are trying to connect and then execute `mysqladmin flush-privileges`. If you are not running MySQL Version 3.22 and you don't know the IP number or host-name of the machine from which you are connecting, you should put an entry with `'%'` as the `Host` column value in the `user` table and restart `mysqld` with the `--log` option on the server machine. After trying to connect from the client machine, the information in the MySQL log will indicate how you really did connect. (Then replace the `'%'` in the `user` table entry with the actual hostname that shows up in the log. Otherwise, you'll have a system that is insecure.)

  Another reason for this error on Linux is that you are using a binary MySQL version that is compiled with a different glibc version than the one you are using. In this case you should either upgrade your OS/glibc or download the source MySQL version and compile this yourself. A source RPM is normally trivial to compile and install, so this isn't a big problem.

- If you get an error message where the hostname is not shown or where the hostname is an IP, even if you try to connect with a hostname:

  ```
  shell> mysqladmin -u root -pxxxx -h some-hostname ver
  Access denied for user: 'root@' (Using password: YES)
  ```

  this means that MySQL got some error when trying to resolve the IP to a hostname. In this case you can execute `mysqladmin flush-hosts` to reset the internal DNS cache. See Section 5.5.5, How MySQL Uses DNS.

  Some permanent solutions are:

  — Try to find out what is wrong with your DNS server and fix this.

  — Specify IPs instead of hostnames in the MySQL privilege tables.

  — Start `mysqld` with `--skip-name-resolve`.

  — Start `mysqld` with `--skip-host-cache`.

  — Connect to `localhost` if you are running the server and the client on the same machine.

  — Put the client machine names in `/etc/hosts`.

- If `mysql -u root test` works but `mysql -h your_hostname -u root test` results in `Access denied`, you may not have the correct name for your host in the user table. A common problem here is that the `Host` value in the user table entry specifies an unqualified hostname, but your system's name resolution routines return a fully qualified domain name (or vice versa). For example, if you have an entry with host `'tcx'` in the user table, but your DNS tells MySQL that your hostname is `'tcx.subnet.se'`, the entry will not work. Try adding an entry to the user table that contains the IP number of your host as the `Host` column value. (Alternatively, you could add an entry to the user table with a `Host` value that contains a wildcard-—for example, `'tcx.%'`. However, use of hostnames ending with `%` is **insecure** and is **not** recommended!)

- If `mysql -u user_name test` works but `mysql -u user_name other_db_name` doesn't work, you don't have an entry for `other_db_name` listed in the `db` table.

- If `mysql -u user_name db_name` works when executed on the server machine, but `mysql -u host_name -u user_name db_name` doesn't work when executed on another client machine, you don't have the client machine listed in the user table or the `db` table.

- If you can't figure out why you get `Access denied`, remove from the user table all entries that have `Host` values containing wildcards (entries that contain `%` or `_`). A very common error is to insert a new entry with `Host='%'` and `User='some user'`, thinking that this will allow you to specify `localhost` to connect from the same machine. The reason that this doesn't work is that the default privileges include an entry with `Host='localhost'` and `User="`. Because that entry has a `Host` value `'localhost'` that is more specific than `'%'`, it is used in preference to the new entry when connecting from `localhost`! The correct procedure is to insert a second entry with `Host='localhost'` and `User='some_user'`, or to remove the entry with `Host='localhost'` and `User="`.

- If you get the following error, you may have a problem with the `db` or host table:

      Access to database denied

  If the entry selected from the `db` table has an empty value in the `Host` column, make sure there are one or more corresponding entries in the host table specifying which hosts the `db` table entry applies to.

  If you get the error when using the SQL commands `SELECT ... INTO OUTFILE` or `LOAD DATA INFILE`, your entry in the user table probably doesn't have the **file** privilege enabled.

- Remember that client programs will use connection parameters specified in configuration files or environment variables. See Appendix E. If a client seems to be sending the wrong default connection parameters when you don't specify them on the

command-line, check your environment and the .my.cnf file in your home directory. You might also check the system-wide MySQL configuration files, though it is
far less likely that client connection parameters will be specified there. See Section
4.1.2, my.cnf Option Files. If you get Access denied when you run a client without any options, make sure you haven't specified an old password in any of your
option files! See Section 4.1.2, my.cnf Option Files.

- If you make changes to the grant tables directly (using an INSERT or UPDATE statement) and your changes seem to be ignored, remember that you must issue a FLUSH
  PRIVILEGES statement or execute a mysqladmin flush-privileges command to
  cause the server to re-read the privilege tables. Otherwise, your changes have no
  effect until the next time the server is restarted. Remember that after you set the
  root password with an UPDATE command, you won't need to specify it until after
  you flush the privileges because the server won't know you've changed the password
  yet!

- If you have access problems with a Perl, PHP, Python, or ODBC program, try to connect to the server with mysql -u user_name db_name or mysql -u user_name
  -pyour_pass db_name. If you are able to connect using the mysql client, there is a
  problem with your program and not with the access privileges. (Note that there is no
  space between -p and the password; you can also use the --password=your_pass
  syntax to specify the password. If you use the -p option alone, MySQL will prompt
  you for the password.)

- For testing, start the mysqld daemon with the --skip-grant-tables option. Then
  you can change the MySQL grant tables and use the mysqlaccess script to check
  whether your modifications have the desired effect. When you are satisfied with your
  changes, execute mysqladmin flush-privileges to tell the mysqld server to
  start using the new grant tables. **Note**: reloading the grant tables overrides the
  --skip-grant-tables option. This allows you to tell the server to begin using the
  grant tables again without bringing it down and restarting it.

- If everything else fails, start the mysqld daemon with a debugging option (for example, --debug=d,general,query). This will print host and user information about
  attempted connections, as well as information about each command issued. See Section D.1.2, Creating Trace Files.

- If you have any other problems with the MySQL grant tables and feel you must post
  the problem to the mailing list, always provide a dump of the MySQL grant tables.
  You can dump the tables with the mysqldump mysql command. As always, post
  your problem using the mysqlbug script. See Section 1.6.2.3, How to report bugs or
  problems. In some cases you may need to restart mysqld with --skip-grant-
  tables to run mysqldump.

4.3 MySQL User Account Management

4.3.1 GRANT and REVOKE Syntax

```
GRANT priv_type [(column_list)] [, priv_type [(column_list)] ...]
    ON {tbl_name | * | *.* | db_name.*}
    TO user_name [IDENTIFIED BY [PASSWORD] 'password']
        [, user_name [IDENTIFIED BY 'password'] ...]
    [REQUIRE
        [{SSL| X509}]
        [CIPHER cipher [AND]]
        [ISSUER issuer [AND]]
        [SUBJECT subject]]
    [WITH [GRANT OPTION | MAX_QUERIES_PER_HOUR=#]]

REVOKE priv_type [(column_list)] [, priv_type [(column_list)] ...]
    ON {tbl_name | * | *.* | db_name.*}
    FROM user_name [, user_name ...]
```

GRANT is implemented in MySQL Version 3.22.11 or later. For earlier MySQL versions, the GRANT statement does nothing.

The GRANT and REVOKE commands allow system administrators to create users and grant and revoke rights to MySQL users at four privilege levels:

Global level

Global privileges apply to all databases on a given server. These privileges are stored in the mysql.user table.

Database level

Database privileges apply to all tables in a given database. These privileges are stored in the mysql.db and mysql.host tables.

Table level

Table privileges apply to all columns in a given table. These privileges are stored in the mysql.tables_priv table.

Column level

Column privileges apply to single columns in a given table. These privileges are stored in the mysql.columns_priv table.

If you give a grant for a user that doesn't exist, that user is created. For examples of how GRANT works, see Section 4.3.5, Adding New Users to MySQL.

For the GRANT and REVOKE statements, priv_type may be specified as any of the following:

```
ALL PRIVILEGES          FILE              RELOAD
ALTER                   INDEX             SELECT
CREATE                  INSERT            SHUTDOWN
DELETE                  PROCESS           UPDATE
DROP                    REFERENCES        USAGE
```

ALL is a synonym for ALL PRIVILEGES. REFERENCES is not yet implemented. USAGE is currently a synonym for "no privileges." It can be used when you want to create a user that has no privileges.

To revoke the **grant** privilege from a user, use a priv_type value of GRANT OPTION:

```
mysql> REVOKE GRANT OPTION ON ... FROM ...;
```

The only priv_type values you can specify for a table are SELECT, INSERT, UPDATE, DELETE, CREATE, DROP, GRANT, INDEX, and ALTER.

The only priv_type values you can specify for a column (that is, when you use a column_list clause) are SELECT, INSERT, and UPDATE.

You can set global privileges by using ON *.* syntax. You can set database privileges by using ON db_name.* syntax. If you specify ON * and you have a current database, you will set the privileges for that database. (**Warning**: if you specify ON * and you **don't** have a current database, you will affect the global privileges!)

In order to accommodate granting rights to users from arbitrary hosts, MySQL supports specifying the user_name value in the form user@host. If you want to specify a user string containing special characters (such as -), or a host string containing special characters or wildcard characters (such as %), you can quote the user or hostname (for example, 'test-user'@'test-hostname').

You can specify wildcards in the hostname. For example, user@"%.loc.gov" applies to user for any host in the loc.gov domain, and user@"144.155.166.%" applies to user for any host in the 144.155.166 class C subnet.

The simple form user is a synonym for user@"%".

MySQL doesn't support wildcards in usernames. Anonymous users are defined by inserting entries with User=" into the mysql.user table or creating an user with an empty name with the GRANT command.

Note: if you allow anonymous users to connect to the MySQL server, you should also grant privileges to all local users as user@localhost because otherwise the anonymous user entry for the local host in the mysql.user table will be used when the user tries to log into the MySQL server from the local machine!

You can verify if this applies to you by executing this query:

```
mysql> SELECT Host,User FROM mysql.user WHERE User='';
```

For the moment, GRANT only supports host, table, database, and column names up to 60 characters long. A username can be up to 16 characters.

The privileges for a table or column are formed from the logical OR of the privileges at each of the four privilege levels. For example, if the mysql.user table specifies that a user has a global **select** privilege, this can't be denied by an entry at the database, table, or column level.

The privileges for a column can be calculated as follows:

```
global privileges
OR (database privileges AND host privileges)
OR table privileges
OR column privileges
```

In most cases, you grant rights to a user at only one of the privilege levels, so life isn't normally as complicated as the previous list would indicate. The details of the privilege-checking procedure are presented in Section 4.2, General Security Issues and the MySQL Access Privilege System.

If you grant privileges for a user/hostname combination that does not exist in the mysql.user table, an entry is added and remains there until deleted with a DELETE command. In other words, GRANT may create user table entries, but REVOKE will not remove them; you must do that explicitly using DELETE.

In MySQL Version 3.22.12 or later, if a new user is created or if you have global grant privileges, the user's password will be set to the password specified by the IDENTIFIED BY clause, if one is given. If the user already had a password, it is replaced by the new one.

If you don't want to send the password in clear text you can use the PASSWORD option followed by a scrambled password from SQL function PASSWORD() or the C API function make_scrambled_password(char *to, const char *password).

Warning: if you create a new user but do not specify an IDENTIFIED BY clause, the user has no password. This is insecure.

Passwords can also be set with the SET PASSWORD command. See Section 5.5.6, SET Syntax.

If you grant privileges for a database, an entry in the mysql.db table is created if needed. When all privileges for the database have been removed with REVOKE, this entry is deleted.

If a user doesn't have any privileges on a table, the table is not displayed when the user requests a list of tables (for example, with a SHOW TABLES statement).

The WITH GRANT OPTION clause gives the user the ability to give to other users any privileges the user has at the specified privilege level. You should be careful to whom you give the **grant** privilege, as two users with different privileges may be able to join privileges!

MAX_QUERIES_PER_HOUR=# limits the number of queries the user can make during one hour. If # is 0, this means that there is no limit of the number of queries. This works by MySQL resetting a user-specific query counter to 0, after it has gone more than one hour since the counter started incrementing.

You cannot grant another user a privilege you don't have yourself; the **grant** privilege allows you to give away only those privileges you possess.

Be aware that when you grant a user the **grant** privilege at a particular privilege level, any privileges the user already possesses (or is given in the future!) at that level are also grantable by that user. Suppose you grant a user the **insert** privilege on a database. If you then grant the **select** privilege on the database and specify WITH GRANT OPTION, the user can give away not only the **select** privilege, but also **insert**. If you then grant the **update** privilege to the user on the database, the user can give away the **insert**, **select**, and **update**.

You should not grant **alter** privileges to a normal user. If you do that, the user can try to subvert the privilege system by renaming tables!

Note that if you are using table or column privileges for even one user, the server examines table and column privileges for all users and this will slow down MySQL a bit.

When mysqld starts, all privileges are read into memory. Database, table, and column privileges take effect at once, and user-level privileges take effect the next time the user connects. Modifications to the grant tables that you perform using GRANT or REVOKE are noticed by the server immediately. If you modify the grant tables manually (using INSERT, UPDATE, etc.), you should execute a FLUSH PRIVILEGES statement or run mysqladmin flush-privileges to tell the server to reload the grant tables. See Section 4.3.3, When Privilege Changes Take Effect.

The biggest differences between the ANSI SQL and MySQL versions of GRANT are:

- In MySQL privileges are given for a username + hostname combination and not only for a username.

- ANSI SQL doesn't have global or database-level privileges, and ANSI SQL doesn't support all privilege types that MySQL supports. MySQL doesn't support the ANSI SQL TRIGGER, EXECUTE, or UNDER privileges.

- ANSI SQL privileges are structured in a hierarchical manner. If you remove a user, all privileges the user has granted are revoked. In MySQL the granted privileges are not automatically revoked. You have to revoke these yourself if needed.

- In MySQL, if you have the **insert** privilege on only some of the columns in a table, you can execute INSERT statements on the table; the columns for which you don't have the **insert** privilege will be set to their default values. ANSI SQL requires you to have the **insert** privilege on all columns.

- When you drop a table in ANSI SQL, all privileges for the table are revoked. If you revoke a privilege in ANSI SQL, all privileges that were granted based on this privilege are also revoked. In MySQL, privileges can be dropped only with explicit REVOKE commands or by manipulating the MySQL grant tables.

For a description of using REQUIRE, see Section 4.3.8, Using Secure Connections.

4.3.2 MySQL Usernames and Passwords

There are several distinctions between the way usernames and passwords are used by MySQL and the way they are used by Unix or Windows:

- Usernames, as used by MySQL for authentication purposes, have nothing to do with Unix usernames (login names) or Windows usernames. Most MySQL clients by default try to log in using the current Unix user name as the MySQL username, but that is for convenience only. Client programs allow a different name to be specified with the -u or --user options. This means that you can't make a database secure in any way unless all MySQL usernames have passwords. Anyone may attempt to connect to the server using any name, and they will succeed if they specify any name that doesn't have a password.

- MySQL usernames can be up to 16 characters long; Unix usernames typically are limited to 8 characters.

- MySQL passwords have nothing to do with Unix passwords. There is no necessary connection between the password you use to log in to a Unix machine and the password you use to access a database on that machine.

- MySQL encrypts passwords using a different algorithm than the one used during the Unix login process. See the descriptions of the PASSWORD() and ENCRYPT() functions in Section 6.3.6.2, Miscellaneous functions. Note that even if the password is stored 'scrambled', and knowing your 'scrambled' password is enough to be able to connect to the MySQL server!

MySQL users and their privileges are normally created with the GRANT command. See Section 4.3.1, GRANT and REVOKE Syntax.

When you log in to a MySQL server with a command-line client you should specify the password with --password=your-password. See Section 4.2.8, Connecting to the MySQL server.

```
mysql --user=monty --password=guess database_name
```

If you want the client to prompt for a password, you should use --password without any argument:

```
mysql --user=monty --password database_name
```

or the short form:

```
mysql -u monty -p database_name
```

Note that in the last example the password is **not** 'database_name'.

If you want to use the -p option to supply a password you should do so like this:

```
mysql -u monty -pguess database_name
```

On some systems, the library call that MySQL uses to prompt for a password will automatically cut the password to 8 characters. Internally MySQL doesn't have any limit for the length of the password.

4.3.3 When Privilege Changes Take Effect

When mysqld starts, all grant table contents are read into memory and become effective at that point.

Modifications to the grant tables that you perform using GRANT, REVOKE, or SET PASSWORD are noticed by the server immediately.

If you modify the grant tables manually (using INSERT, UPDATE, etc.), you should execute a FLUSH PRIVILEGES statement or run mysqladmin flush-privileges or mysqladmin reload to tell the server to reload the grant tables. Otherwise, your changes will have *no effect* until you restart the server. If you change the grant tables manually but forget to reload the privileges, you will be wondering why your changes don't seem to make any difference!

When the server notices that the grant tables have been changed, existing client connections are affected as follows:

- Table and column privilege changes take effect with the client's next request.
- Database privilege changes take effect at the next USE db_name command.
- Global privilege changes and password changes take effect the next time the client connects.

4.3.4 Setting Up the Initial MySQL Privileges

After installing MySQL, you set up the initial access privileges by running `scripts/mysql_install_db`. See Section 2.3.1, Quick Installation Overview. The `mysql_install_db` script starts up the `mysqld` server, then initialises the grant tables to contain the following set of privileges:

- The MySQL `root` user is created as a superuser who can do anything. Connections must be made from the local host.

  Note: The initial `root` password is empty, so anyone can connect as `root` *without a password* and be granted all privileges.

- An anonymous user is created that can do anything with databases that have a name of `'test'` or starting with `'test_'`. Connections must be made from the local host. This means any local user can connect without a password and be treated as the anonymous user.

- Other privileges are denied. For example, normal users can't use `mysqladmin shutdown` or `mysqladmin processlist`.

Note: the default privileges are different for Windows. See Section 2.6.2.3, Running MySQL on Windows.

Because your installation is initially wide open, one of the first things you should do is specify a password for the MySQL `root` user. You can do this as follows (note that you specify the password using the `PASSWORD()` function):

```
shell> mysql -u root mysql
mysql> SET PASSWORD FOR root@localhost=PASSWORD('new_password');
```

If you know what you are doing, you can also directly manipulate the privilege tables:

```
shell> mysql -u root mysql
mysql> UPDATE user SET Password=PASSWORD('new_password')
    ->      WHERE user='root';
mysql> FLUSH PRIVILEGES;
```

Another way to set the password is by using the `mysqladmin` command:

```
shell> mysqladmin -u root password new_password
```

Only users with write/update access to the `mysql` database can change the password for others users. All normal users (not anonymous ones) can only change their own password with either of the preceding commands or with `SET PASSWORD=PASSWORD('new password')`.

Note that if you update the password in the `user` table directly using the first method, you must tell the server to re-read the grant tables (with `FLUSH PRIVILEGES`) because the change will go unnoticed otherwise.

Once the `root` password has been set, thereafter you must supply that password when you connect to the server as `root`.

You may wish to leave the `root` password blank so that you don't need to specify it while you perform additional setup or testing. However, be sure to set it before using your installation for any real production work.

See the `scripts/mysql_install_db` script to see how it sets up the default privileges. You can use this as a basis to see how to add other users.

If you want the initial privileges to be different than those just described, you can modify `mysql_install_db` before you run it.

To re-create the grant tables completely, remove all the `.frm`, `.MYI`, and `.MYD` files in the directory containing the `mysql` database. (This is the directory named `mysql` under the database directory, which is listed when you run `mysqld --help`.) Then run the `mysql_install_db` script, possibly after editing it first to have the privileges you want.

Note: for MySQL versions older than Version 3.22.10, you should not delete the `.frm` files. If you accidentally do this, you should copy them back from your MySQL distribution before running `mysql_install_db`.

4.3.5 Adding New Users to MySQL

You can add users in two different ways: by using GRANT statements or by manipulating the MySQL grant tables directly. The preferred method is to use GRANT statements because they are more concise and less error-prone. See Section 4.3.1, GRANT and REVOKE Syntax.

There are also a lot of contributed programs like `phpmyadmin` that can be used to create and administrate users. See Section 1.6.1, MySQL Portals.

The following examples show how to use the `mysql` client to set up new users. These examples assume that privileges are set up according to the defaults described in the previous section. This means that to make changes, you must be on the same machine where `mysqld` is running, you must connect as the MySQL `root` user, and the `root` user must have the **insert** privilege for the `mysql` database and the **reload** administrative privilege. Also, if you have changed the `root` user password, you must specify it for the following `mysql` commands.

You can add new users by issuing GRANT statements:

```
shell> mysql --user=root mysql
mysql> GRANT ALL PRIVILEGES ON *.* TO monty@localhost
    ->       IDENTIFIED BY 'some_pass' WITH GRANT OPTION;
mysql> GRANT ALL PRIVILEGES ON *.* TO monty@"%"
    ->       IDENTIFIED BY 'some_pass' WITH GRANT OPTION;
mysql> GRANT RELOAD,PROCESS ON *.* TO admin@localhost;
```

```
mysql> GRANT USAGE ON *.* TO dummy@localhost;
```

These GRANT statements set up three new users:

monty

> A full superuser who can connect to the server from anywhere, but who must use a password 'some_pass' to do so. Note that we must issue GRANT statements for both monty@localhost and monty@"%". If we don't add the entry with localhost, the anonymous user entry for localhost that is created by mysql_install_db will take precedence when we connect from the local host because it has a more specific Host field value and thus comes earlier in the user table sort order.

admin

> A user who can connect from localhost without a password and who is granted the **reload** and **process** administrative privileges. This allows the user to execute the mysqladmin reload, mysqladmin refresh, and mysqladmin flush-* commands, as well as mysqladmin processlist. No database-related privileges are granted. (They can be granted later by issuing additional GRANT statements.)

dummy

> A user who can connect without a password, but only from the local host. The global privileges are all set to 'N' —the **usage** privilege type allows you to create a user with no privileges. It is assumed that you will grant database-specific privileges later.

You can also add the same user access information directly by issuing INSERT statements and then telling the server to reload the grant tables:

```
shell> mysql --user=root mysql
mysql> INSERT INTO user VALUES('localhost','monty',PASSWORD('some_pass'),
    ->          'Y','Y','Y','Y','Y','Y','Y','Y','Y','Y','Y','Y','Y','Y');
mysql> INSERT INTO user VALUES('%','monty',PASSWORD('some_pass'),
    ->          'Y','Y','Y','Y','Y','Y','Y','Y','Y','Y','Y','Y','Y','Y');
mysql> INSERT INTO user SET Host='localhost',User='admin',
    ->          Reload_priv='Y', Process_priv='Y';
mysql> INSERT INTO user (Host,User,Password)
    ->          VALUES('localhost','dummy','');
mysql> FLUSH PRIVILEGES;
```

Depending on your MySQL version, you may have to use a different number of 'Y' values (versions prior to Version 3.22.11 had fewer privilege columns). For the admin user, the more readable extended INSERT syntax that is available starting with Version 3.22.11 is used.

Note that to set up a superuser, you need only create a user table entry with the privilege fields set to 'Y'. No db or host table entries are necessary.

The privilege columns in the user table were not set explicitly in the last INSERT statement (for the dummy user), so those columns are assigned the default value of 'N'. This is the same thing that GRANT USAGE does.

The following example adds a user custom who can connect from hosts localhost, server.domain, and whitehouse.gov. He wants to access the bankaccount database only from localhost, the expenses database only from whitehouse.gov, and the customer database from all three hosts. He wants to use the password stupid from all three hosts.

To set up this user's privileges using GRANT statements, run these commands:

```
shell> mysql --user=root mysql
mysql> GRANT SELECT,INSERT,UPDATE,DELETE,CREATE,DROP
    ->      ON bankaccount.*
    ->      TO custom@localhost
    ->      IDENTIFIED BY 'stupid';
mysql> GRANT SELECT,INSERT,UPDATE,DELETE,CREATE,DROP
    ->      ON expenses.*
    ->      TO custom@whitehouse.gov
    ->      IDENTIFIED BY 'stupid';
mysql> GRANT SELECT,INSERT,UPDATE,DELETE,CREATE,DROP
    ->      ON customer.*
    ->      TO custom@'%'
    ->      IDENTIFIED BY 'stupid';
```

We do this to grant statements for the user 'custom' because we want the give the user access to MySQL both from the local machine with Unix sockets and from the remote machine 'whitehouse.gov' over TCP/IP.

To set up the user's privileges by modifying the grant tables directly, run these commands (note the FLUSH PRIVILEGES at the end):

```
shell> mysql --user=root mysql
mysql> INSERT INTO user (Host,User,Password)
    -> VALUES('localhost','custom',PASSWORD('stupid'));
mysql> INSERT INTO user (Host,User,Password)
    -> VALUES('server.domain','custom',PASSWORD('stupid'));
mysql> INSERT INTO user (Host,User,Password)
    -> VALUES('whitehouse.gov','custom',PASSWORD('stupid'));
mysql> INSERT INTO db
    -> (Host,Db,User,Select_priv,Insert_priv,Update_priv,Delete_priv,
    ->  Create_priv,Drop_priv)
    -> VALUES
    -> ('localhost','bankaccount','custom','Y','Y','Y','Y','Y','Y');
mysql> INSERT INTO db
    -> (Host,Db,User,Select_priv,Insert_priv,Update_priv,Delete_priv,
    ->  Create_priv,Drop_priv)
    -> VALUES
    -> ('whitehouse.gov','expenses','custom','Y','Y','Y','Y','Y','Y');
mysql> INSERT INTO db
    -> (Host,Db,User,Select_priv,Insert_priv,Update_priv,Delete_priv,
    ->  Create_priv,Drop_priv)
    -> VALUES('%','customer','custom','Y','Y','Y','Y','Y','Y');
mysql> FLUSH PRIVILEGES;
```

The first three INSERT statements add user table entries that allow user custom to connect from the various hosts with the given password, but grant no permissions to him (all privileges are set to the default value of 'N'). The next three INSERT statements add db table entries that grant privileges to custom for the bankaccount, expenses, and customer databases, but only when accessed from the proper hosts. As usual, when the grant tables are modified directly, the server must be told to reload them (with FLUSH PRIVILEGES) so that the privilege changes take effect.

If you want to give a specific user access from any machine in a given domain, you can issue a GRANT statement like the following:

```
mysql> GRANT ...
    ->     ON *.*
    ->     TO myusername@"%.mydomainname.com"
    ->     IDENTIFIED BY 'mypassword';
```

To do the same thing by modifying the grant tables directly, do this:

```
mysql> INSERT INTO user VALUES ('%.mydomainname.com', 'myusername',
    ->                PASSWORD('mypassword'),...);
mysql> FLUSH PRIVILEGES;
```

You can also use xmysqladmin, mysql_webadmin, and even xmysql to insert, change, and update values in the grant tables. You can find these utilities in the Contrib directory of the MySQL web site (http://www.mysql.com/Downloads/Contrib/).

4.3.6 Setting Up Passwords

In most cases you should use GRANT to set up your users/passwords, so the following only applies for advanced users. See Section 4.3.1, GRANT and REVOKE Syntax.

The examples in the preceding sections illustrate an important principle: when you store a non-empty password using INSERT or UPDATE statements, you must use the PASSWORD() function to encrypt it. This is because the user table stores passwords in encrypted form, not as plaintext. If you forget that fact, you are likely to attempt to set passwords like this:

```
shell> mysql -u root mysql
mysql> INSERT INTO user (Host,User,Password)
    -> VALUES('%','jeffrey','biscuit');
mysql> FLUSH PRIVILEGES;
```

The result is that the plaintext value 'biscuit' is stored as the password in the user table. When the user jeffrey attempts to connect to the server using this password, the mysql client encrypts it with PASSWORD(), generates an authentication vector based on the **encrypted** password and a random number, obtained from the server, and sends the result to the server. The server uses the password value in the user table (that is **not the encrypted** value 'biscuit') to perform the same calculations, and compares results. The comparison fails and the server rejects the connection:

```
shell> mysql -u jeffrey -pbiscuit test
Access denied
```

Passwords must be encrypted when they are inserted in the user table, so the INSERT statement should have been specified like this instead:

```
mysql> INSERT INTO user (Host,User,Password)
    -> VALUES('%','jeffrey',PASSWORD('biscuit'));
```

You must also use the PASSWORD() function when you use SET PASSWORD statements:

```
mysql> SET PASSWORD FOR jeffrey@"%" = PASSWORD('biscuit');
```

If you set passwords using the GRANT ... IDENTIFIED BY statement or the mysqladmin password command, the PASSWORD() function is unnecessary. They both take care of encrypting the password for you, so you would specify a password of 'biscuit' like this:

```
mysql> GRANT USAGE ON *.* TO jeffrey@"%" IDENTIFIED BY 'biscuit';
```

or

```
shell> mysqladmin -u jeffrey password biscuit
```

Note: PASSWORD() does not perform password encryption in the same way that Unix passwords are encrypted. You should not assume that if your Unix password and your MySQL password are the same, that PASSWORD() will result in the same encrypted value as is stored in the Unix password file. See Section 4.3.2, MySQL Usernames and Passwords.

4.3.7 Keeping Your Password Secure

It is inadvisable to specify your password in a way that exposes it to discovery by other users. The methods you can use to specify your password when you run client programs are listed next, along with an assessment of the risks of each method:

- Never give a normal user access to the mysql.user table. Knowing the encrypted password for a user makes it possible to log in as this user. The passwords are only scrambled so that one shouldn't be able to see the real password you used (if you happen to use a similar password with your other applications).

- Use a -pyour_pass or --password=your_pass option on the command line. This is convenient but insecure because your password becomes visible to system status programs (such as ps) that may be invoked by other users to display command-lines. (MySQL clients typically overwrite the command-line argument with zeroes during their initialisation sequence, but there is still a brief interval during which the value is visible.)

- Use a -p or --password option (with no your_pass value specified). In this case, the client program solicits the password from the terminal:

  ```
  shell> mysql -u user_name -p
  Enter password: ********
  ```

  The * characters represent your password.

  It is more secure to enter your password this way than to specify it on the command-line because it is not visible to other users. However, this method of entering a password is suitable only for programs that you run interactively. If you want to invoke a client from a script that runs non-interactively, there is no opportunity to enter the password from the terminal. On some systems, you may even find that the first line of your script is read and interpreted (incorrectly) as your password!

- Store your password in a configuration file. For example, you can list your password in the [client] section of the .my.cnf file in your home directory:

  ```
  [client]
  password=your_pass
  ```

  If you store your password in .my.cnf, the file should not be group or world-readable or writable. Make sure the file's access mode is 400 or 600.

  Section 4.1.2, my.cnf Option Files.

- You can store your password in the MYSQL_PWD environment variable, but this method must be considered extremely insecure and should not be used. Some versions of ps include an option to display the environment of running processes; your password will be in plain sight for all to see if you set MYSQL_PWD. Even on systems without such a version of ps, it is unwise to assume there is no other method to observe process environments. See Appendix E.

All in all, the safest methods are to have the client program prompt for the password or to specify the password in a properly protected .my.cnf file.

4.3.8 Using Secure Connections

4.3.8.1 Basics

MySQL has support for SSL-encrypted connections. To understand how MySQL uses SSL, we need to explain some basics about SSL and X509. People who are already aware of it can skip this part.

By default, MySQL uses unencrypted connections between client and server. This means that someone could watch all your traffic and look at the data being sent/received. Actually, they could even change the data while it is in transit between client and server. Sometimes you need to move really secret data over public networks and in such a case using an unencrypted connection is unacceptable.

SSL is a protocol which uses different encryption algorithms to ensure that data which comes from public networks can be trusted. It has mechanisms to detect any change, loss, or replay of data. SSL also incorporates algorithms to recognise and provide identity verification using the X509 standard.

Encryption is the way to make any kind of data unreadable. In fact, today's practice requires many additional security elements from encryption algorithms. They should resist many kinds of known attacks like just messing with the order of encrypted messages or replaying data twice.

X509 is a standard that makes it possible to identify someone on the Internet. It is most commonly used in e-commerce applications. In basic terms, there should be some company called "Certificate Authority" which assigns electronic certificates to anyone who needs them. Certificates rely on asymmetric encryption algorithms that have two encryption keys—public and secret. A certificate owner can prove his identity by showing his certificate to another party. A certificate consists of his owner's public key. Any data encrypted with this public key can only be decrypted using the corresponding secret key, which is held by the owner of the certificate.

MySQL doesn't use encrypted connections by default because this would make the client/server protocol much slower. Any kind of additional functionality requires the computer to do additional work, and encrypting data is a CPU-intensive operation that requires time and can delay MySQL main tasks. By default MySQL is tuned to be fast as possible.

If you need more information about SSL/X509/encryption, you should use your favourite Internet search engine and search for keywords you are interested in.

4.3.8.2 Requirements

To get secure connections to work with MySQL you must do the following:

1. Install the openssl library. We have tested MySQL with openssl 0.9.6., which you can download from http://www.openssl.org/.

2. Configure MySQL with `--with-vio --with-openssl`.

3. If you are using an old MySQL installation, you have to update your `mysql.user` table with some new columns. You can do this by running the `mysql_fix_privilege_tables.sh` script.

4. You can check if a running mysqld server supports `openssl` by examining if `SHOW VARIABLES LIKE 'have_openssl'` returns `YES`.

4.3.8.3 GRANT **options**

MySQL can check X509 certificate attributes in addition to the normal username/password scheme. All the usual options are still required (username, password, IP address mask, database/table name).

There are different possibilities to limit connections:

- Without any SSL/X509 options, all kinds of encrypted/unencrypted connections are allowed if the username and password are valid.

- REQUIRE SSL option limits the server to allow only SSL-encrypted connections. Note that this option can be omitted if there are any ACL records that allow non-SSL connections.

  ```
  mysql> GRANT ALL PRIVILEGES ON test.* TO root@localhost
      -> IDENTIFIED BY "goodsecret" REQUIRE SSL;
  ```

- REQUIRE X509 means that the client should have a valid certificate but we do not care about the exact certificate, issuer, or subject. The only restriction is that it should be possible to verify its signature with one of the CA certificates.

  ```
  mysql> GRANT ALL PRIVILEGES ON test.* TO root@localhost
      -> IDENTIFIED BY "goodsecret" REQUIRE X509;
  ```

- REQUIRE ISSUER issuer makes the connection more restrictive: now the client must present a valid X509 certificate issued by CA "issuer". Using X509 certificates always implies encryption, so the option "SSL" is not neccessary anymore.

  ```
  mysql> GRANT ALL PRIVILEGES ON test.* TO root@localhost
      -> IDENTIFIED BY "goodsecret"
      -> REQUIRE ISSUER "C=FI, ST=Some-State, L=Helsinki,
      "> O=MySQL Finland AB, CN=Tonu Samuel/Email=tonu@mysql.com";
  ```

- REQUIRE SUBJECT subject requires clients to have a valid X509 certificate with the subject "subject" on it. If the client has a valid certificate but a different "subject," the connection is still not allowed.

  ```
  mysql> GRANT ALL PRIVILEGES ON test.* TO root@localhost
      -> IDENTIFIED BY "goodsecret"
      -> REQUIRE SUBJECT "C=EE, ST=Some-State, L=Tallinn,
      "> O=MySQL demo client certificate,
      "> CN=Tonu Samuel/Email=tonu@mysql.com";
  ```

- REQUIRE CIPHER cipher is needed to ensure that enough strong ciphers and keylengths will be used. SSL itself can be weak if old algorithms with short encryption keys are used. Using this option, we can ask for some exact cipher method to allow a connection.

  ```
  mysql> GRANT ALL PRIVILEGES ON test.* TO root@localhost
      -> IDENTIFIED BY "goodsecret"
      -> REQUIRE CIPHER "EDH-RSA-DES-CBC3-SHA";
  ```

You also can combine these options with each other like this:

```
mysql> GRANT ALL PRIVILEGES ON test.* TO root@localhost
    -> IDENTIFIED BY "goodsecret"
    -> REQUIRE SUBJECT "C=EE, ST=Some-State, L=Tallinn,
    "> O=MySQL demo client certificate,
    "> CN=Tonu Samuel/Email=tonu@mysql.com"
    -> AND ISSUER "C=FI, ST=Some-State, L=Helsinki,
    "> O=MySQL Finland AB, CN=Tonu Samuel/Email=tonu@mysql.com"
    -> AND CIPHER "EDH-RSA-DES-CBC3-SHA";
```

But you cannot use any option twice. Only different options can be mixed.

4.4 Disaster Prevention and Recovery

4.4.1 Database Backups

Because MySQL tables are stored as files, it is easy to do a backup. To get a consistent backup, do a LOCK TABLES on the relevant tables followed by FLUSH TABLES for the tables. See Section 6.7.2, LOCK TABLES/UNLOCK TABLES Syntax, and Section 4.5.3, FLUSH Syntax. You only need a read lock; this allows other threads to continue to query the tables while you are making a copy of the files in the database directory. The FLUSH TABLE is needed to ensure that all the active index pages are written to disk before you start the backup.

If you want to make a SQL-level backup of a table, you can use SELECT INTO OUTFILE or BACKUP TABLE. See Section 6.4.1, SELECT Syntax, and Section 4.4.2, BACKUP TABLE Syntax.

Another way to back up a database is to use the mysqldump program or the mysqlhot-copy script, and Section 4.8.5, mysqldump, Dumping Table Structure and Data. See Section 4.8.6, mysqlhotcopy, Copying MySQL Databases and Tables.

1. Do a full backup of your databases:

    ```
    shell> mysqldump --tab=/path/to/some/dir --opt --full
    ```

    or

    ```
    shell> mysqlhotcopy database /path/to/some/dir
    ```

    You can also simply copy all table files (*.frm, *.MYD, and *.MYI files) as long as the server isn't updating anything. The script mysqlhotcopy does use this method.

2. Stop mysqld if it's running, then start it with the --log-update[=file_name] option. See Section 4.9.3, The Update Log. The update log file(s) provide you with the information you need to replicate changes to the database that are made subsequent to the point at which you executed mysqldump.

If you have to restore something, try to recover your tables using REPAIR TABLE or myisamchk -r first. That should work in 99.9% of all cases. If myisamchk fails, try the following procedure (this will only work if you have started MySQL with --log-update; see Section 4.9.3, The Update Log):

1. Restore the original mysqldump backup.

2. Execute the following command to re-run the updates in the binary log:

    ```
    shell> mysqlbinlog hostname-bin.[0-9]* | mysql
    ```

    If you are using the update log you can use:

    ```
    shell> ls -1 -t -r hostname.[0-9]* | xargs cat | mysql
    ```

ls is used to get all the update log files in the right order.

You can also do selective backups with SELECT * INTO OUTFILE 'file_name' FROM tbl_name and restore with LOAD DATA INFILE 'file_name' REPLACE ... To avoid duplicate records, you need a PRIMARY KEY or a UNIQUE key in the table. The REPLACE keyword causes old records to be replaced with new ones when a new record duplicates an old record on a unique key value.

If you get performance problems in making backups on your system, you can solve this by setting up replication and do the backups on the slave instead of on the master. See Section 4.10.1, Introduction.

If you are using a Veritas filesystem, you can:

1. From a client (or Perl), execute: FLUSH TABLES WITH READ LOCK.

2. From another shell, execute: mount vxfs snapshot.

3. From the first client, execute: UNLOCK TABLES.

4. Copy files from snapshot.

5. Unmount snapshot.

4.4.2 BACKUP TABLE Syntax

```
BACKUP TABLE tbl_name[,tbl_name...] TO '/path/to/backup/directory'
```

Copy to the backup directory the minimum number of table files needed to restore the table. This currently only works for MyISAM tables. For MyISAM tables, copy .frm (definition) and .MYD (data) files. The index file can be rebuilt from those two.

Before using this command, please see Section 4.4.1, Database Backups.

During the backup, read locks will be held for each table, one at time, as they are being backed up. If you want to back up several tables as a snapshot, you must first issue LOCK TABLES obtaining a read lock for each table in the group.

The command returns a table with the following columns:

Column	Value
Table	Table name
Op	Always "backup"
Msg_type	One of status, error, info, or warning.
Msg_text	The message

Note that BACKUP TABLE is only available in MySQL Version 3.23.25 and later.

4.4.3 RESTORE TABLE Syntax

```
RESTORE TABLE tbl_name[,tbl_name...] FROM '/path/to/backup/directory'
```

Restores the table(s) from the backup that was made with BACKUP TABLE. Existing tables will not be overwritten—if you try to restore over an existing table, you will get an error. Restore will take longer than BACKUP due to the need to rebuild the index. The more keys you have, the longer it is going to take. Just as with BACKUP TABLE, RESTORE TABLE currently only works with MyISAM tables.

The command returns a table with the following columns:

Column	Value
Table	Table name
Op	Always "restore"
Msg_type	One of status, error, info, or warning
Msg_text	The message

4.4.4 CHECK TABLE Syntax

```
CHECK TABLE tbl_name[,tbl_name...] [option [option...]]

option = QUICK | FAST | MEDIUM | EXTENDED | CHANGED
```

CHECK TABLE only works on MyISAM and InnoDB tables. On MyISAM tables it's the same thing as running myisamchk -m table_name on the table.

If you don't specify any option, MEDIUM is used.

CHECK TABLE checks the table(s) for errors. For MyISAM tables the key statistics are updated. The command returns a table with the following columns:

Column	Value
Table	Table name
Op	Always "check"
Msg_type	One of status, error, info, or warning
Msg_text	The message

Note that you can get many rows of information for each checked table. The last row will be of Msg_type status and should normally be OK. If you don't get OK, or if you get Not checked, you should normally run a repair of the table. See Section 4.4.6, Using myisamchk for Table Maintenance and Crash Recovery. Not checked means that the table TYPE told MySQL that there wasn't any need to check the table.

The different check types stand for the following:

Type	Meaning
QUICK	Don't scan the rows to check for wrong links.
FAST	Only check tables which haven't been closed properly.
CHANGED	Only check tables which have been changed since the last check or haven't been closed properly.
MEDIUM	Scan rows to verify that deleted links are okay. This also calculates a key checksum for the rows and verifies this with a calculated checksum for the keys.
EXTENDED	Do a full key lookup for all keys for each row. This ensures that the table is 100% consistent, but will take a long time!

For dynamically sized MyISAM tables a started check will always do a MEDIUM check. For statically size rows we skip the row scan for QUICK and FAST as the rows are very seldom corrupted.

You can combine check options as in:

```
CHECK TABLE test_table FAST QUICK;
```

which would simply do a quick check on the table to see whether it was closed properly.

Note: In some case CHECK TABLE will change the table! This happens if the table is marked as 'corrupted' or 'not closed properly' but CHECK TABLE didn't find any problems in the table. In this case CHECK TABLE will mark the table as okay.

If a table is corrupted, it's most likely that the problem is in the indexes and not in the data part. All of the previous check types check the indexes thoroughly and should thus find most errors.

If you just want to check a table that you assume is okay, you should use no check options or the QUICK option. The latter should be used when you are in a hurry and can take the very small risk that QUICK didn't find an error in the data file. (In most cases MySQL should find, under normal usage, any error in the data file. If this happens then the table will be marked as 'corrupted', in which case the table can't be used until it's repaired.)

FAST and CHANGED are mostly intended to be used from a script (for example, to be executed from cron) if you want to check your table from time to time. In most cases FAST is preferred over CHANGED. (The only case when it isn't is when you have found a bug in the MyISAM code.)

EXTENDED is only to be used after you have run a normal check but still get strange errors from a table when MySQL tries to update a row or find a row by key (this is very unlikely if a normal check has succeeded!).

Some things reported by check table can't be corrected automatically:

- Found row where the auto_increment column has the value 0.

  This means that you have in the table a row where the AUTO_INCREMENT index column contains the value 0. (It's possible to create a row where the AUTO_INCREMENT column is 0 by explicitly setting the column to 0 with an UPDATE statement.)

  This isn't an error in itself, but could cause trouble if you decide to dump the table and restore it or do an ALTER TABLE on the table. In this case the AUTO_INCREMENT column will change value, according to the rules of AUTO_INCREMENT columns, which could cause problems like a duplicate key error.

  To get rid of the warning, just execute an UPDATE statement to set the column to some value other than 0.

4.4.5 REPAIR TABLE Syntax

```
REPAIR TABLE tbl_name[,tbl_name...] [QUICK] [EXTENDED] [USE_FRM]
```

REPAIR TABLE only works on MyISAM tables and is the same as running myisamchk -r table_name on the table.

Normally you should never have to run this command, but if disaster strikes you are very likely to get back all your data from a MyISAM table with REPAIR TABLE. If your tables get corrupted a lot you should try to find the reason for this! See Section A.4.1, What to Do if MySQL Keeps Crashing, and Section 7.1.3, MyISAM Table Problems.

REPAIR TABLE repairs a possible corrupted table. The command returns a table with the following columns:

Column	Value
Table	Table name
Op	Always "repair"
Msg_type	One of status, error, info, or warning
Msg_text	The message

Note that you can get many rows of information for each repaired table. The last row will be of Msg_type status and should normally be OK. If you don't get OK, you should try repairing the table with myisamchk -o, as REPAIR TABLE does not yet implement all the options of myisamchk. In the near future, we will make it more flexible.

If QUICK is given, MySQL will try to do a REPAIR of only the index tree.

If you use EXTENDED, MySQL will create the index row by row instead of creating one index at a time with sorting; this may be better than sorting on fixed-length keys if you have long char() keys that compress very well.

As of MySQL 4.0.2 there is a USE_FRM mode for REPAIR. Use it if the .MYI file is missing or if its header is corrupted. In this mode MySQL will re-create the table, using information from the .frm file. This kind of repair cannot be done with myisamchk.

4.4.6 Using myisamchk for Table Maintenance and Crash Recovery

Starting with MySQL Version 3.23.13, you can check MyISAM tables with the CHECK TABLE command. See Section 4.4.4, CHECK TABLE Syntax. You can repair tables with the REPAIR TABLE command. See Section 4.4.5, REPAIR TABLE Syntax.

To check/repair MyISAM tables (.MYI and .MYD) you should use the myisamchk utility. To check/repair ISAM tables (.ISM and .ISD) you should use the isamchk utility. See Chapter 7.

In the following text we will talk about myisamchk, but everything also applies to the old isamchk.

You can use the myisamchk utility to get information about your database tables, check and repair them, or optimise them. The following sections describe how to invoke myisamchk (including a description of its options), how to set up a table maintenance schedule, and how to use myisamchk to perform its various functions.

You can, in most cases, also use the command OPTIMIZE TABLES to optimise and repair tables, but this is not as fast or reliable (in case of real fatal errors) as myisamchk. On the other hand, OPTIMIZE TABLE is easier to use and you don't have to worry about flushing tables. See Section 4.5.1, OPTIMIZE TABLE Syntax.

Even though the repair in myisamchk is quite secure, it's always a good idea to make a backup *before* doing a repair (or anything that could make a lot of changes to a table).

4.4.6.1 myisamchk **invocation syntax**

myisamchk is invoked like this:

```
shell> myisamchk [options] tbl_name
```

The options specify what you want myisamchk to do. They are described next. (You can also get a list of options by invoking myisamchk --help.) With no options, myisamchk simply checks your table. To get more information or to tell myisamchk to take corrective action, specify options as described here and in the following sections.

tbl_name is the database table you want to check/repair. If you run myisamchk somewhere other than in the database directory, you must specify the path to the file because myisamchk has no idea where your database is located. Actually, myisamchk doesn't care whether the files you are working on are located in a database directory; you can copy the files that correspond to a database table into another location and perform recovery operations on them there.

You can name several tables on the myisamchk command-line if you wish. You can also specify a name as an index filename (with the .MYI suffix), which allows you to specify all tables in a directory by using the pattern *.MYI. For example, if you are in a database directory, you can check all the tables in the directory like this:

```
shell> myisamchk *.MYI
```

If you are not in the database directory, you can check all the tables there by specifying the path to the directory:

```
shell> myisamchk /path/to/database_dir/*.MYI
```

You can even check all tables in all databases by specifying a wildcard with the path to the MySQL data directory:

```
shell> myisamchk /path/to/datadir/*/*.MYI
```

The recommended way to quickly check all tables is:

```
myisamchk --silent --fast /path/to/datadir/*/*.MYI
isamchk --silent /path/to/datadir/*/*.ISM
```

If you want to check all tables and repair all tables that are corrupted, you can use the following line:

```
myisamchk --silent --force --fast --update-state -O key_buffer=64M \
          -O sort_buffer=64M -O read_buffer=1M -O write_buffer=1M \
          /path/to/datadir/*/*.MYI
isamchk --silent --force -O key_buffer=64M -O sort_buffer=64M \
```

```
-O read_buffer=1M -O write_buffer=1M /path/to/datadir/*/*.ISM
```

This assumes that you have more than 64M of free space.

Note that if you get an error like:

```
myisamchk: warning: 1 clients is using or hasn't closed the table properly
```

this means that you are trying to check a table that has been updated by the another program (like the mysqld server) that hasn't yet closed the file or that has died without closing the file properly.

If mysqld is running, you must force a sync/close of all tables with FLUSH TABLES and ensure that no one is using the tables while you are running myisamchk. In MySQL Version 3.23 the easiest way to avoid this problem is to use CHECK TABLE instead of myisamchk to check tables.

4.4.6.2 General options for myisamchk

myisamchk supports the following options.

-# or --debug=debug_options
: Output debug log. The debug_options string often is 'd:t:o,filename'.

-? or --help
: Display a help message and exit.

-O var=option, --set-variable var=option
: Set the value of a variable. The possible variables and their default values for myisamchk can be examined with myisamchk --help:

Variable	Value
key_buffer_size	523264
read_buffer_size	262136
write_buffer_size	262136
sort_buffer_size	2097144
sort_key_blocks	16
decode_bits	9

sort_buffer_size is used when the keys are repaired by sorting keys, which is the normal case when you use --recover.

key_buffer_size is used when you are checking the table with --extended-check or when the keys are repaired by inserting keys row by row into the table (like when doing normal inserts). Repairing through the key buffer is used in the following cases:

- If you use `--safe-recover`.

- If the temporary files needed to sort the keys would be more than twice as big as when creating the key file directly. This is often the case when you have big CHAR, VARCHAR, or TEXT keys as the sort needs to store the keys in their entirety during sorting. If you have lots of temporary space and you can force myisam-chk to repair by sorting you can use the `--sort-recover` option.

Reparing through the key buffer takes much less disk space than using sorting, but is also much slower.

If you want a faster repair, set the preceding variables to about 1/4 of your available memory. You can set both variables to big values, as only one of the preceding buffers will be used at a time.

`-s or --silent`
Silent mode. Write output only when errors occur. You can use `-s` twice (`-ss`) to make myisamchk very silent.

`-v or --verbose`
Verbose mode. Print more information. This can be used with `-d` and `-e`. Use `-v` multiple times (`-vv`, `-vvv`) for more verbosity!

`-V or --version`
Print the myisamchk version and exit.

`-w or, --wait`
Instead of giving an error if the table is locked, wait until the table is unlocked before continuing. Note that if you are running mysqld on the table with `--skip-lock-ing`, the table can only be locked by another myisamchk command.

4.4.6.3 Check options for myisamchk

`-c or --check`
Check table for errors. This is the default operation if you are not giving myisamchk any options that override this.

`-e or --extend-check`
Check the table very thoroughly (which is quite slow if you have many indexes). This option should only be used in extreme cases. Normally, myisamchk or myisam-chk `--medium-check` should, in most cases, be able to find out if there are any errors in the table.

If you are using `--extended-check` and have much memory, you should increase the value of key_buffer_size a lot!

`-F or --fast`
> Check only tables that haven't been closed properly.

`-C or --check-only-changed`
> Check only tables that have changed since the last check.

`-f or --force`
> Restart myisamchk with `-r` (repair) on the table, if myisamchk finds any errors in the table.

`-i or --information`
> Print informational statistics about the table that is checked.

`-m or --medium-check`
> Faster than extended-check, but only finds 99.99% of all errors. Should, however, be good enough for most cases.

`-U or --update-state`
> Store in the .MYI file when the table was checked and if the table crashed. This should be used to get the full benefit of the `--check-only-changed` option, but you shouldn't use this option if the mysqld server is using the table and you are running mysqld with `--skip-locking`.

`-T or --read-only`
> Don't mark table as checked. This is useful if you use myisamchk to check a table that is in use by some other application that doesn't use locking (like mysqld `--skip-locking`).

4.4.6.4 Repair options for myisamchk

The following options are used if you start myisamchk with `-r` or `-o`:

`-D # or --data-file-length=#`
> Max length of data file (when re-creating data file when it's "full").

`-e or --extend-check`
> Try to recover every possible row from the data file. Normally this will also find a lot of garbage rows. Don't use this option if you are not totally desperate.

`-f or --force`
> Overwrite old temporary files (table_name.TMD) instead of aborting.

`-k # or keys-used=#`
> If you are using ISAM, this option tells the ISAM table handler to update only the first # indexes. If you are using MyISAM, this option tells which keys to use, where each binary bit stands for one key (first key is bit 0). This can be used to get faster inserts! Deactivated indexes can be reactivated by using myisamchk `-r`. keys.

-l or --no-symlinks
>   Do not follow symbolic links. Normally myisamchk repairs the table a symlink
>   points at. This option doesn't exist in MySQL 4.0, as MySQL 4.0 will not remove
>   symlinks during repair.

-r or --recover
>   Can fix almost anything except unique keys that aren't unique (which is an extremely
>   unlikely error with ISAM/MyISAM tables). If you want to recover a table, this is the
>   option to try first. Only if myisamchk reports that the table can't be recovered by -r,
>   you should then try -o. (Note that in the unlikely case that -r fails, the data file is
>   still intact.) If you have lots of memory, you should increase the size of
>   sort_buffer_size!

-o or --safe-recover
>   Uses an old recovery method (reads through all rows in order and updates all index
>   trees based on the found rows); this is an order of magnitude slower than -r, but can
>   handle a couple of very unlikely cases that -r cannot handle. This recovery method
>   also uses much less disk space than -r. Normally one should always first repair with
>   -r, and only if this fails use -o.
>
>   If you have lots of memory, you should increase the size of key_buffer_size!

-n or --sort-recover
>   Force myisamchk to use sorting to resolve the keys even if the temporary files
>   should be very big.

--character-sets-dir= . . .
>   Directory where character sets are stored.

--set-character-set=name
>   Change the character set used by the index.

-t or --tmpdir=path
>   Path for storing temporary files. If this is not set, myisamchk will use the environ-
>   ment variable TMPDIR for this.

-q or --quick
>   Faster repair by not modifying the data file. One can give a second -q to force
>   myisamchk to modify the original data file in case of duplicate keys.

-u or --unpack
>   Unpack file packed with myisampack.

4.4.6.5 Other options for myisamchk

Other actions that myisamchk can do, besides repair and check tables:

`-a` or `--analyze`

Analyse the distribution of keys. This improves join performance by enabling the join optimiser to better choose in which order it should join the tables and which keys it should use: `myisamchk --describe --verbose table_name`' or using `SHOW KEYS` in MySQL.

`-d` or `--description`

Prints some information about the table.

`-A` or `--set-auto-increment[=value]`

Force `AUTO_INCREMENT` to start at this or a higher value. If no value is given, this sets the next `AUTO_INCREMENT` value to the highest-used value for the auto key + 1.

`-S` or `--sort-index`

Sort the index tree blocks in high-low order. This will optimise seeks and will make table scanning by key faster.

`-R` or `--sort-records=#`

Sorts records according to an index. This makes your data much more localised and may speed up ranged `SELECT` and `ORDER BY` operations on this index. (It may be very slow to do a sort the first time!) To find out a table's index numbers, use `SHOW INDEX`, which shows a table's indexes in the same order that `myisamchk` sees them. Indexes are numbered beginning with 1.

4.4.6.6 `myisamchk` memory usage

Memory allocation is important when you run `myisamchk`. `myisamchk` uses no more memory than you specify with the `-O` options. If you are going to use `myisamchk` on very large files, you should first decide how much memory you want it to use. The default is to use only about 3M to fix things. By using larger values, you can get `myisamchk` to operate faster. For example, if you have more than 32M RAM, you could use options such as these (in addition to any other options you might specify):

```
shell> myisamchk -O sort=16M -O key=16M -O read=1M -O write=1M ...
```

Using `-O sort=16M` should probably be enough for most cases.

Be aware that `myisamchk` uses temporary files in `TMPDIR`. If `TMPDIR` points to a memory filesystem, you may easily get "out of memory" errors. If this happens, set `TMPDIR` to point at some directory with more space and restart `myisamchk`.

When repairing, `myisamchk` will also need a lot of disk space:

- Double the size of the record file (the original one and a copy). This space is not needed if one does a repair with `--quick`, as in this case only the index file will be re-created. This space is needed on the same disk as the original record file!

- Space for the new index file that replaces the old one. The old index file is truncated at start, so one usually ignores this space. This space is needed on the same disk as the original index file!

- When using `--recover` or `--sort-recover` (but not when using `--safe-recover`), you will need space for a sort buffer for: `(largest_key + row_pointer_length)*number_of_rows * 2`. You can check the length of the keys and the row_pointer_length with `myisamchk -dv table`. This space is allocated on the temporary disk (specified by `TMPDIR` or `--tmpdir=#`).

If you have a problem with disk space during repair, you can try to use `--safe-recover` instead of `--recover`.

4.4.6.7 Using `myisamchk` for crash recovery

If you run `mysqld` with `--skip-locking` (which is the default on some systems, like Linux), you can't reliably use `myisamchk` to check a table when `mysqld` is using the same table. If you can be sure that no one is accessing the tables through `mysqld` while you run `myisamchk`, you only have to do `mysqladmin flush-tables` before you start checking the tables. If you can't guarantee this, you must take down `mysqld` while you check the tables. If you run `myisamchk` while `mysqld` is updating the tables, you may get a warning that a table is corrupt even if it isn't.

If you are not using `--skip-locking`, you can use `myisamchk` to check tables at any time. While you do this, all clients that try to update the table will wait until `myisamchk` is ready before continuing.

If you use `myisamchk` to repair or optimise tables, you **must** always ensure that the `mysqld` server is not using the table (this also applies if you are using `--skip-locking`). If you don't take down `mysqld` you should at least do a `mysqladmin flush-tables` before you run `myisamchk`. Your tables **may be corrupted** if the server and `myisamchk` access the tables simultaneously.

This chapter describes how to check for and deal with data corruption in MySQL databases. If your tables get corrupted frequently you should try to find the reason for this! See Section A.4.1, What to Do if MySQL Keeps Crashing.

The `MyISAM` table section contains reasons why a table could be corrupted. See Section 7.1.3, MyISAM Table Problems.

When performing crash recovery, it is important to understand that each table `tbl_name` in a database corresponds to three files in the database directory:

File	Purpose
tbl_name.frm	Table definition (form) file
tbl_name.MYD	Datafile
tbl_name.MYI	Index file

Each of these three file types is subject to corruption in various ways, but problems occur most often in data files and index files.

myisamchk works by creating a copy of the .MYD (data) file row by row. It ends the repair stage by removing the old .MYD file and renaming the new file to the original file-name. If you use --quick, myisamchk does not create a temporary .MYD file, but instead assumes that the .MYD file is correct and only generates a new index file without touching the .MYD file. This is safe because myisamchk automatically detects if the .MYD file is corrupt and aborts the repair in this case. You can also give two --quick options to myisamchk. In this case, myisamchk does not abort on some errors (like duplicate key) but instead tries to resolve them by modifying the .MYD file. Normally the use of two --quick options is useful only if you have too little free disk space to perform a normal repair. In this case you should at least make a backup before running myisamchk.

4.4.6.8 How to check tables for errors

To check a MyISAM table, use the following commands:

myisamchk tbl_name

> This finds 99.99% of all errors. What it can't find is corruption that involves **only** the data file (which is very unusual). If you want to check a table, you should normally run myisamchk without options or with either the -s or --silent option.

myisamchk -m tbl_name

> This finds 99.999% of all errors. It first checks all index entries for errors and then it reads through all rows. It calculates a checksum for all keys in the rows and verifies that the checksum matches the checksum for the keys in the index tree.

myisamchk -e tbl_name

> This does a complete and thorough check of all data (-e means "extended check"). It does a check-read of every key for each row to verify that they indeed point to the correct row. This may take a long time on a big table with many keys. myisamchk will normally stop after the first error it finds. If you want to obtain more informa-tion, you can add the --verbose (-v) option. This causes myisamchk to keep going, up through a maximum of 20 errors. In normal usage, a simple myisamchk (with no arguments other than the table name) is sufficient.

myisamchk -e -i tbl_name

> Like the previous command, but the -i option tells myisamchk to print some infor-mational statistics, too.

4.4.6.9 How to repair tables

In the following section we only talk about using `myisamchk` on `MyISAM` tables (extensions `.MYI` and `.MYD`). If you are using `ISAM` tables (extensions `.ISM` and `.ISD`), you should use `isamchk` instead.

Starting with MySQL Version 3.23.14, you can repair MyISAM tables with the `REPAIR TABLE` command. See Section 4.4.5, `REPAIR TABLE` Syntax.

The symptoms of a corrupted table include queries that abort unexpectedly and observable errors such as these:

- `tbl_name.frm` is locked against change.
- Can't find file `tbl_name.MYI` (Errcode: ###).
- Unexpected end of file.
- Record file is crashed.
- Got error ### from table handler.

  To get more information about the error you can run `perror ###`. Here are the most common errors that indicate a problem with the table:

  ```
  shell> perror 126 127 132 134 135 136 141 144 145
  126 = Index file is crashed / Wrong file format
  127 = Record-file is crashed
  132 = Old database file
  134 = Record was already deleted (or record file crashed)
  135 = No more room in record file
  136 = No more room in index file
  141 = Duplicate unique key or constraint on write or update
  144 = Table is crashed and last repair failed
  145 = Table was marked as crashed and should be repaired
  ```

Note that error 135, No more room in record file, is not an error that can be fixed by a simple repair. In this case you have to do:

```
ALTER TABLE table MAX_ROWS=xxx AVG_ROW_LENGTH=yyy;
```

In the other cases, you must repair your tables. `myisamchk` can usually detect and fix most things that go wrong.

The repair process involves up to four stages, described next. Before you begin, you should `cd` to the database directory and check the permissions of the table files. Make sure they are readable by the Unix user that `mysqld` runs as (and to you because you need to access the files you are checking). If it turns out you need to modify files, they must also be writable by you.

If you are using MySQL Versions 3.23.16 and above, you can (and should) use the `CHECK` and `REPAIR` commands to check and repair `MyISAM` tables. See Section 4.4.4, `CHECK TABLE` Syntax, and Section 4.4.5, `REPAIR TABLE` Syntax.

The manual section about table maintenance includes the options to isamchk/myisamchk. See Section 4.4.6, Using myisamchk for Table Maintenance and Crash Recovery.

The following section is for the cases where the previous command fails or if you want to use the extended features that isamchk/myisamchk provides.

If you are going to repair a table from the command-line, you must first take down the mysqld server. Note that when you do mysqladmin shutdown on a remote server, the mysqld server will still be alive for a while after mysqladmin returns, until all queries are stopped and all keys have been flushed to disk.

Stage 1: Checking your tables

Run myisamchk *.MYI or myisamchk -e *.MYI if you have more time. Use the -s (silent) option to suppress unnecessary information.

If the mysqld server is done you should use the --update option to tell myisamchk to mark the table as 'checked'.

You have to repair only those tables for which myisamchk announces an error. For such tables, proceed to Stage 2.

If you get weird errors when checking (such as out of memory errors), or if myisamchk crashes, go to Stage 3.

Stage 2: Easy safe repair

Note: If you want repairing to go much faster, you should add: -O sort_buffer=# -O key_buffer=# (where # is about 1/4 of the available memory) to all isamchk/myisamchk commands.

First, try myisamchk -r -q tbl_name (-r -q means "quick recovery mode"). This will attempt to repair the index file without touching the data file. If the data file contains everything that it should and the delete links point at the correct locations within the data file, this should work, and the table is fixed. Start repairing the next table. Otherwise, use the following procedure:

1.   Make a backup of the data file before continuing.

2.   Use myisamchk -r tbl_name (-r means "recovery mode"). This will remove incorrect records and deleted records from the data file and reconstruct the index file.

3.   If the preceding step fails, use myisamchk --safe-recover tbl_name. Safe recovery mode uses an old recovery method that handles a few cases that regular recovery mode doesn't (but is slower).

If you get weird errors when repairing (such as out of memory errors), or if myisamchk crashes, go to Stage 3.

Stage 3: Difficult repair

You should only reach this stage if the first 16K block in the index file is destroyed or contains incorrect information, or if the index file is missing. In this case, it's necessary to create a new index file. Do so as follows:

1. Move the data file to some safe place.

2. Use the table description file to create new (empty) data and index files:

    ```
    shell> mysql db_name
    mysql> SET AUTOCOMMIT=1;
    mysql> TRUNCATE TABLE table_name;
    mysql> quit
    ```

    If your SQL version doesn't have TRUNCATE TABLE, use DELETE FROM table_name instead.

3. Copy the old data file back onto the newly created data file. (Don't just move the old file back onto the new file; you want to retain a copy in case something goes wrong.)

Go back to Stage 2. myisamchk -r -q should work now. (This shouldn't be an endless loop.)

As of MySQL 4.0.2 you can also use REPAIR . . . USE_FRM which performs the whole procedure automatically.

Stage 4: Very difficult repair

You should reach this stage only if the description file has also crashed. That should never happen, because the description file isn't changed after the table is created:

1. Restore the description file from a backup and go back to Stage 3. You can also restore the index file and go back to Stage 2. In the latter case, you should start with myisamchk -r.

2. If you don't have a backup but know exactly how the table was created, create a copy of the table in another database. Remove the new data file, then move the description and index files from the other database to your crashed database. This gives you new description and index files, but leaves the data file alone. Go back to Stage 2 and attempt to reconstruct the index file.

4.4.6.10 Table optimisation

To coalesce fragmented records and eliminate wasted space resulting from deleting or updating records, run myisamchk in recovery mode:

```
shell> myisamchk -r tbl_name
```

You can optimise a table in the same way using the SQL OPTIMIZE TABLE statement. OPTIMIZE TABLE does a repair of the table and a key analysis, and sorts the index tree to give faster key lookups. There is also no possibility of unwanted interaction between a utility and the server because the server does all the work when you use OPTIMIZE TABLE. See Section 4.5.1, OPTIMIZE TABLE Syntax.

myisamchk also has a number of other options you can use to improve the performance of a table:

- -S, --sort-index
- -R index_num, --sort-records=index_num
- -a, --analyze

For a full description of the option, see Section 4.4.6.1, myisamchk invocation syntax.

4.4.7 Setting Up a Table Maintenance Regimen

Starting with MySQL Version 3.23.13, you can check MyISAM tables with the CHECK TABLE command. See Section 4.4.4, CHECK TABLE Syntax. You can repair tables with the REPAIR TABLE command. See Section 4.4.5, REPAIR TABLE Syntax.

It is a good idea to perform table checks on a regular basis rather than waiting for problems to occur. For maintenance purposes, you can use myisamchk -s to check tables. The -s option (short for --silent) causes myisamchk to run in silent mode, printing messages only when errors occur.

It's also a good idea to check tables when the server starts up. For example, whenever the machine has done a reboot in the middle of an update, you usually need to check all the tables that could have been affected. (This is an "expected crashed table".) You could add a test to safe_mysqld that runs myisamchk to check all tables that have been modified during the last 24 hours if there is an old .pid (process ID) file left after a reboot. (The .pid file is created by mysqld when it starts up and is removed when it terminates normally. The presence of a .pid file at system startup time indicates that mysqld terminated abnormally.)

An even better test would be to check any table whose last-modified time is more recent than that of the .pid file.

You should also check your tables regularly during normal system operation. At MySQL AB, we run a cron job to check all our important tables once a week, using a line like this in a crontab file:

```
35 0 * * 0 /path/to/myisamchk --fast --silent /path/to/datadir/*/*.MYI
```

This prints out information about crashed tables so that we can examine and repair them when needed.

As we haven't had any unexpectedly crashed tables (tables that become corrupted for reasons other than hardware trouble) for a couple of years now (this is really true), once a week is more than enough for us.

We recommend that to start with, you execute `myisamchk -s` each night on all tables that have been updated during the last 24 hours, until you come to trust MySQL as much as we do.

Normally you don't need to maintain MySQL tables that much. If you are changing tables with dynamic-size rows (tables with VARCHAR, BLOB, or TEXT columns) or have tables with many deleted rows, you may want to from time to time (once a month?) defragment/reclaim space from the tables.

You can do this by using OPTIMIZE TABLE on the tables in question. If you can take the `mysqld` server down for a while do:

```
isamchk -r --silent --sort-index -O sort_buffer_size=16M */*.ISM
myisamchk -r --silent --sort-index  -O sort_buffer_size=16M */*.MYI
```

4.4.8 Getting Information About a Table

To get a description of a table or statistics about it, use the commands shown here. We explain some of the information in more detail later:

myisamchk -d tbl_name

Runs `myisamchk` in "describe mode" to produce a description of your table. If you start MySQL server using the `--skip-locking` option, `myisamchk` may report an error for a table that is updated while it runs. However, because `myisamchk` doesn't change the table in describe mode, there isn't any risk of destroying data.

myisamchk -d -v tbl_name

To produce more information about what `myisamchk` is doing, add `-v` to tell it to run in verbose mode.

myisamchk -eis tbl_name

Shows only the most important information from a table. It is slow because it must read the whole table.

myisamchk -eiv tbl_name

This is like `-eis`, but tells you what is being done.

Example of `myisamchk -d` output:

```
MyISAM file:    company.MYI
Record format:  Fixed length
Data records:   1403698  Deleted blocks:        0
Recordlength:   226

table description:
Key Start Len Index   Type
1   2     8   unique  double
2   15    10  multip. text packed stripped
```

```
3  219   8   multip. double
4   63  10   multip. text packed stripped
5  167   2   multip. unsigned short
6  177   4   multip. unsigned long
7  155   4   multip. text
8  138   4   multip. unsigned long
9  177   4   multip. unsigned long
   193   1           text
```

Example of myisamchk -d -v output:

```
MyISAM file:          company
Record format:        Fixed length
File-version:         1
Creation time:        1999-10-30 12:12:51
Recover time:         1999-10-31 19:13:01
Status:               checked
Data records:               1403698  Deleted blocks:        0
Datafile parts:             1403698  Deleted data:          0
Datafilepointer (bytes):          3  Keyfile pointer (bytes):   3
Max data file length: 3791650815  Max keyfile length: 4294967294
Recordlength:               226
```

```
table description:
Key Start Len Index  Type                     Rec/key    Root Blocksize
1    2   8  unique  double                        1 15845376     1024
2   15  10  multip. text packed stripped          2 25062400     1024
3  219   8  multip. double                       73 40907776     1024
4   63  10  multip. text packed stripped          5 48097280     1024
5  167   2  multip. unsigned short             4840 55200768     1024
6  177   4  multip. unsigned long              1346 65145856     1024
7  155   4  multip. text                       4995 75090944     1024
8  138   4  multip. unsigned long                87 85036032     1024
9  177   4  multip. unsigned long               178 96481280     1024
   193   1          text
```

Example of myisamchk -eis output:

```
Checking MyISAM file: company
Key:  1: Keyblocks used: 97%  Packed:   0%  Max levels:  4
Key:  2: Keyblocks used: 98%  Packed:  50%  Max levels:  4
Key:  3: Keyblocks used: 97%  Packed:   0%  Max levels:  4
Key:  4: Keyblocks used: 99%  Packed:  60%  Max levels:  3
Key:  5: Keyblocks used: 99%  Packed:   0%  Max levels:  3
Key:  6: Keyblocks used: 99%  Packed:   0%  Max levels:  3
Key:  7: Keyblocks used: 99%  Packed:   0%  Max levels:  3
Key:  8: Keyblocks used: 99%  Packed:   0%  Max levels:  3
Key:  9: Keyblocks used: 98%  Packed:   0%  Max levels:  4
Total:   Keyblocks used: 98%  Packed:  17%

Records:              1403698   M.recordlength:       226
Packed:                    0%
Recordspace used:        100%   Empty space:           0%
Blocks/Record:         1.00
Record blocks:        1403698   Delete blocks:         0
```

```
Recorddata:      317235748    Deleted data:        0
Lost space:              0    Linkdata:            0


User time 1626.51, System time 232.36
Maximum resident set size 0, Integral resident set size 0
Non physical pagefaults 0, Physical pagefaults 627, Swaps 0
Blocks in 0 out 0, Messages in 0 out 0, Signals 0
Voluntary context switches 639, Involuntary context switches 28966
```

Example of myisamchk -eiv output:

```
Checking MyISAM file: company
Data records: 1403698    Deleted blocks:          0
- check file-size
- check delete-chain
block_size 1024:
index  1:
index  2:
index  3:
index  4:
index  5:
index  6:
index  7:
index  8:
index  9:
No recordlinks
- check index reference
- check data record references index: 1
Key:  1:  Keyblocks used: 97%  Packed:     0% Max levels:  4
- check data record references index: 2
Key:  2:  Keyblocks used: 98%  Packed:    50% Max levels:  4
- check data record references index: 3
Key:  3:  Keyblocks used: 97%  Packed:     0% Max levels:  4
- check data record references index: 4
Key:  4:  Keyblocks used: 99%  Packed:    60% Max levels:  3
- check data record references index: 5
Key:  5:  Keyblocks used: 99%  Packed:     0% Max levels:  3
- check data record references index: 6
Key:  6:  Keyblocks used: 99%  Packed:     0% Max levels:  3
- check data record references index: 7
Key:  7:  Keyblocks used: 99%  Packed:     0% Max levels:  3
- check data record references index: 8
Key:  8:  Keyblocks used: 99%  Packed:     0% Max levels:  3
- check data record references index: 9
Key:  9:  Keyblocks used: 98%  Packed:     0% Max levels:  4
Total:    Keyblocks used:  9%  Packed:    17%

- check records and index references
[LOTS OF ROW NUMBERS DELETED]

Records:          1403698    M.recordlength:     226  Packed:         0%
Recordspace used:    100%    Empty space:         0% Blocks/Record: 1.00
Record blocks:    1403698    Delete blocks:        0
Recorddata:      317235748    Deleted data:         0
```

```
Lost space:            0   Linkdata:             0

User time 1639.63, System time 251.61
Maximum resident set size 0, Integral resident set size 0
Non physical pagefaults 0, Physical pagefaults 10580, Swaps 0
Blocks in 4 out 0, Messages in 0 out 0, Signals 0
Voluntary context switches 10604, Involuntary context switches 122798
```

Here are the sizes of the data and index files for the table used in the preceding examples:

```
-rw-rw-r--  1 monty   tcx    317235748 Jan 12 17:30 company.MYD
-rw-rw-r--  1 davida  tcx     96482304 Jan 12 18:35 company.MYM
```

Explanations for the types of information myisamchk produces are given here. The "keyfile" is the index file. "Record" and "row" are synonymous:

ISAM file

Name of the ISAM (index) file.

Isam-version

Version of ISAM format. Currently always 2.

Creation time

When the data file was created.

Recover time

When the index/data file was last reconstructed.

Data records

How many records are in the table.

Deleted blocks

How many deleted blocks still have reserved space. You can optimise your table to minimise this space. See Section 4.4.6.10, Table optimisation.

Data file parts

For dynamic record format, this indicates how many data blocks there are. For an optimised table without fragmented records, this is the same as Data records.

Deleted data

How many bytes of non-reclaimed deleted data there are. You can optimise your table to minimise this space. See Section 4.4.6.10, Table optimisation.

Data file pointer

The size of the data file pointer, in bytes. It is usually 2, 3, 4, or 5 bytes. Most tables manage with 2 bytes, but this cannot be controlled from MySQL yet. For fixed tables, this is a record address. For dynamic tables, this is a byte address.

Keyfile pointer

The size of the index file pointer, in bytes. It is usually 1, 2, or 3 bytes. Most tables manage with 2 bytes, but this is calculated automatically by MySQL. It is always a block address.

Max data file length

    How long the table's data file (`.MYD` file) can become, in bytes.

Max keyfile length

    How long the table's keyfile (`.MYI` file) can become, in bytes.

Recordlength

    How much space each record takes, in bytes.

Record format

    The format used to store table rows. The preceding examples use `Fixed length`. Other possible values are `Compressed` and `Packed`.

Table description

    A list of all keys in the table. For each key, some low-level information is presented:

    Key

        This key's number.

    Start

        Where in the record this index part starts.

    Len

        How long this index part is. For packed numbers, this should always be the full length of the column. For strings, it may be shorter than the full length of the indexed column because you can index a prefix of a string column.

    Index

        `unique` or `multip` (multiple). Indicates whether one value can exist multiple times in this index.

    Type

        What datatype this index part has. This is an ISAM datatype with the options `packed`, `stripped` or `empty`.

    Root

        Address of the root index block.

    Blocksize

        The size of each index block. By default this is 1024, but the value may be changed at compile time.

    Rec/key

        This is a statistical value used by the optimiser. It tells how many records there are per value for this key. A unique key always has a value of 1. This may be updated after a table is loaded (or greatly changed) with `myisamchk -a`. If this is not updated at all, a default value of 30 is given.

    In the first preceding example, the 9th key is a multi-part key with two parts.

Keyblocks used

What percentage of the keyblocks are used. Because the table used in the examples had just been reorganised with myisamchk, the values are very high (very near the theoretical maximum).

Packed

MySQL tries to pack keys with a common suffix. This can only be used for CHAR/VARCHAR/DECIMAL keys. For long strings like names, this can significantly reduce the space used. In the third example, the fourth key is 10 characters long and a 60% reduction in space is achieved.

Max levels

How deep the B-tree for this key is. Large tables with long keys get high values.

Records

How many rows are in the table.

M.recordlength

The average record length. For tables with fixed-length records, this is the exact record length.

Packed

MySQL strips spaces from the end of strings. The Packed value indicates the percentage of savings achieved by doing this.

Recordspace used

What percentage of the data file is used.

Empty space

What percentage of the data file is unused.

Blocks/Record

Average number of blocks per record (that is, how many links a fragmented record is composed of). This is always 1.0 for fixed-format tables. This value should stay as close to 1.0 as possible. If it gets too big, you can reorganise the table with myisamchk. See Section 4.4.6.10, Table optimisation.

Recordblocks

How many blocks (links) are used. For fixed format, this is the same as the number of records.

Deleteblocks

How many blocks (links) are deleted.

Recorddata

How many bytes in the data file are used.

Deleted data

How many bytes in the data file are deleted (unused).

Lost space

If a record is updated to a shorter length, some space is lost. This is the sum of all such losses, in bytes.

Linkdata

When the dynamic table format is used, record fragments are linked with pointers (4 to 7 bytes each). `Linkdata` is the sum of the amount of storage used by all such pointers.

If a table has been compressed with `myisampack`, `myisamchk -d` prints additional information about each table column. See Section 4.7.4, `myisampack`, the MySQL Compressed Read-Only Table Generator, for an example of this information and a description of what it means.

4.5 Database Administration Language Reference

4.5.1 OPTIMIZE TABLE Syntax

```
OPTIMIZE TABLE tbl_name[,tbl_name]...
```

`OPTIMIZE TABLE` should be used if you have deleted a large part of a table or if you have made many changes to a table with variable-length rows (tables that have `VARCHAR`, `BLOB`, or `TEXT` columns). Deleted records are maintained in a linked list and subsequent `INSERT` operations reuse old record positions. You can use `OPTIMIZE TABLE` to reclaim the unused space and to defragment the data file.

For the moment, `OPTIMIZE TABLE` only works on `MyISAM` and `BDB` tables. For `BDB` tables, `OPTIMIZE TABLE` is currently mapped to `ANALYZE TABLE`. See Section 4.5.2, `ANALYZE TABLE` Syntax.

You can get `OPTIMIZE TABLE` to work on other table types by starting `mysqld` with `--skip-new` or `--safe-mode`, but in this case `OPTIMIZE TABLE` is just mapped to `ALTER TABLE`.

`OPTIMIZE TABLE` works the following way:

- If the table has deleted or split rows, it repairs the table.
- If the index pages are not sorted, it sorts them.

- If the statistics are not up to date (and the repair couldn't be done by sorting the index), it updates them.

OPTIMIZE TABLE for a MyISAM table is equivalent to running myisamchk --quick --check-only-changed --sort-index --analyze on the table.

Note that the table is locked during the time OPTIMIZE TABLE is running!

4.5.2 ANALYZE TABLE **Syntax**

```
ANALYZE TABLE tbl_name[,tbl_name...]
```

ANALYZE TABLE analyses and stores the key distribution for the table. During the analysis, the table is locked with a read lock. This works on MyISAM and BDB tables.

This is equivalent to running myisamchk -a on the table.

MySQL uses the stored key distribution to decide in which order tables should be joined when one does a join on something other than a constant.

The command returns a table with the following columns:

Column	Value
Table	Table name
Op	Always "analyze"
Msg_type	One of status, error, info, or warning
Msg_text	The message

You can check the stored key distribution with the SHOW INDEX command. See Section 4.5.6.1, Retrieving information about databases, tables, columns, and indexes.

If the table hasn't changed since the last ANALYZE TABLE command, the table will not be analysed again.

4.5.3 FLUSH **Syntax**

```
FLUSH flush_option [,flush_option] ...
```

You should use the FLUSH command if you want to clear some of the internal caches MySQL uses. To execute FLUSH, you must have the **reload** privilege.

`flush_option` can be any of the following:

Option	Description
HOSTS	Empties the host cache tables. You should flush the host tables if some of your hosts change IP number or if you get the error message `Host . . . is blocked`. When more than one `max_connect_errors` error occurs in a row for a given host while connection to MySQL server, MySQL assumes something is wrong and blocks the host from further connection requests. Flushing the host tables allows the host to attempt to connect again. See Section A.2.4, `Host ' . . . ' is blocked` Error. You can start `mysqld` with `-O max_connection_errors=999999999` to avoid this error message.
DES_KEY_FILE	Reloads the DES keys from the file that was specified with the `--des-key-file` option at server startup time.
LOGS	Closes and reopens all log files. If you have specified the update log file or a binary log file without an extension, the extension number of the log file will be incremented by one relative to the previous file. If you have used an extension in the filename, MySQL will close and reopen the update log file. See Section 4.9.3, The Update Log. This is the same thing as sending the `SIGHUP` signal to the `mysqld` server.
PRIVILEGES	Reloads the privileges from the grant tables in the `mysql` database.
QUERY CACHE	Defragment the query cache to better utilise its memory. This command will not remove any queries from the cache, unlike `RESET QUERY CACHE`.
TABLES	Closes all open tables and forces all tables in use to be closed. This also flushes the query cache.
[TABLE	TABLES] tbl_name [,tbl_name . . .]	Flushes only the given tables.
TABLES WITH READ LOCK	Closes all open tables and locks all tables for all databases with a read until one executes `UNLOCK TABLES`. This is a very convenient way to get backups if you have a filesystem, like Veritas, that can take snapshots in time.
STATUS	Resets most status variables to zero. This is something one should only use when debugging a query.

You can also access each of the preceding commands with the `mysqladmin` utility, using the `flush-hosts`, `flush-logs`, `reload`, or `flush-tables` commands.

Also take a look at the `RESET` command used with replication. See Section 4.5.4, `RESET` Syntax.

4.5.4 RESET **Syntax**

```
RESET reset_option [,reset_option] ...
```

The RESET command is used to clear things. It also acts as a stronger version of the FLUSH command. See Section 4.5.3, FLUSH Syntax.

To execute RESET, you must have the **reload** privilege.

Option	Description
MASTER	Deletes all binary logs listed in the index file, resetting the binlog index file to be empty. In pre-3.23.26 versions, FLUSH MASTER (Master).
SLAVE	Makes the slave forget its replication position in the master logs. In pre-3.23.26 versions the command was called FLUSH SLAVE(Slave).
QUERY CACHE	Removes all query results from the query cache.

4.5.5 KILL **Syntax**

```
KILL thread_id
```

Each connection to mysqld runs in a separate thread. You can see which threads are running with the SHOW PROCESSLIST command and kill a thread with the KILL thread_id command.

If you have the **process** privilege, you can see and kill all threads. Otherwise, you can see and kill only your own threads.

You can also use the mysqladmin processlist and mysqladmin kill commands to examine and kill threads.

When you do a KILL, a thread-specific kill flag is set for the thread.

In most cases it may take some time for the thread to die, as the kill flag is only checked at specific intervals.

- In SELECT, ORDER BY, and GROUP BY loops, the flag is checked after reading a block of rows. If the kill flag is set, the statement is aborted.

- When doing an ALTER TABLE, the kill flag is checked before each block of rows is read from the original table. If the kill flag was set, the command is aborted and the temporary table is deleted.

- When doing an UPDATE TABLE and DELETE TABLE, the kill flag is checked after each block is read and after each updated or deleted row. If the kill flag is set the statement is aborted. Note that if you are not using transactions, the changes will not be rolled back!

- GET_LOCK() will abort with NULL.

- An INSERT DELAYED thread will quickly flush all rows it has in memory and die.

- If the thread is in the table lock handler (state: Locked), the table lock will be quickly aborted.

- If the thread is waiting for free disk space in a write call, the write is aborted with a "disk full" error message.

4.5.6 SHOW **Syntax**

```
    SHOW DATABASES [LIKE wild]
or SHOW [OPEN] TABLES [FROM db_name] [LIKE wild]
or SHOW [FULL] COLUMNS FROM tbl_name [FROM db_name] [LIKE wild]
or SHOW INDEX FROM tbl_name [FROM db_name]
or SHOW TABLE STATUS [FROM db_name] [LIKE wild]
or SHOW STATUS [LIKE wild]
or SHOW VARIABLES [LIKE wild]
or SHOW LOGS
or SHOW [FULL] PROCESSLIST
or SHOW GRANTS FOR user
or SHOW CREATE TABLE table_name
or SHOW MASTER STATUS
or SHOW MASTER LOGS
or SHOW SLAVE STATUS
```

SHOW provides information about databases, tables, and columns, as well as status information about the server. If the LIKE wild part is used, the wild string can be a string that uses the SQL % and _ wildcard characters.

4.5.6.1 Retrieving information about databases, tables, columns, and indexes

You can use db_name.tbl_name as an alternative to the tbl_name FROM db_name syntax. These two statements are equivalent:

```
mysql> SHOW INDEX FROM mytable FROM mydb;
mysql> SHOW INDEX FROM mydb.mytable;
```

SHOW DATABASES lists the databases on the MySQL server host. You can also get this list using the mysqlshow command.

SHOW TABLES lists the tables in a given database. You can also get this list using the mysqlshow db_name command.

Note: if a user doesn't have any privileges for a table, the table will not show up in the output from SHOW TABLES or mysqlshow db_name.

SHOW OPEN TABLES lists the tables that are currently open in the table cache. See Section 5.4.7, How MySQL Opens and Closes Tables. The Comment field tells how many times the table is cached and in_use.

SHOW COLUMNS lists the columns in a given table. If you specify the FULL option, you will also get the privileges you have for each column. If the column types are different from what you expect them to be based on a CREATE TABLE statement, note that MySQL sometimes changes column types. See Section 6.5.3.1, Silent column specification changes.

The DESCRIBE statement provides information similar to SHOW COLUMNS. See Section 6.6.2, DESCRIBE Syntax (Get Information About Columns).

SHOW FIELDS is a synonym for SHOW COLUMNS, and SHOW KEYS is a synonym for SHOW INDEX. You can also list a table's columns or indexes with mysqlshow db_name tbl_name or mysqlshow -k db_name tbl_name.

SHOW INDEX returns the index information in a format that closely resembles the SQL-Statistics call in ODBC. The following columns are returned:

Column	Meaning
Table	Name of the table.
Non_unique	0 if the index can't contain duplicates.
Key_name	Name of the index.
Seq_in_index	Column sequence number in index, starting with 1.
Col-umn_name	Column name.
Collation	How the column is sorted in the index. In MySQL, this can have values A (Ascending) or NULL (Not sorted).
Cardinal-ity	Number of unique values in the index. This is updated by running isamchk -a.
Sub_part	Number of indexed characters if the column is only partly indexed. NULL if the entire key is indexed.
Null	Contains 'YES' if the column may contain NULL.
Index_type	Index method used.
Comment	Various remarks. For now, it tells in MySQL < 4.0.2 whether index is FULLTEXT.

Note that as the Cardinality is counted based on statistics stored as integers, it's not necessarily accurate for small tables.

The Null and Index_type columns were added in MySQL 4.0.2.

4.5.6.2 SHOW TABLE STATUS

```
SHOW TABLE STATUS [FROM db_name] [LIKE wild]
```

SHOW TABLE STATUS (new in Version 3.23) works likes SHOW STATUS, but provides a lot of information about each table. You can also get this list using the mysqlshow --status db_name command. The following columns are returned:

Column	Meaning
Name	Name of the table.
Type	Type of table. See Chapter 7.
Row_format	The row storage format (Fixed, Dynamic, or Compressed).
Rows	Number of rows.
Avg_row_length	Average row length.
Data_length	Length of the data file.
Max_data_length	Max length of the data file.
Index_length	Length of the index file.
Data_free	Number of allocated but not used bytes.
Auto_increment	Next auto-increment value.
Create_time	When the table was created.
Update_time	When the data file was last updated.
Check_time	When the table was last checked.
Create_options	Extra options used with CREATE TABLE.
Comment	The comment used when creating the table (or some information why MySQL couldn't access the table information).

InnoDB tables will report the free space in the tablespace in the table comment.

4.5.6.3 SHOW STATUS

SHOW STATUS provides server status information (like mysqladmin extended-status). The output resembles that shown here, though the format and numbers probably differ:

```
+----------------------------+------------+
| Variable_name              | Value      |
+----------------------------+------------+
| Aborted_clients            | 0          |
| Aborted_connects           | 0          |
| Bytes_received             | 155372598  |
| Bytes_sent                 | 1176560426 |
| Connections                | 30023      |
| Created_tmp_disk_tables    | 0          |
| Created_tmp_tables         | 8340       |
| Created_tmp_files          | 60         |
| Delayed_insert_threads     | 0          |
| Delayed_writes             | 0          |
| Delayed_errors             | 0          |
| Flush_commands             | 1          |
| Handler_delete             | 462604     |
| Handler_read_first         | 105881     |
| Handler_read_key           | 27820558   |
| Handler_read_next          | 390681754  |
| Handler_read_prev          | 6022500    |
| Handler_read_rnd           | 30546748   |
| Handler_read_rnd_next      | 246216530  |
| Handler_update             | 16945404   |
```

```
| Handler_write            | 60356676   |
| Key_blocks_used          | 14955      |
| Key_read_requests        | 96854827   |
| Key_reads                | 162040     |
| Key_write_requests       | 7589728    |
| Key_writes               | 3813196    |
| Max_used_connections     | 0          |
| Not_flushed_key_blocks   | 0          |
| Not_flushed_delayed_rows | 0          |
| Open_tables              | 1          |
| Open_files               | 2          |
| Open_streams             | 0          |
| Opened_tables            | 44600      |
| Questions                | 2026873    |
| Select_full_join         | 0          |
| Select_full_range_join   | 0          |
| Select_range             | 99646      |
| Select_range_check       | 0          |
| Select_scan              | 30802      |
| Slave_running            | OFF        |
| Slave_open_temp_tables   | 0          |
| Slow_launch_threads      | 0          |
| Slow_queries             | 0          |
| Sort_merge_passes        | 30         |
| Sort_range               | 500        |
| Sort_rows                | 30296250   |
| Sort_scan                | 4650       |
| Table_locks_immediate    | 1920382    |
| Table_locks_waited       | 0          |
| Threads_cached           | 0          |
| Threads_created          | 30022      |
| Threads_connected        | 1          |
| Threads_running          | 1          |
| Uptime                   | 80380      |
+--------------------------+------------+
```

The preceding status variables have the following meaning:

Variable	Meaning
Aborted_clients	Number of connections aborted because the client died without closing the connection properly. See Section A.2.9, Communication Error/ Aborted Connection.
Aborted_connects	Number of tries to connect to the MySQL server that failed. See Section A.2.9, Communication Error/ Aborted Connection.
Bytes_received	Number of bytes received from all clients.
Bytes_sent	Number of bytes sent to all clients.
Com_xxx	Number of times each xxx command has been executed.
Connections	Number of connection attempts to the MySQL server.
Created_tmp_disk_tables	Number of implicit temporary tables on disk created while executing statements.

Variable	Meaning
Created_tmp_tables	Number of implicit temporary tables in memory created while executing statements.
Created_tmp_files	How many temporary files mysqld has created.
Delayed_insert_threads	Number of delayed insert handler threads in use.
Delayed_writes	Number of rows written with INSERT DELAYED.
Delayed_errors	Number of rows written with INSERT DELAYED for which some error occurred (probably duplicate key).
Flush_commands	Number of executed FLUSH commands.
Handler_delete	Number of times a row was deleted from a table.
Handler_read_first	Number of times the first entry was read from an index. If this is high, it suggests that the server is doing a lot of full index scans for example, SELECT col1 FROM foo, assuming that col1 is indexed.
Handler_read_key	Number of requests to read a row based on a key. If this is high, it is a good indication that your queries and tables are properly indexed.
Handler_read_next	Number of requests to read next row in key order. This will be incremented if you are querying an index column with a range constraint. This also will be incremented if you are doing an index scan.
Handler_read_rnd	Number of requests to read a row based on a fixed position. This will be high if you are doing a lot of queries that require sorting of the result.
Handler_read_rnd_next	Number of requests to read the next row in the data file. This will be high if you are doing a lot of table scans. Generally this suggests that your tables are not properly indexed or that your queries are not written to take advantage of the indexes you have.
Handler_update	Number of requests to update a row in a table.
Handler_write	Number of requests to insert a row in a table.
Key_blocks_used	The number of used blocks in the key cache.
Key_read_requests	The number of requests to read a key block from the cache.
Key_reads	The number of physical reads of a key block from disk.
Key_write_requests	The number of requests to write a key block to the cache.
Key_writes	The number of physical writes of a key block to disk.
Max_used_connections	The maximum number of connections in use simultaneously.
Not_flushed_key_blocks	Keys blocks in the key cache that have changed but haven't yet been flushed to disk.
Not_flushed_delayed_rows	Number of rows waiting to be written in INSERT DELAY queues.
Open_tables	Number of tables that are open.
Open_files	Number of files that are open.
Open_streams	Number of streams that are open (used mainly for logging).
Opened_tables	Number of tables that have been opened.
Select_full_join	Number of joins without keys (should be 0).

Variable	Meaning
Select_full_range_join	Number of joins where we used a range search on reference table.
Select_range	Number of joins where we used ranges on the first table. (It's normally not critical even if this is big.)
Select_scan	Number of joins where we scanned the first table.
Select_range_check	Number of joins without keys where we check for key usage after each row (should be 0).
Questions	Number of queries sent to the server.
Slave_open_temp_tables	Number of temporary tables currently open by the slave thread.
Slow_launch_threads	Number of threads that have taken more than slow_launch_time to connect.
Slow_queries	Number of queries that have taken more than long_query_time. See Section 4.9.5, The Slow Query Log.
Sort_merge_passes	Number of merges the sort has to do. If this value is large you should consider increasing sort_buffer.
Sort_range	Number of sorts that were done with ranges.
Sort_rows	Number of sorted rows.
Sort_scan	Number of sorts that where done by scanning the table.
Table_locks_immediate	Number of times a table lock was acquired immediately. Available after 3.23.33.
Table_locks_waited	Number of times a table lock could not be acquired immediately and a wait was needed. If this is high, and you have performance problems, you should first optimise your queries, and then either split your table(s) or use replication. Available after 3.23.33.
Threads_cached	Number of threads in the thread cache.
Threads_connected	Number of currently open connections.
Threads_created	Number of threads created to handle connections.
Threads_running	Number of threads that are not sleeping.
Uptime	How many seconds the server has been up.

Some comments about the preceding variables:

- If Opened_tables is big, your table_cache variable is probably too small.

- If Key_reads is big, your key_cache is probably too small. The cache hit rate can be calculated with Key_reads/Key_read_requests.

- If Handler_read_rnd is big, you probably have a lot of queries that require MySQL to scan whole tables, or you have joins that don't use keys properly.

- If Threads_created is big, you may want to increase the thread_cache_size variable. The cache hit rate can be calculated with Threads_created/Connections.

- If Created_tmp_disk_tables is big, you may want to increase the tmp_table_size variable to get the temporary tables memory-based instead of disk-based.

4.5.6.4 SHOW VARIABLES

    SHOW VARIABLES [LIKE wild]

SHOW VARIABLES shows the values of some MySQL system variables. You can also get this information using the mysqladmin variables command. If the default values are unsuitable, you can set most of these variables using command-line options when mysqld starts up. See Section 4.1.1, mysqld Command-Line Options.

The output resembles that shown here, though the format and numbers may differ somewhat:

```
+--------------------------------+--------------------------------+
| Variable_name                  | Value                          |
+--------------------------------+--------------------------------+
| ansi_mode                      | OFF                            |
| back_log                       | 50                             |
| basedir                        | /my/monty/                     |
| bdb_cache_size                 | 16777216                       |
| bdb_log_buffer_size            | 32768                          |
| bdb_home                       | /my/monty/data/                |
| bdb_max_lock                   | 10000                          |
| bdb_logdir                     |                                |
| bdb_shared_data                | OFF                            |
| bdb_tmpdir                     | /tmp/                          |
| binlog_cache_size              | 32768                          |
| concurrent_insert              | ON                             |
| connect_timeout                | 5                              |
| datadir                        | /my/monty/data/                |
| delay_key_write                | ON                             |
| delayed_insert_limit           | 100                            |
| delayed_insert_timeout         | 300                            |
| delayed_queue_size             | 1000                           |
| flush                          | OFF                            |
| flush_time                     | 0                              |
| ft_min_word_len                | 4                              |
| ft_max_word_len                | 254                            |
| ft_max_word_len_for_sort       | 20                             |
| ft_boolean_syntax              | + -><()~*                      |
| have_bdb                       | YES                            |
| have_innodb                    | YES                            |
| have_raid                      | YES                            |
| have_openssl                   | NO                             |
| init_file                      |                                |
| interactive_timeout            | 28800                          |
| join_buffer_size               | 131072                         |
| key_buffer_size                | 16776192                       |
| language                       | /my/monty/share/english/       |
| large_files_support            | ON                             |
| log                            | OFF                            |
| log_update                     | OFF                            |
| log_bin                        | OFF                            |
| log_slave_updates              | OFF                            |
| long_query_time                | 10                             |
```

```
| low_priority_updates          | OFF                          |
| lower_case_table_names        | 0                            |
| max_allowed_packet            | 1048576                      |
| max_binlog_cache_size         | 4294967295                   |
| max_connections               | 100                          |
| max_connect_errors            | 10                           |
| max_delayed_threads           | 20                           |
| max_heap_table_size           | 16777216                     |
| max_join_size                 | 4294967295                   |
| max_sort_length               | 1024                         |
| max_tmp_tables                | 32                           |
| max_write_lock_count          | 4294967295                   |
| myisam_bulk_insert_tree_size  | 8388608                      |
| myisam_recover_options        | DEFAULT                      |
| myisam_sort_buffer_size       | 8388608                      |
| net_buffer_length             | 16384                        |
| net_read_timeout              | 30                           |
| net_retry_count               | 10                           |
| net_write_timeout             | 60                           |
| open_files_limit              | 0                            |
| pid_file                      | /my/monty/data/donna.pid     |
| port                          | 3306                         |
| protocol_version              | 10                           |
| record_buffer                 | 131072                       |
| query_buffer_size             | 0                            |
| query_cache_limit             | 1048576                      |
| query_cache_size              | 16768060                     |
| query_cache_startup_type      | 1                            |
| safe_show_database            | OFF                          |
| server_id                     | 0                            |
| skip_locking                  | ON                           |
| skip_networking               | OFF                          |
| skip_show_database            | OFF                          |
| slow_launch_time              | 2                            |
| socket                        | /tmp/mysql.sock              |
| sort_buffer                   | 2097116                      |
| table_cache                   | 64                           |
| table_type                    | MYISAM                       |
| thread_cache_size             | 4                            |
| thread_stack                  | 65536                        |
| tmp_table_size                | 1048576                      |
| tmpdir                        | /tmp/                        |
| version                       | 3.23.29a-gamma-debug         |
| wait_timeout                  | 28800                        |
+-------------------------------+------------------------------+
```

Each option is described here. Values for buffer sizes, lengths, and stack sizes are given in bytes. You can specify values with a suffix of K or M to indicate kilobytes or megabytes. For example, 16M indicates 16 megabytes. The case of suffix letters does not matter; 16M and 16m are equivalent:

ansi_mode

Is ON if mysqld was started with --ansi. See Section 1.7.2, Running MySQL in ANSI Mode.

back_log

The number of outstanding connection requests MySQL can have. This comes into play when the main MySQL thread gets **very** many connection requests in a very short time. It then takes some time (although very little) for the main thread to check the connection and start a new thread. The back_log value indicates how many requests can be stacked during this short time before MySQL momentarily stops answering new requests. You need to increase this only if you expect a large number of connections in a short period of time.

In other words, this value is the size of the listen queue for incoming TCP/IP connections. Your operating system has its own limit on the size of this queue. The manual page for the Unix listen(2) system call should have more details. Check your OS documentation for the maximum value for this variable. Attempting to set back_log higher than your operating system limit will be ineffective.

basedir

The value of the --basedir option.

bdb_cache_size

The buffer that is allocated to cache indexes and rows for BDB tables. If you don't use BDB tables, you should start mysqld with --skip-bdb so as not to waste memory for this cache.

bdb_log_buffer_size

The buffer that is allocated to cache indexes and rows for BDB tables. If you don't use BDB tables, you should set this to 0 or start mysqld with --skip-bdb so as not to waste memory for this cache.

bdb_home

The value of the --bdb-home option.

bdb_max_lock

The maximum number of locks (1000 by default) you can have active on a BDB table. You should increase this if you get errors of type bdb: Lock table is out of available locks or Got error 12 from . . . when you have done long transactions or when mysqld has to examine a lot of rows to calculate the query.

bdb_logdir

The value of the --bdb-logdir option.

bdb_shared_data

Is ON if you are using --bdb-shared-data.

bdb_tmpdir

    The value of the --bdb-tmpdir option.

binlog_cache_size

    The size of the cache to hold the SQL statements for the binary log during a transaction. If you often use big, multi-statement transactions you can increase this to get more performance. See Section 6.7.1, BEGIN/COMMIT/ROLLBACK Syntax.

character_set

    The default character set.

character_sets

    The supported character sets.

concurrent_inserts

    If ON (the default), MySQL will allow you to use INSERT on MyISAM tables at the same time you run SELECT queries on them. You can turn this option off by starting mysqld with --safe or --skip-new.

connect_timeout

    The number of seconds the mysqld server is waiting for a connect packet before responding with Bad handshake.

datadir

    The value of the --datadir option.

delay_key_write

    If enabled (is ON by default), MySQL will honor the DELAY_KEY_WRITE option for CREATE TABLE. This means that the key buffer for tables with this option will not get flushed on every index update, but only when a table is closed. This will speed up writes on keys a lot, but you should add automatic checking of all tables with myisamchk --fast --force if you use this. Note that if you start mysqld with the --delay-key-write-for-all-tables option this means that all tables will be treated as if they were created with the delay_key_write option. You can clear this flag by starting mysqld with --skip-new or --safe-mode.

delayed_insert_limit

    After inserting delayed_insert_limit rows, the INSERT DELAYED handler will check are any SELECT statements pending. If so, it allows these to execute before continuing.

delayed_insert_timeout

    How long an INSERT DELAYED thread should wait for INSERT statements before terminating.

delayed_queue_size

    What size queue (in rows) should be allocated for handling INSERT DELAYED. If the queue becomes full, any client that does INSERT DELAYED will wait until there is room in the queue again.

flush

This is ON if you have started MySQL with the `--flush` option.

flush_time

If this is set to a non-zero value, every `flush_time` seconds all tables will be closed (to free up resources and sync things to disk). We only recommend this option on Windows 9x/Me, or on systems where you have very little resources.

ft_min_word_len

The minimum length of the word to be included in a FULLTEXT index. **Note:** FULL-TEXT indexes must be rebuilt after changing this variable.

ft_max_word_len

The maximum length of the word to be included in a FULLTEXT index. **Note:** FULL-TEXT indexes must be rebuilt after changing this variable.

ft_max_word_len_sort

The maximum length of the word in a FULLTEXT index to be used in fast index re-creation method in REPAIR, CREATE INDEX, or ALTER TABLE. Longer words are inserted the slow way. The rule of thumb is as follows: with `ft_max_word_len_sort` increasing, **MySQL** will create bigger temporary files (thus slowing the process down, due to disk I/O), and will put fewer keys in one sort block (again, decreasing the efficiency). When `ft_max_word_len_sort` is too small, **MySQL** will insert a lot of words into the index the slow way, but short words will be inserted very quickly.

ft_boolean_syntax

List of operators supported by MATCH ... AGAINST(... IN BOOLEAN MODE). See Section 6.8, MySQL Full-Text Search.

have_innodb

YES if mysqld supports InnoDB tables. DISABLED if `--skip-innodb` is used.

have_bdb

YES if mysqld supports Berkeley DB tables. DISABLED if `--skip-bdb` is used.

have_raid

YES if mysqld supports the RAID option.

have_openssl

YES if mysqld supports SSL (encryption) on the client/server protocol.

init_file

The name of the file specified with the `--init-file` option when you start the server. This is a file of SQL statements you want the server to execute when it starts.

interactive_timeout

>The number of seconds the server waits for activity on an interactive connection before closing it. An interactive client is defined as a client that uses the CLIENT_INTERACTIVE option to mysql_real_connect(). See also wait_timeout.

join_buffer_size

>The size of the buffer that is used for full joins (joins that do not use indexes). The buffer is allocated one time for each full join between two tables. Increase this value to get a faster full join when adding indexes is not possible. (Normally the best way to get fast joins is to add indexes.)

key_buffer_size

>Index blocks are buffered and are shared by all threads. key_buffer_size is the size of the buffer used for index blocks.

>Increase this to get better index handling (for all reads and multiple writes) to as much as you can afford; 64M on a 256M machine that mainly runs MySQL is quite common. If you, however, make this too big (for instance more than 50% of your total memory) your system may start to page and become extremely slow. Remember that because MySQL does not cache data reads, you will have to leave some room for the OS filesystem cache.

>You can check the performance of the key buffer by doing show status and examining the variables Key_read_requests, Key_reads, Key_write_requests, and Key_writes. The Key_reads/Key_read_request ratio should normally be < 0.01. The Key_write/Key_write_requests is usually near 1 if you are using mostly updates/deletes but may be much smaller if you tend to do updates that affect many at the same time, or if you are using delay_key_write. See Section 4.5.6, SHOW Syntax.

>To get even more speed when writing many rows at the same time, use LOCK TABLES. See Section 6.7.2, LOCK TABLES/UNLOCK TABLES Syntax.

language

>The language used for error messages.

large_file_support

>If mysqld was compiled with options for big file support.

locked_in_memory

>If mysqld was locked in memory with --memlock.

log

>If logging of all queries is enabled.

`log_update`

    If the update log is enabled.

`log_bin`

    If the binary log is enabled.

`log_slave_updates`

    If the updates from the slave should be logged.

`long_query_time`

    If a query takes longer than this (in seconds), the `Slow_queries` counter will be incremented. If you are using `--log-slow-queries`, the query will be logged to the slow query logfile. See Section 4.9.5, The Slow Query Log.

`lower_case_table_names`

    If set to 1, table names are stored in lowercase on disk and table names will be case-insensitive. See Section 6.1.3, Case Sensitivity in Names.

`max_allowed_packet`

    The maximum size of one packet. The message buffer is initialised to `net_buffer_length` bytes, but can grow up to `max_allowed_packet` bytes when needed. This value by default is small, to catch big (possibly wrong) packets. You must increase this value if you are using big `BLOB` columns. It should be as big as the biggest `BLOB` you want to use. The protocol limits for `max_allowed_packet` are 16M in MySQL 3.23 and 2G in MySQL 4.0.

`max_binlog_cache_size`

    If a multi-statement transaction requires more than this amount of memory, one will get the error "Multi-statement transaction required more than 'max_bin-log_cache_size' bytes of storage".

`max_binlog_size`

    Available after 3.23.33. If a write to the binary (replication) log exceeds the given value, rotate the logs. You cannot set it to less than 1024 bytes, or more than 1G. Default is 1G.

`max_connections`

    The number of simultaneous clients allowed. Increasing this value increases the number of file descriptors that `mysqld` requires. See below for comments on file descriptor limits are covered later in this section. See also Section A.2.5, `Too many connections` Error.

`max_connect_errors`

    If there is more than this number of interrupted connections from a host, this host will be blocked from further connections. You can unblock a host with the command `FLUSH HOSTS`.

max_delayed_threads

Don't start more than this number of threads to handle INSERT DELAYED statements. If you try to insert data into a new table after all INSERT DELAYED threads are in use, the row will be inserted as if the DELAYED attribute wasn't specified.

max_heap_table_size

Don't allow creation of heap tables bigger than this.

max_join_size

Joins that are probably going to read more than max_join_size records return an error. Set this value if your users tend to perform joins that lack a WHERE clause, that take a long time, and that return millions of rows.

max_sort_length

The number of bytes to use when sorting BLOB or TEXT values (only the first max_sort_length bytes of each value are used; the rest are ignored).

max_user_connections

The maximum number of active connections for a single user (0 = no limit).

max_tmp_tables

Maximum number of temporary tables a client can keep open at the same time. (This option doesn't yet do anything.)

max_write_lock_count

After this many write locks, allow some read locks to run in between.

myisam_bulk_insert_tree_size

MySQL uses special tree-like cache to make bulk inserts (that is, INSERT . . . SELECT, INSERT . . . VALUES (. . .), (. . .), . . . , and LOAD DATA INFILE) faster. This variable limits the size of the cache tree in bytes per thread. Setting it to 0 will disable this optimization. **Note**: this cache is only used when adding data to non-empty table. Default value is 8M.

myisam_recover_options

The value of the --myisam-recover option.

myisam_sort_buffer_size

The buffer that is allocated when sorting the index when doing a REPAIR or when creating indexes with CREATE INDEX or ALTER TABLE.

myisam_max_extra_sort_file_size

If the temporary file created for fast index creation would be bigger than using the key cache by the amount specified here, use the key cache method. This is mainly used to force long character keys in large tables to use the slower key cache method to create the index. **Note** that this parameter is given in megabytes!

myisam_max_sort_file_size
> The maximum size of the temporary file MySQL is allowed to use while re-creating the index (during REPAIR, ALTER TABLE, or LOAD DATA INFILE. If the file-size will be bigger than this, the index will be created through the key cache (which is slower). **Note** that this parameter is given in megabytes!

net_buffer_length
> The communication buffer is reset to this size between queries. This should not normally be changed, but if you have very little memory, you can set it to the expected size of a query. (That is, the expected length of SQL statements sent by clients. If statements exceed this length, the buffer is automatically enlarged, up to max_allowed_packet bytes.)

net_read_timeout
> Number of seconds to wait for more data from a connection before aborting the read. Note that when we don't expect data from a connection, the timeout is defined by write_timeout. See also slave_read_timeout.

net_retry_count
> If a read on a communication port is interrupted, retry this many times before giving up. This value should be quite high on FreeBSD as internal interrupts are sent to all threads.

net_write_timeout
> Number of seconds to wait for a block to be written to a connection before aborting the write.

open_files_limit
> If this is not 0, mysqld will use this value to reserve file descriptors to use with setrlimit(). If this value is 0, mysqld will reserve max_connections*5 or max_connections + table_cache*2 (whichever is larger) number of files. You should try increasing this if mysqld gives you the error 'Too many open files'.

pid_file
> The value of the --pid-file option.

port
> The value of the --port option.

protocol_version
> The protocol version used by the MySQL server.

record_buffer
> Each thread that does a sequential scan allocates a buffer of this size for each table it scans. If you do many sequential scans, you may want to increase this value.

record_rnd_buffer

> When reading rows in sorted order after a sort, the rows are read through this buffer to avoid disk seeks. If not set, it's set to the value of record_buffer.

query_buffer_size

> The initial allocation of the query buffer. If most of your queries are long (like when inserting blobs), you should increase this!

query_cache_limit

> Don't cache results that are bigger than this. (Default is 1M).

query_cache_size

> The memory allocated to store results from old queries. If this is 0, the query cache is disabled (default).

query_cache_startup_type

> This may be set (only numeric) as shown in the following table:

Value	Alias	Comment
0	OFF	Don't cache or retrieve results.
1	ON	Cache all results except SELECT SQL_NO_CACHE . . . queries.
2	DEMAND	Cache only SELECT SQL_CACHE . . . queries.

safe_show_database

> Don't show databases for which the user doesn't have any database or table privileges. This can improve security if you're concerned about people being able to see what databases other users have. See also skip_show_database.

server_id

> The value of the --server-id option.

skip_locking

> Is OFF if mysqld uses external locking.

skip_networking

> Is ON if we only allow local (socket) connections.

skip_show_database

> This prevents people from doing SHOW DATABASES if they don't have the **process** privilege. This can improve security if you're concerned about people being able to see what databases other users have. See also safe_show_database.

slave_read_timeout

> Number of seconds to wait for more data from a master/slave connection before aborting the read.

`slow_launch_time`
> If creating the thread takes longer than this value (in seconds), the `Slow_launch_threads` counter will be incremented.

`socket`
> The Unix socket used by the server.

`sort_buffer`
> Each thread that needs to do a sort allocates a buffer of this size. Increase this value for faster `ORDER BY` or `GROUP BY` operations. See Section A.4.4, Where MySQL Stores Temporary Files.

`table_cache`
> The number of open tables for all threads. Increasing this value increases the number of file descriptors that `mysqld` requires. You can check if you need to increase the table cache by checking the `Opened_tables` variable. See Section 4.5.6, `SHOW` Syntax. If this variable is big and you don't do `FLUSH TABLES` a lot (which just forces all tables to be closed and reopened), you should increase the value of this variable.
>
> For more information about the table cache, see Section 5.4.7, How MySQL Opens and Closes Tables.

`table_type`
> The default table type.

`thread_cache_size`
> How many threads we should keep in a cache for reuse. When a client disconnects, the client's threads are put in the cache if there aren't more than `thread_cache_size` threads from before. All new threads are first taken from the cache, and only when the cache is empty is a new thread created. This variable can be increased to improve performance if you have a lot of new connections. (Normally this doesn't give a notable performance improvement if you have a good thread implementation.) By examining the difference between the `Connections` and `Threads_created` you can see how efficient the current thread cache is for you.

`thread_concurrency`
> On Solaris, `mysqld` will call `thr_setconcurrency()` with this value. `thr_setconcurrency()` permits the application to give the threads system a hint for the desired number of threads that should be run at the same time.

`thread_stack`
> The stack size for each thread. Many of the limits detected by the `crash-me` test are dependent on this value. The default is large enough for normal operation. See Section 5.1.4, The MySQL Benchmark Suite.

timezone
>   The timezone for the server.

tmp_table_size
>   If an in-memory temporary table exceeds this size, MySQL will automatically con-
>   vert it to an on-disk MyISAM table. Increase the value of tmp_table_size if you do
>   many advanced GROUP BY queries and you have lots of memory.

tmpdir
>   The directory used for temporary files and temporary tables.

version
>   The version number for the server.

wait_timeout
>   The number of seconds the server waits for activity on a connection before closing it.
>   See also interactive_timeout.

For information on how to tune these variables, see Section 5.5.2, Tuning Server Parameters.

4.5.6.5 SHOW LOGS

SHOW LOGS shows you status information about existing log files. It currently only displays information about Berkeley DB log files.

File
>   Shows the full path to the log file.

Type
>   Shows the type of the log file (BDB for Berkeley DB log files).

Status
>   Shows the status of the log file (FREE if the file can be removed, or IN USE if the file
>   is needed by the transaction subsystem).

4.5.6.6 SHOW PROCESSLIST

SHOW [FULL] PROCESSLIST shows you which threads are running. You can also get
this information using the mysqladmin processlist command. If you have the **process** privilege, you can see all threads. Otherwise, you can see only your own threads. See
Section 4.5.5, KILL Syntax. If you don't use the FULL option, only the first 100 characters
of each query will be shown.

This command is very useful if you get the 'too many connections' error message and
want to find out what's going on. MySQL reserves one extra connection for a client with
the **process** privilege to ensure that you should always be able to log in and check the system (assuming you are not giving this privilege to all your users).

Some states commonly seen in mysqladmin processlist include the following:

Checking table
> The thread is performing an [automatic] check of the table.

Closing tables
> Means that the thread is flushing the changed table data to disk and closing the used tables. This should be a fast operation. If not, you should check that you don't have a full disk or that the disk is not in very heavy use.

Connect out
> Slave connecting to master.

Copying to tmp table on disk
> The temporary result set was larger than tmp_table_size and the thread is now changing the in memory-based temporary table to a disk-based one to save memory.

Creating tmp table
> The thread is creating a temporary table to hold a part of the result for the query.

deleting from main table
> When executing the first part of a multi-table delete and you are only deleting from the first table.

deleting from reference tables
> When executing the second part of a multi-table delete and we are deleting the matched rows from the other tables.

Flushing tables
> The thread is executing FLUSH TABLES and is waiting for all threads to close their tables.

Killed
> Someone has sent a kill to the thread and it should abort next time it checks the kill flag. The flag is checked in each major loop in MySQL, but in some cases it may still take a short time for the thread to die. If the thread is locked by some other thread, the kill will take effect as soon as the other thread releases its lock.

Sending data
> The thread is processing rows for a SELECT statement and is also sending data to the client.

Sorting for group
> The thread is doing a sort to satisfy a GROUP BY.

Sorting for order
> The thread is doing a sort to satisfy an ORDER BY.

Opening tables

> This simply means that the thread is trying to open a table. This should be a very fast procedure, unless something prevents it from opening. For example an ALTER TABLE or a LOCK TABLE can prevent opening a table until the command is finished.

Removing duplicates

> The query was using SELECT DISTINCT in such a way that MySQL couldn't optimize that distinct away at an early stage. Because of this MySQL has to do an extra stage to remove all duplicated rows before sending the result to the client.

Reopen table

> The thread got a lock for the table, but noticed after getting the lock that the underlying table structure changed. It has freed the lock, closed the table, and is now trying to reopen it.

Repair by sorting

> The repair code is using sorting to create indexes.

Repair with keycache

> The repair code is creating keys one by one through the key cache. This is much slower than Repair by sorting.

Searching rows for update

> The thread is doing a first phase to find all matching rows before updating them. This has to be done if the UPDATE is changing the index that is used to find the involved rows.

Sleeping

> The thread is wating for the client to send a new command to it.

System lock

> The thread is waiting to get an external system lock for the table. If you are not using multiple mysqld servers that are accessing the same tables, you can disable system locks with the --skip-locking option.

Upgrading lock

> The INSERT DELAYED handler is trying to get a lock for the table to insert rows.

Updating

> The thread is searching for rows to update and is updating them.

User Lock

> The thread is waiting on a GET_LOCK().

Waiting for tables

> The thread got a notification that the underlying structure for a table has changed and it needs to reopen the table to get the new structure. To be able to reopen the table it must, however, wait until all other threads have closed the table in question.

> This notification happens if another thread has used FLUSH TABLES or one of the following commands on the table in question: FLUSH TABLES table_name, ALTER TABLE, RENAME TABLE, REPAIR TABLE, ANALYZE TABLE, or OPTIMIZE TABLE.

waiting for handler insert

> The INSERT DELAYED handler has processed all inserts and is waiting to get new ones.

Most states are very quick operations. If threads last in any of these states for many seconds, there may be a problem that needs to be investigated.

There are some other states that are not mentioned previously, but most of these are only useful to find bugs in mysqld.

4.5.6.7 SHOW GRANTS FOR

SHOW GRANTS FOR user lists the grant commands that must be issued to duplicate the grants for a user.

```
mysql> SHOW GRANTS FOR root@localhost;
+-----------------------------------------------------------------------+
| Grants for root@localhost                                             |
+-----------------------------------------------------------------------+
| GRANT ALL PRIVILEGES ON *.* TO 'root'@'localhost' WITH GRANT OPTION |
+-----------------------------------------------------------------------+
```

4.5.6.8 SHOW CREATE TABLE

Shows a CREATE TABLE statement that will create the given table:

```
mysql> SHOW CREATE TABLE t\G
*************************** 1. row ***************************
       Table: t
Create Table: CREATE TABLE t (
  id int(11) default NULL auto_increment,
  s char(60) default NULL,
  PRIMARY KEY (id)
) TYPE=MyISAM
```

SHOW CREATE TABLE will quote table and column names according to the SQL_QUOTE_SHOW_CREATE option. See Section 5.5.6, SET Syntax.

4.6   MySQL Localisation and International Usage

4.6.1   The Character Set Used for Data and Sorting

By default, MySQL uses the ISO-8859-1 (Latin1) character set with sorting according to Swedish/Finnish. This is the character set suitable in the USA and Western Europe.

All standard MySQL binaries are compiled with `--with-extra-charsets=complex`. This will add code to all standard programs to be able to handle `latin1` and all multi-byte character sets within the binary. Other character sets will be loaded from a character-set definition file when needed.

The character set determines what characters are allowed in names and how things are sorted by the `ORDER BY` and `GROUP BY` clauses of the `SELECT` statement.

You can change the character set with the `--default-character-set` option when you start the server. The character sets available depend on the `--with-charset=charset` and `--with-extra-charset= list-of-charset | complex | all` options to `configure`, and the character set configuration files listed in `SHAREDIR/charsets/Index`. See Section 2.3.3, Typical `configure` Options.

If you change the character set when running MySQL (which may also change the sort order), you must run `myisamchk -r -q` on all tables. Otherwise, your indexes may not be ordered correctly.

When a client connects to a MySQL server, the server sends the default character set in use to the client. The client will switch to use this character set for this connection.

One should use `mysql_real_escape_string()` when escaping strings for a SQL query. `mysql_real_escape_string()` is identical to the old `mysql_escape_string()` function, except that it takes the MySQL connection handle as the first parameter.

If the client is compiled with different paths than where the server is installed and the user who configured MySQL didn't include all character sets in the MySQL binary, one must specify for the client where it can find the additional character sets it will need if the server runs with a different character set than the client.

One can specify this by putting in a MySQL option file:

```
[client]
character-sets-dir=/usr/local/mysql/share/mysql/charsets
```

where the path points to the directory in which the dynamic MySQL character sets are stored.

One can force the client to use specific character set by specifying:

```
[client]
default-character-set=character-set-name
```

but normally this is never needed.

4.6.1.1 German character set

To get German sorting order, you should start `mysqld` with `--default-character-set=latin_de`. This will give you the following characteristics.

When sorting and comparing strings the following mapping is done on the strings before doing the comparison:

```
ä  ->  ae
ö  ->  oe
ü  ->  ue
ß  ->  ss
```

All accented characters are converted to their unaccented uppercase counterparts. All letters are converted to uppercase.

When comparing strings with `LIKE` the one -> two character mapping is not done. All letters are converted to uppercase. Accents are removed from all letters except: Ü, ü, Ö, ö, Ä, and ä.

4.6.2 Non-English Error Messages

`mysqld` can issue error messages in the following languages: Czech, Danish, Dutch, English (the default), Estonian, French, German, Greek, Hungarian, Italian, Japanese, Korean, Norwegian, Norwegian-ny, Polish, Portuguese, Romanian, Russian, Slovak, Spanish, and Swedish.

To start `mysqld` with a particular language, use either the `--language=lang` or `-L lang` options. For example:

```
shell> mysqld --language=swedish
```

or:

```
shell> mysqld --language=/usr/local/share/swedish
```

Note that all language names are specified in lowercase.

The language files are located (by default) in `mysql_base_dir/share/LANGUAGE/`.

To update the error message file, you should edit the `errmsg.txt` file and execute the following command to generate the `errmsg.sys` file:

```
shell> comp_err errmsg.txt errmsg.sys
```

If you upgrade to a newer version of MySQL, remember to repeat your changes with the new `errmsg.txt` file.

4.6.3 Adding a New Character Set

To add another character set to MySQL, use the following procedure.

Decide if the set is simple or complex. If the character set does not need to use special string collating routines for sorting and does not need multi-byte character support, it is simple. If it needs either of those features, it is complex.

For example, `latin1` and `danish` are simple character sets while `big5` or `czech` are complex character sets.

In the following section, we have assumed that you named your character set `MYSET`.

For a simple character set do the following:

1.   Add MYSET to the end of the `sql/share/charsets/Index` file. Assign a unique number to it.

2.   Create the file `sql/share/charsets/MYSET.conf`. (You can use `sql/share/charsets/latin1.conf` as a base for this.)

     The syntax for the file is very simple:

     •   Comments start with a '#' character and proceed to the end of the line.

     •   Words are separated by arbitrary amounts of whitespace.

     •   When defining the character set, every word must be a number in hexadecimal format.

     •   The `ctype` array takes up the first 257 words. The `to_lower`, `to_upper`, and `sort_order` arrays take up 256 words each after that.

     Section 4.6.4, The Character Definition Arrays.

3.   Add the character set name to the `CHARSETS_AVAILABLE` and `COMPILED_CHARSETS` lists in `configure.in`.

4.   Reconfigure, recompile, and test.

For a complex character set do the following:

1.   Create the file `strings/ctype-MYSET.c` in the MySQL source distribution.

2.   Add MYSET to the end of the `sql/share/charsets/Index` file. Assign a unique number to it.

3. Look at one of the existing `ctype-*.c` files to see what needs to be defined—for example, `strings/ctype-big5.c`. Note that the arrays in your file must have names like `ctype_MYSET`, `to_lower_MYSET`, and so on. This corresponds to the arrays in the simple character set. See Section 4.6.4, The Character Definition Arrays.

4. Near the top of the file, place a special comment like this:

    ```
    /*
     * This comment is parsed by configure to create ctype.c,
     * so don't change it unless you know what you are doing.
     *
     * .configure. number_MYSET=MYNUMBER
     * .configure. strxfrm_multiply_MYSET=N
     * .configure. mbmaxlen_MYSET=N
     */
    ```

    The `configure` program uses this comment to include the character set into the MySQL library automatically.

    The strxfrm_multiply and mbmaxlen lines will be explained in the following sections. Only include these if you need the string collating functions or the multi-byte character set functions, respectively.

5. You should then create some of the following functions:

    *   `my_strncoll_MYSET()`

    *   `my_strcoll_MYSET()`

    *   `my_strxfrm_MYSET()`

    *   `my_like_range_MYSET()`

    Section 4.6.5, String Collating Support.

6. Add the character set name to the `CHARSETS_AVAILABLE` and `COMPILED_CHARSETS` lists in `configure.in`.

7. Reconfigure, recompile, and test.

The file `sql/share/charsets/README` includes some more instructions.

If you want to have the character set included in the MySQL distribution, mail a patch to *internals@lists.mysql.com*.

4.6.4 The Character Definition Arrays

`to_lower[]` and `to_upper[]` are simple arrays that hold the lowercase and uppercase characters corresponding to each member of the character set. For example:

```
to_lower['A'] should contain 'a'
to_upper['a'] should contain 'A'
```

sort_order[] is a map indicating how characters should be ordered for comparison and sorting purposes. For many character sets, this is the same as to_upper[] (which means sorting will be case-insensitive). MySQL will sort characters based on the value of sort_order[character]. For more complicated sorting rules, see Section 4.6.5, String Collating Support.

ctype[] is an array of bit values, with one element for one character. (Note that to_lower[], to_upper[], and sort_order[] are indexed by character value, but ctype[] is indexed by character value + 1. This is an old legacy to be able to handle EOF.)

You can find the following bitmask definitions in m_ctype.h:

```
#define _U    01      /* Uppercase */
#define _L    02      /* Lowercase */
#define _N    04      /* Numeral (digit) */
#define _S    010     /* Spacing character */
#define _P    020     /* Punctuation */
#define _C    040     /* Control character */
#define _B    0100    /* Blank */
#define _X    0200    /* heXadecimal digit */
```

The ctype[] entry for each character should be the union of the applicable bitmask values that describe the character. For example, 'A' is an uppercase character (_U) as well as a hexadecimal digit (_X), so ctype['A'+1] should contain the value:

```
_U + _X = 01 + 0200 = 0201
```

4.6.5 String Collating Support

If the sorting rules for your language are too complex to be handled with the simple sort_order[] table, you need to use the string collating functions.

Right now the best documentation on this is the character sets that are already implemented. Look at the big5, czech, gbk, sjis, and tis160 character sets for examples.

You must specify the strxfrm_multiply_MYSET=N value in the special comment at the top of the file. N should be set to the maximum ratio to which the strings may grow during my_strxfrm_MYSET (it must be a positive integer).

4.6.6 Multi-Byte Character Support

If you want to add support for a new character set that includes multi-byte characters, you need to use the multi-byte character functions.

Right now the best documentation on this is the character sets that are already implemented. Look at the euc_kr, gb2312, gbk, sjis, and ujis character sets for examples. These are implemented in the ctype-'charset'.c files in the strings directory.

You must specify the mbmaxlen_MYSET=N value in the special comment at the top of the source file. N should be set to the size in bytes of the largest character in the set.

4.6.7 Problems with Character Sets

If you try to use a character set that is not compiled into your binary, you can run into a couple of different problems:

- Your program has a wrong path to where the character sets are stored. (The default is /usr/local/mysql/share/mysql/charsets.) This can be fixed by using the --character-sets-dir option to the program in question.

- The character set is a multi-byte-character set that can't be loaded dynamically. In this case you have to recompile the program with the support for the character set.

- The character set is a dynamic character set, but you don't have a configure file for it. In this case you should install the configure file for the character set from a new MySQL distribution.

- Your Index file doesn't contain the name for the character set.

  ```
  ERROR 1105: File '/usr/local/share/mysql/charsets/?.conf' not found
  (Errcode: 2)
  ```

  In this case you should either get a new Index file or add by hand the name of any missing character sets.

For MyISAM tables, you can check the character set name and number for a table with myisamchk -dvv table_name.

4.7 MySQL Server-Side Scripts and Utilities

4.7.1 Overview of the Server-Side Scripts and Utilities

All MySQL clients that communicate with the server using the mysqlclient library use the following environment variables:

Name	Description
MYSQL_UNIX_PORT	The default socket; used for connections to localhost
MYSQL_TCP_PORT	The default TCP/IP port
MYSQL_PWD	The default password
MYSQL_DEBUG	Debug-trace options when debugging
TMPDIR	The directory where temporary tables/files are created

Use of MYSQL_PWD is insecure. See Section 4.2.8, Connecting to the MySQL server.

The mysql client uses the file named in the MYSQL_HISTFILE environment variable to save the command-line history. The default value for the history file is $HOME/.mysql_history, where $HOME is the value of the HOME environment variable. See Appendix E.

All MySQL programs take many different options. However, every MySQL program provides a --help option that you can use to get a full description of the program's different options. For example, try mysql --help.

You can override default options for all standard client programs with an option file. See Section 4.1.2, my.cnf Option Files.

The following list briefly describes the MySQL programs:

myisamchk

Utility to describe, check, optimise, and repair MySQL tables. Because myisamchk has many functions, it is described in its own chapter. See Section 4.4.6, Using myisamchk for Table Maintenance and Crash Recovery.

make_binary_distribution

Makes a binary release of a compiled MySQL. This could be sent by FTP to /pub/mysql/Incoming on support.mysql.com for the convenience of other MySQL users.

msql2mysql

A shell script that converts mSQL programs to MySQL. It doesn't handle all cases, but it gives a good start when converting.

mysqlaccess

A script that checks the access privileges for a host, user, and database combination.

mysqladmin

Utility for performing administrative operations, such as creating or dropping databases, reloading the grant tables, flushing tables to disk, and reopening log files. mysqladmin can also be used to retrieve version, process, and status information from the server. See Section 4.8.3, mysqladmin, Administrating a MySQL Server.

mysqlbug
> The MySQL bug report script. This script should always be used when filing a bug report to the MySQL list.

mysqld
> The SQL daemon. This should always be running.

mysqldump
> Dumps a MySQL database into a file as SQL statements or as tab-separated text files. Enhanced freeware originally by Igor Romanenko. See Section 4.8.5, mysqldump, Dumping Table Structure and Data.

mysqlimport
> Imports text files into their respective tables using LOAD DATA INFILE. See Section 4.8.7, mysqlimport, Importing Data from Text Files.

mysqlshow
> Displays information about databases, tables, columns, and indexes.

mysql_install_db
> Creates the MySQL grant tables with default privileges. This is usually executed only once, when first installing MySQL on a system.

replace
> A utility program that is used by msql2mysql, but that has more general applicability as well. replace changes strings in place in files or on the standard input. Uses a finite-state machine to match longer strings first. Can be used to swap strings. For example, this command swaps a and b in the given files:
>
>   shell> replace a b b a—file1 file2 ...

4.7.2 safe_mysqld, the Wrapper Around mysqld

safe_mysqld is the recommended way to start a mysqld daemon on Unix. safe_mysqld adds some safety features such as restarting the server when an error occurs and logging runtime information to a log file.

If you don't use --mysqld=#, or --mysqld-version=# safe_mysqld will use an executable named mysqld-max if it exists. If not, safe_mysqld will start mysqld. This makes it very easy to test to use mysqld-max instead of mysqld; just copy mysqld-max to where you have mysqld and it will be used.

Normally one should never edit the safe_mysqld script, but instead put the options to safe_mysqld in the [safe_mysqld] section in the my.cnf file. safe_mysqld will read all options from the [mysqld], [server], and [safe_mysqld] sections from the option files. See Section 4.1.2, my.cnf Option Files.

Note that all options on the command-line to safe_mysqld are passed to mysqld. If you wants to use any options in safe_mysqld that mysqld doesn't support, you must specify these in the option file.

Most of the options to safe_mysqld are the same as the options to mysqld. See Section 4.1.1, mysqld Command-Line Options.

safe_mysqld supports the following options:

--basedir=path
--core-file-size=#
> Size of the core file mysqld should be able to create. Passed to ulimit -c.

--datadir=path
--defaults-extra-file=path
--defaults-file=path
--err-log=path
--ledir=path
> Path to mysqld

--log=path
--mysqld=mysqld-version
> Name of the mysqld version in the ledir directory you want to start.

--mysqld-version=version
> Similar to --mysqld=, but here you only give the suffix for mysqld. For example, if you use --mysqld-version=max, safe_mysqld will start the ledir/mysqld-max version. If the argument to --mysqld-version is empty, ledir/mysqld will be used.

--no-defaults
--open-files-limit=#
> Number of files mysqld should be able to open. Passed to ulimit -n. Note that you need to start safe_mysqld as root for this to work properly!

--pid-file=path
--port=#
--socket=path
--timezone=#
> Set the timezone (the TZ) variable to the value of this parameter.

--user=#
> The safe_mysqld script is written so that it normally is able to start a server that was installed from either a source or a binary version of MySQL, even if these install the server in slightly different locations. safe_mysqld expects one of these conditions to be true:

•   The server and databases can be found relative to the directory from which safe_mysqld is invoked. safe_mysqld looks under its working directory for bin and data directories (for binary distributions) or for libexec and var directories (for source distributions). This condition should be met if you execute safe_mysqld from your MySQL installation directory (for example, /usr/local/mysql for a binary distribution).

- If the server and databases cannot be found relative to the working directory, safe_mysqld attempts to locate them by absolute pathnames. Typical locations are /usr/local/libexec and /usr/local/var. The actual locations are determined when the distribution was built from which safe_mysqld comes. They should be correct if MySQL was installed in a standard location.

Because safe_mysqld will try to find the server and databases relative to its own working directory, you can install a binary distribution of MySQL anywhere, as long as you start safe_mysqld from the MySQL installation directory:

```
shell> cd mysql_installation_directory
shell> bin/safe_mysqld &
```

If safe_mysqld fails, even when invoked from the MySQL installation directory, you can modify it to use the path to mysqld and the pathname options that are correct for your system. Note that if you upgrade MySQL in the future, your modified version of safe_mysqld will be overwritten, so you should make a copy of your edited version that you can reinstall.

4.7.3 mysqld_multi, Program for Managing Multiple MySQL servers

mysqld_multi is meant for managing several mysqld processes running in different Unix sockets and TCP/IP ports.

The program will search for group(s) named [mysqld#] from my.cnf (or the given —config-file=...), where # can be any positive number starting from 1. These groups should be the same as the usual [mysqld] group (e.g., options to mysqld; see the MySQL manual for detailed information about this group), but with those port, socket, etc., options that are wanted for each separate mysqld process. The number in the group name has another function; it can be used for starting, stopping, or reporting some specific mysqld servers with this program. See the following usage and option for more details.

```
Usage: mysqld_multi [OPTIONS] {start|stop|report} [GNR,GNR,GNR...]
or     mysqld_multi [OPTIONS] {start|stop|report} [GNR-GNR,GNR,GNR-GNR,...]
```

The GNR in the preceding example means the group number. You can start, stop, or report any GNR, or several of them at the same time. (See example.) The GNRs list can be comma-separated or combined with a dash, of which the latter means that all the GNRs between GNR1-GNR2 will be affected. Without the GNR argument all the found groups will be either started, stopped, or reported. Note that you must not have any whitespace in the GNR list. Anything after a whitespace is ignored.

`mysqld_multi` supports the following options:

`--config-file= . . .`

Alternative config file. Note: This will not affect this program's own options (group [`mysqld_multi`]), but only groups [mysqld#]. Without this option everything will be searched from the ordinary my.cnf file.

`--example`

Give an example of a config file.

`--help`

Print this help and exit.

`--log= . . .`

Log file. Full path to and the name for the log file. Note: If the file exists, everything will be appended.

`--mysqladmin= . . .`

`mysqladmin` binary to be used for a server shutdown.

`--mysqld= . . .`

`mysqld` binary to be used. Note that you can give `safe_mysqld` to this option also. The options are passed to `mysqld`. Just make sure you have `mysqld` in your environment variable `PATH` or fix `safe_mysqld`.

`--no-log`

Print to stdout instead of the log file. By default, the log file is turned on.

`--password= . . .`

Password for user for `mysqladmin`.

`--tcp-ip`

Connect to the MySQL server(s) via the TCP/IP port instead of the Unix socket. This affects stopping and reporting. If a socket file is missing, the server may still be running, but can be accessed only via the TCP/IP port. By default connecting is done via the Unix socket.

`--user= . . .`

MySQL user for `mysqladmin`.

`--version`

Print the version number and exit.

Some notes about `mysqld_multi`:

• Make sure that the MySQL user who is stopping the `mysqld` services (e.g., using the `mysqladmin`) has the same password and username for all the data directories accessed (to the 'mysql' database) And make sure that the user has the 'Shutdown_priv' privilege! If you have many data directories and many different 'mysql' databases with different passwords for the MySQL 'root' user, you may want to create a common 'multi_admin' user for each using the same password. Here's how to do it:

```
shell> mysql -u root -S /tmp/mysql.sock -proot_password -e
"GRANT SHUTDOWN ON *.* TO multi_admin@localhost IDENTIFIED BY 'multipass'"
Section 4.2.6, How the Privilege System Works.
```

You will have to do this for each `mysqld` running in each data directory that you have (just change the socket, -S=...).

- `pid-file` is very important if you are using `safe_mysqld` to start `mysqld` (e.g., `--mysqld=safe_mysqld`). Every `mysqld` should have its own `pid-file`. The advantage using `safe_mysqld` instead of `mysqld` directly is that `safe_mysqld` 'guards' every `mysqld` process and will restart it, if a `mysqld` process fails due to signal kill -9, or similar failure (like segmentation fault, which MySQL should never do, of course). Please note that the `safe_mysqld` script may require that you start it from a certain place. This means that you may have to `cd` to a certain directory before you start the `mysqld_multi`. If you have problems starting, please see the `safe_mysqld` script. Check especially the lines:

```
------------------------------------------------------------------------
MY_PWD=`pwd` Check if we are starting this relative (for the binary
release) if test -d /data/mysql -a -f ./share/mysql/english/errmsg.sys
-a -x ./bin/mysqld
------------------------------------------------------------------------
Section 4.7.2, safe_mysqld, the Wrapper Around mysqld.
```

This test should be successful. If it isn't, you may encounter the following problems:

- Beware of the dangers starting multiple `mysqld`s in the same data directory. Use separate data directories, unless you **know** what you are doing!

- The socket file and the TCP/IP port must be different for every `mysqld`.

- The first and fifth `mysqld` group were intentionally left out from the example. You may have 'gaps' in the config file. This gives you more flexibility. The order in which the `mysqld`s are started or stopped depends on the order in which they appear in the config file.

- When you want to refer to a certain group using GNR with this program, just use the number in the end of the group name ([mysqld# <==).

- You may want to use option '--user' for `mysqld`, but in order to do this you need to be root when you start the `mysqld_multi` script. Having the option in the config file doesn't matter; you will just get a warning, if you are not the superuser and the `mysqld`s are started under **your** Unix account. **Important**: Make sure that the `pid-file` and the data directory are read+write (+execute for the latter one) accessible for **that** Unix user, who the specific `mysqld` process is started as. **Do not** use the Unix root account for this, unless you **know** what you are doing!

- **Most important**: Make sure that you understand the meanings of the options that are passed to the mysqlds and **why one would want** to have separate mysqld processes. Starting multiple mysqlds in one data directory **will not** give you extra performance in a threaded system!

See Section 4.1.4, Running Multiple MySQL Servers on the Same Machine.

This is an example of the config file on behalf of mysqld_multi:

```
# This file should probably be in your home dir (~/.my.cnf) or /etc/my.cnf
# Version 2.1 by Jani Tolonen

[mysqld_multi]
mysqld      = /usr/local/bin/safe_mysqld
mysqladmin  = /usr/local/bin/mysqladmin
user        = multi_admin
password    = multipass

[mysqld2]
socket      = /tmp/mysql.sock2
port        = 3307
pid-file    = /usr/local/mysql/var2/hostname.pid2
datadir     = /usr/local/mysql/var2
language    = /usr/local/share/mysql/english
user        = john

[mysqld3]
socket      = /tmp/mysql.sock3
port        = 3308
pid-file    = /usr/local/mysql/var3/hostname.pid3
datadir     = /usr/local/mysql/var3
language    = /usr/local/share/mysql/swedish
user        = monty

[mysqld4]
socket      = /tmp/mysql.sock4
port        = 3309
pid-file    = /usr/local/mysql/var4/hostname.pid4
datadir     = /usr/local/mysql/var4
language    = /usr/local/share/mysql/estonia
user        = tonu

[mysqld6]
socket      = /tmp/mysql.sock6
port        = 3311
pid-file    = /usr/local/mysql/var6/hostname.pid6
datadir     = /usr/local/mysql/var6
language    = /usr/local/share/mysql/japanese
user        = jani
```

See Section 4.1.2, my.cnf Option Files.

4.7.4 `myisampack`, the MySQL Compressed Read-Only Table Generator

`myisampack` is used to compress MyISAM tables, and `pack_isam` is used to compress ISAM tables. Because ISAM tables are deprecated, we will only discuss `myisampack` here, but everything said about `myisampack` should also be true for `pack_isam`.

`myisampack` works by compressing each column in the table separately. The information needed to decompress columns is read into memory when the table is opened. This results in much better performance when accessing individual records because you only have to uncompress exactly one record, not a much larger disk block as when using Stacker on MS-DOS. Usually, `myisampack` packs the data file 40%-70%.

MySQL uses memory mapping (`mmap()`) on compressed tables and falls back to normal read/write file usage if `mmap()` doesn't work.

There are currently two limitations with `myisampack`:

*   After packing, the table is read-only.

*   `myisampack` can also pack `BLOB` or `TEXT` columns. The older `pack_isam` could not do this.

Fixing these limitations is on our TODO list but with low priority.

`myisampack` is invoked like this:

```
shell> myisampack [options] filename ...
```

Each filename should be the name of an index (`.MYI`) file. If you are not in the database directory, you should specify the pathname to the file. It is permissible to omit the `.MYI` extension.

`myisampack` supports the following options:

`-b, --backup`
Make a backup of the table as `tbl_name.OLD`.

`-#, --debug=debug_options`
Output the debug log. The `debug_options` string often is `'d:t:o,filename'`.

`-f, --force`
Force packing of the table even if it becomes bigger or if the temporary file exists. `myisampack` creates a temporary file named `tbl_name.TMD` while it compresses the table. If you kill `myisampack`, the `.TMD` file may not be deleted. Normally, `myisampack` exits with an error if it finds that `tbl_name.TMD` exists. With `--force`, `myisampack` packs the table anyway.

`-?, --help`

Display a help message and exit.

`-j big_tbl_name, --join=big_tbl_name`

Join all tables named on the command-line into a single table `big_tbl_name`. All tables that are to be combined **must** be identical (same column names and types, same indexes, etc.).

`-p #, --packlength=#`

Specify the record length storage size, in bytes. The value should be 1, 2, or 3. (`myisampack` stores all rows with length pointers of 1, 2, or 3 bytes. In most normal cases, `myisampack` can determine the right length value before it begins packing the file, but it may notice during the packing process that it could have used a shorter length. In this case, `myisampack` will print a note that the next time you pack the same file, you could use a shorter record length.)

`-s, --silent`

Silent mode. Write output only when errors occur.

`-t, --test`

Don't actually pack table, just test packing it.

`-T dir_name, --tmp_dir=dir_name`

Use the named directory as the location in which to write the temporary table.

`-v, --verbose`

Verbose mode. Write information about progress and packing result.

`-V, --version`

Display version information and exit.

`-w, --wait`

Wait and retry if table is in use. If the `mysqld` server was invoked with the `--skip-locking` option, it is not a good idea to invoke `myisampack` if the table might be updated during the packing process.

The sequence of commands shown here illustrates a typical table compression session:

```
shell> ls -l station.*
-rw-rw-r--   1 monty    my        994128 Apr 17 19:00 station.MYD
-rw-rw-r--   1 monty    my         53248 Apr 17 19:00 station.MYI
-rw-rw-r--   1 monty    my          5767 Apr 17 19:00 station.frm

shell> myisamchk -dvv station

MyISAM file:     station
Isam-version:  2
Creation time: 1996-03-13 10:08:58
Recover time:  1997-02-02 3:06:43
Data records:               1192  Deleted blocks:         0
Datafile: Parts:            1192  Deleted data:           0
```

```
Datafile pointer (bytes):     2  Keyfile pointer (bytes):     2
Max data file length:   54657023  Max keyfile length:   33554431
Recordlength:               834
Record format: Fixed length
```

```
table description:
Key Start Len Index    Type                     Root  Blocksize  Rec/key
1    2     4  unique   unsigned long            1024   1024          1
2   32    30  multip.  text                    10240   1024          1
```

```
Field Start Length Type
1     1     1
2     2     4
3     6     4
4    10     1
5    11    20
6    31     1
7    32    30
8    62    35
9    97    35
10   132   35
11   167    4
12   171   16
13   187   35
14   222    4
15   226   16
16   242   20
17   262   20
18   282   20
19   302   30
20   332    4
21   336    4
22   340    1
23   341    8
24   349    8
25   357    8
26   365    2
27   367    2
28   369    4
29   373    4
30   377    1
31   378    2
32   380    8
33   388    4
34   392    4
35   396    4
36   400    4
37   404    1
38   405    4
39   409    4
40   413    4
41   417    4
42   421    4
43   425    4
```

```
44    429   20
45    449   30
46    479   1
47    480   1
48    481   79
49    560   79
50    639   79
51    718   79
52    797   8
53    805   1
54    806   1
55    807   20
56    827   4
57    831   4
```

```
shell> myisampack station.MYI
Compressing station.MYI: (1192 records)
- Calculating statistics
```

```
normal:      20  empty-space:      16  empty-zero:      12  empty-fill: 11
pre-space:    0  end-space:        12  table-lookups:    5  zero:        7
Original trees: 57  After join: 17
- Compressing file
87.14%
```

```
shell> ls -l station.*
-rw-rw-r--   1 monty     my          127874 Apr 17 19:00 station.MYD
-rw-rw-r--   1 monty     my           55296 Apr 17 19:04 station.MYI
-rw-rw-r--   1 monty     my            5767 Apr 17 19:00 station.frm
```

```
shell> myisamchk -dvv station
```

```
MyISAM file:       station
Isam-version:  2
Creation time: 1996-03-13 10:08:58
Recover time:  1997-04-17 19:04:26
Data records:               1192  Deleted blocks:          0
Datafile: Parts:            1192  Deleted data:            0
Datafilepointer (bytes):       3  Keyfile pointer (bytes): 1
Max data file length:   16777215  Max keyfile length:      131071
Recordlength:                834
Record format: Compressed
```

```
table description:
Key Start Len Index    Type              Root  Blocksize  Rec/key
1   2    4    unique   unsigned long     10240 1024       1
2   32   30   multip.  text              54272 1024       1
```

```
Field Start Length Type                  Huff tree  Bits
1     1     1      constant                  1        0
2     2     4      zerofill(1)               2        9
3     6     4      no zeros, zerofill(1)     2        9
4     10    1                                3        9
5     11    20     table-lookup              4        0
```

6	31	1		3	9
7	32	30	no endspace, not_always	5	9
8	62	35	no endspace, not_always, no empty	6	9
9	97	35	no empty	7	9
10	132	35	no endspace, not_always, no empty	6	9
11	167	4	zerofill(1)	2	9
12	171	16	no endspace, not_always, no empty	5	9
13	187	35	no endspace, not_always, no empty	6	9
14	222	4	zerofill(1)	2	9
15	226	16	no endspace, not_always, no empty	5	9
16	242	20	no endspace, not_always	8	9
17	262	20	no endspace, no empty	8	9
18	282	20	no endspace, no empty	5	9
19	302	30	no endspace, no empty	6	9
20	332	4	always zero	2	9
21	336	4	always zero	2	9
22	340	1		3	9
23	341	8	table-lookup	9	0
24	349	8	table-lookup	10	0
25	357	8	always zero	2	9
26	365	2		2	9
27	367	2	no zeros, zerofill(1)	2	9
28	369	4	no zeros, zerofill(1)	2	9
29	373	4	table-lookup	11	0
30	377	1		3	9
31	378	2	no zeros, zerofill(1)	2	9
32	380	8	no zeros	2	9
33	388	4	always zero	2	9
34	392	4	table-lookup	12	0
35	396	4	no zeros, zerofill(1)	13	9
36	400	4	no zeros, zerofill(1)	2	9
37	404	1		2	9
38	405	4	no zeros	2	9
39	409	4	always zero	2	9
40	413	4	no zeros	2	9
41	417	4	always zero	2	9
42	421	4	no zeros	2	9
43	425	4	always zero	2	9
44	429	20	no empty	3	9
45	449	30	no empty	3	9
46	479	1		14	4
47	480	1		14	4
48	481	79	no endspace, no empty	15	9
49	560	79	no empty	2	9
50	639	79	no empty	2	9
51	718	79	no endspace	16	9
52	797	8	no empty	2	9
53	805	1		17	1
54	806	1		3	9
55	807	20	no empty	3	9
56	827	4	no zeros, zerofill(2)	2	9
57	831	4	no zeros, zerofill(1)	2	9

The information printed by `myisampack` is described here:

`normal`

 The number of columns for which no extra packing is used.

`empty-space`

 The number of columns containing values that are only spaces; these will occupy 1 bit.

`empty-zero`

 The number of columns containing values that are only binary 0s; these will occupy 1 bit.

`empty-fill`

 The number of integer columns that don't occupy the full byte range of their type; these are changed to a smaller type (for example, an `INTEGER` column may be changed to `MEDIUMINT`).

`pre-space`

 The number of decimal columns that are stored with leading spaces. In this case, each value will contain a count for the number of leading spaces.

`end-space`

 The number of columns that have a lot of trailing spaces. In this case, each value will contain a count for the number of trailing spaces.

`table-lookup`

 The column had only a small number of different values, which were converted to an `ENUM` before Huffman compression.

`zero`

 The number of columns for which all values are zero.

`original trees`

 The initial number of Huffman trees.

`after join`

 The number of distinct Huffman trees left after joining trees to save some header space.

After a table has been compressed, `myisamchk -dvv` prints additional information about each field:

`type`

 The field type may contain the following descriptors:

 `constant`

  All rows have the same value.

no endspace
> Don't store endspace.

no endspace, not_always
> Don't store endspace and don't do end space compression for all values.

no endspace, no empty
> Don't store endspace. Don't store empty values.

table-lookup
> The column was converted to an ENUM.

zerofill(n)
> The most significant n bytes in the value are always 0 and are not stored.

no zeros
> Don't store zeros.

always zero
> 0 values are stored in 1 bit.

Huff tree
> The Huffman tree associated with the field.

bits
> The number of bits used in the Huffman tree.

After you have run pack_isam/myisampack you must run isamchk/myisamchk to re-create the index. At this time you can also sort the index blocks and create statistics needed for the MySQL optimiser to work more efficiently:

```
myisamchk -rq --analyze --sort-index table_name.MYI
isamchk   -rq --analyze --sort-index table_name.ISM
```

After you have installed the packed table into the MySQL database directory you should do mysqladmin flush-tables to force mysqld to start using the new table.

If you want to unpack a packed table, you can do this with the --unpack option to isamchk or myisamchk.

4.7.5 mysqld-max, an Extended mysqld Server

mysqld-max is the MySQL server (mysqld) configured with the following configure options:

Option	Comment
—with-server-suffix=-max	Add a suffix to the mysqld version string.
—with-innodb	Support for InnoDB tables.
—with-bdb	Support for Berkeley DB (BDB) tables.
CFLAGS=-DUSE_SYMDIR	Symbolic links support for Windows.

You can find the MySQL-max binaries at http://www.mysql.com/downloads/mysql-max-3.23.html.

The Windows MySQL binary distributions include both the standard mysqld.exe binary and the mysqld-max.exe binary. See http://www.mysql.com/downloads/mysql-3.23.html. See also Section 2.1.2, Installing MySQL on Windows.

Note that as InnoDB and Berkeley DB are not available for all platforms, some of the Max binaries may not have support for both of these. You can check which table types are supported by doing the following query:

```
mysql> SHOW VARIABLES LIKE "have_%";
+----------------+-------+
| Variable_name  | Value |
+----------------+-------+
| have_bdb       | YES   |
| have_innodb    | NO    |
| have_isam      | YES   |
| have_raid      | NO    |
| have_openssl   | NO    |
+----------------+-------+
```

The meanings of the values are:

Value	Meaning
YES	The option is activated and usable.
NO	MySQL is not compiled with support for this option.
DISABLED	The xxxx option is disabled because one started mysqld with --skip-xxxx or because one didn't start mysqld with all needed options to enable the option. In this case the hostname.err file should contain a reason why the option is disabled.

Note: To be able to create InnoDB tables you **must** edit your startup options to include at least the innodb_data_file_path option. See Section 7.5.2, InnoDB Startup Options.

To get better performance for BDB tables, you should add some configuration options for these too. See Section 7.6.3, BDB Startup Options.

safe_mysqld will automatically try to start any mysqld binary with the -max prefix. This makes it very easy to test out another mysqld binary in an existing installation. Just run configure with the options you want and then install the new mysqld binary as mysqld-max in the same directory where your old mysqld binary is. See Section 4.7.2, safe_mysqld, the Wrapper Around mysqld.

The mysqld-max RPM uses the aforementioned safe_mysqld feature. It just installs the mysqld-max executable and safe_mysqld will automatically use this executable when safe_mysqld is restarted.

The following table shows which table types our standard **MySQL-Max** binaries include:

System	BDB	InnoDB
AIX 4.3	N	Y
HP-UX 11.0	N	Y
Linux-Alpha	N	Y
Linux-Intel	Y	Y
Linux-Ia64	N	Y
Solaris-Intel	N	Y
Solaris-SPARC	Y	Y
Caldera (SCO) OSR5	Y	Y
UnixWare	Y	Y
Windows/NT	Y	Y

4.8 MySQL Client-Side Scripts and Utilities

4.8.1 Overview of the Client-Side Scripts and Utilities

All MySQL clients that communicate with the server using the mysqlclient library use the following environment variables:

Name	Description
MYSQL_UNIX_PORT	The default socket; used for connections to localhost
MYSQL_TCP_PORT	The default TCP/IP port
MYSQL_PWD	The default password
MYSQL_DEBUG	Debug-trace options when debugging
TMPDIR	The directory where temporary tables/files are created

Use of MYSQL_PWD is insecure. See Section 4.2.8, Connecting to the MySQL server.

The mysql client uses the file named in the MYSQL_HISTFILE environment variable to save the command-line history. The default value for the history file is $HOME/.mysql_history, where $HOME is the value of the HOME environment variable. See Appendix E.

All MySQL programs take many different options. However, every MySQL program provides a `--help` option that you can use to get a full description of the program's different options. For example, try `mysql --help`.

You can override default options for all standard client programs with an option file. See Section 4.1.2, `my.cnf` Option Files.

The following list briefly describes the MySQL programs:

`myisamchk`

> Utility to describe, check, optimise, and repair MySQL tables. Because `myisamchk` has many functions, it is described in its own chapter. See Chapter 4.

`make_binary_distribution`

> Makes a binary release of a compiled MySQL. This could be sent by FTP to `/pub/mysql/Incoming` on `support.mysql.com` for the convenience of other MySQL users.

`msql2mysql`

> A shell script that converts mSQL programs to MySQL. It doesn't handle all cases, but it gives a good start when converting.

`mysqlaccess`

> A script that checks the access privileges for a host, user, and database combination.

`mysqladmin`

> Utility for performing administrative operations, such as creating or dropping databases, reloading the grant tables, flushing tables to disk, and reopening log files. `mysqladmin` can also be used to retrieve version, process, and status information from the server. See Section 4.8.3, `mysqladmin`, Administrating a MySQL Server.

`mysqlbug`

> The MySQL bug report script. This script should always be used when filing a bug report to the MySQL list.

`mysqld`

> The SQL daemon. This should always be running.

`mysqldump`

> Dumps a MySQL database into a file as SQL statements or as tab-separated text files. Enhanced freeware originally by Igor Romanenko. See Section 4.8.5, `mysqldump`, Dumping Table Structure and Data.

`mysqlimport`

> Imports text files into their respective tables using LOAD DATA INFILE. See Section 4.8.7, `mysqlimport`, Importing Data from Text Files.

`mysqlshow`

Displays information about databases, tables, columns, and indexes.

`mysql_install_db`

Creates the MySQL grant tables with default privileges. This is usually executed only once, when first installing MySQL on a system.

`replace`

A utility program that is used by `msql2mysql`, but that has more general applicability as well. `replace` changes strings in place in files or on the standard input. Uses a finite state machine to match longer strings first. Can be used to swap strings. For example, this command swaps a and b in the given files:

```
shell> replace a b b a—file1 file2 ...
```

4.8.2 The Command-Line Tool

`mysql` is a simple SQL shell (with GNU `readline` capabilities). It supports interactive and non-interactive use. When used interactively, query results are presented in an ASCII-table format. When used non-interactively (for example, as a filter), the result is presented in tab-separated format. (The output format can be changed using command-line options.) You can run scripts simply like this:

```
shell> mysql database < script.sql > output.tab
```

If you have problems due to insufficient memory in the client, use the `--quick` option! This forces `mysql` to use `mysql_use_result()` rather than `mysql_store_result()` to retrieve the result set.

Using `mysql` is very easy. Just start it as follows: `mysql database` or `mysql --user=user_name --password=your_password database`. Type a SQL statement, end it with `;`, `\g`, or `\G`, and press Enter.

`mysql` supports the following options:

`-?, --help`

Display this help and exit.

`-A, --no-auto-rehash`

No automatic rehashing. One has to use 'rehash' to get table and field completion. This gives a quicker start of mysql.

`-B, --batch`

Print results with a tab as separator, each row on a new line. Doesn't use history file.

`--character-sets-dir= ...`

Directory where character sets are located.

-C, --compress
>   Use compression in server/client protocol.

-#, --debug[= . . .]
>   Debug log. Default is 'd:t:o,/tmp/mysql.trace'.

-D, --database= . . .
>   Database to use. This is mainly useful in the my.cnf file.

--default-character-set= . . .
>   Set the default character set.

-e, --execute= . . .
>   Execute command and quit. (Output like with —batch.)

-E, --vertical
>   Print the output of a query (rows) vertically. Without this option you can also force
>   this output by ending your statements with \G.

-f, --force
>   Continue even in case of a SQL error.

-g, --no-named-commands
>   Named commands are disabled. Use * form only, or use named commands only in
>   the beginning of a line ending with a semicolon (;). Since Version 10.9, the client
>   now starts with this option **enabled** by default! With the -g option, long-format com-
>   mands will still work from the first line, however.

-G, --enable-named-commands
>   Named commands are **enabled**. Long-format commands are allowed as well as
>   shortened * commands.

-i, --ignore-space
>   Ignore space after function names.

-h, --host= . . .
>   Connect to the given host.

-H, --html
>   Produce HTML output.

-L, --skip-line-numbers
>   Don't write line number for errors. Useful when one wants to compare result files
>   that include error messages.

--no-pager
>   Disable pager and print to stdout. See interactive help (\h) also.

--no-tee
>   Disable outfile. See interactive help (\h) also.

`-n, --unbuffered`
Flush buffer after each query.

`-N, --skip-column-names`
Don't write column names in results.

`-O, --set-variable var=option`
Give a variable a value. `--help` lists variables.

`-o, --one-database`
Only update the default database. This is useful for skipping updates to other databases in the update log.

`--pager[=. . .]0]`
Output type. Default is your ENV variable PAGER. Valid pagers are less, more, cat [> filename], etc. See interactive help (\h) also. This option does not work in batch mode. Pager works only in Unix.

`-p[password], --password[=. . .]`
Password to use when connecting to the server. If a password is not given on the command-line, you will be prompted for it. Note that if you use the short form `-p` you can't have a space between the option and the password.

`-P --port=. . .`
TCP/IP port number to use for connection.

`-q, --quick`
Don't cache result, print it row-by-row. This may slow down the server if the output is suspended. Doesn't use history file.

`-r, --raw`
Write column values without escape conversion. Used with `--batch`.

`-s, --silent`
Be more silent.

`-S --socket=. . .`
Socket file to use for connection.

`-t --table`
Output in table format. This is default in non-batch mode.

`-T, --debug-info`
Print some debug information at exit.

`--tee=. . .`
Append everything into outfile. See interactive help (\h) also. Does not work in batch mode.

`-u, --user=#`

    User for login if not current user.

`-U, --safe-updates[=#], --i-am-a-dummy[=#]`

    Only allow UPDATE and DELETE that uses keys. More information about this option is provided later in this section. You can reset this option if you have it in your `my.cnf` file by using `--safe-updates=0`.

`-v, --verbose`

    More verbose output (-v -v -v gives the table output format).

`-V, --version`

    Output version information and exit.

`-w, --wait`

    Wait and retry if connection is down instead of aborting.

You can also set the following variables with `-O` or `--set-variable`:

Variable Name	Default	Description
connect_timeout	0	Number of seconds before timeout connection.
max_allowed_packet	16777216	Max packet length to send/receive from to server.
net_buffer_length	16384	Buffer for TCP/IP and socket communication.
select_limit	1000	Automatic limit for SELECT when using —i-am-a-dummy.
max_join_size	1000000	Automatic limit for rows in a join when using —i-am-a-dummy.

If you type 'help' on the command-line, `mysql` will print out the commands that it supports:

```
mysql> help

MySQL commands:
help      (\h)   Display this text.
?         (\h)   Synonym for 'help'.
clear     (\c)   Clear command.
connect   (\r)   Reconnect to the server.
                 Optional arguments are db and host.
edit      (\e)   Edit command with $EDITOR.
ego       (\G)   Send command to mysql server,
                 display result vertically.
exit      (\q)   Exit mysql. Same as quit.
go        (\g)   Send command to mysql server.
nopager   (\n)   Disable pager, print to stdout.
notee     (\t)   Don't write into outfile.
pager     (\P)   Set PAGER [to_pager].
                 Print the query results via PAGER.
print     (\p)   Print current command.
quit      (\q)   Quit mysql.
rehash    (\#)   Rebuild completion hash.
```

```
source   (\.)    Execute a SQL script file.
                 Takes a file name as an argument.
status   (\s)    Get status information from the server.
tee      (\T)    Set outfile [to_outfile].
                 Append everything into given outfile.
use      (\u)    Use another database.
                 Takes database name as argument.
```

The pager command works only in Unix.

The status command gives you some information about the connection and the server you are using. If you are running in the --safe-updates mode, status will also print the values for the mysql variables that affect your queries.

A useful startup option for beginners (introduced in MySQL Version 3.23.11) is --safe-updates (or --i-am-a-dummy for users that have at some time done a DELETE FROM table_name but forgot the WHERE clause). When using this option, mysql sends the following command to the MySQL server when opening the connection:

```
SET SQL_SAFE_UPDATES=1,SQL_SELECT_LIMIT=#select_limit#,
    SQL_MAX_JOIN_SIZE=#max_join_size#"
```

where #select_limit# and #max_join_size# are variables that can be set from the mysql command-line. See Section 5.5.6, SET Syntax.

This results in the following:

- You are not allowed to do an UPDATE or DELETE statement if you don't have a key constraint in the WHERE part. One can, however, force an UPDATE/DELETE by using LIMIT:

    ```
    UPDATE table_name SET not_key_column=# WHERE not_key_column=# LIMIT 1;
    ```

- All big results are automatically limited to #select_limit# rows.

- SELECT's that will probably need to examine more than #max_join_size row combinations will be aborted.

Some useful hints about the mysql client:

Some data is much more readable when displayed vertically, instead of the usual horizontal box-type output. For example, longer text, which includes new lines, is often much easier to read with vertical output.

```
mysql> SELECT * FROM mails WHERE LENGTH(txt) < 300 lIMIT 300,1\G
*************************** 1. row ***************************
  msg_nro: 3068
     date: 2000-03-01 23:29:50
time_zone: +0200
mail_from: Monty
    reply: monty@no.spam.com
  mail_to: "Thimble Smith" <tim@no.spam.com>
      sbj: UTF-8
```

```
       txt: >>>>> "Thimble" == Thimble Smith writes:

Thimble> Hi.  I think this is a good idea.  Is anyone familiar with UTF-8
Thimble> or Unicode? Otherwise, I'll put this on my TODO list and see what
Thimble> happens.

Yes, please do that.

Regards,
Monty
       file: inbox-jani-1
       hash: 190402944
1 row in set (0.09 sec)
```

- For logging, you can use the tee option. The tee can be started with option
  --tee=..., or from the command-line interactively with command tee. All the
  data displayed on the screen will also be appended into a given file. This can be very
  useful for debugging purposes also. The tee can be disabled from the command-line
  with command notee. Executing tee again starts logging again. Without a parameter the previous file will be used. Note that tee will flush the results into the file after
  each command, just before the command-line appears again waiting for the next
  command.

- Browsing, or searching the results in interactive mode in Unix less, more, or any
  other similar program, is now possible with option --pager[=...]. Without this
  argument, mysql client will look for the environment variable PAGER and set pager
  to that. pager can be started from the interactive command-line with command
  pager and disabled with command nopager. The command takes an argument
  optionally and the pager will be set to that. Command pager can be called without
  an argument, but this requires that the option --pager was used, or the pager will
  default to stdout. pager works only in Unix, since it uses the popen() function,
  which doesn't exist in Windows. In Windows, the tee option can be used instead,
  although it may not be as handy as pager can be in some situations.

- Here are a few tips about pager: you can use it to write to a file:

  ```
  mysql> pager cat > /tmp/log.txt
  ```

  and the results will only go to a file. You can also pass any options for the programs
  that you want to use with the pager:

  ```
  mysql> pager less -n -i -S
  ```

  Note the option '-S'. You may find it very useful when browsing the results; try the
  option with horizontal output (end commands with '\g' or ';') and with vertical output (end commands with '\G'). Sometimes a very wide result set is hard to read from
  the screen. With option -S set to *less* you can browse the results within the interactive *less* from left to right, preventing lines longer than your screen from being con-
  tinued to the next line. This can make the result set much more readable. You can

switch the mode between on and off within the interactive *less* with '-S'. See the 'h' for more help about *less*.

- Last (unless you already understood this from the previous examples) you can combine very complex methods to handle the results—for example, the following would send the results to two files in two different directories, on two different hard disks mounted on /dr1 and /dr2, yet let the results still be seen on the screen via less:

```
mysql> pager cat | tee /dr1/tmp/res.txt | \
tee /dr2/tmp/res2.txt | less -n -i -S
```

- You can also combine these two functions; have the tee enabled and set the pager to 'less', and you will be able to browse the results in Unix 'less' and still have everything appended into a file the same time. The difference between Unix tee used with the pager and the mysql client built-in tee is that the built-in tee works even if you don't have the Unix tee available. The built-in tee also logs everything that is printed on the screen, where the Unix tee used with pager doesn't log quite that much. Last, but not least, the interactive tee is easier to switch on and off, when you want to log something into a file but want to be able to turn the feature off sometimes.

4.8.3 mysqladmin, Administrating a MySQL Server

This is a utility for performing administrative operations. The syntax is:

```
shell> mysqladmin [OPTIONS] command [command-option] command ...
```

You can get a list of the options your version of mysqladmin supports by executing mysqladmin --help.

The current mysqladmin supports the following commands:

create databasename
    Create a new database.

drop databasename
    Delete a database and all its tables.

extended-status
    Gives an extended status message from the server.

flush-hosts
    Flush all cached hosts.

flush-logs
    Flush all logs.

`flush-tables`

Flush all tables.

`flush-privileges`

Reload grant tables (same as reload).

`kill id,id, . . .`

Kill mysql threads.

`password`

Set a new password. Change old password to new-password.

`ping`

Check if mysqld is alive.

`processlist`

Show list of active threads in server.

`reload`

Reload grant tables.

`refresh`

Flush all tables and close and open log files.

`shutdown`

Take server down.

`slave-start`

Start slave replication thread.

`slave-stop`

Stop slave replication thread.

`status`

Gives a short status message from the server.

`variables`

Prints variables available.

`version`

Get version info from server.

All commands can be shortened to their unique prefix. For example:

```
shell> mysqladmin proc stat
+----+-------+-----------+----+-------------+------+-------+------+
| Id | User  | Host      | db | Command     | Time | State | Info |
+----+-------+-----------+----+-------------+------+-------+------+
| 6  | monty | localhost |    | Processlist | 0    |       |      |
+----+-------+-----------+----+-------------+------+-------+------+
Uptime: 10077  Threads: 1  Questions: 9  Slow queries: 0
Opens: 6 Flush tables: 1  Open tables: 2
Memory in use: 1092K  Max memory used: 1116K
```

The mysqladmin status command result has the following columns:

Column	Description
Uptime	Number of seconds the MySQL server has been up.
Threads	Number of active threads (clients).
Questions	Number of questions from clients since mysqld was started.
Slow queries	Queries that have taken more than long_query_time seconds. See Section 4.9.5, The Slow Query Log.
Opens	How many tables mysqld has opened.
Flush tables	Number of flush . . . , refresh, and reload commands.
Open tables	Number of tables that are open now.
Memory in use	Memory allocated directly by the mysqld code (only available when MySQL is compiled with --with-debug=full).
Max memory used	Maximum memory allocated directly by the mysqld code (only available when MySQL is compiled with --with-debug=full).

If you do myslqadmin shutdown on a socket (in other words, on the computer where mysqld is running), mysqladmin will wait until the MySQL pid-file is removed to ensure that the mysqld server has stopped properly.

4.8.4 Using mysqlcheck for Table Maintenance and Crash Recovery

Since MySQL Version 3.23.38 you can use a new checking and repairing tool for MyISAM tables. The difference between this tool and myisamchk is that mysqlcheck should be used when the mysqld server is running, where as myisamchk should be used when it is not. The benefit is that you no longer have to take the server down for checking or repairing your tables.

mysqlcheck uses MySQL server commands CHECK, REPAIR, ANALYZE, and OPTIMIZE in a convenient way for the user.

There are three alternative ways to invoke mysqlcheck:

```
shell> mysqlcheck [OPTIONS] database [tables]
shell> mysqlcheck [OPTIONS] --databases DB1 [DB2 DB3...]
shell> mysqlcheck [OPTIONS] --all-databases
```

In this way, mysqlcheck can be used in a similar way as mysqldump when it comes to what databases and tables you want to choose.

mysqlcheck does have a special feature compared to the other clients; the default behavior, checking tables (-c), can be changed by renaming the binary. So if you want to have a tool that repairs tables by default, you should just copy mysqlcheck to your hard drive with a new name, mysqlrepair, or alternatively make a symbolic link to mysqlrepair and name the symbolic link mysqlrepair. If you invoke mysqlrepair now, it will repair tables by default.

The names that you can use to change `mysqlcheck` default behavior are as follows:

```
mysqlrepair:   The default option will be -r
mysqlanalyze:  The default option will be -a
mysqloptimize: The default option will be -o
```

The options available for `mysqlcheck` are listed here. Please check what your version
supports with `mysqlcheck --help`.

`-A, --all-databases`
Check all the databases. This will be the same as —databases with all databases
selected.

`-1, --all-in-1`
Instead of making one query for each table, execute all queries in 1 query separately
for each database. Table names will be in a comma-separated list.

`-a, --analyze`
Analyse given tables.

`--auto-repair`
If a checked table is corrupted, automatically fix it. Repairing will be done after all
tables have been checked, if corrupted ones were found.

`-#, --debug= . . .`
Output debug log. Often this is 'd:t:o,filename'.

`--character-sets-dir= . . .`
Directory where character sets are located.

`-c, --check`
Check table for errors.

`-C, --check-only-changed`
Check only tables that have changed since last check or haven't been closed properly.

`--compress`
Use compression in server/client protocol.

`-?, --help`
Display this help message and exit.

`-B, --databases`
To check several databases. Note the difference in usage; in this case no tables are
given. All name arguments are regarded as database names.

`--default-character-set= . . .`
Set the default character set.

-F, --fast

Check only tables that haven't been closed properly.

-f, --force

Continue even if we get an sql-error.

-e, --extended

If you are using this option with CHECK TABLE, it will ensure that the table is 100% consistent, but will take a long time.

If you are using this option with REPAIR TABLE, it will run an extended repair on the table, which may not only take a long time to execute, but may also produce a lot of garbage rows!

-h, --host= . . .

Connect to host.

-m, --medium-check

Faster than extended-check, but only finds 99.99% of all errors. Should be good enough for most cases.

-o, --optimize

Optimise tables.

-p, --password[= . . .]

Password to use when connecting to server. If password is not given it's solicited on the tty.

-P, --port= . . .

Port number to use for connection.

-q, --quick

If you are using this option with CHECK TABLE, it prevents the check from scanning the rows to check for wrong links. This is the fastest check.

If you are using this option with REPAIR TABLE, it will try to repair only the index tree. This is the fastest repair method for a table.

-r, --repair

Can fix almost anything except unique keys that aren't reallyunique.

-s, --silent

Print only error messages.

-S, --socket= . . .

Socket file to use for connection.

--tables

Overrides option —databases (-B).

`-u, --user=#`

   User for login if not current user.

`-v, --verbose`

   Print info about the various stages.

`-V, --version`

   Output version information and exit.

4.8.5 `mysqldump`, Dumping Table Structure and Data

`mysqldump` is a utility to dump a database or a collection of databases for backup or for transferring the data to another SQL server (not necessarily a MySQL server). The dump will contain SQL statements to create the table and/or populate the table.

If you are doing a backup on the server, you should consider using the `mysqlhotcopy` instead. See Section 4.8.6, `mysqlhotcopy`, Copying MySQL Databases and Tables.

```
shell> mysqldump [OPTIONS] database [tables]
OR      mysqldump [OPTIONS] --databases [OPTIONS] DB1 [DB2 DB3...]
OR      mysqldump [OPTIONS] --all-databases [OPTIONS]
```

If you don't give any tables or use the `--databases` or `--all-databases`, the whole database(s) will be dumped.

You can get a list of the options your version of `mysqldump` supports by executing `mysqldump --help`.

Note that if you run `mysqldump` without `--quick` or `--opt`, `mysqldump` will load the whole result set into memory before dumping the result. This will probably be a problem if you are dumping a big database.

Note that if you are using a new copy of the `mysqldump` program and you are going to do a dump that will be read into a very old MySQL server, you should not use the `--opt` or `-e` options.

`mysqldump` supports the following options:

`--add-locks`

   Add LOCK TABLES before and UNLOCK TABLES after each table dump (to get faster inserts into MySQL).

`--add-drop-table`

   Add a `drop table` before each create statement.

`-A, --all-databases`

   Dump all the databases. This will be the same as `--databases` with all databases selected.

`-a, --all`

Include all MySQL-specific create options.

`--allow-keywords`

Allows creation of column names that are keywords. This works by prefixing each column name with the table name.

`-c, --complete-insert`

Use complete insert statements (with column names).

`-C, --compress`

Compress all information between the client and the server if both support compression.

`-B, --databases`

To dump several databases. Note the difference in usage. In this case no tables are given. All name arguments are regarded as database names. USE db_name; will be included in the output before each new database.

`--delayed`

Insert rows with the INSERT DELAYED command.

`-e, --extended-insert`

Use the new multi-line INSERT syntax. (Gives more compact and faster insert statements.)

`-#, --debug[=option_string]`

Trace usage of the program (for debugging).

`--help`

Display a help message and exit.

`--fields-terminated-by= . . .`
`--fields-enclosed-by= . . .`
`--fields-optionally-enclosed-by= . . .`
`--fields-escaped-by= . . .`
`--lines-terminated-by= . . .`

These options are used with the -T option and have the same meaning as the corresponding clauses for LOAD DATA INFILE. See Section 6.4.9, LOAD DATA INFILE Syntax.

`-F, --flush-logs`

Flush log file in the MySQL server before starting the dump.

`-f, --force,`

Continue even in case of a SQL error during a table dump.

`-h, --host=..`

Dump data from the MySQL server on the named host. The default host is local-host.

`-l, --lock-tables`

Lock all tables before starting the dump. The tables are locked with READ LOCAL to allow concurrent inserts in the case of MyISAM tables.

`-K, --disable-keys`

/*!40000 ALTER TABLE tb_name DISABLE KEYS */; and /*!40000 ALTER TABLE tb_name ENABLE KEYS */; will be put in the output.

`-n, --no-create-db`

CREATE DATABASE /*!32312 IF NOT EXISTS*/ db_name; will not be put in the output. This line will be added otherwise, if —databases or —all-databases option were given.

`-t, --no-create-info`

Don't write table creation information (the CREATE TABLE statement).

`-d, --no-data`

Don't write any row information for the table. This is very useful if you just want to get a dump of the structure for a table!

`--opt`

Same as `--quick` `--add-drop-table` `--add-locks` `--extended-insert` `—lock-tables`. Should give you the fastest possible dump for reading into a MySQL server.

`-pyour_pass, --password[=your_pass]`

The password to use when connecting to the server. If you specify no =your_pass part, mysqldump you will be prompted for a password.

`-P port_num, --port=port_num`

The TCP/IP port number to use for connecting to a host. (This is used for connections to hosts other than localhost, for which Unix sockets are used.)

`-q, --quick`

Don't buffer query, dump directly to stdout. Uses mysql_use_result() to do this.

`-r, --result-file= . . .`

Direct output to a given file. This option should be used in MS-DOS because it prevents new line '\n' from being converted to '\n\r' (new line + carriage return).

`-S /path/to/socket, --socket=/path/to/socket`

The socket file to use when connecting to localhost (which is the default host).

`--tables`

Overrides option —databases (-B).

`-T, --tab=path-to-some-directory`

Creates a `table_name.sql` file that contains the SQL CREATE commands, and a `table_name.txt` file that contains the data, for each give table. **Note**: This only works if `mysqldump` is run on the same machine as the `mysqld` daemon. The format of the `.txt` file is made according to the `--fields-xxx` and `--lines--xxx` options.

`-u user_name, --user=user_name`

The MySQL username to use when connecting to the server. The default value is your Unix login name.

`-O var=option, --set-variable var=option`

Set the value of a variable. The possible variables are listed below.

`-v, --verbose`

Verbose mode. Print out more information on what the program does.

`-V, --version`

Print version information and exit.

`-w, --where='where-condition'`

Dump only selected records. Note that quotes are mandatory.

`-X, --xml`

Dumps a database as well-formed XML.

`-x, --first-slave`

Locks all tables across all databases.

```
"--where=user='jimf'" "-wuserid>1" "-wuserid<1"
```

`-O net_buffer_length=#, where # < 16M`

When creating multi-row-insert statements (as with option `--extended-insert` or `--opt`), `mysqldump` will create rows up to `net_buffer_length` length. If you increase this variable, you should also ensure that the `max_allowed_packet` variable in the MySQL server is bigger than the `net_buffer_length`.

The most normal use of `mysqldump` is probably for making a backup of whole databases. See Section 4.4.1, Database Backups.

```
mysqldump --opt database > backup-file.sql
```

You can read this back into MySQL with:

```
mysql database < backup-file.sql
```

or

```
mysql -e "source /patch-to-backup/backup-file.sql" database
```

However, it's also very useful to populate another MySQL server with information from a database:

```
mysqldump --opt database | mysql ---host=remote-host -C database
```

It is possible to dump several databases with one command:

```
mysqldump --databases database1 [database2 ...] > my_databases.sql
```

If all the databases are wanted, one can use:

```
mysqldump --all-databases > all_databases.sql
```

4.8.6 `mysqlhotcopy`, Copying MySQL Databases and Tables

`mysqlhotcopy` is a Perl script that uses LOCK TABLES, FLUSH TABLES, and `cp` or `scp` to quickly make a backup of a database. It's the fastest way to make a backup of a database of single tables, but it can only be run on the same machine where the database directories are.

```
mysqlhotcopy db_name [/path/to/new_directory]
```

```
mysqlhotcopy db_name_1 ... db_name_n /path/to/new_directory
```

```
mysqlhotcopy db_name./regex/
```

`mysqlhotcopy` supports the following options:

`-?, --help`
    Display a help screen and exit.

`-u, --user=#`
    User for database login.

`-p, --password=#`
    Password to use when connecting to server.

`-P, --port=#`
    Port to use when connecting to local server.

`-S, --socket=#`
    Socket to use when connecting to local server.

`--allowold`
    Don't abort if target already exists (rename it _old).

`--keepold`

Don't delete previous (now renamed) target when done.

`--noindices`

Don't include full index files in copy to make the backup smaller and faster. The indexes can later be reconstructed with `myisamchk -rq`.

`--method=#`

Method for copy (`cp` or `scp`).

`-q, --quiet`

Be silent except for errors.

`--debug`

Enable debug.

`-n, --dryrun`

Report actions without doing them.

`--regexp=#`

Copy all databases with names matching regexp.

`--suffix=#`

Suffix for names of copied databases.

`--checkpoint=#`

Insert checkpoint entry into specified db.table.

`--flushlog`

Flush logs once all tables are locked.

`--tmpdir=#`

Temporary directory (instead of /tmp).

You can use `perldoc mysqlhotcopy` to get ore complete documentation for `mysql-hotcopy`.

`mysqlhotcopy` reads the groups `[client]` and `[mysqlhotcopy]` from the option files.

To be able to execute `mysqlhotcopy` you need write access to the backup directory, the **select** privilege for the tables you are about to copy, and the MySQL **reload** privilege (to be able to execute FLUSH TABLES).

4.8.7 `mysqlimport`, Importing Data from Text Files

`mysqlimport` provides a command-line interface to the LOAD DATA INFILE SQL statement. Most options to `mysqlimport` correspond directly to the same options to LOAD DATA INFILE. See Section 6.4.9, LOAD DATA INFILE Syntax.

mysqlimport is invoked like this:

```
shell> mysqlimport [options] database textfile1 [textfile2 ...]
```

For each text file named on the command-line, mysqlimport strips any extension from the filename and uses the result to determine which table to import the file's contents into. For example, files named patient.txt, patient.text, and patient would all be imported into a table named patient.

mysqlimport supports the following options:

-c, --columns=...

> This option takes a comma-separated list of field names as an argument. The field list is used to create a proper LOAD DATA INFILE command, which is then passed to MySQL. See Section 6.4.9, LOAD DATA INFILE Syntax.

-C, --compress

> Compress all information between the client and the server if both support compression.

-#, --debug[=option_string]

> Trace usage of the program (for debugging).

-d, --delete

> Empty the table before importing the text file.

--fields-terminated-by=...
--fields-enclosed-by=...
--fields-optionally-enclosed-by=...
--fields-escaped-by=...
--lines-terminated-by=...

> These options have the same meaning as the corresponding clauses for LOAD DATA INFILE. See Section 6.4.9, LOAD DATA INFILE Syntax.

-f, --force

> Ignore errors. For example, if a table for a text file doesn't exist, continue processing any remaining files. Without --force, mysqlimport exits if a table doesn't exist.

--help

> Display a help message and exit.

-h host_name, --host=host_name

> Import data to the MySQL server on the named host. The default host is localhost.

-i, --ignore

> See the description for the --replace option.

`-l, --lock-tables`

Lock **all** tables for writing before processing any text files. This ensures that all tables are synchronised on the server.

`-L, --local`

Read input files from the client. By default, text files are assumed to be on the server if you connect to `localhost` (which is the default host).

`-pyour_pass, --password[=your_pass]`

The password to use when connecting to the server. If you specify no `=your_pass` part, `mysqlimport` you will be prompted for a password.

`-P port_num, --port=port_num`

The TCP/IP port number to use for connecting to a host. (This is used for connections to hosts other than `localhost`, for which Unix sockets are used.)

`-r, --replace`

The `--replace` and `--ignore` options control handling of input records that duplicate existing records on unique key values. If you specify `--replace`, new rows replace existing rows that have the same unique key value. If you specify `--ignore`, input rows that duplicate an existing row on a unique key value are skipped. If you don't specify either option, an error occurs when a duplicate key value is found, and the rest of the text file is ignored.

`-s, --silent`

Silent mode. Write output only when errors occur.

`-S /path/to/socket, --socket=/path/to/socket`

The socket file to use when connecting to `localhost` (which is the default host).

`-u user_name, --user=user_name`

The MySQL username to use when connecting to the server. The default value is your Unix login name.

`-v, --verbose`

Verbose mode. Print out more information regarding what the program does.

`-V, --version`

Print version information and exit.

Here is a sample run using `mysqlimport`:

```
$ mysql --version
mysql  Ver 9.33 Distrib 3.22.25, for pc-linux-gnu (i686)
$ uname -a
Linux xxx.com 2.2.5-15 #1 Mon Apr 19 22:21:09 EDT 1999 i586 unknown
$ mysql -e 'CREATE TABLE imptest(id INT, n VARCHAR(30))' test
$ ed
a
100     Max Sydow
101     Count Dracula
```

```
w imptest.txt
32
q
$ od -c imptest.txt
0000000   1   0   0  \t   M   a   x       S   y   d   o   w  \n   1   0
0000020   1  \t   C   o   u   n   t       D   r   a   c   u   l   a  \n
0000040
$ mysqlimport --local test imptest.txt
test.imptest: Records: 2  Deleted: 0  Skipped: 0  Warnings: 0
$ mysql -e 'SELECT * FROM imptest' test
+------+---------------+
| id   | n             |
+------+---------------+
|  100 | Max Sydow     |
|  101 | Count Dracula |
+------+---------------+
```

4.8.8 Showing Databases, Tables, and Columns

mysqlshow can be used to quickly look at which databases exist, their tables, and the tables' columns.

With the mysql program you can get the same information with the SHOW commands. See Section 4.5.6, SHOW Syntax.

mysqlshow is invoked like this:

```
shell> mysqlshow [OPTIONS] [database [table [column]]]
```

- If no database is given, all matching databases are shown.
- If no table is given, all matching tables in the database are shown.
- If no column is given, all matching columns and column types in the table are shown.

Note that in newer MySQL versions, you only see those databases/tables/columns for which you have some privileges.

If the last argument contains a shell or SQL wildcard (*, ?, % or _), only what's matched by the wildcard is shown. This may cause some confusion when you try to display the columns for a table with a _, as in this case mysqlshow only shows you the table names that match the pattern. This is easily fixed by adding an extra % last on the command-line (as a separate argument).

4.8.9 perror, Explaining Error Codes

For most system errors MySQL will, in addition to an internal text message, also print the system error code in one of the following styles: message . . . (errno: #) or message . . . (Errcode: #).

You can find out what the error code means by either examining the documentation for your system or using the perror utility.

perror prints a description for a system error code, or a MyISAM/ISAM table handler error code.

perror is invoked like this:

```
shell> perror [OPTIONS] [ERRORCODE [ERRORCODE...]]

Example:

shell> perror 13 64
Error code  13:  Permission denied
Error code  64:  Machine is not on the network
```

Note that the error messages are mostly system-dependent!

4.8.10 How to Run SQL Commands from a Text File

The mysql client typically is used interactively, like this:

```
shell> mysql database
```

However, it's also possible to put your SQL commands in a file and tell mysql to read its input from that file. To do so, create a text file text_file that contains the commands you wish to execute. Then invoke mysql as shown here:

```
shell> mysql database < text_file
```

You can also start your text file with a USE db_name statement. In this case, it is unnecessary to specify the database name on the command line:

```
shell> mysql < text_file
```

If you are already running mysql, you can execute a SQL script file using the source command:

```
mysql> source filename;
```

For more information about batch mode, see Section 3.6, Using mysql in Batch Mode.

4.9 The MySQL Log Files

MySQL has several different log files that can help you find out what's going on inside mysqld:

Log file	Description
The error log	Problems encountered when starting, running, or stopping mysqld.
The isam log	Logs all changes to the ISAM tables. Used only for debugging the isam code.
The query log	Established connections and executed queries.
The update log	Deprecated: stores all statements that change data.
The binary log	Stores all statements that change something. Used also for replication.
The slow log	Stores all queries that took more than long_query_time to execute or didn't use indexes.

All logs can be found in the mysqld data directory. You can force mysqld to reopen the log files (or in some cases switch to a new log) by executing FLUSH LOGS. See Section 4.5.3, FLUSH Syntax.

4.9.1 The Error Log

mysqld writes all errors to the stderr, which the safe_mysqld script redirects to a file called 'hostname'.err. (On Windows, mysqld writes this directly to \mysql\data\mysql.err.)

This contains information indicating when mysqld was started and stopped and also any critical errors found when running. If mysqld dies unexpectedly and safe_mysqld needs to restart mysqld, safe_mysqld will write a restarted mysqld row in this file. This log also holds a warning if mysqld notices a table that needs to be automatically checked or repaired.

On some operating systems, the error log will contain a stack trace that can be used to find out where mysqld died. See Section D.1.4, Using a Stack Trace.

4.9.2 The General Query Log

If you want to know what happens within mysqld, you should start it with --log[=file]. This will log all connections and queries to the log file (by default named 'hostname'.log). This log can be very useful when you suspect an error in a client and want to know exactly what mysqld thought the client sent to it.

By default, the mysql.server script starts the MySQL server with the -l option. If you need better performance when you start using MySQL in a production environment, you can remove the -l option from mysql.server or change it to --log-bin.

The entries in this log are written as mysqld receives the questions. This may be different from the order in which the statements are executed. This is in contrast to the update log and the binary log which are written after the query is executed, but before any locks are released.

4.9.3 The Update Log

Note: the update log is replaced by the binary log. See Section 4.9.4, The Binary Update Log. With this you can do anything that you can do with the update log.

When started with the `--log-update[=file_name]` option, `mysqld` writes a log file containing all SQL commands that update data. If no filename is given, it defaults to the name of the host machine. If a filename is given, but it doesn't contain a path, the file is written in the data directory. If `file_name` doesn't have an extension, `mysqld` will create log file names like so: `file_name.###`, where `###` is a number that is incremented each time you execute `mysqladmin refresh`, execute `mysqladmin flush-logs`, execute the `FLUSH LOGS` statement, or restart the server.

Note: For the previous scheme to work, you must not create your own files with the same filename as the update log + some extensions that may be regarded as a number, in the directory used by the update log!

If you use the `--log` or `-l` options, `mysqld` writes a general log with a filename of `hostname.log`. Restarts and refreshes do not cause a new log file to be generated (although it is closed and reopened). In this case you can copy it (on Unix) by doing:

```
mv hostname.log hostname-old.log
mysqladmin flush-logs
cp hostname-old.log to-backup-directory
rm hostname-old.log
```

Update logging is smart because it logs only statements that really update data. So an `UPDATE` or a `DELETE` with a `WHERE` that finds no rows is not written to the log. It even skips `UPDATE` statements that set a column to the value it already has.

The update logging is done immediately after a query completes but before any locks are released or any commit is done. This ensures that the log will be logged in the execution order.

If you want to update a database from update log files, you could do the following (assuming your update logs have names of the form `file_name.###`):

```
shell> ls -1 -t -r file_name.[0-9]* | xargs cat | mysql
```

`ls` is used to get all the log files in the right order.

This can be useful if you have to revert to backup files after a crash and you want to redo the updates that occurred between the time of the backup and the crash.

4.9.4 The Binary Update Log

The intention is that the binary log should replace the update log, so we recommend you switch to this log format as soon as possible!

The binary log contains all information that is available in the update log in a more efficient format. It also contains information about how long every query that updated the database took.

The binary log is also used when you are replicating a slave from a master. See Section 4.10, Replication in MySQL.

When started with the `--log-bin[=file_name]` option, `mysqld` writes a log file containing all SQL commands that update data. If no filename is given, it defaults to the name of the host machine followed by `-bin`. If a filename is given, but it doesn't contain a path, the file is written in the data directory.

If you supply an extension to `--log-bin=filename.extension`, the extension will be silently removed.

To the binary log filename, `mysqld` will append an extension that is a number that is incremented each time you execute `mysqladmin refresh`, execute `mysqladmin flush-logs`, execute the `FLUSH LOGS` statement, or restart the server. A new binary log will also automatically be created when it reaches `max_bin_log_size`. You can delete all inactive binary log files with the `RESET MASTER` command. See Section 4.5.4, `RESET` Syntax.

You can use the following options to `mysqld` to affect what is logged to the binary log:

Option	Description
`binlog-do-db=database_name`	Tells the master it should log updates for the specified database, and exclude all others not explicitly mentioned. (Example: `binlog-do-db=some_database`.)
`binlog-ignore-db=database_name`	Tells the master that updates to the given database should not be logged to the binary log. (Example: `binlog-ignore-db=some_database`.)

To determine which different binary log files have been used, `mysqld` will also create a binary log index file that contains the name of all used binary log files. By default this has the same name as the binary log file, with the extension `'.index'`. You can change the name of the binary log index file with the `--log-bin-index=[filename]` option.

If you are using replication, you should not delete old binary log files until you are sure that no slave will ever need to use them. One way to do this is to do `mysqladmin flush-logs` once a day and then remove any logs that are more than 3 days old.

You can examine the binary log file with the `mysqlbinlog` command. For example, you can update a MySQL server from the binary log as follows:

```
mysqlbinlog log-file | mysql -h server_name
```

You can also use the `mysqlbinlog` program to read the binary log directly from a remote MySQL server!

`mysqlbinlog --help` will give you more information on how to use this program!

If you are using `BEGIN [WORK]` or `SET AUTOCOMMIT=0`, you must use the MySQL binary log for backups instead of the old update log.

The binary logging is done immediately after a query completes but before any locks are released or any commit is done. This ensures that the log will be logged in the execution order.

All updates (`UPDATE`, `DELETE`, or `INSERT`) that change a transactional table (like BDB tables) are cached until a `COMMIT`. Any updates to a non-transactional table are stored in the binary log at once. Every thread will, on start, allocate a buffer of `binlog_cache_size` to buffer queries. If a query is bigger than this, the thread will open a temporary file to handle the bigger cache. The temporary file will be deleted when the thread ends.

The `max_binlog_cache_size` can be used to restrict the total size used to cache a multi-transaction query.

If you are using the update or binary log, concurrent inserts will not work together with `CREATE ... INSERT` and `INSERT ... SELECT`. This is to ensure that you can re-create an exact copy of your tables by applying the log on a backup.

4.9.5 The Slow Query Log

When started with the `--log-slow-queries[=file_name]` option, `mysqld` writes a log file containing all SQL commands that took more than `long_query_time` to execute. The time to get the initial table locks is not counted as execution time.

The slow query log is logged after the query is executed and after all locks have been released. This may be different from the order in which the statements are executed.

If no filename is given, it defaults to the name of the host machine suffixed with `-slow.log`. If a filename is given, but doesn't contain a path, the file is written in the data directory.

The slow query log can be used to find queries that take a long time to execute and are thus candidates for optimisation. With a large log, that can become a difficult task. You can pipe the slow query log through the `mysqldumpslow` command to get a summary of the queries that appear in the log.

If you are using `--log-long-format`, queries that are not using indexes are also printed. See Section 4.1.1, `mysqld` Command-Line Options.

4.9.6 Log File Maintenance

MySQL has a lot of log files, which makes it easy to see what is going on. See Section 4.9, The MySQL Log Files. One must, however, from time to time clean up after MySQL to ensure that the logs don't take up too much disk space.

When using MySQL with log files, you will, from time to time, want to remove/back up old log files and tell MySQL to start logging on new files. See Section 4.4.1, Database Backups.

On a Linux (`RedHat`) installation, you can use the `mysql-log-rotate` script for this. If you installed MySQL from an RPM distribution, the script should have been installed automatically. Note that you should be careful with this if you are using the log for replication!

On other systems you must install a short script yourself that you start from `cron` to handle log files.

You can force MySQL to start using new log files by using `mysqladmin flush-logs` or by using the SQL command `FLUSH LOGS`. If you are using MySQL Version 3.21 you must use `mysqladmin refresh`.

The preceding command does the following:

- If standard logging (`--log`) or slow query logging (`--log-slow-queries`) is used, it closes and reopens the log file (`mysql.log` and `'hostname'-slow.log` as default).

- If update logging (`--log-update`) is used, it closes the update log and opens a new log file with a higher sequence number.

If you are using only an update log, you only have to flush the logs and then move away the old update log files to a backup. If you are using normal logging, you can do something like:

```
shell> cd mysql-data-directory
shell> mv mysql.log mysql.old
shell> mysqladmin flush-logs
```

and then take a backup and remove `mysql.old`.

4.10 Replication in MySQL

This section describes the various replication features in MySQL. It serves as a reference to the options available with replication. You will be introduced to replication and learn how to implement it. Toward the end, there are some frequently asked questions and descriptions of problems and how to solve them.

We suggest that you visit our web site at http://www.mysql.com/ often and read updates to this section. Replication is constantly being improved, and we update the manual frequently with the most current information.

4.10.1 Introduction

One way replication can be used is to increase both robustness and speed. For robustness you can have two systems and can switch to the backup if you have problems with the master. The extra speed is achieved by sending a part of the non-updating queries to the replica server. Of course, this only works if non-updating queries dominate, but that is the normal case.

Starting in Version 3.23.15, MySQL supports one-way replication internally. One server acts as the master, while the other acts as the slave. Note that one server could play the roles of master in one pair and slave in the other. The master server keeps a binary log of updates (see Section 4.9.4, The Binary Update Log) and an index file to binary logs to keep track of log rotation. The slave, upon connecting, informs the master where it left off since the last successfully propagated update, catches up on the updates, and then blocks and waits for the master to notify it of the new updates.

Note that if you are replicating a database, all updates to this database should be done through the master!

Another benefit of using replication is that one can get live backups of the system by doing a backup on a slave instead of doing it on the master. See Section 4.4.1, Database Backups.

4.10.2 Replication Implementation Overview

MySQL replication is based on the server keeping track of all changes to your database (updates, deletes, etc.) in the binary log (see Section 4.9.4, The Binary Update Log) and the slave server(s) reading the saved queries from the master server's binary log so that the slave can execute the same queries on its copy of the data.

It is **very important** to realise that the binary log is simply a record starting from a fixed point in time (the moment you enable binary logging). Any slaves that you set up will need copies of all the data from your master as it existed the moment that you enabled binary logging on the master. If you start your slaves with data that doesn't agree with what was on the master **when the binary log was started**, your slaves may fail.

Starting in 4.0.0, one can use LOAD DATA FROM MASTER to set up a slave. Note that 4.0.0 slaves cannot communicate with 3.23 masters, but 4.0.1 and later version slaves can. 3.23 slaves cannot talk to 4.0 masters.

You must also be aware that LOAD DATA FROM MASTER currently works only if all the tables on the master are MyISAM type, and will acquire a global read lock, so no writes are possible while the tables are being transferred from the master. This limitation is of a temporary nature, and is due to the fact that we have not yet implement hot lock-free table backup. It will be removed in the future 4.0 branch versions once we implemented hot backup enabling LOAD DATA FROM MASTER to work without blocking master updates.

Due to the aforementioned limitation, we recommend that at this point you use LOAD DATA FROM MASTER only if the dataset on the master is relatively small, or if a prolonged read lock on the master is acceptable. While the actual speed of LOAD DATA FROM MAS-TER may vary from system to system, a good rule for a rough estimate of how long it is going to take is 1 second per 1M of the data file. You will get close to the estimate if both master and slave are equivalent to 700MHz Pentium, are connected through 100Mit/s network, and your index file is about half the size of your data file. Of course, your mileage will vary from system to system. This rule just gives you a rough order of magnitude estimate.

Once a slave is properly configured and running, it will simply connect to the master and wait for updates to process. If the master goes away or the slave loses connectivity with your master, it will keep trying to connect every master-connect-retry seconds until it is able to reconnect and resume listening for updates.

Each slave keeps track of where it left off. The master server has no knowledge of how many slaves there are or which ones are up-to-date at any given time.

The next section explains the master/slave setup process in more detail.

4.10.3 How to Set Up Replication

Here is a quick description of how to set up complete replication on your current MySQL server. It assumes you want to replicate all your databases and have not configured replication before. You will need to shut down your master server briefly to complete the following steps.

While this method is the most straightforward way to set up a slave, it is not the only one. For example, if you already have a snapshot of the master, and the master already has server id set and binary logging enabled, you can set up a slave without shutting the master down or even blocking the updates. For more details, please see Section 4.10.7, Replication FAQ.

If you want to become a real MySQL replication guru, we suggest that you begin by studying, pondering, and trying all commands mentioned in Section 4.10.6, SQL Commands Related to Replication. You should also familiarize yourself with replication startup options in my.cnf in Section 4.10.5, Replication Options in my.cnf.

1. Make sure you have a recent version of MySQL installed on the master and slave(s).

    Use Version 3.23.29 or higher. Previous releases used a different binary log format and had bugs which have been fixed in newer releases. Please, do not report bugs until you have verified that the problem is present in the latest release.

2. Set up a special replication user on the master with the FILE privilege and permission to connect from all the slaves. If the user is only doing replication (which is recommended), you don't need to grant any additional privileges.

    For example, to create a usernamed repl which can access your master from any host, you might use this command:

    ```
    mysql> GRANT FILE ON *.* TO repl@"%" IDENTIFIED BY '<password>';
    ```

3. Shut down MySQL on the master.

    ```
    mysqladmin -u root -p<password> shutdown
    ```

4. Snapshot all the data on your master server.

    The easiest way to do this (on Unix) is to simply use **tar** to produce an archive of your entire data directory. The exact data directory location depends on your installation.

    ```
    tar -cvf /tmp/mysql-snapshot.tar /path/to/data-dir
    ```

    Windows users can use WinZIP or similar software to create an archive of the data directory.

5. In my.cnf on the master add log-bin and server-id=unique number to the [mysqld] section and restart it. It is very important that the id of the slave is different from the id of the master. Think of server-id as something similar to the IP address—it uniquely identifies the server instance in the community of replication partners.

    ```
    [mysqld]
    log-bin
    server-id=1
    ```

6. Restart MySQL on the master.

7. Add the following to my.cnf on the slave(s):

    ```
    master-host=<hostname of the master>
    master-user=<replication username>
    master-password=<replication user password>
    master-port=<TCP/IP port for master>
    server-id=<some unique number between 2 and 2^32-1>
    ```

replacing the values in <> with what is relevant to your system.

server-id must be different for each server participating in replication. If you don't specify a server-id, it will be set to 1 if you have not defined master-host. Otherwise, it will be set to 2. Note that in the case of server-id omission the master will refuse connections from all slaves, and the slave will refuse to connect to a master. Thus, omitting server-id is only good for backup with a binary log.

8. Copy the snapshot data into your data directory on your slave(s). Make sure that the privileges on the files and directories are correct. The user that MySQL runs as needs to be able to read and write to them, just as on the master.

9. Restart the slave(s).

After you have done this, the slave(s) should connect to the master and catch up on any updates that happened since the snapshot was taken.

If you have forgotten to set server-id for the slave you will get the following error in the error log file:

```
Warning: one should set server_id to a non-0 value if master_host is set.
The server will not act as a slave.
```

If you have forgotten to do this for the master, the slaves will not be able to connect to the master.

If a slave is not able to replicate for any reason, you will find error messages in the error log on the slave.

Once a slave is replicating, you will find a file called master.info in the same directory as your error log. The master.info file is used by the slave to keep track of how much of the master's binary log it has processed. **Do not** remove or edit the file, unless you really know what you are doing. Even in that case, it is preferred that you use CHANGE MASTER TO command.

4.10.4 Replication Features and Known Problems

The following is an explanation of what is supported and what is not:

*   Replication will be done correctly with AUTO_INCREMENT, LAST_INSERT_ID(), and TIMESTAMP values.

*   RAND() in updates does not replicate properly. Use RAND(some_non_rand_expr) if you are replicating updates with RAND(). You can, for example, use UNIX_TIMESTAMP() for the argument to RAND().

- You have to use the same character set (--default-character-set) on the master and the slave. If not, you may get duplicate key errors on the slave because a key that is regarded as unique on the master may not be that in the other character set.

- In 3.23, LOAD DATA INFILE will be handled properly as long as the file still resides on the master server at the time of update propagation. LOAD LOCAL DATA INFILE will be skipped. In 4.0, this limitation is not present—all forms of LOAD DATA INFILE are properly replicated.

- Update queries that use user variables are not replication-safe (yet).

- FLUSH commands are not stored in the binary log and therefore are not replicated to the slaves. This is not normally a problem, as FLUSH doesn't change anything. This does, however, mean that if you update the MySQL privilege tables directly without using the the GRANT statement and you replicate the mysql privilege database, you must do a FLUSH PRIVILEGES on your slaves to put the new privileges into effect.

- Temporary tables starting in 3.23.29 are replicated properly except when you shut down the slave server (not just the slave thread), you have some temporary tables open, and they are used in subsequent updates. To deal with this problem shutting down the slave, do SLAVE STOP, check Slave_open_temp_tables variable to see if it is 0, then issue mysqladmin shutdown. If the number is not 0, restart the slave thread with SLAVE START and see if you have better luck next time. There will be a cleaner solution, but it has to wait until version 4.0. In earlier versions temporary tables are not replicated properly—we recommend that you either upgrade, or execute SET SQL_LOG_BIN=0 on your clients before all queries with temp tables.

- MySQL only supports one master and many slaves. In 4.x, we will add a voting algorithm to automatically change master if something goes wrong with the current master. We will also introduce 'agent' processes to help perform load balancing by sending select queries to different slaves.

- Starting in Version 3.23.26, it is safe to connect servers in a circular master-slave relationship with log-slave-updates enabled. Note, however, that many queries will not work right in this kind of setup unless your client code is written to take care of the potential problems that can happen from updates that occur in different sequences on different servers.

  This means that you can do a setup like the following:

  ```
  A -> B -> C -> A
  ```

  This setup will work only if you do non-conflicting updates between the tables. In other words, if you insert data in A and C, you should never inserted a row in A that may have a conflicting key with a row insert in C. You should also not update the same rows on two servers if the order in which the updates are applied matters.

  Note that the log format has changed in Version 3.23.26 so that pre-3.23.26 slaves will not be able to read it.

- If the query on the slave gets an error, the slave thread will terminate, and a message will appear in the .err file. You should then connect to the slave manually, fix the cause of the error (for example, non-existent table), and then run the SLAVE START SQL command (available starting in Version 3.23.16). In Version 3.23.15, you will have to restart the server.

- If connection to the master is lost, the slave will retry immediately, and then, in case of failure, every master-connect-retry (default 60 seconds). Because of this, it is safe to shut down the master, and then restart it after a while. The slave will also be able to deal with network connectivity outages.

- Shutting down the slave (cleanly) is also safe, as it keeps track of where it left off. Unclean shutdowns might produce problems, especially if disk cache was not synced before the system died. Your system fault tolerance will be greatly increased if you have a good UPS.

- If the master is listening on a non-standard port, you will also need to specify this with master-port parameter in my.cnf.

- In Version 3.23.15, all of the tables and databases will be replicated. Starting in Version 3.23.16, you can restrict replication to a set of databases with replicate-do-db directives in my.cnf or just exclude a set of databases with replicate-ignore-db. Note that up until Version 3.23.23, there was a bug that did not properly deal with LOAD DATA INFILE if you did it in a database that was excluded from replication.

- Starting in Version 3.23.16, SET SQL_LOG_BIN = 0 will turn off replication (binary) logging on the master, and SET SQL_LOG_BIN = 1 will turn it back on. You must have the **process** privilege to do this.

- Starting in Version 3.23.19, you can clean up stale replication leftovers when something goes wrong and you want a clean start with FLUSH MASTER and FLUSH SLAVE commands. In Version 3.23.26 we have renamed them to RESET MASTER and RESET SLAVE, respectively, to clarify what they do. The old FLUSH variants still work, though, for compatibility.

- Starting in Version 3.23.23, you can change masters and adjust log position with CHANGE MASTER TO.

- Starting in Version 3.23.23, you tell the master that updates in certain databases should not be logged to the binary log with binlog-ignore-db.

- Starting in Version 3.23.26, you can use replicate-rewrite-db to tell the slave to apply updates from one database on the master to the one with a different name on the slave.

- Starting in Version 3.23.28, you can use PURGE MASTER LOGS TO 'log-name' to get rid of old logs while the slave is running.

- Due to the non-transactional nature of MyISAM tables, it is possible to have a query that will only partially update a table and return an error code. This can happen, for example, on a multi-row insert that has one row violating a key constraint, or if a long update query is killed after updating some of the rows. If that happens on the master, the slave thread will exit and wait for the DBA to decide what to do about it unless the error code is legitimate and the query execution results in the same error code. If this error code validation behaviour is not desirable, some (or all) errors could be masked out with the `slave-skip-errors` option starting in Version 3.23.47.

- While individual tables can be excluded from replication with `replicate-do-table`/`replicate-ignore-table` or `replicate-wild-do-table`/`replicate-wild-ignore-table`, there are currently some design deficiencies that in some rather rare cases produce unexpected results. The replication protocol does not inform the slave explicitly which tables are going to be modified by the query—so the slave has to parse the query to know this. To avoid redundant parsing for queries that will end up actually being executed, table exclusion is currently implemented by sending the query to the standard MySQL parser, which will short-circuit the query and report success if it detects that the table should be ignored. In addition to several inefficiencies, this approach is also more bug-prone, and there are two known bugs as of Version 3.23.49—because the parser automatically opens the table when parsing some queries, the ignored table has to exist on the slave. The other bug is that if the ignored table gets partially updated, the slave thread will not notice that the table actually should have been ignored and will suspend the replication process. While these bugs are conceptually very simple to fix, we have not yet found a way to do this without a significant code change that would compromise the stability status of the 3.23 branch. There exists a workaround for both if in the rare case it happens to affect your application—use `slave-skip-errors`.

4.10.5 Replication Options in `my.cnf`

If you are using replication, we recommend that you use MySQL Version 3.23.30 or later. Older versions work, but they do have some bugs and are missing some features. Some of the options mentioned here may not be available in your version if it is not the most recent one. For all options specific to the the 4.0 branch, there is a note indicating so. Otherwise, if you discover that the option you are interested in is not available in your 3.23 version, and you really need it, please upgrade to the most recent 3.23 branch.

Please be aware that 4.0 branch is still in alpha, so some things may not be working as smoothly as you would like. If you really would like to try the new features of 4.0, we recommend you do it in such a way that in case there is a problem, your mission-critical applications will not be disrupted.

On both master and slave you need to use the `server-id` option. This sets an unique replication id. You should pick a unique value in the range between 1 to 2^32-1 for each master and slave. Example: `server-id=3`.

The following table describes the options you can use for the MASTER:

Option	Description
`log-bin=filename`	Write to a binary update log to the specified location. Note that if you give it a parameter with an extension (for example, `log-bin=/mysql/logs/replication.log`) versions up to 3.23.24 will not work right during replication if you do FLUSH LOGS. The problem is fixed in Version 3.23.25. If you are using this kind of log name, FLUSH LOGS will be ignored on binlog. To clear the log, run FLUSH MASTER, and do not forget to run FLUSH SLAVE on all slaves. In Versions 3.23.26 and later, you should use RESET MASTER and RESET SLAVE.
`log-bin-index=filename`	Because the user could issue the FLUSH LOGS command, we need to know which log is currently active and which ones have been rotated out and in what sequence. This information is stored in the binary log index file. The default is `'hostname'.index`. You should not need to change this. Example: `log-bin-index=db.index`
`sql-bin-update-same`	If set, setting SQL_LOG_BIN to a value will automatically set SQL_LOG_UPDATE to the same value, and vice versa.
`binlog-do-db=database_name`	Tells the master that it should log updates to the binary log if the current database is `database_name`. All other databases are ignored. Note that if you use this, you should ensure that you do updates only in the current database. Example: `binlog-do-db=sales`
`binlog-ignore-db=database_name`	Tells the master that updates where the current database is `database_name` should not be stored in the binary log. Note that if you use this, you should ensure that you do updates only in the current database. Example: `binlog-ignore-db=accounting`.

The following table describes the options you can use for the SLAVE:

Option	Description
master-host=host	Master hostname or IP address for replication. If not set, the slave thread will not be started. Note that the setting of master-host will be ignored if there exists a valid master.info file. Probably a better name for this option would have been something like bootstrap-master-host, but it is too late to change now. Example: master-host=db-master.mycompany.com
master-user=username	The username the slave thread will use for authentication when connecting to the master. The user must have the **file** privilege. If the master user is not set, user test is assumed. The value in master.info will take precedence if it can be read. Example: master-user=scott
master-password=password	The password the slave thread will authenticate with when connecting to the master. If not set, an empty password is assumed.The value in master.info will take precedence if it can be read. Example: master-password=tiger
master-port=portnumber	The port the master is listening on. If not set, the compiled setting of MYSQL_PORT is assumed. If you have not tinkered with configure options, this should be 3306. The value in master.info will take precedence if it can be read. Example: master-port=3306
master-connect-retry=seconds	The number of seconds the slave thread will sleep before retrying to connect to the master in case the master goes down or the connection is lost. Default is 60. Example: master-connect-retry=60
master-ssl	Available after 4.0.0. Turn SSL on for replication. Be warned that this is a relatively new feature. Example: master-ssl
master-ssl-key	Available after 4.0.0. Master SSL keyfile name. Only applies if you have enabled master-ssl. Example: master-ssl-key=SSL/master-key.pem
master-ssl-cert	Available after 4.0.0. Master SSL certificate file name. Only applies if you have enabled master-ssl. Example: master-ssl-key=SSL/master-cert.pem
master-info-file=filename	The location of the file that remembers where we left off on the master during the replication process. The default is master.info in the data directory. You should not need to change this. Example: master-info-file=master.info
report-host	Available after 4.0.0. Hostname or IP of the slave to be reported to the master during slave registration. Will appear in the output of SHOW SLAVE HOSTS. Leave unset if you do not want the slave to register itself with the master. Note that it is not sufficient for the master to simply read the IP of the slave off the socket once the slave connects. Due to NAT and other routing issues, that IP may not be valid for connecting to the slave from the master or other hosts. Example: report-host=slave1.mycompany.com.

Option	Description
report-port	Available after 4.0.0. Port for connecting to slave reported to the master during slave registration. Set it only if the slave is listening on a non-default port or if you have a special tunnel from the master or other clients to the slave. If not sure, leave this option unset.
replicate-do-table=db_name.table_name	Tells the slave thread to restrict replication to the specified table. To specify more than one table, use the directive multiple times, once for each table. This will work for cross-database updates, in contrast to replicate-do-db. Example: replicate-do-table=some_db.some_table
replicate-ignore-table=db_name.table_name	Tells the slave thread to not replicate to the specified table. To specify more than one table to ignore, use the directive multiple times, once for each table. This will work for cross-datbase updates, in contrast to replicate-ignore-db. Example: replicate-ignore-table=db_name.some_table
replicate-wild-do-table=db_name.table_name	Tells the slave thread to restrict replication to the tables that match the specified wildcard pattern. To specify more than one table, use the directive multiple times, once for each table. This will work for cross-database updates. Example: replicate-wild-do-table=foo%.bar% will replicate only updates to tables in all databases that start with foo and whose table names start with bar.
replicate-wild-ignore-table=db_name.table_name	Tells the slave thread to not replicate to the tables that match the given wildcard pattern. To specify more than one table to ignore, use the directive multiple times, once for each table. This will work for cross-database updates. Example: replicate-wild-ignore-table=foo%.bar% will not do updates to tables in databases that start with foo and whose table names start with bar.
replicate-ignore-db=database_name	Tells the slave thread to not replicate to the specified database. To specify more than one database to ignore, use the directive multiple times, once for each database. This option will not work if you use cross-database updates. If you need cross database updates to work, make sure you have 3.23.28 or later, and use replicate-wild-ignore-table=db_name.%. Example: replicate-ignore-db=some_db
replicate-do-db=database_name	Tells the slave thread to restrict replication to the specified database. To specify more than one database, use the directive multiple times, once for each database. Note that this will only work if you do not use cross-database queries such as UPDATE some_db.some_table SET foo='bar' while having selected a different or no database. If you need cross-database updates to work, make sure you have 3.23.28 or later, and use replicate-wild-do-table=db_name.%. Example: replicate-do-db=some_db

Option	Description
`log-slave-updates`	Tells the slave to log the updates from the slave thread to the binary log. Off by default. You will need to turn it on if you plan to daisy-chain the slaves.
`replicate-rewrite-db=from_name->to_name`	Updates to a database with a different name than the original. Example: `replicate-rewrite-db=master_db_name->slave_db_name`
`slave-skip-errors=err_code1,err_code2, . . .`	Available only in 3.23.47 and later. Tells the slave thread to continue replication when a query returns an error from the provided list. Normally, replication will discontinue when an error is encountered, giving the user a chance to resolve the inconsistency in the data manually. Do not use this option unless you fully understand why you are getting the errors. If there are no bugs in your replication setup and client programs, and no bugs in MySQL itself, you should never get an abort with error. Indiscriminate use of this option will result in slaves being hopelessly out of sync with the master and you having no idea how the problem happened. For error codes, you should use the numbers provided by the error message in your slave error log and in the output of `SHOW SLAVE STATUS`. A full list of error messages can be found in the source distribution in `Docs/mysqld_error.txt`. You can (but should not) also use a very non-recommended value of `all` which will ignore all error messages and keep barging along regardless. Needless to say, if you use it, we make no promises regarding your data integrity. Please do not complain if your data on the slave is not anywhere close to what it is on the master in this case—you have been warned. Example: `slave-skip-errors=1062,1053` or `slave-skip-errors=all`.
`skip-slave-start`	Tells the slave server not to start the slave on the startup. The user can start it later with `SLAVE START`.
`slave_read_timeout=#`	Number of seconds to wait for more data from the master before aborting the read.

4.10.6 SQL Commands Related to Replication

Replication can be controlled through the SQL interface. Here is the summary of commands:

Command	Description
`SLAVE START`	Starts the slave thread. (Slave)
`SLAVE STOP`	Stops the slave thread. (Slave)
`SET SQL_LOG_BIN=0`	Disables update logging if the user has the **process** privilege. Ignored otherwise. (Master)
`SET SQL_LOG_BIN=1`	Re-enables update logging if the user has the **process** privilege. Ignored otherwise. (Master)

Command	Description
SET SQL_SLAVE_SKIP_COUNTER=n	Skip the next n events from the master. Only valid when the slave thread is not running; otherwise, gives an error. Useful for recovering from replication glitches.
RESET MASTER	Deletes all binary logs listed in the index file, resetting the binlog index file to be empty. In pre-3.23.26 versions, use FLUSH MASTER. (Master)
RESET SLAVE	Makes the slave forget its replication position in the master logs. In pre-3.23.26 versions, the command was called FLUSH SLAVE. (Slave)
LOAD TABLE tblname FROM MASTER	Downloads a copy of the table from master to the slave. Implemented mainly for debugging of LOAD DATA FROM MASTER, but some "gourmet" users might find it useful for other things. Do not use it if you consider yourself the average "non-hacker" type user. (Slave)
LOAD DATA FROM MASTER	Available starting in 4.0.0. Takes a snapshot of the master and copies it to the slave. Updates the values of MASTER_LOG_FILE and MASTER_LOG_POS so that the slave will start replicating from the correct position. Will honor table and database exclusion rules specified with replicate-* options. So far works only with MyISAM tables and acquires a global read lock on the master while taking the snapshot. In the future it is planned to make it work with InnoDB tables and to remove the need for global read lock using the non-blocking online backup feature.

CHANGE MASTER TO master_def_list	Changes the master parameters to the values specified in master_def_list and restarts the slave thread. master_def_list is a comma-separated list of master_def where master_def is one of the following: MASTER_HOST, MASTER_USER, MASTER_PASSWORD, MASTER_PORT, MASTER_CONNECT_RETRY, MASTER_LOG_FILE, or MASTER_LOG_POS. For example:
	
	`CHANGE MASTER TO`
	`    MASTER_HOST='master2.mycompany.com',`
	`    MASTER_USER='replication',`
	`    MASTER_PASSWORD='bigs3cret',`
	`    MASTER_PORT=3306,`
	`    MASTER_LOG_FILE='master2-bin.001',`
	`    MASTER_LOG_POS=4;`

Command	Description
CHANGE MASTER TO master_def_list *(continued)*	You only need to specify the values that need to be changed. The values that you omit will stay the same with the exception of when you change the host or the port. In that case, the slave will assume that since you are connecting to a different host or a different port, the master is different. Therefore, the old values of log and position are not applicable anymore, and will automatically be reset to an empty string and 0, respectively (the startvalues). Note that if you restart the slave, it will remember its last master. If this is not desirable, you should delete the master.info file before restarting, and the slave will read its master from my.cnf or the command-line.This command is useful for setting up a slave when you have the snapshot of the master and have recorded the log and the offset on the master that the snapshot corresponds to. You can run CHANGE MASTER TO MASTER_LOG_FILE='log_name_on_master', MASTER_LOG_POS=log_offset_on_master on the slave after restoring the snapshot.(Slave)
SHOW MASTER STATUS	Provides status information on the binlog of the master. (Master)
SHOW SLAVE HOSTS	Available after 4.0.0. Gives a listing of slaves currently registered with the master. (Master)
SHOW SLAVE STATUS	Provides status information on essential parameters of the slave thread. (Slave)
SHOW MASTER LOGS	Only available starting in Version 3.23.28. Lists the binary logs on the master. You should use this command prior to PURGE MASTER LOGS TO to find out how far you should go. (Master)
SHOW BINLOG EVENTS [IN 'log-name'] [FROM pos] [LIMIT [offset,] rows]	Shows the events in the binary update log. Primarily used for testing/debugging, but can also be used by regular clients that for some reason need to read the binary log contents. (Master)
SHOW NEW MASTER FOR SLAVE WITH MASTER_LOG_FILE='logfile' AND MASTER_LOG_POS=pos AND MASTER_LOG_SEQ=log_seq AND MASTER_SERVER_ID=server_id	This command is used when a slave of a possibly dead/unavailable master needs to be switched to replicate off another slave that has been replicating the same master. The command will return recalculated replication coordinates, and the output can be used in a subsequent CHANGE MASTER TO command. Normal users should never need to run this command. It is primarily reserved for internal use by the fail-safe replication code. We may later change the syntax if we find a more intuitive way to describe this operation.

Command	Description
PURGE MASTER LOGS TO 'logname'	Available starting in Version 3.23.28. Deletes all the replication logs that are listed in the log index as being prior to the specified log, and removes them from the log index, so that the given log now becomes the first. Example: PURGE MASTER LOGS TO 'mysql-bin.010' This command will do nothing and fail with an error if you have an active slave that is currently reading one of the logs you are trying to delete. However, if you have a dormant slave, and happen to purge one of the logs it wants to read, the slave will be unable to replicate once it comes up. The command is safe to run while slaves are replicating—you do not need to stop them. You must first check all the slaves with SHOW SLAVE STATUS to see which log they are on, then do a listing of the logs on the master with SHOW MASTER LOGS, find the earliest log among all the slaves (if all the slaves are up to date, this will be the last log on the list), back up all the logs you are about to delete (optional), and purge up to the target log.

4.10.7 Replication FAQ

Q: How do I configure a slave if the master is already running and I do not want to stop it?

A: There are several options. If you have taken a backup of the master at some point and recorded the binlog name and offset (from the output of SHOW MASTER STATUS) corresponding to the snapshot, do the following:

* Make sure a unique server id is assigned to the slave.

* Execute CHANGE MASTER TO MASTER_HOST='master-host-name', MAS-
  TER_USER='master-user-name', MASTER_PASSWORD='master-pass', MAS-
  TER_LOG_FILE='recorded-log-name',   MAS-
  TER_LOG_POS=recorded_log_pos.

* Execute SLAVE START.

If you do not have a backup of the master already, here is a quick way to do it consistently:

* FLUSH TABLES WITH READ LOCK.

* gtar zcf /tmp/backup.tar.gz /var/lib/mysql (or a variation of this).

- SHOW MASTER STATUS—make sure to record the output, as you will need it later.

- UNLOCK TABLES.

Afterward, follow the instructions for the case when you have a snapshot and have recorded the log name and offset. You can use the same snapshot to set up several slaves. As long as the binary logs of the master are left intact, you can wait as long as several days or in some cases maybe a month to set up a slave once you have the snapshot of the master. In theory the waiting gap can be infinite. The two practical limitations are the disk space of the master getting filled with old logs, and the amount of time it will take the slave to catch up.

In Versions 4.0.0 and newer, you can also use LOAD DATA FROM MASTER. This is a convenient command that will take a snapshot, restore it to the slave, and adjust the log name and offset on the slave all at once. In the future, LOAD DATA FROM MASTER will be the recommended way to set up a slave. Be warned, however, that the read lock may be held for a long time if you use this command. It is not yet implemented as efficiently as we would like to have it. If you have large tables, the preferred method at this time is still with a local tar snapshot after executing FLUSH TABLES WITH READ LOCK.

Q: Does the slave need to be connected to the master all the time?

A: No, it does not. You can have the slave go down or stay disconnected for hours or even days, then reconnect, catch up on the updates, and then disconnect or go down for a while again. So you can, for example, use the master-slave setup over a dial-up link that is up only for short periods of time. The implications of that are that at any given time the slave is not guaranteed to be in sync with the master unless you take some special measures. In the future, we will have the option to block the master until at least one slave is in sync.

Q: How do I force the master to block updates until the slave catches up?

A: Execute the following commands:

- Master: FLUSH TABLES WITH READ LOCK.

- Master: SHOW MASTER STATUS—record the log name and the offset.

- Slave: SELECT   MASTER_POS_WAIT('recorded_log_name', recorded_log_offset). When the select returns, the slave is currently in sync with the master.

- Master: UNLOCK TABLES—now the master will continue updates.

Q: Why do I sometimes see more than one Binlog_Dump thread on the master after I have restarted the slave?

A: Binlog_Dump is a continuous process that is handled by the server in the following way:

- Catch up on the updates.

- Once there are no more updates left, go into pthread_cond_wait(), from which we can be awakened either by an update or a kill.

- On wake-up, check the reason. If we are not supposed to die, continue the Binlog_dump loop.

- If there is some fatal error, such as detecting a dead client, terminate the loop.

So if the slave thread stops on the slave, the corresponding Binlog_Dump thread on the master will not notice it until after at least one update to the master (or a kill), which is needed to wake it up from pthread_cond_wait(). In the meantime, the slave could have opened another connection, which resulted in another Binlog_Dump thread.

The preceding problem should not be present in Versions 3.23.26 and later. In Version 3.23.26 we added server-id to each replication server, and now all the old zombie threads are killed on the master when a new replication thread connects from the same slave.

Q: How do I rotate replication logs?

A: In Version 3.23.28 you should use the PURGE MASTER LOGS TO command after determining which logs can be deleted, and optionally backing them up first. In earlier versions the process is much more painful, and cannot be safely done without stopping all the slaves in the case that you plan to re-use log names. You will need to stop the slave threads, edit the binary log index file, delete all the old logs, restart the master, start slave threads, and then remove the old log files.

Q: How do I upgrade on a hot replication setup?

A: If you are upgrading pre-3.23.26 versions, you should just lock the master tables, let the slave catch up, run FLUSH MASTER on the master and FLUSH SLAVE on the slave to reset the logs, then restart new versions of the master and the slave. Note that the slave can stay down for some time. Since the master is logging all the updates, the slave will be able to catch up once it is up and can connect.

After 3.23.26, we have locked the replication protocol for modifications, so you can upgrade masters and slaves on the fly to a newer 3.23 versions and you can have different versions of MySQL running on the slave and the master, as long as they are both newer than 3.23.26.

Q: What issues should I be aware of when setting up two-way replication?

A: MySQL replication currently does not support any locking protocol between master and slave to guarantee the atomicity of a distributed (cross-server) update. In other words, it is possible for client A to make an update to co-master 1, and in the meantime, before it propagates to co-master 2, client B could make an update to co-master 2 that will make the update of client A work differently than it did on co-master 1. Thus, when the update of client A will make it to co-master 2, it will produce tables that will be different from what you have on co-master 1, even after all the updates from co-master 2 have also prop-agated. So you should not co-chain two servers in a two-way replication relationship, unless you are sure that your updates can safely happen in any order, or unless you take care of mis-ordered updates somehow in the client code.

You must also realise that two-way replication actually does not improve performance very much, if at all, as far as updates are concerned. Both servers need to do the same amount of updates each, as you would have one server do. The only difference is that there will be a little less lock contention because the updates originating on another server will be serialised in one slave thread. This benefit, though, might be offset by network delays.

Q: How can I use replication to improve performance of my system?

A: You should set up one server as the master, direct all writes to it, and configure as many slaves as you have the money and rackspace for, distributing the reads among the master and the slaves. You can also start the slaves with `--skip-bdb`, `--low-prior-ity-updates` and `--delay-key-write-for-all-tables` to get speed improvements for the slave. In this case the slave will use non-transactional `MyISAM` tables instead of `BDB` tables to get more speed.

Q: What should I do to prepare my client code to use performance-enhancing replication?

A: If the part of your code that is responsible for database access has been properly abstracted/modularised, converting it to run with the replicated setup should be very smooth and easy. Just change the implementation of your database access to read from some slave or the master, and to always write to the master. If your code does not have this level of abstraction, setting up a replicated system will give you an opportunity/moti-vation to it clean up. You should start by creating a wrapper library /module with the fol-lowing functions:

- `safe_writer_connect()`
- `safe_reader_connect()`
- `safe_reader_query()`
- `safe_writer_query()`

`safe_` means that the function will take care of handling all the error conditions.

You should then convert your client code to use the wrapper library. It may be a painful and scary process at first, but it will pay off in the long run. All applications that follow the preceding pattern will be able to take advantage of one-master/many-slaves solution. The code will be a lot easier to maintain, and adding troubleshooting options will be triv-ial. You will just need to modify one or two functions, for example, to log how long each query took, or which query, among your many thousands, gave you an error. If you have written a lot of code already, you may want to automate the conversion task by using Monty's `replace` utility, which comes with the standard distribution of MySQL, or just write your own Perl script. Hopefully, your code follows some recognisable pattern. If not, you are probably better off rewriting it anyway, or at least going through and manually beating it into a pattern.

Note that, of course, you can use different names for the functions. What is important is having a unified interface for connecting for reads, connecting for writes, doing a read, and doing a write.

Q: When and how much can MySQL replication improve the performance of my system?

A: MySQL replication is most beneficial for a system with frequent reads and not-so-frequent writes. In theory, by using a one-master/many-slaves setup you can scale by adding more slaves until you either run out of network bandwidth, or your update load grows to the point that the master cannot handle it.

In order to determine how many slaves you can get before the added benefits begin to level out, and how much you can improve performance of your site, you need to know your query patterns, and empirically (by benchmarking) determine the relationship between the throughput on reads (reads per second, or `max_reads`) and on writes `max_writes`) on a typical master and a typical slave. The following example will show you a rather simplified calculation of what you can get with replication for our imagined system.

Let's say our system load consists of 10% writes and 90% reads, and we have determined that `max_reads` = 1200 - 2 * `max_writes`, or in other words, our system can do 1200 reads per second with no writes, our average write is twice as slow as our average read, and the relationship is linear. Let us suppose that our master and slave are of the same capacity, and we have N slaves and 1 master. Then we have for each server (master or slave):

*   `reads = 1200 - 2 * writes` (from benchmarks)
*   `reads = 9* writes / (N + 1)`   (reads split, but writes go to all servers)
*   `9*writes/(N+1) + 2 * writes = 1200`
*   `writes = 1200/(2 + 9/(N+1)`

So if N = 0, which means we have no replication, our system can handle 1200/11, or about 109 writes per second (which means we will have 9 times as many reads due to the nature of our application).

*   If N = 1, we can get up to 184 writes per second.
*   If N = 8, we get up to 400 writes.

- If N = 17, we get 480 writes.

Eventually as N approaches infinity (and our budget negative infinity), we can get very close to 600 writes per second, increasing system throughput by about 5.5 times. However, with only 8 servers, we increased it almost 4 times already.

Note that our computations assumed infinite network bandwidth, and neglected several other factors that could turn out to be significant on your system. In many cases, you may not be able to make a computation similar to the preceding one that will accurately predict what will happen on your system if you add N replication slaves. However, answering the following questions should help you decide whether and how much, if at all, the replication will improve the performance of your system:

- What is the read/write ratio on your system?
- How much more write load can one server handle if you reduce the reads?
- How many slaves do you have bandwidth for on your network?

Q: How can I use replication to provide redundancy/high availability?

A: With the currently available features, you would have to set up a master and a slave (or several slaves), write a script that will monitor the master to see if it is up, and instruct your applications and the slaves of the master change in case of failure. Some suggestions:

- To tell a slave to change the master, use the `CHANGE MASTER TO` command.
- A good way to keep your applications informed as to the location of the master is to have a dynamic DNS entry for the master. With `bind` you can use `nsupdate` to dynamically update your DNS.
- You should run your slaves with the `log-bin` option and without `log-slave-updates`. This way the slave will be ready to become a master as soon as you issue `STOP SLAVE`, `RESET MASTER`, and `CHANGE MASTER TO` on the other slaves. It will also help you catch spurious updates that may happen because of misconfiguration of the slave (ideally, you want to configure access rights so that no client can update the slave, except for the slave thread) combined with the bugs in your client programs (they should never update the slave directly).

We are currently working on integrating an automatic master election system into MySQL, but until it is ready, you will have to create your own monitoring tools.

4.10.8 Troubleshooting Replication

If you have followed the instructions and your replication setup is not working, first eliminate the user-error factor by checking the following:

- Is the master logging to the binary log? Check with SHOW MASTER STATUS. If it is, Position will be non-zero. If not, verify that you have given the master log-bin option and have set server-id.

- Is the slave running? Check with SHOW SLAVE STATUS. The answer is found in Slave_running column. If not, verify slave options and check the error log for messages.

- If the slave is running, did it establish connection with the master? Do SHOW PROCESSLIST, find the thread with the system user value in the User column and none in the Host column, and check the State column. If it says connecting to master, verify the privileges for the replication user on the master, master hostname, your DNS setup, whether the master is actually running, whether it is reachable from the slave, and if all that seems okay, read the error logs.

- If the slave was running but then stopped, look at SHOW SLAVE STATUS output and check the error logs. It usually happens when some query that succeeded on the master fails on the slave. This should never happen if you have taken a proper snapshot of the master, and have never modified the data on the slave outside of the slave thread. If it does, it is a bug. Report it as described later.

- If a query that succeeded on the master refuses to run on the slave, and a full database resync (the proper thing to do) does not seem feasible, try the following:

  — First see if there is some stray record in the way. Understand how it got there, then delete it and run SLAVE START.

  — If that does not work or does not apply, try to understand if it would be safe to make the update manually (if needed) and then ignore the next query from the master.

  — If you have decided you can skip the next query, do SET SQL_SLAVE_SKIP_COUNTER=1; SLAVE START; to skip a query that does not use AUTO_INCREMENT or use LAST_INSERT_ID(), or SET SQL_SLAVE_SKIP_COUNTER=2; SLAVE START; otherwise. The reason queries that use AUTO_INCREMENT or LAST_INSERT_ID() are different is that they take two events in the binary log of the master.

  — If you are sure the slave started out perfectly in sync with the master, and no one has updated the tables involved outside of the slave thread, report the bug, so you will not have to do perform these tricks again.

- Make sure you are not running into an old bug by upgrading to the most recent version.

- If all else fails, read the error logs. If they are big, perform grep -i slave /path/to/your-log.err on the slave. There is no generic pattern to search for on the master, as the only errors it logs are general system errors. If it can, it will send the error to the slave when things go wrong.

When you have determined that there is no user error involved, and replication still either does not work at all or is unstable, it is time to start working on a bug report. We need to get as much info as possible from you to be able to track down the bug. Please spend some time and effort preparing a good bug report. Ideally, we would like to have a test case in the format found in the `mysql-test/t/rpl*` directory of the source tree. If you submit a test case like that, you can expect a patch within a day or two in most cases, although, of course, your mileage may vary depending on a number of factors.

The second best option is to write a simple program with easily configurable connection arguments for the master and the slave that will demonstrate the problem on our systems. You can write one in Perl or in C, depending on which language you know better.

If you use one of these methods to demonstrate the bug, use `mysqlbug` to prepare a bug report and send it to *bugs@lists.mysql.com*. If you have a phantom, a problem that does occur but that you cannot duplicate "at will":

- Verify that there is no user error involved. For example, if you update the slave outside of the slave thread, the data will be out of sync, and you can have unique key violations on updates, in which case the slave thread will stop and wait for you to clean up the tables manually to bring them in sync.

- Run slave with `log-slave-updates` and `log-bin`. This will keep a log of all updates on the slave.

- Save all evidence before resetting the replication. If we have no or only sketchy information, it will take us a while to track down the problem. Collect the following evidence:

  — All binary logs on the master

  — All binary logs on the slave

  — The output of `SHOW MASTER STATUS` on the master at the time you have discovered the problem

  — The output of `SHOW SLAVE STATUS` on the master at the time you have discovered the problem

  — Error logs on the master and on the slave

- Use `mysqlbinlog` to examine the binary logs. The following should be helpful to find the trouble query, for example:

  ```
  mysqlbinlog -j pos_from_slave_status /path/to/log_from_slave_status | head
  ```

Once you have collected the evidence on the phantom problem, try hard to isolate it into a separate test case first. Then report the problem to *bugs@lists.mysql.com* with as much info as possible.

5

MySQL Optimisation

Optimisation is a complicated task because it ultimately requires understanding of the whole system. While it may be possible to do some local optimisations with little knowledge of your system or application, the more optimal you want your system to become the more you will have to know about it.

This chapter will try to explain and give some examples of different ways to optimise MySQL. Remember, however, that there are always some (increasingly harder) additional ways to make the system even faster.

5.1 Optimisation Overview

The most important part in speeding up a system is, of course, the basic design. You also need to know what your system will be doing, and what your bottlenecks are.

The most common bottlenecks are:

- Disk seeks. It takes time for the disk to find a piece of data. With modern disks in 1999, the mean time for this is usually lower than 10ms, so we can in theory do about 100 seeks a second. This time improves slowly with new disks and is very hard to optimise for a single table. The way to optimise this is to spread the data on more than one disk.

- Disk reading/writing. When the disk is at the correct position we need to read the data. With modern disks in 1999, one disk delivers something like 10-20M/s. This is easier to optimise than seeks because you can read in parallel from multiple disks.

- CPU cycles. When we have the data in main memory (or if it already was there) we need to process it to get to our result. Having small tables compared to the memory is the most common limiting factor. But then, with small tables speed is usually not the problem.

- Memory bandwidth. When the CPU needs more data than can fit in the CPU cache the main memory bandwidth becomes a bottleneck. This is an uncommon bottleneck for most systems, but one should be aware of it.

5.1.1 MySQL Design Limitations/Tradeoffs

When using the MyISAM table handler, MySQL uses extremely fast table locking (multiple readers/single writers). The biggest problem with this table type is if you have a mix of a steady stream of updates and slow selects on the same table. If this is a problem with some tables, you can use another table type for these. See Chapter 7.

MySQL can work with both transactional and non-transactional tables. To be able to work smoothly with non-transactional tables (which can't roll back if something goes wrong), MySQL has the following rules:

- All columns have default values.

- If you insert a 'wrong' value in a column—for instance, a NULL in a NOT NULL column or a numerical value that's too big in a numerical column—MySQL will, instead of giving an error, set the column to the 'best possible value'. For numerical values this is 0, the smallest possible values, or the largest possible value. For strings this is either the empty string or the longest possible string that can be in the column.

- All calculated expressions return a value that can be used instead of signaling an error condition. For example. 1/0 returns NULL.

The reason for these rules is that we can't check these conditions before the query starts to execute. If we encounter a problem after updating a few rows, we can't just rollback, as the table type may not support this. We can't stop because in that case the update would be 'half done' which is probably the worst possible scenario. In this case it's better to 'do the best you can' and then continue as if nothing happened.

This means that one should not use MySQL to check field content, but one should do this in the application.

5.1.2 Portability

Because all SQL servers implement different parts of SQL, it takes work to write portable SQL applications. For very simple selects/inserts it is very easy, but the more you need the harder it gets. If you want an application that is fast with many databases, it becomes even harder!

To make a complex application portable you need to choose a number of SQL servers that it should work with.

You can use the MySQL crash-me program/web page (http://www.mysql.com/information/crash-me.php) to find functions, types, and limits you can use with a selection of database servers. Crash-me now tests far from everything possible, but it is still comprehensive with about 450 things tested.

For example, you shouldn't have column names longer than 18 characters if you want to be able to use Informix or DB2.

Both the MySQL benchmarks and crash-me programs are very database-independent. By taking a look at how we have handled this, you can get a feeling for what you have to do to write your application so that it is database-independent. The benchmarks themselves can be found in the sql-bench directory in the MySQL source distribution. They are written in Perl with a DBI database interface (which solves the access part of the problem).

See http://www.mysql.com/information/benchmarks.html for the results from this benchmark.

As you can see in these results, all databases have some weak points. That is, they have different design compromises that lead to different behavior.

If you strive for database independence, you need to get a good feeling for each SQL server's bottlenecks. MySQL is very fast at retrieving and updating things, but will have a problem mixing slow readers/writers on the same table. Oracle, on the other hand, has a big problem when you try to access rows that you have recently updated (until they are flushed to disk). Transaction databases in general are not very good at generating summary tables from log tables, as in this case row locking is almost useless.

To get your application *really* database-independent, you need to define an easily extendable interface through which you manipulate your data. As C++ is available on most systems, it makes sense to use a C++ classes interface to the databases.

If you use some specific feature for some database (like the REPLACE command in MySQL), you should code a method for the other SQL servers to implement the same feature (but slower). With MySQL you can use the /*! */ syntax to add MySQL-specific keywords to a query. The code inside /**/ will be treated as a comment (ignored) by most other SQL servers.

If high performance is more important than exactness, as in some Web applications, it is possibile to create an application layer that caches all results to give you even higher performance. By letting old results 'expire' after a while, you can keep the cache reasonably fresh. This provides a method to handle high-load spikes, in which case you can dynamically increase the cache and set the expire timeout higher until things get back to normal.

In this case the table creation information should contain information on the initial size of the cache and how often the table should normally be refreshed.

5.1.3 What Have We Used MySQL for?

During MySQL initial development, the features of MySQL were made to fit our largest customer. They handle data warehousing for a couple of the biggest retailers in Sweden.

From all stores, we get weekly summaries of all bonus-card transactions, and we are expected to provide useful information for the store owners to help them find how their advertisement campaigns are affecting their customers.

The data is quite huge (about 7 million summary transactions per month), and we have data for 4-10 years that we need to present to the users. We got weekly requests from the customers that they want to get 'instant' access to new reports from this data.

We solved this by storing all information per month in compressed 'transaction' tables. We have a set of simple macros (script) that generate summary tables grouped by different criteria (product group, customer id, store ...) from the transaction tables. The reports are web pages that are dynamically generated by a small Perl script that parses a web page, executes the SQL statements in it, and inserts the results. We would have used PHP or mod_perl instead, but they were not available at that time.

For graphical data we wrote a simple tool in C that can produce GIFs based on the result of a SQL query (with some processing of the result). This is also dynamically executed from the Perl script that parses the HTML files.

In most cases a new report can simply be done by copying an existing script and modifying the SQL query in it. In some cases, we will need to add more fields to an existing summary table or generate a new one, but this is also quite simple, as we keep all transaction tables on disk. (Currently we have at least 50G of transaction tables and 200G of other customer data.)

We also let our customers access the summary tables directly with ODBC so that the advanced users can themselves experiment with the data.

We haven't had any problems handling this with quite modest Sun Ultra SPARCstation (2x200 Mhz). We recently upgraded one of our servers to a 2-CPU 400Mhz UltraSPARC, and we are now planning to start handling transactions on the product level, which would mean a tenfold increase of data. We think we can keep up with this by just adding more disks to our systems.

We are also experimenting with Intel-Linux to be able to get more CPU power cheaper. Now that we have the binary portable database format (new in Version 3.23), we will start to use this for some parts of the application.

Our initial feelings are that Linux will perform much better on low to medium loads and Solaris will perform better when you start to get a high load because of extreme disk I/O, but we don't yet have anything conclusive about this. After some discussion with a Linux Kernel developer, this might be a side effect of Linux giving so much resources to the batch job that the interactive performance gets very low. This makes the machine feel very slow and unresponsive while big batches are going. Hopefully this will be better handled in future Linux Kernels.

5.1.4 The MySQL Benchmark Suite

This should contain a technical description of the MySQL benchmark suite (and `crash-me`), but that description is not written yet. Currently, you can get a good idea of the benchmark by looking at the code and results in the `sql-bench` directory in any MySQL source distributions.

This benchmark suite is meant to be a benchmark that will tell any user what things a given SQL implementation performs well or poorly.

Note that this benchmark is single-threaded, so it measures the minimum time for the operations. We plan to in the future add a lot of multi-threaded tests to the benchmark suite.

For example, (run on the same NT 4.0 machine):

Reading 2000000 rows by index	Seconds	Seconds
mysql	367	249
mysql_odbc	464	
db2_odbc	1206	
informix_odbc	121126	
ms-sql_odbc	1634	
oracle_odbc	20800	
solid_odbc	877	
sybase_odbc	17614	

Inserting (350768) rows	Seconds	Seconds
mysql	381	206
mysql_odbc	619	
db2_odbc	3460	
informix_odbc	2692	
ms-sql_odbc	4012	
oracle_odbc	11291	
solid_odbc	1801	
sybase_odbc	4802	

In this test MySQL was run with an 8M index cache.

We have gathered some more benchmark results at http://www.mysql.com/information/benchmarks.html.

Note that Oracle is not included because they asked to be removed. All Oracle bench-marks have to be passed by Oracle! We believe that makes Oracle benchmarks **very** biased because the preceding benchmarks are supposed to show what a standard installa-tion can do for a single client.

To run the benchmark suite, you have to download a MySQL source distribution, install the Perl DBD driver for the database you want to test, and then do:

```
cd sql-bench
perl run-all-tests --server=#
```

where # is one of the supported servers. You can get a list of all options and supported servers by doing `run-all-tests --help`.

`crash-me` tries to determine what features a database supports and what its capabilities and limitations are by actually running queries. For example, it determines:

- What column types are supported
- How many indexes are supported
- What functions are supported
- How big a query can be
- How big a `VARCHAR` column can be

We can find the result from crash-me on a lot of different databases at http://www.mysql.com/information/crash-me.php.

5.1.5 Using Your Own Benchmarks

You should definitely benchmark your application and database to find out where the bot-tlenecks are. By fixing it (or by replacing the bottleneck with a 'dummy module') you can then easily identify the next bottleneck (and so on). Even if the overall performance for your application is sufficient, you should at least make a plan for each bottleneck, and decide how to solve it if someday you really need the extra performance.

For an example of portable benchmark programs, look at the MySQL benchmark suite. See Section 5.1.4, The MySQL Benchmark Suite. You can take any program from this suite and modify it to suit your needs. By doing this, you can try different solutions to your problem and test which is really the fastest solution for you.

It is very common that some problems only occur when the system is very heavily loaded. We have had many customers who contact us when they have a (tested) system in production and have encountered load problems. In every one of these cases so far, it has been problems with basic design (table scans are **not good** at high load) or OS/Library issues. Most of this would be a **lot** easier to fix if the systems were not already in produc-tion.

To avoid problems like this, you should put some effort into benchmarking your whole application under the worst possible load! You can use Super Smack for this. It is available at http://www.mysql.com/Downloads/super-smack/super-smack-1.0.tar.gz. As the name suggests, it can bring your system down to its knees if you ask it, so make sure to use it only on your development systems.

5.2 Optimising SELECTs and Other Queries

First, one thing that affects all queries: the more complex permission system setup you have, the more overhead you get.

If you do not have any GRANT statements done, MySQL will optimise the permission checking somewhat. So if you have a very high volume it may be worth the time to avoid grants. Otherwise, more permission checks result in a larger overhead.

If your problem is with some explicit MySQL function, you can always time this in the MySQL client:

```
mysql> SELECT BENCHMARK(1000000,1+1);
+------------------------+
| BENCHMARK(1000000,1+1) |
+------------------------+
|                      0 |
+------------------------+
1 row in set (0.32 sec)
```

This shows that MySQL can execute 1,000,000 + expressions in 0.32 second on a Pentium II 400MHz.

All MySQL functions should be very optimised, but there may be some exceptions, and the BENCHMARK(loop_count,expression) is a great tool to find out if this is a problem with your query.

5.2.1 EXPLAIN Syntax (Get Information About a SELECT)

```
    EXPLAIN tbl_name
or  EXPLAIN SELECT select_options
```

EXPLAIN tbl_name is a synonym for DESCRIBE tbl_name or SHOW COLUMNS FROM tbl_name.

When you precede a SELECT statement with the keyword EXPLAIN, MySQL explains how it would process the SELECT, providing information about how tables are joined and in which order.

With the help of EXPLAIN, you can see when you must add indexes to tables to get a
faster SELECT that uses indexes to find the records. You can also see if the optimiser joins
the tables in an optimal order. To force the optimiser to use a specific join order for a
SELECT statement, add a STRAIGHT_JOIN clause.

For non-simple joins, EXPLAIN returns a row of information for each table used in the
SELECT statement. The tables are listed in the order they would be read. MySQL resolves
all joins using a single-sweep multi-join method. This means that MySQL reads a row
from the first table, then finds a matching row in the second table, then in the third table,
and so on. When all tables are processed, it outputs the selected columns and backtracks
through the table list until a table is found for which there are more matching rows. The
next row is read from this table and the process continues with the next table.

Output from EXPLAIN includes the following columns:

table
> The table to which the row of output refers.

type
> The join type. Information about the various types is given below.

possible_keys
> The possible_keys column indicates which indexes MySQL could use to find the
> rows in this table. Note that this column is totally independent of the order of the
> tables. That means that some of the keys in possible_keys may not be usable in prac-
> tice with the generated table order.

> If this column is empty, there are no relevant indexes. In this case, you may be able
> to improve the performance of your query by examining the WHERE clause to see if it
> refers to some column or columns that would be suitable for indexing. If so, create
> an appropriate index and check the query with EXPLAIN again. See Section 6.5.4,
> ALTER TABLE Syntax.

> To see what indexes a table has, use SHOW INDEX FROM tbl_name.

key
> The key column indicates the key (index) that MySQL actually decided to use. The
> key is NULL if no index was chosen. If MySQL chooses the wrong index, you can
> probably force MySQL to use another index by using myisamchk --analyze. See
> Section 4.4.6.1, myisamchk invocation syntax. Or you could use USE INDEX/
> IGNORE INDEX. See Section 6.4.1, SELECT Syntax.

key_len
> The key_len column indicates the length of the key that MySQL decided to use.
> The length is NULL if the key is NULL. Note that this tells us how many parts of a
> multi-part key MySQL will actually use.

ref

> The ref column shows which columns or constants are used with the key to select rows from the table.

rows

> The rows column indicates the number of rows MySQL believes it must examine to execute the query.

Extra

> This column contains additional information on how MySQL will resolve the query. Here is an explanation of the different text strings that can be found in this column:

Distinct

> MySQL will not continue searching for more rows for the current row combination after it has found the first matching row.

Not exists

> MySQL was able to do a LEFT JOIN optimisation on the query and will not examine more rows in this table for the previous row combination after it finds one row that matches the LEFT JOIN criteria.
>
> Here is an example of this:
>
> ```
> SELECT * FROM t1 LEFT JOIN t2 ON t1.id=t2.id WHERE t2.id IS NULL;
> ```
>
> Assume that t2.id is defined with NOT NULL. In this case MySQL will scan t1 and look up the rows in t2 through t1.id. If MySQL finds a matching row in t2, it knows that t2.id can never be NULL, and will not scan through the rest of the rows in t2 that have the same id. In other words, for each row in t1, MySQL only needs to do a single lookup in t2, independent of how many matching rows there are in t2.

range checked for each record (index map: #)0]

> MySQL didn't find a real good index to use. It will, instead, for each row combination in the preceding tables, do a check on which index to use (if any), and use this index to retrieve the rows from the table. This isn't very fast but is faster than having to do a join without an index.

Using filesort

> MySQL will need to do an extra pass to find out how to retrieve the rows in sorted order. The sort is done by going through all rows according to the join type and storing the sort key + pointer to the row for all rows that match the WHERE. Then the keys are sorted. Finally the rows are retrieved in sorted order.

Using index

> The column information is retrieved from the table using only information in the index tree without having to do an additional seek to read the actual row. This can be done when all the used columns for the table are part of the same index.

Using temporary

To resolve the query MySQL will need to create a temporary table to hold the result. This typically happens if you do an ORDER BY on a different column set than you did a GROUP BY on.

Where used

A WHERE clause will be used to restrict which rows will be matched against the next table or sent to the client. If you don't have this information and the table is of type ALL or index, you may have something wrong in your query (if you don't intend to fetch/examine all rows from the table).

If you want to get your queries as fast as possible, you should look out for Using filesort and Using temporary.

The different join types are listed here, ordered from best to worst type:

system

The table has only one row (= system table). This is a special case of the const join type.

const

The table has, at most, a one matching row, which will be read at the start of the query. Because there is only one row, values from the column in this row can be regarded as constants by the rest of the optimiser. const tables are very fast, as they are read only once!

eq_ref

One row will be read from this table for each combination of rows from the previous tables. This is the best possible join type, other than the const types. It is used when all parts of an index are used by the join and the index is UNIQUE or a PRIMARY KEY.

ref

All rows with matching index values will be read from this table for each combination of rows from the previous tables. ref is used if the join uses only a leftmost prefix of the key, or if the key is not UNIQUE or a PRIMARY KEY (in other words, if the join cannot select a single row based on the key value). If the key that is used matches only a few rows, this join type is good.

range

Only rows that are in a given range will be retrieved, using an index to select the rows. The key column indicates which index is used. The key_len contains the longest key part that was used. The ref column will be NULL for this type.

index

This is the same as ALL, except that only the index tree is scanned. This is usually faster than ALL, as the index file is usually smaller than the data file.

ALL

A full table scan will be done for each combination of rows from the previous tables. This is normally not good if the table is the first table not marked const, and usually **very** bad in all other cases. You normally can avoid ALL by adding more indexes so that the row can be retrieved based on constant values or column values from earlier tables.

You can get a good indication of how good a join is by multiplying all values in the rows column of the EXPLAIN output. This should tell you roughly how many rows MySQL must examine to execute the query. This number is also used when you restrict queries with the max_join_size variable. See Section 5.5.2, Tuning Server Parameters.

The following example shows how a JOIN can be optimised progressively using the information provided by EXPLAIN.

Suppose you have the SELECT statement shown here, that you examine using EXPLAIN:

```
EXPLAIN SELECT tt.TicketNumber, tt.TimeIn,
               tt.ProjectReference, tt.EstimatedShipDate,
               tt.ActualShipDate, tt.ClientID,
               tt.ServiceCodes, tt.RepetitiveID,
               tt.CurrentProcess, tt.CurrentDPPerson,
               tt.RecordVolume, tt.DPPrinted, et.COUNTRY,
               et_1.COUNTRY, do.CUSTNAME
        FROM tt, et, et AS et_1, do
        WHERE tt.SubmitTime IS NULL
            AND tt.ActualPC = et.EMPLOYID
            AND tt.AssignedPC = et_1.EMPLOYID
            AND tt.ClientID = do.CUSTNMBR;
```

For this example, assume that:

*   The columns being compared have been declared as follows:

Table	Column	Column type
tt	ActualPC	CHAR(10)
tt	AssignedPC	CHAR(10)
tt	ClientID	CHAR(10)
et	EMPLOYID	CHAR(15)
do	CUSTNMBR	CHAR(15)

*   The tables have the indexes shown here:

Table	Index
tt	ActualPC
tt	AssignedPC
tt	ClientID

Table	Index
et	EMPLOYID (primary key)
do	CUSTNMBR (primary key)

- The tt.ActualPC values aren't evenly distributed.

Initially, before any optimisations have been performed, the EXPLAIN statement produces the following information:

```
table type possible_keys                    key  key_len ref  rows  Extra
et    ALL  PRIMARY                           NULL NULL    NULL 74
do    ALL  PRIMARY                           NULL NULL    NULL 2135
et_1  ALL  PRIMARY                           NULL NULL    NULL 74
tt    ALL  AssignedPC,ClientID,ActualPC NULL NULL    NULL 3872
      range checked for each record (key map: 35)
```

Because type is ALL for each table, this output indicates that MySQL is doing a full join for all tables! This will take quite a long time, as the product of the number of rows in each table must be examined! For the case at hand, this is 74 * 2135 * 74 * 3872 = 45,268,558,720 rows. If the tables were bigger, you can only imagine how long it would take.

One problem here is that MySQL can't (yet) use indexes on columns efficiently if they are declared differently. In this context, VARCHAR and CHAR are the same unless they are declared as different lengths. Because tt.ActualPC is declared as CHAR(10) and et.EMPLOYID is declared as CHAR(15), there is a length mismatch.

To fix this disparity between column lengths, use ALTER TABLE to lengthen ActualPC from 10 characters to 15 characters:

```
mysql> ALTER TABLE tt MODIFY ActualPC VARCHAR(15);
```

Now tt.ActualPC and et.EMPLOYID are both VARCHAR(15). Executing the EXPLAIN statement again produces this result:

```
table type    possible_keys        key     key_len ref         rows  Extra
tt    ALL     AssignedPC,ClientID,ActualPC NULL NULL NULL 3872  where used
do    ALL     PRIMARY              NULL    NULL    NULL        2135
      range checked for each record (key map: 1)
et_1  ALL     PRIMARY              NULL    NULL    NULL        74
      range checked for each record (key map: 1)
et    eq_ref  PRIMARY              PRIMARY 15      tt.ActualPC 1
```

This is not perfect, but is much better (the product of the rows values is now less by a factor of 74). This version is executed in a couple of seconds.

A second alteration can be made to eliminate the column length mismatches for the tt.AssignedPC = et_1.EMPLOYID and tt.ClientID = do.CUSTNMBR comparisons:

```
mysql> ALTER TABLE tt MODIFY AssignedPC VARCHAR(15),
    ->                   MODIFY ClientID    VARCHAR(15);
```

Now EXPLAIN produces this output:

table	type	possible_keys	key	key_len	ref	rows	Extra
et	ALL	PRIMARY	NULL	NULL	NULL	74	
tt	ref	AssignedPC, ClientID, ActualPC	ActualPC	15	et.EMPLOYID	52	where used
et_1	eq_ref	PRIMARY	PRIMARY	15	tt.AssignedPC	1	
do	eq_ref	PRIMARY	PRIMARY	15	tt.ClientID	1	

This is almost as good as it can get.

The remaining problem is that, by default, MySQL assumes that values in the tt.ActualPC column are evenly distributed, and that isn't the case for the tt table. Fortunately, it is easy to tell MySQL about this:

```
shell> myisamchk --analyze PATH_TO_MYSQL_DATABASE/tt
shell> mysqladmin refresh
```

Now the join is perfect, and EXPLAIN produces this result:

table	type	possible_keys	key	key_len	ref	rows	Extra
tt	ALL	AssignedPC, ClientID, ActualPC	NULL	NULL	NULL	3872	where used
et	eq_ref	PRIMARY	PRIMARY	15	tt.ActualPC	1	
et_1	eq_ref	PRIMARY	PRIMARY	15	tt.AssignedPC	1	
do	eq_ref	PRIMARY	PRIMARY	15	tt.ClientID	1	

Note that the rows column in the output from EXPLAIN is an educated guess from the MySQL join optimiser. To optimise a query, you should check if the numbers are even close to the truth. If not, you may get better performance by using STRAIGHT_JOIN in your SELECT statement and trying to list the tables in a different order in the FROM clause.

5.2.2 Estimating Query Performance

In most cases you can estimate the performance by counting disk seeks. For small tables, you can usually find the row in 1 disk seek (as the index is probably cached). For bigger tables, you can estimate that (using B++ tree indexes) you will need: log(row_count) / log(index_block_length / 3 * 2 / (index_length + data_pointer_length)) + 1 seeks to find a row.

In MySQL an index block is usually 1024 bytes and the data pointer is usually 4 bytes. A 500,000-row table with an index length of 3 (medium integer) gives you: log(500,000)/log(1024/3*2/(3+4)) + 1 = 4 seeks.

As this index would require about 500,000 * 7 * 3/2 = 5.2M (assuming that the index buffers are filled to 2/3, which is typical), you will probably have much of the index in memory and you will probably only need 1-2 calls to read data from the OS to find the row.

For writes, however, you will need 4 seek requests (as noted previously) to find where to place the new index and normally 2 seeks to update the index and write the row.

Note that this doesn't mean that your application will slowly degenerate by N log N! As long as everything is cached by the OS or SQL server things will only go marginally slower while the table gets bigger. After the data gets too big to be cached, things will start to go much slower until your applications are only bound by disk-seeks (which increase by N log N). To avoid this, increase the index cache as the data grows. See Section 5.5.2, Tuning Server Parameters.

5.2.3 Speed of SELECT Queries

In general, when you want to make a slow SELECT ... WHERE faster, the first thing to check is whether you can add an index. See Section 5.4.3, How MySQL Uses Indexes. All references between different tables should usually be done with indexes. You can use the EXPLAIN command to determine which indexes are used for a SELECT. See Section 5.2.1, EXPLAIN Syntax (Get Information About a SELECT).

Some general tips:

- To help MySQL optimise queries better, run myisamchk -analyze on a table after it has been loaded with relevant data. This updates a value for each index part that indicates the average number of rows that have the same value. (For unique indexes, this is always 1, of course.) MySQL will use this to decide which index to choose when you connect two tables with 'a non-constant expression'. You can check the result from the analyze run by doing SHOW INDEX FROM table_name and examining the Cardinality column.

- To sort an index and data according to an index, use myisamchk -sort-index -sort-records=1 (if you want to sort on index 1). If you have a unique index from which you want to read all records in order according to that index, this is a good way to make that faster. Note, however, that this sorting isn't written optimally and will take a long time for a large table!

5.2.4 How MySQL Optimises WHERE Clauses

The WHERE optimisations are put in the SELECT part here because they are mostly used with SELECT, but the same optimisations apply for WHERE in DELETE and UPDATE statements.

Also note that this section is incomplete. MySQL does many optimisations, and we have not had time to document them all.

Some of the optimisations performed by MySQL are listed here:

* Removal of unnecessary parentheses:

  ```
  ((a AND b) AND c OR (((a AND b) AND (c AND d))))
  -> (a AND b AND c) OR (a AND b AND c AND d)
  ```

* Constant folding:

  ```
  (a<b AND b=c) AND a=5
  -> b>5 AND b=c AND a=5
  ```

* Constant condition removal (needed because of constant folding):

  ```
  (B>=5 AND B=5) OR (B=6 AND 5=5) OR (B=7 AND 5=6)
  -> B=5 OR B=6
  ```

* Constant expressions used by indexes are evaluated only once.

* COUNT(*) on a single table without a WHERE is retrieved directly from the table information for MyISAM and HEAP tables. This is also done for any NOT NULL expression when used with only one table.

* Early detection of invalid constant expressions. MySQL quickly detects that some SELECT statements are impossible and returns no rows.

* HAVING is merged with WHERE if you don't use GROUP BY or group functions (COUNT(), MIN() ...).

* For each sub-join, a simpler WHERE is constructed to get a fast WHERE evaluation for each sub-join and also to skip records as soon as possible.

* All constant tables are read first, before any other tables in the query. A constant table is:

  — An empty table or a table with 1 row.

  — A table that is used with a WHERE clause on a UNIQUE index, or a PRIMARY KEY, where all index parts are used with constant expressions and the index parts are defined as NOT NULL.

  All the following tables are used as constant tables:

  ```
  mysql> SELECT * FROM t WHERE primary_key=1;
  mysql> SELECT * FROM t1,t2
      ->          WHERE t1.primary_key=1 AND t2.primary_key=t1.id;
  ```

* The best join combination to join the tables is found by trying all possibilities. If all columns in ORDER BY and in GROUP BY come from the same table, this table is preferred first when joining.

* If there is an ORDER BY clause and a different GROUP BY clause, or if the ORDER BY or GROUP BY contains columns from tables other than the first table in the join queue, a temporary table is created.

- If you use SQL_SMALL_RESULT, MySQL will use an in-memory temporary table.

- Each table index is queried, and the best index that spans fewer than 30% of the rows is used. If no such index can be found, a quick table scan is used.

- In some cases, MySQL can read rows from the index without even consulting the data file. If all columns used from the index are numeric, only the index tree is used to resolve the query.

- Before each record is output, those that do not match the HAVING clause are skipped.

Some examples of queries that are very fast:

```
mysql> SELECT COUNT(*) FROM tbl_name;
mysql> SELECT MIN(key_part1),MAX(key_part1) FROM tbl_name;
mysql> SELECT MAX(key_part2) FROM tbl_name
    ->           WHERE key_part_1=constant;
mysql> SELECT ... FROM tbl_name
    ->           ORDER BY key_part1,key_part2,... LIMIT 10;
mysql> SELECT ... FROM tbl_name
    ->           ORDER BY key_part1 DESC,key_part2 DESC,... LIMIT 10;
```

The following queries are resolved using only the index tree (assuming the indexed columns are numeric):

```
mysql> SELECT key_part1,key_part2 FROM tbl_name WHERE key_part1=val;
mysql> SELECT COUNT(*) FROM tbl_name
    ->           WHERE key_part1=val1 AND key_part2=val2;
mysql> SELECT key_part2 FROM tbl_name GROUP BY key_part1;
```

The following queries use indexing to retrieve the rows in sorted order without a separate sorting pass:

```
mysql> SELECT ... FROM tbl_name
    ->           ORDER BY key_part1,key_part2,... ;
mysql> SELECT ... FROM tbl_name
    ->           ORDER BY key_part1 DESC,key_part2 DESC,... ;
```

5.2.5 How MySQL Optimises DISTINCT

DISTINCT is converted to a GROUP BY on all columns. DISTINCT combined with ORDER BY will in many cases also need a temporary table.

When combining LIMIT # with DISTINCT, MySQL will stop as soon as it finds # unique rows.

If you don't use columns from all used tables, MySQL will stop scanning the unused tables as soon as it has found the first match.

```
SELECT DISTINCT t1.a FROM t1,t2 where t1.a=t2.a;
```

In this case, assuming t1 is used before t2 (check with EXPLAIN), MySQL will stop reading from t2 (for that particular row in t1) when the first row in t2 is found.

5.2.6 How MySQL Optimises LEFT JOIN
and RIGHT JOIN

A LEFT JOIN B in MySQL is implemented as follows:

* The table B is set to be dependent on table A and all tables that A is dependent on.

* The table A is set to be dependent on all tables (except B) that are used in the LEFT JOIN condition.

* All LEFT JOIN conditions are moved to the WHERE clause.

* All standard join optimisations are done, with the exception that a table is always read after all tables it is dependent on. If there is a circular dependence, MySQL will issue an error.

* All standard WHERE optimisations are done.

* If there is a row in A that matches the WHERE clause, but there wasn't any row in B that matched the LEFT JOIN condition, an extra B row is generated with all columns set to NULL.

* If you use LEFT JOIN to find rows that don't exist in some table and you have the test, column_name IS NULL in the WHERE part, where column_name is a column that is declared as NOT NULL, MySQL will stop searching after more rows (for a particular key combination) after it has found one row that matches the LEFT JOIN condition.

RIGHT JOIN is implemented analogously as LEFT JOIN.

The table read order forced by LEFT JOIN and STRAIGHT JOIN will help the join optimiser (which calculates in which order tables should be joined) to do its work much more quickly, as there are fewer table permutations to check.

Note that this means that if you do a query of type:

```
SELECT * FROM a,b LEFT JOIN c ON (c.key=a.key) LEFT JOIN d (d.key=a.key)
        WHERE b.key=d.key
```

MySQL will do a full scan on b as the LEFT JOIN will force it to be read before d.

The fix in this case is to change the query to:

```
SELECT * FROM b,a LEFT JOIN c ON (c.key=a.key) LEFT JOIN d (d.key=a.key)
        WHERE b.key=d.key
```

5.2.7 How MySQL Optimises ORDER BY

In some cases MySQL can use an index to satisfy an ORDER BY or GROUP BY request without doing any extra sorting.

The index can also be used even if the ORDER BY doesn't match the index exactly, as long as all the unused index parts and all the extra ORDER BY columns are constants in the WHERE clause. The following queries will use the index to resolve the ORDER BY / GROUP BY part:

```
SELECT * FROM t1 ORDER BY key_part1,key_part2,...
SELECT * FROM t1 WHERE key_part1=constant ORDER BY key_part2
SELECT * FROM t1 WHERE key_part1=constant GROUP BY key_part2
SELECT * FROM t1 ORDER BY key_part1 DESC,key_part2 DESC
SELECT * FROM t1 WHERE key_part1=1 ORDER BY key_part1 DESC,key_part2 DESC
```

Some cases where MySQL can *cannot* use indexes to resolve the ORDER BY (note that MySQL will still use indexes to find the rows that match the WHERE clause):

- You are doing an ORDER BY on different keys:

  ```
  SELECT * FROM t1 ORDER BY key1,key2
  ```

- You are doing an ORDER BY using non-consecutive key parts:

  ```
  SELECT * FROM t1 WHERE key2=constant ORDER BY key_part2
  ```

- You are mixing ASC and DESC:

  ```
  SELECT * FROM t1 ORDER BY key_part1 DESC,key_part2 ASC
  ```

- The key used to fetch the rows is not the same one that is used to do the ORDER BY:

  ```
  SELECT * FROM t1 WHERE key2=constant ORDER BY key1
  ```

- You are joining many tables and the columns you are doing an ORDER BY on are not all from the first not-const table that is used to retrieve rows (this is the first table in the EXPLAIN output which doesn't use a const row fetch method).

- You have different ORDER BY and GROUP BY expressions.

- The used table index is an index type that doesn't store rows in order (like the HASH index in HEAP tables).

- The index colum may contain NULL values and one is using ORDER BY ... DESC. This is because in SQL NULL values is always sorted before normal values, whether or not you are using DESC.

In the cases where MySQL has to sort the result, it uses the following algorithm:

- Read all rows according to key or by table scanning. Rows that don't match the WHERE clause are skipped.

- Store the sort-key in a buffer (of size sort_buffer).

- When the buffer gets full, run a qsort on it and store the result in a temporary file. Save a pointer to the sorted block. (In the case where all rows fit into the sort buffer, no temporary file is created.)

- Repeat this until all rows have been read.

- Do a multi-merge of up to MERGEBUFF (7) regions to one block in another temporary file. Repeat until all blocks from the first file are in the second file.

- Repeat the following until there is less than MERGEBUFF2 (15) blocks left.

- On the last multi-merge, only the pointer to the row (last part of the sort-key) is written to a result file.

- Now the code in sql/records.cc will be used to read through them in sorted order by using the row pointers in the result file. To optimize this, we read in a big block of row pointers, sort them and then read the rows in the sorted order into a row buffer (record_rnd_buffer).

With EXPLAIN SELECT ... ORDER BY you can check if MySQL can use indexes to resolve the query. If you get Using filesort in the extra column, MySQL can't use indexes to resolve the ORDER BY. See Section 5.2.1, EXPLAIN Syntax (Get Information About a SELECT).

If you want to have a higher ORDER BY speed, you should first see if you can get MySQL to use indexes instead of having to do an extra sorting phase. If this is not possible, you can:

- Increase the size of the sort_buffer variable.

- Increase the size of the record_rnd_buffer variable.

- Change tmpdir to point to a dedicated disk with lots of empty space.

5.2.8 How MySQL Optimises LIMIT

In some cases MySQL will handle the query differently when you are using LIMIT # and not using HAVING:

- If you are selecting only a few rows with LIMIT, MySQL will use indexes in some cases when it normally would prefer to do a full table scan.

- If you use LIMIT # with ORDER BY, MySQL will end the sorting as soon as it has found the first # lines instead of sorting the whole table.

- When combining LIMIT # with DISTINCT, MySQL will stop as soon as it finds # unique rows.

- In some cases a GROUP BY can be resolved by reading the key in order (or do a sort on the key) and then calculating summaries until the key value changes. In this case LIMIT # will not calculate any unnecessary GROUP BYs.

- As soon as MySQL has sent the first # rows to the client, it will abort the query (if you are not using SQL_CALC_FOUND_ROWS).

- LIMIT 0 will always quickly return an empty set. This is useful to check the query and to get the column types of the result columns.

- When the server uses temporary tables to resolve the query, the LIMIT # is used to calculate how much space is required.

5.2.9 Speed of INSERT Queries

The time to insert a record is approximately as follows:

- Connect: (3)
- Sending query to server: (2)
- Parsing query: (2)
- Inserting record: (1 x size of record)
- Inserting indexes: (1 x number of indexes)
- Close: (1)

where the numbers are somewhat proportional to the overall time. This does not take into consideration the initial overhead to open tables (which is done once for each concurrently running query).

The size of the table slows down the insertion of indexes by N log N (B-trees).

Some ways to speed up inserts:

- If you are inserting many rows from the same client at the same time, use multiple value list INSERT statements. This is much faster (many times, in some cases) than using separate INSERT statements. If you are adding data to non-empty tables, you may tune up the myisam_bulk_insert_tree_size variable to make it even faster. See Section 4.5.6.4, SHOW VARIABLES.

- If you are inserting a lot of rows from different clients, you can get higher speed by using the INSERT DELAYED statement. See Section 6.4.3, INSERT Syntax.

- Note that with MyISAM tables you can insert rows at the same time SELECTs are running if there are no deleted rows in the tables.

- When loading a table from a text file, use LOAD DATA INFILE. This is usually 20 times faster than using a lot of INSERT statements. See Section 6.4.9, LOAD DATA INFILE Syntax.

- It is possible with some extra work to make LOAD DATA INFILE run even faster when the table has many indexes. Use the following procedure:

    1. Optionally create the table with CREATE TABLE. For example, use mysql or Perl-DBI.

    2. Execute a FLUSH TABLES statement or the shell command mysqladmin flush-tables.

    3. Use myisamchk --keys-used=0 -rq /path/to/db/tbl_name. This will remove all usage of all indexes from the table.

    4. Insert data into the table with LOAD DATA INFILE. This will not update any indexes and will therefore be very fast.

    5. If you are going to only read the table in the future, run myisampack on it to make it smaller. See Section 7.1.2.3, Compressed table characteristics.

    6. Re-create the indexes with myisamchk -r -q /path/to/db/tbl_name. This will create the index tree in memory before writing it to disk, which is much faster because it avoids lots of disk seeks. The resulting index tree is also perfectly balanced.

    7. Execute a FLUSH TABLES statement or the shell command mysqladmin flush-tables.

    Note that LOAD DATA INFILE also performs this optimization if you insert into an empty table; the main difference with the preceding procedure is that you can let myisamchk allocate much more temporary memory for the index creation that you may want MySQL to allocate for every index re-creation.

    Since **MySQL 4.0** you can also use ALTER TABLE tbl_name DISABLE KEYS instead of myisamchk --keys-used=0 -rq /path/to/db/tbl_name and ALTER TABLE tbl_name ENABLE KEYS instead of myisamchk -r -q /path/to/db/tbl_name. This way you can also skip the FLUSH TABLES steps.

- You can speed up insertions that are done over multiple statements by locking your tables:

    ```
    mysql> LOCK TABLES a WRITE;
    mysql> INSERT INTO a VALUES (1,23),(2,34),(4,33);
    mysql> INSERT INTO a VALUES (8,26),(6,29);
    mysql> UNLOCK TABLES;
    ```

    The main speed difference is that the index buffer is flushed to disk only once, after all INSERT statements have completed. Normally there would be as many index buffer flushes as there are different INSERT statements. Locking is not needed if you can insert all rows with a single statement.

    For transactional tables, you should use BEGIN/COMMIT instead of LOCK TABLES to get a speedup.

Locking will also lower the total time of multi-connection tests, but the maximum wait time for some threads will go up (because they wait for locks). For example:

```
thread 1 does 1000 inserts
thread 2, 3, and 4 does 1 insert
thread 5 does 1000 inserts
```

If you don't use locking, 2, 3, and 4 will finish before 1 and 5. If you use locking, 2, 3, and 4 probably will not finish before 1 or 5, but the total time should be about 40% faster.

As INSERT, UPDATE, and DELETE operations are very fast in MySQL, you will obtain better overall performance by adding locks around everything that does more than about 5 inserts or updates in a row. If you do very many inserts in a row, you could do a LOCK TABLES followed by an UNLOCK TABLES once in a while (about each 1000 rows) to allow other threads access to the table. This would still result in a nice performance gain.

Of course, LOAD DATA INFILE is much faster for loading data.

To get some more speed for both LOAD DATA INFILE and INSERT, enlarge the key buffer. See Section 5.5.2, Tuning Server Parameters.

5.2.10 Speed of UPDATE Queries

Update queries are optimised as a SELECT query with the additional overhead of a write. The speed of the write is dependent on the size of the data that is being updated and the number of indexes that are updated. Indexes that are not changed will not be updated.

Also, another way to get fast updates is to delay updates and then do many updates in a row later. Doing many updates in a row is much quicker than doing one at a time if you lock the table.

Note that, with the dynamic record format, updating a record to a longer total length may split the record. So if you do this often, it is very important to perform an OPTIMIZE TABLE sometimes. See Section 4.5.1, OPTIMIZE TABLE Syntax.

5.2.11 Speed of DELETE Queries

If you want to delete all rows in the table, you should use TRUNCATE TABLE table_name. See Section 6.4.7, TRUNCATE Syntax.

The time to delete a record is exactly proportional to the number of indexes. To delete records more quickly, you can increase the size of the index cache. See Section 5.5.2, Tuning Server Parameters.

5.2.12 Other Optimisation Tips

Unsorted tips for faster systems:

- Use persistent connections to the database to avoid the connection overhead. If you can't use persistent connections and you are doing a lot of new connections to the database, you may want to change the value of the thread_cache_size variable. See Section 5.5.2, Tuning Server Parameters.

- Always check that all your queries really use the indexes you have created in the tables. In MySQL you can do this with the EXPLAIN command.

- Try to avoid complex SELECT queries on MyISAM tables that are updated a lot. This is to avoid problems with table locking.

- The new MyISAM tables can insert rows in a table without deleted rows at the same time another table is reading from it. If this is important for you, you should consider methods where you don't have to delete rows, or run OPTIMIZE TABLE after you have deleted a lot of rows.

- Use ALTER TABLE ... ORDER BY expr1,expr2 ... if you mostly retrieve rows in expr1,expr2 ... order. By using this option after big changes to the table, you may be able to get higher performance.

- In some cases it may make sense to introduce a column that is "hashed' based on information from other columns. If this column is short and reasonably unique it may be much faster than a big index on many columns. In MySQL it's very easy to use this extra column: SELECT * FROM table_name WHERE hash=MD5(CON-CAT(col1,col2)) AND col_1='constant' AND col_2='constant'.

- For tables that change a lot you should try to avoid all VARCHAR or BLOB columns. You will get a dynamic row length as soon as you are using a single VARCHAR or BLOB column. See Chapter 7.

- It's not normally useful to split a table into different tables just because the rows get 'big'. To access a row, the biggest performance hit is the disk seek to find the first byte of the row. After finding the data most new disks can read the whole row fast enough for most applications. The only cases where it really matters to split up a table are if it's a dynamic row size table (as noted earlier) that you can change to a fixed row size, or if you very often need to scan the table and don't need most of the columns. See Chapter 7.

- If you very often need to calculate things based on information from a lot of rows (like counts of things), it's probably much better to introduce a new table and update the counter in real time. An update of type UPDATE table set count=count+1 where index_column=constant is very fast!

This is really important when you use databases like MySQL that only have table locking (multiple readers/single writers). This will also give better performance with most databases, as the row-locking manager in this case will have less to do.

- If you need to collect statistics from big log tables, use summary tables instead of scanning the whole table. Maintaining the summaries should be much faster than trying to do statistics 'live'. It's much faster to regenerate new summary tables from the logs when things change (depending on business decisions) than to have to change the running application!

- If possible, one should classify reports as 'live' or 'statistical', where data needed for statistical reports is only generated based on summary tables that are generated from the actual data.

- Take advantage of the fact that columns have default values. Insert values explicitly only when the value to be inserted differs from the default. This reduces the parsing that MySQL needs to do and improves the insert speed.

- In some cases it's convenient to pack and store data into a blob. In this case you have to add some extra code in your application to pack/unpack things in the blob, but this may save a lot of accesses at some stage. This is practical when you have data that doesn't conform to a static table structure.

- Normally you should try to keep all data non-redundant (what is called third normal form in database theory), but you should not be afraid of duplicating things or creating summary tables if you need these to gain more speed.

- Stored procedures or UDF (user-defined functions) may be a good way to get more performance. In this case you should, however, always have a way to do this in some other (slower) way if you use a database that doesn't support this.

- You can always gain something by caching queries/answers in your application and trying to do many inserts/updates at the same time. If your database supports lock tables (like MySQL and Oracle), this should help to ensure that the index cache is only flushed once after all updates.

- Use INSERT /*! DELAYED */ when you do not need to know when your data is written. This speeds things up because many records can be written with a single disk write.

- Use INSERT /*! LOW_PRIORITY */ when you want your selects to be more important.

- Use SELECT /*! HIGH_PRIORITY */ to get selects that jump the queue. That is, the select is done even if there is somebody waiting to do a write.

- Use the multi-line INSERT statement to store many rows with one SQL command (many SQL servers support this).

- Use LOAD DATA INFILE to load bigger amounts of data. This is faster than normal inserts and will be even faster when myisamchk is integrated in mysqld.

- Use AUTO_INCREMENT columns to make unique values.

- Use OPTIMIZE TABLE once in a while to avoid fragmentation when using the dynamic table format. See Section 4.5.1, OPTIMIZE TABLE Syntax.

- Use HEAP tables to get more speed when possible. See Chapter 7.

- When using a normal web server setup, images should be stored as files. That is, store only a file reference in the database. The main reason for this is that a normal web server is much better at caching files than database contents. So it's much easier to get a fast system if you are using files.

- Use in-memory tables for non-critical data that is accessed often (like information about the last shown banner for users that don't have cookies).

- Columns with identical information in different tables should be declared identical and have identical names. Before Version 3.23 you got slow joins otherwise.

  Try to keep the names simple (use name instead of customer_name in the customer table). To make your names portable to other SQL servers you should keep them shorter than 18 characters.

- If you need really high speed, you should take a look at the low-level interfaces for data storage that the different SQL servers support! For example, by accessing the MySQL MyISAM directly, you could get a speed increase of 2-5 times compared to using the SQL interface. To be able to do this the data must be on the same server as the application, and usually it should only be accessed by one process (because external file locking is really slow). One could eliminate the aforementioned problems by introducing low-level MyISAM commands in the MySQL server (this could be one easy way to get more performance if needed). By carefully designing the database interface, it should be quite easy to support this type of optimisation.

- In many cases it's faster to access data from a database (using a live connection) than from a text file, just because the database is likely to be more compact than the text file (if you are using numerical data), and this will involve fewer disk accesses. You will also save code because you don't have to parse your text files to find line and column boundaries.

- You can also use replication to speed things up. See Section 4.10, Replication in MySQL.

- Declaring a table with DELAY_KEY_WRITE=1 will make the updating of indexes faster, as these are not logged to disk until the file is closed. The downside is that you should run myisamchk on these tables before you start mysqld to ensure that they are okay if something killed mysqld in the middle. As the key information can always be generated from the data, you should not lose anything by using DELAY_KEY_WRITE.

5.3 Locking Issues

5.3.1 How MySQL Locks Tables

You can find a discussion about different locking methods in the appendix. See Section D.4, Locking Methods.

All locking in MySQL is deadlock-free, except for InnoDB and BDB type tables. This is managed by always requesting all needed locks at once at the beginning of a query and always locking the tables in the same order.

InnoDB type tables automatically acquire their row locks and BDB type tables their page locks during the processing of SQL statements, not at the start of the transaction.

The locking method MySQL uses for WRITE locks works as follows:

*   If there are no locks on the table, put a write lock on it.

*   Otherwise, put the lock request in the write lock queue.

The locking method MySQL uses for READ locks works as follows:

*   If there are no write locks on the table, put a read lock on it.

*   Otherwise, put the lock request in the read lock queue.

When a lock is released, the lock is made available to the threads in the write lock queue, then to the threads in the read lock queue.

This means that if you have many updates on a table, SELECT statements will wait until there are no more updates.

To work around this for the case where you want to do many INSERT and SELECT operations on a table, you can insert rows in a temporary table and update the real table with the records from the temporary table once in a while.

This can be done with the following code:

```
mysql> LOCK TABLES real_table WRITE, insert_table WRITE;
mysql> INSERT INTO real_table SELECT * FROM insert_table;
mysql> TRUNCATE TABLE insert_table;
mysql> UNLOCK TABLES;
```

You can use the LOW_PRIORITY options with INSERT, UPDATE, or DELETE, or HIGH_PRIORITY with SELECT if you want to prioritise retrieval in some specific cases. You can also start mysqld with --low-priority-updates to get the same behavior.

Using SQL_BUFFER_RESULT can also help make table locks shorter. See Section 6.4.1, SELECT Syntax.

You could also change the locking code in mysys/thr_lock.c to use a single queue. In this case, write locks and read locks would have the same priority, which might help some applications.

5.3.2 Table Locking Issues

The table locking code in MySQL is deadlock free.

MySQL uses table locking (instead of row locking or column locking) on all table types, except InnoDB and BDB tables, to achieve a very high lock speed. For large tables, table locking is much better than row locking for most applications, but there are, of course, some pitfalls.

For InnoDB and BDB tables, MySQL only uses table locking if you explicitly lock the table with LOCK TABLES. For these table types we recommend that you not use LOCK TABLES at all because InnoDB uses automatic row-level locking and BDB uses page-level locking to ensure transaction isolation.

In MySQL Versions 3.23.7 and above, you can insert rows into MyISAM tables at the same time other threads are reading from the table. Note that currently this only works if there are no holes after deleted rows in the table at the time the insert is made. When all holes have been filled with new data, concurrent inserts will automatically be enabled again.

Table locking enables many threads to read from a table at the same time, but if a thread wants to write to a table, it must first get exclusive access. During the update, all other threads that want to access this particular table will wait until the update is ready.

As updates on tables normally are considered to be more important than SELECT, all statements that update a table have higher priority than statements that retrieve information from a table. This should ensure that updates are not 'starved' because one issues a lot of heavy queries against a specific table. (You can change this by using LOW_PRIORITY with the statement that does the update or HIGH_PRIORITY with the SELECT statement.)

Starting from MySQL Version 3.23.7 one can use the max_write_lock_count variable to force MySQL to temporary give all SELECT statements that wait for a table a higher priority after a specific number of inserts on a table.

Table locking is, however, not very good under the following scenario:

- A client issues a SELECT that takes a long time to run.

- Another client then issues an UPDATE on a used table. This client will wait until the SELECT is finished.

- Another client issues another SELECT statement on the same table. As UPDATE has higher priority than SELECT, this SELECT will wait for the UPDATE to finish. It will also wait for the first SELECT to finish!

- A thread is waiting for something like full disk, in which case all threads that want to access the problem table will also be put in a waiting state until more disk space is made available.

Some possible solutions to this problem are:

- Try to get the SELECT statements to run faster. You may have to create some summary tables to do this.

- Start mysqld with --low-priority-updates. This will give all statements that update (modify) a table lower priority than a SELECT statement. In this case the last SELECT statement in the previous scenario would execute before the INSERT statement.

- You can give a specific INSERT, UPDATE, or DELETE statement lower priority with the LOW_PRIORITY attribute.

- Start mysqld with a low value for **max_write_lock_count** to give READ locks after a certain number of WRITE locks.

- You can specify that all updates from a specific thread should be done with low priority by using the SQL command SET SQL_LOW_PRIORITY_UPDATES=1. See Section 5.5.6, SET Syntax.

- You can specify that a specific SELECT is very important with the HIGH_PRIORITY attribute. See Section 6.4.1, SELECT Syntax.

- If you have problems with INSERT combined with SELECT, switch to use the new MyISAM tables, as these support concurrent SELECTs and INSERTs.

- If you mainly mix INSERT and SELECT statements, the DELAYED attribute to INSERT will probably solve your problems. See Section 6.4.3, INSERT Syntax.

- If you have problems with SELECT and DELETE, the LIMIT option to DELETE may help. See Section 6.4.6, DELETE Syntax.

5.4 Optimising Database Structure

5.4.1 Design Choices

MySQL keeps row data and index data in separate files. Many (almost all) other databases mix row and index data in the same file. We believe that the MySQL choice is better for a very wide range of modern systems.

Another way to store the row data is to keep the information for each column in a separate area (examples are SDBM and Focus). This will cause a performance hit for every query that accesses more than one column. Because this degenerates so quickly when more than one column is accessed, we believe that this model is not good for general-purpose databases.

The more common case is that the index and data are stored together (like in Oracle/ Sybase et al.). In this case you will find the row information at the leaf page of the index. The good thing with this layout is that, depending on how well the index is cached, it saves a disk read. The bad things with this layout are:

- Table scanning is much slower because you have to read through the indexes to get at the data.

- You can't use only the index table to retrieve data for a query.

- You lose a lot of space, as you must duplicate indexes from the nodes (because you can't store the row in the nodes).

- Deletes will degenerate the table over time (as indexes in nodes are usually not updated on delete).

- It's harder to cache only the index data.

5.4.2 Get Your Data as Small as Possible

One of the most basic optimisation is to get your data (and indexes) to take as little space on the disk (and in memory) as possible. This can give huge improvements because disk reads are faster, and normally, less main memory will be used. Indexing also takes fewer resources if done on smaller columns.

MySQL supports a lot of different table types and row formats. Choosing the right table format may give you a big performance gain. See Chapter 7.

You can get better performance on a table and minimise storage space using the following techniques:

- Use the most efficient (smallest) types possible. MySQL has many specialised types that save disk space and memory.

- Use the smaller integer types if possible to get smaller tables. For example, MEDIU-MINT is often better than INT.

- Declare columns to be NOT NULL if possible. It makes everything faster and you save one bit per column. Note that if you really need NULL in your application you should definitely use it. Just avoid having it on all columns by default.

- If you don't have any variable-length columns (VARCHAR, TEXT, or BLOB columns), a fixed-size record format is used. This is faster but unfortunately may waste some space. See Section 7.1.2, MyISAM Table Formats.

- The primary index of a table should be as short as possible. This makes identification of one row easy and efficient.

- For each table, you have to decide which storage/index method to use. See Chapter 7.

- Only create the indexes that you really need. Indexes are good for retrieval but bad when you need to store things fast. If you mostly access a table by searching on a combination of columns, make an index on them. The first index part should be the most-used column. If you are **always** using many columns, you should use the column with more duplicates first to get better compression of the index.

- If it's very likely that a column has a unique prefix on the first number of characters, it's better to only index this prefix. MySQL supports an index on a part of a character column. Shorter indexes are faster, not only because they take less disk space, but also because they will give you more hits in the index cache and, thus, fewer disk seeks. See Section 5.5.2, Tuning Server Parameters.

- In some circumstances it can be beneficial to split into two a table that is scanned very often. This is especially true if it is a dynamic-format table and it is possible to use a smaller static-format table that can be used to find the relevant rows when scanning the table.

5.4.3 How MySQL Uses Indexes

Indexes are used to find rows with a specific value of one column fast. Without an index MySQL has to start with the first record and then read through the whole table until it finds the relevant rows. The bigger the table, the more this costs. If the table has an index for the columns in question, MySQL can quickly get a position to seek to in the middle of the data file without having to look at all the data. If a table has 1000 rows, this is at least 100 times faster than reading sequentially. Note that if you need to access almost all 1000 rows it is faster to read sequentially because you then avoid disk seeks.

All MySQL indexes (PRIMARY, UNIQUE, and INDEX) are stored in B-trees. Strings are automatically prefix- and end-space compressed. See Section 6.5.7, CREATE INDEX Syntax.

Indexes are used to:

- Quickly find the rows that match a WHERE clause.

- Retrieve rows from other tables when performing joins.

- Find the MAX() or MIN() value for a specific indexed column. This is optimised by a preprocessor that checks if you are using WHERE key_part_# = constant on all key parts < N. In this case MySQL will do a single key lookup and replace the MIN() expression with a constant. If all expressions are replaced with constants, the query will return at once:

  ```
  SELECT MIN(key_part2),MAX(key_part2) FROM table_name where key_part1=10
  ```

- Sort or group a table if the sorting or grouping is done on a leftmost prefix of a usable key (for example, ORDER BY key_part_1,key_part_2). The key is read in reverse order if all key parts are followed by DESC. See Section 5.2.7, How MySQL

Optimises ORDER BY.

- In some cases a query can be optimised to retrieve values without consulting the data file. If all used columns for some table are numeric and form a leftmost prefix for some key, the values may be retrieved from the index tree for greater speed:

```
SELECT key_part3 FROM table_name WHERE key_part1=1
```

Suppose you issue the following SELECT statement:

```
mysql> SELECT * FROM tbl_name WHERE col1=val1 AND col2=val2;
```

If a multiple-column index exists on col1 and col2, the appropriate rows can be fetched directly. If separate single-column indexes exist on col1 and col2, the optimiser tries to find the most restrictive index by deciding which index will find fewer rows and using that index to fetch the rows.

If the table has a multiple-column index, any leftmost prefix of the index can be used by the optimiser to find rows. For example, if you have a three-column index on (col1,col2,col3), you have indexed search capabilities on (col1), (col1,col2), and (col1,col2,col3).

MySQL can't use a partial index if the columns don't form a leftmost prefix of the index. Suppose you have the following SELECT statements:

```
mysql> SELECT * FROM tbl_name WHERE col1=val1;
mysql> SELECT * FROM tbl_name WHERE col2=val2;
mysql> SELECT * FROM tbl_name WHERE col2=val2 AND col3=val3;
```

If an index exists on (col1,col2,col3), only the first query shown in the preceding statements uses the index. The second and third queries do involve indexed columns, but (col2) and (col2,col3) are not leftmost prefixes of (col1,col2,col3).

MySQL also uses indexes for LIKE comparisons if the argument to LIKE is a constant string that doesn't start with a wildcard character. For example, the following SELECT statements use indexes:

```
mysql> SELECT * FROM tbl_name WHERE key_col LIKE "Patrick%";
mysql> SELECT * FROM tbl_name WHERE key_col LIKE "Pat%_ck%";
```

In the first statement, only rows with Patrick' <= key_col < "Patricl" are considered. In the second statement, only rows with "Pat" <= key_col < "Pau" are considered.

The following SELECT statements will not use indexes:

```
mysql> SELECT * FROM tbl_name WHERE key_col LIKE "%Patrick%";
mysql> SELECT * FROM tbl_name WHERE key_col LIKE other_col;
```

In the first statement, the LIKE value begins with a wildcard character. In the second statement, the LIKE value is not a constant.

Searching using `column_name IS NULL` will use indexes if column_name is an index.

MySQL normally uses the index that finds the least number of rows. An index is used for columns that you compare with the following operators: =, >, >=, <, <=, BETWEEN, and a LIKE with a non-wildcard prefix like `'something%'`.

Any index that doesn't span all AND levels in the WHERE clause is not used to optimise the query. In other words, to be able to use an index, a prefix of the index must be used in every AND group.

The following WHERE clauses use indexes:

```
... WHERE index_part1=1 AND index_part2=2 AND other_column=3
... WHERE index=1 OR A=10 AND index=2        /* index = 1 OR index = 2 */
... WHERE index_part1='hello' AND index_part_3=5
        /* optimised like "index_part1='hello'" */
... WHERE index1=1 and index2=2 or index1=3 and index3=3;
        /* Can use index on index1 but not on index2 or index 3 */
```

These WHERE clauses do **NOT** use indexes:

```
... WHERE index_part2=1 AND index_part3=2  /* index_part_1 is not used */
... WHERE index=1 OR A=10                  /* Index is not used in
                                              both AND parts */
... WHERE index_part1=1 OR index_part2=10  /* No index spans all rows  */
```

Note that in some cases MySQL will not use an index, even if one would be available. Some of the cases where this happens are:

• If the use of the index would require MySQL to access more than 30% of the rows in the table. (In this case a table scan is probably much faster, as this will require us to do much fewer seeks.) Note that if such a query uses LIMIT to only retrieve part of the rows, MySQL will use an index anyway, as it can much more quickly find the few rows to return in the result.

• If the index range may contain NULL values and you are using ORDER BY ... DESC

5.4.4 Column Indexes

All MySQL column types can be indexed. Use of indexes on the relevant columns is the best way to improve the performance of SELECT operations.

The maximum number of keys and the maximum index length are defined per table handler. See Chapter 7. You can with all table handlers have at least 16 keys and a total index length of at least 256 bytes.

For CHAR and VARCHAR columns, you can index a prefix of a column. This is much faster and requires less disk space than indexing the whole column. The syntax to use in the CREATE TABLE statement to index a column prefix looks like this:

```
KEY index_name (col_name(length))
```

The following example creates an index for the first 10 characters of the name column:

```
mysql> CREATE TABLE test (
    ->         name CHAR(200) NOT NULL,
    ->         KEY index_name (name(10)));
```

For BLOB and TEXT columns, you must index a prefix of the column. You cannot index the entire column.

In MySQL Versions 3.23.23 or later, you can also create special **FULLTEXT** indexes. They are used for full-text searches. Only the MyISAM table type supports FULLTEXT indexes. They can be created only from VARCHAR and TEXT columns. Indexing always happens over the entire column and partial indexing is not supported. See Section 6.8, MySQL Full-Text Search for details.

5.4.5 Multiple-Column Indexes

MySQL can create indexes on multiple columns. An index may consist of up to 15 columns. (On CHAR and VARCHAR columns you can also use a prefix of the column as a part of an index.)

A multiple-column index can be considered a sorted array containing values that are created by concatenating the values of the indexed columns.

MySQL uses multiple-column indexes in such a way that queries are fast when you specify a known quantity for the first column of the index in a WHERE clause, even if you don't specify values for the other columns.

Suppose a table is created using the following specification:

```
mysql> CREATE TABLE test (
    ->         id INT NOT NULL,
    ->         last_name CHAR(30) NOT NULL,
    ->         first_name CHAR(30) NOT NULL,
    ->         PRIMARY KEY (id),
    ->         INDEX name (last_name,first_name));
```

In this case, the index name is an index over last_name and first_name. The index will be used for queries that specify values in a known range for last_name, or for both last_name and first_name. Therefore, the name index will be used in the following queries:

```
mysql> SELECT * FROM test WHERE last_name="Widenius";

mysql> SELECT * FROM test WHERE last_name="Widenius"
    ->                         AND first_name="Michael";

mysql> SELECT * FROM test WHERE last_name="Widenius"
    ->                         AND (first_name="Michael" OR first_name="Monty");
```

```
mysql> SELECT * FROM test WHERE last_name="Widenius"
    ->                          AND first_name >="M" AND first_name < "N";
```

However, the name index will *not* be used in the following queries:

```
mysql> SELECT * FROM test WHERE first_name="Michael";
```

```
mysql> SELECT * FROM test WHERE last_name="Widenius"
    ->                          OR first_name="Michael";
```

For more information on the manner in which MySQL uses indexes to improve query performance, see Section 5.4.3, How MySQL Uses Indexes.

5.4.6 Why So Many Open tables?

When you run mysqladmin status, you'll see something like this:

```
Uptime: 426 Running threads: 1 Questions: 11082 Reloads: 1 Open tables: 12
```

This can be somewhat perplexing if you only have 6 tables.

MySQL is multi-threaded, so it may have many queries on the same table simultaneously. To minimise the problem with two threads having different states on the same file, the table is opened independently by each concurrent thread. This takes some memory but will normally increase performance. Wth ISAM and MyISAM tables this also requires one extra file descriptor for the data file. With these table types the index file descriptor is shared between all threads.

You can read more about this topic in the next section. See Section 5.4.7, How MySQL Opens and Closes Tables.

5.4.7 How MySQL Opens and Closes Tables

table_cache, max_connections, and max_tmp_tables affect the maximum number of files the server keeps open. If you increase one or both of these values, you may run up against a limit imposed by your operating system on the per-process number of open file descriptors. However, you can increase the limit on many systems. Consult your OS documentation to find out how to do this because the method for changing the limit varies widely from system to system.

table_cache is related to max_connections. For example, for 200 concurrent running connections, you should have a table cache of at least 200 * n, where n is the maximum number of tables in a join. You also need to reserve some extra file descriptors for temporary tables and files.

Make sure that your operating system can handle the number of open file descriptors implied by the table_cache setting. If table_cache is set too high, MySQL may run out of file descriptors and refuse connections, fail to perform queries, and be very unreliable. You also have to take into account that the MyISAM table handler needs two file descriptors for each unique open table. You can increase the number of file descriptors available for MySQL with the `--open-files-limit=#` startup option. See Section A.2.16, File Not Found.

The cache of open tables will be kept at a level of `table_cache` entries (default 64; this can be changed with the `-O table_cache=#` option to `mysqld`). Note that MySQL may temporarily open even more tables to be able to execute queries.

An unused table is closed and removed from the table cache under the following circumstances:

- When the cache is full and a thread tries to open a table that is not in the cache.
- When the cache contains more than `table_cache` entries and a thread is no longer using a table.
- When someone executes `mysqladmin refresh` or `mysqladmin flush-tables`.
- When someone executes 'FLUSH TABLES.'

When the table cache fills up, the server uses the following procedure to locate a cache entry to use:

- Tables that are not currently in use are released, in least-recently-used order.
- If the cache is full and no tables can be released, but a new table needs to be opened, the cache is temporarily extended as necessary.
- If the cache is in a temporarily extended state and a table goes from in-use to not-in-use state, the table is closed and released from the cache.

A table is opened for each concurrent access. This means that if you have two threads accessing the same table, or if you access the table twice in the same query (with `AS`) the table needs to be opened twice. The first open of any table takes two file descriptors; each additional use of the table takes only one file descriptor. The extra descriptor for the first open is used for the index file; this descriptor is shared among all threads.

If you are opening a table with the `HANDLER table_name OPEN` statement, a dedicated table object is allocated for the thread. This table object is not shared by other threads and will not be closed until the thread calls `HANDLER table_name CLOSE`, or until the thread dies. See Section 6.4.2, `HANDLER` Syntax. When this happens, the table is put back in the table_cache (if it isn't full).

You can check if your table cache is too small by checking the mysqld variable `Opened_tables`. If this is quite big, even if you haven't done a lot of `FLUSH TABLES`, you should increase your table cache. See Section 4.5.6.3, `SHOW STATUS`.

5.4.8 Drawbacks to Creating Large Numbers of Tables in the Same Database

If you have many files in a directory, open, close, and create operations will be slow. If you execute SELECT statements on many different tables, there will be a little overhead when the table cache is full because for every table that has to be opened, another must be closed. You can reduce this overhead by making the table cache larger.

5.5 Optimising the MySQL Server

5.5.1 System/Compile Time and Startup Parameter Tuning

We start with the system-level things since some of these decisions have to be made very early. In other cases a fast look at this part may suffice because it is not that important for the big gains. However, it is always nice to have a feeling about how much one could gain by changing things at this level.

The default OS to use is really important! To get the most use of multiple-CPU machines one should use Solaris (because the threads works really well) or Linux (because the 2.2 kernel has really good SMP support). Also, on 32-bit machines Linux has a 2G file-size limit by default. Hopefully this will be fixed soon when new filesystems are released (XFS/Reiserfs). If you have a desperate need for files bigger than 2G on Linux-Intel 32 bit, you should get the LFS patch for the ext2 filesystem.

Because we have not run MySQL in production on that many platforms, we advise you to test your intended platform before choosing it, if possible.

Other tips:

- If you have enough RAM, you could remove all swap devices. Some operating systems will use a swap device in some contexts even if you have free memory.

- Use the --skip-locking MySQL option to avoid external locking. Note that this will not impact MySQL's functionality as long as you only run one server. Just remember to take down the server (or lock relevant parts) before you run myisam-chk. On some systems this switch is mandatory because the external locking does not work in any case.

  The --skip-locking option is on by default when compiling with MIT-pthreads, because flock() isn't fully supported by MIT-pthreads on all platforms. It's also on default for Linux, as Linux file locking is not yet safe.

  The only case when you can't use --skip-locking is if you run multiple MySQL *servers* (not clients) on the same data, or run myisamchk on the table without first flushing and locking the mysqld server tables first.

You can still use LOCK TABLES/UNLOCK TABLES even if you are using --skip-locking.

5.5.2 Tuning Server Parameters

You can get the default buffer sizes used by the mysqld server with this command:

```
shell> mysqld --help
```

This command produces a list of all mysqld options and configurable variables. The output includes the default values and looks something like this:

```
Possible variables for option --set-variable (-O) are:
back_log                   current value: 5
bdb_cache_size             current value: 1048540
binlog_cache_size          current value: 32768
connect_timeout            current value: 5
delayed_insert_timeout     current value: 300
delayed_insert_limit       current value: 100
delayed_queue_size         current value: 1000
flush_time                 current value: 0
interactive_timeout        current value: 28800
join_buffer_size           current value: 131072
key_buffer_size            current value: 1048540
lower_case_table_names     current value: 0
long_query_time            current value: 10
max_allowed_packet         current value: 1048576
max_binlog_cache_size      current value: 4294967295
max_connections            current value: 100
max_connect_errors         current value: 10
max_delayed_threads        current value: 20
max_heap_table_size        current value: 16777216
max_join_size              current value: 4294967295
max_sort_length            current value: 1024
max_tmp_tables             current value: 32
max_write_lock_count       current value: 4294967295
myisam_sort_buffer_size    current value: 8388608
net_buffer_length          current value: 16384
net_retry_count            current value: 10
net_read_timeout           current value: 30
net_write_timeout          current value: 60
query_buffer_size          current value: 0
record_buffer              current value: 131072
record_rnd_buffer          current value: 131072
slow_launch_time           current value: 2
sort_buffer                current value: 2097116
table_cache                current value: 64
thread_concurrency         current value: 10
tmp_table_size             current value: 1048576
thread_stack               current value: 131072
wait_timeout               current value: 28800
```

If a `mysqld` server is currently running, you can see what values it actually is using for the variables by executing this command:

```
shell> mysqladmin variables
```

You can find a full description of all variables in the SHOW VARIABLES section of this manual. See Section 4.5.6.4, SHOW VARIABLES.

You can also see some statistics from a running server by issuing the command SHOW STATUS. See Section 4.5.6.3, SHOW STATUS.

MySQL uses algorithms that are very scalable, so you can usually run with very little memory. If you, however, give MySQL more memory, you will normally also get better performance.

When tuning a MySQL server, the two most important variables to use are `key_buffer_size` and `table_cache`. You should first feel confident that you have these right before trying to change any of the other variables.

If you have much memory (>=256M) and many tables and want maximum performance with a moderate number of clients, you should use something like this:

```
shell> safe_mysqld -O key_buffer=64M -O table_cache=256 \
            -O sort_buffer=4M -O record_buffer=1M &
```

If you have only 128M and only a few tables, but you still do a lot of sorting, you can use something like this:

```
shell> safe_mysqld -O key_buffer=16M -O sort_buffer=1M
```

If you have little memory and lots of connections, use something like this:

```
shell> safe_mysqld -O key_buffer=512k -O sort_buffer=100k \
            -O record_buffer=100k &
```

or even:

```
shell> safe_mysqld -O key_buffer=512k -O sort_buffer=16k \
            -O table_cache=32 -O record_buffer=8k -O net_buffer=1K &
```

If you are doing a GROUP BY or ORDER BY on files that are much bigger than your available memory you should increase the value of `record_rnd_buffer` to speed up the reading of rows after the sorting is done.

When you have installed MySQL, the `support-files` directory will contain some different `my.cnf` example files: `my-huge.cnf`, `my-large.cnf`, `my-medium.cnf`, and `my-small.cnf`. You can use these as a base to optimise your system.

If there are very many connections, "swapping problems" may occur unless `mysqld` has been configured to use very little memory for each connection. `mysqld` performs better if you have enough memory for all connections, of course.

Note that if you change an option to mysqld, it remains in effect only for that instance of the server.

To see the effects of a parameter change, do something like this:

```
shell> mysqld -O key_buffer=32m --help
```

Make sure that the --help option is last; otherwise, the effect of any options listed after it on the command-line will not be reflected in the output.

5.5.3 How Compiling and Linking Affects the Speed of MySQL

Most of the following tests are done on Linux with the MySQL benchmarks, but they should give some indication for other operating systems and workloads.

You get the fastest executable when you link with -static.

On Linux, you will get the fastest code when compiling with pgcc and -O3. To compile sql_yacc.cc with these options, you need about 200M of memory because gcc/pgcc needs a lot of memory to make all functions inline. You should also set CXX=gcc when configuring MySQL to avoid inclusion of the libstdc++ library (it is not needed). Note that with some versions of pgcc, the resulting code will only run on true Pentium processors, even if you use the compiler option indicating that you want the resulting code to be working on all x586-type processors (like AMD).

By just using a better compiler and/or better compiler options you can get a 10-30% speed increase in your application. This is particularly important if you compile the SQL server yourself!

We have tested both the Cygnus CodeFusion and Fujitsu compilers, but when we tested them, neither was sufficiently bug-free to allow MySQL to be compiled with optimisations on.

When you compile MySQL you should only include support for the character sets that you are going to use. (Option --with-charset=xxx.) The standard MySQL binary distributions are compiled with support for all character sets.

Here is a list of some measurements that we have done:

- If you use pgcc and compile everything with -O6, the mysqld server is 1% faster than with gcc 2.95.2.

- If you link dynamically (without -static), the result is 13% slower on Linux. Note that you still can use a dynamic linked MySQL library. It is only the server that is critical for performance.

- If you strip your mysqld binary with strip libexec/mysqld, the resulting binary can be up to 4% faster.

- If you connect using TCP/IP rather than Unix sockets, the result is 7.5% slower on the same computer. (If you are connecting to localhost, MySQL will, by default, use sockets.)

- If you connect using TCP/IP from another computer over a 100M Ethernet, things will be 8-11% slower.

- If you compile with --with-debug=full, you will lose 20% for most queries, but some queries may take substantially longer (the MySQL benchmarks ran 35% slower). If you use --with-debug, you will only lose 15%. By starting a mysqld version compiled with --with-debug=full with --skip-safemalloc the end result should be close to when configuring with --with-debug.

- On a Sun SPARCstation 20, SunPro C++ 4.2 is 5% faster than gcc 2.95.2.

- Compiling with gcc 2.95.2 for UltraSPARC with the option -mcpu=v8 -Wa,-xarch=v8plusa gives 4% more performance.

- On Solaris 2.5.1, MIT-pthreads is 8-12% slower than Solaris native threads on a single processor. With more load/CPUs the difference should get bigger.

- Running with --log-bin makes **MySQL** 1% slower.

- Compiling on Linux-x86 using gcc without frame pointers -fomit-frame-pointer or -fomit-frame-pointer -ffixed-ebp makes mysqld 1–4% faster.

The MySQL-Linux distribution provided by MySQL AB used to be compiled with pgcc, but we had to go back to regular gcc because of a bug in pgcc that would generate the code that does not run on AMD. We will continue using gcc until that bug is resolved. In the meantime, if you have a non-AMD machine, you can get a faster binary by compiling with pgcc. The standard MySQL Linux binary is linked statically to get it faster and more portable.

5.5.4 How MySQL Uses Memory

The following list indicates some of the ways that the mysqld server uses memory. Where applicable, the name of the server variable relevant to the memory use is given:

- The key buffer (variable key_buffer_size) is shared by all threads; other buffers used by the server are allocated as needed. See Section 5.5.2, Tuning Server Parameters.

- Each connection uses some thread-specific space: a stack (default 64K, variable thread_stack), a connection buffer (variable net_buffer_length), and a result buffer (variable net_buffer_length). The connection buffer and result buffer are dynamically enlarged up to max_allowed_packet when needed. When a query is running, a copy of the current query string is also allocated.

- All threads share the same base memory.

- Only the compressed ISAM/MyISAM tables are memory-mapped. This is because the 32-bit memory space of 4G is not large enough for most big tables. When systems with a 64-bit address space become more common we may add general support for memory mapping.

- Each request doing a sequential scan over a table allocates a read buffer (variable `record_buffer`).

- When reading rows in 'random' order (for example, after a sort) a random-read buffer is allocated to avoid disk seeks (variable `record_rnd_buffer`).

- All joins are done in one pass, and most joins can be done without even using a temporary table. Most temporary tables are memory-based (HEAP) tables. Temporary tables with a big record length (calculated as the sum of all column lengths) or that contain BLOB columns are stored on disk.

  One problem in MySQL versions before Version 3.23.2 is that if a HEAP table exceeds the size of `tmp_table_size`, you get the error `The table tbl_name is full`. In newer versions this is handled by automatically changing the in-memory (HEAP) table to a disk-based (MyISAM) table as necessary. To work around this problem, you can increase the temporary table size by setting the `tmp_table_size` option to `mysqld`, or by setting the SQL option `SQL_BIG_TABLES` in the client program. See Section 5.5.6, `SET` Syntax. In MySQL Version 3.20, the maximum size of the temporary table was `record_buffer*16`, so if you are using this version, you have to increase the value of `record_buffer`. You can also start `mysqld` with the `--big-tables` option to always store temporary tables on disk. However, this will affect the speed of many complicated queries.

- Most requests doing a sort allocate a sort buffer and 0-2 temporary files depending on the result set size. See Section A.4.4, Where MySQL Stores Temporary Files.

- Almost all parsing and calculating are done in a local memory store. No memory overhead is needed for small items, and the normal slow memory allocation and freeing are avoided. Memory is allocated only for unexpectedly large strings (this is done with `malloc()` and `free()`).

- Each index file is opened once and the data file is opened once for each concurrently running thread. For each concurrent thread, a table structure, column structures for each column, and a buffer of size 3 * n are allocated (where n is the maximum row length, not counting BLOB columns). A BLOB uses 5 to 8 bytes plus the length of the BLOB data. The ISAM/MyISAM table handlers will use one extra row buffer for internal usage.

- For each table having BLOB columns, a buffer is enlarged dynamically to read in larger BLOB values. If you scan a table, a buffer as large as the largest BLOB value is allocated.

- Table handlers for all in-use tables are saved in a cache and managed as a FIFO. Normally the cache has 64 entries. If a table has been used by two running threads at the same time, the cache contains two entries for the table. See Section 5.4.7, How MySQL Opens and Closes Tables.

- A mysqladmin flush-tables command closes all tables that are not in use and marks all in-use tables to be closed when the currently executing thread finishes. This will effectively free most in-use memory.

ps and other system status programs may report that mysqld uses a lot of memory. This may be caused by thread-stacks on different memory addresses. For example, the Solaris version of ps counts the unused memory between stacks as used memory. You can verify this by checking available swap with swap -s. We have tested mysqld with commercial memory-leakage detectors, so there should be no memory leaks.

5.5.5 How MySQL Uses DNS

When a new thread connects to mysqld, mysqld will span a new thread to handle the request. This thread will first check if the hostname is in the hostname cache. If not, the thread will call gethostbyaddr_r() and gethostbyname_r() to resolve the hostname.

If the operating system doesn't support these thread-safe calls, the thread will lock a mutex and call gethostbyaddr() and gethostbyname() instead. Note that in this case no other thread can resolve other hostnames that are not in the hostname cache until the first thread is ready.

You can disable DNS host lookup by starting mysqld with --skip-name-resolve. In this case you can, however, only use IP names in the MySQL privilege tables.

If you have a very slow DNS and many hosts, you can get more performance by either disabling DNS lookup with --skip-name-resolve or by increasing the HOST_CACHE_SIZE define (default: 128) and recompiling mysqld.

You can disable the hostname cache with --skip-host-cache. You can clear the hostname cache with FLUSH HOSTS or mysqladmin flush-hosts.

If you don't want to allow connections over TCP/IP, you can do this by starting mysqld with --skip-networking.

5.5.6 SET Syntax

```
SET [OPTION] SQL_VALUE_OPTION= value, ...
```

SET OPTION sets various options that affect the operation of the server or your client. Any option you set remains in effect until the current session ends, or until you set the option to a different value.

CHARACTER SET character_set_name | DEFAULT

This maps all strings from and to the client with the given mapping. Currently the only option for character_set_name is cp1251_koi8, but you can easily add new mappings by editing the sql/convert.cc file in the MySQL source distribution. The default mapping can be restored by using a character_set_name value of DEFAULT.

Note that the syntax for setting the CHARACTER SET option differs from the syntax for setting the other options.

PASSWORD = PASSWORD('some password')

Set the password for the current user. Any non-anonymous user can change his own password!

PASSWORD FOR user = PASSWORD('some password')

Set the password for a specific user on the current server host. Only a user with access to the mysql database can do this. The user should be given in user@hostname format, where user and hostname are exactly as they are listed in the User and Host columns of the mysql.user table entry. For example, if you had an entry with User and Host fields of 'bob' and '%.loc.gov', you would write:

```
mysql> SET PASSWORD FOR bob@"%.loc.gov" = PASSWORD("newpass");
```

or

```
mysql> UPDATE mysql.user SET password=PASSWORD("newpass")
    ->                   WHERE user="bob" AND host="%.loc.gov";
```

SQL_AUTO_IS_NULL = 0 | 1

If set to 1 (default), one can find the last inserted row for a table with an AUTO_INCREMENT column with the following construct: WHERE auto_increment_column IS NULL. This is used by some ODBC programs like Access.

AUTOCOMMIT= 0 | 1

If set to 1, all changes to a table will be done at once. To start a multi-command transaction, you have to use the BEGIN statement. See Section 6.7.1, BEGIN/COMMIT/ROLLBACK Syntax. If set to 0, you have to use COMMIT / ROLLBACK to accept/ revoke that transaction. See Section 6.7.1, BEGIN/COMMIT/ROLLBACK Syntax. Note that when you change from not AUTOCOMMIT mode to AUTOCOMMIT mode, MySQL will do an automatic COMMIT on any open transactions.

SQL_BIG_TABLES = 0 | 1

If set to 1, all temporary tables are stored on disk rather than in memory. This will be a little slower, but you will not get the error The table tbl_name is full for big SELECT operations that require a large temporary table. The default value for a new connection is 0 (that is, use in-memory temporary tables).

SQL_BIG_SELECTS = 0 | 1

> If set to 0, MySQL will abort if a SELECT is attempted that probably will take a very long time. This is useful when an inadvisable WHERE statement has been issued. A big query is defined as a SELECT that probably will have to examine more than max_join_size rows. The default value for a new connection is 1 (which will allow all SELECT statements).

SQL_BUFFER_RESULT = 0 | 1

> SQL_BUFFER_RESULT will force the result from SELECTs to be put into a temporary table. This will help MySQL free the table locks early and will help in cases where it takes a long time to send the result set to the client.

SQL_LOW_PRIORITY_UPDATES = 0 | 1

> If set to 1, all INSERT, UPDATE, DELETE, and LOCK TABLE WRITE statements wait until there is no pending SELECT or LOCK TABLE READ on the affected table.

SQL_MAX_JOIN_SIZE = value | DEFAULT

> Don't allow SELECTs that will probably need to examine more than value row combinations. By setting this value, you can catch SELECTs where keys are not used properly and that would probably take a long time. Setting this to a value other than DEFAULT will reset the SQL_BIG_SELECTS flag. If you set the SQL_BIG_SELECTS flag again, the SQL_MAX_JOIN_SIZE variable will be ignored. You can set a default value for this variable by starting mysqld with -O max_join_size=#.

SQL_QUERY_CACHE_TYPE = OFF | ON | DEMAND
SQL_QUERY_CACHE_TYPE = 0 | 1 | 2

> Set query cache setting for this thread.

Option	Description
0 or OFF	Don't cache or retrieve results.
1 or ON	Cache all results except SELECT SQL_NO_CACHE . . . queries.
2 or DEMAND	Cache only SELECT SQL_CACHE . . . queries.

SQL_SAFE_UPDATES = 0 | 1

> If set to 1, MySQL will abort if an UPDATE or DELETE is attempted that doesn't use a key or LIMIT in the WHERE clause. This makes it possible to catch wrong updates when creating SQL commands by hand.

SQL_SELECT_LIMIT = value | DEFAULT

> The maximum number of records to return from SELECT statements. If a SELECT has a LIMIT clause, the LIMIT takes precedence over the value of SQL_SELECT_LIMIT. The default value for a new connection is "unlimited." If you have changed the limit, the default value can be restored by using a SQL_SELECT_LIMIT value of DEFAULT.

SQL_LOG_OFF = 0 | 1

> If set to 1, no logging will be done to the standard log for this client, if the client has the **process** privilege. This does not affect the update log!

SQL_LOG_UPDATE = 0 | 1

> If set to 0, no logging will be done to the update log for the client, if the client has the **process** privilege. This does not affect the standard log!

SQL_QUOTE_SHOW_CREATE = 0 | 1

> If set to 1, SHOW CREATE TABLE will quote table and column names. This is **on** by default, for replication of tables with fancy column names to work. See Section 4.5.6.8, SHOW CREATE TABLE.

TIMESTAMP = timestamp_value | DEFAULT

> Set the time for this client. This is used to get the original timestamp if you use the update log to restore rows. timestamp_value should be a Unix epoch timestamp, not a MySQL timestamp.

LAST_INSERT_ID = #

> Set the value to be returned from LAST_INSERT_ID(). This is stored in the update log when you use LAST_INSERT_ID() in a command that updates a table.

INSERT_ID = #

> Set the value to be used by the following INSERT or ALTER TABLE command when inserting an AUTO_INCREMENT value. This is mainly used with the update log.

See Section 6.7.3, SET TRANSACTION Syntax.

5.6 Disk Issues

- As mentioned before, disks seeks are a big performance bottleneck. This problem gets more and more apparent when the data starts to grow so large that effective caching becomes impossible. For large databases, where you access data more or less randomly, you can be sure that you will need at least one disk seek to read and a couple of disk seeks to write things. To minimise this problem, use disks with low seek times.

- Increase the number of available disk spindles (and thereby reduce the seek overhead) by either symlink files to different disks or striping the disks.

  Using symbolic links

  > This means that you symlink the index and/or data file(s) from the normal data directory to another disk (that may also be striped). This makes both the seek and read times better (if the disks are not used for other things). See Section 5.6.1, Using Symbolic Links.

Striping

> Striping means that you have many disks and put the first block on the first disk, the second block on the second disk, the Nth on the (N mod number_of_disks) disk, and so on. This means if your normal data size is less than the stripe size (or perfectly aligned) you will get much better performance. Note that striping is very dependent on the OS and stripe size. So benchmark your application with different stripe-sizes. See Section 5.1.5, Using Your Own Benchmarks.

> Note that the speed difference for striping is **very** dependent on the parameters. Depending on how you set the striping parameters and number of disks you may get a difference in orders of magnitude. Note that you have to choose to optimise for random or sequential access.

- For reliability you may want to use RAID 0+1 (striping + mirroring), but in this case you will need 2*N drives to hold N drives of data. This is probably the best option if you have the money for it! You may, however, also have to invest in some volume-management software to handle it efficiently.

- A good option is to have semi-important data (that can be regenerated) on a RAID 0 disk while storing really important data (like host information and logs) on a RAID 0+1 or RAID N disk. RAID N can be a problem if you have many writes because of the time it takes to update the parity bits.

- You may also set the parameters for the filesystem that the database uses. One easy change is to mount the filesystem with the noatime option. That makes it skip the updating of the last access time in the inode and, therefore, will avoid some disk seeks.

- On Linux, you can get much more performance (up to 100% under load is not uncommon) by using hdpram to configure your disk's interface! The following should be a good hdparm option for MySQL (and probably many other applications):

```
hdparm -m 16 -d 1
```

Note that the performance/reliability when using this option depends on your hardware, so we strongly suggest that you test your system thoroughly after using hdparm! Please consult the hdparm manpage for more information! If hdparm is not used wisely, filesystem corruption may result. Back up everything before experimenting!

- On many operating systems you can mount the disks with the 'async' flag to set the filesystem to be updated asynchronously. If your computer is reasonablly stable, this should give you more performance without sacrificing too much reliability. (This flag is on by default on Linux.)

- If you don't need to know when a file was last accessed (which is not really useful on a database server), you can mount your filesystems with the noatime flag.

5.6.1 Using Symbolic Links

You can move tables and databases from the database directory to other locations and replace them with symbolic links to the new locations. You might want to do this, for example, to move a database to a file system with more free space or increase the speed of your system by spreading your tables to different disks.

The recommended way to do this is to just symlink databases to a different disk and only symlink tables as a last resort.

5.6.1.1 Using symbolic links for databases

The way to symlink a database is to first create a directory on some disk where you have free space and then create a symlink to it from the MySQL database directory.

```
shell> mkdir /dr1/databases/test
shell> ln -s /dr1/databases/test mysqld-datadir
```

MySQL doesn't support linking of one directory to multiple databases. Replacing a database directory with a symbolic link will work fine as long as you don't make a symbolic link between databases. Suppose you have a database db1 under the MySQL data directory, and then make a symlink db2 that points to db1:

```
shell> cd /path/to/datadir
shell> ln -s db1 db2
```

Now, for any table tbl_a in db1, there is also a table tbl_a in db2. If one thread updates db1.tbl_a and another thread updates db2.tbl_a, there will be problems.

If you really need this, you must change the following code in mysys/mf_format.c:

```
if (flag & 32 || (!lstat(to,&stat_buff) && S_ISLNK(stat_buff.st_mode)))
```

to

```
if (1)
```

On Windows you can use internal symbolic links to directories by compiling MySQL with -DUSE_SYMDIR. This allows you to put different databases on different disks. See Section 2.6.2.5, Splitting data across different disks on windows.

5.6.1.2 Using symbolic links for tables

On MySQL versions pror to 4.0 you should not symlink tables, if you are not very careful with them. The problem is that if you run ALTER TABLE, REPAIR TABLE, or OPTIMIZE TABLE on a symlinked table, the symlinks will be removed and replaced by the original files. This happens because the previous command works by creating a temporary file in the database directory, and when the command is complete, it replaces the original file with the temporary file.

You should not symlink tables on systems that don't have a fully working `realpath()` call. (At least Linux and Solaris support `realpath()`).

In MySQL 4.0 symlinks are only fully supported for `MyISAM` tables. For other table types you will probably get strange problems when doing any of the above mentioned commands.

The handling of symbolic links in MySQL 4.0 works the following way (this is mostly relevant only for `MyISAM` tables):

- In the data directory you will always have the table definition file and the data/index files.

- You can symlink the index file and the data file to different directories independent of the other.

- The symlinking can be done from the operating system (if `mysqld` is not running) or with the `INDEX/DATA DIRECTORY="path-to-dir"` command in `CREATE TABLE`. See Section 6.5.3, `CREATE TABLE` Syntax.

- `myisamchk` will not replace a symlink with the index/file but will work directly on the files the symlink points to. Any temporary files will be created in the same directory where the data/index file is.

- When you drop a table that is using symlinks, both the symlink and the file the symlink points to is dropped. This is a good reason why you should **not** run `mysqld` as root and not allow persons to have write access to the MySQL database directories.

- If you rename a table with `ALTER TABLE RENAME` and you don't change the database, the symlink in the database directory will be renamed to the new name and the data/index file will be renamed accordingly.

- If you use `ALTER TABLE RENAME` to move a table to another database, the table will be moved to the other database directory and the old symlinks and the files they pointed to will be deleted.

- If you are not using symlinks you should use the `--skip-symlink` option to `mysqld` to ensure that no one can drop or rename a file outside of the `mysqld` data directory.

Things that are not yet supported:

- `ALTER TABLE` ignores all `INDEX/DATA DIRECTORY="path"` options.

- `CREATE TABLE` doesn't report if the table has symbolic links.

- `mysqldump` doesn't include the symbolic links information in the output.

- `BACKUP TABLE` and `RESTORE TABLE` don't respect symbolic links.

6

MySQL Language Reference

MySQL has a very complex but intuitive and easy-to-learn SQL interface. This chapter describes the various commands, types, and functions you will need to know in order to use MySQL efficiently and effectively. This chapter also serves as a reference to all functionality included in MySQL. In order to use this chapter effectively, you may find it useful to refer to the various indexes.

6.1 Language Structure

6.1.1 Literals: How to Write Strings and Numbers

This section describes the various ways to write strings and numbers in MySQL. It also covers the various nuances and "gotchas" that you may run into when dealing with these basic types in MySQL.

6.1.1.1 Strings

A string is a sequence of characters, surrounded by either single quote (') or double quote (") characters (only the single quote if you run in ANSI mode). Examples:

```
'a string'
"another string"
```

Within a string, certain sequences have special meaning. Each of these sequences begins with a backslash (\), known as the *escape character*. MySQL recognises the following escape sequences:

\0 An ASCII 0 (NUL) character.

\' A single quote (') character.

\" A double quote (") character.

\b A backspace character.

\n A newline character.

\r A carriage return character.

\t A tab character.

\z ASCII(26) (Control-Z). This character can be encoded to allow you to work around the problem that ASCII(26) stands for END-OF-FILE on Windows. (ASCII(26) will cause problems if you try to use `mysql database < filename`.)

\\ A backslash (\) character.

\% A % character. This is used to search for literal instances of % in contexts where % would otherwise be interpreted as a wildcard character. See Section 6.3.2.1, String comparison functions.

_ A _ character. This is used to search for literal instances of _ in contexts where _ would otherwise be interpreted as a wildcard character. See Section 6.3.2.1, String comparison functions.

Note that if you use \% or _ in some string contexts, these will return the strings \% and _ and not % and _.

There are several ways to include quotes within a string:

• A ' inside a string quoted with ' may be written as ".

• A " inside a string quoted with " may be written as "".

• You can precede the quote character with an escape character (\).

• A ' inside a string quoted with " needs no special treatment and need not be doubled or escaped. In the same way, " inside a string quoted with ' needs no special treatment.

The SELECT statements shown here demonstrate how quoting and escaping work:

```
mysql> SELECT 'hello', '"hello"', '""hello""', 'hel''lo', '\'hello';
+-------+---------+-----------+--------+--------+
| hello | "hello" | ""hello"" | hel'lo | 'hello |
+-------+---------+-----------+--------+--------+

mysql> SELECT "hello", "'hello'", "''hello''", "hel""lo", "\"hello";
+-------+---------+-----------+--------+--------+
| hello | 'hello' | ''hello'' | hel"lo | "hello |
+-------+---------+-----------+--------+--------+

mysql> SELECT "This\nIs\nFour\nlines";
+--------------------+
| This
Is
Four
lines |
+--------------------+
```

If you want to insert binary data into a string column (such as a BLOB), the following characters must be represented by escape sequences:

NUL

ASCII 0. You should represent this by \0 (a backslash and an ASCII 0 character).

\   ASCII 92, backslash. Represent this by \\.

'   ASCII 39, single quote. Represent this by \'.

"   ASCII 34, double quote. Represent this by \".

If you write C code, you can use the C API function mysql_real_escape_string() to escape characters for the INSERT statement. See Section 8.4.2, C API Function Overview. In Perl, you can use the quote method of the DBI package to convert special characters to the proper escape sequences. See Section 8.2.2, The DBI Interface.

You should use an escape function on any string that might contain any of the special characters listed previously!

Alternatively, many MySQL APIs provide some sort of placeholder capability that allows you to insert special markers into a query string, and then bind data values to them when you issue the query. In this case, the API takes case of escaping special characters in the values for you automatically.

6.1.1.2 Numbers

Integers are represented as a sequence of digits. Floats use . as a decimal separator. Either type of number may be preceded by - to indicate a negative value.

Examples of valid integers:

```
1221
0
-32
```

Examples of valid floating-point numbers:

```
294.42
-32032.6809e+10
148.00
```

An integer may be used in a floating-point context; it is interpreted as the equivalent floating-point number.

6.1.1.3 Hexadecimal values

MySQL supports hexadecimal values. In numeric context these act like an integer (64-bit precision). In string context these act like a binary string where each pair of hex digits is converted to a character:

```
mysql> SELECT x'FF'
          -> 255
mysql> SELECT 0xa+0;
          -> 10
mysql> SELECT 0x5061756c;
          -> Paul
```

The x'hexstring' syntax (new in 4.0) is based on ANSI SQL and the 0x syntax is based on ODBC. Hexadecimal strings are often used by ODBC to supply values for BLOB columns. You can convert a string or a number to hexadecimal with the HEX() function.

6.1.1.4 NULL values

The NULL value means "no data" and is different from values such as 0 for numeric types or the empty string for string types. See Section A.5.3, Problems with NULL Values.

NULL may be represented by \N when using the text file import or export formats (LOAD DATA INFILE, SELECT ... INTO OUTFILE). See Section 6.4.9, LOAD DATA INFILE Syntax.

6.1.2 Database, Table, Index, Column, and Alias Names

Database, table, index, column, and alias names all follow the same rules in MySQL. The following table shows the lengths and characters allowed.

Note that the rules changed starting with MySQL Version 3.23.6 when we introduced quoting of identifiers (database, table, and column names) with '. " will also work to quote identifiers if you run in ANSI mode. See Section 1.7.2, Running MySQL in ANSI Mode.

Identifier	Max length	Allowed characters
Database	64	Any character that is allowed in a directory name except / or .
Table	64	Any character that is allowed in a filename, except / or .
Column	64	All characters
Alias	255	All characters

Note that in addition to this, you can't have ASCII(0) or ASCII(255) or the quoting character in an identifier.

Note that if the identifier is a restricted word or contains special characters, you must always quote it with ' when you use it:

```
mysql> SELECT * FROM 'select' WHERE 'select'.id > 100;
```

In previous versions of MySQL, the name rules are as follows:

- A name may consist of alphanumeric characters from the current character set as well as _ and $. The default character set is ISO-8859-1 Latin1; this may be changed with the --default-character-set option to mysqld. See Section 4.6.1, The Character Set Used for Data and Sorting.

- A name may start with any character that is legal in a name. In particular, a name may start with a digit (this differs from many other database systems!). However, a name cannot consist *only* of digits.

- You cannot use the . character in names because it is used to extend the format by which you can refer to columns.

It is recommended that you do not use names like 1e because an expression like 1e+1 is ambiguous. It may be interpreted as the expression 1e + 1 or as the number 1e+1.

In MySQL you can refer to a column using any of the following forms:

Column reference	Meaning
col_name	Column col_name from whichever table used in the query contains a column of that name.
tbl_name.col_name	Column col_name from table tbl_name of the current database.
db_name.tbl_name. col_name	Column col_name from table tbl_name of the database db_name. This form is available in MySQL Versions 3.22 or later.
'column_name'	A column that is a keyword or contains special characters.

You need not specify a tbl_name or db_name.tbl_name prefix for a column reference in a statement unless the reference would be ambiguous. For example, suppose tables t1 and t2 each contain a column c, and you retrieve c in a SELECT statement that uses both t1 and t2. In this case, c is ambiguous because it is not unique among the tables used in the statement, so you must indicate which table you mean by writing t1.c or t2.c. Similarly, if you are retrieving from a table t in database db1 and from a table t in database db2, you must refer to columns in those tables as db1.t.col_name and db2.t.col_name.

The syntax .tbl_name means the table tbl_name in the current database. This syntax is accepted for ODBC compatibility because some ODBC programs prefix table names with a . character.

6.1.3 Case Sensitivity in Names

In MySQL, databases and tables correspond to directories and files within those directories. Consequently, the case sensitivity of the underlying operating system determines the case sensitivity of database and table names. This means database and table names are case-insensitive in Windows and case-sensitive in most varieties of Unix (Mac OS X being an exception). See Section 1.7.3, MySQL Extensions to ANSI SQL92.

Note: although database and table names are case-insensitive for Windows, you should not refer to a given database or table using different cases within the same query. The following query would not work because it refers to a table both as my_table and as MY_TABLE:

```
mysql> SELECT * FROM my_table WHERE MY_TABLE.col=1;
```

Column names and column aliases are case-insensitive in all cases.

Aliases on tables are case-sensitive. The following query would not work because it refers to the alias both as a and as A:

```
mysql> SELECT col_name FROM tbl_name AS a
    ->                 WHERE a.col_name = 1 OR A.col_name = 2;
```

If you have trouble remembering the lettercase for database and table names, adopt a consistent convention, such as always creating databases and tables using lowercase names.

One way to avoid this problem is to start mysqld with -O lower_case_table_names=1. By default this option is 1 on Windows and 0 on Unix.

If lower_case_table_names is 1 MySQL will convert all table names to lowercase on storage and lookup. Note that if you change this option, you need to first convert your old table names to lowercase before starting mysqld.

6.1.4 User Variables

MySQL supports thread-specific variables with the @variablename syntax. A variable name may consist of alphanumeric characters from the current character set and also _, $, and . . The default character set is ISO-8859-1 Latin1; this may be changed with the --default-character-set option to mysqld. See Section 4.6.1, The Character Set Used for Data and Sorting.

Variables don't have to be initialised. They contain NULL by default and can store an integer, real, or string value. All variables for a thread are automatically freed when the thread exits.

You can set a variable with the SET syntax:

```
SET @variable= { integer expression | real expression | string expression }
[,@variable= ...].
```

You can also assign a value to a variable in statements other than SET. However, in this case the assignment operator is := rather than = because = is reserved for comparisons in non-SET statements:

```
mysql> SELECT @t1:=(@t2:=1)+@t3:=4,@t1,@t2,@t3;
+----------------------+------+------+------+
| @t1:=(@t2:=1)+@t3:=4 | @t1  | @t2  | @t3  |
+----------------------+------+------+------+
|                    5 |    5 |    1 |    4 |
+----------------------+------+------+------+
```

User variables may be used where expressions are allowed. Note that this does not currently include contexts where a number is explicitly required, such as in the LIMIT clause of a SELECT statement, or the IGNORE number LINES clause of a LOAD DATA statement.

Note: in a SELECT statement, each expression is evaluated only when it's sent to the client. This means that in the HAVING, GROUP BY, or ORDER BY clause, you can't refer to an expression that involves variables that are set in the SELECT part. For example, the following statement will not work as expected:

```
mysql> SELECT (@aa:=id) AS a, (@aa+3) AS b FROM table_name HAVING b=5;
```

The reason is that @aa will not contain the value of the current row, but the value of id for the previously accepted row.

6.1.5 Comment Syntax

The MySQL server supports the # to end of line, -- to end of line, and /* in-line or multiple-line */ comment styles:

```
mysql> SELECT 1+1;     # This comment continues to the end of line
mysql> SELECT 1+1;     --This comment continues to the end of line
mysql> SELECT 1 /* this is an in-line comment */ + 1;
mysql> SELECT 1+
/*
this is a
multiple-line comment
*/
1;
```

Note that the -- (double-dash) comment style requires you to have at least one space after the second dash!

Although the server understands the comment syntax just described, there are some limitations on the way that the mysql client parses /* ... */ comments:

- Single-quote and double-quote characters are taken to indicate the beginning of a quoted string, even within a comment. If the quote is not matched by a second quote within the comment, the parser doesn't realise the comment has ended. If you are running mysql interactively, you can tell that it has gotten confused like this because the prompt changes from mysql> to '> or ">.

- A semicolon is taken to indicate the end of the current SQL statement and anything following it to indicate the beginning of the next statement.

These limitations apply both when you run mysql interactively and when you put commands in a file and tell mysql to read its input from that file with mysql < some-file.

MySQL supports the – ANSI SQL comment style only if the second dash is followed by a space. See Section 1.7.4.7, – as the start of a comment.

6.1.6 Is MySQL Picky About Reserved Words?

A common problem stems from trying to create a table with column names that use the names of datatypes or functions built into MySQL, such as TIMESTAMP or GROUP. You're allowed to do it (for example, ABS is an allowed column name), but whitespace is not allowed between a function name and the immediately following (when using functions whose names are also column names.

The following words are explicitly reserved in MySQL. Most of them are forbidden by ANSI SQL92 as column and/or table names (for example, GROUP). A few are reserved because MySQL needs them and is (currently) using a yacc parser:

Word	Word	Word
ADD	ALL	ALTER
ANALYZE	AND	AS
ASC	AUTO_INCREMENT	BDB
BERKELEYDB	BETWEEN	BIGINT
BINARY	BLOB	BOTH
BY	CASCADE	CASE
CHANGE	CHAR	CHARACTER
COLUMN	COLUMNS	CONSTRAINT
CREATE	CROSS	CURRENT_DATE
CURRENT_TIME	CURRENT_TIMESTAMP	DATABASE
DATABASES	DAY_HOUR	DAY_MINUTE
DAY_SECOND	DEC	DECIMAL
DEFAULT	DELAYED	DELETE
DESC	DESCRIBE	DISTINCT

Word	Word	Word
DISTINCTROW	DOUBLE	DROP
ELSE	ENCLOSED	ESCAPED
EXISTS	EXPLAIN	FIELDS
FLOAT	FOR	FOREIGN
FROM	FULLTEXT	FUNCTION
GRANT	GROUP	HAVING
HIGH_PRIORITY	HOUR_MINUTE	HOUR_SECOND
IF	IGNORE	IN
INDEX	INFILE	INNER
INNODB	INSERT	INSERT_ID
INT	INTEGER	INTERVAL
INTO	IS	JOIN
KEY	KEYS	KILL
LAST_INSERT_ID	LEADING	LEFT
LIKE	LIMIT	LINES
LOAD	LOCK	LONG
LONGBLOB	LONGTEXT	LOW_PRIORITY
MASTER_SERVER_ID	MATCH	MEDIUMBLOB
MEDIUMINT	MEDIUMTEXT	MIDDLEINT
MINUTE_SECOND	MRG_MYISAM	NATURAL
NOT	NULL	NUMERIC
ON	OPTIMIZE	OPTION
OPTIONALLY	OR	ORDER
OUTER	OUTFILE	PARTIAL
PRECISION	PRIMARY	PRIVILEGES
PROCEDURE	PURGE	READ
REAL	REFERENCES	REGEXP
RENAME	REPLACE	REQUIRE
RESTRICT	RETURNS	REVOKE
RIGHT	RLIKE	SELECT
SET	SHOW	SMALLINT
SONAME	SQL_AUTO_IS_NULL	SQL_BIG_RESULT
SQL_BIG_SELECTS	SQL_BIG_TABLES	SQL_BUFFER_RESULT
SQL_CALC_FOUND_ROWS	SQL_LOG_BIN	SQL_LOG_OFF
SQL_LOG_UPDATE	SQL_LOW_PRIOR-ITY_UPDATES	SQL_MAX_JOIN_SIZE
SQL_QUOTE_SHOW_CREATE	SQL_SAFE_UPDATES	SQL_SELECT_LIMIT
SQL_SLAVE_SKIP_COUNTER	SQL_SMALL_RESULT	SQL_WARNINGS
SSL	STARTING	STRAIGHT_JOIN
STRIPED	TABLE	TABLES
TERMINATED	THEN	TINYBLOB
TINYINT	TINYTEXT	TO
TRAILING	UNION	UNIQUE

Word	Word	Word
UNLOCK	UNSIGNED	UPDATE
USAGE	USE	USING
VALUES	VARBINARY	VARCHAR
VARYING	WHEN	WHERE
WITH	WRITE	YEAR_MONTH
ZEROFILL		

The following symbols (from the preceding table) are disallowed by ANSI SQL but allowed by MySQL as column/table names. This is because some of these names are very natural names and a lot of people have already used them.

- ACTION

- BIT

- DATE

- ENUM

- NO

- TEXT

- TIME

- TIMESTAMP

6.2 Column Types

MySQL supports a number of column types, which may be grouped into three categories: numeric types, date and time types, and string (character) types. This section first gives an overview of the types available and summarises the storage requirements for each column type, then provides a more detailed description of the properties of the types in each category. The overview is intentionally brief. The more detailed descriptions should be consulted for additional information about particular column types, such as the allowable formats in which you can specify values.

The column types supported by MySQL are listed next. The following code letters are used in the descriptions:

M   Indicates the maximum display size. The maximum legal display size is 255.

D   Applies to floating-point types and indicates the number of digits following the decimal point. The maximum possible value is 30, but should be no greater than M-2.

Square brackets ([and]) indicate parts of type specifiers that are optional.

Note that if you specify ZEROFILL for a column, MySQL will automatically add the UNSIGNED attribute to the column.

Warning: you should be aware that when you use subtraction between integer values where one is of type UNSIGNED, the result will be unsigned! See Section 6.3.5, Cast Functions.

TINYINT[(M)] [UNSIGNED] [ZEROFILL]
> A very small integer. The signed range is –128 to 127. The unsigned range is 0 to 255.

BIT
BOOL
> These are synonyms for TINYINT(1).

SMALLINT[(M)] [UNSIGNED] [ZEROFILL]
> A small integer. The signed range is –32768 to 32767. The unsigned range is 0 to 65535.

MEDIUMINT[(M)] [UNSIGNED] [ZEROFILL]
> A medium-size integer. The signed range is –8388608 to 8388607. The unsigned range is 0 to 16777215.

INT[(M)] [UNSIGNED] [ZEROFILL]
> A normal-size integer. The signed range is –2147483648 to 2147483647. The unsigned range is 0 to 4294967295.

INTEGER[(M)] [UNSIGNED] [ZEROFILL]
> This is a synonym for INT.

BIGINT[(M)] [UNSIGNED] [ZEROFILL]
> A large integer. The signed range is –9223372036854775808 to 9223372036854775807. The unsigned range is 0 to 18446744073709551615.

Some things you should be aware of with respect to BIGINT columns:

- All arithmetic is done using signed BIGINT or DOUBLE values, so you shouldn't use unsigned big integers larger than 9223372036854775807 (63 bits) except with bit functions! If you do that, some of the last digits in the result may be wrong because of rounding errors when converting the BIGINT to a DOUBLE.

  MySQL 4.0 can handle BIGINT in the following cases:

  — Use integers to store big unsigned values in a BIGINT column.

  — In MIN(big_int_column) and MAX(big_int_column).

  — When using operators (+, –, *, etc.) where both operands are integers.

- You can always store an exact integer value in a BIGINT column by storing it as a string. In this case, MySQL will perform a string-to-number conversion that involves no intermediate double representation.

- -, +, and * will use BIGINT arithmetic when both arguments are integer values! This means that if you multiply two big integers (or results from functions that return integers), you may get unexpected results when the result is larger than 9223372036854775807.

FLOAT(precision) [UNSIGNED] [ZEROFILL]

A floating-point number. precision can be <=24 for a single-precision floating-point number and between 25 and 53 for a double-precision floating-point number. These types are like the FLOAT and DOUBLE types described next. FLOAT(X) has the same range as the corresponding FLOAT and DOUBLE types, but the display size and number of decimals are undefined.

In MySQL Version 3.23, this is a true floating-point value. In earlier MySQL versions, FLOAT(precision) always has 2 decimals.

Note that using FLOAT may give you some unexpected problems, as all calculations in MySQL are done with double precision. See Section A.5.6, Solving Problems with No Matching Rows.

This syntax is provided for ODBC compatibility.

FLOAT[(M,D)] [UNSIGNED] [ZEROFILL]

A small (single-precision) floating-point number. Allowable values are -3.402823466E+38 to -1.175494351E-38, 0, and 1.175494351E-38 to 3.402823466E+38. If UNSIGNED is specified, negative values are disallowed. The M is the display width and D is the number of decimals. FLOAT without arguments or FLOAT(X) where X <= 24 stands for a single-precision floating-point number.

DOUBLE[(M,D)] [UNSIGNED] [ZEROFILL]

A normal-size (double-precision) floating-point number. Allowable values are -1.7976931348623157E+308 to -2.2250738585072014E-308, 0, and 2.2250738585072014E-308 to 1.7976931348623157E+308. If UNSIGNED is specified, negative values are disallowed. The M is the display width and D is the number of decimals. DOUBLE without arguments or FLOAT(X) where 25 <= X <= 53 stands for a double-precision floating-point number.

DOUBLE PRECISION[(M,D)] [UNSIGNED] [ZEROFILL]
REAL[(M,D)] [UNSIGNED] [ZEROFILL]

These are synonyms for DOUBLE.

DECIMAL[(M[,D])] [UNSIGNED] [ZEROFILL]

An unpacked floating-point number. Behaves like a CHAR column: "unpacked" means the number is stored as a string, using one character for each digit of the value. The decimal point and, for negative numbers, the - sign are not counted in M (but space for these is reserved). If D is 0, values will have no decimal point or fractional part. The maximum range of DECIMAL values is the same as for DOUBLE, but the actual range for a given DECIMAL column may be constrained by the choice of M and D. If

UNSIGNED is specified, negative values are disallowed.

If D is omitted, the default is 0. If M is omitted, the default is 10.

In MySQL versions prior to Version 3.23, the M argument must include the space needed for the sign and the decimal point.

```
DEC[(M[,D])] [UNSIGNED] [ZEROFILL]
NUMERIC[(M[,D])] [UNSIGNED] [ZEROFILL]
```

These are synonyms for DECIMAL.

DATE

A date. The supported range is '1000-01-01' to '9999-12-31'. MySQL displays DATE values in YYYY-MM-DD format, but allows you to assign values to DATE columns using either strings or numbers. See Section 6.2.2.2, The DATETIME, DATE, and TIMESTAMP types.

DATETIME

A date and time combination. The supported range is '1000-01-01 00:00:00' to '9999-12-31 23:59:59'. MySQL displays DATETIME values in YYYY-MM-DD HH:MM:SS format, allowing you to assign values to DATETIME columns with strings or numbers. See Section 6.2.2.2, The DATETIME, DATE, and TIMESTAMP types.

TIMESTAMP[(M)]

A timestamp. The range is '1970-01-01 00:00:00' to sometime in the year 2037. MySQL displays TIMESTAMP values in YYYYMMDDHHMMSS, YYMMDDHHMMSS, YYYYM-MDD, or YYMMDD format, depending on whether M is 14 (or missing), 12, 8, or 6, but allows you to assign values to TIMESTAMP columns using either strings or numbers. A TIMESTAMP column is useful for recording the date and time of an INSERT or UPDATE operation because it is automatically set to the date and time of the most recent operation if you don't give it a value yourself. You can also set it to the current date and time by assigning it a NULL value. See Section 6.2.2, Date and Time Types.

The M argument affects only how a TIMESTAMP column is displayed; its values always are stored using 4 bytes each.

Note that TIMESTAMP(M) columns where M is 8 or 14 are reported to be numbers while other TIMESTAMP(M) columns are reported to be strings. This is just to ensure that one can reliably dump and restore the table with these types! See Section 6.2.2.2, The DATETIME, DATE, and TIMESTAMP types.

TIME

A time. The range is '-838:59:59' to '838:59:59'. MySQL displays TIME values in HH:MM:SS format, but allows you to assign values to TIME columns using either strings or numbers. See Section 6.2.2.3, The TIME type.

YEAR[(2|4)]

A year in 2- or 4-digit format (default is 4-digit). The allowable values are 1901 to 2155, 0000 in the 4-digit year format, and 1970-2069 if you use the 2-digit format (70-69). MySQL displays YEAR values in YYYY format, but allows you to assign values to YEAR columns using either strings or numbers. (The YEAR type is unavailable prior to MySQL Version 3.22.) See Section 6.2.2.4, The YEAR type.

[NATIONAL] CHAR(M) [BINARY]

A fixed-length string that is always right-padded with spaces to the specified length when stored. The range of M is 0 to 255 characters (1 to 255 prior to MySQL Version 3.23). Trailing spaces are removed when the value is retrieved. CHAR values are sorted and compared in case-insensitive fashion according to the default character set unless the BINARY keyword is given.

NATIONAL CHAR (or its equivalent short form, NCHAR) is the ANSI SQL way to define that a CHAR column should use the default CHARACTER set. This is the default in MySQL.

CHAR is shorthand for CHARACTER.

MySQL allows you to create a column of type CHAR(0). This is mainly useful when you have to be compliant with some old applications that depend on the existence of a column but that do not actually use the value. This is also quite nice when you need a column that only can take 2 values: a CHAR(0), that is not defined as NOT NULL, will occupy only one bit and can take only 2 values: NULL or " ". See Section 6.2.3.1, The CHAR and VARCHAR types.

CHAR

This is a synonym for CHAR(1).

[NATIONAL] VARCHAR(M) [BINARY]

A variable-length string. **Note**: trailing spaces are removed when the value is stored (this differs from the ANSI SQL specification). The range of M is 0 to 255 characters (1 to 255 prior to MySQL Version 4.0.2). VARCHAR values are sorted and compared in case-insensitive fashion unless the BINARY keyword is given. See Section 6.5.3.1, Silent column specification changes.

VARCHAR is shorthand for CHARACTER VARYING. See Section 6.2.3.1, The CHAR and VARCHAR types.

TINYBLOB
TINYTEXT

A BLOB or TEXT column with a maximum length of 255 ($2^8 - 1$) characters. See Section 6.5.3.1, Silent column specification changes. See Section 6.2.3.2, The BLOB and TEXT types.

BLOB

TEXT

> A BLOB or TEXT column with a maximum length of 65535 (2^16 - 1) characters. See Section 6.5.3.1, Silent column specification changes. See Section 6.2.3.2, The BLOB and TEXT types.

MEDIUMBLOB

MEDIUMTEXT

> A BLOB or TEXT column with a maximum length of 16777215 (2^24 - 1) characters. See Section 6.5.3.1, Silent column specification changes. See Section 6.2.3.2, The BLOB and TEXT types.

LONGBLOB

LONGTEXT

> A BLOB or TEXT column with a maximum length of 4294967295 (2^32 - 1) characters. See Section 6.5.3.1, Silent column specification changes. Note that because the server/client protocol and MyISAM tables currently have a limit of 16M per communication packet/table row, you can't yet use the whole range of this type. See Section 6.2.3.2, The BLOB and TEXT types.

ENUM('value1','value2',...)

> An enumeration. A string object that can have only one value, chosen from the list of values 'value1', 'value2', ..., NULL, or the special "" error value. An ENUM can have a maximum of 65535 distinct values. See Section 6.2.3.3, The ENUM type.

SET('value1','value2',...)

> A set. A string object that can have zero or more values, each of which must be chosen from the list of values 'value1', 'value2', ... A SET can have a maximum of 64 members. See Section 6.2.3.4, The SET type.

6.2.1 Numeric Types

MySQL supports all of the ANSI/ISO SQL92 numeric types. These types include the exact numeric datatypes (NUMERIC, DECIMAL, INTEGER, and SMALLINT), as well as the approximate numeric datatypes (FLOAT, REAL, and DOUBLE PRECISION). The keyword INT is a synonym for INTEGER, and the keyword DEC is a synonym for DECIMAL.

The NUMERIC and DECIMAL types are implemented as the same type by MySQL, as permitted by the SQL92 standard. They are used for values for which it is important to preserve exact precision— for example, with monetary data. When declaring a column of one of these types the precision and scale can be (and usually are) specified. For example:

```
salary DECIMAL(9,2)
```

In this example, 9 (precision) represents the number of significant decimal digits that will be stored for values, and 2 (scale) represents the number of digits that will be stored following the decimal point. In this case, therefore, the range of values that can be stored in the salary column is from -9999999.99 to 9999999.99. (MySQL can actually store numbers up to 9999999.99 in this column because it doesn't have to store the sign for positive numbers.)

In ANSI/ISO SQL92, the syntax DECIMAL(p) is equivalent to DECIMAL(p,0). Similarly, the syntax DECIMAL is equivalent to DECIMAL(p,0), where the implementation is allowed to decide the value of p. MySQL does not currently support either of these variant forms of the DECIMAL/NUMERIC datatypes. This is not generally a serious problem, as the principal benefits of these types derive from the ability to control both precision and scale explicitly.

DECIMAL and NUMERIC values are stored as strings, rather than as binary floating-point numbers, in order to preserve the decimal precision of those values. One character is used for each digit of the value, the decimal point (if scale > 0), and the - sign (for negative numbers). If scale is 0, DECIMAL and NUMERIC values contain no decimal point or fractional part.

The maximum range of DECIMAL and NUMERIC values is the same as for DOUBLE, but the actual range for a given DECIMAL or NUMERIC column can be constrained by the precision or scale for a given column. When such a column is assigned a value with more digits following the decimal point than are allowed by the specified scale, the value is rounded to that scale. When a DECIMAL or NUMERIC column is assigned a value whose magnitude exceeds the range implied by the specified (or defaulted) precision and scale, MySQL stores the value representing the corresponding end point of that range.

As an extension to the ANSI/ISO SQL92 standard, MySQL also supports the integer types TINYINT, MEDIUMINT, and BIGINT as listed in the preceding tables. Another extension is supported by MySQL for optionally specifying the display width of an integer value in parentheses following the base keyword for the type (for example, INT(4)). This optional width specification is used to left-pad the display of values whose width is less than the width specified for the column, but does not constrain the range of values that can be stored in the column, nor the number of digits that will be displayed for values whose width exceeds that specified for the column. When used in conjunction with the optional extension attribute ZEROFILL, the default padding of spaces is replaced with zeroes. For example, for a column declared as INT(5) ZEROFILL, a value of 4 is retrieved as 00004. Note that if you store larger values than the display width in an integer column, you may experience problems when MySQL generates temporary tables for some complicated joins, as in these cases MySQL trusts that the data did fit into the original column width.

All integer types can have an optional (non-standard) attribute UNSIGNED. Unsigned values can be used when you want to allow only positive numbers in a column and you need a little bigger numeric range for the column.

As of MySQL 4.0.2, floating-point types also can be UNSIGNED. As with integer types, this attribute prevents negative values from being stored in the column. Unlike the integer types, the upper range of column values remains the same.

The FLOAT type is used to represent approximate numeric data types. The ANSI/ISO SQL92 standard allows an optional specification of the precision (but not the range of the exponent) in bits following the keyword FLOAT in parentheses. The MySQL implementation also supports this optional precision specification. When the keyword FLOAT is used for a column type without a precision specification, MySQL uses four bytes to store the values. A variant syntax is also supported, with two numbers given in parentheses following the FLOAT keyword. With this option, the first number continues to represent the storage requirements for the value in bytes, and the second number specifies the number of digits to be stored and displayed following the decimal point (as with DECIMAL and NUMERIC). When MySQL is asked to store a number for such a column with more decimal digits following the decimal point than specified for the column, the value is rounded to eliminate the extra digits when the value is stored.

The REAL and DOUBLE PRECISION types do not accept precision specifications. As an extension to the ANSI/ISO SQL92 standard, MySQL recognises DOUBLE as a synonym for the DOUBLE PRECISION type. In contrast with the standard's requirement that the precision for REAL be smaller than that used for DOUBLE PRECISION, MySQL implements both as 8-byte double-precision floating-point values (when not running in "ANSI mode"). For maximum portability, code requiring storage of approximate numeric data values should use FLOAT or DOUBLE PRECISION with no specification of precision or number of decimal points.

When asked to store a value in a numeric column that is outside the column type's allowable range, MySQL clips the value to the appropriate endpoint of the range and stores the resulting value instead.

For example, the range of an INT column is -2147483648 to 2147483647. If you try to insert -9999999999 into an INT column, the value is clipped to the lower endpoint of the range, and -2147483648 is stored instead. Similarly, if you try to insert 9999999999, 2147483647 is stored instead.

If the INT column is UNSIGNED, the size of the column's range is the same but its endpoints shift up to 0 and 4294967295. If you try to store -9999999999 and 9999999999, the values stored in the column become 0 and 4294967296.

Conversions that occur due to clipping are reported as "warnings" for ALTER TABLE, LOAD DATA INFILE, UPDATE, and multi-row INSERT statements.

6.2.2 Date and Time Types

The date and time types are DATETIME, DATE, TIMESTAMP, TIME, and YEAR. Each of these has a range of legal values, as well as a "zero" value that is used when you specify a really illegal value. Note that MySQL allows you to store certain "not strictly" legal date values—for example, 1999-11-31. The reason for this is that we think it's the responsibility of the application to handle date checking, not the SQL servers. To make the date checking "fast", MySQL only checks that the month is in the range of 0-12 and the day is in the range of 0-31. These ranges are defined this way because MySQL allows you to store, in a DATE or DATETIME column, dates where the day or month-day is zero. This is extremely useful for applications that need to store a birthdate for which you don't know the exact date. In this case you simply store the date like 1999-00-00 or 1999-01-00. (You cannot expect to get a correct value from functions like DATE_SUB() or DATE_ADD for dates like these.)

Here are some general considerations to keep in mind when working with date and time types:

- MySQL retrieves values for a given date or time type in a standard format, but it attempts to interpret a variety of formats for values that you supply (for example, when you specify a value to be assigned to or compared to a date or time type). Nevertheless, only the formats described in the following sections are supported. It is expected that you will supply legal values, and unpredictable results may occur if you use values in other formats.

- Although MySQL tries to interpret values in several formats, it always expects the year part of date values to be leftmost. Dates must be given in year-month-day order (for example, '98-09-04'), rather than in the month-day-year or day-month-year orders commonly used elsewhere (for example, '09-04-98', '04-09-98').

- MySQL automatically converts a date or time type value to a number if the value is used in a numeric context, and vice versa.

- When MySQL encounters a value for a date or time type that is out of range or otherwise illegal for the type (see the start of this section), it converts the value to the "zero" value for that type. (The exception is that out-of-range TIME values are clipped to the appropriate endpoint of the TIME range.) The following table shows the format of the "zero" value for each type:

Column type	"Zero" value
DATETIME	'0000-00-00 00:00:00'
DATE	'0000-00-00'
TIMESTAMP	00000000000000 (length depends on display size)
TIME	'00:00:00'
YEAR	0000

- The "zero" values are special, but you can store or refer to them explicitly using the values shown in the table. You can also do this using the values '0' or 0, which are easier to write.

- "Zero" date or time values used through MyODBC are converted automatically to NULL in MyODBC Versions 2.50.12 and above because ODBC can't handle such values.

6.2.2.1 Y2K issues and datetypes

MySQL itself is Y2K-safe (see Section 1.2.5, Year 2000 Compliance), but input values presented to MySQL may not be. Any input containing 2-digit year values is ambiguous because the century is unknown. Such values must be interpreted into 4-digit form because MySQL stores years internally using four digits.

For DATETIME, DATE, TIMESTAMP, and YEAR types, MySQL interprets dates with ambiguous year values using the following rules:

- Year values in the range 00-69 are converted to 2000-2069.

- Year values in the range 70-99 are converted to 1970-1999.

Remember that these rules provide only reasonable guesses as to what your data means. If the heuristics used by MySQL don't produce the correct values, you should provide unambiguous input containing 4-digit year values.

ORDER BY will sort 2-digit YEAR/DATE/DATETIME types properly.

Note also that some functions like MIN() and MAX() will convert a TIMESTAMP/DATE to a number. This means that a timestamp with a 2-digit year will not work properly with these functions. The fix in this case is to convert the TIMESTAMP/DATE to 4-digit year format or use something like MIN(DATE_ADD(timestamp,INTERVAL 0 DAYS)).

6.2.2.2 The DATETIME, DATE, and TIMESTAMP types

The DATETIME, DATE, and TIMESTAMP types are related. This section describes their characteristics, how they are similar, and how they differ.

The DATETIME type is used when you need values that contain both date and time information. MySQL retrieves and displays DATETIME values in YYYY-MM-DD HH:MM:SS format. The supported range is '1000-01-01 00:00:00' to '9999-12-31 23:59:59'. ("Supported" means that although earlier values might work, there is no guarantee that they will.)

The DATE type is used when you need only a date value, without a time part. MySQL retrieves and displays DATE values in YYYY-MM-DD format. The supported range is '1000-01-01' to '9999-12-31'.

The TIMESTAMP column type provides a type that you can use to automatically mark INSERT or UPDATE operations with the current date and time. If you have multiple

TIMESTAMP columns, only the first one is updated automatically.

Automatic updating of the first TIMESTAMP column occurs under any of the following conditions:

- The column is not specified explicitly in an INSERT or LOAD DATA INFILE statement.

- The column is not specified explicitly in an UPDATE statement and some other column changes value. (Note that an UPDATE that sets a column to the value it already has will not cause the TIMESTAMP column to be updated because if you set a column to its current value, MySQL ignores the update for efficiency.)

- You explicitly set the TIMESTAMP column to NULL.

TIMESTAMP columns other than the first may also be set to the current date and time. Just set the column to NULL or to NOW().

You can set any TIMESTAMP column to a value different from the current date and time by setting it explicitly to the desired value. This is true even for the first TIMESTAMP column. You can use this property if, for example, you want a TIMESTAMP to be set to the current date and time when you create a row, but not to be changed whenever the row is updated later:

- Let MySQL set the column when the row is created. This will initialise it to the current date and time.

- When you perform subsequent updates to other columns in the row, set the TIME-STAMP column explicitly to its current value.

On the other hand, you may find it just as easy to use a DATETIME column that you initialise to NOW() when the row is created and leave alone for subsequent updates.

TIMESTAMP values may range from the beginning of 1970 to sometime in the year 2037, with a resolution of one second. Values are displayed as numbers.

The format in which MySQL retrieves and displays TIMESTAMP values depends on the display size, as illustrated in the following table. The "full" TIMESTAMP format is 14 digits, but TIMESTAMP columns may be created with shorter display sizes:

Column type	Display format
TIMESTAMP(14)	YYYYMMDDHHMMSS
TIMESTAMP(12)	YYMMDDHHMMSS
TIMESTAMP(10)	YYMMDDHHMM
TIMESTAMP(8)	YYYYMMDD
TIMESTAMP(6)	YYMMDD
TIMESTAMP(4)	YYMM
TIMESTAMP(2)	YY

All TIMESTAMP columns have the same storage size, regardless of display size. The most common display sizes are 6, 8, 12, and 14. You can specify an arbitrary display size at table creation time, but values of 0 or greater than 14 are coerced to 14. Odd-valued sizes in the range from 1 to 13 are coerced to the next higher even number.

You can specify DATETIME, DATE, and TIMESTAMP values using any of a common set of formats:

- As a string in either YYYY-MM-DD HH:MM:SS or YY-MM-DD HH:MM:SS format. A "relaxed" syntax is allowed---any punctuation character may be used as the delimiter between date parts or time parts. For example, '98-12-31 11:30:45', '98.12.31 11+30+45', '98/12/31 11*30*45', and '98@12@31 11^30^45' are equivalent.

- As a string in either YYYY-MM-DD or YY-MM-DD format. A "relaxed" syntax is allowed here, too. For example, '98-12-31', '98.12.31', '98/12/31', and '98@12@31' are equivalent.

- As a string with no delimiters in either YYYYMMDDHHMMSS or YYMMDDHHMMSS format, provided that the string makes sense as a date. For example, '19970523091528' and '970523091528' are interpreted as '1997-05-23 09:15:28', but '971122129015' is illegal (it has a nonsensical minute part) and becomes '0000-00-00 00:00:00'.

- As a string with no delimiters in either YYYYMMDD or YYMMDD format, provided that the string makes sense as a date. For example, '19970523' and '970523' are interpreted as '1997-05-23', but '971332' is illegal (it has nonsensical month and day parts) and becomes '0000-00-00'.

- As a number in either YYYYMMDDHHMMSS or YYMMDDHHMMSS format, provided that the number makes sense as a date. For example, 19830905132800 and 830905132800 are interpreted as '1983-09-05 13:28:00'.

- As a number in either YYYYMMDD or YYMMDD format, provided that the number makes sense as a date. For example, 19830905 and 830905 are interpreted as '1983-09-05'.

- As the result of a function that returns a value that is acceptable in a DATETIME, DATE, or TIMESTAMP context, such as NOW() or CURRENT_DATE.

Illegal DATETIME, DATE, or TIMESTAMP values are converted to the "zero" value of the appropriate type ('0000-00-00 00:00:00', '0000-00-00', or 00000000000000).

For values specified as strings that include date part delimiters, it is not necessary to specify two digits for month or day values that are less than 10. '1979-6-9' is the same as '1979-06-09'. Similarly, for values specified as strings that include time part delimiters, it is not necessary to specify two digits for hour, month, or second values that are less than 10. '1979-10-30 1:2:3' is the same as '1979-10-30 01:02:03'.

Values specified as numbers should be 6, 8, 12, or 14 digits long. If the number is 8 or 14 digits long, it is assumed to be in YYYYMMDD or YYYYMMDDHHMMSS format and that the year is given by the first 4 digits. If the number is 6 or 12 digits long, it is assumed to be in YYMMDD or YYMMDDHHMMSS format and that the year is given by the first 2 digits. Numbers that are not one of these lengths are interpreted as though padded with leading zeros to the closest length.

Values specified as non-delimited strings are interpreted using their length as given. If the string is 8 or 14 characters long, the year is assumed to be given by the first 4 characters. Otherwise, the year is assumed to be given by the first 2 characters. The string is interpreted from left to right to find year, month, day, hour, minute, and second values, for as many parts as are present in the string. This means you should not use strings that have fewer than 6 characters. For example, if you specify '9903', thinking that will represent March, 1999, you will find that MySQL inserts a "zero" date into your table. This is because the year and month values are 99 and 03, but the day part is missing (zero), so the value is not a legal date.

TIMESTAMP columns store legal values using the full precision with which the value was specified, regardless of the display size. This has several implications:

- Always specify year, month, and day, even if your column types are TIMESTAMP(4) or TIMESTAMP(2). Otherwise, the value will not be a legal date and 0 will be stored.

- If you use ALTER TABLE to widen a narrow TIMESTAMP column, information will be displayed that previously was "hidden".

- Similarly, narrowing a TIMESTAMP column does not cause information to be lost, except in the sense that less information is shown when the values are displayed.

- Although TIMESTAMP values are stored to full precision, the only function that operates directly on the underlying stored value is UNIX_TIMESTAMP(). Other functions operate on the formatted retrieved value. This means you cannot use functions such as HOUR() or SECOND() unless the relevant part of the TIMESTAMP value is included in the formatted value. For example, the HH part of a TIMESTAMP column is not displayed unless the display size is at least 10, so trying to use HOUR() on shorter TIMESTAMP values produces a meaningless result.

You can to some extent assign values of one date type to an object of a different date type. However, there may be some alteration of the value or loss of information:

- If you assign a DATE value to a DATETIME or TIMESTAMP object, the time part of the resulting value is set to '00:00:00' because the DATE value contains no time information.

- If you assign a DATETIME or TIMESTAMP value to a DATE object, the time part of the resulting value is deleted because the DATE type stores no time information.

- Remember that although DATETIME, DATE, and TIMESTAMP values all can be specified using the same set of formats, the types do not all have the same range of values. For example, TIMESTAMP values cannot be earlier than 1970 or later than 2037. This means that a date such as '1968-01-01', while legal as a DATETIME or DATE value, is not a valid TIMESTAMP value and will be converted to 0 if assigned to such an object.

Be aware of certain pitfalls when specifying date values:

- The relaxed format allowed for values specified as strings can be deceiving. For example, a value such as '10:11:12' might look like a time value because of the : delimiter, but if used in a date context will be interpreted as the year '2010-11-12'. The value '10:45:15' will be converted to '0000-00-00' because '45' is not a legal month.

- Year values specified as two digits are ambiguous because the century is unknown. MySQL interprets 2-digit year values using the following rules:

  — Year values in the range 00–69 are converted to 2000–2069.

  — Year values in the range 70–99 are converted to 1970–1999.

6.2.2.3 The TIME type

MySQL retrieves and displays TIME values in HH:MM:SS format (or HHH:MM:SS format for large hour values). TIME values may range from '-838:59:59' to '838:59:59'. The reason the hours part may be so large is that the TIME type may be used not only to represent a time of day (which must be less than 24 hours), but also elapsed time or a time interval between two events (which may be much greater than 24 hours, or even negative).

You can specify TIME values in a variety of formats:

- As a string in D HH:MM:SS.fraction format. (Note that MySQL doesn't yet store the fraction for the time column.) One can also use one of the following "relaxed" syntaxes:

  HH:MM:SS.fraction, HH:MM:SS, HH:MM, D HH:MM:SS, D HH:MM, D HH, or SS. Here D is days between 0-33.

- As a string with no delimiters in HHMMSS format, provided that it makes sense as a time. For example, '101112' is understood as '10:11:12', but '109712' is illegal (it has a nonsensical minute part) and becomes '00:00:00'.

- As a number in HHMMSS format, provided that it makes sense as a time. For example, 101112 is understood as '10:11:12'. The following alternative formats are also understood: SS, MMSS, HHMMSS, and HHMMSS.fraction. Note that MySQL doesn't yet store the fraction part.

- As the result of a function that returns a value that is acceptable in a TIME context, such as CURRENT_TIME.

For TIME values specified as strings that include a time part delimiter, it is not necessary to specify two digits for hours, minutes, or seconds values that are less than 10. '8:3:2' is the same as '08:03:02'.

Be careful about assigning "short" TIME values to a TIME column. Without colons, MySQL interprets values using the assumption that the rightmost digits represent seconds. (MySQL interprets TIME values as elapsed time rather than as time of day.) For example, you might think of '1112' and 1112 as meaning '11:12:00' (12 minutes after 11 o'clock), but MySQL interprets them as '00:11:12' (11 minutes, 12 seconds). Similarly, '12' and 12 are interpreted as '00:00:12'. TIME values with colons, by contrast, are always treated as time of the day. That is, '11:12' will mean '11:12:00', not '00:11:12'.

Values that lie outside the TIME range but are otherwise legal are clipped to the appropriate endpoint of the range. For example, '-850:00:00' and '850:00:00' are converted to '-838:59:59' and '838:59:59'.

Illegal TIME values are converted to '00:00:00'. Note that because '00:00:00' is itself a legal TIME value, there is no way to tell, from a value of '00:00:00' stored in a table, whether the original value was specified as '00:00:00' or whether it was illegal.

6.2.2.4 The YEAR type

The YEAR type is a 1-byte type used for representing years.

MySQL retrieves and displays YEAR values in YYYY format. The range is 1901 to 2155.

You can specify YEAR values in a variety of formats:

- As a four-digit string in the range '1901' to '2155'.

- As a four-digit number in the range 1901 to 2155.

- As a two-digit string in the range '00' to '99'. Values in the ranges '00' to '69' and '70' to '99' are converted to YEAR values in the ranges 2000 to 2069 and 1970 to 1999.

- As a two-digit number in the range 1 to 99. Values in the ranges 1 to 69 and 70 to 99 are converted to YEAR values in the ranges 2001 to 2069 and 1970 to 1999. Note that the range for two-digit numbers is slightly different from the range for two-digit strings, because you cannot specify zero directly as a number and have it be interpreted as 2000. You **must** specify it as a string '0' or '00' or it will be interpreted as 0000.

- As the result of a function that returns a value that is acceptable in a YEAR context, such as NOW().

Illegal YEAR values are converted to 0000.

6.2.3 String Types

The string types are CHAR, VARCHAR, BLOB, TEXT, ENUM, and SET. This section describes how these types work, their storage requirements, and how to use them in your queries.

6.2.3.1 The CHAR and VARCHAR types

The CHAR and VARCHAR types are similar, but differ in the way they are stored and retrieved.

The length of a CHAR column is fixed to the length that you declare when you create the table. The length can be any value between 1 and 255. (As of MySQL Version 3.23, the length of CHAR may be 0 to 255.) When CHAR values are stored, they are right-padded with spaces to the specified length. When CHAR values are retrieved, trailing spaces are removed.

Values in VARCHAR columns are variable-length strings. You can declare a VARCHAR column to be any length between 1 and 255, just as for CHAR columns. However, in contrast to CHAR, VARCHAR values are stored using only as many characters as are needed, plus one byte to record the length. Values are not padded; instead, trailing spaces are removed when values are stored. (This space removal differs from the ANSI SQL specification.)

If you assign a value to a CHAR or VARCHAR column that exceeds the column's maximum length, the value is truncated to fit.

The following table illustrates the differences between the two types of columns by showing the result of storing various string values into CHAR(4) and VARCHAR(4) columns:

Value	CHAR(4)	Storage required	VAR-CHAR(4)	Storage required
"	' '	4 bytes	"	1 byte
'ab'	'ab '	4 bytes	'ab'	3 bytes
'abcd'	'abcd'	4 bytes	'abcd'	5 bytes
'abcde-fgh'	'abcd'	4 bytes	'abcd'	5 bytes

The values retrieved from the CHAR(4) and VARCHAR(4) columns will be the same in each case because trailing spaces are removed from CHAR columns upon retrieval.

Values in CHAR and VARCHAR columns are sorted and compared in case-insensitive fashion, unless the BINARY attribute was specified when the table was created. The BINARY attribute means that column values are sorted and compared in case-sensitive fashion according to the ASCII order of the machine where the MySQL server is running. BINARY doesn't affect how the column is stored or retrieved.

The BINARY attribute is sticky. This means that if a column marked BINARY is used in an expression, the whole expression is compared as a BINARY value.

MySQL may silently change the type of a CHAR or VARCHAR column at table creation time. See Section 6.5.3.1, Silent column specification changes.

6.2.3.2 The BLOB and TEXT types

A BLOB is a binary large object that can hold a variable amount of data. The four BLOB types—TINYBLOB, BLOB, MEDIUMBLOB, and LONGBLOB—differ only in the maximum length of the values they can hold. See Section 6.2.6, Column Type Storage Requirements.

The four TEXT types—TINYTEXT, TEXT, MEDIUMTEXT, and LONGTEXT—correspond to the four BLOB types and have the same maximum lengths and storage requirements. The only difference between the BLOB and TEXT types is that sorting and comparison are performed in case-sensitive fashion for BLOB values and case-insensitive fashion for TEXT values. In other words, a TEXT is a case-insensitive BLOB.

If you assign a value to a BLOB or TEXT column that exceeds the column type's maximum length, the value is truncated to fit.

In most respects, you can regard a TEXT column as a VARCHAR column that can be as big as you like. Similarly, you can regard a BLOB column as a VARCHAR BINARY column. The differences are:

- You can have indexes on BLOB and TEXT columns with MySQL Versions 3.23.2 and newer. Older versions of MySQL did not support this.

- There is no trailing-space removal for BLOB and TEXT columns when values are stored, as there is for VARCHAR columns.

- BLOB and TEXT columns cannot have DEFAULT values.

MyODBC defines BLOB values as LONGVARBINARY and TEXT values as LONGVARCHAR.

Because BLOB and TEXT values may be extremely long, you may run up against some constraints when using them:

- If you want to use GROUP BY or ORDER BY on a BLOB or TEXT column, you must convert the column value into a fixed-length object. The standard way to do this is with the SUBSTRING function. For example:

```
mysql> SELECT comment FROM tbl_name,SUBSTRING(comment,20) AS substr
    ->                    ORDER BY substr;
```

If you don't do this, only the first `max_sort_length` bytes of the column are used when sorting. The default value of `max_sort_length` is 1024; this value can be changed using the `-O` option when starting the `mysqld` server. You can group on an expression involving BLOB or TEXT values by specifying the column position or by using an alias:

```
mysql> SELECT id,SUBSTRING(blob_col,1,100) FROM tbl_name GROUP BY 2;
mysql> SELECT id,SUBSTRING(blob_col,1,100) AS b FROM tbl_name GROUP BY b;
```

- The maximum size of a BLOB or TEXT object is determined by its type, but the largest value you can actually transmit between the client and server is determined by the amount of available memory and the size of the communications buffers. You can change the message buffer size, but you must do so on both the server and client ends. See Section 5.5.2, Tuning Server Parameters.

Note that each BLOB or TEXT value is represented internally by a separately allocated object. This is in contrast to all other column types, for which storage is allocated once per column when the table is opened.

6.2.3.3 The ENUM type

An ENUM is a string object whose value normally is chosen from a list of allowed values that are enumerated explicitly in the column specification at table creation time.

The value may also be the empty string (" ") or NULL under certain circumstances:

- If you insert an invalid value into an ENUM (that is, a string not present in the list of allowed values), the empty string is inserted instead as a special error value. This string can be distinguished from a "normal" empty string by the fact that this string has the numerical value 0. More about this later.

- If an ENUM is declared NULL, NULL is also a legal value for the column, and the default value is NULL. If an ENUM is declared NOT NULL, the default value is the first element of the list of allowed values.

Each enumeration value has an index:

- Values from the list of allowable elements in the column specification are numbered beginning with 1.

- The index value of the empty string error value is 0. This means that you can use the following SELECT statement to find rows into which invalid ENUM values were assigned:

```
mysql> SELECT * FROM tbl_name WHERE enum_col=0;
```

- The index of the NULL value is NULL.

For example, a column specified as ENUM("one", "two", "three") can have any of the values shown in the following table. The index of each value is also shown:

Value	Index
NULL	NULL
" "	0
"one"	1
"two"	2
"three"	3

An enumeration can have a maximum of 65535 elements.

Lettercase is irrelevant when you assign values to an ENUM column. However, values retrieved from the column later have lettercase matching the values that were used to specify the allowable values at table creation time.

If you retrieve an ENUM in a numeric context, the column value's index is returned. For example, you can retrieve numeric values from an ENUM column like this:

```
mysql> SELECT enum_col+0 FROM tbl_name;
```

If you store a number into an ENUM, the number is treated as an index, and the value stored is the enumeration member with that index. (However, this will not work with LOAD DATA, which treats all input as strings.)

ENUM values are sorted according to the order in which the enumeration members were listed in the column specification. (In other words, ENUM values are sorted according to their index numbers.) For example, "a" sorts before "b" for ENUM("a", "b"), but "b" sorts before "a" for ENUM("b", "a"). The empty string sorts before non-empty strings, and NULL values sort before all other enumeration values.

If you want to get all possible values for an ENUM column, you should use SHOW COLUMNS FROM table_name LIKE enum_column_name and parse the ENUM definition in the second column.

6.2.3.4 The SET type

A SET is a string object that can have zero or more values, each of which must be chosen from a list of allowed values specified when the table is created. SET column values that consist of multiple set members are specified with members separated by commas (,). A consequence of this is that SET member values cannot themselves contain commas.

For example, a column specified as SET("one", "two") NOT NULL can have any of these values:

```
" "
"one"
"two"
"one,two"
```

A SET can have a maximum of 64 different members.

MySQL stores SET values numerically, with the low-order bit of the stored value corresponding to the first set member. If you retrieve a SET value in a numeric context, the value retrieved has bits set corresponding to the set members that make up the column value. For example, you can retrieve numeric values from a SET column like this:

```
mysql> SELECT set_col+0 FROM tbl_name;
```

If a number is stored into a SET column, the bits that are set in the binary representation of the number determine the set members in the column value. Suppose a column is specified as SET("a","b","c","d"). Then the members have the following bit values:

SET member	Decimal value	Binary value
a	1	0001
b	2	0010
c	4	0100
d	8	1000

If you assign a value of 9 to this column, that is 1001 in binary, so the first and fourth SET value members "a" and "d" are selected and the resulting value is "a,d".

For a value containing more than one SET element, it does not matter what order the elements are listed in when you insert the value. It also does not matter how many times a given element is listed in the value. When the value is retrieved later, each element in the value will appear once, with elements listed according to the order in which they were specified at table creation time. For example, if a column is specified as SET("a","b","c","d"), "a,d", "d,a", and "d,a,a,d,d" will all appear as "a,d" when retrieved.

If you set a SET column to an unsupported value, the value will be ignored.

SET values are sorted numerically. NULL values sort before non-NULL SET values.

Normally, you perform a SELECT on a SET column using the LIKE operator or the FIND_IN_SET() function:

```
mysql> SELECT * FROM tbl_name WHERE set_col LIKE '%value%';
mysql> SELECT * FROM tbl_name WHERE FIND_IN_SET('value',set_col)>0;
```

But the following will also work:

```
mysql> SELECT * FROM tbl_name WHERE set_col = 'val1,val2';
mysql> SELECT * FROM tbl_name WHERE set_col & 1;
```

The first of these statements looks for an exact match. The second looks for values containing the first set member.

If you want to get all possible values for a SET column, you should use SHOW COLUMNS FROM table_name LIKE set_column_name and parse the SET definition in the second column.

6.2.4 Choosing the Right Type for a Column

For the most efficient use of storage, try to use the most precise type in all cases. For example, if an integer column will be used for values in the range between 1 and 99999, MEDIUMINT UNSIGNED is the best type.

Accurate representation of monetary values is a common problem. In MySQL, you should use the DECIMAL type. This is stored as a string, so no loss of accuracy should occur. If accuracy is not too important, the DOUBLE type may also be good enough.

For high precision, you can always convert to a fixed-point type stored in a BIGINT. This allows you to do all calculations with integers and convert results back to floating-point values only when necessary.

6.2.5 Using Column Types from Other Database Engines

To make it easier to use code written for SQL implementations from other vendors, MySQL maps column types as shown in the following table. These mappings make it easier to move table definitions from other database engines to MySQL:

Other vendor type	MySQL type
BINARY (NUM)	CHAR (NUM) BINARY
CHAR VARYING (NUM)	VARCHAR (NUM)
FLOAT4	FLOAT
FLOAT8	DOUBLE
INT1	TINYINT
INT2	SMALLINT
INT3	MEDIUMINT
INT4	INT
INT8	BIGINT
LONG VARBINARY	MEDIUMBLOB
LONG VARCHAR	MEDIUMTEXT
MIDDLEINT	MEDIUMINT
VARBINARY (NUM)	VARCHAR (NUM) BINARY

Column type mapping occurs at table creation time. If you create a table with types used by other vendors and then issue a DESCRIBE tbl_name statement, MySQL reports the table structure using the equivalent MySQL types.

6.2.6 Column Type Storage Requirements

The storage requirements for each of the column types supported by MySQL are listed in the following sections.

6.2.6.1 Storage requirements for numeric types

Column type	Storage required
TINYINT	1 byte
SMALLINT	2 bytes
MEDIUMINT	3 bytes
INT	4 bytes
INTEGER	4 bytes
BIGINT	8 bytes
FLOAT(X)	4 if X <= 24 or 8 if 25 <= X <= 53
FLOAT	4 bytes
DOUBLE	8 bytes
DOUBLE PRECISION	8 bytes
REAL	8 bytes
DECIMAL(M,D)	M+2 bytes if D > 0, M+1 bytes if D = 0 (D+2, if M < D)
NUMERIC(M,D)	M+2 bytes if D > 0, M+1 bytes if D = 0 (D+2, if M < D)

6.2.6.2 Storage requirements for date and time types

Column type	Storage required
DATE	3 bytes
DATETIME	8 bytes
TIMESTAMP	4 bytes
TIME	3 bytes
YEAR	1 byte

6.2.6.3 Storage requirements for string types

Column type	Storage required
CHAR(M)	M bytes, 1 <= M <= 255
VARCHAR(M)	L+1 bytes, where L <= M and 1 <= M <= 255
TINYBLOB, TINYTEXT	L+1 bytes, where $L < 2^8$
BLOB, TEXT	L+2 bytes, where $L < 2^{16}$
MEDIUMBLOB, MEDIUMTEXT	L+3 bytes, where $L < 2^{24}$
LONGBLOB, LONGTEXT	L+4 bytes, where $L < 2^{32}$
ENUM('value1', 'value2', . . .)	1 or 2 bytes, depending on the number of enumeration values (65535 values maximum)
SET('value1', 'value2', . . .)	1, 2, 3, 4, or 8 bytes, depending on the number of set members (64 members maximum)

VARCHAR and the BLOB and TEXT types are variable-length types, for which the storage requirements depend on the actual length of column values (represented by L in the preceding table), rather than on the type's maximum possible size. For example, a VAR-CHAR(10) column can hold a string with a maximum length of 10 characters. The actual storage required is the length of the string (L), plus 1 byte to record the length of the string. For the string 'abcd', L is 4 and the storage requirement is 5 bytes.

The BLOB and TEXT types require 1, 2, 3, or 4 bytes to record the length of the column value, depending on the maximum possible length of the type. See Section 6.2.3.2, The BLOB and TEXT types.

If a table includes any variable-length column types, the record format will also be variable-length. Note that when a table is created, MySQL may, under certain conditions, change a column from a variable-length type to a fixed-length type, or vice versa. See Section 6.5.3.1, Silent column specification changes.

The size of an ENUM object is determined by the number of different enumeration values. One byte is used for enumerations with up to 255 possible values. Two bytes are used for enumerations with up to 65535 values. See Section 6.2.3.3, The ENUM type.

The size of a SET object is determined by the number of different set members. If the set size is N, the object occupies (N+7)/8 bytes, rounded up to 1, 2, 3, 4, or 8 bytes. A SET can have a maximum of 64 members. See Section 6.2.3.4, The SET type.

6.3 Functions for Use in SELECT and WHERE Clauses

A select_expression or where_definition in a SQL statement can consist of any expression using the functions described next.

An expression that contains NULL always produces a NULL value unless otherwise indicated in the documentation for the operators and functions involved in the expression.

Note: there must be no whitespace between a function name and the parentheses following it. This helps the MySQL parser distinguish between function calls and references to tables or columns that happen to have the same name as a function. Spaces around arguments are permitted, though.

You can force MySQL to accept spaces after the function name by starting mysqld with --ansi or using the CLIENT_IGNORE_SPACE to mysql_connect(), but in this case all function names will become reserved words. See Section 1.7.2, Running MySQL in ANSI Mode.

For the sake of brevity, examples display the output from the mysql program in abbreviated form. So this:

```
mysql> SELECT MOD(29,9);
1 rows in set (0.00 sec)

+-----------+
| mod(29,9) |
+-----------+
|         2 |
+-----------+
```

is displayed like this:

```
mysql> SELECT MOD(29,9);
        -> 2
```

6.3.1 Non-Type-Specific Operators and Functions

6.3.1.1 Parentheses

```
( ... )
```

Use parentheses to force the order of evaluation in an expression. For example:

```
mysql> SELECT 1+2*3;
        -> 7
mysql> SELECT (1+2)*3;
        -> 9
```

6.3.1.2 Comparison operators

Comparison operations result in a value of 1 (TRUE), 0 (FALSE), or NULL. These functions work for both numbers and strings. Strings are automatically converted to numbers and numbers to strings as needed (as in Perl).

MySQL performs comparisons using the following rules:

- If one or both arguments are NULL, the result of the comparison is NULL, except for the <=> operator.

- If both arguments in a comparison operation are strings, they are compared as strings.

- If both arguments are integers, they are compared as integers.

- Hexadecimal values are treated as binary strings if not compared to a number.

- If one of the arguments is a TIMESTAMP or DATETIME column and the other argument is a constant, the constant is converted to a timestamp before the comparison is performed. This is done to be more ODBC-friendly.

- In all other cases, the arguments are compared as floating-point (real) numbers.

By default, string comparisons are done in case-independent fashion using the current character set (ISO-8859-1 Latin1 by default, which also works excellently for English).

The following examples illustrate conversion of strings to numbers for comparison operations:

```
mysql> SELECT 1 > '6x';
        -> 0
mysql> SELECT 7 > '6x';
        -> 1
mysql> SELECT 0 > 'x6';
        -> 0
mysql> SELECT 0 = 'x6';
        -> 1
```

=

Equal:

```
mysql> SELECT 1 = 0;
        -> 0
mysql> SELECT '0' = 0;
        -> 1
mysql> SELECT '0.0' = 0;
        -> 1
mysql> SELECT '0.01' = 0;
        -> 0
mysql> SELECT '.01' = 0.01;
        -> 1
```

<>
!=

Not equal:

```
mysql> SELECT '.01' <> '0.01';
        -> 1
mysql> SELECT .01 <> '0.01';
        -> 0
mysql> SELECT 'zapp' <> 'zappp';
        -> 1
```

<=   Less than or equal:

```
mysql> SELECT 0.1 <= 2;
        -> 1
```

<

Less than:

```
mysql> SELECT 2 < 2;
        -> 0
```

>=   Greater than or equal:

```
mysql> SELECT 2 >= 2;
        -> 1
```

>

Greater than:

```
mysql> SELECT 2 > 2;
        -> 0
```

<=>

NULL safe equal:

```
mysql> SELECT 1 <=> 1, NULL <=> NULL, 1 <=> NULL;
        -> 1 1 0
```

IS NULL
IS NOT NULL

Test whether a value is or is not NULL:

```
mysql> SELECT 1 IS NULL, 0 IS NULL, NULL IS NULL;
        -> 0 0 1
mysql> SELECT 1 IS NOT NULL, 0 IS NOT NULL, NULL IS NOT NULL;
        -> 1 1 0
```

To be able to work well with other programs, MySQL supports the following extra features when using IS NULL:

- You can find the last inserted row with:

  ```
  SELECT * FROM tbl_name WHERE auto_col IS NULL
  ```

  This can be disabled by setting SQL_AUTO_IS_NULL=0. See Section 5.5.6, SET Syntax.

- For NOT NULL DATE and DATETIME columns you can find the special date 0000-00-00 by using:

  ```
  SELECT * FROM tbl_name WHERE date_column IS NULL
  ```

  This is needed to get some ODBC applications to work (as ODBC doesn't support a 0000-00-00 date).

expr BETWEEN min AND max

If expr is greater than or equal to min and expr is less than or equal to max, BETWEEN returns 1, otherwise it returns 0. This is equivalent to the expression (min <= expr AND expr <= max) if all the arguments are of the same type. The first argument (expr) determines how the comparison is performed as follows:

- If expr is a TIMESTAMP, DATE, or DATETIME column, MIN() and MAX() are formatted to the same format if they are constants.

- If expr is a case-insensitive string expression, a case-insensitive string comparison is done.

- If expr is a case-sensitive string expression, a case-sensitive string comparison is done.

- If expr is an integer expression, an integer comparison is done.

- Otherwise, a floating-point (real) comparison is done.

```
mysql> SELECT 1 BETWEEN 2 AND 3;
        -> 0
mysql> SELECT 'b' BETWEEN 'a' AND 'c';
        -> 1
mysql> SELECT 2 BETWEEN 2 AND '3';
        -> 1
mysql> SELECT 2 BETWEEN 2 AND 'x-3';
        -> 0
```

expr NOT BETWEEN min AND max

Same as NOT (expr BETWEEN min AND max).

expr IN (value, . . .)

Returns 1 if expr is any of the values in the IN list, otherwise returns 0. If all values are constants, all values are evaluated according to the type of expr and sorted. The search for the item is then done using a binary search. This means IN is very quick if the IN value list consists entirely of constants. If expr is a case-sensitive string expression, the string comparison is performed in case-sensitive fashion:

```
mysql> SELECT 2 IN (0,3,5,'wefwf');
        -> 0
mysql> SELECT 'wefwf' IN (0,3,5,'wefwf');
        -> 1
```

expr NOT IN (value, . . .)

Same as NOT (expr IN (value, . . .)).

ISNULL(expr)

If expr is NULL, ISNULL() returns 1, otherwise it returns 0:

```
mysql> SELECT ISNULL(1+1);
        -> 0
mysql> SELECT ISNULL(1/0);
        -> 1
```

Note that a comparison of NULL values using = will always be false!

COALESCE(list)

Returns first non-NULL element in list:

```
mysql> SELECT COALESCE(NULL,1);
        -> 1
mysql> SELECT COALESCE(NULL,NULL,NULL);
        -> NULL
```

INTERVAL(N,N1,N2,N3, . . .)

Returns 0 if N < N1, 1 if N < N2, and so on. All arguments are treated as integers. It is required that N1 < N2 < N3 < . . . < Nn for this function to work correctly. This is because a binary search is used (very fast):

```
mysql> SELECT INTERVAL(23, 1, 15, 17, 30, 44, 200);
        -> 3
mysql> SELECT INTERVAL(10, 1, 10, 100, 1000);
        -> 2
mysql> SELECT INTERVAL(22, 23, 30, 44, 200);
        -> 0
```

If you are comparing a case-sensitive string with any of the standard operators (=, <> . . . , but not LIKE) the end space will be ignored.

```
mysql> SELECT "a" ="A ";
        -> 1
```

6.3.1.3 Logical operators

All logical functions return 1 (TRUE), 0 (FALSE), or NULL (unknown, which is in most cases the same as FALSE):

NOT
!

Logical NOT. Returns 1 if the argument is 0, otherwise returns 0. Exception: NOT NULL returns NULL:

```
mysql> SELECT NOT 1;
        -> 0
mysql> SELECT NOT NULL;
        -> NULL
mysql> SELECT ! (1+1);
        -> 0
mysql> SELECT ! 1+1;
        -> 1
```

The last example returns 1 because the expression evaluates the same way as (!1)+1.

OR
|| Logical OR. Returns 1 if either argument is not 0 and not NULL:

```
mysql> SELECT 1 || 0;
        -> 1
mysql> SELECT 0 || 0;
        -> 0
mysql> SELECT 1 || NULL;
        -> 1
```

AND

&& Logical AND. Returns 0 if either argument is 0 or NULL, otherwise returns 1:

```
mysql> SELECT 1 && NULL;
        -> 0
mysql> SELECT 1 && 0;
        -> 0
```

6.3.1.4 Control flow functions

IFNULL(expr1,expr2)

If expr1 is not NULL, IFNULL() returns expr1, otherwise it returns expr2. IFNULL() returns a numeric or string value, depending on the context in which it is used:

```
mysql> SELECT IFNULL(1,0);
        -> 1
mysql> SELECT IFNULL(NULL,10);
        -> 10
mysql> SELECT IFNULL(1/0,10);
        -> 10
mysql> SELECT IFNULL(1/0,'yes');
        -> 'yes'
```

NULLIF(expr1,expr2)

If expr1 = expr2 is true, return NULL, otherwise return expr1. This is the same as CASE WHEN x = y THEN NULL ELSE x END:

```
mysql> SELECT NULLIF(1,1);
        -> NULL
mysql> SELECT NULLIF(1,2);
        -> 1
```

Note that expr1 is evaluated twice in MySQL if the arguments are equal.

IF(expr1,expr2,expr3)

If expr1 is TRUE (expr1 <> 0 and expr1 <> NULL), IF() returns expr2, otherwise it returns expr3. IF() returns a numeric or string value, depending on the context in which it is used:

```
mysql> SELECT IF(1>2,2,3);
        -> 3
mysql> SELECT IF(1<2,'yes','no');
        -> 'yes'
mysql> SELECT IF(STRCMP('test','test1'),'no','yes');
        -> 'no'
```

expr1 is evaluated as an integer value, which means that if you are testing floating-point or string values, you should do so using a comparison operation:

```
mysql> SELECT IF(0.1,1,0);
       -> 0
mysql> SELECT IF(0.1<>0,1,0);
       -> 1
```

In the first case, IF(0.1) returns 0 because 0.1 is converted to an integer value, resulting in a test of IF(0). This may not be what you expect. In the second case, the comparison tests the original floating-point value to see whether it is non-zero. The result of the comparison is used as an integer.

The default return type of IF() (which may matter when it is stored into a temporary table) is calculated in MySQL Version 3.23 as follows:

Expression	Return value
expr2 or expr3 returns a string	string
expr2 or expr3 returns a floating-point value	floating-point
expr2 or expr3 returns an integer	integer

If expr2 and expr3 are strings, then the result is case-sensitive if both strings are case-sensitive. (Starting from 3.23.51)

```
CASE value WHEN [compare-value] THEN result [WHEN [compare-value]
THEN result ...] [ELSE result] END
CASE WHEN [condition] THEN result [WHEN [condition] THEN result
...] [ELSE result] END
```

The first version returns the result where value=compare-value. The second version returns the result for the first condition, which is true. If there was no matching result value, the result after ELSE is returned. If there is no ELSE part, NULL is returned:

```
mysql> SELECT CASE 1 WHEN 1 THEN "one"
             WHEN 2 THEN "two" ELSE "more" END;
       -> "one"
mysql> SELECT CASE WHEN 1>0 THEN "true" ELSE "false" END;
       -> "true"
mysql> SELECT CASE BINARY "B" WHEN "a" THEN 1 WHEN "b" THEN 2 END;
       -> NULL
```

The type of the return value (INTEGER, DOUBLE or STRING) is the same as the type of the first returned value (the expression after the first THEN).

6.3.2 String Functions

String-valued functions return NULL if the length of the result would be greater than the max_allowed_packet server parameter. See Section 5.5.2, Tuning Server Parameters.

For functions that operate on string positions, the first position is numbered 1.

ASCII(str)

Returns the ASCII code value of the leftmost character of the string str. Returns 0 if str is the empty string. Returns NULL if str is NULL:

```
mysql> SELECT ASCII('2');
        -> 50
mysql> SELECT ASCII(2);
        -> 50
mysql> SELECT ASCII('dx');
        -> 100
```

See also the ORD() function.

ORD(str)

If the leftmost character of the string str is a multi-byte character, returns the code for that character, calculated from the ASCII code values of its constituent characters using this formula: ((first byte ASCII code)*256+(second byte ASCII code))[*256+third byte ASCII code...]. If the leftmost character is not a multi-byte character, returns the same value that the ASCII() function does:

```
mysql> SELECT ORD('2');
        -> 50
```

CONV(N,from_base,to_base)

Converts numbers between different number bases. Returns a string representation of the number N, converted from base from_base to base to_base. Returns NULL if any argument is NULL. The argument N is interpreted as an integer, but may be specified as an integer or a string. The minimum base is 2 and the maximum base is 36. If to_base is a negative number, N is regarded as a signed number. Otherwise, N is treated as unsigned. CONV works with 64-bit precision:

```
mysql> SELECT CONV("a",16,2);
        -> '1010'
mysql> SELECT CONV("6E",18,8);
        -> '172'
mysql> SELECT CONV(-17,10,-18);
        -> '-H'
mysql> SELECT CONV(10+"10"+'10'+0xa,10,10);
        -> '40'
```

BIN(N)

Returns a string representation of the binary value of N, where N is a longlong (BIGINT) number. This is equivalent to CONV(N,10,2). Returns NULL if N is NULL:

```
mysql> SELECT BIN(12);
        -> '1100'
```

OCT(N)

Returns a string representation of the octal value of N, where N is a longlong number. This is equivalent to CONV(N,10,8). Returns NULL if N is NULL:

```
mysql> SELECT OCT(12);
        -> '14'
```

HEX(N_or_S)

If N_OR_S is a number, returns a string representation of the hexadecimal value of N, where N is a longlong (BIGINT) number. This is equivalent to CONV(N,10,16).

If N_OR_S is a string, returns a hexadecimal string of N_OR_S where each character in N_OR_S is converted to 2 hexadecimal digits. This is the inverse of the 0xff strings.

```
mysql> SELECT HEX(255);
        -> 'FF'
mysql> SELECT HEX("abc");
        -> 616263
mysql> SELECT 0x616263;
        -> "abc"
```

CHAR(N, . . .)

CHAR() interprets the arguments as integers and returns a string consisting of the characters given by the ASCII code values of those integers. NULL values are skipped:

```
mysql> SELECT CHAR(77,121,83,81,'76');
        -> 'MySQL'
mysql> SELECT CHAR(77,77.3,'77.3');
        -> 'MMM'
```

CONCAT(str1,str2, . . .)

Returns the string that results from concatenating the arguments. Returns NULL if any argument is NULL. May have more than 2 arguments. A numeric argument is converted to the equivalent string form:

```
mysql> SELECT CONCAT('My', 'S', 'QL');
        -> 'MySQL'
mysql> SELECT CONCAT('My', NULL, 'QL');
        -> NULL
mysql> SELECT CONCAT(14.3);
        -> '14.3'
```

CONCAT_WS(separator, str1, str2, . . .)

CONCAT_WS() stands for CONCAT With Separator and is a special form of CONCAT(). The first argument is the separator for the rest of the arguments. The separator can be a string as well as the rest of the arguments. If the separator is NULL, the result will be NULL. The function will skip any NULLs and empty strings, after the separator argument. The separator will be added between the strings to be concatenated:

```
mysql> SELECT CONCAT_WS(",","First name","Second name","Last Name");
        -> 'First name,Second name,Last Name'
mysql> SELECT CONCAT_WS(",","First name",NULL,"Last Name");
        -> 'First name,Last Name'
```

LENGTH(str)
OCTET_LENGTH(str)
CHAR_LENGTH(str)
CHARACTER_LENGTH(str)

Returns the length of the string str:

```
mysql> SELECT LENGTH('text');
      -> 4
mysql> SELECT OCTET_LENGTH('text');
      -> 4
```

Note that for CHAR_LENGTH() and CHARACTER_LENGTH(), multi-byte characters are only counted once.

BIT_LENGTH(str)

Returns the length of the string str in bits:

```
mysql> SELECT BIT_LENGTH('text');
      -> 32
```

LOCATE(substr,str)
POSITION(substr IN str)

Returns the position of the first occurrence of substring substr in string str. Returns 0 if substr is not in str:

```
mysql> SELECT LOCATE('bar', 'foobarbar');
      -> 4
mysql> SELECT LOCATE('xbar', 'foobar');
      -> 0
```

This function is multi-byte safe. In MySQL 3.23 this function is case- insensitive, while in 4.0 it's only case-insensitive if either argument is a binary string.

LOCATE(substr,str,pos)

Returns the position of the first occurrence of substring substr in string str, starting at position pos. Returns 0 if substr is not in str:

```
mysql> SELECT LOCATE('bar', 'foobarbar',5);
      -> 7
```

This function is multi-byte safe. In MySQL 3.23 this function is case- insensitive, while in 4.0 it's only case-insensitive if either argument is a binary string.

INSTR(str,substr)

Returns the position of the first occurrence of substring substr in string str. This is the same as the two-argument form of LOCATE(), except that the arguments are swapped:

```
mysql> SELECT INSTR('foobarbar', 'bar');
      -> 4
mysql> SELECT INSTR('xbar', 'foobar');
      -> 0
```

This function is multi-byte safe. In MySQL 3.23 this function is case- insensitive, while in 4.0 it's only case-insensitive if either argument is a binary string.

LPAD(str,len,padstr)

Returns the string str, left-padded with the string padstr until str is len characters long. If str is longer than len' it will be shortened to len characters.

```
mysql> SELECT LPAD('hi',4,'??');
        -> '??hi'
```

RPAD(str,len,padstr)

Returns the string str, right-padded with the string padstr until str is len characters long. If str is longer than len' then it will be shortened to len characters.

```
mysql> SELECT RPAD('hi',5,'?');
        -> 'hi???'
```

LEFT(str,len)

Returns the leftmost len characters from the string str:

```
mysql> SELECT LEFT('foobarbar', 5);
        -> 'fooba'
```

This function is multi-byte safe.

RIGHT(str,len)

Returns the rightmost len characters from the string str:

```
mysql> SELECT RIGHT('foobarbar', 4);
        -> 'rbar'
```

This function is multi-byte safe.

SUBSTRING(str,pos,len)
SUBSTRING(str FROM pos FOR len)
MID(str,pos,len)

Returns a substring len characters long from string str, starting at position pos. The variant form that uses FROM is ANSI SQL92 syntax:

```
mysql> SELECT SUBSTRING('Quadratically',5,6);
        -> 'ratica'
```

This function is multi-byte safe.

SUBSTRING(str,pos)
SUBSTRING(str FROM pos)

Returns a substring from string str starting at position pos:

```
mysql> SELECT SUBSTRING('Quadratically',5);
        -> 'ratically'
mysql> SELECT SUBSTRING('foobarbar' FROM 4);
        -> 'barbar'
```

This function is multi-byte safe.

SUBSTRING_INDEX(str,delim,count)

Returns the substring from string str before count occurrences of the delimiter delim. If count is positive, everything to the left of the final delimiter (counting from the left) is returned. If count is negative, everything to the right of the final delimiter (counting from the right) is returned:

```
mysql> SELECT SUBSTRING_INDEX('www.mysql.com', '.', 2);
        -> 'www.mysql'
mysql> SELECT SUBSTRING_INDEX('www.mysql.com', '.', -2);
        -> 'mysql.com'
```

This function is multi-byte safe.

LTRIM(str)

Returns the string str with leading space characters removed:

```
mysql> SELECT LTRIM('  barbar');
        -> 'barbar'
```

RTRIM(str)

Returns the string str with trailing space characters removed:

```
mysql> SELECT RTRIM('barbar   ');
        -> 'barbar'
```

This function is multi-byte safe.

TRIM([[BOTH | LEADING | TRAILING] [remstr] FROM] str)

Returns the string str with all remstr prefixes and/or suffixes removed. If none of the specifiers BOTH, LEADING or TRAILING is given, BOTH is assumed. If remstr is not specified, spaces are removed:

```
mysql> SELECT TRIM('  bar   ');
        -> 'bar'
mysql> SELECT TRIM(LEADING 'x' FROM 'xxxbarxxx');
        -> 'barxxx'
mysql> SELECT TRIM(BOTH 'x' FROM 'xxxbarxxx');
        -> 'bar'
mysql> SELECT TRIM(TRAILING 'xyz' FROM 'barxxyz');
        -> 'barx'
```

This function is multi-byte safe.

SOUNDEX(str)

Returns a soundex string from str. Two strings that sound almost the same should have identical soundex strings. A standard soundex string is 4 characters long, but the SOUNDEX() function returns an arbitrarily long string. You can use SUBSTRING() on the result to get a standard soundex string. All non-alphanumeric characters are ignored in the given string. All international alpha characters outside the A-Z range are treated as vowels:

```
mysql> SELECT SOUNDEX('Hello');
        -> 'H400'
mysql> SELECT SOUNDEX('Quadratically');
        -> 'Q36324'
```

SPACE(N)

Returns a string consisting of N space characters:

```
mysql> SELECT SPACE(6);
        -> '      '
```

REPLACE(str,from_str,to_str)

Returns the string str with all occurrences of the string from_str replaced by the string to_str:

```
mysql> SELECT REPLACE('www.mysql.com', 'w', 'Ww');
        -> 'WwWwWw.mysql.com'
```

This function is multi-byte safe.

REPEAT(str,count)

Returns a string consisting of the string str repeated count times. If count <= 0, returns an empty string. Returns NULL if str or count are NULL:

```
mysql> SELECT REPEAT('MySQL', 3);
        -> 'MySQLMySQLMySQL'
```

REVERSE(str)

Returns the string str with the order of the characters reversed:

```
mysql> SELECT REVERSE('abc');
        -> 'cba'
```

This function is multi-byte safe.

INSERT(str,pos,len,newstr)

Returns the string str, with the substring beginning at position pos and len characters long replaced by the string newstr:

```
mysql> SELECT INSERT('Quadratic', 3, 4, 'What');
        -> 'QuWhattic'
```

This function is multi-byte safe.

ELT(N,str1,str2,str3, ...)

Returns str1 if N = 1, str2 if N = 2, and so on. Returns NULL if N is less than 1 or greater than the number of arguments. ELT() is the complement of FIELD():

```
mysql> SELECT ELT(1, 'ej', 'Heja', 'hej', 'foo');
        -> 'ej'
mysql> SELECT ELT(4, 'ej', 'Heja', 'hej', 'foo');
        -> 'foo'
```

`FIELD(str,str1,str2,str3, ... )`

Returns the index of `str` in the `str1`, `str2`, `str3`, . . . list. Returns 0 if `str` is not found. `FIELD()` is the complement of `ELT()`:

```
mysql> SELECT FIELD('ej', 'Hej', 'ej', 'Heja', 'hej', 'foo');
        -> 2
mysql> SELECT FIELD('fo', 'Hej', 'ej', 'Heja', 'hej', 'foo');
        -> 0
```

`FIND_IN_SET(str,strlist)`

Returns a value 1 to N if the string `str` is in the list `strlist` consisting of N substrings. A string list is a string composed of substrings separated by , characters. If the first argument is a constant string and the second is a column of type `SET`, the `FIND_IN_SET()` function is optimised to use bit arithmetic! Returns 0 if `str` is not in `strlist` or if `strlist` is the empty string. Returns `NULL` if either argument is `NULL`. This function will not work properly if the first argument contains a ,:

```
mysql> SELECT FIND_IN_SET('b','a,b,c,d');
        -> 2
```

`MAKE_SET(bits,str1,str2, ... )`

Returns a set (a string containing substrings separated by , characters) consisting of the strings that have the corresponding bit in `bits` set. `str1` corresponds to bit 0, `str2` to bit 1, etc. `NULL` strings in `str1`, `str2`, . . . are not appended to the result:

```
mysql> SELECT MAKE_SET(1,'a','b','c');
        -> 'a'
mysql> SELECT MAKE_SET(1 | 4,'hello','nice','world');
        -> 'hello,world'
mysql> SELECT MAKE_SET(0,'a','b','c');
        -> ''
```

`EXPORT_SET(bits,on,off,[separator, [number_of_bits]])`

Returns a string where for every bit set in 'bit', you get an 'on' string and for every reset bit you get an 'off' string. Each string is separated with 'separator' (default ',') and only 'number_of_bits' (default 64) of 'bits' is used:

```
mysql> SELECT EXPORT_SET(5,'Y','N',',',4)
        -> Y,N,Y,N
```

`LCASE(str)`

`LOWER(str)`

Returns the string `str` with all characters changed to lowercase according to the current character set mapping (the default is ISO-8859-1 Latin1):

```
mysql> SELECT LCASE('QUADRATICALLY');
        -> 'quadratically'
```

This function is multi-byte safe.

UCASE(str)
UPPER(str)

> Returns the string str with all characters changed to uppercase according to the current character set mapping (the default is ISO-8859-1 Latin1):

```
mysql> SELECT UCASE('Hej');
        -> 'HEJ'
```

> This function is multi-byte safe.

LOAD_FILE(file_name)

> Reads the file and returns the file contents as a string. The file must be on the server, you must specify the full pathname to the file, and you must have the **file** privilege. The file must be readable by all and be smaller than max_allowed_packet.

> If the file doesn't exist or can't be read due to one of these reasons, the function returns NULL:

```
mysql> UPDATE tbl_name
          SET blob_column=LOAD_FILE("/tmp/picture")
          WHERE id=1;
```

If you are not using MySQL Version 3.23, you have to read the file inside your application and create an INSERT statement to update the database with the file information. One way to do this, if you are using the MySQL++ library, can be found at http://www.mysql.com/documentation/mysql++/mysql++-examples.html.

MySQL automatically converts numbers to strings as necessary, and vice versa:

```
mysql> SELECT 1+"1";
        -> 2
mysql> SELECT CONCAT(2,' test');
        -> '2 test'
```

If you want to convert a number to a string explicitly, pass it as the argument to CON-CAT().

If a string function is given a binary string as an argument, the resulting string is also a binary string. A number converted to a string is treated as a binary string. This only affects comparisons.

6.3.2.1 String comparison functions

Normally, if any expression in a string comparison is case-sensitive, the comparison is performed in case-sensitive fashion.

expr LIKE pat [ESCAPE 'escape-char']

> Pattern matching using SQL simple regular expression comparison. Returns 1 (TRUE) or 0 (FALSE). With LIKE you can use the following two wildcard characters in the pattern:

Char	Description
%	Matches any number of characters, even zero characters
_	Matches exactly one character

```
mysql> SELECT 'David!' LIKE 'David_';
        -> 1
mysql> SELECT 'David!' LIKE '%D%v%';
        -> 1
```

To test for literal instances of a wildcard character, precede the character with the escape character. If you don't specify the ESCAPE character, \ is assumed:

String	Description
\%	Matches one % character
_	Matches one _ character

```
mysql> SELECT 'David!' LIKE 'David\_';
        -> 0
mysql> SELECT 'David_' LIKE 'David\_';
        -> 1
```

To specify a different escape character, use the ESCAPE clause:

```
mysql> SELECT 'David_' LIKE 'David|_' ESCAPE '|';
        -> 1
```

The following two statements illustrate that string comparisons are case-insensitive unless one of the operands is a binary string:

```
mysql> SELECT 'abc' LIKE 'ABC';
        -> 1
mysql> SELECT 'abc' LIKE BINARY 'ABC';
        -> 0
```

LIKE is allowed on numeric expressions! (This is a MySQL extension to the ANSI SQL LIKE.)

```
mysql> SELECT 10 LIKE '1%';
        -> 1
```

Note: because MySQL uses the C escape syntax in strings (for example, \n), you must double any \ that you use in your LIKE strings. For example, to search for \n, specify it as \\n. To search for \, specify it as \\\\ (the backslashes are stripped once by the parser and another time when the pattern match is done, leaving a single backslash to be matched).

`expr NOT LIKE pat [ESCAPE 'escape-char']`

Same as NOT (expr LIKE pat [ESCAPE 'escape-char']).

`expr REGEXP pat`

`expr RLIKE pat`

Performs a pattern match of a string expression expr against a pattern pat. The pattern can be an extended regular expression. See Appendix F. Returns 1 if expr matches pat, otherwise returns 0. RLIKE is a synonym for REGEXP, provided for mSQL compatibility. Note: because MySQL uses the C escape syntax in strings (for example, \n), you must double any \ that you use in your REGEXP strings. As of MySQL Version 3.23.4, REGEXP is case-insensitive for normal (not binary) strings:

```
mysql> SELECT 'Monty!' REGEXP 'm%y%%';
        -> 0
mysql> SELECT 'Monty!' REGEXP '.*';
        -> 1
mysql> SELECT 'new*\n*line' REGEXP 'new\\*.\\*line';
        -> 1
mysql> SELECT "a" REGEXP "A", "a" REGEXP BINARY "A";
        -> 1  0
mysql> SELECT "a" REGEXP "^[a-d]";
        -> 1
```

REGEXP and RLIKE use the current character set (ISO-8859-1 Latin1 by default) when deciding the type of a character.

`expr NOT REGEXP pat`

`expr NOT RLIKE pat`

Same as NOT (expr REGEXP pat).

`STRCMP(expr1,expr2)`

STRCMP() returns 0 if the strings are the same, −1 if the first argument is smaller than the second according to the current sort order, and 1 otherwise:

```
mysql> SELECT STRCMP('text', 'text2');
        -> -1
mysql> SELECT STRCMP('text2', 'text');
        -> 1
mysql> SELECT STRCMP('text', 'text');
        -> 0
```

`MATCH (col1,col2,...) AGAINST (expr)`

`MATCH (col1,col2,...) AGAINST (expr IN BOOLEAN MODE)`

MATCH ... AGAINST() is used for full-text search and returns a relevance similarity measure between the text in columns (col1,col2,...) and the query expr. Relevance is a positive floating-point number. Zero relevance means no similarity. MATCH ... AGAINST() is available in MySQL Versions 3.23.23 or later. IN BOOLEAN MODE extension was added in Version 4.0.1. For details and usage examples, see Section 6.8, MySQL Full-Text Search.

6.3.2.2 Case sensitivity

BINARY0]

The BINARY operator casts the string following it to a binary string. This is an easy way to force a column comparison to be case-sensitive even if the column isn't defined as BINARY or BLOB:

```
mysql> SELECT "a" = "A";
        -> 1
mysql> SELECT BINARY "a" = "A";
        -> 0
```

BINARY string is shorthand for CAST(string AS BINARY). See Section 6.3.5, Cast Functions. BINARY was introduced in MySQL Version 3.23.0.

Note that in some context MySQL will not be able to use the index efficiently when you cast an indexed column to BINARY.

If you want to compare a blob case-insensitively you can always convert the blob to uppercase before doing the comparison:

```
SELECT 'A' LIKE UPPER(blob_col) FROM table_name;
```

We plan to soon introduce casting between different character sets to make string comparison even more flexible.

6.3.3 Numeric Functions

6.3.3.1 Arithmetic operations

The usual arithmetic operators are available. Note that in the case of −, +, and *, the result is calculated with BIGINT (64-bit) precision if both arguments are integers! If one of the arguments is an unsigned integer, and the other argument is also an integer, the result will be an unsigned integer. See Section 6.3.5, Cast Functions.

+   Addition:

```
mysql> SELECT 3+5;
        -> 8
```

−   Subtraction:

```
mysql> SELECT 3-5;
        -> -2
```

*   Multiplication:

```
mysql> SELECT 3*5;
        -> 15
mysql> SELECT 18014398509481984*18014398509481984.0;
        -> 324518553658426726783156020576256.0
mysql> SELECT 18014398509481984*18014398509481984;
        -> 0
```

The result of the last expression is incorrect because the result of the integer multiplication exceeds the 64-bit range of BIGINT calculations.

/   Division:

```
mysql> SELECT 3/5;
        -> 0.60
```

Division by zero produces a NULL result:

```
mysql> SELECT 102/(1-1);
        -> NULL
```

A division will be calculated with BIGINT arithmetic only if performed in a context where its result is converted to an integer!

6.3.3.2 Mathematical functions

All mathematical functions return NULL in case of an error.

–   Unary minus. Changes the sign of the argument:

```
mysql> SELECT - 2;
        -> -2
```

Note that if this operator is used with a BIGINT, the return value is a BIGINT! This means that you should avoid using – on integers that may have the value of -2^{63}!

ABS(X)

Returns the absolute value of X:

```
mysql> SELECT ABS(2);
        -> 2
mysql> SELECT ABS(-32);
        -> 32
```

This function is safe to use with BIGINT values.

SIGN(X)

Returns the sign of the argument as –1, 0, or 1, depending on whether X is negative, zero, or positive:

```
mysql> SELECT SIGN(-32);
        -> -1
mysql> SELECT SIGN(0);
        -> 0
mysql> SELECT SIGN(234);
        -> 1
```

MOD(N,M)

%   Modulo (like the % operator in C). Returns the remainder of N divided by M:

```
mysql> SELECT MOD(234, 10);
        -> 4
mysql> SELECT 253 % 7;
```

```
                    -> 1
mysql> SELECT MOD(29,9);
                    -> 2
```

This function is safe to use with BIGINT values.

FLOOR(X)

Returns the largest integer value not greater than X:

```
mysql> SELECT FLOOR(1.23);
       -> 1
mysql> SELECT FLOOR(-1.23);
       -> -2
```

Note that the return value is converted to a BIGINT!

CEILING(X)

Returns the smallest integer value not less than X:

```
mysql> SELECT CEILING(1.23);
       -> 2
mysql> SELECT CEILING(-1.23);
       -> -1
```

Note that the return value is converted to a BIGINT!

ROUND(X)

Returns the argument X, rounded to the nearest integer:

```
mysql> SELECT ROUND(-1.23);
       -> -1
mysql> SELECT ROUND(-1.58);
       -> -2
mysql> SELECT ROUND(1.58);
       -> 2
```

Note that the behavior of ROUND() when the argument is halfway between two integers depends on the C library implementation. Some round to the nearest even number, always up, always down, or always toward zero. If you need one kind of rounding, you should use a well-defined function like TRUNCATE() or FLOOR() instead.

ROUND(X,D)

Returns the argument X, rounded to a number with D decimals. If D is 0, the result will have no decimal point or fractional part:

```
mysql> SELECT ROUND(1.298, 1);
       -> 1.3
mysql> SELECT ROUND(1.298, 0);
       -> 1
```

EXP(X)

Returns the value of e (the base of natural logarithms) raised to the power of X:

```
mysql> SELECT EXP(2);
       -> 7.389056
mysql> SELECT EXP(-2);
       -> 0.135335
```

LOG(X)

Returns the natural logarithm of X:

```
mysql> SELECT LOG(2);
       -> 0.693147
mysql> SELECT LOG(-2);
       -> NULL
```

If you want the log of a number X to some arbitary base B, use the formula LOG(X)/LOG(B).

LOG10(X)

Returns the base-10 logarithm of X:

```
mysql> SELECT LOG10(2);
       -> 0.301030
mysql> SELECT LOG10(100);
       -> 2.000000
mysql> SELECT LOG10(-100);
       -> NULL
```

POW(X,Y)
POWER(X,Y)

Returns the value of X raised to the power of Y:

```
mysql> SELECT POW(2,2);
       -> 4.000000
mysql> SELECT POW(2,-2);
       -> 0.250000
```

SQRT(X)

Returns the non-negative square root of X:

```
mysql> SELECT SQRT(4);
       -> 2.000000
mysql> SELECT SQRT(20);
       -> 4.472136
```

PI()

Returns the value of PI. The default shown number of decimals is 5, but MySQL internally uses the full double precision for PI.

```
mysql> SELECT PI();
       -> 3.141593
mysql> SELECT PI()+0.000000000000000000;
       -> 3.141592653589793116
```

COS(X)

Returns the cosine of X, where X is given in radians:

```
mysql> SELECT COS(PI());
        -> -1.000000
```

SIN(X)

Returns the sine of X, where X is given in radians:

```
mysql> SELECT SIN(PI());
        -> 0.000000
```

TAN(X)

Returns the tangent of X, where X is given in radians:

```
mysql> SELECT TAN(PI()+1);
        -> 1.557408
```

ACOS(X)

Returns the arc cosine of X—that is, the value whose cosine is X. Returns NULL if X is not in the range −1 to 1:

```
mysql> SELECT ACOS(1);
        -> 0.000000
mysql> SELECT ACOS(1.0001);
        -> NULL
mysql> SELECT ACOS(0);
        -> 1.570796
```

ASIN(X)

Returns the arc sine of X—that is, the value whose sine is X. Returns NULL if X is not in the range −1 to 1:

```
mysql> SELECT ASIN(0.2);
        -> 0.201358
mysql> SELECT ASIN('foo');
        -> 0.000000
```

ATAN(X)

Returns the arc tangent of X—that is, the value whose tangent is X:

```
mysql> SELECT ATAN(2);
        -> 1.107149
mysql> SELECT ATAN(-2);
        -> -1.107149
```

ATAN(Y,X)
ATAN2(Y,X)

Returns the arc tangent of the two variables X and Y. It is similar to calculating the arc tangent of Y / X, except that the signs of both arguments are used to determine the quadrant of the result:

```
mysql> SELECT ATAN(-2,2);
        -> -0.785398
mysql> SELECT ATAN2(PI(),0);
        -> 1.570796
```

COT(X)

Returns the cotangent of X:

```
mysql> SELECT COT(12);
        -> -1.57267341
mysql> SELECT COT(0);
        -> NULL
```

RAND()
RAND(N)

Returns a random floating-point value in the range 0 to 1.0. If an integer argument N is specified, it is used as the seed value:

```
mysql> SELECT RAND();
        -> 0.9233482386203
mysql> SELECT RAND(20);
        -> 0.15888261251047
mysql> SELECT RAND(20);
        -> 0.15888261251047
mysql> SELECT RAND();
        -> 0.63553050033332
mysql> SELECT RAND();
        -> 0.70100469486881
```

You can't use a column with RAND() values in an ORDER BY clause because ORDER BY would evaluate the column multiple times. In MySQL Version 3.23, you can, however, do SELECT * FROM table_name ORDER BY RAND().

This is useful to get a random sample of a set SELECT * FROM table1, table2 WHERE a=b AND c<d ORDER BY RAND() LIMIT 1000.

Note that a RAND() in a WHERE clause will be re-evaluated every time the WHERE is executed.

RAND() is not meant to be a perfect random generator, but instead a fast way to generate ad hoc random numbers that will be portable between platforms for the same MySQL version.

LEAST(X,Y, . . .)

With two or more arguments, returns the smallest (minimum-valued) argument. The arguments are compared using the following rules:

- If the return value is used in an INTEGER context, or all arguments are integer-valued, they are compared as integers.

- If the return value is used in a REAL context, or all arguments are real-valued, they are compared as reals.

- If any argument is a case-sensitive string, the arguments are compared as case-sensitive strings.

- In other cases, the arguments are compared as case-insensitive strings:

```
mysql> SELECT LEAST(2,0);
        -> 0
mysql> SELECT LEAST(34.0,3.0,5.0,767.0);
        -> 3.0
mysql> SELECT LEAST("B","A","C");
        -> "A"
```

In MySQL versions prior to Version 3.22.5, you can use MIN() instead of LEAST.

GREATEST(X,Y, . . .)

Returns the largest (maximum-valued) argument. The arguments are compared using the same rules as for LEAST:

```
mysql> SELECT GREATEST(2,0);
        -> 2
mysql> SELECT GREATEST(34.0,3.0,5.0,767.0);
        -> 767.0
mysql> SELECT GREATEST("B","A","C");
        -> "C"
```

In MySQL versions prior to Version 3.22.5, you can use MAX() instead of GREAT-EST.

DEGREES(X)

Returns the argument X, converted from radians to degrees:

```
mysql> SELECT DEGREES(PI());
        -> 180.000000
```

RADIANS(X)

Returns the argument X, converted from degrees to radians:

```
mysql> SELECT RADIANS(90);
        -> 1.570796
```

TRUNCATE(X,D)

Returns the number X, truncated to D decimals. If D is 0, the result will have no decimal point or fractional part:

```
mysql> SELECT TRUNCATE(1.223,1);
        -> 1.2
mysql> SELECT TRUNCATE(1.999,1);
        -> 1.9
mysql> SELECT TRUNCATE(1.999,0);
        -> 1
```

Note that as decimal numbers are normally not stored as exact numbers in computers, but as double values, you may be fooled by the following result:

```
mysql> SELECT TRUNCATE(10.28*100,0);
        -> 1027
```

This happens because 10.28 is actually stored as something like 10.2799999999999999.

6.3.4 Date and Time Functions

See Section 6.2.2, Date and Time Types, for a description of the range of values each type has and the valid formats in which date and time values may be specified.

Here is an example that uses date functions. The following query selects all records with a date_col value from within the last 30 days:

```
mysql> SELECT something FROM tbl_name
            WHERE TO_DAYS(NOW()) - TO_DAYS(date_col) <= 30;
```

DAYOFWEEK(date)

Returns the weekday index

for date (1 = Sunday, 2 = Monday, ... 7 = Saturday). These index values correspond to the ODBC standard:

```
mysql> SELECT DAYOFWEEK('1998-02-03');
        -> 3
```

WEEKDAY(date)

Returns the weekday index for date (0 = Monday, 1 = Tuesday, ... 6 = Sunday):

```
mysql> SELECT WEEKDAY('1997-10-04 22:23:00');
        -> 5
mysql> SELECT WEEKDAY('1997-11-05');
        -> 2
```

DAYOFMONTH(date)

Returns the day of the month for date, in the range 1 to 31:

```
mysql> SELECT DAYOFMONTH('1998-02-03');
        -> 3
```

DAYOFYEAR(date)

Returns the day of the year for date, in the range 1 to 366:

```
mysql> SELECT DAYOFYEAR('1998-02-03');
        -> 34
```

MONTH(date)

Returns the month for date, in the range 1 to 12:

```
mysql> SELECT MONTH('1998-02-03');
        -> 2
```

`DAYNAME(date)`

Returns the name of the weekday for date:

```
mysql> SELECT DAYNAME("1998-02-05");
        -> 'Thursday'
```

`MONTHNAME(date)`

Returns the name of the month for date:

```
mysql> SELECT MONTHNAME("1998-02-05");
        -> 'February'
```

`QUARTER(date)`

Returns the quarter of the year for date, in the range 1 to 4:

```
mysql> SELECT QUARTER('98-04-01');
        -> 2
```

`WEEK(date)`
`WEEK(date,first)`

With a single argument, returns the week for date, in the range 0 to 53 (yes, there may be the beginnings of a week 53), for locations where Sunday is the first day of the week. The two-argument form of `WEEK()` allows you to specify whether the week starts on Sunday or Monday. The week starts on Sunday if the second argument is 0, on Monday if the second argument is 1:

```
mysql> SELECT WEEK('1998-02-20');
        -> 7
mysql> SELECT WEEK('1998-02-20',0);
        -> 7
mysql> SELECT WEEK('1998-02-20',1);
        -> 8
mysql> SELECT WEEK('1998-12-31',1);
        -> 53
```

Note: in Version 4.0, `WEEK(#,0)` was changed to match the calendar in the USA.

`YEAR(date)`

Returns the year for date, in the range 1000 to 9999:

```
mysql> SELECT YEAR('98-02-03');
        -> 1998
```

`YEARWEEK(date)`
`YEARWEEK(date,first)`

Returns year and week for a date. The second arguments works exactly like the second argument to `WEEK()`. Note that the year may be different from the year in the date argument for the first and the last week of the year:

```
mysql> SELECT YEARWEEK('1987-01-01');
        -> 198653
```

HOUR(time)

Returns the hour for time, in the range 0 to 23:

```
mysql> SELECT HOUR('10:05:03');
        -> 10
```

MINUTE(time)

Returns the minute for time, in the range 0 to 59:

```
mysql> SELECT MINUTE('98-02-03 10:05:03');
        -> 5
```

SECOND(time)

Returns the second for time, in the range 0 to 59:

```
mysql> SELECT SECOND('10:05:03');
        -> 3
```

PERIOD_ADD(P,N)

Adds N months to period P (in the format YYMM or YYYYMM). Returns a value in the format YYYYMM.

Note that the period argument P is **not** a date value:

```
mysql> SELECT PERIOD_ADD(9801,2);
        -> 199803
```

PERIOD_DIFF(P1,P2)

Returns the number of months between periods P1 and P2. P1 and P2 should be in the format YYMM or YYYYMM.

Note that the period arguments P1 and P2 are **not** date values:

```
mysql> SELECT PERIOD_DIFF(9802,199703);
        -> 11
```

DATE_ADD(date,INTERVAL expr type)
DATE_SUB(date,INTERVAL expr type)
ADDDATE(date,INTERVAL expr type)
SUBDATE(date,INTERVAL expr type)

These functions perform date arithmetic. They are new for MySQL Version 3.22. ADDDATE() and SUBDATE() are synonyms for DATE_ADD() and DATE_SUB().

In MySQL Version 3.23, you can use + and – instead of DATE_ADD() and DATE_SUB() if the expression on the right side is a date or datetime column. (See example below.)

date is a DATETIME or DATE value specifying the starting date. expr is an expression specifying the interval value to be added or subtracted from the starting date. expr is a string; it may start with a – for negative intervals. type is a keyword indicating how the expression should be interpreted.

The related function EXTRACT(type FROM date) returns the 'type' interval from the date.

The following table shows how the type and expr arguments are related:

type value	Expected expr format
SECOND	SECONDS
MINUTE	MINUTES
HOUR	HOURS
DAY	DAYS
MONTH	MONTHS
YEAR	YEARS
MINUTE_SECOND	"MINUTES:SECONDS"
HOUR_MINUTE	"HOURS:MINUTES"
DAY_HOUR	"DAYS HOURS"
YEAR_MONTH	"YEARS-MONTHS"
HOUR_SECOND	"HOURS:MINUTES:SECONDS"
DAY_MINUTE	"DAYS HOURS:MINUTES"
DAY_SECOND	"DAYS HOURS:MINUTES:SECONDS"

MySQL allows any punctuation delimiter in the expr format. Those shown in the table are the suggested delimiters. If the date argument is a DATE value and your calculations involve only YEAR, MONTH, and DAY parts (that is, no time parts), the result is a DATE value. Otherwise, the result is a DATETIME value:

```
mysql> SELECT "1997-12-31 23:59:59" + INTERVAL 1 SECOND;
        -> 1998-01-01 00:00:00
mysql> SELECT INTERVAL 1 DAY + "1997-12-31";
        -> 1998-01-01
mysql> SELECT "1998-01-01" - INTERVAL 1 SECOND;
        -> 1997-12-31 23:59:59
mysql> SELECT DATE_ADD("1997-12-31 23:59:59",
    ->                 INTERVAL 1 SECOND);
        -> 1998-01-01 00:00:00
mysql> SELECT DATE_ADD("1997-12-31 23:59:59",
    ->                 INTERVAL 1 DAY);
        -> 1998-01-01 23:59:59
mysql> SELECT DATE_ADD("1997-12-31 23:59:59",
    ->                 INTERVAL "1:1" MINUTE_SECOND);
        -> 1998-01-01 00:01:00
mysql> SELECT DATE_SUB("1998-01-01 00:00:00",
    ->                 INTERVAL "1 1:1:1" DAY_SECOND);
        -> 1997-12-30 22:58:59
mysql> SELECT DATE_ADD("1998-01-01 00:00:00",
    ->                 INTERVAL "-1 10" DAY_HOUR);
        -> 1997-12-30 14:00:00
mysql> SELECT DATE_SUB("1998-01-02", INTERVAL 31 DAY);
        -> 1997-12-02
```

If you specify an interval value that is too short (does not include all the interval parts that would be expected from the type keyword), MySQL assumes you have left out the leftmost parts of the interval value. For example, if you specify a type of DAY_SECOND, the value of expr is expected to have days, hours, minutes, and seconds parts. If you specify a value like "1:10", MySQL assumes that the days and hours parts are missing and the value represents minutes and seconds. In other words, "1:10" DAY_SECOND is interpreted in such a way that it is equivalent to "1:10" MINUTE_SECOND. This is analogous to the way that MySQL interprets TIME values as representing elapsed time rather than as time of day.

Note that if you add or subtract a date value against something that contains a time part, the date value will be automatically converted to a datetime value:

```
mysql> SELECT DATE_ADD("1999-01-01", INTERVAL 1 DAY);
        -> 1999-01-02
mysql> SELECT DATE_ADD("1999-01-01", INTERVAL 1 HOUR);
        -> 1999-01-01 01:00:00
```

If you use really incorrect dates, the result is NULL. If you add MONTH, YEAR_MONTH, or YEAR and the resulting date has a day that is larger than the maximum day for the new month, the day is adjusted to the maximum days in the new month:

```
mysql> SELECT DATE_ADD('1998-01-30', INTERVAL 1 MONTH);
        -> 1998-02-28
```

Note from the preceding example that the word INTERVAL and the type keyword are not case-sensitive.

EXTRACT(type FROM date)

The EXTRACT() function uses the same kinds of interval type specifiers as DATE_ADD() or DATE_SUB(), but extracts parts from the date rather than performing date arithmetic:

```
mysql> SELECT EXTRACT(YEAR FROM "1999-07-02");
        -> 1999
mysql> SELECT EXTRACT(YEAR_MONTH FROM "1999-07-02 01:02:03");
        -> 199907
mysql> SELECT EXTRACT(DAY_MINUTE FROM "1999-07-02 01:02:03");
        -> 20102
```

TO_DAYS(date)

Given a date date, returns a daynumber (the number of days since year 0):

```
mysql> SELECT TO_DAYS(950501);
        -> 728779
mysql> SELECT TO_DAYS('1997-10-07');
        -> 729669
```

TO_DAYS() is not intended for use with values that precede the advent of the Gregorian calendar (1582) because it doesn't take into account the days that were lost when the calendar was changed.

FROM_DAYS (N)

Given a daynumber N, returns a DATE value:

```
mysql> SELECT FROM_DAYS(729669);
        -> '1997-10-07'
```

FROM_DAYS() is not intended for use with values that precede the advent of the Gregorian calendar (1582) because it doesn't take into account the days that were lost when the calendar was changed.

DATE_FORMAT(date, format)

Formats the date value according to the format string. The following specifiers may be used in the format string:

Specifier	Description
%M	Month name (January..December)
%W	Weekday name (Sunday..Saturday)
%D	Day of the month with English suffix (1st, 2nd, 3rd, etc.)
%Y	Year, numeric, 4 digits
%y	Year, numeric, 2 digits
%X	Year for the week where Sunday is the first day of the week, numeric, 4 digits, used with '%V'
%x	Year for the week, where Monday is the first day of the week, numeric, 4 digits, used with '%v'
%a	Abbreviated weekday name (Sun..Sat)
%d	Day of the month, numeric (00..31)
%e	Day of the month, numeric (0..31)
%m	Month, numeric (01..12)
%c	Month, numeric (1..12)
%b	Abbreviated month name (Jan..Dec)
%j	Day of year (001..366)
%H	Hour (00..23)
%k	Hour (0..23)
%h	Hour (01..12)
%I	Hour (01..12)
%l	Hour (1..12)
%i	Minutes, numeric (00..59)
%r	Time, 12-hour (hh:mm:ss [AP]M)
%T	Time, 24-hour (hh:mm:ss)
%S	Seconds (00..59)
%s	Seconds (00..59)
%p	AM or PM
%w	Day of the week (0=Sunday..6=Saturday)
%U	Week (0..53), where Sunday is the first day of the week
%u	Week (0..53), where Monday is the first day of the week

Specifier	Description
%V	Week (1..53), where Sunday is the first day of the week; used with '%X'
%v	Week (1..53), where Monday is the first day of the week; used with '%x'
%%	A literal %

All other characters are just copied to the result without interpretation:

```
mysql> SELECT DATE_FORMAT('1997-10-04 22:23:00', '%W %M %Y');
        -> 'Saturday October 1997'
mysql> SELECT DATE_FORMAT('1997-10-04 22:23:00', '%H:%i:%s');
        -> '22:23:00'
mysql> SELECT DATE_FORMAT('1997-10-04 22:23:00',
                          '%D %y %a %d %m %b %j');
        -> '4th 97 Sat 04 10 Oct 277'
mysql> SELECT DATE_FORMAT('1997-10-04 22:23:00',
                          '%H %k %I %r %T %S %w');
        -> '22 22 10 10:23:00 PM 22:23:00 00 6'
mysql> SELECT DATE_FORMAT('1999-01-01', '%X %V');
        -> '1998 52'
```

As of MySQL Version 3.23, the % character is required before format specifier characters. In earlier versions of MySQL, % was optional.

TIME_FORMAT(time,format)

This is used like the preceding DATE_FORMAT() function, but the format string may contain only those format specifiers that handle hours, minutes, and seconds. Other specifiers produce a NULL value or 0.

CURDATE()

CURRENT_DATE

Returns today's date as a value in 'YYYY-MM-DD' or YYYYMMDD format, depending on whether the function is used in a string or numeric context:

```
mysql> SELECT CURDATE();
        -> '1997-12-15'
mysql> SELECT CURDATE() + 0;
        -> 19971215
```

CURTIME()

CURRENT_TIME

Returns the current time as a value in 'HH:MM:SS' or HHMMSS format, depending on whether the function is used in a string or numeric context:

```
mysql> SELECT CURTIME();
        -> '23:50:26'
mysql> SELECT CURTIME() + 0;
        -> 235026
```

`NOW()`

`SYSDATE()`

`CURRENT_TIMESTAMP`

Returns the current date and time as a value in `'YYYY-MM-DD HH:MM:SS'` or `YYYYMMDDHHMMSS` format, depending on whether the function is used in a string or numeric context:

```
mysql> SELECT NOW();
        -> '1997-12-15 23:50:26'
mysql> SELECT NOW() + 0;
        -> 19971215235026
```

`UNIX_TIMESTAMP()`

`UNIX_TIMESTAMP(date)`

If called with no argument, returns a Unix timestamp (seconds since `'1970-01-01 00:00:00'` GMT) as an unsigned integer. If `UNIX_TIMESTAMP()` is called with a date argument, it returns the value of the argument as seconds since `'1970-01-01 00:00:00'` GMT. date may be a `DATE` string, a `DATETIME` string, a `TIMESTAMP`, or a number in the format YYMMDD or YYYYMMDD in local time:

```
mysql> SELECT UNIX_TIMESTAMP();
        -> 882226357
mysql> SELECT UNIX_TIMESTAMP('1997-10-04 22:23:00');
        -> 875996580
```

When `UNIX_TIMESTAMP` is used on a `TIMESTAMP` column, the function will return the internal timestamp value directly, with no implicit "string-to-unix-time- stamp" conversion. If you give `UNIX_TIMESTAMP()` a wrong or out-of-range date, it will return 0.

If you want to subtract `UNIX_TIMESTAMP()` columns, you may want to cast the result to signed integers. See Section 6.3.5, Cast Functions.

`FROM_UNIXTIME(unix_timestamp)`

Returns a representation of the `unix_timestamp` argument as a value in `'YYYY-MM-DD HH:MM:SS'` or `YYYYMMDDHHMMSS` format, depending on whether the function is used in a string or numeric context:

```
mysql> SELECT FROM_UNIXTIME(875996580);
        -> '1997-10-04 22:23:00'
mysql> SELECT FROM_UNIXTIME(875996580) + 0;
        -> 19971004222300
```

`FROM_UNIXTIME(unix_timestamp,format)`

Returns a string representation of the Unix timestamp, formatted according to the `format` string. `format` may contain the same specifiers as those listed in the entry for the `DATE_FORMAT()` function:

```
mysql> SELECT FROM_UNIXTIME(UNIX_TIMESTAMP(),
                            '%Y %D %M %h:%i:%s %x');
        -> '1997 23rd December 03:43:30 1997'
```

SEC_TO_TIME(seconds)

Returns the seconds argument, converted to hours, minutes, and seconds, as a value in 'HH:MM:SS' or HHMMSS format, depending on whether the function is used in a string or numeric context:

```
mysql> SELECT SEC_TO_TIME(2378);
        -> '00:39:38'
mysql> SELECT SEC_TO_TIME(2378) + 0;
        -> 3938
```

TIME_TO_SEC(time)

Returns the time argument, converted to seconds:

```
mysql> SELECT TIME_TO_SEC('22:23:00');
        -> 80580
mysql> SELECT TIME_TO_SEC('00:39:38');
        -> 2378
```

6.3.5 Cast Functions

The syntax of the CAST function is:

```
CAST(expression AS type)
```

or

```
CONVERT(expression,type)
```

Where type is one of:

- BINARY
- DATE
- DATETIME
- SIGNED {INTEGER}
- TIME
- UNSIGNED {INTEGER}

CAST() is ANSI SQL99 syntax and CONVERT() is ODBC syntax.

The cast function is mainly useful when you want to create a column with a specific type in a CREATE ... SELECT:

```
CREATE TABLE new_table SELECT CAST('2000-01-01' AS DATE);
```

CAST(string AS BINARY) is the same thing as BINARY string.

To cast a string to a numeric value, you don't normally have to do anything; just use the string value as if it were a number:

```
mysql> SELECT 1+'1';
        -> 2
```

MySQL supports arithmetic with both signed and unsigned 64-bit values. If you are using numerical operations (like +) and one of the operands is unsigned integer, the result will be unsigned. You can override this by using the SIGNED and UNSIGNED cast operators, which will cast the operation to a signed or unsigned 64-bit integer, respectively.

```
mysql> SELECT CAST(1-2 AS UNSIGNED)
        -> 18446744073709551615
mysql> SELECT CAST(CAST(1-2 AS UNSIGNED) AS SIGNED);
        -> -1
```

Note that if either operation is a floating-point value (in this context DECIMAL() is regarded as a floating-point value), the result will be a floating-point value and is not affected by the preceding rule.

```
mysql> SELECT CAST(1 AS UNSIGNED) -2.0
        -> -1.0
```

If you are using a string in an arithmetic operation, this is converted to a floating-point number.

The CAST() and CONVERT() functions were added in MySQL 4.0.2.

The handing of unsigned values was changed in MySQL 4.0 to be able to support BIG-INT values properly. If you have some code that you want to run in both MySQL 4.0 and 3.23 (in which case you probably can't use the CAST function), you can use the following trick to get a signed result when subtracting two unsigned integer columns:

```
SELECT (unsigned_column_1+0.0)-(unsigned_column_2+0.0);
```

The idea is that the columns are converted to floating-point before doing the subtraction.

If you get a problem with UNSIGNED columns in your old MySQL application when porting to MySQL 4.0, you can use the --sql-mode=NO_UNSIGNED_SUBTRACTION option when starting mysqld. Note, however, that as long as you use this, you will not be able to make efficient use of the UNSIGNED BIGINT column type.

6.3.6 Other Functions

6.3.6.1 Bit functions

MySQL uses BIGINT (64-bit) arithmetic for bit operations, so these operators have a maximum range of 64 bits:

Bitwise OR:

```
mysql> SELECT 29 | 15;
        -> 31
```

The result is an unsigned 64-bit integer.

&

Bitwise AND:

```
mysql> SELECT 29 & 15;
        -> 13
```

The result is an unsigned 64-bit integer.

<< Shifts a longlong (BIGINT) number to the left:

```
mysql> SELECT 1 << 2;
        -> 4
```

The result is an unsigned 64-bit integer.

>> Shifts a longlong (BIGINT) number to the right:

```
mysql> SELECT 4 >> 2;
        -> 1
```

The result is an unsigned 64-bit integer.

~

Invert all bits:

```
mysql> SELECT 5 & ~1;
        -> 4
```

The result is an unsigned 64-bit integer.

BIT_COUNT(N)

Returns the number of bits that are set in the argument N:

```
mysql> SELECT BIT_COUNT(29);
        -> 4
```

6.3.6.2 Miscellaneous functions

DATABASE()

Returns the current database name:

```
mysql> SELECT DATABASE();
        -> 'test'
```

If there is no current database, DATABASE() returns the empty string.

USER()
SYSTEM_USER()
SESSION_USER()

Returns the current MySQL username:

```
mysql> SELECT USER();
        -> 'davida@localhost'
```

In MySQL Versions 3.22.11 or later, this includes the client hostname as well as the username. You can extract just the username part like this (which works whether the value includes a hostname part):

```
mysql> SELECT SUBSTRING_INDEX(USER(),"@",1);
        -> 'davida'
```

PASSWORD(str)

Calculates a password string from the plaintext password str. This is the function that is used for encrypting MySQL passwords for storage in the Password column of the user grant table:

```
mysql> SELECT PASSWORD('badpwd');
        -> '7f84554057dd964b'
```

PASSWORD() encryption is non-reversible.

PASSWORD() does not perform password encryption in the same way that Unix passwords are encrypted. You should not assume that if your Unix password and your MySQL password are the same, PASSWORD() will result in the same encrypted value as is stored in the Unix password file. See ENCRYPT().

ENCRYPT(str[,salt])

Encrypt str using the Unix crypt() system call. The salt argument should be a string with two characters (as of MySQL Version 3.22.16, salt may be longer than two characters):

```
mysql> SELECT ENCRYPT("hello");
        -> 'VxuFAJXVARROc'
```

If crypt() is not available on your system, ENCRYPT() always returns NULL.

ENCRYPT() ignores all but the first 8 characters of str, at least on some systems. This will be determined by the behavior of the underlying crypt() system call.

ENCODE(str,pass_str)

Encrypt str using pass_str as the password. To decrypt the result, use DECODE().

The result is a binary string of the same length as string. If you want to save it in a column, use a BLOB column type.

DECODE(crypt_str,pass_str)

Descrypts the encrypted string crypt_str using pass_str as the password. crypt_str should be a string returned from ENCODE().

MD5(string)

Calculates an MD5 checksum for the string. Value is returned as a 32 long hex number that may, for example, be used as a hash key:

```
mysql> SELECT MD5("testing");
        -> 'ae2b1fca515949e5d54fb22b8ed95575'
```

This is an "RSA Data Security, Inc. MD5 Message-Digest Algorithm".

DES_ENCRYPT(string_to_encrypt [, (key_number | key_string)])

Encrypts the string with the given key using the DES algorithm, which provides strong encryption.

Note that this function only works if you have configured MySQL with SSL support. See Section 4.3.8, Using Secure Connections.

The encryption key to use is chosen the following way:

Argument	Description
Only one argument	The first key from des-key-file is used.
Key number	The given key (0-9) from the des-key-file is used.
String	The given key_string will be used to crypt string_to_encrypt.

The return string will be a binary string where the first character will be CHAR(128 | key_number).

The 128 is added to make it easier to recognize an encrypted key. If you use a string key, key_number will be 127.

On error, this function returns NULL.

The string length for the result will be new_length= org_length + (8-(org_length % 8))+1.

The des-key-file has the following format:

```
key_number des_key_string
key_number des_key_string
```

Each key_number must be a number in the range from 0 to 9. Lines in the file may be in any order. des_key_string is the string that will be used to encrypt the message. Between the number and the key there should be at least one space. The first key is the default key that will be used if you don't specify any key argument to DES_ENCRYPT().

You can tell MySQL to read new key values from the key file with the FLUSH DES_KEY_FILE command. This requires the Reload_priv privilege.

One benefit of having a set of default keys is that it gives applications a way to check for the existence of encrypted column values, without giving the end user the right to decrypt those values.

```
mysql> SELECT customer_address FROM customer_table WHERE
        crypted_credit_card = DES_ENCRYPT("credit_card_number");
```

DES_DECRYPT(string_to_decrypt [, key_string])

Decrypts a string encrypted with DES_ENCRYPT().

Note that this function only works if you have configured MySQL with SSL support. See Section 4.3.8, Using Secure Connections.

If no key_string argument is given, DES_DECRYPT() examines the first byte of the encrypted string to determine the DES key number that was used to encrypt the original string, then reads the key from the des-key-file to decrypt the message. For this to work the user must have the **process** privilege.

If you pass this function a key_string argument, that string is used as the key for decrypting the message.

If the string_to_decrypt doesn't look like an encrypted string, MySQL will return the given string_to_decrypt.

On error, this function returns NULL.

LAST_INSERT_ID([expr])

Returns the last automatically generated value that was inserted into an AUTO_INCREMENT column. See Section 8.4.3.126, mysql_insert_id().

```
mysql> SELECT LAST_INSERT_ID();
        -> 195
```

The last ID that was generated is maintained in the server on a per-connection basis. It will not be changed by another client. It will not even be changed if you update another AUTO_INCREMENT column with a non-magic value (that is, a value that is not NULL and not 0).

If you insert many rows at the same time with an insert statement, LAST_INSERT_ID() returns the value for the first inserted row. The reason for this is so that you can easily reproduce the same INSERT statement against some other server.

If expr is given as an argument to LAST_INSERT_ID(), the value of the argument is returned by the function, is set as the next value to be returned by LAST_INSERT_ID(), and is used as the next AUTO_INCREMENT value. This can be used to simulate sequences.

First create the table:

```
mysql> CREATE TABLE sequence (id INT NOT NULL);
mysql> INSERT INTO sequence VALUES (0);
```

Then the table can be used to generate sequence numbers like this:

```
mysql> UPDATE sequence SET id=LAST_INSERT_ID(id+1);
```

You can generate sequences without calling LAST_INSERT_ID(), but the utility of using the function this way is that the ID value is maintained in the server as the last automatically generated value. You can retrieve the new ID as you would read any normal AUTO_INCREMENT value in MySQL. For example, LAST_INSERT_ID() (without an argument) will return the new ID. The C API function mysql_insert_id() can also be used to get the value.

Note that as mysql_insert_id() is only updated after INSERT and UPDATE statements, you can't use this function to retrieve the value for LAST_INSERT_ID(expr) after executing other SQL statements like SELECT or SET.

FORMAT(X,D)

Formats the number X to a format like '#,###,###.##', rounded to D decimals. If D is 0, the result will have no decimal point or fractional part:

```
mysql> SELECT FORMAT(12332.123456, 4);
        -> '12,332.1235'
mysql> SELECT FORMAT(12332.1,4);
        -> '12,332.1000'
mysql> SELECT FORMAT(12332.2,0);
        -> '12,332'
```

VERSION()

Returns a string indicating the MySQL server version:

```
mysql> SELECT VERSION();
        -> '3.23.13-log'
```

Note that if your version ends with -log this means that logging is enabled.

CONNECTION_ID()

Returns the connection id (thread_id) for the connection. Every connection has its own unique id:

```
mysql> SELECT CONNECTION_ID();
        -> 1
```

GET_LOCK(str,timeout)

Tries to obtain a lock with a name given by the string str, with a timeout of timeout seconds. Returns 1 if the lock was obtained successfully, 0 if the attempt timed out, or NULL if an error occurred (such as running out of memory or the thread was killed with mysqladmin kill). A lock is released when you execute RELEASE_LOCK(), execute a new GET_LOCK(), or the thread terminates. This function can be used to implement application locks or to simulate record locks. It blocks requests by other clients for locks with the same name; clients that agree on a given lock string name can use the string to perform cooperative advisory locking:

```
mysql> SELECT GET_LOCK("lock1",10);
        -> 1
mysql> SELECT GET_LOCK("lock2",10);
        -> 1
mysql> SELECT RELEASE_LOCK("lock2");
        -> 1
mysql> SELECT RELEASE_LOCK("lock1");
        -> NULL
```

Note that the second RELEASE_LOCK() call returns NULL because the lock "lock1" was automatically released by the second GET_LOCK() call.

RELEASE_LOCK(str)

Releases the lock named by the string str that was obtained with GET_LOCK(). Returns 1 if the lock was released, 0 if the lock wasn't locked by this thread (in which case the lock is not released), and NULL if the named lock didn't exist. The lock will not exist if it was never obtained by a call to GET_LOCK() or if it already has been released.

The DO statement is convenient to use with RELEASE_LOCK(). See Section 6.4.10, DO Syntax.

BENCHMARK(count,expr)

The BENCHMARK() function executes the expression expr repeatedly count times. It may be used to time how fast MySQL processes the expression. The result value is always 0. The intended use is in the mysql client, which reports query execution times:

```
mysql> SELECT BENCHMARK(1000000,ENCODE("hello","goodbye"));
+----------------------------------------------+
| BENCHMARK(1000000,ENCODE("hello","goodbye")) |
+----------------------------------------------+
|                                            0 |
+----------------------------------------------+
1 row in set (4.74 sec)
```

The time reported is the elapsed time on the client end, not the CPU time on the server end. It may be advisable to execute BENCHMARK() several times, and interpret the result with regard to how heavily loaded the server machine is.

INET_NTOA(expr)

Given a numeric network address (4 or 8 bytes), returns the dotted-quad representation of the address as a string:

```
mysql> SELECT INET_NTOA(3520061480);
        ->   "209.207.224.40"
```

INET_ATON(expr)

Given the dotted-quad representation of a network address as a string, returns an integer that represents the numeric value of the address. Addresses may be 4- or 8-byte addresses:

```
mysql> SELECT INET_ATON("209.207.224.40");
       -> 3520061480
```

The generated number is always in network byte order; for example, the previous number is calculated as 209*256^3 + 207*256^2 + 224*256 +40.

MASTER_POS_WAIT(log_name, log_pos)

Blocks until the slave reaches the specified position in the master log during replication. If master information is not initialised, returns NULL. If the slave is not running, will block and wait until it is started and goes to or passes the specified position. If the slave is already past the specified position, returns immediately. The return value is the number of log events it had to wait to get to the specified position, or NULL in case of error. Useful for control of master-slave synchronisation, but was originally written to facilitate replication testing.

FOUND_ROWS()

Returns the number of rows that the last SELECT SQL_CALC_FOUND_ROWS ... command would have returned, if wasn't restricted with LIMIT.

```
mysql> SELECT SQL_CALC_FOUND_ROWS * FROM tbl_name
       WHERE id > 100 LIMIT 10;
mysql> SELECT FOUND_ROWS();
```

The second SELECT will return a number indicating how many rows the first SELECT would have returned had it been written without the LIMIT clause.

Note that if you are using SELECT SQL_CALC_FOUND_ROWS ... MySQL has to calculate all rows in the result set. However, this is faster than if you did not use LIMIT, as the result set need not be sent to the client.

6.3.7 Functions for Use with GROUP BY Clauses

If you use a group function in a statement containing no GROUP BY clause, it is equivalent to grouping on all rows.

COUNT(expr)

Returns a count of the number of non-NULL values in the rows retrieved by a SELECT statement:

```
mysql> SELECT student.student_name,COUNT(*)
    ->         FROM student,course
    ->         WHERE student.student_id=course.student_id
    ->         GROUP BY student_name;
```

COUNT(*) is somewhat different in that it returns a count of the number of rows retrieved, whether they contain NULL values.

COUNT(*) is optimised to return very quickly if the SELECT retrieves from one table, no other columns are retrieved, and there is no WHERE clause. For example:

```
mysql> SELECT COUNT(*) FROM student;
```

COUNT(DISTINCT expr, [expr . . .])

Returns a count of the number of different non-NULL values:

```
mysql> SELECT COUNT(DISTINCT results) FROM student;
```

In MySQL you can get the number of distinct expression combinations that don't contain NULL by giving a list of expressions. In ANSI SQL you would have to do a concatenation of all expressions inside CODE(DISTINCT . . .).

AVG(expr)

Returns the average value of expr:

```
mysql> SELECT student_name, AVG(test_score)
    ->         FROM student
    ->         GROUP BY student_name;
```

MIN(expr)

MAX(expr)

Returns the minimum or maximum value of expr. MIN() and MAX() may take a string argument; in such cases they return the minimum or maximum string value. See Section 5.4.3, How MySQL Uses Indexes.

```
mysql> SELECT student_name, MIN(test_score), MAX(test_score)
    ->         FROM student
    ->         GROUP BY student_name;
```

SUM(expr)

Returns the sum of expr. Note that if the return set has no rows, it returns NULL!

STD(expr)

STDDEV(expr)

Returns the standard deviation of expr. This is an extension to ANSI SQL. The STDDEV() form of this function is provided for Oracle compatibility.

BIT_OR(expr)

Returns the bitwise OR of all bits in expr. The calculation is performed with 64-bit (BIGINT) precision.

BIT_AND(expr)

Returns the bitwise AND of all bits in expr. The calculation is performed with 64-bit (BIGINT) precision.

MySQL has extended the use of GROUP BY. You can use columns or calculations in the SELECT expressions that don't appear in the GROUP BY part. This stands for *any possible value for this group.* You can use this to get better performance by avoiding sorting and grouping on unnecessary items. For example, you don't need to group on `cus-tomer.name` in the following query:

```
mysql> SELECT order.custid,customer.name,MAX(payments)
    ->        FROM order,customer
    ->        WHERE order.custid = customer.custid
    ->        GROUP BY order.custid;
```

In ANSI SQL, you would have to add `customer.name` to the `GROUP BY` clause. In MySQL, the name is redundant if you don't run in ANSI mode.

Don't use this feature if the columns you omit from the `GROUP BY` part aren't unique in the group! You will get unpredictable results.

In some cases, you can use `MIN()` and `MAX()` to obtain a specific column value even if it isn't unique. The following gives the value of `column` from the row containing the smallest value in the `sort` column:

```
SUBSTR(MIN(CONCAT(RPAD(sort,6,' '),column)),7)
```

See Section 3.5.4, The Rows Holding the Group-Wise Maximum of a Certain Field.

Note that if you are using MySQL Version 3.22 (or earlier) or if you are trying to follow ANSI SQL, you can't use expressions in `GROUP BY` or `ORDER BY` clauses. You can work around this limitation by using an alias for the expression:

```
mysql> SELECT id,FLOOR(value/100) AS val FROM tbl_name
    ->        GROUP BY id,val ORDER BY val;
```

In MySQL Version 3.23 you can do:

```
mysql> SELECT id,FLOOR(value/100) FROM tbl_name ORDER BY RAND();
```

6.4 Data Manipulation: SELECT, INSERT, UPDATE, DELETE

6.4.1 SELECT Syntax

```
SELECT [STRAIGHT_JOIN]
       [SQL_SMALL_RESULT] [SQL_BIG_RESULT] [SQL_BUFFER_RESULT]
       [SQL_CACHE | SQL_NO_CACHE] [SQL_CALC_FOUND_ROWS] [HIGH_PRIORITY]
       [DISTINCT | DISTINCTROW | ALL]
    select_expression,...
    [INTO {OUTFILE | DUMPFILE} 'file_name' export_options]
    [FROM table_references
      [WHERE where_definition]
      [GROUP BY {unsigned_integer | col_name | formula} [ASC | DESC], ...]
      [HAVING where_definition]
```

```
[ORDER BY {unsigned_integer | col_name | formula} [ASC | DESC] ,...]
[LIMIT [offset,] rows]
[PROCEDURE procedure_name]
[FOR UPDATE | LOCK IN SHARE MODE]]
```

SELECT is used to retrieve rows selected from one or more tables. select_expression indicates the columns you want to retrieve. SELECT may also be used to retrieve rows computed without reference to any table. For example:

```
mysql> SELECT 1 + 1;
       -> 2
```

All keywords used must be given in exactly the order shown in the preceding example. For instance, a HAVING clause must come after any GROUP BY clause and before any ORDER BY clause.

- A SELECT expression may be given an alias using AS. The alias is used as the expression's column name and can be used with ORDER BY or HAVING clauses. For example:

  ```
  mysql> SELECT CONCAT(last_name,', ',first_name) AS full_name
      FROM mytable ORDER BY full_name;
  ```

- You cannot use a column alias in a WHERE clause because the column value may not yet be determined when the WHERE clause is executed. See Section A.5.4, Problems with alias.

- The FROM table_references clause indicates the tables from which to retrieve rows. If you name more than one table, you are performing a join. For information on join syntax, see Section 6.4.1.1, JOIN syntax. For each table specified, you may optionally specify an alias:

  ```
  table_name [[AS] alias] [USE INDEX (key_list)] [IGNORE INDEX (key_list)]
  ```

  As of MySQL Version 3.23.12, you can give hints about which index MySQL should use when retrieving information from a table. This is useful if EXPLAIN shows that MySQL is using the wrong index. By specifying USE INDEX (key_list), you can tell MySQL to use only one of the specified indexes to find rows in the table. The alternative syntax IGNORE INDEX (key_list) can be used to tell MySQL to not use some particular index. USE/IGNORE KEY are synonyms for USE/IGNORE INDEX.

- You can refer to a column as col_name, tbl_name.col_name, or db_name.tbl_name.col_name. You need not specify a tbl_name or db_name.tbl_name prefix for a column reference in a SELECT statement unless the reference would be ambiguous. See Section 6.1.2, Database, Table, Index, Column, and Alias Names, for examples of ambiguity that require the more explicit column reference forms.

- A table reference may be aliased using `tbl_name [AS] alias_name`:

```
mysql> SELECT t1.name, t2.salary FROM employee AS t1, info AS t2
    ->         WHERE t1.name = t2.name;
mysql> SELECT t1.name, t2.salary FROM employee t1, info t2
    ->         WHERE t1.name = t2.name;
```

- Columns selected for output may be referred to in ORDER BY and GROUP BY clauses using column names, column aliases, or column positions. Column positions begin with 1:

```
mysql> SELECT college, region, seed FROM tournament
    ->       ORDER BY region, seed;
mysql> SELECT college, region AS r, seed AS s FROM tournament
    ->       ORDER BY r, s;
mysql> SELECT college, region, seed FROM tournament
    ->       ORDER BY 2, 3;
```

To sort in reverse order, add the DESC (descending) keyword to the name of the column in the ORDER BY clause that you are sorting by. The default is ascending order; this may be specified explicitly using the ASC keyword.

- You can in the WHERE clause use any of the functions that MySQL supports. See Section 6.3, Functions for Use in SELECT and WHERE Clauses.

- The HAVING clause can refer to any column or alias named in the `select_expression`. It is applied last, just before items are sent to the client, with no optimisation. Don't use HAVING for items that should be in the WHERE clause. For example, do not write this:

```
mysql> SELECT col_name FROM tbl_name HAVING col_name > 0;
```

Write this instead:

```
mysql> SELECT col_name FROM tbl_name WHERE col_name > 0;
```

In MySQL Version 3.22.5 or later, you can also write queries like this:

```
mysql> SELECT user,MAX(salary) FROM users
    ->       GROUP BY user HAVING MAX(salary)>10;
```

In older MySQL versions, you can write this instead:

```
mysql> SELECT user,MAX(salary) AS sum FROM users
    ->       group by user HAVING sum>10;
```

- The options DISTINCT, DISTINCTROW, and ALL specify whether duplicate rows should be returned. The default is (ALL), in which case all matching rows are returned. DISTINCT and DISTINCTROW are synonyms and specify that duplicate rows in the result set should be removed.

- All options beginning with SQL_, STRAIGHT_JOIN, and HIGH_PRIORITY are MySQL extensions to ANSI SQL.

- HIGH_PRIORITY will give the SELECT higher priority than a statement that updates a table. You should only use this for queries that are very fast and must be done at once. A SELECT HIGH_PRIORITY query will run if the table is locked for read even if an update statement is waiting for the table to be free.

- SQL_BIG_RESULT can be used with GROUP BY or DISTINCT to tell the optimiser that the result set will have many rows. In this case, MySQL will directly use disk-based temporary tables if needed. MySQL will also, in this case, prefer sorting to doing a temporary table with a key on the GROUP BY elements.

- SQL_BUFFER_RESULT will force the result to be put into a temporary table. This will help MySQL free the table locks early and will help in cases where it takes a long time to send the result set to the client.

- SQL_SMALL_RESULT, a MySQL-specific option, can be used with GROUP BY or DISTINCT to tell the optimiser that the result set will be small. In this case, MySQL will use fast temporary tables to store the resulting table instead of using sorting. In MySQL Version 3.23 this shouldn't normally be needed.

- SQL_CALC_FOUND_ROWS tells MySQL to calculate how many rows there would be in the result, disregarding any LIMIT clause. The number of rows can be obtained with SELECT FOUND_ROWS(). See Section 6.3.6.2, Miscellaneous functions.

- SQL_CACHE tells MySQL to store the query result in the query cache if you are using SQL_QUERY_CACHE_TYPE=2 (DEMAND). See Section 6.9, MySQL Query Cache.

- SQL_NO_CACHE tells MySQL to not allow the query result to be stored in the query cache. See Section 6.9, MySQL Query Cache.

- If you use GROUP BY, the output rows will be sorted according to the GROUP BY as if you would have had an ORDER BY over all the fields in the GROUP BY. MySQL has extended the GROUP BY so that you can also specify ASC and DESC to GROUP BY:

  ```
  SELECT a,COUNT(b) FROM test_table GROUP BY a DESC
  ```

- MySQL has extended the use of GROUP BY to allow you to select fields which are not mentioned in the GROUP BY clause. If you are not getting the results you expect from your query, please read the GROUP BY description. See Section 6.3.7, Functions for Use with GROUP BY Clauses.

- STRAIGHT_JOIN forces the optimiser to join the tables in the order in which they are listed in the FROM clause. You can use this to speed up a query if the optimiser joins the tables in non-optimal order. See Section 5.2.1, EXPLAIN Syntax (Get Information About a SELECT).

- The LIMIT clause can be used to constrain the number of rows returned by the SELECT statement. LIMIT takes one or two numeric arguments. The arguments must be integer constants.

If two arguments are given, the first specifies the offset of the first row to return, and the second specifies the maximum number of rows to return. The offset of the initial row is 0 (not 1):

```
mysql> SELECT * FROM table LIMIT 5,10;   # Retrieve rows 6-15
```

If one argument is given, it indicates the maximum number of rows to return:

```
mysql> SELECT * FROM table LIMIT 5;      # Retrieve first 5 rows
```

In other words, LIMIT n is equivalent to LIMIT 0,n.

• The SELECT ... INTO OUTFILE 'file_name' form of SELECT writes the selected rows to a file. The file is created on the server host and cannot already exist (among other things, this prevents database tables and files such as /etc/passwd from being destroyed). You must have the **file** privilege on the server host to use this form of SELECT.

SELECT ... INTO OUTFILE is mainly intended to let you very quickly dump a table on the server machine. If you want to create the resulting file on some host other than the server host you can't use SELECT ... INTO OUTFILE. In this case you should instead use some client program like mysqldump --tab or mysql -e "SELECT ... " > outfile to generate the file.

SELECT ... INTO OUTFILE is the complement of LOAD DATA INFILE; the syntax for the export_options part of the statement consists of the same FIELDS and LINES clauses that are used with the LOAD DATA INFILE statement. See Section 6.4.9, LOAD DATA INFILE Syntax.

In the resulting text file, only the following characters are escaped by the ESCAPED BY character:

— The ESCAPED BY character

— The first character in FIELDS TERMINATED BY

— The first character in LINES TERMINATED BY

Additionally, ASCII 0 is converted to ESCAPED BY followed by 0 (ASCII 48).

This is because you **must** escape any FIELDS TERMINATED BY, ESCAPED BY, or LINES TERMINATED BY characters to reliably be able to read the file back. ASCII 0 is escaped to make it easier to view with some pagers.

As the resulting file doesn't have to conform to the SQL syntax, nothing else need be escaped.

Here is an example of getting a file in the format used by many old programs:

```
SELECT a,b,a+b INTO OUTFILE "/tmp/result.text"
FIELDS TERMINATED BY ',' OPTIONALLY ENCLOSED BY '"'
LINES TERMINATED BY "\n"
FROM test_table;
```

- If you use INTO DUMPFILE instead of INTO OUTFILE, MySQL will only write one row into the file, without any column or line terminations and without any escaping. This is useful if you want to store a blob in a file.

- Note that any file created by INTO OUTFILE and INTO DUMPFILE is going to be readable for all users! The reason is that MySQL server can't create a file that is owned by anyone other than the user it's running as (you should never run mysqld as root). Therefore, the file has to be word-readable so that you can retrieve the rows.

- If you are using FOR UPDATE on a table handler with page/row locks, the examined rows will be write-locked.

6.4.1.1 JOIN syntax

MySQL supports the following JOIN syntaxes for use in SELECT statements:

```
table_reference, table_reference
table_reference [CROSS] JOIN table_reference
table_reference INNER JOIN table_reference join_condition
table_reference STRAIGHT_JOIN table_reference
table_reference LEFT [OUTER] JOIN table_reference join_condition
table_reference LEFT [OUTER] JOIN table_reference
table_reference NATURAL [LEFT [OUTER]] JOIN table_reference
{ oj table_reference LEFT OUTER JOIN table_reference ON conditional_expr }
table_reference RIGHT [OUTER] JOIN table_reference join_condition
table_reference RIGHT [OUTER] JOIN table_reference
table_reference NATURAL [RIGHT [OUTER]] JOIN table_reference
```

Where table_reference is defined as:

```
table_name [[AS] alias] [USE INDEX (key_list)] [IGNORE INDEX (key_list)]
```

and join_condition is defined as:

```
ON conditional_expr |
USING (column_list)
```

You should never have any conditions in the ON part that are used to restrict which rows you have in the result set. If you want to restrict which rows should be in the result, you have to do this in the WHERE clause.

Note that in versions before Version 3.23.17, the INNER JOIN didn't take a join_condition!

The last LEFT OUTER JOIN syntax shown in the preceding example exists only for compatibility with ODBC:

- A table reference may be aliased using tbl_name AS alias_name or tbl_name alias_name:

```
mysql> SELECT t1.name, t2.salary FROM employee AS t1, info AS t2
    ->         WHERE t1.name = t2.name;
```

- The ON conditional is any conditional of the form that may be used in a WHERE clause.

- If there is no matching record for the right table in the ON or USING part in a LEFT JOIN, a row with all columns set to NULL is used for the right table. You can use this fact to find records in a table that have no counterpart in another table:

```
mysql> SELECT table1.* FROM table1
    ->         LEFT JOIN table2 ON table1.id=table2.id
    ->         WHERE table2.id IS NULL;
```

This example finds all rows in table1 with an id value that is not present in table2 (that is, all rows in table1 with no corresponding row in table2). This assumes that table2.id is declared NOT NULL, of course. See Section 5.2.6, How MySQL Optimises LEFT JOIN and RIGHT JOIN.

- The USING (column_list) clause names a list of columns that must exist in both tables. A USING clause such as:

```
A LEFT JOIN B USING (C1,C2,C3,...)
```

is defined to be semantically identical to an ON expression like this:

```
A.C1=B.C1 AND A.C2=B.C2 AND A.C3=B.C3,...
```

- The NATURAL [LEFT] JOIN of two tables is defined to be semantically equivalent to an INNER JOIN or a LEFT JOIN with a USING clause that names all columns that exist in both tables.

- INNER JOIN and , (comma) are semantically equivalent. Both do a full join between the tables used. Normally, you specify how the tables should be linked in the WHERE condition.

- RIGHT JOIN works analogously to LEFT JOIN. To keep code portable across databases, it's recommended to use LEFT JOIN instead of RIGHT JOIN.

- STRAIGHT_JOIN is identical to JOIN, except that the left table is always read before the right table. This can be used for those (few) cases where the join optimiser puts the tables in the wrong order.

- As of MySQL Version 3.23.12, you can give hints about which index MySQL should use when retrieving information from a table. This is useful if EXPLAIN shows that MySQL is using the wrong index. By specifying USE INDEX (key_list), you can tell MySQL to use only one of the specified indexes to find rows in the table. The alternative syntax IGNORE INDEX (key_list) can be used to tell MySQL to not use some particular index. USE/IGNORE KEY are synonyms for USE/IGNORE INDEX.

Some examples:

```
mysql> SELECT * FROM table1,table2 WHERE table1.id=table2.id;
mysql> SELECT * FROM table1 LEFT JOIN table2 ON table1.id=table2.id;
mysql> SELECT * FROM table1 LEFT JOIN table2 USING (id);
mysql> SELECT * FROM table1 LEFT JOIN table2 ON table1.id=table2.id
    ->             LEFT JOIN table3 ON table2.id=table3.id;
mysql> SELECT * FROM table1 USE INDEX (key1,key2)
    ->             WHERE key1=1 AND key2=2 AND key3=3;
mysql> SELECT * FROM table1 IGNORE INDEX (key3)
    ->             WHERE key1=1 AND key2=2 AND key3=3;
```

See Section 5.2.6, How MySQL Optimises LEFT JOIN and RIGHT JOIN.

6.4.1.2 UNION **syntax**

```
SELECT ...
UNION [ALL]
SELECT ...
  [UNION
    SELECT ...]
```

UNION is implemented in MySQL 4.0.0.

UNION is used to combine the result from many SELECT statements into one result set.

The SELECT commands are normal select commands, but with the following restrictions:

• Only the last SELECT command can have INTO OUTFILE.

If you don't use the keyword ALL for the UNION, all returned rows will be unique, as if you had done a DISTINCT for the total result set. If you specify ALL, you will get all matching rows from all the used SELECT statements.

If you want to use an ORDER BY for the total UNION result, you should use parentheses:

```
(SELECT a FROM table_name WHERE a=10 AND B=1 ORDER BY a LIMIT 10)
UNION
(SELECT a FROM table_name WHERE a=11 AND B=2 ORDER BY a LIMIT 10)
ORDER BY a;
```

6.4.2 HANDLER **Syntax**

```
HANDLER tbl_name OPEN [ AS alias ]
HANDLER tbl_name READ index_name { = | >= | <= | < } (value1,value2,...)
    [ WHERE ... ] [LIMIT ... ]
HANDLER tbl_name READ index_name { FIRST | NEXT | PREV | LAST }
    [ WHERE ... ] [LIMIT ... ]
HANDLER tbl_name READ { FIRST | NEXT }
    [ WHERE ... ] [LIMIT ... ]
HANDLER tbl_name CLOSE
```

The HANDLER statement provides direct access to the MyISAM table handler interface, bypassing the SQL optimiser. Thus, it is faster than SELECT.

The first form of the HANDLER statement opens a table, making it accessible via subsequent HANDLER . . . READ statements. This table object is not shared by other threads and will not be closed until the thread calls HANDLER tbl_name CLOSE or the thread dies.

The second form fetches one row (or more, specified by the LIMIT clause) where the index specified complies to the condition and the WHERE condition is met. If the index consists of several parts (spans over several columns), the values are specified in comma-separated lists. Providing values only for the few first columns is possible.

The third form fetches one row (or more, specified by the LIMIT clause) from the table in index order, matching the WHERE condition.

The fourth form (without index specification) fetches one row (or more, specified by the LIMIT clause) from the table in natural row order (as stored in the data file) matching the WHERE condition. It is faster than HANDLER tbl_name READ index_name when a full table scan is desired.

HANDLER . . . CLOSE closes a table that was opened with HANDLER . . . OPEN.

HANDLER is a somewhat low-level statement. For example, it does not provide consistency. That is, HANDLER . . . OPEN does **not** take a snapshot of the table, and does **not** lock the table. This means that after a HANDLER . . . OPEN is issued, table data can be modified (by this or another thread) and these modifications may appear only partially in HANDLER . . . NEXT or HANDLER . . . PREV scans.

6.4.3 INSERT **Syntax**

```
INSERT [LOW_PRIORITY | DELAYED] [IGNORE]
    [INTO] tbl_name [(col_name,...)]
    VALUES (expression,...),(...),...
or  INSERT [LOW_PRIORITY | DELAYED] [IGNORE]
    [INTO] tbl_name [(col_name,...)]
    SELECT ...
or  INSERT [LOW_PRIORITY | DELAYED] [IGNORE]
    [INTO] tbl_name
    SET col_name=expression, col_name=expression, ...
```

INSERT inserts new rows into an existing table. The INSERT . . . VALUES form of the statement inserts rows based on explicitly specified values. The INSERT . . . SELECT form inserts rows selected from another table or tables. The INSERT . . . VALUES form with multiple value lists is supported in MySQL Version 3.22.5 or later. The col_name=expression syntax is supported in MySQL Version 3.22.10 or later.

tbl_name is the table into which rows should be inserted. The column name list or the SET clause indicates which columns the statement specifies values for:

- If you specify no column list for INSERT ... VALUES or INSERT ...
  SELECT, values for all columns must be provided in the VALUES() list or by the
  SELECT. If you don't know the order of the columns in the table, use DESCRIBE
  tbl_name to find out.

- Any column not explicitly given a value is set to its default value. For example, if
  you specify a column list that doesn't name all the columns in the table, unnamed
  columns are set to their default values. Default value assignment is described in Section 6.5.3, CREATE TABLE Syntax.

  MySQL always has a default value for all fields. This is something that is imposed
  on MySQL to be able to work with both transactional and non-transactional tables.

  Our view is that field content checks should be done in the application and not in the
  database server.

- An expression may refer to any column that was set earlier in a value list. For
  example, you can say this:

  ```
  mysql> INSERT INTO tbl_name (col1,col2) VALUES(15,col1*2);
  ```

  but not this:

  ```
  mysql> INSERT INTO tbl_name (col1,col2) VALUES(col2*2,15);
  ```

- If you specify the keyword LOW_PRIORITY, execution of the INSERT is delayed until
  no other clients are reading from the table. In this case the client has to wait until the
  insert statement is completed, which may take a long time if the table is in heavy use.
  This is in contrast to INSERT DELAYED, which lets the client continue at once. See
  Section 6.4.4, INSERT DELAYED Syntax. Note that LOW_PRIORITY should normally
  not be used with MyISAM tables, as this disables concurrent inserts. See Section 7.1,
  MyISAM Tables.

- If you specify the keyword IGNORE in an INSERT with many value rows, any rows
  that duplicate an existing PRIMARY or UNIQUE key in the table are ignored and are
  not inserted. If you do not specify IGNORE, the insert is aborted if any row duplicates
  an existing key value. You can determine with the C API function mysql_info()
  how many rows were inserted into the table.

- If MySQL was configured using the DONT_USE_DEFAULT_FIELDS option, INSERT
  statements generate an error unless you explicitly specify values for all columns that
  require a non-NULL value. See Section 2.3.3, Typical configure Options.

- You can find the value used for an AUTO_INCREMENT column with the
  mysql_insert_id function. See Section 8.4.3.126, mysql_insert_id().

If you use INSERT ... SELECT or an INSERT ... VALUES statement with multiple value lists, you can use the C API function mysql_info() to get information about
the query. The format of the information string is shown here:

```
Records: 100 Duplicates: 0 Warnings: 0
```

Duplicates indicates the number of rows that couldn't be inserted because they would duplicate some existing unique index value. Warnings indicates the number of attempts to insert column values that were problematic in some way. Warnings can occur under any of the following conditions:

- Inserting NULL into a column that has been declared NOT NULL. The column is set to its default value.

- Setting a numeric column to a value that lies outside the column's range. The value is clipped to the appropriate endpoint of the range.

- Setting a numeric column to a value such as '10.34 a'. The trailing garbage is stripped and the remaining numeric part is inserted. If the value doesn't make sense as a number, the column is set to 0.

- Inserting a string into a CHAR, VARCHAR, TEXT, or BLOB column that exceeds the column's maximum length. The value is truncated to the column's maximum length.

- Inserting a value into a date or time column that is illegal for the column type. The column is set to the appropriate zero value for the type.

6.4.3.1 INSERT . . . SELECT syntax

```
INSERT [LOW_PRIORITY] [IGNORE] [INTO] tbl_name [(column list)] SELECT ...
```

With the INSERT . . . SELECT statement you can quickly insert many rows into a table from one or many tables:

```
INSERT INTO tblTemp2 (fldID) SELECT tblTemp1.fldOrder_ID FROM tblTemp1 WHERE
tblTemp1.fldOrder_ID > 100;
```

The following conditions hold for an INSERT . . . SELECT statement:

- The target table of the INSERT statement cannot appear in the FROM clause of the SELECT part of the query because it's forbidden in ANSI SQL to SELECT from the same table into which you are inserting. (The problem is that the SELECT possibly would find records that were inserted earlier during the same run. When using subselect clauses, the situation could easily be very confusing!)

- AUTO_INCREMENT columns work as usual.

- You can use the C API function mysql_info() to get information about the query. See Section 6.4.3, INSERT Syntax.

- To ensure that the update log/binary log can be used to re-create the original tables, MySQL will not allow concurrent inserts during INSERT . . . SELECT.

You can, of course, also use REPLACE instead of INSERT to overwrite old rows.

6.4.4 INSERT DELAYED Syntax

```
INSERT DELAYED ...
```

The DELAYED option for the INSERT statement is a MySQL-specific option that is very useful if you have clients that can't wait for the INSERT to complete. This is a common problem when you use MySQL for logging and you also periodically run SELECT and UPDATE statements that take a long time to complete. DELAYED was introduced in MySQL Version 3.22.15. It is a MySQL extension to ANSI SQL92.

INSERT DELAYED only works with ISAM and MyISAM tables. Note that as MyISAM tables support concurrent SELECT and INSERT, if there are no free blocks in the middle of the data file you very seldom need to use INSERT DELAYED with MyISAM. See Section 7.1, MyISAM Tables.

When you use INSERT DELAYED, the client will get an OK at once and the row will be inserted when the table is not in use by any other thread.

Another major benefit of using INSERT DELAYED is that inserts from many clients are bundled together and written in one block. This is much faster than doing many separate inserts.

Note that currently the queued rows are only stored in memory until they are inserted into the table. This means that if you kill mysqld the hard way (kill -9) or if mysqld dies unexpectedly, any queued rows that weren't written to disk are lost!

The following describes in detail what happens when you use the DELAYED option to INSERT or REPLACE. In this description, the "thread" is the thread that received an INSERT DELAYED command and "handler" is the thread that handles all INSERT DELAYED statements for a particular table.

- When a thread executes a DELAYED statement for a table, a handler thread is created to process all DELAYED statements for the table, if no such handler already exists.

- The thread checks whether the handler has acquired a DELAYED lock already; if not, it tells the handler thread to do so. The DELAYED lock can be obtained even if other threads have a READ or WRITE lock on the table. However, the handler will wait for all ALTER TABLE locks or FLUSH TABLES to ensure that the table structure is up to date.

- The thread executes the INSERT statement, but instead of writing the row to the table, it puts a copy of the final row into a queue that is managed by the handler thread. Any syntax errors are noticed by the thread and reported to the client program.

- The client can't report the number of duplicates or the AUTO_INCREMENT value for the resulting row; it can't obtain them from the server because the INSERT returns before the insert operation has been completed. If you use the C API, the mysql_info() function doesn't return anything meaningful, for the same reason.

- The update log is updated by the handler thread when the row is inserted into the table. In case of multiple-row inserts, the update log is updated when the first row is inserted.

- After every delayed_insert_limit row is written, the handler checks whether any SELECT statements are still pending. If so, it allows these to execute before continuing.

- When the handler has no more rows in its queue, the table is unlocked. If no new INSERT DELAYED commands are received within delayed_insert_timeout seconds, the handler terminates.

- If more than delayed_queue_size rows are pending already in a specific handler queue, the thread requesting INSERT DELAYED waits until there is room in the queue. This is done to ensure that the mysqld server doesn't use all memory for the delayed memory queue.

- The handler thread will show up in the MySQL process list with delayed_insert in the Command column. It will be killed if you execute a FLUSH TABLES command or kill it with KILL thread_id. However, it will first store all queued rows into the table before exiting. During this time it will not accept any new INSERT commands from another thread. If you execute an INSERT DELAYED command after this, a new handler thread will be created.

  Note that this means that INSERT DELAYED commands have higher priority than normal INSERT commands if an INSERT DELAYED handler is already running! Other update commands will have to wait until the INSERT DELAYED queue is empty, someone kills the handler thread (with KILL thread_id), or someone executes FLUSH TABLES.

- The following status variables provide information about INSERT DELAYED commands:

Variable	Meaning
Delayed_insert_threads	Number of handler threads
Delayed_writes	Number of rows written with INSERT DELAYED
Not_flushed_delayed_rows	Number of rows waiting to be written

You can view these variables by issuing a SHOW STATUS statement or by executing a mysqladmin extended-status command.

Note that INSERT DELAYED is slower than a normal INSERT if the table is not in use. There is also the additional overhead for the server to handle a separate thread for each table on which you use INSERT DELAYED. This means that you should only use INSERT DELAYED when you are really sure you need it!

6.4.5 UPDATE **Syntax**

```
UPDATE [LOW_PRIORITY] [IGNORE] tbl_name
    SET col_name1=expr1 [, col_name2=expr2, ...]
    [WHERE where_definition]
    [LIMIT #]
```

UPDATE updates columns in existing table rows with new values. The SET clause indicates which columns to modify and the values they should be given. The WHERE clause, if given, specifies which rows should be updated. Otherwise, all rows are updated. If the ORDER BY clause is specified, the rows will be updated in the order that is specified.

If you specify the keyword LOW_PRIORITY, execution of the UPDATE is delayed until no other clients are reading from the table.

If you specify the keyword IGNORE, the update statement will not abort even if we get duplicate key errors during the update. Rows that would cause conflicts will not be updated.

If you access a column from tbl_name in an expression, UPDATE uses the current value of the column. For example, the following statement sets the age column to one more than its current value:

```
mysql> UPDATE persondata SET age=age+1;
```

UPDATE assignments are evaluated from left to right. For example, the following statement doubles the age column, then increments it:

```
mysql> UPDATE persondata SET age=age*2, age=age+1;
```

If you set a column to the value it currently has, MySQL notices this and doesn't update it.

UPDATE returns the number of rows that were actually changed. In MySQL Version 3.22 or later, the C API function mysql_info() returns the number of rows that were matched and updated and the number of warnings that occurred during the UPDATE.

In MySQL Version 3.23, you can use LIMIT # to ensure that only a given number of rows are changed.

6.4.6 DELETE **Syntax**

```
DELETE [LOW_PRIORITY | QUICK] FROM table_name
    [WHERE where_definition]
    [ORDER BY ...]
    [LIMIT rows]
```

or

```
DELETE [LOW_PRIORITY | QUICK] table_name[.*] [,table_name[.*] ...]
    FROM table-references
```

```
            [WHERE where_definition]
```

or

```
DELETE [LOW_PRIORITY | QUICK]
        FROM table_name[.*], [table_name[.*] ...]
        USING table-references
        [WHERE where_definition]
```

DELETE deletes rows from table_name that satisfy the condition given by where_definition, and returns the number of records deleted.

If you issue a DELETE with no WHERE clause, all rows are deleted. If you do this in AUTO-COMMIT mode, this works as TRUNCATE. See Section 6.4.7, TRUNCATE Syntax. In MySQL 3.23, DELETE without a WHERE clause will return zero as the number of affected records.

If you really want to know how many records are deleted when you are deleting all rows, and are willing to suffer a speed penalty, you can use a DELETE statement of this form:

```
mysql> DELETE FROM table_name WHERE 1>0;
```

Note that this is much slower than DELETE FROM table_name with no WHERE clause because it deletes rows one at a time.

If you specify the keyword LOW_PRIORITY, execution of the DELETE is delayed until no other clients are reading from the table.

If you specify the word QUICK, the table handler will not merge index leaves during delete, which may speed up certain kinds of deletes.

In MyISAM tables, deleted records are maintained in a linked list and subsequent INSERT operations reuse old record positions. To reclaim unused space and reduce file-sizes, use the OPTIMIZE TABLE statement or the myisamchk utility to reorganise tables. OPTIMIZE TABLE is easier, but myisamchk is faster. See Section 4.5.1, OPTIMIZE TABLE Syntax and Section 4.4.6.10, Table optimisation.

The first multi-table delete format is supported starting from MySQL 4.0.0. The second multi-table delete format is supported starting from MySQL 4.0.2.

The idea is that only matching rows from the tables listed **before** the FROM or before the USING clause are deleted. The effect is that you can delete rows from many tables at the same time and also have additional tables that are used for searching.

The .* after the table names is there just to be compatible with Access:

```
DELETE t1,t2 FROM t1,t2,t3 WHERE t1.id=t2.id AND t2.id=t3.id
```

or

```
DELETE FROM t1,t2 USING t1,t2,t3 WHERE t1.id=t2.id AND t2.id=t3.id
```

In the preceding case we delete matching rows just from tables t1 and t2.

ORDER BY and the use of multiple tables in the DELETE statement are supported in MySQL 4.0.

If an ORDER BY clause is used, the rows will be deleted in that order. This is really only useful in conjunction with LIMIT. For example:

```
DELETE FROM somelog
WHERE user = 'jcole'
ORDER BY timestamp
LIMIT 1
```

This will delete the oldest entry (by timestamp) where the row matches the WHERE clause.

The MySQL-specific LIMIT rows option to DELETE tells the server the maximum number of rows to be deleted before control is returned to the client. This can be used to ensure that a specific DELETE command doesn't take too much time. You can simply repeat the DELETE command until the number of affected rows is less than the LIMIT value.

6.4.7 TRUNCATE **Syntax**

```
TRUNCATE TABLE table_name
```

In 3.23 TRUNCATE TABLE is mapped to COMMIT ; DELETE FROM table_name. See Section 6.4.6, DELETE Syntax.

TRUNCATE TABLE differs from DELETE FROM . . . in the following ways:

- Truncate operations drop and re-create the table, which is much faster than deleting rows one by one.

- Not transaction-safe; you will get an error if you have an active transaction or an active table lock.

- Doesn't return the number of deleted rows.

- As long as the table definition file table_name.frm is valid, the table can be re-created this way, even if the data or index files have become corrupted.

TRUNCATE is an Oracle SQL extension.

6.4.8 REPLACE **Syntax**

```
     REPLACE [LOW_PRIORITY | DELAYED]
         [INTO] tbl_name [(col_name,...)]
         VALUES (expression,...),(...),...
or   REPLACE [LOW_PRIORITY | DELAYED]
         [INTO] tbl_name [(col_name,...)]
         SELECT ...
```

```
or  REPLACE [LOW_PRIORITY | DELAYED]
        [INTO] tbl_name
        SET col_name=expression, col_name=expression,...
```

REPLACE works exactly like INSERT, except that if an old record in the table has the same value as a new record on a unique index, the old record is deleted before the new record is inserted. See Section 6.4.3, INSERT Syntax.

In other words, you can't access the values of the old row from a REPLACE statement. In some old MySQL versions it appeared that you could do this, but that was a bug that has been corrected.

When you use a REPLACE command, mysql_affected_rows() will return 2 if the new row replaced an old row. This is because one row was inserted and then the duplicate was deleted.

This fact makes it easy to determine whether REPLACE added or replaced a row: check whether the affected-rows value is 1 (added) or 2 (replaced).

6.4.9 LOAD DATA INFILE Syntax

```
LOAD DATA [LOW_PRIORITY | CONCURRENT] [LOCAL] INFILE 'file_name.txt'
    [REPLACE | IGNORE]
    INTO TABLE tbl_name
    [FIELDS
        [TERMINATED BY '\t']
        [[OPTIONALLY] ENCLOSED BY '']
        [ESCAPED BY '\\' ]
    ]
    [LINES TERMINATED BY '\n']
    [IGNORE number LINES]
    [(col_name,...)]
```

The LOAD DATA INFILE statement reads rows from a text file into a table at a very high speed. If the LOCAL keyword is specified, the file is read from the client host. If LOCAL is not specified, the file must be located on the server. (LOCAL is available in MySQL Version 3.22.6 or later.)

For security reasons, when reading text files located on the server, the files must either reside in the database directory or be readable by all. Also, to use LOAD DATA INFILE on server files, you must have the **file** privilege on the server host. See Section 4.2.7, Privileges Provided by MySQL.

In MySQL 3.23.49 and MySQL 4.0.2 LOCAL will only work if you have not started mysqld with --local-infile=0 or if you have not enabled your client to support LOCAL. See Section 4.2.4, Security Issues with LOAD DATA LOCAL.

If you specify the keyword LOW_PRIORITY, execution of the LOAD DATA statement is delayed until no other clients are reading from the table.

If you specify the keyword CONCURRENT with a MyISAM table, other threads can retrieve data from the table while LOAD DATA is executing. Using this option will, of course, affect the performance of LOAD DATA a bit even if no other thread is using the table at the same time.

Using LOCAL will be a bit slower than letting the server access the files directly because the contents of the file must travel from the client host to the server host. On the other hand, you do not need the **file** privilege to load local files.

If you are using MySQL before Version 3.23.24 you can't read from a FIFO with LOAD DATA INFILE. If you need to read from a FIFO (for example, the output from gunzip), use LOAD DATA LOCAL INFILE instead.

You can also load data files by using the mysqlimport utility; it operates by sending a LOAD DATA INFILE command to the server. The --local option causes mysqlimport to read data files from the client host. You can specify the --compress option to get better performance over slow networks if the client and server support the compressed protocol.

When locating files on the server host, the server uses the following rules:

*   If an absolute pathname is given, the server uses the pathname as is.

*   If a relative pathname with one or more leading components is given, the server searches for the file relative to the server's data directory.

*   If a filename with no leading components is given, the server looks for the file in the database directory of the current database.

Note that these rules mean a file given as ./myfile.txt is read from the server's data directory, whereas a file given as myfile.txt is read from the database directory of the current database. For example, the following LOAD DATA statement reads the file data.txt from the database directory for db1 because db1 is the current database, even though the statement explicitly loads the file into a table in the db2 database:

```
mysql> USE db1;
mysql> LOAD DATA INFILE "data.txt" INTO TABLE db2.my_table;
```

The REPLACE and IGNORE keywords control handling of input records that duplicate existing records on unique key values. If you specify REPLACE, new rows replace existing rows that have the same unique key value. If you specify IGNORE, input rows that duplicate an existing row on a unique key value are skipped. If you don't specify either option, an error occurs when a duplicate key value is found, and the rest of the text file is ignored.

If you load data from a local file using the LOCAL keyword, the server has no way to stop transmission of the file in the middle of the operation, so the default bahavior is the same as if IGNORE were specified.

If you use LOAD DATA INFILE on an empty MyISAM table, all non-unique indexes are created in a separate batch (like in REPAIR). This normally makes LOAD DATA INFILE much faster when you have many indexes.

LOAD DATA INFILE is the complement of SELECT . . . INTO OUTFILE. See Section 6.4.1, SELECT Syntax. To write data from a database to a file, use SELECT . . . INTO OUTFILE. To read the file back into the database, use LOAD DATA INFILE. The syntax of the FIELDS and LINES clauses is the same for both commands. Both clauses are optional, but FIELDS must precede LINES if both are specified.

If you specify a FIELDS clause, each of its subclauses (TERMINATED BY, [OPTIONALLY] ENCLOSED BY, and ESCAPED BY) is also optional, except that you must specify at least one of them.

If you don't specify a FIELDS clause, the defaults are the same as if you had written this:

```
FIELDS TERMINATED BY '\t' ENCLOSED BY '' ESCAPED BY '\\'
```

If you don't specify a LINES clause, the default is the same as if you had written this:

```
LINES TERMINATED BY '\n'
```

In other words, the defaults cause LOAD DATA INFILE to act as follows when reading input:

- Look for line boundaries at newlines.

- Break lines into fields at tabs.

- Do not expect fields to be enclosed within any quoting characters.

- Interpret occurrences of tab, newline, or \ preceded by \ as literal characters that are part of field values.

Conversely, the defaults cause SELECT . . . INTO OUTFILE to act as follows when writing output:

- Write tabs between fields.

- Do not enclose fields within any quoting characters.

- Use \ to escape instances of tab, newline, or \ that occur within field values.

- Write newlines at the ends of lines.

Note that to write FIELDS ESCAPED BY '\\', you must specify two backslashes for the value to be read as a single backslash.

The IGNORE number LINES option can be used to ignore a header of column names at the start of the file:

```
mysql> LOAD DATA INFILE "/tmp/file_name" INTO TABLE test IGNORE 1 LINES;
```

When you use SELECT ... INTO OUTFILE in tandem with LOAD DATA INFILE to write data from a database into a file and then read the file back into the database later, the field and line handling options for both commands must match. Otherwise, LOAD DATA INFILE will not interpret the contents of the file properly. Suppose you use SELECT ... INTO OUTFILE to write a file with fields delimited by commas:

```
mysql> SELECT * INTO OUTFILE 'data.txt'
    ->           FIELDS TERMINATED BY ','
    ->           FROM ...;
```

To read the comma-delimited file back in, the correct statement would be:

```
mysql> LOAD DATA INFILE 'data.txt' INTO TABLE table2
    ->           FIELDS TERMINATED BY ',';
```

If instead you tried to read in the file with the following statement, it wouldn't work because it instructs LOAD DATA INFILE to look for tabs between fields:

```
mysql> LOAD DATA INFILE 'data.txt' INTO TABLE table2
    ->           FIELDS TERMINATED BY '\t';
```

The likely result is that each input line would be interpreted as a single field.

LOAD DATA INFILE can be used to read files obtained from external sources, too. For example, a file in dBASE format will have fields separated by commas and enclosed in double quotes. If lines in the file are terminated by newlines, the following command illustrates the field and line handling options you would use to load the file:

```
mysql> LOAD DATA INFILE 'data.txt' INTO TABLE tbl_name
    ->           FIELDS TERMINATED BY ',' ENCLOSED BY '"'
    ->           LINES TERMINATED BY '\n';
```

Any of the field or line handling options may specify an empty string ("). If not empty, the FIELDS [OPTIONALLY] ENCLOSED BY and FIELDS ESCAPED BY values must be a single character. The FIELDS TERMINATED BY and LINES TERMINATED BY values may be more than one character. For example, to write lines that are terminated by carriage return-linefeed pairs, or to read a file containing such lines, specify a LINES TERMI-NATED BY '\r\n' clause.

For example, to read into a SQL table a file of jokes that are separated with a line of %%, you can do:

```
CREATE TABLE jokes (a INT NOT NULL AUTO_INCREMENT PRIMARY KEY, joke TEXT
NOT NULL);
LOAD DATA INFILE "/tmp/jokes.txt" INTO TABLE jokes FIELDS TERMINATED BY ""
LINES TERMINATED BY "\n%%\n" (joke);
```

FIELDS [OPTIONALLY] ENCLOSED BY controls quoting of fields. For output (SELECT ... INTO OUTFILE), if you omit the word OPTIONALLY, all fields are enclosed by the

ENCLOSED BY character. An example of such output (using a comma as the field delimiter) is shown here:

```
"1","a string","100.20"
"2","a string containing a , comma","102.20"
"3","a string containing a \" quote","102.20"
"4","a string containing a \", quote and comma","102.20"
```

If you specify OPTIONALLY, the ENCLOSED BY character is used only to enclose CHAR and VARCHAR fields:

```
1,"a string",100.20
2,"a string containing a , comma",102.20
3,"a string containing a \" quote",102.20
4,"a string containing a \", quote and comma",102.20
```

Note that occurrences of the ENCLOSED BY character within a field value are escaped by prefixing them with the ESCAPED BY character. Also note that if you specify an empty ESCAPED BY value, it is possible to generate output that cannot be read properly by LOAD DATA INFILE. For example, the preceding output would appear as follows if the escape character is empty. Observe that the second field in the fourth line contains a comma following the quote, which (erroneously) appears to terminate the field:

```
1,"a string",100.20
2,"a string containing a , comma",102.20
3,"a string containing a " quote",102.20
4,"a string containing a ", quote and comma",102.20
```

For input, the ENCLOSED BY character, if present, is stripped from the ends of field values. (This is true whether OPTIONALLY is specified; OPTIONALLY has no effect on input interpretation.) Occurrences of the ENCLOSED BY character preceded by the ESCAPED BY character are interpreted as part of the current field value. In addition, duplicated ENCLOSED BY characters occurring within fields are interpreted as single ENCLOSED BY characters if the field itself starts with that character. For example, if ENCLOSED BY '"' is specified, quotes are handled as shown here:

```
"The ""BIG"" boss"  -> The "BIG" boss
The "BIG" boss       -> The "BIG" boss
The ""BIG"" boss     -> The ""BIG"" boss
```

FIELDS ESCAPED BY controls how to write or read special characters. If the FIELDS ESCAPED BY character is not empty, it is used to prefix the following characters on output:

- The FIELDS ESCAPED BY character.

- The FIELDS [OPTIONALLY] ENCLOSED BY character.

- The first character of the FIELDS TERMINATED BY and LINES TERMINATED BY values.

- ASCII 0 (what is actually written following the escape character is ASCII '0', not a zero-valued byte).

If the FIELDS ESCAPED BY character is empty, no characters are escaped. It is probably not a good idea to specify an empty escape character, particularly if field values in your data contain any of the characters in the list just given.

For input, if the FIELDS ESCAPED BY character is not empty, occurrences of that character are stripped and the following character is taken literally as part of a field value. The exceptions are an escaped 0 or N (for example, \0 or \N if the escape character is \). These sequences are interpreted as ASCII 0 (a zero-valued byte) and NULL.

For more information about \-escape syntax, see Section 6.1.1, Literals: How to Write Strings and Numbers.

In certain cases, field and line handling options interact:

- If LINES TERMINATED BY is an empty string and FIELDS TERMINATED BY is non-empty, lines are also terminated with FIELDS TERMINATED BY.

- If the FIELDS TERMINATED BY and FIELDS ENCLOSED BY values are both empty ("), a fixed-row (non-delimited) format is used. With fixed-row format, no delimiters are used between fields. Instead, column values are written and read using the "display" widths of the columns. For example, if a column is declared as INT(7), values for the column are written using 7-character fields. On input, values for the column are obtained by reading 7 characters. Fixed-row format also affects handling of NULL values. Note that fixed-size format will not work if you are using a multi-byte character set.

Handling of NULL values varies, depending on the FIELDS and LINES options you use:

- For the default FIELDS and LINES values, NULL is written as \N for output and \N is read as NULL for input (assuming the ESCAPED BY character is \).

- If FIELDS ENCLOSED BY is not empty, a field containing the literal word NULL as its value is read as a NULL value (this differs from the word NULL enclosed within FIELDS ENCLOSED BY characters, which is read as the string 'NULL').

- If FIELDS ESCAPED BY is empty, NULL is written as the word NULL.

- With fixed-row format (which happens when FIELDS TERMINATED BY and FIELDS ENCLOSED BY are both empty), NULL is written as an empty string. Note that this causes both NULL values and empty strings in the table to be indistinguishable when written to the file because they are both written as empty strings. If you need to be able to tell the two apart when reading the file back in, you should not use fixed-row format.

Some cases are not supported by LOAD DATA INFILE:

- Fixed-size rows (FIELDS TERMINATED BY and FIELDS ENCLOSED BY both empty) and BLOB or TEXT columns.

- If you specify one separator that is the same as or a prefix of another, LOAD DATA INFILE won't be able to interpret the input properly. For example, the following FIELDS clause would cause problems:

```
FIELDS TERMINATED BY '"' ENCLOSED BY '"'
```

- If FIELDS ESCAPED BY is empty, a field value that contains an occurrence of FIELDS ENCLOSED BY or LINES TERMINATED BY followed by the FIELDS TER-MINATED BY value will cause LOAD DATA INFILE to stop reading a field or line too early. This happens because LOAD DATA INFILE cannot properly determine where the field or line value ends.

The following example loads all columns of the persondata table:

```
mysql> LOAD DATA INFILE 'persondata.txt' INTO TABLE persondata;
```

No field list is specified, so LOAD DATA INFILE expects input rows to contain a field for each table column. The default FIELDS and LINES values are used.

If you wish to load only some of a table's columns, specify a field list:

```
mysql> LOAD DATA INFILE 'persondata.txt'
    ->              INTO TABLE persondata (col1,col2,...);
```

You must also specify a field list if the order of the fields in the input file differs from the order of the columns in the table. Otherwise, MySQL cannot tell how to match up input fields with table columns.

If a row has too few fields, the columns for which no input field is present are set to default values. Default value assignment is described in Section 6.5.3, CREATE TABLE Syntax.

An empty field value is interpreted differently than if the field value is missing:

- For string types, the column is set to the empty string.

- For numeric types, the column is set to 0.

- For date and time types, the column is set to the appropriate "zero" value for the type. See Section 6.2.2, Date and Time Types.

Note that these are the same values that result if you assign an empty string explicitly to a string, numeric, or date, or if you assign a time type explicitly in an INSERT or UPDATE statement.

TIMESTAMP columns are only set to the current date and time if there is a NULL value for the column, or (for the first TIMESTAMP column only) if the TIMESTAMP column is left out from the field list when a field list is specified.

If an input row has too many fields, the extra fields are ignored and the number of warnings is incremented.

LOAD DATA INFILE regards all input as strings, so you can't use numeric values for ENUM or SET columns the way you can with INSERT statements. All ENUM and SET values must be specified as strings!

If you are using the C API, you can get information about the query by calling the API function mysql_info() when the LOAD DATA INFILE query finishes. The format of the information string is shown here:

```
Records: 1  Deleted: 0  Skipped: 0  Warnings: 0
```

Warnings occur under the same circumstances as when values are inserted via the INSERT statement (see Section 6.4.3, INSERT Syntax), except that LOAD DATA INFILE also generates warnings when there are too few or too many fields in the input row. The warnings are not stored anywhere; the number of warnings can only be used as an indication if everything went well. If you get warnings and want to know exactly why you got them, one way to do this is to use SELECT . . . INTO OUTFILE into another file and compare this to your original input file.

If you need LOAD DATA to read from a pipe, you can use the following trick:

```
mkfifo /mysql/db/x/x
chmod 666 /mysql/db/x/x
cat < /dev/tcp/10.1.1.12/4711 > /nt/mysql/db/x/x
mysql -e "LOAD DATA INFILE 'x' INTO TABLE x" x
```

If you are using a version of MySQL older than 3.23.25 you can only do this with LOAD DATA LOCAL INFILE.

For more information about the efficiency of INSERT versus LOAD DATA INFILE and speeding up LOAD DATA INFILE, see Section 5.2.9, Speed of INSERT Queries.

6.4.10 DO Syntax

```
DO expression, [expression, ...]
```

Execute the expression but don't return any results. This is a shorthand of SELECT expression, expression, but has the advantage that it's slightly faster when you don't care about the result.

This is mainly useful with functions that have side effects, like RELEASE_LOCK.

6.5 Data Definition: CREATE, DROP, ALTER

6.5.1 CREATE DATABASE Syntax

```
CREATE DATABASE [IF NOT EXISTS] db_name
```

CREATE DATABASE creates a database with the given name. Rules for allowable database names are given in Section 6.1.2, Database, Table, Index, Column, and Alias Names. An error occurs if the database already exists and you didn't specify IF NOT EXISTS.

Databases in MySQL are implemented as directories containing files that correspond to tables in the database. Because there are no tables in a database when it is initially created, the CREATE DATABASE statement only creates a directory under the MySQL data directory.

You can also create databases with mysqladmin. See Section 4.8, MySQL Client-Side Scripts and Utilities.

6.5.2 DROP DATABASE Syntax

```
DROP DATABASE [IF EXISTS] db_name
```

DROP DATABASE drops all tables in the database and deletes the database. If you do a DROP DATABASE on a symbolic linked database, both the link and the original database are deleted. **Be very careful with this command!**

DROP DATABASE returns the number of files that were removed from the database directory. Normally, this is three times the number of tables because normally each table corresponds to a .MYD file, a .MYI file, and a .frm file.

The DROP DATABASE command removes from the given database directory all files with the following extensions:

Ext	Ext	Ext	Ext
.BAK	.DAT	.HSH	.ISD
.ISM	.ISM	.MRG	.MYD
.MYI	.db	.frm	

All subdirectories that consists of 2 digits (RAID directories) are also removed.

In MySQL Version 3.22 or later, you can use the keywords IF EXISTS to prevent an error from occurring if the database doesn't exist.

You can also drop databases with mysqladmin. See Section 4.8, MySQL Client-Side Scripts and Utilities.

6.5.3 CREATE TABLE **Syntax**

```
CREATE [TEMPORARY] TABLE [IF NOT EXISTS] tbl_name [(create_definition,...)]
[table_options] [select_statement]

create_definition:
    col_name type [NOT NULL | NULL] [DEFAULT default_value] [AUTO_INCREMENT]
            [PRIMARY KEY] [reference_definition]
    or  PRIMARY KEY (index_col_name,...)
    or  KEY [index_name] (index_col_name,...)
    or  INDEX [index_name] (index_col_name,...)
    or  UNIQUE [INDEX] [index_name] (index_col_name,...)
    or  FULLTEXT [INDEX] [index_name] (index_col_name,...)
    or  [CONSTRAINT symbol] FOREIGN KEY [index_name] (index_col_name,...)
            [reference_definition]
    or  CHECK (expr)

type:
        TINYINT[(length)] [UNSIGNED] [ZEROFILL]
    or  SMALLINT[(length)] [UNSIGNED] [ZEROFILL]
    or  MEDIUMINT[(length)] [UNSIGNED] [ZEROFILL]
    or  INT[(length)] [UNSIGNED] [ZEROFILL]
    or  INTEGER[(length)] [UNSIGNED] [ZEROFILL]
    or  BIGINT[(length)] [UNSIGNED] [ZEROFILL]
    or  REAL[(length,decimals)] [UNSIGNED] [ZEROFILL]
    or  DOUBLE[(length,decimals)] [UNSIGNED] [ZEROFILL]
    or  FLOAT[(length,decimals)] [UNSIGNED] [ZEROFILL]
    or  DECIMAL(length,decimals) [UNSIGNED] [ZEROFILL]
    or  NUMERIC(length,decimals) [UNSIGNED] [ZEROFILL]
    or  CHAR(length) [BINARY]
    or  VARCHAR(length) [BINARY]
    or  DATE
    or  TIME
    or  TIMESTAMP
    or  DATETIME
    or  TINYBLOB
    or  BLOB
    or  MEDIUMBLOB
    or  LONGBLOB
    or  TINYTEXT
    or  TEXT
    or  MEDIUMTEXT
    or  LONGTEXT
    or  ENUM(value1,value2,value3,...)
    or  SET(value1,value2,value3,...)

index_col_name:
        col_name [(length)]

reference_definition:
        REFERENCES tbl_name [(index_col_name,...)]
                [MATCH FULL | MATCH PARTIAL]
                [ON DELETE reference_option]
                [ON UPDATE reference_option]
```

```
reference_option:
        RESTRICT | CASCADE | SET NULL | NO ACTION | SET DEFAULT

table_options:
        TYPE = {BDB | HEAP | ISAM | InnoDB | MERGE | MRG_MYISAM | MYISAM }
or      AUTO_INCREMENT = #
or      AVG_ROW_LENGTH = #
or      CHECKSUM = {0 | 1}
or      COMMENT = "string"
or      MAX_ROWS = #
or      MIN_ROWS = #
or      PACK_KEYS = {0 | 1 | DEFAULT}
or      PASSWORD = "string"
or      DELAY_KEY_WRITE = {0 | 1}
or      ROW_FORMAT= { default | dynamic | fixed | compressed }
or      RAID_TYPE= {1 | STRIPED | RAID0 } RAID_CHUNKS=#  RAID_CHUNKSIZE=#
or      UNION = (table_name,[table_name...])
or      INSERT_METHOD= {NO | FIRST | LAST }
or      DATA DIRECTORY="absolute path to directory"
or      INDEX DIRECTORY="absolute path to directory"

select_statement:
        [IGNORE | REPLACE] SELECT ...  (Some legal select statement)
```

CREATE TABLE creates a table with the given name in the current database. Rules for allowable table names are given in Section 6.1.2, Database, Table, Index, Column, and Alias Names. An error occurs if there is no current database or if the table already exists.

In MySQL Version 3.22 or later, the table name can be specified as db_name.tbl_name. This works whether there is a current database.

In MySQL Version 3.23, you can use the TEMPORARY keyword when you create a table. A temporary table will automatically be deleted if a connection dies and the name is per connection. This means that two different connections can both use the same temporary table name without conflicting with each other or with an existing table of the same name. (The existing table is hidden until the temporary table is deleted.)

In MySQL Version 3.23 or later, you can use the keywords IF NOT EXISTS so that an error does not occur if the table already exists. Note that there is no verification that the table structures are identical.

Each table tbl_name is represented by some files in the database directory. In the case of MyISAM-type tables you will get:

File	Purpose
tbl_name.frm	Table definition (form) file
tbl_name.MYD	Datafile
tbl_name.MYI	Index file

Here is some more information on the properties of the various column types (see also Section 6.2, Column Types):

- If neither NULL nor NOT NULL is specified, the column is treated as though NULL had been specified.

- An integer column may have the additional attribute AUTO_INCREMENT. When you insert a value of NULL (recommended) or 0 into an AUTO_INCREMENT column, the column is set to value+1, where value is the largest value for the column currently in the table. AUTO_INCREMENT sequences begin with 1. See Section 8.4.3.126, mysql_insert_id().

  If you delete the row containing the maximum value for an AUTO_INCREMENT column, the value will be reused with an ISAM or BDB table but not with a MyISAM or InnoDB table. If you delete all rows in the table with DELETE FROM table_name (without a WHERE) in AUTOCOMMIT mode, the sequence starts over for all table types.

  Note: There can be only one AUTO_INCREMENT column per table, and it must be indexed. MySQL Version 3.23 will also only work properly if the AUTO_INCREMENT column only has positive values. Inserting a negative number is regarded as inserting a very large positive number. This is done to avoid precision problems when numbers "wrap" over from positive to negative and also to ensure that one doesn't accidentally get an AUTO_INCREMENT column that contains 0.

  In MyISAM and BDB tables you can specify AUTO_INCREMENT secondary columns in a multi-column key. See Section 3.5.9, Using AUTO_INCREMENT.

  To make MySQL compatible with some ODBC applications, you can find the last inserted row with the following query:

  ```
  SELECT * FROM tbl_name WHERE auto_col IS NULL
  ```

- NULL values are handled differently for TIMESTAMP columns than for other column types. You cannot store a literal NULL in a TIMESTAMP column; setting the column to NULL sets it to the current date and time. Because TIMESTAMP columns behave this way, the NULL and NOT NULL attributes do not apply in the normal way and are ignored if you specify them.

  On the other hand, to make it easier for MySQL clients to use TIMESTAMP columns, the server reports that such columns may be assigned NULL values (which is true), even though TIMESTAMP never actually will contain a NULL value. You can see this when you use DESCRIBE tbl_name to get a description of your table.

  Note that setting a TIMESTAMP column to 0 is not the same as setting it to NULL because 0 is a valid TIMESTAMP value.

- If no DEFAULT value is specified for a column, MySQL automatically assigns one.

  If the column may take NULL as a value, the default value is NULL.

If the column is declared as NOT NULL, the default value depends on the column type:

— For numeric types other than those declared with the AUTO_INCREMENT attribute, the default is 0. For an AUTO_INCREMENT column, the default value is the next value in the sequence.

— For date and time types other than TIMESTAMP, the default is the appropriate zero value for the type. For the first TIMESTAMP column in a table, the default value is the current date and time. See Section 6.2.2, Date and Time Types.

— For string types other than ENUM, the default value is the empty string. For ENUM, the default is the first enumeration value (if you haven't explicitly specified another default value with the DEFAULT directive).

Default values must be constants. This means, for example, that you cannot set the default for a date column to be the value of a function such as NOW() or CURRENT_DATE.

- KEY is a synonym for INDEX.

- In MySQL, a UNIQUE key can have only distinct values. An error occurs if you try to add a new row with a key that matches an existing row.

- A PRIMARY KEY is a unique KEY with the extra constraint that all key columns must be defined as NOT NULL. In MySQL the key is named PRIMARY. A table can have only one PRIMARY KEY. If you don't have a PRIMARY KEY and some applications ask for the PRIMARY KEY in your tables, MySQL will return the first UNIQUE key, which doesn't have any NULL columns, as the PRIMARY KEY.

- A PRIMARY KEY can be a multiple-column index. However, you cannot create a multiple-column index using the PRIMARY KEY key attribute in a column specification. Doing so will mark only that single column as primary. You must use the PRIMARY KEY(index_col_name, . . .) syntax.

- If the PRIMARY or UNIQUE key consists of only one column and this is of type integer, you can also refer to it as _rowid (new in Version 3.23.11).

- If you don't assign a name to an index, the index will be assigned the same name as the first index_col_name, with an optional suffix (_2, _3, . . .) to make it unique. You can see index names for a table using SHOW INDEX FROM tbl_name. See Section 4.5.6, SHOW Syntax.

- Only the MyISAM, InnoDB, and BDB table types support indexes on columns that can have NULL values. In other cases you must declare such columns NOT NULL or an error results.

- With col_name(length) syntax, you can specify an index that uses only a part of a CHAR or VARCHAR column. This can make the index file much smaller. See Section 5.4.4, Column Indexes.

- Only the MyISAM table type supports indexing on BLOB and TEXT columns. When putting an index on a BLOB or TEXT column you *must* always specify the length of the index:

  ```
  CREATE TABLE test (blob_col BLOB, INDEX(blob_col(10)));
  ```

- When you use ORDER BY or GROUP BY with a TEXT or BLOB column, only the first max_sort_length bytes are used. See Section 6.2.3.2, The BLOB and TEXT types.

- In MySQL Version 3.23.23 or later, you can also create special **FULLTEXT** indexes. They are used for full-text searches. Only the MyISAM table type supports FULLTEXT indexes. They can be created only from VARCHAR and TEXT columns. Indexing always happens over the entire column; partial indexing is not supported. See Section 6.8, MySQL Full-Text Search, for details of operation.

- The FOREIGN KEY, CHECK, and REFERENCES clauses don't actually do anything. The syntax for them is provided only for compatibility, to make it easier to port code from other SQL servers and to run applications that create tables with references. See Section 1.7.4, MySQL Differences Compared to ANSI SQL92.

- Each NULL column takes one bit extra, rounded up to the nearest byte.

- The maximum record length in bytes can be calculated as follows:

  ```
  row length = 1
              + (sum of column lengths)
              + (number of NULL columns + 7)/8
              + (number of variable-length columns)
  ```

- The table_options and SELECT options are only implemented in MySQL Versions 3.23 and higher.

  The different table types are:

Table type	Description
BDB or Berkeley_db	Transaction-safe tables with page locking. See Section 7.6, BDB or Berkeley_DB Tables.
HEAP	The data for this table is only stored in memory. See Section 7.4, HEAP Tables.
ISAM	The original table handler. See Section 7.3, ISAM Tables.
InnoDB	Transaction-safe tables with row locking. See Section 7.5, InnoDB Tables.
MERGE	A collection of MyISAM tables used as one table. See Section 7.2, MERGE Tables.
MRG_MyISAM	An alias for MERGE tables.
MyISAM	The new binary portable table handler that is replacing ISAM. See Section 7.1, MyISAM Tables.

See Chapter 7.

If a table type is specified and that particular type is not available, MySQL will choose the closest table type to the one that you have specified. For example, if TYPE=BDB is specified and that distribution of MySQL does not support BDB tables, the table will be created as MyISAM instead.

The other table options are used to optimise the behavior of the table. In most cases, you don't have to specify any of them. The options work for all table types, if not otherwise indicated:

Option	Description
AUTO_INCREMENT	The next AUTO_INCREMENT value you want to set for your table (MyISAM).
AVG_ROW_LENGTH	An approximation of the average row length for your table. You only need to set this for large tables with variable-size records.
CHECKSUM	Set this to 1 if you want MySQL to maintain a checksum for all rows (makes the table a little slower to update but makes it easier to find corrupted tables) (MyISAM).
COMMENT	A 60-character comment for your table.
MAX_ROWS	Maximum number of rows you plan to store in the table.
MIN_ROWS	Minimum number of rows you plan to store in the table.
PACK_KEYS	Set this to 1 if you want to have a smaller index. This usually makes updates slower and reads faster (MyISAM, ISAM). Setting this to 0 will disable all packing of keys. Setting this to DEFAULT (MySQL 4.0) will tell the table handler to only pack long CHAR/VARCHAR columns.
PASSWORD	Encrypt the .frm file with a password. This option doesn't do anything in the standard MySQL version.
DELAY_KEY_WRITE	Set this to 1 if you want to delay key table updates until the table is closed (MyISAM).
ROW_FORMAT	Defines how the rows should be stored. Currently this option only works with MyISAM tables, which support the DYNAMIC and FIXED row formats. See Section 7.1.2, MyISAM Table Formats.

When you use a MyISAM table, MySQL uses the product of max_rows * avg_row_length to decide how big the resulting table will be. If you don't specify any of the preceding options, the maximum size for a table will be 4G (or 2G if your operating system only supports 2G tables). The reason for this is just to keep down the pointer sizes to make the index smaller and faster if you don't really need big files.

If you don't use PACK_KEYS, the default is to only pack strings, not numbers. If you use PACK_KEYS=1, numbers will be packed as well.

When packing binary number keys, MySQL will use prefix compression. This means that you will only get a big benefit of this if you have many numbers that are the same. Prefix compression means that every key needs one extra byte to indicate how many bytes of the previous key are the same for the next key (note that the pointer to the row is stored in high-byte-first-order directly after the key, to improve compression). This means that if you have many equal keys on two rows in a row, all following "same" keys will usually only take 2 bytes (including the pointer to the row). Compare this to the ordinary case where the following keys will take storage_size_for_key + pointer_size (usually 4). On the other hand, if all keys are totally different, you will lose 1 byte per key, if the key isn't a key that can have NULL values. (In this case the packed key length will be stored in the same byte that is used to mark if a key is NULL.)

- If you specify a SELECT after the CREATE statement, MySQL will create new fields for all elements in the SELECT. For example:

```
mysql> CREATE TABLE test (a INT NOT NULL AUTO_INCREMENT,
    ->           PRIMARY KEY (a), KEY(b))
    ->           TYPE=MyISAM SELECT b,c FROM test2;
```

This will create a MyISAM table with three columns: a, b, and c. Notice that the columns from the SELECT statement are appended to the right side of the table, not overlapped onto it. Take the following example:

```
mysql> SELECT * FROM foo;
+---+
| n |
+---+
| 1 |
+---+

mysql> CREATE TABLE bar (m INT) SELECT n FROM foo;
Query OK, 1 row affected (0.02 sec)
Records: 1  Duplicates: 0  Warnings: 0

mysql> SELECT * FROM bar;
+------+---+
| m    | n |
+------+---+
| NULL | 1 |
+------+---+
1 row in set (0.00 sec)
```

For each row in table foo, a row is inserted in bar with the values from foo and default values for the new columns.

CREATE TABLE ... SELECT will not automatically create any indexes for you. This is done intentionally to make the command as flexible as possible. If you want to have indexes in the created table, you should specify these before the SELECT statement:

```
mysql> CREATE TABLE bar (UNIQUE (n)) SELECT n FROM foo;
```

If any errors occur while copying the data to the table, it will automatically be deleted.

To ensure that the update log/binary log can be used to re-create the original tables, MySQL will not allow concurrent inserts during CREATE TABLE ... SELECT.

- The RAID_TYPE option will help you to break the 2G/4G limit for the MyISAM data file (not the index file) on operating systems that don't support big files. Note that this option is not recommended for filesystem that support big files!

  You can get more speed from the I/O bottleneck by putting RAID directories on different physical disks. RAID_TYPE will work on any OS, as long as you have configured MySQL with --with-raid. For now the only allowed RAID_TYPE is STRIPED (1 and RAID0 are aliases for this).

  If you specify RAID_TYPE=STRIPED for a MyISAM table, MyISAM will create RAID_CHUNKS subdirectories named 00, 01, 02 in the database directory. In each of these directories MyISAM will create a table_name.MYD. When writing data to the data file, the RAID handler will map the first RAID_CHUNKSIZE *1024 bytes to the first file, the next RAID_CHUNKSIZE *1024 bytes to the next file, and so on.

- UNION is used when you want to use a collection of identical tables as one. This only works with MERGE tables. See Section 7.2, MERGE Tables.

  For the moment you need to have **select**, **update**, and **delete** privileges on the tables you map to a MERGE table. All mapped tables must be in the same database as the MERGE table.

- If you want to insert data in a MERGE table, you have to specify with INSERT_METHOD into table the row should be inserted. See Section 7.2, MERGE Tables. This option was introduced in MySQL 4.0.0.

- In the created table the PRIMARY key will be placed first, followed by all UNIQUE keys and then the normal keys. This helps the MySQL optimiser to prioritise which key to use and also to more quickly detect duplicated UNIQUE keys.

- By using DATA DIRECTORY="directory" or INDEX DIRECTORY="directory" you can specify where the table handler should put its table and index files. Note that the directory should be a full path to the directory (not a relative path).

  This only works for MyISAM tables in MySQL 4.0, when you are not using the --skip-symlink option. See Section 5.6.1.2, Using symbolic links for tables.

6.5.3.1 Silent column specification changes

In some cases, MySQL silently changes a column specification from that given in a CREATE TABLE statement (this may also occur with ALTER TABLE):

- VARCHAR columns with a length less than four are changed to CHAR.

- If any column in a table has a variable length, the entire row is variable-length as a result. Therefore, if a table contains any variable-length columns (VARCHAR, TEXT, or BLOB), all CHAR columns longer than three characters are changed to VARCHAR columns. This doesn't affect how you use the columns in any way; in MySQL, VAR-CHAR is just a different way to store characters. MySQL performs this conversion because it saves space and makes table operations faster. See Chapter 7.

- TIMESTAMP display sizes must be even and in the range from 2 to 14. If you specify a display size of 0 or greater than 14, the size is coerced to 14. Odd-valued sizes in the range from 1 to 13 are coerced to the next higher even number.

- You cannot store a literal NULL in a TIMESTAMP column; setting it to NULL sets it to the current date and time. Because TIMESTAMP columns behave this way, the NULL and NOT NULL attributes do not apply in the normal way and are ignored if you specify them. DESCRIBE tbl_name always reports that a TIMESTAMP column may be assigned NULL values.

- MySQL maps certain column types used by other SQL database vendors to MySQL types. See Section 6.2.5, Using Column Types from Other Database Engines.

If you want to see whether MySQL used a column type other than the one you specified, issue a DESCRIBE tbl_name statement after creating or altering your table.

Certain other column type changes may occur if you compress a table using myisam-pack. See Section 7.1.2.3, Compressed table characteristics.

6.5.4 ALTER TABLE Syntax

```
ALTER [IGNORE] TABLE tbl_name alter_spec [, alter_spec ...]

alter_specification:
        ADD [COLUMN] create_definition [FIRST | AFTER column_name ]
    or  ADD [COLUMN] (create_definition, create_definition,...)
    or  ADD INDEX [index_name] (index_col_name,...)
    or  ADD PRIMARY KEY (index_col_name,...)
    or  ADD UNIQUE [index_name] (index_col_name,...)
    or  ADD FULLTEXT [index_name] (index_col_name,...)
    or  ADD [CONSTRAINT symbol] FOREIGN KEY index_name (index_col_name,...)
            [reference_definition]
    or  ALTER [COLUMN] col_name {SET DEFAULT literal | DROP DEFAULT}
    or  CHANGE [COLUMN] old_col_name create_definition
                [FIRST | AFTER column_name]
    or  MODIFY [COLUMN] create_definition [FIRST | AFTER column_name]
    or  DROP [COLUMN] col_name
    or  DROP PRIMARY KEY
    or  DROP INDEX index_name
    or  DISABLE KEYS
    or  ENABLE KEYS
    or  RENAME [TO] new_tbl_name
    or  ORDER BY col
    or  table_options
```

ALTER TABLE allows you to change the structure of an existing table. For example, you can add or delete columns, create or destroy indexes, change the type of existing columns, or rename columns or the table itself. You can also change the comment for the table and type of the table. See Section 6.5.3, CREATE TABLE Syntax.

If you use ALTER TABLE to change a column specification but DESCRIBE tbl_name indicates that your column was not changed, it is possible that MySQL ignored your modification for one of the reasons described in Section 6.5.3.1, Silent column specification changes. For example, if you try to change a VARCHAR column to CHAR, MySQL will still use VARCHAR if the table contains other variable-length columns.

ALTER TABLE works by making a temporary copy of the original table. The alteration is performed on the copy, then the original table is deleted and the new one is renamed. This is done in such a way that all updates are automatically redirected to the new table without any failed updates. While ALTER TABLE is executing, the original table is readable by other clients. Updates and writes to the table are stalled until the new table is ready.

Note that if you use any option to ALTER TABLE other than RENAME, MySQL will always create a temporary table, even if the data wouldn't strictly need to be copied (like when you change the name of a column). We plan to fix this in the future, but as one doesn't normally do ALTER TABLE that often this isn't that high on our TODO. For MyISAM tables, you can speed up the index recreation part (which is the slowest part of the recreation process) by setting the myisam_sort_buffer_size variable to a high value.

- To use ALTER TABLE, you need **alter**, **insert**, and **create** privileges on the table.

- IGNORE is a MySQL extension to ANSI SQL92. It controls how ALTER TABLE works if there are duplicates on unique keys in the new table. If IGNORE isn't specified, the copy is aborted and rolled back. If IGNORE is specified, then for rows with duplicates on a unique key, only the first row is used; the others are deleted.

- You can issue multiple ADD, ALTER, DROP, and CHANGE clauses in a single ALTER TABLE statement. This is a MySQL extension to ANSI SQL92, which allows only one of each clause per ALTER TABLE statement.

- CHANGE col_name, DROP col_name, and DROP INDEX are MySQL extensions to ANSI SQL92.

- MODIFY is an Oracle extension to ALTER TABLE.

- The optional word COLUMN is a pure noise word and can be omitted.

- If you use ALTER TABLE tbl_name RENAME TO new_name without any other options, MySQL simply renames the files that correspond to the table tbl_name. There is no need to create the temporary table. See Section 6.5.5, RENAME TABLE Syntax.

- create_definition clauses use the same syntax for ADD and CHANGE as for CREATE TABLE. Note that this syntax includes the column name, not just the column type. See Section 6.5.3, CREATE TABLE Syntax.

- You can rename a column using a `CHANGE old_col_name create_definition` clause. To do so, specify the old and new column names and the type that the column currently has. For example, to rename an `INTEGER` column from a to b, you can do this:

  ```
  mysql> ALTER TABLE t1 CHANGE a b INTEGER;
  ```

  If you want to change a column's type but not the name, `CHANGE` syntax still requires two column names even if they are the same. For example:

  ```
  mysql> ALTER TABLE t1 CHANGE b b BIGINT NOT NULL;
  ```

  However, as of MySQL Version 3.22.16a, you can also use `MODIFY` to change a column's type without renaming it:

  ```
  mysql> ALTER TABLE t1 MODIFY b BIGINT NOT NULL;
  ```

- If you use `CHANGE` or `MODIFY` to shorten a column for which an index exists on part of the column (for instance, if you have an index on the first 10 characters of a VAR-CHAR column), you cannot make the column shorter than the number of characters that are indexed.

- When you change a column type using `CHANGE` or `MODIFY`, MySQL tries to convert data to the new type as accurately as possible.

- In MySQL Version 3.22 or later, you can use `FIRST` or `ADD ... AFTER col_name` to add a column at a specific position within a table row. The default is to add the column last.

- `ALTER COLUMN` specifies a new default value for a column or removes the old default value. If the old default is removed and the column can be `NULL`, the new default is `NULL`. If the column cannot be `NULL`, MySQL assigns a default value, as described in Section 6.5.3, `CREATE TABLE` Syntax.

- `DROP INDEX` removes an index. This is a MySQL extension to ANSI SQL92. See Section 6.5.8, `DROP INDEX` Syntax.

- If columns are dropped from a table, the columns are also removed from any index of which they are a part. If all columns that make up an index are dropped, the index is dropped as well.

- If a table contains only one column, the column cannot be dropped. If you intend to remove the table, use `DROP TABLE` instead.

- `DROP PRIMARY KEY` drops the primary index. If no such index exists, it drops the first `UNIQUE` index in the table. (MySQL marks the first `UNIQUE` key as the `PRIMARY KEY` if no `PRIMARY KEY` was specified explicitly.)

  If you add a `UNIQUE INDEX` or `PRIMARY KEY` to a table, this is stored before any not `UNIQUE` index so that MySQL can detect duplicate keys as early as possible.

- ORDER BY allows you to create the new table with the rows in a specific order. Note that the table will not remain in this order after inserts and deletes. In some cases, it may make sorting easier for MySQL if the table is in order by the column that you wish to order it by later. This option is mainly useful when you know that you are mostly going to query the rows in a certain order. by using this option after big changes to the table, you may be able to get higher performance.

- If you use ALTER TABLE on a MyISAM table, all non-unique indexes are created in a separate batch (like in REPAIR). This should make ALTER TABLE much faster when you have many indexes.

- Since **MySQL 4.0** the preceding feature can be activated explicitly. ALTER TABLE . . . DISABLE KEYS makes MySQL stop updating non-unique indexes for MyISAM table. ALTER TABLE . . . ENABLE KEYS then should be used to re-create missing indexes. As MySQL does it with a special algorithm that is much faster than inserting keys one by one, disabling keys could give a considerable speedup on bulk inserts.

- With the C API function mysql_info(), you can find out how many records were copied, and (when IGNORE is used) how many records were deleted due to duplication of unique key values.

- The FOREIGN KEY, CHECK, and REFERENCES clauses don't actually do anything. The syntax for them is provided only for compatibility, to make it easier to port code from other SQL servers and to run applications that create tables with references. See Section 1.7.4, MySQL Differences Compared to ANSI SQL92.

Here is an example that shows some of the uses of ALTER TABLE. We begin with a table t1 that is created as follows:

```
mysql> CREATE TABLE t1 (a INTEGER,b CHAR(10));
```

To rename the table from t1 to t2:

```
mysql> ALTER TABLE t1 RENAME t2;
```

To change column a from INTEGER to TINYINT NOT NULL (leaving the name the same), and to change column b from CHAR(10) to CHAR(20) as well as renaming it from b to c:

```
mysql> ALTER TABLE t2 MODIFY a TINYINT NOT NULL, CHANGE b c CHAR(20);
```

To add a new TIMESTAMP column named d:

```
mysql> ALTER TABLE t2 ADD d TIMESTAMP;
```

To add an index on column d, and make column a the primary key:

```
mysql> ALTER TABLE t2 ADD INDEX (d), ADD PRIMARY KEY (a);
```

To remove column c:

```
mysql> ALTER TABLE t2 DROP COLUMN c;
```

To add a new AUTO_INCREMENT integer column named c:

```
mysql> ALTER TABLE t2 ADD c INT UNSIGNED NOT NULL AUTO_INCREMENT,
            ADD INDEX (c);
```

Note that we indexed c because AUTO_INCREMENT columns must be indexed, and also that we declare c as NOT NULL because indexed columns cannot be NULL.

When you add an AUTO_INCREMENT column, column values are filled in with sequence numbers for you automatically. You can set the first sequence number by executing SET INSERT_ID=# before ALTER TABLE or using the AUTO_INCREMENT = # table option. See Section 5.5.6, SET Syntax.

With MyISAM tables, if you don't change the AUTO_INCREMENT column, the sequence number will not be affected. If you drop an AUTO_INCREMENT column and then add another AUTO_INCREMENT column, the numbers will start from 1 again.

See Section A.6.1, Problems with ALTER TABLE

6.5.5 RENAME TABLE Syntax

```
RENAME TABLE tbl_name TO new_tbl_name[, tbl_name2 TO new_tbl_name2,...]
```

The rename is done atomically, which means that no other thread can access any of the tables while the rename is running. This makes it possible to replace a table with an empty one:

```
CREATE TABLE new_table (...);
RENAME TABLE old_table TO backup_table, new_table TO old_table;
```

The rename is done from left to right, which means that if you want to swap two table names, you have to:

```
RENAME TABLE old_table    TO backup_table,
             new_table    TO old_table,
             backup_table TO new_table;
```

As long as two databases are on the same disk you can also rename from one database to another:

```
RENAME TABLE current_db.tbl_name TO other_db.tbl_name;
```

When you execute RENAME, you can't have any locked tables or active transactions. You must also have the **alter** and **drop** privileges on the original table, and the **create** and **insert** privileges on the new table.

If MySQL encounters any errors in a multiple-table rename, it will do a reverse rename for all renamed tables to get everything back to the original state.

RENAME TABLE was added in MySQL 3.23.23.

6.5.6 DROP TABLE Syntax

```
DROP TABLE [IF EXISTS] tbl_name [, tbl_name,...] [RESTRICT | CASCADE]
```

DROP TABLE removes one or more tables. All table data and the table definition are *removed*, so **be careful** with this command!

In MySQL Version 3.22 or later, you can use the keywords IF EXISTS to prevent an error from occurring for tables that don't exist.

RESTRICT and CASCADE are allowed to make porting easier. For the moment they don't do anything.

Note: DROP TABLE will automatically commit current active transaction.

6.5.7 CREATE INDEX Syntax

```
CREATE [UNIQUE|FULLTEXT] INDEX index_name
      ON tbl_name (col_name[(length)],... )
```

The CREATE INDEX statement doesn't do anything in MySQL prior to Version 3.22. In Version 3.22 or later, CREATE INDEX is mapped to an ALTER TABLE statement to create indexes. See Section 6.5.4, ALTER TABLE Syntax.

Normally, you create all indexes on a table at the time the table itself is created with CRE-ATE TABLE. See Section 6.5.3, CREATE TABLE Syntax. CREATE INDEX allows you to add indexes to existing tables.

A column list of the form (col1,col2, . . .) creates a multiple-column index. Index values are formed by concatenating the values of the given columns.

For CHAR and VARCHAR columns, indexes can be created that use only part of a column, using col_name(length) syntax. (On BLOB and TEXT columns the length is required.) The following statement creates an index using the first 10 characters of the name column:

```
mysql> CREATE INDEX part_of_name ON customer (name(10));
```

Because most names usually differ in the first 10 characters, this index should not be much slower than an index created from the entire name column. Also, using partial columns for indexes can make the index file much smaller, which could save a lot of disk space and might also speed up INSERT operations!

Note that you can only add an index on a column that can have NULL values or on a BLOB/TEXT column if you are using MySQL Versions 3.23.2 or newer and are using the MyISAM table type.

For more information about how MySQL uses indexes, see Section 5.4.3, How MySQL Uses Indexes.

FULLTEXT indexes can index only VARCHAR and TEXT columns, and only in MyISAM tables. FULLTEXT indexes are available in MySQL Version 3.23.23 and later. See Section 6.8, MySQL Full-Text Search.

6.5.8 DROP INDEX Syntax

```
DROP INDEX index_name ON tbl_name
```

DROP INDEX drops the index named index_name from the table tbl_name. DROP INDEX doesn't do anything in MySQL prior to Version 3.22. In Version 3.22 or later, DROP INDEX is mapped to an ALTER TABLE statement to drop the index. See Section 6.5.4, ALTER TABLE Syntax.

6.6 Basic MySQL User Utility Commands

6.6.1 USE Syntax

```
USE db_name
```

The USE db_name statement tells MySQL to use the db_name database as the default database for subsequent queries. The database remains current until the end of the session or until another USE statement is issued:

```
mysql> USE db1;
mysql> SELECT COUNT(*) FROM mytable;      # selects from db1.mytable
mysql> USE db2;
mysql> SELECT COUNT(*) FROM mytable;      # selects from db2.mytable
```

Making a particular database current by means of the USE statement does not preclude you from accessing tables in other databases. The following example accesses the author table from the db1 database and the editor table from the db2 database:

```
mysql> USE db1;
mysql> SELECT author_name,editor_name FROM author,db2.editor
    ->        WHERE author.editor_id = db2.editor.editor_id;
```

The USE statement is provided for Sybase compatibility.

6.6.2 DESCRIBE Syntax (Get Information About Columns)

```
{DESCRIBE | DESC} tbl_name {col_name | wild}
```

DESCRIBE is a shortcut for SHOW COLUMNS FROM. See Section 4.5.6.1, Retrieving information about databases, tables, columns, and indexes.

DESCRIBE provides information about a table's columns. col_name may be a column name or a string containing the SQL % and _ wildcard characters.

If the column types are different from what you expect them to be based on a CREATE TABLE statement, note that MySQL sometimes changes column types. See Section 6.5.3.1, Silent column specification changes.

This statement is provided for Oracle compatibility.

The SHOW statement provides similar information. See Section 4.5.6, SHOW Syntax.

6.7 MySQL Transactional and Locking Commands

6.7.1 BEGIN/COMMIT/ROLLBACK Syntax

By default, MySQL runs in autocommit mode. This means that as soon as you execute an update, MySQL will store the update on disk.

If you are using transaction-safe tables (like InnoDB and BDB) you can put MySQL into non-autocommit mode with the following command:

```
SET AUTOCOMMIT=0
```

After this you must use COMMIT to store your changes to disk or ROLLBACK if you want to ignore the changes you have made since the beginning of your transaction.

If you want to switch from AUTOCOMMIT mode for one series of statements, you can use the BEGIN or BEGIN WORK statement:

```
BEGIN;
SELECT @A:=SUM(salary) FROM table1 WHERE type=1;
UPDATE table2 SET summary=@A WHERE type=1;
COMMIT;
```

Note that if you are using non-transaction-safe tables, the changes will be stored at once, independent of the status of the autocommit mode.

If you do a ROLLBACK when you have updated a non-transactional table you will get an error (ER_WARNING_NOT_COMPLETE_ROLLBACK) as a warning. All transactional safe tables will be restored but any non-transactional table will not change.

If you are using BEGIN or SET AUTOCOMMIT=0, you should use the MySQL binary log for backups instead of the older update log. Transactions are stored in the binary log in one chunk, upon COMMIT, to ensure that transactions which are rolled back are not stored. See Section 4.9.4, The Binary Update Log.

The following commands automatically end a transaction (as if you had done a COMMIT before executing the command):

Command	Command	Command
ALTER TABLE	BEGIN	CREATE INDEX
DROP DATABASE	DROP TABLE	RENAME TABLE
TRUNCATE		

You can change the isolation level for transactions with SET TRANSACTION ISOLATION LEVEL . . . . See Section 6.7.3, SET TRANSACTION Syntax.

6.7.2 LOCK TABLES/UNLOCK TABLES **Syntax**

```
LOCK TABLES tbl_name [AS alias] {READ | [READ LOCAL] | [LOW_PRIORITY] WRITE}
               [, tbl_name {READ | [LOW_PRIORITY] WRITE} ...]
...
UNLOCK TABLES
```

LOCK TABLES locks tables for the current thread. UNLOCK TABLES releases any locks held by the current thread. All tables that are locked by the current thread are automatically unlocked when the thread issues another LOCK TABLES, or when the connection to the server is closed.

The main reasons to use LOCK TABLES are for emulating transactions or getting more speed when updating tables. This is explained in more detail later.

If a thread obtains a READ lock on a table, that thread (and all other threads) can only read from the table. If a thread obtains a WRITE lock on a table, only the thread holding the lock can READ from or WRITE to the table. Other threads are blocked.

The difference between READ LOCAL and READ is that READ LOCAL allows non-conflicting INSERT statements to execute while the lock is held. This can't, however, be used if you are going to manipulate the database files outside MySQL while you hold the lock.

When you use LOCK TABLES, you must lock all tables that you are going to use and you must use the same alias that you are going to use in your queries! If you are using a table multiple times in a query (with aliases), you must get a lock for each alias!

WRITE locks normally have higher priority than READ locks, to ensure that updates are processed as soon as possible. This means that if one thread obtains a READ lock and then another thread requests a WRITE lock, subsequent READ lock requests will wait until the

WRITE thread has gotten the lock and released it. You can use LOW_PRIORITY WRITE locks to allow other threads to obtain READ locks while the thread is waiting for the WRITE lock. You should only use LOW_PRIORITY WRITE locks if you are sure that there will eventually be a time when no threads will have a READ lock.

LOCK TABLES works as follows:

1. Sort all tables to be locked in an internally defined order (from the user standpoint the order is undefined).

2. If a table is locked with a read and a write lock, put the write lock before the read lock.

3. Lock one table at a time until the thread gets all locks.

This policy ensures that table locking is deadlock-free. There are, however, other things one needs to be aware of with this schema.

If you are using a LOW_PRIORITY_WRITE lock for a table, this means only that MySQL will wait for this particular lock until there are no threads that want a READ lock. When the thread has got the WRITE lock and is waiting to get the lock for the next table in the lock table list, all other threads will wait for the WRITE lock to be released. If this becomes a serious problem with your application, you should consider converting some of your tables to transaction-safe tables.

You can safely kill a thread that is waiting for a table lock with KILL. See Section 4.5.5, KILL Syntax.

Note that you should **not** lock any tables that you are using with INSERT DELAYED because in this case the INSERT is done by a separate thread.

Normally, you don't have to lock tables, as all single UPDATE statements are atomic; no other thread can interfere with any other currently executing SQL statement. There are a few cases when you would like to lock tables anyway:

*   If you are going to run many operations on a bunch of tables, it's much faster to lock the tables you are going to use. The downside is, of course, that no other thread can update a READ-locked table and no other thread can read a WRITE-locked table.

    The reason some things are faster under LOCK TABLES is that MySQL will not flush the key cache for the locked tables until UNLOCK TABLES is called (normally the key cache is flushed after each SQL statement). This speeds up inserting/updating/deletes on MyISAM tables.

*   If you are using a table handler in MySQL that doesn't support transactions, you must use LOCK TABLES if you want to ensure that no other thread comes between a SELECT and an UPDATE. The following example requires LOCK TABLES in order to execute safely:

```
mysql> LOCK TABLES trans READ, customer WRITE;
mysql> SELECT SUM(value) FROM trans WHERE customer_id=some_id;
mysql> UPDATE customer SET total_value=sum_from_previous_statement
    ->           WHERE customer_id=some_id;
mysql> UNLOCK TABLES;
```

Without LOCK TABLES, there is a chance that another thread might insert a new row in the trans table between execution of the SELECT and UPDATE statements.

By using incremental updates (UPDATE customer SET value=value+new_value) or the LAST_INSERT_ID() function, you can avoid using LOCK TABLES in many cases.

You can also solve some cases by using the user-level lock functions GET_LOCK() and RELEASE_LOCK(). These locks are saved in a hash table in the server and implemented with pthread_mutex_lock() and pthread_mutex_unlock() for high speed. See Section 6.3.6.2, Miscellaneous functions.

See Section 5.3.1, How MySQL Locks Tables, for more information on locking policy.

You can lock all tables in all databases with read locks with the FLUSH TABLES WITH READ LOCK command. See Section 4.5.3, FLUSH Syntax. This is a very convenient way to get backups if you have a filesystem, like Veritas, that can take snapshots in time.

Note: LOCK TABLES is not transaction-safe and will automatically commit any active transactions before attempting to lock the tables.

6.7.3 SET TRANSACTION **Syntax**

```
SET [GLOBAL | SESSION] TRANSACTION ISOLATION LEVEL
{ READ UNCOMMITTED | READ COMMITTED | REPEATABLE READ | SERIALIZABLE }
```

Sets the transaction isolation level for the global, whole session or the next transaction.

The default behavior is to set the isolation level for the next (not started) transaction.

If you set the GLOBAL privilege it will affect all newly created threads. You will need the **process** privilege to do do this.

Setting the SESSION privilege will affect the following and all future transactions.

You can set the default isolation level for mysqld with --transaction-isolation= . . . . See Section 4.1.1, mysqld Command-Line Options.

6.8 MySQL Full-Text Search

As of Version 3.23.23, MySQL has support for full-text indexing and searching. Full-text indexes in MySQL are an index of type FULLTEXT. FULLTEXT indexes can be created from VARCHAR and TEXT columns at CREATE TABLE time or added later with ALTER TABLE or CREATE INDEX. For large datasets, it will be much faster to load your data into a table that has no FULLTEXT index, then create the index with ALTER TABLE (or CREATE INDEX). Loading data into a table that already has a FULLTEXT index will be slower.

Full-text searching is performed with the MATCH() function:

```
mysql> CREATE TABLE articles (
    ->   id INT UNSIGNED AUTO_INCREMENT NOT NULL PRIMARY KEY,
    ->   title VARCHAR(200),
    ->   body TEXT,
    ->   FULLTEXT (title,body)
    -> );
Query OK, 0 rows affected (0.00 sec)

mysql> INSERT INTO articles VALUES
    -> (0,'MySQL Tutorial', 'DBMS stands for DataBase ...'),
    -> (0,'How To Use MySQL Efficiently', 'After you went through a ...'),
    -> (0,'Optimising MySQL','In this tutorial we will show ...'),
    -> (0,'1001 MySQL Trick','1. Never run mysqld as root. 2. ...'),
    -> (0,'MySQL vs. YourSQL', 'In the following database comparison ...'),
    -> (0,'MySQL Security', 'When configured properly, MySQL ...');
Query OK, 6 rows affected (0.00 sec)
Records: 6  Duplicates: 0  Warnings: 0

mysql> SELECT * FROM articles
    ->           WHERE MATCH (title,body) AGAINST ('database');
+----+-------------------+-------------------------------------------+
| id | title             | body                                      |
+----+-------------------+-------------------------------------------+
|  5 | MySQL vs. YourSQL | In the following database comparison ...   |
|  1 | MySQL Tutorial    | DBMS stands for DataBase ...              |
+----+-------------------+-------------------------------------------+
2 rows in set (0.00 sec)
```

The MATCH() function performs a natural-language search for a string against a text collection (a set of one or more columns included in a FULLTEXT index). The search string is given as the argument to AGAINST(). The search is performed in case-insensitive fashion. For every row in the table, MATCH() returns a relevance value—that is, a similarity measure between the search string and the text in that row in the columns named in the MATCH() list.

When MATCH() is used in a WHERE clause (see the previous example) the rows returned are automatically sorted with highest relevance first. Relevance values are non-negative floating-point numbers. Zero relevance means no similarity. Relevance is computed based on the number of words in the row, the number of unique words in that row, the total number of words in the collection, and the number of documents (rows) that contain a particular word.

It is also possible to perform a boolean mode search. This is explained later in this section.

The preceding example is a basic illustration showing how to use the MATCH() function. Rows are returned in order of decreasing relevance.

The next example shows how to retrieve the relevance values explicitly. As neither WHERE nor ORDER BY clauses are present, returned rows are not ordered.

```
mysql> SELECT id,MATCH (title,body) AGAINST ('Tutorial') FROM articles;
+----+------------------------------------------+
| id | MATCH (title,body) AGAINST ('Tutorial')  |
+----+------------------------------------------+
|  1 |                        0.64840710366884  |
|  2 |                                       0  |
|  3 |                        0.66266459031789  |
|  4 |                                       0  |
|  5 |                                       0  |
|  6 |                                       0  |
+----+------------------------------------------+
6 rows in set (0.00 sec)
```

The following example is more complex. The query returns the relevance and still sorts the rows in order of decreasing relevance. To achieve this result, you should specify MATCH() twice. This will cause no additional overhead because the MySQL optimiser will notice that the two MATCH() calls are identical and invoke the full-text search code only once.

```
mysql> SELECT id, body, MATCH (title,body) AGAINST
    -> ('Security implications of running MySQL as root') AS score
    -> FROM articles WHERE MATCH (title,body) AGAINST
    -> ('Security implications of running MySQL as root');
+----+--------------------------------------+----------------+
| id | body                                 | score          |
+----+--------------------------------------+----------------+
|  4 | 1. Never run mysqld as root. 2. ...  | 1.5055546709332 |
|  6 | When configured properly, MySQL ...  |  1.31140957288  |
+----+--------------------------------------+----------------+
2 rows in set (0.00 sec)
```

MySQL uses a very simple parser to split text into words. A "word" is any sequence of characters consisting of letters, numbers, ', and _. Any "word" that is present in the stop-word list or is just too short (3 characters or less) is ignored.

Every correct word in the collection and in the query is weighted according to its significance in the query or collection. This way, a word that is present in many documents will have lower weight (and may even have a zero weight) because it has lower semantic value in this particular collection. Otherwise, if the word is rare, it will receive a higher weight. The weights of the words are then combined to compute the relevance of the row.

Such a technique works best with large collections (in fact, it was carefully tuned this way). For very small tables, word distribution does not reflect adequately their semantic value, and this model may sometimes produce bizarre results.

```
mysql> SELECT * FROM articles WHERE MATCH (title,body) AGAINST ('MySQL');
Empty set (0.00 sec)
```

The search for the word MySQL produces no results in the previous example because that word is present in more than half the rows. As such, it is effectively treated as a stopword (that is, a word with zero semantic value). This is the most desirable behavior—a natural language query should not return every second row from a 1GB table.

A word that matches half of the rows in a table is less likely to locate relevant documents. In fact, it will most likely find plenty of irrelevant documents. We all know this happens far too often when we are trying to find something on the Internet with a search engine. It is with this reasoning that such rows have been assigned a low semantic value in **this particular dataset**.

As of Version 4.0.1, MySQL can also perform boolean full-text searches using the IN BOOLEAN MODE modifier.

```
mysql> SELECT * FROM articles WHERE MATCH (title,body)
    ->     AGAINST ('+MySQL -YourSQL' IN BOOLEAN MODE);
+----+-------------------------------+-------------------------------------+
| id | title                         | body                                |
+----+-------------------------------+-------------------------------------+
|  1 | MySQL Tutorial                | DBMS stands for DataBase ...        |
|  2 | How To Use MySQL Efficiently  | After you went through a ...        |
|  3 | Optimising MySQL              | In this tutorial we will show ...   |
|  4 | 1001 MySQL Trick              | 1. Never run mysqld as root. 2. ... |
|  6 | MySQL Security                | When configured properly, MySQL ... |
+----+-------------------------------+-------------------------------------+
```

This query retrieved all the rows that contain the word MySQL (note: the 50% threshold is not used), but that do **not** contain the word YourSQL. Note that a boolean mode search does not auto-magically sort rows in order of decreasing relevance. You can see this from the result of the preceding query, where the row with the highest relevance (the one that contains MySQL twice) is listed last, not first. A boolean full-text search can also work even without a FULLTEXT index, although it would be **slow**.

The boolean full-text search capability supports the following operators:

+

A leading plus sign indicates that this word **must be** present in every row returned.

−

A leading minus sign indicates that this word **must not be** present in any row returned.

By default (when neither plus nor minus is specified) the word is optional, but the rows that contain it will be rated higher. This mimics the behaviour of MATCH() ... AGAINST() without the IN BOOLEAN MODE modifier.

`< >`

These two operators are used to change a word's contribution to the relevance value that is assigned to a row. The < operator decreases the contribution and the > operator increases it.

`( )`

Parentheses are used to group words into subexpressions.

`~`

A leading tilde acts as a negation operator, causing the word's contribution to the row relevance to be negative. It's useful for marking noise words. A row that contains such a word will be rated lower than others, but will not be excluded altogether, as it would be with the – operator.

`*`

An asterisk is the truncation operator. Unlike the other operators, it should be **appended** to the word, not prepended.

`"`

The phrase, that is enclosed in double quotes `"`, matches only rows that contain this phrase **literally, as it was typed**.

And here are some examples:

`apple banana`

find rows that contain at least one of these words.

`+apple +juice`

. . . both words.

`+apple macintosh.`

. . . word "apple", but rank it higher if it also contain "macintosh".

`+apple -macintosh`

. . . word "apple" but not "macintosh".

`+apple +(>pie <strudel)`

. . . "apple" and "pie", or "apple" and "strudel" (in any order), but rank "apple pie" higher than "apple strudel".

`apple*`

. . . "apple", "apples", "applesauce", and "applet".

`"some words"`

. . . "some words of wisdom", but not "some noise words".

6.8.1 Full-Text Restrictions

- All parameters to the MATCH() function must be columns from the same table that is part of the same FULLTEXT index, unless the MATCH() is IN BOOLEAN MODE.

- The MATCH() column list must exactly match the column list in some FULLTEXT index definition for the table, unless this MATCH() is IN BOOLEAN MODE.

- The argument to AGAINST() must be a constant string.

6.8.2 Fine-Tuning MySQL Full-Text Search

Unfortunately, full-text search has few user-tunable parameters yet, although adding some is very high on the TODO. If you have a MySQL source distribution (see Section 2.3, Installing a MySQL Source Distribution), you can exert more control over full-text searching behavior.

Note that full-text search was carefully tuned for the best searching effectiveness. Modifying the default behavior will, in most cases, only make the search results worse. Do not alter the MySQL sources unless you know what you are doing!

- The minimum length of words to be indexed is defined by the MySQL variable ft_min_word_length. See Section 4.5.6.4, SHOW VARIABLES. Change it to the value you prefer, and rebuild your FULLTEXT indexes.

- The stopword list is defined in myisam/ft_static.c Modify it to your taste, recompile MySQL, and rebuild your FULLTEXT indexes.

- The 50% threshold is determined by the particular weighting scheme chosen. To disable it, change the following line in myisam/ftdefs.h:

```
#define GWS_IN_USE GWS_PROB
```

to:

```
#define GWS_IN_USE GWS_FREQ
```

Then recompile MySQL. There is no need to rebuild the indexes in this case. **Note**: by doing this you **severely** decrease MySQL's ability to provide adequate relevance values for the MATCH() function. If you really need to search for such common words, it would be better to search using IN BOOLEAN MODE instead, which does not observe the 50% threshold.

- Sometimes the search engine maintainer would like to change the operators used for boolean full-text searches. These are defined by the ft_boolean_syntax variable. See Section 4.5.6.4, SHOW VARIABLES. Still, this variable is read-only, so its value is set in myisam/ft_static.c.

6.8.3 Full-Text Search TODO

- Make all operations with FULLTEXT index **faster**.

- Proximity operators.

- Support for "always-index words". They could be any strings the user wants to treat as words. Examples are "C++", "AS/400", "TCP/IP", etc.

- Support for full-text search in MERGE tables.

- Support for multi-byte charsets.

- Make stopword list to depend on the language of the data.

- Stemming (dependent on the language of the data, of course).

- Generic user-suppliable UDF preparser.

- Make the model more flexible (by adding some adjustable parameters to FULLTEXT in CREATE/ALTER TABLE).

6.9 MySQL Query Cache

From Version 4.0.1, MySQL server features a Query Cache. When in use, the query cache stores the text of a SELECT query together with the corresponding result that is sent to a client. If another identical query is received, the server can then retrieve the results from the query cache rather than parsing and executing the same query again.

The query cache is extremely useful in an environment where (some) tables don't change very often and you have a lot of identical queries. This is a typical situation for many web servers that use a lot of dynamic content.

Following is some performance data for the query cache (we got this by running the MySQL benchmark suite on a Linux Alpha 2x500MHz with 2G of RAM and a 64M query cache):

- If you want to disable the query cache code, set query_cache_size=0. By disabling the query cache code there is no noticeable overhead. (query cache can be excluded from code with help of configure option --without-query-cache)

- If all of the queries you're preforming are simple (such as selecting a row from a table with one row),but still differ so that the queries cannot be cached, the overhead for having the query cache active is 13%. This could be regarded as the worst-case scenario. However, in real life, queries are much more complicated than our simple example, so the overhead is normally significantly lower.

- Searches after one row in a one-row table are 238% faster. This can be regarded as close to the minimum speedup to be expected for a query that is cached.

6.9.1 How the Query Cache Operates

Queries are compared before parsing. Thus:

```
SELECT * FROM TABLE
```

and

```
Select * from table
```

are regarded as different queries for query cache, so queries need to be exactly the same (byte for byte) to be seen as identical. In addition, a query may be seen as different if for instance, one client is using a new communication protocol format or a character set different from that used by another client.

Queries that use different databases, use different protocol versions, or default character sets are considered different queries and are cached separately.

The cache does work for SELECT CALC_ROWS . . . and SELECT FOUND_ROWS() . . . type queries because the number of found rows is also stored in the cache.

If a table changes (INSERT, UPDATE, DELETE, TRUNCATE, ALTER, or DROP TABLE|DATABASE), all cached queries that used this table (possibly through a MRG_MyISAM table!) become invalid and are removed from the cache.

Transactional InnoDB tables that have been changed will be invalidated when a COMMIT is performed.

A query cannot be cached if it contains one of these functions:

Function	Function	Function	Function
User-Defined Functions	CONNECTION_ID	FOUND_ROWS	GET_LOCK
RELEASE_LOCK	LOAD_FILE	MASTER_POS_WAIT	NOW
SYSDATE	CURRENT_TIME- STAMP	CURDATE	CURRENT_DATE
CURTIME	CURRENT_TIME	DATABASE	ENCRYPT (with one parameter)
LAST_INSERT_ID	RAND	UNIX_TIME- STAMP (without parameters)	USER
BENCHMARK			

Nor can a query be cached if it contains user variables, or if it is of the forms SELECT . . . IN SHARE MODE or SELECT * FROM AUTOINCREMENT_FIELD IS NULL (to retrieve last insert id - ODBC workaround).

However, FOUND_ROWS() will return the correct value, even if the preceding query was fetched from the cache.

Queries that don't use any tables, or in cases where the user has a column privilege for any of the involved tables, are not cached.

Before a query is fetched from the query cache, MySQL will check that the user has the SELECT privilege to all the involved databases and tables. If this is not the case, the cached result will not be used.

6.9.2 Query Cache Configuration

The query cache adds a few MySQL system variables for mysqld which may be set in a configuration file, on the command-line when starting mysqld:

query_cache_limit
> Don't cache results that are bigger than this. (Default 1M.)

query_cache_size
> The memory allocated to store results from old queries. If this is 0, the query cache is disabled (default).

query_cache_startup_type
> This may be set (only numeric) to:

Option	Description
0	OFF (don't cache or retrieve results)
1	ON (cache all results except SELECT SQL_NO_CACHE . . . queries)
2	DEMAND (cache only SELECT SQL_CACHE . . . queries)

Inside a thread (connection), the behaviour of the query cache can be changed from the default. The syntax is as follows:

```
SQL_QUERY_CACHE_TYPE = OFF | ON | DEMAND
SQL_QUERY_CACHE_TYPE = 0   | 1  | 2
```

Option	Description
0 or OFF	Don't cache or retrieve results.
1 or ON	Cache all results except SELECT SQL_NO_CACHE . . . queries.
2 or DEMAND	Cache only SELECT SQL_CACHE . . . queries.

SQL_QUERY_CACHE_TYPE depends on the value of query_cache_startup_type when the thread was created. This is the default.

6.9.3 Query Cache Options in SELECT

There are two possible query cache-related parameters that may be specified in a SELECT query:

Option	Description
SQL_CACHE	If SQL_QUERY_CACHE_TYPE is DEMAND, allow the query to be cached. If SQL_QUERY_CACHE_TYPE is ON, this is the default. If SQL_QUERY_CACHE_TYPE is OFF, do nothing.
SQL_NO_CACHE	Make this query non-cachable don't allow this query to be stored in the cache.

6.9.4 Query Cache Status and Maintenance

With the FLUSH QUERY CACHE command you can defragment the query cache to better utilise its memory. This command will not remove any queries from the cache. FLUSH TABLES also flushes the query cache.

The RESET QUERY CACHE command removes all query results from the query cache.

You can monitor query cache performance in SHOW STATUS:

Variable	Description
Qcache_queries_in_cache	Number of queries registered in the cache
Qcache_inserts	Number of queries added to the cache
Qcache_hits	Number of cache hits
Qcache_not_cached	Number of non-cached queries (not cachable, or due to SQL_QUERY_CACHE_TYPE)
Qcache_free_memory	Amount of free memory for query cache
Qcache_total_blocks	Total number of blocks in query cache
Qcache_free_blocks	Number of free memory blocks in query cache

Total number of queries = Qcache_inserts + Qcache_hits + Qcache_not_cached.

The query cache uses variable-length blocks, so Qcache_total_blocks and Qcache_free_blocks may indicate query cache memory fragmentation. After FLUSH QUERY CACHE only a single (big) free block remains.

Note: Every query needs a minimum of two blocks (one for the query text and one or more for the query results). Also, every table that is used by a query needs one block, but if two or more queries use the same table only one block needs to be allocated.

7

MySQL Table Types

As of MySQL Version 3.23.6, you can choose between three basic table formats: ISAM, HEAP, and MyISAM. Newer MySQL may support additional table types (InnoDB, or BDB), depending on how you compile it.

When you create a new table, you can tell MySQL which table type it should use for the table. MySQL will always create a .frm file to hold the table and column definitions. Depending on the table type, the index and data will be stored in other files.

Note that to use InnoDB tables you have to use at least the innodb_data_file_path startup option. See Section 7.5.2, InnoDB Startup Options.

The default table type in MySQL is MyISAM. If you are trying to use a table type that is not compiled-in or activated, MySQL will instead create a table of type MyISAM. This is a very useful feature when you want to copy tables between different SQL servers that support different table types (like copying tables to a slave that is optimised for speed by not having transactional tables). This automatic table changing can, however, also be very confusing for new MySQL users. We plan to fix this by introducing warnings in MySQL 4.0 and giving a warning when a table type is automatically changed.

You can convert tables between different types with the ALTER TABLE statement. See Section 6.5.4, ALTER TABLE Syntax.

Note that MySQL supports two different kinds of tables: transaction-safe tables (InnoDB and BDB) and non-transaction-safe tables (HEAP, ISAM, MERGE, and MyISAM).

Advantages of transaction-safe tables (TST):

- Safer. Even if MySQL crashes or you get hardware problems, you can get your data back, either by automatic recovery or from a backup + the transaction log.

- You can combine many statements and accept these all in one go with the COMMIT command.

- You can execute ROLLBACK to ignore your changes (if you are not running in auto commit mode).

- If an update fails, all your changes will be restored. (With NTST tables all changes that have taken place are permanent)

Advantages of non-transaction-safe tables (NTST):

- Much faster, as there is no transaction overhead.

- Will use less disk space, as there is no overhead of transactions.

- Will use less memory to do updates.

You can combine TST and NTST tables in the same statements to get the best of both worlds.

7.1 MyISAM Tables

MyISAM is the default table type in MySQL Version 3.23. It's based on the ISAM code and has a lot of useful extensions.

The index is stored in a file with the .MYI (MYIndex) extension, and the data is stored in a file with the .MYD (MYData) extension. You can check/repair MyISAM tables with the myisamchk utility. See Section 4.4.6.7, Using myisamchk for crash recovery. You can compress MyISAM tables with myisampack to take up much less space. See Section 4.7.4, myisampack, the MySQL Compressed Read-Only Table Generator.

The following is new in MyISAM:

- There is a flag in the MyISAM file that indicates whether the table was closed correctly. If mysqld is started with --myisam-recover, MyISAM tables will automatically be checked and/or repaired on open if the table wasn't closed properly.

- You can INSERT new rows in a table that doesn't have free blocks in the middle of the data file, at the same time other threads are reading from the table (concurrent insert). A free block can come from an update of a dynamic length row with much data to a row with less data, or when deleting rows. When all free blocks are used up, all future inserts will be concurrent again.

- Support for big files (63-bit) on filesystems/operating systems that support big files.

- All data is stored with the low byte first. This makes the data machine and OS independent. The only requirement is that the machine uses two's-complement signed integers (as every machine for the last 20 years has) and IEEE floating-point format (also totally dominant among mainstream machines). The only type of machines that may not support binary compatibility are embedded systems (because they sometimes have peculiar processors).

There is no big speed penalty in storing data low byte first; the bytes in a table row are normally unaligned, and it doesn't take that much more power to read an unaligned byte in order than in reverse order. The actual fetch-column-value code is also not time-critical compared to other code.

- All number keys are stored with high byte first to give better index compression.

- Internal handling of one AUTO_INCREMENT column. MyISAM will automatically update this on INSERT/UPDATE. The AUTO_INCREMENT value can be reset with myisamchk. This will make AUTO_INCREMENT columns faster (at least 10%) and old numbers will not be reused as with the old ISAM. Note that when an AUTO_INCRE-MENT is defined on the end of a multi-part key the old behavior is still present.

- When inserted in sorted order (as when you are using an AUTO_INCREMENT column) the key tree will be split so that the high node only contains one key. This will improve the space utilisation in the key tree.

- BLOB and TEXT columns can be indexed.

- NULL values are allowed in indexed columns. This takes 0-1 bytes/key.

- Maximum key length is 500 bytes by default (can be changed by recompiling). In cases of keys longer than 250 bytes, a bigger key block size than the default of 1024 bytes is used for this key.

- Maximum number of keys/table is 32 as default. This can be enlarged to 64 without having to recompile myisamchk.

- myisamchk will mark tables as checked if one runs it with --update-state. myisamchk --fast will only check those tables that don't have this mark.

- myisamchk -a stores statistics for key parts (and not only for whole keys, as in ISAM).

- Dynamic size-rows will now be much less fragmented when mixing deletes with updates and inserts. This is done by automatically combining adjacent deleted blocks and by extending blocks if the next block is deleted.

- myisampack can pack BLOB and VARCHAR columns.

- You can put the data file and index file on different directories to get more speed (with the DATA/INDEX DIRECTORY="path" option to CREATE TABLE). See Section 6.5.3, CREATE TABLE Syntax.

MyISAM also supports the following things, which MySQL will be able to use in the near future:

- Support for a true VARCHAR type; a VARCHAR column starts with a length stored in 2 bytes.

- Tables with VARCHAR may have fixed or dynamic record lengths.

- VARCHAR and CHAR may be up to 64K. All key segments have their own language definition. This will enable MySQL to have different language definitions per column.

- A hashed computed index can be used for UNIQUE. This will allow you to have UNIQUE on any combination of columns in a table. (You can't search on a UNIQUE computed index, however.)

Note that index files are usually much smaller with MyISAM than with ISAM. This means that MyISAM will normally use fewer system resources than ISAM, but will need more CPU space time when inserting data into a compressed index.

The following options to mysqld can be used to change the behavior of MyISAM tables. See Section 4.5.6.4, SHOW VARIABLES.

Option	Description
--myisam-recover=#	Automatic recovery of crashed tables.
-O myisam_sort_buffer_size=#	Buffer used when recovering tables.
--delay-key-write-for-all-tables	Don't flush key buffers between writes for any MyISAM table.
-O myisam_max_extra_sort_file_size=#	Used to help MySQL decide when to use the slow but safe key cache index create method. **Note** that this parameter is given in megabytes!
-O myisam_max_sort_file_size=#	Don't use the fast sort index method to create index if the temporary file would get bigger than this. **Note** that this parameter is given in megabytes!
-O myisam_bulk_insert_tree_size=#	Size of tree cache used in bulk insert optimisation. **Note** that this is a limit **per thread**!

The automatic recovery is activated if you start mysqld with --myisam-recover=#. See Section 4.1.1, mysqld Command-Line Options. On open, the table is checked if it's marked as crashed or if the open count variable for the table is not 0 and you are running with --skip-locking. If either of these is true the following happens.

- The table is checked for errors.

- If an error is found, try to do a fast repair (with sorting and without re-creating the data file) of the table.

- If the repair fails because of an error in the data file (for example, a duplicate key error), try again, but this time re-create the data file.

- If the repair fails, retry once more with the old repair option method (write row by row without sorting), which should be able to repair any type of error with little disk requirements.

If the recover wouldn't be able to recover all rows from a previous completed statement and you didn't specify FORCE as an option to myisam-recover, the automatic repair will abort with an error message in the error file:

```
Error: Couldn't repair table: test.g00pages
```

If you in this case had used the FORCE option you would instead have gotten a warning in the error file:

```
Warning: Found 344 of 354 rows when repairing ./test/g00pages
```

Note that if you run automatic recover with the BACKUP option, you should have a cron script that automatically moves files with names like tablename-datetime.BAK from the database directories to backup media.

Section 4.1.1, mysqld Command-Line Options.

7.1.1 Space Needed for Keys

MySQL can support different index types, but the normal type is ISAM or MyISAM. These use a B-tree index, and you can roughly calculate the size for the index file as (key_length+4)/0.67, summed over all keys. (This is for the worst case, when all keys are inserted in sorted order and we don't have any compressed keys.)

String indexes are space-compressed. If the first index part is a string, it will also be prefix-compressed. Space compression makes the index file smaller than the preceding figures if the string column has a lot of trailing space or is a VARCHAR column that is not always used to the full length. Prefix compression is used on keys that start with a string. Prefix compression helps if there are many strings with an identical prefix.

In MyISAM tables, you can also prefix-compress numbers by specifying PACK_KEYS=1 when you create the table. This helps when you have many integer keys that have an identical prefix when the numbers are stored high byte first.

7.1.2 MyISAM Table Formats

MyISAM supports 3 different table types. Two of them are chosen automatically depending on the type of columns you are using. The third, compressed tables, can only be created with the myisampack tool.

When you CREATE or ALTER a table you can, for tables that don't have BLOBs, force the table format to DYNAMIC or FIXED with the ROW_FORMAT=# table option. In the future you will be able to compress/decompress tables by specifying ROW_FORMAT=compressed | default to ALTER TABLE. See Section 6.5.3, CREATE TABLE Syntax.

7.1.2.1 Static (fixed-length) table characteristics

This is the default format. It's used when the table contains no VARCHAR, BLOB, or TEXT columns.

This is the simplest and most secure format. It is also the fastest of the on-disk formats. The speed comes from the easy way data can be found on disk. When looking up something with an index and static format it is very simple. Just multiply the row number by the row length.

Also, when scanning a table it is very easy to read a constant number of records with each disk read.

The security is evidenced if your computer crashes when writing to a fixed-size MyISAM file, in which case myisamchk can easily figure out where each row starts and ends. So it can usually reclaim all records except the partially written one. Note that in MySQL all indexes can always be reconstructed:

- All CHAR, NUMERIC, and DECIMAL columns are space-padded to the column width.

- Very quick.

- Easy to cache.

- Easy to reconstruct after a crash because records are located in fixed positions.

- Doesn't have to be reorganised (with myisamchk) unless a huge number of records are deleted and you want to return free disk space to the operating system.

- Usually requires more disk space than dynamic tables.

7.1.2.2 Dynamic table characteristics

This format is used if the table contains any VARCHAR, BLOB, or TEXT columns or if the table was created with ROW_FORMAT=dynamic.

This format is a little more complex because each row has to have a header that says how long it is. One record can also end up at more than one location when it is made longer at an update.

You can use OPTIMIZE table or myisamchk to defragment a table. If you have static data that you access/change a lot in the same table as some VARCHAR or BLOB columns, it might be a good idea to move the dynamic columns to other tables just to avoid fragmentation:

- All string columns are dynamic (except those with a length less than 4).

- Each record is preceded by a bitmap indicating which columns are empty (") for string columns, or zero for numeric columns. (This isn't the same as columns containing NULL values.) If a string column has a length of zero after removal of trailing spaces, or a numeric column has a value of zero, it is marked in the bitmap and not saved to disk. Non-empty strings are saved as a length byte plus the string contents.

- Usually takes much less disk space than fixed-length tables.

- Each record uses only as much space as is required. If a record becomes larger, it is split into as many pieces as are required. This results in record fragmentation.

- If you update a row with information that extends the row length, the row will be fragmented. In this case, you may have to run myisamchk -r from time to time to get better performance. Use myisamchk -ei tbl_name for some statistics.

- Not as easy to reconstruct after a crash because a record may be fragmented into many pieces and a link (fragment) may be missing.

- The expected row length for dynamic-sized records is:

```
3
+ (number of columns + 7) / 8
+ (number of char columns)
+ packed size of numeric columns
+ length of strings
+ (number of NULL columns + 7) / 8
```

There is a penalty of 6 bytes for each link. A dynamic record is linked whenever an update causes an enlargement of the record. Each new link will be at least 20 bytes, so the next enlargement will probably go in the same link. If not, there will be another link. You may check how many links there are with myisamchk -ed. All links may be removed with myisamchk -r.

7.1.2.3 Compressed table characteristics

This is a read-only type that is generated with the optional myisampack tool (pack_isam for ISAM tables):

- All MySQL distributions, even those that existed before MySQL went GPL, can read tables that were compressed with myisampack.

- Compressed tables take very little disk space. This minimises disk usage, which is very nice when using slow disks (like CD-ROMs).

- Each record is compressed separately (very little access overhead). The header for a record is fixed (1-3 bytes) depending on the biggest record in the table. Each column is compressed differently. Some of the compression types are:

  — There is usually a different Huffman table for each column.

  — Suffix space compression.

  — Prefix space compression.

  — Numbers with value 0 are stored using 1 bit.

— If values in an integer column have a small range, the column is stored using the smallest possible type. For example, a BIGINT column (8 bytes) may be stored as a TINYINT column (1 byte) if all values are in the range 0 to 255.

— If a column has only a small set of possible values, the column type is converted to ENUM.

— A column may use a combination of the preceding compressions.

• Can handle fixed- or dynamic-length records.

• Can be uncompressed with myisamchk.

7.1.3 MyISAM Table Problems

The file format that MySQL uses to store data has been extensively tested, but there are always circumstances that may cause database tables to become corrupted.

7.1.3.1 Corrupted MyISAM tables

Even if the MyISAM table format is very reliable (all changes to a table are written before the SQL statements returns), you can still get corrupted tables if some of the following things happen:

• The mysqld process is killed in the middle of a write.

• Unexpected shutdown of the computer (for example, if the computer is turned off).

• A hardware error.

• You are using an external program (like myisamchk) on a live table.

• A software bug in the MySQL or MyISAM code.

Typical symptoms for a corrupt table are:

• You get the error Incorrect key file for table: '...'. Try to repair it while selecting data from the table.

• Queries don't find rows in the table or return incomplete data.

You can check if a table is okay with the command CHECK TABLE. See Section 4.4.4, CHECK TABLE Syntax.

You can repair a corrupted table with REPAIR TABLE. See Section 4.4.5, REPAIR TABLE Syntax. You can also repair a table when mysqld is not running with the myisamchk command, myisamchk syntax.

If your tables get corrupted a lot you should try to find the reason for this! See Section A.4.1, What to Do if MySQL Keeps Crashing.

In this case the most important thing to know is if the table got corrupted if the mysqld died (one can easily verify this by checking if there is a recent row restarted mysqld in the mysqld error file). If this isn't the case, you should try to make a test case of this. See Section D.1.6, Making a Test Case When You Experience Table Corruption.

7.1.3.2 Client is using or hasn't closed the table properly

Each MyISAM .MYI file has in the header a counter that can be used to check if a table has been closed properly.

If you get the following warning from CHECK TABLE or myisamchk:

```
# client is using or hasn't closed the table properly
```

this means that this counter has come out of sync. This doesn't mean that the table is corrupted, but means that you should at least do a check on the table to verify that it's okay.

The counter works as follows:

*   The first time a table is updated in MySQL, a counter in the header of the index files is incremented.

*   The counter is not changed during further updates.

*   When the last instance of a table is closed (because of a FLUSH or because there isn't room in the table cache) the counter is decremented if the table has been updated at any point.

*   When you repair the table or check the table and it was okay, the counter is reset to 0.

*   To avoid problems with interaction with other processes that may do a check on the table, the counter is not decremented on close if it was 0.

In other words, the only ways this can go out of sync are:

*   The MyISAM tables are copied without a LOCK and FLUSH TABLES.

*   MySQL has crashed between an update and the final close. (Note that the table may still be okay, as MySQL always issues writes for everything between each statement.)

*   Someone has done a myisamchk --repair or myisamchk --update-state on a table that was in use by mysqld.

*   Many mysqld servers are using the table and one has done a REPAIR or CHECK of the table while it was in use by another server. In this setup the CHECK is safe to do (even if you will get the warning from other servers), but REPAIR should be avoided, as it currently replaces the data file with a new one, which is not signaled to the other servers.

7.2 MERGE Tables

MERGE tables are new in MySQL Version 3.23.25. The code is still in gamma, but should be reasonable stable.

A MERGE table (also known as a MRG_MyISAM table) is a collection of identical MyISAM tables that can be used as one. You can only SELECT, DELETE, and UPDATE from the collection of tables. If you DROP the MERGE table, you are only dropping the MERGE specification.

Note that DELETE FROM merge_table used without a WHERE will only clear the mapping for the table, not delete everything in the mapped tables. (We plan to fix this in 4.1.)

With identical tables we mean that all tables are created with identical column and key information. You can't put a MERGE over tables where the columns are packed differently, don't have exactly the same columns, or have the keys in a different order. Some of the tables can, however, be compressed with myisampack. See Section 4.7.4, myisampack, the MySQL Compressed Read-Only Table Generator.

When you create a MERGE table, you will get a .frm table definition file and a .MRG table list file. The .MRG just contains a list of the index files (.MYI files) that should be used as one. All used tables must be in the same database as the MERGE table itself.

For the moment, you need to have **select**, **update**, and **delete** privileges on the tables you map to a MERGE table.

MERGE tables can help you solve the following problems:

- Easily manage a set of log tables. For example, you can put data from different months into separate files, compress some of them with myisampack, and then create a MERGE to use these as one.

- Give you more speed. You can split a big read-only table based on some criteria and then put the different table part on different disks. A MERGE table on this could be much faster than using the big table. (You can, of course, also use a RAID to get the same kind of benefits.)

- Do more efficient searches. If you know exactly what you are looking for, you can search in just one of the split tables for some queries and use **MERGE** table for others. You can even have many different MERGE tables active, with possible overlapping files.

- More efficient repairs. It's easier to repair the individual files that are mapped to a MERGE file than trying to repair a real big file.

- Instant mapping of many files as one. A MERGE table uses the index of the individual tables. It doesn't need to maintain an index of one. This makes MERGE table collections *very* fast to make or remap. Note that you must specify the key definitions when you create a MERGE table!

- If you have a set of tables that you join to a big table on demand or batch, you should instead create a MERGE table on them on demand. This is much faster and will save a lot of disk space.

- Go around the file-size limit for the operating system.

- You can create an alias/synonym for a table by just using MERGE over one table. There shouldn't be any really notable performance impacts of doing this (only a couple of indirect calls and memcpys for each read).

The disadvantages with MERGE tables are:

- You can only use identical MyISAM tables for a MERGE table.

- AUTO_INCREMENT columns are not automatically updated on INSERT.

- REPLACE doesn't work.

- MERGE tables uses more file descriptors. If you are using a **MERGE** that maps over 10 tables and 10 users are using this, you are using 10*10 + 10 file descriptors. (10 data files for 10 users and 10 shared index files.)

- Key reads are slower. When you do a read on a key, the MERGE handler will need to issue a read on all underlying tables to check which one most closely matches the given key. If you then do a 'read-next,' the merge table handler will need to search the read buffers to find the next key. Only when one key buffer is used up will the handler need to read the next key block. This makes MERGE keys much slower on eq_ref searches, but not much slower on ref searches. See Section 5.2.1, EXPLAIN Syntax (Get Information About a SELECT).

- You can't do DROP TABLE, ALTER TABLE, or DELETE FROM table_name without a WHERE clause on any of the tables that are mapped by a MERGE table that is 'open'. If you do this, the MERGE table may still refer to the original table and you will get unexpected results.

When you create a MERGE table you have to specify with UNION(list-of-tables) which tables you want to use as one. Optionally you can specify with INSERT_METHOD if you want insert for the MERGE table to happen in the first or last table in the UNION list. If you don't specify INSERT_METHOD or specify NO, all INSERT commands on the MERGE table will return an error.

The following example shows you how to use MERGE tables:

```
CREATE TABLE t1 (a INT AUTO_INCREMENT PRIMARY KEY, message CHAR(20));
CREATE TABLE t2 (a INT AUTO_INCREMENT PRIMARY KEY, message CHAR(20));
INSERT INTO t1 (message) VALUES ("Testing"),("table"),("t1");
INSERT INTO t2 (message) VALUES ("Testing"),("table"),("t2");
CREATE TABLE total (a INT NOT NULL, message CHAR(20), KEY(a))
        TYPE=MERGE UNION=(t1,t2) INSERT_METHOD=LAST;
```

Note that we didn't create a UNIQUE or PRIMARY KEY in the total table, as the key isn't going to be unique in the total table.

Note that you can also manipulate the .MRG file directly from the outside of the MySQL server:

```
shell> cd /mysql-data-directory/current-database
shell> ls -1 t1.MYI t2.MYI > total.MRG
shell> mysqladmin flush-tables
```

Now you can do things like:

```
mysql> SELECT * FROM total;
+---+---------+
| a | message |
+---+---------+
| 1 | Testing |
| 2 | table   |
| 3 | t1      |
| 1 | Testing |
| 2 | table   |
| 3 | t2      |
+---+---------+
```

To remap a MERGE table you can do one of the following:

- DROP the table and re-create it.

- Use ALTER TABLE table_name UNION(. . .).

- Change the .MRG file and issue a FLUSH TABLE on the MERGE table and all underlying tables to force the handler to read the new definition file.

7.2.1 MERGE Table Problems

The following are the known problems with MERGE tables:

- MERGE tables cannot maintain UNIQUE constraints over the whole table. When you do INSERT, the data goes into the first or last table (according to INSERT_METHOD=xxx) and this MyISAM table ensures that the data is unique, but it knows nothing about the first MyISAM table.

- DELETE FROM merge_table used without a WHERE will only clear the mapping for the table, not delete everything in the mapped tables.

- RENAME TABLE on a table used in an active MERGE table may corrupt the table. This will be fixed in MySQL 4.0.x.

- Creation of a table of type MERGE doesn't check if the underlying tables are of compatible types. If you use MERGE tables in this fashion, you are very likely to run into strange problems.

- If you use ALTER TABLE to first add a UNIQUE index to a table used in a MERGE table and then use ALTER TABLE to add a normal index on the MERGE table, the key order will be different for the tables if there was an old non-unique key in the table. This is because ALTER TABLE puts UNIQUE keys before normal keys to be able to detect duplicate keys as early as possible.

- The range optimizer can't yet use MERGE table efficiently and may sometimes produce non-optimal joins. This will be fixed in MySQL 4.0.x.

- DROP TABLE on a table that is in use by a MERGE table will not work on Windows because the MERGE handler does the table mapping hidden from the upper layer of MySQL. Because Windows doesn't allow you to drop files that are open, you first must flush all MERGE tables (with FLUSH TABLES) or drop the MERGE table before dropping the table. We will fix this at the same time we introduce VIEWs.

7.3 ISAM Tables

You can also use the deprecated ISAM table type. This will disappear rather soon (probably in MySQL 4.1) because MyISAM is a better implementation of the same thing. ISAM uses a B-tree index. The index is stored in a file with the .ISM extension, and the data is stored in a file with the .ISD extension. You can check/repair ISAM tables with the isam-chk utility. See Section 4.4.6.7, Using myisamchk for crash recovery.

ISAM has the following features/properties:

- Compressed and fixed-length keys.
- Fixed and dynamic record length.
- 16 keys with 16 key parts/key.
- Max key length 256 (default).
- Data is stored in machine format; this is fast, but is machine/OS-dependent.

Most of the things true for MyISAM tables are also true for ISAM tables. See Section 7.1, MyISAM Tables. The major differences compared to MyISAM tables are:

- ISAM tables are not binary-portable across OS/platforms.
- Can't handle tables > 4G.
- Only support prefix compression on strings.
- Smaller key limits.
- Dynamic tables get more fragmented.
- Tables are compressed with pack_isam rather than with myisampack.

If you want to convert an ISAM table to a MyISAM table so that you can use utilities such as mysqlcheck, use an ALTER TABLE statement:

```
mysql> ALTER TABLE tbl_name TYPE = MYISAM;
```

The embedded MySQL versions doesn't support ISAM tables.

7.4 HEAP Tables

HEAP tables use a hashed index and are stored in memory. This makes them very fast, but if MySQL crashes you will lose all data stored in them. HEAP is very useful for temporary tables!

The MySQL internal HEAP tables use 100% dynamic hashing without overflow areas. There is no extra space needed for free lists. HEAP tables also don't have problems with delete + inserts, which normally is common with hashed tables:

```
mysql> CREATE TABLE test TYPE=HEAP SELECT ip,SUM(downloads) AS down
    ->                    FROM log_table GROUP BY ip;
mysql> SELECT COUNT(ip),AVG(down) FROM test;
mysql> DROP TABLE test;
```

Here are some things you should consider when you use HEAP tables:

- You should always specify MAX_ROWS in the CREATE statement to ensure that you accidentally do not use all memory.

- Indexes will only be used with = and <=> (but are *very* fast).

- HEAP tables can only use whole keys to search for a row; compare this to MyISAM tables where any prefix of the key can be used to find rows.

- HEAP tables use a fixed record length format.

- HEAP doesn't support BLOB/TEXT columns.

- HEAP doesn't support AUTO_INCREMENT columns.

- HEAP doesn't support an index on a NULL column.

- You can have non-unique keys in a HEAP table (this isn't common for hashed tables).

- HEAP tables are shared between all clients (just like any other table).

- You can't search for the next entry in order (that is, to use the index to do an ORDER BY).

- Data for HEAP tables is allocated in small blocks. The tables are 100% dynamic (on inserting). No overflow areas and no extra key space are needed. Deleted rows are put in a linked list and are reused when you insert new data into the table.

- You need enough extra memory for all HEAP tables that you want to use at the same time.

- To free memory, you should execute DELETE FROM heap_table, TRUNCATE heap_table, or DROP TABLE heap_table.

- MySQL cannot find out approximately how many rows there are between two values (this is used by the range optimiser to decide which index to use). This may affect some queries if you change a MyISAM table to a HEAP table.

- To ensure that you accidentally don't do anything foolish, you can't create HEAP tables bigger than max_heap_table_size.

The memory needed for one row in a HEAP table is:

```
SUM_OVER_ALL_KEYS(max_length_of_key + sizeof(char*) * 2)
+ ALIGN(length_of_row+1, sizeof(char*))
```

sizeof(char*) is 4 on 32-bit machines and 8 on 64-bit machines.

7.5 InnoDB Tables

7.5.1 InnoDB Tables Overview

InnoDB provides MySQL with a transaction-safe (ACID-compliant) table handler with commit, rollback, and crash recovery capabilities. InnoDB does locking on row level and also provides an Oracle-style consistent non-locking read in SELECTs. These features increase multi-user concurrency and performance. There is no need for lock escalation in InnoDB because row level locks in InnoDB fit in very little space. InnoDB tables support FOREIGN KEY constraints as the first table type in MySQL.

InnoDB has been designed for maximum performance when processing large data volumes. Its CPU efficiency is probably not matched by any other disk-based relational database engine.

Technically, InnoDB is a complete database backend placed under MySQL. InnoDB has its own buffer pool for caching data and indexes in main memory. InnoDB stores its tables and indexes in a tablespace, which may consist of several files. This is different from, for example, MyISAM tables, where each table is stored as a separate file. InnoDB tables can be of any size also on those operating systems where file-size is limited to 2G.

You can find the latest information about InnoDB at http://www.innodb.com/. The most up-to-date version of the InnoDB manual is always placed there, and you can also order commercial licenses and support for InnoDB.

InnoDB is currently (October 2001) used in production at several large database sites requiring high performance. The famous Internet news site Slashdot.org runs on InnoDB. Mytrix, Inc. stores over 1TB of data in InnoDB, and another site handles an average load of 800 inserts/updates per second in InnoDB.

InnoDB tables are included in the MySQL source distribution starting from 3.23.34a and are activated in the MySQL -Max binary. For Windows the -Max binaries are contained in the standard distribution.

If you have downloaded a binary version of MySQL that includes support for InnoDB, simply follow the instructions of the MySQL manual for installing a binary version of MySQL. If you already have MySQL-3.23 installed, then the simplest way to install MySQL -Max is to replace the server executable mysqld with the corresponding executable in the -Max distribution. MySQL and MySQL -Max differ only in the server executable. See Section 2.2.7, Installing a MySQL Binary Distribution. See Section 4.7.5, mysqld-max, an Extended mysqld Server.

To compile MySQL with InnoDB support, download MySQL-3.23.34a or newer version from http://www.mysql.com/ and configure MySQL with the --with-innodb option. See the MySQL manual about installing a MySQL source distribution. See Section 2.3, Installing a MySQL Source Distribution.

```
cd /path/to/source/of/mysql-3.23.37
./configure --with-innodb
```

To use InnoDB you have to specify InnoDB startup options in your my.cnf or my.ini file. The minimal way to modify it is to add to the [mysqld] section the line

```
innodb_data_file_path=ibdata:30M
```

but to get good performance it is best that you specify options as recommended. See Section 7.5.2, InnoDB Startup Options.

InnoDB is distributed under the GNU GPL License Version 2 (of June 1991). In the source distribution of MySQL, InnoDB appears as a subdirectory.

7.5.2 InnoDB Startup Options

To use InnoDB tables in MySQL-Max-3.23 you MUST specify configuration parameters in the [mysqld] section of the configuration file my.cnf, or on Windows optionally in my.ini.

At the minimum, in 3.23 you must specify innodb_data_file_path. In MySQL-4.0 you do not need to specify even innodb_data_file_path: the default for it is to create an auto-extending 16M file ibdata1 to the datadir of MySQL. (In MySQL-4.0.0 and 4.0.1 the data file is 64M and not auto-extending.)

But to get good performance you MUST explicitly set the InnoDB parameters listed in the following examples.

Starting from versions 3.23.50 and 4.0.2 InnoDB allows the last data file on the innodb_data_file_path line to be specified as **auto-extending**. The syntax for innodb_data_file_path is then the following:

```
pathtodata file:sizespecification;pathtodata file:sizespecification;...
...  ;pathtodata file:sizespecification[:autoextend[:max:sizespecification]]
```

If you specify the last data file with the autoextend option, InnoDB will extend the last data file if it runs out of free space in the tablespace. The increment is 8M at a time. An example:

```
innodb_data_file_path = /ibdata/ibdata1:100M:autoextend
```

instructs InnoDB to create just a single data file whose initial size is 100M and which is extended in 8M blocks when space runs out. If the disk becomes full you may want to add another data file to another disk, for example. Then you have to look at the size of ibdata1, round the size downward to the closest multiple of 1024 * 1024 bytes (= 1M), and specify the rounded size of ibdata1 explicitly in innodb_data_file_path. After that you can add another data file:

```
innodb_data_file_path = /ibdata/ibdata1:988M;/disk2/ibdata2:50M:autoextend
```

Be cautious on filesystems where the maximum file-size is 2G! InnoDB is not aware of the OS maximum file-size. On those filesystems you might want to specify the max size for the data file:

```
innodb_data_file_path = /ibdata/ibdata1:100M:autoextend:max:2000M
```

Suppose you have a Windows NT computer with 128M of RAM and a single 1G hard disk. The following is an example of possible configuration parameters in my.cnf or my.ini for InnoDB:

```
[mysqld]
# You can write your other MySQL server options here
# ...
#
innodb_data_home_dir = c:\ibdata
#                                 Datafiles must be able to
#                                 hold your data and indexes
innodb_data_file_path = ibdata1:2000M;ibdata2:2000M
#                                 Set buffer pool size to 50 - 80 %
#                                 of your computer's memory
set-variable = innodb_buffer_pool_size=70M
set-variable = innodb_additional_mem_pool_size=10M
innodb_log_group_home_dir = c:\iblogs
#                                 .._log_arch_dir must be the same
#                                 as .._log_group_home_dir
innodb_log_arch_dir = c:\iblogs
innodb_log_archive=0
set-variable = innodb_log_files_in_group=3
#                                 Set the log file-size to about
#                                 15 % of the buffer pool size
set-variable = innodb_log_file_size=10M
set-variable = innodb_log_buffer_size=8M
#                                 Set ..flush_log_at_trx_commit to
#                                 0 if you can afford losing
#                                 a few last transactions
innodb_flush_log_at_trx_commit=1
set-variable = innodb_file_io_threads=4
set-variable = innodb_lock_wait_timeout=50
```

Note that InnoDB **does not create directories: you must create them yourself.** Use the Unix or MS-DOS mkdir command to create the data and log group home directories. Check also that the MySQL server has **the right to create files** in the directories you specify.

Note that data files must be < 2G in some filesystems! The combined size of data files must be >= 10M. The combined size of the log files must be < 4G.

If you do not specify innodb_data_home_dir, the default is that InnoDB creates its data files to the datadir of MySQL. Then you cannot use absolute file paths in innodb_data_file_path.

When you create an InnoDB database for the first time, it is best that you start the MySQL server from the command prompt. Then InnoDB will print the information about the database creation to the screen, and you see what is happening. For example, in Windows you can start mysqld-max.exe with:

```
your-path-to-mysqld>mysqld-max --standalone --console
```

For information about what the printout should look like, see Section 7.5.3, Creating InnoDB Tablespace.

Where to put my.cnf or my.ini in Windows? The rules for Windows are the following:

- Only one my.cnf or my.ini file should be created.

- The my.cnf file should be placed in the root directory of the drive C:.

- The my.ini file should be placed in the WINDIR directory—e.g, C:\WINDOWS or C:\WINNT. You can use the SET command of MS-DOS to print the value of WINDIR.

- If your PC uses a boot loader where the C: drive is not the boot drive, your only option is to use the my.ini file.

Where to specify options in Unix? On Unix mysqld reads options from the following files, if they exist, in the following order:

/etc/my.cnf
> Global options

COMPILATION_DATADIR/my.cnf
> Server-specific options

defaults-extra-file
> The file specified with --defaults-extra-file=...

~/.my.cnf
> User-specific options

COMPILATION_DATADIR is the MySQL data directory which was specified as a ./con-figure option when mysqld was compiled (typically /usr/local/mysql/data for a binary installation or /usr/local/var for a source installation).

If you are not sure from where mysqld reads its my.cnf or my.ini, you can give the path as the first command-line option to the server: mysqld --defaults-file=your_path_to_my_cnf.

Suppose you have a Linux computer with 512M of RAM and three 20G hard disks (at directory paths '/', '/dr2', and '/dr3'). Here is an example of possible configuration parameters in my.cnf for InnoDB:

```
[mysqld]
# You can write your other MySQL server options here
# ...
#
innodb_data_home_dir = /
#                                   Datafiles must be able to
#                                   hold your data and indexes
innodb_data_file_path = ibdata/ibdata1:2000M;dr2/ibdata/ibdata2:2000M
#                                   Set buffer pool size to 50 - 80 %
#                                   of your computer's memory, but
#                                   make sure on Linux x86 total
#                                   memory usage is < 2 GB
set-variable = innodb_buffer_pool_size=350M
set-variable = innodb_additional_mem_pool_size=20M
innodb_log_group_home_dir = /dr3/iblogs
#                                   .._log_arch_dir must be the same
#                                   as .._log_group_home_dir
innodb_log_arch_dir = /dr3/iblogs
innodb_log_archive=0
set-variable = innodb_log_files_in_group=3
#                                   Set the log file-size to about
#                                   15 % of the buffer pool size
set-variable = innodb_log_file_size=50M
set-variable = innodb_log_buffer_size=8M
#                                   Set ..flush_log_at_trx_commit to
#                                   0 if you can afford losing
#                                   a few last transactions
innodb_flush_log_at_trx_commit=1
set-variable = innodb_file_io_threads=4
set-variable = innodb_lock_wait_timeout=50
#innodb_flush_method=fdatasync
#innodb_fast_shutdown=1
#set-variable = innodb_thread_concurrency=5
```

Note that we have placed the two data files on different disks. The reason for the name innodb_data_file_path is that you can also specify paths to your data files, and inn-odb_data_home_dir is just textually catenated before your data file paths, adding a pos-sible slash or backslash in between. InnoDB will fill the tablespace formed by the data files from the bottom up. In some cases it will improve the performance of the database if all data is not placed on the same physical disk. Putting log files on a different disk from data is very often beneficial for performance. You can also use **raw disk partitions** (raw devices) as data files. In some Unix systems they speed up I/O. See the manual section on InnoDB file space management about how to specify them in my.cnf.

Warning: On Linux x86 you must be careful **not to set memory usage too high.** glibc will allow the process heap to grow over thread stacks, which will crash your server. It is a risk if the value of:

```
innodb_buffer_pool_size + key_buffer +
max_connections * (sort_buffer + record_buffer) + max_connections * 2 M
```

is close to or exceeds 2G. Each thread will use a stack (often 2M, but in MySQL AB binaries only 256 kB) and, in the worst case, also sort_buffer + record_buffer additional memory.

How to tune other mysqld server parameters? Typical values which suit most users are:

```
set-variable = max_connections=200
set-variable = record_buffer=1M
set-variable = sort_buffer=1M
#                                  Set key_buffer to 5 - 50 %
#                                  of your RAM depending on how
#                                  much you use MyISAM tables, but
#                                  keep key_buffer + InnoDB
#                                  buffer pool size < 80 % of
#                                  your RAM
set-variable = key_buffer=...
```

Note that some parameters are given using the numeric my.cnf parameter format—set-variable = innodb... = 123—others (string and boolean parameters) with another format—innodb_... = ...

The meanings of the configuration parameters are as follows:

Option	Description
innodb_data_home_dir	The common part of the directory path for all InnoDB data files. The default for this parameter is the datadir of MySQL.
innodb_data_file_path	Paths to individual data files and their sizes. The full directory path to each data file is acquired by concatenating innodb_data_home_dir to the paths specified here. The file-sizes are specified in megabytes, hence the M after the size specification. InnoDB also understands the abbreviation G; 1G meaning 1024M. Starting from 3.23.44 you can set the file-size bigger than 4G on those operating systems which support big files. On some operating systems files must be < 2G. The sum of the sizes of the files must be at least 10M.
innodb_mirrored_log_groups	Number of identical copies of log groups we keep for the database. Currently this should be set to 1.

Option	Description
`innodb_log_group_home_dir`	Directory path to InnoDB log files.
`innodb_log_files_in_group`	Number of log files in the log group. InnoDB writes to the files in a circular fashion. Value 3 is recommended here.
`innodb_log_file_size`	Size of each log file in a log group in megabytes. Sensible values range from 1M to 1/nth of the size of the buffer pool specified below, where n is the number of log files in the group. The bigger the value, the less checkpoint flush activity is needed in the buffer pool, saving disk I/O. But bigger log files also mean that recovery will be slower in case of a crash. The combined size of log files must be < 4G on 32-bit computers.
`innodb_log_buffer_size`	The size of the buffer which InnoDB uses to write logs to the log files on disk. Sensible values range from 1M to half the combined size of the log files. A big log buffer allows large transactions to run without a need to write the log to disk until the transactions commit. Thus, if you have big transactions, making the log buffer big will save disk I/O.
`innodb_flush_log_at_trx_commit`	Normally this is set to 1, meaning that at a transaction commit the log is flushed to disk, and the modifications made by the transaction become permanent and survive a database crash. If you are willing to compromise this safety, and you are running small transactions, you may set this to 0 to reduce disk I/O to the logs.
`innodb_log_arch_dir`	The directory where fully written log files would be archived if we used log archiving. The value of this parameter should currently be set the same as `innodb_log_group_home_dir`.
`innodb_log_archive`	This value should currently be set to 0. As recovery from a backup is done by MySQL using its own log files, there is currently no need to archive InnoDB log files.
`innodb_buffer_pool_size`	The size of the memory buffer InnoDB uses to cache data and indexes of its tables. The bigger you set this the less disk I/O is needed to access data in tables. On a dedicated database server you may set this parameter up to 80% of the machine's physical memory size. Do not set it too large, though, because competition of the physical memory may cause paging in the operating system.
`innodb_additional_mem_pool_size`	Size of a memory pool InnoDB uses to store data dictionary information and other internal data structures. A sensible value for this might be 2M, but the more tables you have in your application the more you will need to allocate here. If InnoDB runs out of memory in this pool, it will start to allocate memory from the operating system and write warning messages to the MySQL error log.
`innodb_file_io_threads`	Number of file I/O threads in InnoDB. Normally, this should be 4, but on Windows disk I/O may benefit from a larger number.

Option	Description
innodb_lock_wait_timeout	Timeout in seconds an InnoDB transaction may wait for a lock before being rolled back. InnoDB automatically detects transaction deadlocks in its own lock table and rolls back the transaction. If you use the LOCK TABLES command, or transaction-safe table handlers other than InnoDB in the same transaction, a deadlock may arise which InnoDB cannot notice. In cases like this the timeout is useful to resolve the situation.
innodb_flush_method	(Available from 3.23.40 up.) The default value for this is fdatasync. Another option is O_DSYNC.

7.5.3 Creating InnoDB Tablespace

Suppose you have installed MySQL and have edited my.cnf so that it contains the necessary InnoDB configuration parameters. Before starting MySQL you should check that the directories you have specified for InnoDB data files and log files exist and that you have access rights to those directories. InnoDB cannot create directories, only files. Check also that you have enough disk space for the data and log files.

When you now start MySQL, InnoDB will start creating your data files and log files. InnoDB will print something like the following:

```
~/mysqlm/sql > mysqld
InnoDB: The first specified data file /home/heikki/data/ibdata1
did not exist:
InnoDB: a new database to be created!
InnoDB: Setting file /home/heikki/data/ibdata1 size to 134217728
InnoDB: Database physically writes the file full: wait...
InnoDB: data file /home/heikki/data/ibdata2 did not exist:
new to be created
InnoDB: Setting file /home/heikki/data/ibdata2 size to 262144000
InnoDB: Database physically writes the file full: wait...
InnoDB: Log file /home/heikki/data/logs/ib_logfile0 did not exist:
new to be created
InnoDB: Setting log file /home/heikki/data/logs/ib_logfile0 size to 5242880
InnoDB: Log file /home/heikki/data/logs/ib_logfile1 did not exist:
new to be created
InnoDB: Setting log file /home/heikki/data/logs/ib_logfile1 size to 5242880
InnoDB: Log file /home/heikki/data/logs/ib_logfile2 did not exist:
new to be created
InnoDB: Setting log file /home/heikki/data/logs/ib_logfile2 size to 5242880
InnoDB: Started
mysqld: ready for connections
```

A new InnoDB database has now been created. You can connect to the MySQL server with the usual MySQL client programs like mysql. When you shut down the MySQL server with mysqladmin shutdown, InnoDB output will be like the following:

```
010321 18:33:34  mysqld: Normal shutdown
010321 18:33:34  mysqld: Shutdown Complete
InnoDB: Starting shutdown...
InnoDB: Shutdown completed
```

You can now look at the data files and log directories and you will see the files created. The log directory will also contain a small file named ib_arch_log_0000000000. That file resulted from the database creation, after which InnoDB switched off log archiving. When MySQL is again started, the output will be like the following:

```
~/mysqlm/sql > mysqld
InnoDB: Started
mysqld: ready for connections
```

7.5.3.1 If something goes wrong in database creation

If InnoDB prints an operating system error in a file operation, usually the problem is one of the following:

- You did not create InnoDB data or log directories.

- mysqld does not have the rights to create files in those directories.

- mysqld does not read the right my.cnf or my.ini file, and consequently does not see the options you specified.

- The disk is full or a disk quota is exceeded.

- You have created a subdirectory whose name is equal to a data file you specified.

- There is a syntax error in innodb_data_home_dir or innodb_data_file_path.

If something goes wrong in an InnoDB database creation, you should delete all files created by InnoDB. This means all data files, all log files, the small archived log file, and in the case you already did create some InnoDB tables, delete also the corresponding .frm files for these tables from the MySQL database directories. Then you can try the InnoDB database creation again.

7.5.4 Creating InnoDB Tables

Suppose you have started the MySQL client with the command mysql test. To create a table in the InnoDB format you must specify TYPE = InnoDB in the table creation SQL command:

```
CREATE TABLE CUSTOMER (A INT, B CHAR (20), INDEX (A)) TYPE = InnoDB;
```

This SQL command will create a table and an index on column A into the InnoDB tablespace consisting of the data files you specified in my.cnf. In addition MySQL will create a file CUSTOMER.frm to the MySQL database directory test. Internally, InnoDB will add to its own data dictionary an entry for table 'test/CUSTOMER'. Thus you can create a table of the same name CUSTOMER in another database of MySQL, and the table names will not collide inside InnoDB.

You can query the amount of free space in the InnoDB tablespace by issuing the table sta-tus command of MySQL for any table you have created with `TYPE = InnoDB`. Then the amount of free space in the tablespace appears in the table comment section in the output of `SHOW`. An example:

```
SHOW TABLE STATUS FROM test LIKE 'CUSTOMER'
```

Note that the statistics `SHOW` gives about InnoDB tables are only approximate: they are used in SQL optimisation. Table and index reserved sizes in bytes are accurate, though.

7.5.4.1 Converting MyISAM tables to InnoDB

InnoDB does not have a special optimisation for separate index creation. Therefore, it does not pay to export and import the table and create indexes afterward. The fastest way to alter a table to InnoDB is to do the inserts directly to an InnoDB table—that is, use `ALTER TABLE ... TYPE=INNODB`, or create an empty InnoDB table with identical definitions and insert the rows with `INSERT INTO ... SELECT * FROM ....`

To get better control over the insertion process, it may be good to insert big tables in pieces:

```
INSERT INTO newtable SELECT * FROM oldtable
    WHERE yourkey > something AND yourkey <= somethingelse;
```

After all data has been inserted you can rename the tables.

During the conversion of big tables you should make the InnoDB buffer pool size large to reduce disk I/O. Do not set it larger than 80% of the physical memory, though. You should make InnoDB log files and the log buffer large.

Make sure you do not run out of tablespace: InnoDB tables take a lot more space than MyISAM tables. If an `ALTER TABLE` runs out of space, it will start a rollback, and that can take hours if it is disk-bound. In inserts InnoDB uses the insert buffer to merge sec-ondary index records to indexes in batches. That saves a lot of disk I/O. In rollback no such mechanism is used, and the rollback can take 30 times longer than the insertion.

In the case of a runaway rollback, if you do not have valuable data in your database, it is better that you kill the database process and delete all InnoDB data and log files and all InnoDB table `.frm` files, and start your job again, rather than wait for millions of disk I/Os to complete.

7.5.4.2 Foreign key constraints

Starting from Version 3.23.43b InnoDB features foreign key constraints. InnoDB is the first MySQL table type which allows you to define foreign key constraints to guard the integrity of your data.

The syntax of a foreign key constraint definition in InnoDB is as follows:

```
FOREIGN KEY (index_col_name, ...)
                    REFERENCES table_name (index_col_name, ...)
                    [ON DELETE CASCADE | ON DELETE SET NULL]
```

Both tables have to be of the InnoDB type and **there must be an index where the foreign key and the referenced key are listed as the first columns**. InnoDB does not auto-create indexes on foreign keys or referenced keys: you have to create them explicitly.

Corresponding columns in the foreign key and the referenced key must have similar internal data types inside InnoDB so that they can be compared without a type conversion. The size and the signedness of integer types has to be the same. The length of string types need not be the same.

Starting from Version 3.23.50 you can also associate the ON DELETE CASCADE or ON DELETE SET NULL clause with the foreign key constraint.

If ON DELETE CASCADE is specified, and a row in the parent table is deleted, then InnoDB automatically deletes also all those rows in the child table whose foreign key values are equal to the referenced key value in the parent row. If ON DELETE SET NULL is specified, the child rows are automatically updated so that the columns in the foreign key are set to the SQL NULL value.

Starting from version 3.23.50, InnoDB does not check foreign key constraints on those foreign key or referenced key values which contain a NULL column.

Starting from version 3.23.50 the InnoDB parser allows you to use backquotes (') around table and column names in the above definition but the InnoDB parser is not yet aware of possible variable lower_case_table_names you give in my.cnf.

An example:

```
CREATE TABLE parent(id INT NOT NULL, PRIMARY KEY (id)) TYPE=INNODB;
CREATE TABLE child(id INT, parent_id INT, INDEX par_ind (parent_id),
          FOREIGN KEY (parent_id) REFERENCES parent(id)
          ON DELETE SET NULL
) TYPE=INNODB;
```

If MySQL gives the error number 1005 from a CREATE TABLE statement, the error message string refers to errno 150, then the table creation failed because a foreign key constraint was not correctly formed. Similarly, if an ALTER TABLE fails and it refers to errno 150, that means a foreign key definition would be incorrectly formed for the altered table.

Starting from Version 3.23.50 InnoDB allows you to add a new foreign key constraint to a table through

```
ALTER TABLE yourtablename
    ADD CONSTRAINT FOREIGN KEY (...) REFERENCES anothertablename(...)
```

Remember to create the required indexes first, though.

In InnoDB versions < 3.23.50 ALTER TABLE or CREATE INDEX should not be used in connection with tables that have foreign key constraints or are referenced in foreign key constraints: any ALTER TABLE removes all foreign key constraints defined for the table. You should not use ALTER TABLE to the referenced table either, but use DROP TABLE and CREATE TABLE to modify the schema. When MySQL does an ALTER TABLE it may internally use RENAME TABLE, and that will confuse the foreign key constraints that refer to the table. A CREATE INDEX statement in MySQL is processed as an ALTER TABLE, and these restrictions also apply to it.

When doing foreign key checks InnoDB sets shared row level locks on child or parent records it has to look at. InnoDB checks foreign key constraints immediately: the check is not deferred to transaction commit.

InnoDB allows you to drop any table even though that would break the foreign key constraints that reference the table. When you drop a table the constraints that were defined in its create statement are also dropped.

If you re-create a table that was dropped, it has to have a definition that conforms to the foreign key constraints referencing it. It must have the right column names and types, and it must have indexes on the referenced keys, as stated previously. If these are not satisfied, MySQL returns error number 1005 and refers to errno 150 in the error message string.

Starting from Version 3.23.50 InnoDB returns the foreign key definitions of a table when you call

```
SHOW CREATE TABLE yourtablename
```

Then also mysqldump produces correct definitions of tables to the dump file, and does not forget about the foreign keys.

You can also list the foreign key constraints for a table T with:

```
SHOW TABLE STATUS FROM yourdatabasename LIKE 'T'
```

The foreign key constraints are listed in the table comment of the output.

InnoDB does not yet support ON DELETE CASCADE or other special options on the constraints.

7.5.5 Adding and Removing InnoDB Data and Log Files

You cannot increase the size of an InnoDB data file. To add more into your tablespace you have to add a new data file. To do this you have to shut down your MySQL database, edit the my.cnf file, add a new file to innodb_data_file_path, and then start MySQL again.

Currently you cannot remove a data file from InnoDB. To decrease the size of your database you have to use mysqldump to dump all your tables, create a new database, and import your tables to the new database.

If you want to change the number or the size of your InnoDB log files, you have to shut down MySQL and make sure that it shuts down without errors. Then copy the old log files into a safe place just in case something went wrong in the shutdown and you will need them to recover the database. Delete the old log files from the log file directory, edit my.cnf, and start MySQL again. InnoDB will tell you at the startup that it is creating new log files.

7.5.6 Backing up and Recovering an InnoDB Database

The key to safe database management is taking regular backups.

InnoDB Hot Backup is an online backup tool you can use to back up your InnoDB database while it is running. InnoDB Hot Backup does not require you to shut down your database and it does not set any locks or disturb your normal database processing. InnoDB Hot Backup is an additional tool that is not included in the standard MySQL distribution. See the InnoDB Hot Backup homepage at http://www.innodb.com/ hotbackup.html for detailed information and screenshots.

If you are able to shut down your MySQL server, to take a 'binary' backup of your database you have to do the following:

*   Shut down your MySQL database and make sure it shuts down without errors.
*   Copy all your data files into a safe place.
*   Copy all your InnoDB log files to a safe place.
*   Copy your my.cnf configuration file(s) to a safe place.
*   Copy all the .frm files for your InnoDB tables into a safe place.

There is currently no online or incremental backup tool available for InnoDB, though they are in the TODO list.

In addition to taking the binary backups just described, you should also regularly take dumps of your tables with mysqldump. This is because a binary file may be corrupted without you noticing it. Dumped tables are stored into text files that are human-readable and much simpler than database binary files. Seeing table corruption from dumped files is easier, and since their format is simpler, the chance for serious data corruption in them is smaller.

A good idea is to take the dumps at the same time you take a binary backup of your database. You have to shut out all clients from your database to get a consistent snapshot of all your tables into your dumps. Then you can take the binary backup, and you will then have a consistent snapshot of your database in two formats.

To be able to recover your InnoDB database to the present from the binary backup just described, you have to run your MySQL database with the general logging and log archiving of MySQL switched on. Here by the general logging we mean the logging mechanism of the MySQL server that is independent of InnoDB logs.

To recover from a crash of your MySQL server process, the only thing you have to do is restart it. InnoDB will automatically check the logs and perform a roll-forward of the database to the present. InnoDB will automatically roll back uncommitted transactions that were present at the time of the crash. During recovery, InnoDB will print out something like the following:

```
~/mysqlm/sql > mysqld
InnoDB: Database was not shut down normally.
InnoDB: Starting recovery from log files...
InnoDB: Starting log scan based on checkpoint at
InnoDB: log sequence number 0 13674004
InnoDB: Doing recovery: scanned up to log sequence number 0 13739520
InnoDB: Doing recovery: scanned up to log sequence number 0 13805056
InnoDB: Doing recovery: scanned up to log sequence number 0 13870592
InnoDB: Doing recovery: scanned up to log sequence number 0 13936128
...
InnoDB: Doing recovery: scanned up to log sequence number 0 20555264
InnoDB: Doing recovery: scanned up to log sequence number 0 20620800
InnoDB: Doing recovery: scanned up to log sequence number 0 20664692
InnoDB: 1 uncommitted transaction(s) which must be rolled back
InnoDB: Starting rollback of uncommitted transactions
InnoDB: Rolling back trx no 16745
InnoDB: Rolling back of trx no 16745 completed
InnoDB: Rollback of uncommitted transactions completed
InnoDB: Starting an apply batch of log records to the database...
InnoDB: Apply batch completed
InnoDB: Started
mysqld: ready for connections
```

If your database gets corrupted or your disk fails, you have to do the recovery from a backup. In the case of corruption, you should first find a backup that is not corrupted. From a backup do the recovery from the general log files of MySQL according to instructions in the MySQL manual.

7.5.6.1 Checkpoints

InnoDB implements a checkpoint mechanism called a fuzzy checkpoint. InnoDB will flush modified database pages from the buffer pool in small batches. There is no need to flush the buffer pool in one single batch, which would, in practice, stop processing user SQL statements for a while.

In crash recovery InnoDB looks for a checkpoint label written to the log files. It knows that all modifications to the database before the label are already present on the disk image of the database. Then InnoDB scans the log files forward from the place of the checkpoint, applying the logged modifications to the database.

InnoDB writes to the log files in a circular fashion. All committed modifications that make the database pages in the buffer pool different from the images on disk must be available in the log files in case InnoDB has to do a recovery. This means that when InnoDB starts to reuse a log file in the circular fashion, it has to make sure that the database page images on disk already contain the modifications logged in the log file InnoDB is going to reuse. In other words, InnoDB has to make a checkpoint, and often this involves flushing of modified database pages to disk.

This explains why making your log files very big may save disk I/O in checkpointing. It can make sense to set the total size of the log files as big as the buffer pool, or even bigger. The drawback in big log files is that crash recovery can last longer because there will be more log to apply to the database.

7.5.7 Moving an InnoDB Database to Another Machine

InnoDB data and log files are binary-compatible on all platforms if the floating-point number format on the machines is the same. You can move an InnoDB database simply by copying all the relevant files, which we already listed in the previous section on backing up a database. If the floating-point formats on the machines are different but you have not used FLOAT or DOUBLE data types in your tables, the procedure is the same: just copy the relevant files. If the formats are different and your tables contain floating-point data, you have to use mysqldump and mysqlimport to move those tables.

A performance tip is to switch off the auto commit when you import data into your database, assuming your tablespace has enough space for the big rollback segment the big import transaction will generate. Do the commit only after importing a whole table or a segment of a table.

7.5.8 InnoDB Transaction Model

In the InnoDB transaction model the goal has been to combine the best properties of a multi-versioning database to traditional two-phase locking. InnoDB does locking on row level and runs queries by default as non-locking consistent reads, in the style of Oracle. The lock table in InnoDB is stored so space-efficiently that lock escalation is not needed: typically several users are allowed to lock every row in the database, or any random subset of the rows, without InnoDB running out of memory.

In InnoDB all user activity happens inside transactions. If the auto-commit mode is used in MySQL, each SQL statement will form a single transaction. If the auto commit mode is switched off, we can think that a user always has a transaction open. If he issues the SQL COMMIT or ROLLBACK statement, that ends the current transaction, and a new one starts. Both statements will release all InnoDB locks that were set during the current transaction. A COMMIT means that the changes made in the current transaction are made permanent and become visible to other users. A ROLLBACK, on the other hand, cancels all modifications made by the current transaction.

7.5.8.1 Consistent read

A consistent read means that InnoDB uses its multi-versioning to present to a query a snapshot of the database at a point in time. The query will see the changes made by exactly those transactions that committed before that point of time, and no changes made by later or uncommitted transactions. The exception to this rule is that the query will see the changes made by the transaction that issues the query.

When a transaction issues its first consistent read, InnoDB assigns the snapshot, or the point of time, which all consistent reads in the same transaction will use. In the snapshot are all transactions that committed before assigning the snapshot. Thus, the consistent reads within the same transaction will also be consistent with respect to each other. You can get a fresher snapshot for your queries by committing the current transaction, and after that, issuing new queries.

Consistent read is the default mode in which InnoDB processes SELECT statements. A consistent read does not set any locks on the tables it accesses, and therefore other users are free to modify those tables at the same time a consistent read is being performed on the table.

7.5.8.2 Locking reads

A consistent read is not convenient in some circumstances. Suppose you want to add a new row into your table CHILD, and make sure that the child already has a parent in table PARENT.

Suppose you use a consistent read to read the table PARENT and indeed see the parent of the child in the table. Can you now safely add the child row to table CHILD? No because it may happen that meanwhile some other user has deleted the parent row from the table PARENT, and you are not aware of that.

The solution is to perform the SELECT in a locking mode, LOCK IN SHARE MODE:

```
SELECT * FROM PARENT WHERE NAME = 'Jones' LOCK IN SHARE MODE;
```

Performing a read in share mode means that we read the latest available data, and set a shared mode lock on the rows we read. If the latest data belongs to a yet uncommitted transaction of another user, we will wait until that transaction commits. A shared mode lock prevents others from updating or deleting the row we have read. After we see that the above query returns the parent 'Jones', we can safely add his child to table CHILD, and commit our transaction. This example shows how to implement referential integrity in your application code.

Let us look at another example: we have an integer counter field in a table CHILD_CODES which we use to assign a unique identifier to each child we add to table CHILD. Obviously, using a consistent read or a shared mode read to read the present value of the counter is not a good idea, since then two users of the database may see the same value for the counter, and we will get a duplicate key error when we add the two children with the same identifier to the table.

In this case there are two good ways to implement the reading and incrementing of the counter: (1) update the counter first by incrementing it by 1 and only after that read it, or (2) read the counter first with a lock mode FOR UPDATE, and increment after that:

```
SELECT COUNTER_FIELD FROM CHILD_CODES FOR UPDATE;
UPDATE CHILD_CODES SET COUNTER_FIELD = COUNTER_FIELD + 1;
```

A SELECT ... FOR UPDATE will read the latest available data, setting exclusive locks on each row it reads. Thus, it sets the same locks a searched SQL UPDATE would set on the rows.

7.5.8.3 Next-key locking: Avoiding the phantom problem

In row level locking InnoDB uses an algorithm called next-key locking. InnoDB does the row level locking so that when it searches or scans an index of a table, it sets shared or exclusive locks on the index records it encounters. Thus, the row level locks are more precisely called index record locks.

The locks InnoDB sets on index records also affect the 'gap' before that index record. If a user has a shared or exclusive lock on record R in an index, another user cannot insert a new index record immediately before R in the index order. This locking of gaps is done to prevent the so-called phantom problem. Suppose I want to read and lock all children with an identifier bigger than 100 from table CHILD, and update some field in the selected rows:

```
SELECT * FROM CHILD WHERE ID > 100 FOR UPDATE;
```

Suppose there is an index on table CHILD on column ID. Our query will scan that index starting from the first record where ID is bigger than 100. Now, if the locks set on the index records would not lock out inserts made in the gaps, a new child might meanwhile be inserted to the table. If in my transaction I now execute:

```
SELECT * FROM CHILD WHERE ID > 100 FOR UPDATE;
```

again, I will see a new child in the result set the query returns. This is against the isolation principle of transactions: a transaction should be able to run so that the data it has read does not change during the transaction. If we regard a set of rows as a data item, the new 'phantom' child would break this isolation principle.

When InnoDB scans an index it can also lock the gap after the last record in the index. Just that happens in the previous example: the locks set by InnoDB will prevent any insert to the table where ID would be bigger than 100.

You can use next-key locking to implement a uniqueness check in your application: if you read your data in share mode and do not see a duplicate for a row you are going to insert, you can safely insert your row. The next-key lock set on the successor of your row during the read will prevent anyone from inserting a duplicate for your row in the meantime. Thus, the next-key locking allows you to 'lock' the non-existence of something in your table.

7.5.8.4 Locks set by different SQL statements in InnoDB

SELECT . . . FROM . . .
> This is a consistent read, reading a snapshot of the database and setting no locks.

SELECT . . . FROM . . . LOCK IN SHARE MODE
> Sets shared next-key locks on all index records the read encounters.

SELECT . . . FROM . . . FOR UPDATE
> Sets exclusive next-key locks on all index records the read encounters.

INSERT INTO . . . VALUES (. . .)
> Sets an exclusive lock on the inserted row; note that this lock is not a next-key lock and does not prevent other users from inserting to the gap before the inserted row. If a duplicate key error occurs, sets a shared lock on the duplicate index record.

INSERT INTO T SELECT . . . FROM S WHERE . . .
> Sets an exclusive (non-next-key) lock on each row inserted into T. Does the search on S as a consistent read, but sets shared next-key locks on S if the MySQL logging is on. InnoDB has to set locks in the latter case because in roll-forward recovery from a backup every SQL statement has to be executed in exactly the same way as it was done originally.

CREATE TABLE . . . SELECT . . .
> Performs the SELECT as a consistent read or with shared locks, like in the previous item.

REPLACE
> Is done like an insert if there is no collision on a unique key. Otherwise, an exclusive next-key lock is placed on the row which has to be updated.

UPDATE . . . SET . . . WHERE . . .
> Sets an exclusive next-key lock on every record the search encounters.

DELETE FROM . . . WHERE . . .
> Sets an exclusive next-key lock on every record the search encounters.

FOREIGN KEY

> If this constraint is defined on a table, any insert, update, or delete which requires checking of the constraint condition sets shared record level locks on the records it looks at to check the constraint. Also in the case where the constraint fails, InnoDB sets these locks.

LOCK TABLES ...

> Sets table locks. In the implementation the MySQL layer of code sets these locks. The automatic deadlock detection of InnoDB cannot detect deadlocks where such table locks are involved: see the following section. Also, since MySQL does know about row level locks, it is possible that you get a table lock on a table where another user currently has row level locks. But that does not put transaction integerity into danger. See Section 7.5.14, Restrictions on InnoDB Tables.

7.5.8.5 Deadlock detection and rollback

InnoDB automatically detects a deadlock of transactions and rolls back the transaction whose lock request was the last one to build a deadlock—that is, a cycle in the waits-for graph of transactions. InnoDB cannot detect deadlocks where a lock set by a MySQL LOCK TABLES statement is involved, or if a lock set in a table handler other than InnoDB is involved. You have to resolve these situations using innodb_lock_wait_timeout set in my.cnf.

When InnoDB performs a complete rollback of a transaction, all the locks of the transaction are released. However, if just a single SQL statement is rolled back as a result of an error, some of the locks set by the SQL statement may be preserved. This is because InnoDB stores row locks in a format where it cannot afterward know which was set by which SQL statement.

7.5.8.6 An example of how the consistent read works in InnoDB

When you issue a consistent read—that is, an ordinary SELECT statement—InnoDB will give your transaction a timepoint according to when your query sees the database. Thus, if transaction B deletes a row and commits after your timepoint was assigned, you will not see the row deleted. The same is true with inserts and updates.

You can advance your timepoint by committing your transaction and then doing another SELECT.

This is called multi-versioned concurrency control:

```
                  User A                    User B

                  SET AUTOCOMMIT=0;          SET AUTOCOMMIT=0;
time
 |                SELECT * FROM t;
 |                empty set
```

```
|                                    INSERT INTO t VALUES (1, 2);
|
v                  SELECT * FROM t;
                   empty set

                                    COMMIT;

                   SELECT * FROM t;
                   empty set;

                   COMMIT;

                   SELECT * FROM t;
                   ---------------------
                   |   1   |   2   |
                   ---------------------
```

Thus, user A sees the row inserted by B only when B has committed the insert, and A has committed his own transaction so that the timepoint is advanced past the commit of B.

If you want to see the "freshest" state of the database, you should use a locking read:

```
SELECT * FROM t LOCK IN SHARE MODE;
```

7.5.9 Performance Tuning Tips

1. If the Unix `top` or the Windows `Task Manager` shows that the CPU usage percentage with your workload is less than 70%, your workload is probably disk-bound. Maybe you are making too many transaction commits, or the buffer pool is too small. Making the buffer pool bigger can help, but do not set it bigger than 80% of your physical memory.

2. Wrap several modifications into one transaction. InnoDB must flush the log to disk at each transaction commit, if that transaction made modifications to the database. Since the rotation speed of a disk is typically, at most, 167 revolutions/second, that constrains the number of commits to the same 167/second if the disk does not fool the operating system.

3. If you can afford the loss of some latest committed transactions, you can set the `my.cnf` parameter `innodb_flush_log_at_trx_commit` to zero. InnoDB tries to flush the log anyway once per second, though the flush is not guaranteed.

4. Make your log files big, even as big as the buffer pool. When InnoDB has written the log files full, it has to write the modified contents of the buffer pool to disk in a checkpoint. Small log files will cause many unnecessary disk writes. The drawback in big log files is that recovery time will be longer.

5. Also the log buffer should be quite big—say 8 M.

6. (Relevant from 3.23.39 up.) In some versions of Linux and Unix, flushing files to disk with the Unix `fdatasync` and other similar methods is surprisingly slow. The default method InnoDB uses is the `fdatasync` function. If you are not satisfied with the database write performance, you may try setting `innodb_flush_method` in `my.cnf` to

O_DSYNC, though O_DSYNC seems to be slower on most systems.

7. In importing data to InnoDB, make sure that MySQL does not have `autocommit=1` on. Then every insert requires a log flush to disk. Put before your plain SQL import file line:

```
SET AUTOCOMMIT=0;
```

and after it:

```
COMMIT;
```

If you use the `mysqldump` option `--opt`, you will get dump files that are fast to import also to an InnoDB table, even without wrapping them to the preceding `SET AUTOCOM-MIT=0; ... COMMIT;` wrappers.

8. Beware of big rollbacks of mass inserts: InnoDB uses the insert buffer to save disk I/O in inserts, but in a corresponding rollback no such mechanism is used. A disk-bound rollback can take 30 times the time of the corresponding insert. Killing the database process will not help because the rollback will start again at database startup. The only way to get rid of a runaway rollback is to increase the buffer pool so that the rollback becomes CPU-bound and runs fast, or delete the whole InnoDB database.

9. Beware also of other big disk-bound operations. Use `DROP TABLE` or `TRUNCATE` (from MySQL 4.0 up) to empty a table, not `DELETE FROM yourtable`.

10. Use the multi-line `INSERT` to reduce communication overhead between the client and the server if you need to insert many rows:

```
INSERT INTO yourtable VALUES (1, 2), (5, 5);
```

This tip is, of course, valid for inserts into any table type, not just InnoDB.

7.5.9.1 The InnoDB monitor

Starting from Version 3.23.41 InnoDB includes the InnoDB Monitor, which prints information on the InnoDB internal state. When switched on, InnoDB Monitor will make the MySQL server `mysqld` print data (note: the MySQL client will not print anything) to the standard output about once every 15 seconds. This data is useful in performance tuning. On Windows you must start `mysqld-max` from an MS-DOS prompt with the `--stan-dalone --console` options to direct the output to the MS-DOS prompt window.

There is a separate `innodb_lock_monitor` which prints the same information as `inn-odb_monitor` plus information on locks set by each transaction.

The printed information includes data on:

- Lock waits of a transactions

- Semaphore waits of threads

- Pending file I/O requests

- Buffer pool statistics

- Purge and insert buffer merge activity of the main thread of InnoDB

You can start InnoDB Monitor through the following SQL command:

```
CREATE TABLE innodb_monitor(a int) type = innodb;
```

and stop it by:

```
DROP TABLE innodb_monitor;
```

The CREATE TABLE syntax is just a way to pass a command to the InnoDB engine through the MySQL SQL parser: the created table is not relevant at all for InnoDB Monitor. If you shut down the database when the monitor is running, and you want to start the monitor again, you have to drop the table before you can issue a new CREATE TABLE to start the monitor. This syntax may change in a future release.

A sample output of the InnoDB Monitor:

```
================================
010809 18:45:06 INNODB MONITOR OUTPUT
================================
--------------------------
LOCKS HELD BY TRANSACTIONS
--------------------------
LOCK INFO:
Number of locks in the record hash table 1294
LOCKS FOR TRANSACTION ID 0 579342744
TABLE LOCK table test/mytable trx id 0 582333343 lock_mode IX

RECORD LOCKS space id 0 page no 12758 n bits 104 table test/mytable index
PRIMARY trx id 0 582333343 lock_mode X
Record lock, heap no 2 PHYSICAL RECORD: n_fields 74; 1-byte offs FALSE;
info bits 0
 0: len 4; hex 0001a801; asc ;; 1: len 6; hex 000022b5b39f; asc ";;
 2: len 7; hex 000002001e03ec; asc ;; 3: len 4; hex 00000001;
 ...
-------------------------------------------------
CURRENT SEMAPHORES RESERVED AND SEMAPHORE WAITS
-------------------------------------------------
SYNC INFO:
Sorry, cannot give mutex list info in non-debug version!
Sorry, cannot give rw-lock list info in non-debug version!
-------------------------------------------------------
SYNC ARRAY INFO: reservation count 6041054, signal count 2913432
4a239430 waited for by thread 49627477 op. S-LOCK file NOT KNOWN line 0
Mut ex 0 sp 5530989 r 62038708 sys 2155035;
rws 0 8257574 8025336; rwx 0 1121090 1848344
```

```
--------------------------------------------------------
CURRENT PENDING FILE I/O'S
--------------------------
Pending normal aio reads:
Reserved slot, messages 40157658 4a4a40b8
Reserved slot, messages 40157658 4a477e28
...
Reserved slot, messages 40157658 4a4424a8
Reserved slot, messages 40157658 4a39ea38
Total of 36 reserved aio slots
Pending aio writes:
Total of 0 reserved aio slots
Pending insert buffer aio reads:
Total of 0 reserved aio slots
Pending log writes or reads:
Reserved slot, messages 40158c98 40157f98
Total of 1 reserved aio slots
Pending synchronous reads or writes:
Total of 0 reserved aio slots
-----------
BUFFER POOL
-----------
LRU list length 8034
Free list length 0
Flush list length 999
Buffer pool size in pages 8192
Pending reads 39
Pending writes: LRU 0, flush list 0, single page 0
Pages read 31383918, created 51310, written 2985115
----------------------------
END OF INNODB MONITOR OUTPUT
============================
010809 18:45:22 InnoDB starts purge
010809 18:45:22 InnoDB purged 0 pages
```

Some notes on the output:

- If the section LOCKS HELD BY TRANSACTIONS reports lock waits, your application may have lock contention. The output can also help to trace reasons for transaction deadlocks.

- Section SYNC INFO will report reserved semaphores if you compile InnoDB with UNIV_SYNC_DEBUG defined in univ.i.

- Section SYNC ARRAY INFO reports threads waiting for a semaphore and statistics on how many times threads have needed a spin or a wait on a mutex or an rw-lock semaphore. A big number of threads waiting for semaphores may be a result of disk I/O, or contention problems inside InnoDB. Contention can be due to heavy parallelism of queries, or problems in operating system thread scheduling.

- Section CURRENT PENDING FILE I/O'S lists pending file I/O requests. A large number of these indicates that the workload is disk I/O-bound.

- Section BUFFER POOL gives you statistics on pages read and written. You can calculate from these numbers how many data file I/Os your queries are currently doing.

7.5.10 Implementation of Multi-Versioning

Since InnoDB is a multi-versioned database, it must keep information of old versions of rows in the tablespace. This information is stored in a data structure we call a rollback segment after an analogous data structure in Oracle.

InnoDB internally adds two fields to each row stored in the database. A 6-byte field tells the transaction identifier for the last transaction that inserted or updated the row. Also a deletion is internally treated as an update where a special bit in the row is set to mark it as deleted. Each row also contains a 7-byte field called the roll pointer. The roll pointer points to an undo log record written to the rollback segment. If the row was updated, the undo log record contains the information necessary to rebuild the content of the row before it was updated.

InnoDB uses the information in the rollback segment to perform the undo operations needed in a transaction rollback. It also uses the information to build earlier versions of a row for a consistent read.

Undo logs in the rollback segment are divided into insert and update undo logs. Insert undo logs are only needed in transaction rollback and can be discarded as soon as the transaction commits. Update undo logs are used also in consistent reads, and they can be discarded only after there is no transaction present for which InnoDB has assigned a snapshot that in a consistent read could need the information in the update undo log to build an earlier version of a database row.

You must remember to commit your transactions regularly, including those transactions that only issue consistent reads. Otherwise InnoDB cannot discard data from the update undo logs, and the rollback segment may grow too big, filling up your tablespace.

The physical size of an undo log record in the rollback segment is typically smaller than the corresponding inserted or updated row. You can use this information to calculate the space needed for your rollback segment.

In our multi-versioning scheme a row is not physically removed from the database immediately when you delete it with an SQL statement. Only when InnoDB can discard the update undo log record written for the deletion can it also physically remove the corresponding row and its index records from the database. This removal operation is called a purge, and it is quite fast, usually taking the same order of time as the SQL statement which did the deletion.

7.5.11 Table and Index Structures

MySQL stores its data dictionary information of tables in `.frm` files in database directories. But every InnoDB type table also has its own entry in InnoDB internal data dictionaries inside the tablespace. When MySQL drops a table or a database, it has to delete both a `.frm` file or files, and the corresponding entries inside the InnoDB data dictionary. This is the reason why you cannot move InnoDB tables between databases simply by moving the `.frm` files, and why DROP DATABASE did not work for InnoDB type tables in MySQL versions <= 3.23.43.

Every InnoDB table has a special index called the clustered index where the data of the rows is stored. If you define a PRIMARY KEY on your table, the index of the primary key will be the clustered index.

If you do not define a primary key for your table, InnoDB will internally generate a clustered index where the rows are ordered by the row id InnoDB assigns to the rows in such a table. The row id is a 6-byte field which monotonically increases as new rows are inserted. Thus, the rows ordered by the row id will be physically in the insertion order.

Accessing a row through the clustered index is fast because the row data will be on the same page where the index search leads us. In many databases the data is traditionally stored on a different page from the index record. If a table is large, the clustered index architecture often saves disk I/O when compared to the traditional solution.

The records in non-clustered indexes (we also call them secondary indexes) in InnoDB contain the primary key value for the row. InnoDB uses this primary key value to search for the row from the clustered index. Note that if the primary key is long, the secondary indexes will use more space.

7.5.11.1 Physical structure of an index

All indexes in InnoDB are B-trees where the index records are stored in the leaf pages of the tree. The default size of an index page is 16 kB. When new records are inserted, InnoDB tries to leave 1 / 16 of the page free for future insertions and updates of the index records.

If index records are inserted in a sequential (ascending or descending) order, the resulting index pages will be about 15/16 full. If records are inserted in a random order, the pages will be 1/2 - 15/16 full. If the fill factor of an index page drops below 1/2, InnoDB will try to contract the index tree to free the page.

7.5.11.2 Insert buffering

It is a common situation in a database application that the primary key is a unique identifier and new rows are inserted in the ascending order of the primary key. Thus, the insertions to the clustered index do not require random reads from a disk.

On the other hand, secondary indexes are usually non-unique and insertions happen in a relatively random order. This would cause a lot of random disk I/Os without a special mechanism used in InnoDB.

If an index record should be inserted to a non-unique secondary index, InnoDB checks if the secondary index page is already in the buffer pool. If that is the case, InnoDB will do the insertion directly to the index page. But, if the index page is not found from the buffer pool, InnoDB inserts the record to a special insert buffer structure. The insert buffer is kept so small that it entirely fits in the buffer pool, and insertions can be made to it very fast.

The insert buffer is periodically merged to the secondary index trees in the database. Often we can merge several insertions on the same page of the index tree, and hence save disk I/Os. It has been measured that the insert buffer can speed up insertions to a table up to 15 times.

7.5.11.3 Adaptive hash indexes

If a database fits almost entirely in main memory, the fastest way to perform queries on it is to use hash indexes. InnoDB has an automatic mechanism which monitors index searches made to the indexes defined for a table, and if InnoDB notices that queries could benefit from building a hash index, such an index is automatically built.

But note that the hash index is always built based on an existing B-tree index on the table. InnoDB can build a hash index on a prefix of any length of the key defined for the B-tree, depending on what search pattern InnoDB observes on the B-tree index. A hash index can be partial: it is not required that the whole B-tree index is cached in the buffer pool. InnoDB will build hash indexes on demand to often-accessed pages of the index.

In a sense, through the adaptive hash index mechanism InnoDB adapts itself to ample main memory, coming closer to the architecture of main memory databases.

7.5.11.4 Physical Record Structure

- Each index record in InnoDB contains a header of 6 bytes. The header is used to link consecutive records together, and also in the row level locking.

- Records in the clustered index contain fields for all user-defined columns. In addition, there is a 6-byte field for the transaction id and a 7-byte field for the roll pointer.

- If the user has not defined a primary key for a table, then each clustered index record contains also a 6-byte row id field.

- Each secondary index record contains also all the fields defined for the clustered index key.

- A record contains also a pointer to each field of the record. If the total length of the fields in a record is < 128 bytes, then the pointer is 1 byte, else 2 bytes.

7.5.11.5 How an auto-increment column works in InnoDB

After a database startup, when a user first does an insert to a table T where an auto-increment column has been defined, and the user does not provide an explicit value for the column, then InnoDB executes `SELECT MAX(auto-inc-column) FROM T`, and assigns that value incremented by one to the column and the auto-increment counter of the table. We say that the auto-increment counter for table T has been initialised.

InnoDB follows the same procedure in initializing the auto-increment counter for a freshly created table.

Note that if the user specifies in an insert the value 0 to the auto-increment column, then InnoDB treats the row like the value would not have been specified.

After the auto-increment counter has been initialised, if a user inserts a row where he explicitly specifies the column value, and the value is bigger than the current counter value, then the counter is set to the specified column value. If the user does not explicitly specify a value, then InnoDB increments the counter by one and assigns its new value to the column.

The auto-increment mechanism, when assigning values from the counter, bypasses locking and transaction handling. Therefore you may also get gaps in the number sequence if you roll back transactions that got numbers from the counter.

The behavior of auto-increment is not defined if a user gives a negative value to the column or if the value becomes bigger than the maximum integer that can be stored in the specified integer type.

7.5.12 File Space Management and Disk I/O

7.5.12.1 Disk I/O

In disk I/O InnoDB uses asynchronous I/O. On Windows NT it uses the native asynchronous I/O provided by the operating system. On Unix, InnoDB uses simulated asynchronous I/O built into InnoDB: InnoDB creates a number of I/O threads to take care of I/O operations, such as read-ahead. In a future version we will add support for simulated I/O on Windows NT and native aio on those versions of Unix that have one.

On Windows NT InnoDB uses non-buffered I/O. That means that the disk pages InnoDB reads or writes are not buffered in the operating system file cache. This saves some memory bandwidth.

Starting from 3.23.41 InnoDB uses a novel file flush technique called doublewrite. It adds safety to crash recovery after an operating system crash or a power outage, and improves performance on most Unix flavors by reducing the need for fsync operations.

Doublewrite means that before writing pages to a data file InnoDB first writes them to a contiguous tablespace area called the doublewrite buffer. Only after the write and the flush to the doublewrite buffer have completed, does InnoDB write the pages to their proper positions in the data file. If the operating system crashes in the middle of a page write, InnoDB will, in recovery, find a good copy of the page from the doublewrite buffer.

Starting from 3.23.41 you can also use a raw disk partition as a data file, though this has not been tested yet. When you create a new data file you have to put the keyword newraw immediately after the data file-size in innodb_data_file_path. The partition must be >= than you specify as the size. Note that 1M in InnoDB is 1024x1024 bytes, while in disk specifications 1M usually means 1 million bytes.

```
innodb_data_file_path=hdd1:5Gnewraw;hdd2:2Gnewraw
```

When you start the database again you **must** change the keyword to raw. Otherwise, InnoDB will write over your partition!

```
innodb_data_file_path=hdd1:5Graw;hdd2:2Graw
```

By using a raw disk you can, on some Unix sysytems, perform unbuffered I/O.

There are two read-ahead heuristics in InnoDB: sequential read-ahead and random read-ahead. In sequential read-ahead InnoDB notices that the access pattern to a segment in the tablespace is sequential. Then InnoDB will post in advance a batch of reads of database pages to the I/O system. In random read-ahead InnoDB notices that some area in a tablespace seems to be in the process of being fully read into the buffer pool. Then InnoDB posts the remaining reads to the I/O system.

7.5.12.2 File space management

The data files you define in the configuration file form the tablespace of InnoDB. The files are simply catenated to form the tablespace. There is no striping in use. Currently you cannot directly instruct where the space is allocated for your tables, except by using the following fact: from a newly created tablespace InnoDB will allocate space starting from the low end.

The tablespace consists of database pages whose default size is 16 kB. The pages are grouped into extents of 64 consecutive pages. The 'files' inside a tablespace are called segments in InnoDB. The name of the rollback segment is somewhat misleading because it actually contains many segments in the tablespace.

For each index in InnoDB we allocate two segments: one is for non-leaf nodes of the B-tree, the other is for leaf nodes. The idea here is to achieve better sequentiality for the leaf nodes, which contain the data.

When a segment grows inside the tablespace, InnoDB allocates the first 32 pages to it individually. After that InnoDB starts to allocate whole extents to the segment. InnoDB can add to a large segment up to 4 extents at a time to ensure good sequentiality of data.

Some pages in the tablespace contain bitmaps of other pages, and therefore a few extents in an InnoDB tablespace cannot be allocated to segments as a whole, but only as individual pages.

When you issue a query SHOW TABLE STATUS FROM ... LIKE ... to ask for available free space in the tablespace, InnoDB will report the extents which are definitely free in the tablespace. InnoDB always reserves some extents for clean-up and other internal purposes; these reserved extents are not included in the free space.

When you delete data from a table, InnoDB will contract the corresponding B-tree indexes. Individual pages or extents to the tablespace are freed from depending on the pattern of deletes, so that the freed space is available for other users. Dropping a table or deleting all rows from it is guaranteed to release the space to other users, but remember that deleted rows can be physically removed only in a purge operation after they are no longer needed in transaction rollback or consistent read.

7.5.12.3 Defragmenting a table

If there are random insertions or deletions in the indexes of a table, the indexes may become fragmented. By fragmentation we mean that the physical ordering of the index pages on the disk is not close to the alphabetical ordering of the records on the pages, or that there are many unused pages in the 64-page blocks that were allocated to the index.

You can speed up index scans if you periodically use mysqldump to dump the table to a text file, drop the table, and reload it from the dump. Another way to do the defragmenting is to ALTER the table type to MyISAM and back to InnoDB again. Note that a MyISAM table must fit in a single file on your operating system.

If the insertions to an index are always ascending and records are deleted only from the end, the file space management algorithm of InnoDB guarantees that fragmentation in the index will not occur.

7.5.13 Error Handling

The error handling in InnoDB is not always the same as specified in the ANSI SQL standards. According to the ANSI standard, any error during an SQL statement should cause the rollback of that statement. InnoDB sometimes rolls back only part of the statement, and other times the whole transaction. The following list specifies the error handling of InnoDB:

- If you run out of file space in the tablespace, you will get the MySQL `'Table is full'` error and InnoDB rolls back the SQL statement.

- A transaction deadlock or a timeout in a lock wait make InnoDB roll back the whole transaction.

- A duplicate key error only rolls back the insert of that particular row, even in a statement like `INSERT INTO ... SELECT ....` This will probably change so that the SQL statement will be rolled back if you have not specified the `IGNORE` option in your statement.

- A 'row too long' error rolls back the SQL statement.

- Other errors are mostly detected by the MySQL layer of code, and they roll back the corresponding SQL statement.

7.5.14 Restrictions on InnoDB Tables

- **Warning**: Do **not** convert MySQL system tables from MyISAM to InnoDB tables! This is not supported. If you do this MySQL will not restart until you restore the old system tables from a backup or regenerate them with the mysql_install_db script.

- `SHOW TABLE STATUS` does not give accurate statistics on InnoDB tables, except for the physical size reserved by the table. The row count is only a rough estimate used in SQL optimisation.

- If you try to create a unique index on a prefix of a column you will get an error:

  ```
  CREATE TABLE T (A CHAR(20), B INT, UNIQUE (A(5))) TYPE = InnoDB;
  ```

  If you create a non-unique index on a prefix of a column, InnoDB will create an index over the whole column.

- `INSERT DELAYED` is not supported for InnoDB tables.

- The MySQL `LOCK TABLES` operation does not know of InnoDB row level locks set in already completed SQL statements: this means that you can get a table lock on a table even if there still exist transactions of other users that have row level locks on the same table. Thus, your operations on the table may have to wait if they collide with these locks of other users. Also, a deadlock is possible. However, this does not endanger transaction integrity because the row level locks set by InnoDB will always take care of the integrity. Also, a table lock prevents other transactions from acquiring more row level locks (in a conflicting lock mode) on the table.

- You cannot have a key on a `BLOB` or `TEXT` column.

- A table cannot contain more than 1000 columns.

- `DELETE FROM TABLE` does not regenerate the table but instead deletes all rows, one by one, which is not that fast. In future versions of MySQL you can use `TRUNCATE`, which is fast.

- The default database page size in InnoDB is 16 kB. By recompiling the code one can set it from 8 kB to 64 kB. The maximun row length is slightly less than half of a database page in versions up to 3.23.40 of InnoDB. Starting from source release 3.23.41 BLOB and TEXT columns are allowed to be less than 4G. The total row length must also be less than 4G. InnoDB does not store fields whose size is less than or equal to 128 bytes on separate pages. After InnoDB has modified the row by storing long fields on separate pages, the remaining length of the row must be less than half a database page. The maximun key length is 7000 bytes.

- On some operating systems data files must be less than 2G. The combined size of log files must be less than 4G on 32-bit computers.

- The maximum tablespace size is 4 billion database pages. This is also the maximum size for a table. The minimum tablespace size is 10M.

7.5.15 InnoDB Contact Information

To contact Innobase Oy, producer of the InnoDB engine. visit http://www.innodb.com/ or email *Heikki.Tuuri@innodb.com*.

phone: 358-9-6969 3250 (office) 358-40-5617367 (mobile)
Innobase Oy Inc.
World Trade Center Helsinki
Aleksanterinkatu 17
P.O.Box 800
00101 Helsinki
Finland

7.6 BDB or Berkeley_DB Tables

7.6.1 Overview of BDB Tables

Support for BDB tables is included in the MySQL source distribution starting from Version 3.23.34 and is activated in the MySQL-Max binary.

BerkeleyDB, available at http://www.sleepycat.com/, has provided MySQL with a transactional table handler. BerkeleyDB tables may have a greater chance of surviving crashes, and also provide COMMIT and ROLLBACK on transactions. The MySQL source distribution comes with a BDB distribution that has a couple of small patches to make it work more smoothly with MySQL. You can't use a non-patched BDB version with MySQL.

We at MySQL AB are working in close cooperation with Sleepycat to keep the quality of the MySQL/BDB interface high.

When it comes to supporting BDB tables, we are committed to helping our users locate the problem and create a reproducible test case for any problems involving BDB tables. Any such test case will be forwarded to Sleepycat, who in turn will help us find and fix the problem. As this is a two-stage operation, any problems with BDB tables may take a little longer for us to fix than for other table handlers. However, as the BerkeleyDB code itself has been used by many other applications, we don't envision any big problems with this. See Section 1.4.1, Support Offered by MySQL AB.

7.6.2 Installing BDB

If you have downloaded a binary version of MySQL that includes support for BerkeleyDB, simply follow the instructions for installing a binary version of MySQL. See Section 2.2.7, Installing a MySQL Binary Distribution, and Section 4.7.5, mysqld-max, an Extended mysqld Server.

To compile MySQL with BerkeleyDB support, download MySQL Version 3.23.34 or newer and configure MySQL with the --with-berkeley-db option. See Section 2.3, Installing a MySQL Source Distribution.

```
cd /path/to/source/of/mysql-3.23.34
./configure --with-berkeley-db
```

Please refer to the manual provided with the BDB distribution for more updated information.

Even though BerkeleyDB is in itself very tested and reliable, the MySQL interface is still considered beta quality. We are actively improving and optimising it to get it stable very soon.

7.6.3 BDB Startup Options

If you are running with AUTOCOMMIT=0, your changes in BDB tables will not be updated until you execute COMMIT. Instead of COMMIT you can execute ROLLBACK to forget your changes. See Section 6.7.1, BEGIN/COMMIT/ROLLBACK Syntax.

If you are running with AUTOCOMMIT=1 (the default), your changes will be committed immediately. You can start an extended transaction with the BEGIN WORK SQL command, after which your changes will not be committed until you execute COMMIT (or decide to ROLLBACK the changes).

The following options to mysqld can be used to change the behavior of BDB tables:

Option	Description
--bdb-home=directory	Base directory for BDB tables. This should be the same directory you use for —datadir.
--bdb-lock-detect=#	Berkeley lock detect. One of (DEFAULT, OLDEST, RANDOM, or YOUNGEST).
--bdb-logdir=directory	Berkeley DB log file directory.

Option	Description
--bdb-no-sync	Don't synchronously flush logs.
--bdb-no-recover	Don't start BerkeleyDB in recover mode.
--bdb-shared-data	Start BerkeleyDB in multi-process mode (don't use DB_PRIVATE when initialising Berkeley DB).
--bdb-tmpdir=directory	BerkeleyDB tempfile name.
--skip-bdb	Don't use BerkeleyDB.
-O bdb_max_lock=1000	Set the maximum number of locks possible. See Section 4.5.6.4, SHOW VARIABLES.

If you use --skip-bdb, MySQL will not initialise the Berkeley DB library and this will save a lot of memory. Of course, you cannot use BDB tables if you are using this option.

Normally you should start mysqld without --bdb-no-recover if you intend to use BDB tables. This may, however, give you problems when you try to start mysqld if the BDB log files are corrupted. See Section 2.4.2, Problems Starting the MySQL server.

With bdb_max_lock you can specify the maximum number of locks (10,000 by default) that you can have active on a BDB table. You should increase this if you get errors of type bdb: Lock table is out of available locks or Got error 12 from . . . when you have to do long transactions or when mysqld has to examine a lot of rows to calculate the query.

You may also want to change binlog_cache_size and max_binlog_cache_size if you are using big multi-line transactions. See Section 6.7.1, BEGIN/COMMIT/ROLLBACK Syntax.

7.6.4 Characteristics of BDB Tables

- To be able to roll back transactions, BDB maintains log files. For maximum performance you should place these on a different disk from your databases by using the --bdb_log_dir options.

- MySQL performs a checkpoint each time a new BDB log file is started, and removes any log files that are not needed for current transactions. One can also run FLUSH LOGS at any time to checkpoint the BerkeleyDB tables.

  For disaster recovery, one should use table backups plus MySQL's binary log. See Section 4.4.1, Database Backups.

  Warning: If you delete old log files that are in use, BDB will not be able to do recovery at all and you may lose data if something goes wrong.

- MySQL requires a PRIMARY KEY in each BDB table to be able to refer to previously read rows. If you don't create one, MySQL will create and maintain a hidden PRIMARY KEY for you. The hidden key has a length of 5 bytes and is incremented for each insert attempt.

- If all columns you access in a BDB table are part of the same index or part of the primary key, MySQL can execute the query without having to access the actual row. In a MyISAM table this holds only if the columns are part of the same index.

- The PRIMARY KEY will be faster than any other key, as the PRIMARY KEY is stored together with the row data. As the other keys are stored as the key data + the PRIMARY KEY, it's important to keep the PRIMARY KEY as short as possible to save disk space and get better speed.

- LOCK TABLES works on BDB tables as with other tables. If you don't use LOCK TABLE, MySQL will issue an internal multiple-write lock on the table to ensure that the table will be properly locked if another thread issues a table lock.

- Internal locking in BDB tables is done on page level.

- SELECT COUNT(*) FROM table_name is slow, as BDB tables don't maintain a count of the number of rows in the table.

- Scanning is slower than with MyISAM tables, as one has data in BDB tables stored in B-trees and not in a separate data file.

- The application must always be prepared to handle cases where any change of a BDB table may make an automatic rollback and any read may fail with a deadlock error.

- Keys are not compressed to previous keys, as with ISAM or MyISAM tables. In other words, the key information will take a little more space in BDB tables compared to MyISAM tables, which don't use PACK_KEYS=0.

- There are often holes in the BDB table to allow you to insert new rows in the middle of the key tree. This makes BDB tables somewhat larger than MyISAM tables.

- The optimiser needs to know an approximation of the number of rows in the table. MySQL solves this by counting inserts and maintaining this in a separate segment in each BDB table. If you don't issue a lot of DELETE or ROLLBACK statements, this number should be accurate enough for the MySQL optimiser, but as MySQL only stores the number on close, it may be incorrect if MySQL dies unexpectedly. It should not be fatal even if this number is not 100% correct. One can update the number of rows by executing ANALYZE TABLE or OPTIMIZE TABLE. See Section 4.5.2, ANALYZE TABLE Syntax, and Section 4.5.1, OPTIMIZE TABLE Syntax.

- If you get a full disk with a BDB table, you will get an error (probably error 28) and the transaction should roll back. This is in contrast with MyISAM and ISAM tables, where mysqld will wait for enough free disk space before continuing.

7.6.5 Things We Need to Fix for BDB in the Near Future

- It's very slow to open many BDB tables at the same time. If you are going to use BDB tables, you should not have a very big table cache (as in, >256) and you should use --no-auto-rehash with the mysql client. We plan to partly fix this in 4.0.

- SHOW TABLE STATUS doesn't yet provide that much information for BDB tables.

- Optimise performance.

- Change to not use page locks at all when we are scanning tables.

7.6.6 Operating Systems Supported by BDB

If, after building MySQL with support for BDB tables, you get the following error in the log file when you start mysqld:

```
bdb: architecture lacks fast mutexes: applications cannot be threaded
Can't init databases
```

this means that BDB tables are not supported for your architecture. In this case you have to rebuild MySQL without BDB table support.

Note: the following list is not complete; we will update it as we receive more information about this.

Currently we know that BDB tables work with the following operating systems:

- Linux 2.x Intel
- Solaris SPARC
- Caldera (SCO) OpenServer
- Caldera (SCO) UnixWare 7.0.1

It doesn't work with the following operating systems:

- Linux 2.x Alpha
- Max OS X

7.6.7 Restrictions on BDB Tables

Here are the restrictions you have when using BDB tables:

- BDB tables store in the .db file the path to the file as it was created This was done to be able to detect locks in a multi-user environment that supports symlinks).

   The effect of this is that BDB tables are not movable between directories!

- When taking backups of BDB tables, you have to either use mysqldump or take a backup of all table_name.db files and the BDB log files. The BDB log files are the files in the base data directory named log.XXXXXX (6 digits). The BDB table handler stores unfinished transactions in the log files and requires these to be present when mysqld starts.

7.6.8 Errors that May Occur When Using BDB Tables

- If you get the following error in the hostname.err log when starting mysqld:

  ```
  bdb:  Ignoring log file: .../log.XXXXXXXXXX: unsupported log version #
  ```

  it means that the new BDB version doesn't support the old log file format. In this case you have to delete all BDB logs from your database directory (the files that have the format log.XXXXXXXXXX) and restart mysqld. We also recommend you do a mysqldump --opt of your old BDB tables, delete the old table, and restore the dump.

- If you are running in not auto_commit mode and delete a table you are using by another thread, you may get the following error messages in the MySQL error file:

  ```
  001119 23:43:56  bdb:  Missing log fileid entry
  001119 23:43:56  bdb:  txn_abort: Log undo failed for LSN:
                         1 3644744: Invalid
  ```

  This is not fatal, but we don't recommend that you delete tables if you are not in auto_commit mode, until this problem is fixed (the fix is not trivial).

8

MySQL APIs

This chapter describes the APIs available for MySQL, where to get them, and how to use them. The C API is the most extensively covered, as it was developed by the MySQL team and is the basis for most of the other APIs.

8.1 MySQL PHP API

PHP is a server-side, HTML-embedded scripting language that may be used to create dynamic web pages. It contains support for accessing several databases, including MySQL. PHP may be run as a separate program or compiled as a module for use with the Apache web server.

The distribution and documentation are available at the PHP web site (http://www.php.net/).

8.1.1 Common Problems with MySQL and PHP

- Error: "Maximum Execution Time Exceeded." This is a PHP limit. Go into the `php3.ini` file and set the maximum execution time up from 30 seconds to something higher, as needed. It is also not a bad idea to double the RAM allowed per script to 16M instead of 8M.

- Error: "Fatal error: Call to unsupported or undefined function mysql_connect() in .." This means that your PHP version isn't compiled with MySQL support. You can either compile a dynamic MySQL module and load it into PHP or recompile PHP with built-in MySQL support. This is described in detail in the PHP manual.

- Error: "undefined reference to 'uncompress'." This means that the client library is compiled with support for a compressed client/server protocol. The fix is to add `-lz` last when linking with `-lmysqlclient`.

8.2 MySQL Perl API

This section documents the Perl `DBI` interface. The former interface was called `mysqlperl`. DBI/DBD now is the recommended Perl interface, so `mysqlperl` is obsolete and is not documented here.

8.2.1 `DBI` with `DBD::mysql`

`DBI` is a generic interface for many databases. That means that you can write a script that works with many different database engines without change. You need a dataBase driver (DBD) defined for each database type. For MySQL, this driver is called `DBD::mysql`.

For more information on the Perl5 DBI, please visit the `DBI` web page and read the documentation:

```
http://www.symbolstone.org/technology/perl/DBI/
```

For more information on object oriented programming (OOP) as defined in Perl5, see the Perl OOP page:

```
http://language.perl.com/info/documentation.html
```

Note that if you want to use transactions with Perl, you need to have `Msql-Mysql-modules` Version 1.2216 or newer.

Installation instructions for MySQL Perl support are given in Section 2.7, Perl Installation Comments.

8.2.2 The `DBI` Interface

8.2.2.1 Portable DBI methods

Method	Description
`connect`	Establishes a connection to a database server
`disconnect`	Disconnects from the database server
`prepare`	Prepares an SQL statement for execution
`execute`	Executes prepared statements
`do`	Prepares and executes an SQL statement
`quote`	Quotes string or `BLOB` values to be inserted
`fetchrow_array`	Fetches the next row as an array of fields
`fetchrow_arrayref`	Fetches the next row as a reference array of fields
`fetchrow_hashref`	Fetches the next row as a reference to a hashtable
`fetchall_arrayref`	Fetches all data as an array of arrays
`finish`	Finishes a statement and lets the system free resources
`rows`	Returns the number of rows affected
`data_sources`	Returns an array of databases available on localhost
`ChopBlanks`	Controls whether `fetchrow_*` methods trim spaces

Method	Description
NUM_OF_PARAMS	The number of placeholders in the prepared statement
NULLABLE	Which columns can be NULL
trace	Perform tracing for debugging

8.2.2.2 MySQL-specific methods

Method	Description
insertid	The latest AUTO_INCREMENT value.
is_blob	Which columns are BLOB values.
is_key	Which columns are keys.
is_num	Which columns are numeric.
is_pri_key	Which columns are primary keys.
is_not_null	Which columns CANNOT be NULL. See NULLABLE.
length	Maximum possible column sizes.
max_length	Maximum column sizes actually present in result.
NAME	Column names.
NUM_OF_FIELDS	Number of fields returned.
table	Table names in returned set.
type	All column types.

The Perl methods are described in more detail in the following sections. Variables used for method return values have these meanings:

$dbh
> Database handle

$sth
> Statement handle

$rc
> Return code (often a status)

$rv
> Return value (often a row count)

8.2.2.3 Portable DBI methods

connect($data_source, $username, $password)
> Use the connect method to make a database connection to the data source. The $data_source value should begin with DBI:driver_name:. Example uses of connect with the DBD::mysql driver:

```
$dbh = DBI->connect("DBI:mysql:$database", $user, $password);
$dbh = DBI->connect("DBI:mysql:$database:$hostname",
                    $user, $password);
$dbh = DBI->connect("DBI:mysql:$database:$hostname:$port",
```

```
                        $user, $password);
```

If the username and/or password are undefined, DBI uses the values of the DBI_USER and DBI_PASS environment variables, respectively. If you don't specify a hostname, it defaults to 'localhost'. If you don't specify a port number, it defaults to the default MySQL port (3306).

As of Msql-Mysql-modules Version 1.2009, the $data_source value allows certain modifiers:

mysql_read_default_file=file_name

> Read filename as an option file. For information on option files, see Section 4.1.2, my.cnf Option Files.

mysql_read_default_group=group_name

> The default group when reading an option file is normally the [client] group. By specifying the mysql_read_default_group option, the default group becomes the [group_name] group.

mysql_compression=1

> Use compressed communication between the client and server (MySQL Version 3.22.3 or later).

mysql_socket=/path/to/socket

> Specify the pathname of the Unix socket that is used to connect to the server (MySQL Version 3.21.15 or later).

Multiple modifiers may be given; each must be preceded by a semicolon.

For example, if you want to avoid hardcoding the username and password into a DBI script, you can take them from the user's ~/.my.cnf option file instead by writing your connect call like this:

```
$dbh = DBI->connect("DBI:mysql:$database"
              . ";mysql_read_default_file=$ENV{HOME}/.my.cnf",
              $user, $password);
```

This call will read options defined for the [client] group in the option file. If you wanted to do the same thing but use options specified for the [perl] group as well, you could use this:

```
$dbh = DBI->connect("DBI:mysql:$database"
              . ";mysql_read_default_file=$ENV{HOME}/.my.cnf"
              . ";mysql_read_default_group=perl",
              $user, $password);
```

disconnect

> The disconnect method disconnects the database handle from the database. This is typically called right before you exit from the program. Example:

```
$rc = $dbh->disconnect;
```

prepare($statement)

Prepares an SQL statement for execution by the database engine and returns a state-ment handle ($sth), which you can use to invoke the execute method. Typically you handle SELECT statements (and SELECT-like statements such as SHOW, DESCRIBE, and EXPLAIN) by means of prepare and execute. Example:

```
$sth = $dbh->prepare($statement)
    or die "Can't prepare $statement: $dbh->errstr\n";
```

execute

The execute method executes a prepared statement. For non-SELECT statements, execute returns the number of rows affected. If no rows are affected, execute returns "0E0", which Perl treats as zero but regards as true. If an error occurs, exe-cute returns undef. For SELECT statements, execute only starts the SQL query in the database; you need to use one of the fetch_* methods described later to retrieve the data. Example:

```
$rv = $sth->execute
        or die "can't execute the query: $sth->errstr;
```

do($statement)

The do method prepares and executes an SQL statement and returns the number of rows affected. If no rows are affected, do returns "0E0", which Perl treats as zero but regards as true. This method is generally used for non-SELECT statements that cannot be prepared in advance (due to driver limitations) or that do not need to be executed more than once (inserts, deletes, etc.). Example:

```
$rv = $dbh->do($statement)
        or die "Can't execute $statement: $dbh- >errstr\n";
```

Generally the 'do' statement is much faster (and is preferable) than prepare/execute for statements that don't contain parameters.

quote($string)

The quote method is used to "escape" any special characters contained in the string and to add the required outer quotation marks. Example:

```
$sql = $dbh->quote($string)
```

fetchrow_array

This method fetches the next row of data and returns it as an array of field values. Example:

```
while(@row = $sth->fetchrow_array) {
        print qw($row[0]\t$row[1]\t$row[2]\n);
}
```

`fetchrow_arrayref`

This method fetches the next row of data and returns it as a reference to an array of field values. Example:

```
while($row_ref = $sth->fetchrow_arrayref) {
        print qw($row_ref->[0]\t$row_ref->[1]\t$row_ref->[2]\n);
}
```

`fetchrow_hashref`

This method fetches a row of data and returns a reference to a hash table containing field name/value pairs. This method is not nearly as efficient as using array references as demonstrated earlier. Example:

```
while($hash_ref = $sth->fetchrow_hashref) {
        print qw($hash_ref->{firstname}\t$hash_ref->{lastname}\t\
                $hash_ref- > title}\n);
}
```

`fetchall_arrayref`

This method is used to get all the data (rows) to be returned from the SQL statement. It returns a reference to an array of references to arrays for each row. You access or print the data by using a nested loop. Example:

```
my $table = $sth->fetchall_arrayref
                    or die "$sth->errstr\n";
my($i, $j);
for $i ( 0 .. $#{$table} ) {
        for $j ( 0 .. $#{$table->[$i]} ) {
                print "$table->[$i][$j]\t";
        }
        print "\n";
}
```

`finish`

Indicates that no more data will be fetched from this statement handle. You call this method to free up the statement handle and any system resources associated with it. Example:

```
$rc = $sth->finish;
```

`rows`

Returns the number of rows changed (updated, deleted, etc.) by the last command. This is usually used after a non-SELECT execute statement. Example:

```
$rv = $sth->rows;
```

`NULLABLE`

Returns a reference to an array of boolean values; for each element of the array, a value of TRUE indicates that this column may contain NULL values. Example:

```
        $null_possible = $sth->{NULLABLE};
```

NUM_OF_FIELDS

> This attribute indicates the number of fields returned by a SELECT or SHOW FIELDS statement. You may use this for checking whether a statement returned a result: a zero value indicates a non-SELECT statement like INSERT, DELETE, or UPDATE. Example:

```
        $nr_of_fields = $sth->{NUM_OF_FIELDS};
```

data_sources($driver_name)

> This method returns an array containing names of databases available to the MySQL server on the host 'localhost'. Example:

```
        @dbs = DBI->data_sources("mysql");
```

ChopBlanks

> This attribute determines whether the fetchrow_* methods will chop leading and trailing blanks from the returned values. Example:

```
        $sth->{'ChopBlanks'} =1;
```

trace($trace_level)
trace($trace_level, $trace_filename)

> The trace method enables or disables tracing. When invoked as a DBI class method, it affects tracing for all handles. When invoked as a database or statement handle method, it affects tracing for the given handle (and any future children of the handle). Setting $trace_level to 2 provides detailed trace information. Setting $trace_level to 0 disables tracing. Trace output goes to the standard error output by default. If $trace_filename is specified, the file is opened in append mode and output for **all** traced handles is written to that file. Example:

```
        DBI->trace(2);                  # trace everything
        DBI->trace(2,"/tmp/dbi.out");   # trace everything to
                                        # /tmp/dbi.out
        $dth->trace(2);                 # trace this database handle
        $sth->trace(2);                 # trace this statement handle
```

> You can also enable DBI tracing by setting the DBI_TRACE environment variable. Setting it to a numeric value is equivalent to calling DBI->(value). Setting it to a pathname is equivalent to calling DBI->(2,value).

8.2.2.4 MySQL-specific methods

The following methods are MySQL-specific and not part of the DBI standard. Several of them are now deprecated: is_blob, is_key, is_num, is_pri_key, is_not_null, length, max_length, and table. Where DBI-standard alternatives exist, they are noted:

insertid

> If you use the AUTO_INCREMENT feature of MySQL, the new auto-incremented values will be stored here. Example:
>
> $new_id = $sth->{insertid};
>
> As an alternative, you can use $dbh->{'mysql_insertid'}.

is_blob

> Returns a reference to an array of boolean values; for each element of the array, a value of TRUE indicates that the respective column is a BLOB. Example:
>
> $keys = $sth->{is_blob};

is_key

> Returns a reference to an array of boolean values; for each element of the array, a value of TRUE indicates that the respective column is a key. Example:
>
> $keys = $sth->{is_key};

is_num

> Returns a reference to an array of boolean values; for each element of the array, a value of TRUE indicates that the respective column contains numeric values. Example:
>
> $nums = $sth->{is_num};

is_pri_key

> Returns a reference to an array of boolean values; for each element of the array, a value of TRUE indicates that the respective column is a primary key. Example:
>
> $pri_keys = $sth->{is_pri_key};

is_not_null

> Returns a reference to an array of boolean values; for each element of the array, a value of FALSE indicates that this column may contain NULL values. Example:
>
> $not_nulls = $sth->{is_not_null};
>
> is_not_null is deprecated; it is preferable to use the NULLABLE attribute (described earlier), because that is a DBI standard.

length

max_length

> Each of these methods returns a reference to an array of column sizes. The length array indicates the maximum possible sizes that each column may be (as declared in the table description). The max_length array indicates the maximum sizes actually present in the result table. Example:

```
$lengths = $sth->{length};
$max_lengths = $sth->{max_length};
```

NAME

Returns a reference to an array of column names. Example:

```
$names = $sth->{NAME};
```

table

Returns a reference to an array of table names. Example:

```
$tables = $sth->{table};
```

type

Returns a reference to an array of column types. Example:

```
$types = $sth->{type};
```

8.2.3 More DBI/DBD Information

You can use the `perldoc` command to get more information about DBI.

```
perldoc DBI
perldoc DBI::FAQ
perldoc DBD::mysql
```

You can also use the pod2man, pod2html, etc., tools to translate to other formats.

You can find the latest DBI information at the DBI web page: http://www.symbol-stone.org/technology/perl/DBI/

8.3 MySQL ODBC Support

MySQL provides support for ODBC by means of the MyODBC program. This section will teach you how to install MyODBC, and how to use it. Here, you will also find a list of common programs that are known to work with MyODBC.

8.3.1 How to Install MyODBC

MyODBC is a 32-bit ODBC (2.50) level 0 (with level 1 and level 2 features) driver for connecting an ODBC-aware application to MySQL. MyODBC works on Windows 9x/Me/NT/2000/XP and most Unix platforms.

MyODBC is in public domain, and you can find the newest version at http://www.mysql.com/downloads/api-myodbc.html.

If you have problems with MyODBC and your program also works with OLEDB, you should try the OLEDB driver.

Normally you only need to install MyODBC on Windows machines. You only need MyODBC for Unix if you have a program like ColdFusion that is running on the Unix machine and uses ODBC to connect to the databases.

If you want to install MyODBC on a Unix box, you will also need an ODBC manager. MyO-
DBC is known to work with most of the Unix ODBC managers. See Section 1.6.1,
MySQL Portals.

To install MyODBC on Windows, you should download the appropriate MyODBC .zip file,
unpack it with WinZIP or some similar program, and execute the SETUP.EXE file.

On Windows/NT/XP you may get the following error when trying to install MyODBC:

```
An error occurred while copying C:\WINDOWS\SYSTEM\MFC30.DLL. Restart
Windows and try installing again (before running any applications which
use ODBC)
```

The problem in this case is that some other program is using ODBC and because of how
Windows is designed, you may not in this case be able to install a new ODBC driver with
Microsoft's ODBC setup program. In most cases you can continue by just pressing
Ignore to copy the rest of the MyODBC files and the final installation should still work.
If this doesn't work, the solution is to reboot your computer in "safe mode" (choose this
by pressing F8 just before your machine starts Windows during rebooting), install MyO-
DBC, and reboot to normal mode.

- To make a connection to a Unix box from a Windows box, with an ODBC application (one that doesn't support MySQL natively), you must first install MyODBC on the
  Windows machine.

- The user and Windows machines must have the access privileges to the MySQL
  server on the Unix machine. This is set up with the GRANT command. See Section
  4.3.1, GRANT and REVOKE Syntax.

- You must create an ODBC DSN entry as follows:

  — Open the Control Panel on the Windows machine.

  — Double-click the ODBC Data Sources 32-bit icon.

  — Click the tab User DSN.

  — Click the button Add.

  — Select MySQL in the screen Create New Data Source and click the Finish but-
    ton.

  — The MySQL Driver default configuration screen is shown. See Section 8.3.2,
    How to Fill in the Various Fields in the ODBC Administrator Program.

- Now start your application and select the ODBC driver with the DSN you specified
  in the ODBC administrator.

Notice that there are other configuration options on the screen of MySQL (trace, don't
prompt on connect, etc.) that you can try if you run into problems.

8.3.2 How to Fill in the Various Fields in the ODBC Administrator Program

There are three possibilities for specifying the server name on Windows 95:

- Use the IP address of the server.

- Add a file \windows\lmhosts with the following information:

      ip hostname

   For example:

      194.216.84.21 my_hostname

- Configure the PC to use DNS.

Example of how to fill in the ODBC setup:

```
Windows DSN name:    test
Description:         This is my test database
MySql Database:      test
Server:              194.216.84.21
User:                monty
Password:            my_password
Port:
```

The value for the Windows DSN name field is any name that is unique in your Windows ODBC setup.

You don't have to specify values for the Server, User, Password, or Port fields in the ODBC setup screen. However, if you do, the values will be used as the defaults later when you attempt to make a connection. You have the option of changing the values at that time.

If the port number is not given, the default port (3306) is used.

If you specify the option Read options from C:\my.cnf, the groups client and odbc will be read from the C:\my.cnf file. You can use all options that are usable by mysql_options(). See Section 8.4.3.159, mysql_options().

8.3.3 Connect Parameters for MyODBC

One can specify the following parameters for MyODBC on the [Servername] section of an ODBC.INI file or through the InConnectionString argument in the SQLDriver-Connect() call:

Parameter	Default value	Comment
user	ODBC (on Windows)	The username used to connect to MySQL.
server	localhost	The hostname of the MySQL server.
database		The default database.
option	0	An integer by which you can specify how MyODBC should work. See next table.
port	3306	The TCP/IP port to use if server is not localhost.
stmt		A statement that will be executed upon connection to MySQL.
password		The password for the server user combination.
socket		The socket or Windows pipe to connect to.

The option argument is used to tell MyODBC that the client isn't 100% ODBC-compliant. On Windows, one normally sets the option flag by toggling the different options on the connection screen, but one can also set this in the opton argument. The following options are listed in the same order as they appear in the MyODBC connect screen:

Bit	Description
1	The client can't handle that MyODBC returns the real width of a column.
2	The client can't handle that MySQL returns the true value of affected rows. If this flag is set, MySQL returns 'found rows' instead. One must have MySQL 3.21.14 or newer to get this to work.
4	Make a debug log in c:\myodbc.log. This is the same as putting MYSQL_DEBUG=d:t:O,c::\myodbc.log in AUTOEXEC.BAT.
8	Don't set any packet limit for results and parameters.
16	Don't prompt for questions even if the driver would like to prompt.
32	Simulate an ODBC 1.0 driver in some context.
64	Ignore the use of database name in 'database.table.column'.
128	Force the use of ODBC manager cursors (experimental).
256	Disable the use of extended fetch (experimental).
512	Pad CHAR fields to full column length.
1024	SQLDescribeCol() will return fully qualifed column names.
2048	Use the compressed server/client protocol.
4096	Tell server to ignore space after function name and before ' (' (needed by Power-Builder). This will make all function names keywords!
8192	Connect with named pipes to a mysqld server running on NT.
16384	Change LONGLONG columns to INT columns (some applications can't handle LONGLONG).
32768	Return 'user' as Table_qualifier and Table_owner from SQLTables (experimental).
65536	Read parameters from the client and odbc groups from my.cnf.
131072	Add some extra safety checks (should not be needed but ...).

If you want to have many options, you should add these flags. For example, setting option to 12 (4+8) gives you debugging without package limits.

The default MYODBC.DLL is compiled for optimal performance. If you want to debug MyODBC (for example, to enable tracing), you should instead use MYODBCD.DLL. To install this file, copy MYODBCD.DLL over the installed MYODBC.DLL file.

8.3.4 How to Report Problems with MyODBC

MyODBC has been tested with Access, Admndemo.exe, C++-Builder, Borland Builder 4, Centura Team Developer (formerly Gupta SQL/Windows), ColdFusion (on Solaris and NT with svc pack 5), Crystal Reports, DataJunction, Delphi, ERwin, Excel, iHTML, File-Maker Pro, FoxPro, Notes 4.5/4.6, SBSS, Perl DBD-ODBC, Paradox, Powerbuilder, Powerdesigner 32 bit, VC++, and Visual Basic.

If you know of any other applications that work with MyODBC, please send mail to *myo-dbc@lists.mysql.com* about this!

With some programs you may get an error like: Another user has modified the record that you have modified. In most cases this can be solved by doing one of the following things:

- Add a primary key for the table if there isn't one already.

- Add a timestamp column if there isn't one already.

- Only use double float fields. Some programs may fail when they compare single floats.

If the this doesn't help, you should do a MyODBC trace file and try to figure out why things go wrong.

8.3.5 Programs Known to Work with MyODBC

Most programs should work with MyODBC, but for each of those in the following list, we have tested it ourselves or received confirmation from some user that it works:

Access

   To make Access work:

- If you are using Access 2000, you should get and install the newest (Version 2.6 or above) Microsoft MDAC (Microsoft Data Access Components) from http://www.microsoft.com/data/. This will fix the following bug in Access: when you export data to MySQL, the table and column names aren't specified. Another way around this bug is to upgrade to MyODBC Version 2.50.33 and MySQL Version 3.23.x, which together provide a workaround for this bug!

   You should also get and apply the Microsoft Jet 4.0 Service Pack 5 (SP5) (http://support.microsoft.com/support/kb/articles/Q 239/1/14.ASP). This will fix some cases where columns are marked as #deleted# in Access.

Note that if you are using MySQL Version 3.22, you must apply the MDAC patch and use MyODBC 2.50.32 or 2.50.34 and above to go around this problem.

- For all Access versions, you should enable the MyODBC option flag Return matching rows. For Access 2.0, you should additionally enable Simulate ODBC 1.0.

- You should have a timestamp in all tables you want to be able to update. For maximum portability TIMESTAMP(14) or simple TIMESTAMP is recommended instead of other TIMESTAMP(X) variations.

- You should have a primary key in the table. If not, new or updated rows may show up as #DELETED#.

- Only use DOUBLE float fields. Access fails when comparing with single floats. The symptom usually is that new or updated rows may show up as #DELETED# or that you can't find or update rows.

- If you are linking a table through MyODBC, which has BIGINT as one of the column, the results will be displayed as #DELETED. The workaround solution is:

  — Have one more dummy column with TIMESTAMP as the datatype, preferably TIMESTAMP(14).

  — Check the 'Change BIGINT columns to INT' in the connection options dialog in ODBC DSN Administrator.

  — Delete the table link from Access and re-create it.

  It still displays the previous records as #DELETED#, but newly added/updated records will be displayed properly.

- If you still get the error Another user has changed your data after adding a TIMESTAMP column, the following trick may help you:

  Don't use table data sheet view. Create instead a form with the fields you want, and use that form data sheet view. You should set the DefaultValue property for the TIMESTAMP column to NOW(). It may be a good idea to hide the TIMES-TAMP column from view so that your users are not confused.

- In some cases, Access may generate illegal SQL queries that MySQL can't understand. You can fix this by selecting "Query|SQLSpecific|Pass-Through" from the Access menu.

- Access on NT will report BLOB columns as OLE OBJECTS. If you want to have MEMO columns instead, you should change the column to TEXT with ALTER TABLE.

- Access can't always handle DATE columns properly. If you have a problem with these, change the columns to DATETIME.

- If you have in Access a column defined as BYTE, Access will try to export this as TINYINT instead of TINYINT UNSIGNED. This will give you problems if you have values > 127 in the column!

ADO

When you are coding with the ADO API and MyODBC you need to put attention in some default properties that aren't supported by the MySQL server. For example, using the CursorLocation Property as adUseServer will return for the RecordCount Property a result of -1. To have the right value, you need to set this property to adUseClient, similar to waht is shown in the following VB code:

```
Dim myconn As New ADODB.Connection
Dim myrs As New Recordset
Dim mySQL As String
Dim myrows As Long

myconn.Open "DSN=MyODBCsample"
mySQL = "SELECT * from user"
myrs.Source = mySQL
Set myrs.ActiveConnection = myconn
myrs.CursorLocation = adUseClient
myrs.Open
myrows = myrs.RecordCount

myrs.Close
myconn.Close
```

Another workaround is to use a SELECT COUNT(*) statement for a similar query to get the correct row count.

Active server pages (ASP)

You should use the option flag Return matching rows.

BDE applications

To get these to work, you should set the option flags Don't optimize column widths and Return matching rows.

Borland Builder 4

When you start a query you can use the property Active or use the method Open. Note that Active will start by automatically issuing a SELECT * FROM . . . query that may not be a good thing if your tables are big!

ColdFusion (On Unix)

The following information is taken from the ColdFusion documentation:

Use the following information to configure ColdFusion Server for Linux to use the unixODBC driver with MyODBC for MySQL data sources. Allaire has verified that MyODBC Version 2.50.26 works with MySQL Version 3.22.27 and ColdFusion for

Linux. (Any newer version should also work.) You can download MyODBC at http://www.mysql.com/downloads/api-myodbc.html.

ColdFusion Version 4.5.1 allows you to use the ColdFusion Administrator to add the MySQL data source. However, the driver is not included with ColdFusion Version 4.5.1. Before the MySQL driver will appear in the ODBC data sources drop-down list, you must build and copy the MyODBC driver to /opt/coldfusion/lib/libmy-odbc.so.

The Contrib directory contains the program mydsn-xxx.zip, which allows you to build and remove the DSN registry file for the MyODBC driver on ColdFusion applications.

DataJunction

You have to change it to output VARCHAR rather than ENUM, as it exports the latter in a manner that causes MySQL grief.

Excel

Works. A few tips:

* If you have problems with dates, try to select them as strings using the CON-CAT() function. For example:

```
select CONCAT(rise_time), CONCAT(set_time)
    from sunrise_sunset;
```

Values retrieved as strings this way should be correctly recognised as time values by Excel97.

The purpose of CONCAT() in this example is to fool ODBC into thinking the column is of "string type". Without the CONCAT(), ODBC knows the column is of time type, and Excel does not understand that.

Note that this is a bug in Excel because it automatically converts a string to a time. This would be great if the source were a text file, but is plain stupid when the source is an ODBC connection that reports exact types for each column.

Word

To retrieve data from MySQL to Word/Excel documents, you need to use the MyODBC driver and the Add-in Microsoft Query help.

For example, to create a db with a table containing 2 columns of text:

1. Insert rows using the mysql client command-line tool.

2. Create a DSN file using the ODBC manager—for example, my for the preceding db.

3. Open the Word application.

4. Create a new blank document.

5. Using the toolbar called Database, press the button Insert Database.

6. Press the button Get Data.

7. At the right hand of the screen Get Data, press the button Ms Query.

8. In the Ms Query create a New Data Source using the DSN file my.

9. Select the new query.

10. Select the columns that you want.

11. Make a Filter if you want.

12. Make a Sort if you want.

13. Select Return Data to Microsoft Word.

14. Click Finish.

15. Click Insert Data and select the records.

16. Click OK and you see the rows in your Word document.

odbcadmin

Test program for ODBC.

Delphi

You must use BDE Version 3.2 or newer. Set the `Don't optimize column width` option field when connecting to MySQL.

Also, here is some potentially useful Delphi code that sets up both an ODBC entry and a BDE entry for `MyODBC` (the BDE entry requires a BDE Alias Editor that is free at a Delphi Super Page near you. (Thanks to Bryan Brunton *bryan@flesherfab.com* for this):

```
fReg:= TRegistry.Create;
  fReg.OpenKey('\Software\ODBC\ODBC.INI\DocumentsFab', True);
  fReg.WriteString('Database', 'Documents');
  fReg.WriteString('Description', ' ');
  fReg.WriteString('Driver', 'C:\WINNT\System32\myodbc.dll');
  fReg.WriteString('Flag', '1');
  fReg.WriteString('Password', '');
  fReg.WriteString('Port', ' ');
  fReg.WriteString('Server', 'xmark');
  fReg.WriteString('User', 'winuser');
  fReg.OpenKey('\Software\ODBC\ODBC.INI\ODBC Data Sources', True);
  fReg.WriteString('DocumentsFab', 'MySQL');
  fReg.CloseKey;
  fReg.Free;

  Memo1.Lines.Add('DATABASE NAME=');
  Memo1.Lines.Add('USER NAME=');
  Memo1.Lines.Add('ODBC DSN=DocumentsFab');
  Memo1.Lines.Add('OPEN MODE=READ/WRITE');
```

```
Memo1.Lines.Add('BATCH COUNT=200');
Memo1.Lines.Add('LANGDRIVER=');
Memo1.Lines.Add('MAX ROWS=-1');
Memo1.Lines.Add('SCHEMA CACHE DIR=');
Memo1.Lines.Add('SCHEMA CACHE SIZE=8');
Memo1.Lines.Add('SCHEMA CACHE TIME=-1');
Memo1.Lines.Add('SQLPASSTHRU MODE=SHARED AUTOCOMMIT');
Memo1.Lines.Add('SQLQRYMODE=');
Memo1.Lines.Add('ENABLE SCHEMA CACHE=FALSE');
Memo1.Lines.Add('ENABLE BCD=FALSE');
Memo1.Lines.Add('ROWSET SIZE=20');
Memo1.Lines.Add('BLOBS TO CACHE=64');
Memo1.Lines.Add('BLOB SIZE=32');

AliasEditor.Add('DocumentsFab','MySQL',Memo1.Lines);
```

C++ Builder

Tested with BDE Version 3.0. The only known problem is that when the table schema changes, query fields are not updated. BDE, however, does not seem to recognise primary keys, only the index PRIMARY, though this has not been a problem.

Vision

You should use the option flag `Return matching rows`.

Visual Basic

To be able to update a table, you must define a primary key for the table.

Visual Basic with ADO can't handle big integers. This means that some queries like `SHOW PROCESSLIST` will not work properly. The fix is to set add the option `OPTION=16834` in the ODBC connect string or set the `Change BIGINT columns to INT` option in the MyODBC connect screen. You may also want to set the `Return matching rows` option.

VisualInterDev

If you get the error `[Microsoft][ODBC Driver Manager] Driver does not support this parameter` the reason may be that you have a `BIGINT` in your result. Try setting the `Change BIGINT columns to INT` option in the MyODBC connect screen.

Visual Objects

You should use the option flag `Don't optimize column widths`.

8.3.6 How to Get the Value of an AUTO_INCREMENT Column in ODBC

A common problem is how to get the value of an automatically generated ID from an INSERT. With ODBC, you can do something like this (assuming that auto is an AUTO_INCREMENT field):

```
INSERT INTO foo (auto,text) VALUES(NULL,'text');
SELECT LAST_INSERT_ID();
```

Or, if you are just going to insert the ID into another table, you can do this:

```
INSERT INTO foo (auto,text) VALUES(NULL,'text');
INSERT INTO foo2 (id,text) VALUES(LAST_INSERT_ID(),'text');
```

Section 8.4.6.3, How can I get the unique ID for the last inserted row?

For the benefit of some ODBC applications (at least Delphi and Access), the following query can be used to find a newly inserted row:

```
SELECT * FROM tbl_name WHERE auto IS NULL;
```

8.3.7 Reporting Problems with MyODBC

If you encounter difficulties with MyODBC, you should start by making a log file from the ODBC manager (the log you get when requesting logs from ODBCADMIN) and a MyO-DBC log.

To get a MyODBC log, you need to do the following:

1. Ensure that you are using myodbcd.dll and not myodbc.dll. The easiest way to do this is to get myodbcd.dll from the MyODBC distribution and copy it over the myodbc.dll, which is probably in your C:\windows\system32 or C:\winnt\system32 directory.

    Note that you probably want to restore the old myodbc.dll file when you have finished testing, as this is a lot faster than myodbcd.dll.

2. Tag the 'Trace MyODBC' option flag in the MyODBC connect/configure screen. The log will be written to file C:\myodbc.log.

    If the trace option is not remembered when you are going back to this screen, it means that you are not using the myodbcd.dll driver (see Step 1).

3. Start your application and try to get it to fail.

Check the MyODBC trace file to find out what could be wrong. You should be able to find out the issued queries by searching after the string >mysql_real_query in the myo-dbc.log file.

You should also try duplicating the queries in the mysql monitor or admndemo to find out if the error is with MyODBC or MySQL.

If you find out something is wrong, please only send the relevant rows (max 40 rows) to *myodbc@lists.mysql.com*. Please never send the whole MyODBC or ODBC log file!

If you are unable to find out what's wrong, the last option is to make an archive (tar or zip) that contains a MyODBC trace file, the ODBC log file, and a README file that explains the problem. You can send this to ftp://support.mysql.com/pub/mysql/secret/.

Only we at MySQL AB will have access to the files you upload, and we will be very discrete with the data!

If you can create a program that also shows this problem, please upload this too!

If the program works with some other SQL server, you should make an ODBC log file where you do exactly the same thing in the other SQL server.

Remember that the more information you can supply to us, the more likely it is that we can fix the problem!

8.4 MySQL C API

The C API code is distributed with MySQL. It is included in the `mysqlclient` library and allows C programs to access a database.

Many of the clients in the MySQL source distribution are written in C. If you are looking for examples that demonstrate how to use the C API, take a look at these clients. You can find these in the `clients` directory in the MySQL source distribution.

Most of the other client APIs (all except Java) use the `mysqlclient` library to communicate with the MySQL server. This means that, for example, you can take advantage of many of the same environment variables that are used by other client programs because they are referenced from the library. See Section 4.8, MySQL Client-Side Scripts and Utilities, for a list of these variables.

The client has a maximum communication buffer size. The size of the buffer that is allocated initially (16K bytes) is automatically increased up to the maximum size (the maximum is 16M). Because buffer sizes are increased only as demand warrants, simply increasing the default maximum limit does not in itself cause more resources to be used. This size check is mostly a check for erroneous queries and communication packets.

The communication buffer must be large enough to contain a single SQL statement (for client-to-server traffic) and one row of returned data (for server-to-client traffic). Each thread's communication buffer is dynamically enlarged to handle any query or row up to the maximum limit. For example, if you have BLOB values that contain up to 16M of data, you must have a communication buffer limit of at least 16M (in both server and client). The client's default maximum is 16M, but the default maximum in the server is 1M. You can increase this by changing the value of the `max_allowed_packet` parameter when the server is started. See Section 5.5.2, Tuning Server Parameters.

MySQL server shrinks each communication buffer to `net_buffer_length` bytes after each query. For clients, the size of the buffer associated with a connection is not decreased until the connection is closed, at which time client memory is reclaimed.

For programming with threads, see Section 8.4.8, How to Make a Threaded Client. For creating a stand-alone application that includes the "server" and "client" in the same program (and does not communicate with an external MySQL server), see Section 8.4.9, libmysqld, the Embedded MySQL Server Library.

8.4.1 C API Datatypes

MYSQL

> This structure represents a handle to one database connection. It is used for almost all MySQL functions.

MYSQL_RES

> This structure represents the result of a query that returns rows (SELECT, SHOW, DESCRIBE, EXPLAIN). The information returned from a query is called the *result set* in the remainder of this section.

MYSQL_ROW

> This is a type-safe representation of one row of data. It is currently implemented as an array of counted byte strings. (You cannot treat these as null-terminated strings if field values may contain binary data because such values may contain null bytes internally.) Rows are obtained by calling mysql_fetch_row().

MYSQL_FIELD

> This structure contains information about a field, such as the field's name, type, and size. Its members are described in more detail later. You may obtain the MYSQL_FIELD structures for each field by calling mysql_fetch_field() repeatedly. Field values are not part of this structure; they are contained in a MYSQL_ROW structure.

MYSQL_FIELD_OFFSET

> This is a type-safe representation of an offset into a MySQL field list (used by mysql_field_seek()). Offsets are field numbers within a row, beginning at zero.

my_ulonglong

> The type used for the number of rows and for mysql_affected_rows(), mysql_num_rows(), and mysql_insert_id(). This type provides a range of 0 to 1.84e19.

> On some systems, attempting to print a value of type my_ulonglong will not work. To print such a value, convert it to unsigned long and use a %lu print format. Example:

```
printf (Number of rows: %lu\n", (unsigned long) mysql_num_rows(result));
```

The MYSQL_FIELD structure contains the following members:

char * name

> The name of the field, as a null-terminated string.

`char * table`

The name of the table containing this field, if it isn't a calculated field. For calculated fields, the `table` value is an empty string.

`char * def`

The default value of this field, as a null-terminated string. This is set only if you use `mysql_list_fields()`.

`enum enum_field_types type`

The type of the field. The `type` value may be one of the following:

Type value	Type description
FIELD_TYPE_TINY	TINYINT field
FIELD_TYPE_SHORT	SMALLINT field
FIELD_TYPE_LONG	INTEGER field
FIELD_TYPE_INT24	MEDIUMINT field
FIELD_TYPE_LONGLONG	BIGINT field
FIELD_TYPE_DECIMAL	DECIMAL or NUMERIC field
FIELD_TYPE_FLOAT	FLOAT field
FIELD_TYPE_DOUBLE	DOUBLE or REAL field
FIELD_TYPE_TIMESTAMP	TIMESTAMP field
FIELD_TYPE_DATE	DATE field
FIELD_TYPE_TIME	TIME field
FIELD_TYPE_DATETIME	DATETIME field
FIELD_TYPE_YEAR	YEAR field
FIELD_TYPE_STRING	String (CHAR or VARCHAR) field
FIELD_TYPE_BLOB	BLOB or TEXT field (use `max_length` to determine the maximum length)
FIELD_TYPE_SET	SET field
FIELD_TYPE_ENUM	ENUM field
FIELD_TYPE_NULL	NULL-type field
FIELD_TYPE_CHAR	Deprecated; use FIELD_TYPE_TINY instead

You can use the `IS_NUM()` macro to test whether a field has a numeric type. Pass the `type` value to `IS_NUM()` and it will evaluate to TRUE if the field is numeric:

```
if (IS_NUM(field->type))
    printf("Field is numeric\n");
```

`unsigned int length`

The width of the field, as specified in the table definition.

`unsigned int max_length`

The maximum width of the field for the result set (the length of the longest field value for the rows actually in the result set). If you use `mysql_store_result()` or `mysql_list_fields()`, this contains the maximum length for the field. If you use `mysql_use_result()`, the value of this variable is zero.

`unsigned int flags`

> Different bit-flags for the field. The `flags` value may have zero or more of the following bits set:

Flag value	Flag description
NOT_NULL_FLAG	Field can't be NULL.
PRI_KEY_FLAG	Field is part of a primary key.
UNIQUE_KEY_FLAG	Field is part of a unique key.
MULTIPLE_KEY_FLAG	Field is part of a non-unique key.
UNSIGNED_FLAG	Field has the UNSIGNED attribute.
ZEROFILL_FLAG	Field has the ZEROFILL attribute.
BINARY_FLAG	Field has the BINARY attribute.
AUTO_INCREMENT_FLAG	Field has the AUTO_INCREMENT attribute.
ENUM_FLAG	Field is an ENUM (deprecated).
SET_FLAG	Field is a SET (deprecated).
BLOB_FLAG	Field is a BLOB or TEXT (deprecated).
TIMESTAMP_FLAG	Field is a TIMESTAMP (deprecated).

> Use of the BLOB_FLAG, ENUM_FLAG, SET_FLAG, and TIMESTAMP_FLAG flags is deprecated because they indicate the type of a field rather than an attribute of its type. It is preferable to test field->type against FIELD_TYPE_BLOB, FIELD_TYPE_ENUM, FIELD_TYPE_SET, or FIELD_TYPE_TIMESTAMP instead.

> The following example illustrates a typical use of the `flags` value:

```
if (field->flags & NOT_NULL_FLAG)
    printf("Field can't be null\n");
```

> You may use the following convenience macros to determine the boolean status of the `flags` value:

Flag status	Description
IS_NOT_NULL(flags)	True if this field is defined as NOT NULL
IS_PRI_KEY(flags)	True if this field is a primary key
IS_BLOB(flags)	True if this field is a BLOB or TEXT (deprecated; test field->type instead)

`unsigned int decimals`

> The number of decimals for numeric fields.

8.4.2 C API Function Overview

The functions available in the C API are listed next and are described in greater detail in a later section. See Section 8.4.3, C API Function Descriptions.

Function	Description
mysql_affected_rows()	Returns the number of rows changed/deleted/inserted by the last UPDATE, DELETE, or INSERT query.
mysql_change_user()	Changes user and database on an open connection.
mysql_charac-ter_set_name()	Returns the name of the default character set for the connection.
mysql_close()	Closes a server connection.
mysql_connect()	Connects to a MySQL server. This function is deprecated; use mysql_real_connect() instead.
mysql_create_db()	Creates a database. This function is deprecated; use the SQL command CREATE DATABASE instead.
mysql_data_seek()	Seeks to an arbitrary row in a query result set.
mysql_debug()	Does a DBUG_PUSH with the given string.
mysql_drop_db()	Drops a database. This function is deprecated; use the SQL command DROP DATABASE instead.
mysql_dump_debug_info()	Makes the server write debug information to the log.
mysql_eof()	Determines whether the last row of a result set has been read. This function is deprecated; mysql_errno() or mysql_error() may be used instead.
mysql_errno()	Returns the error number for the most recently invoked MySQL function.
mysql_error()	Returns the error message for the most recently invoked MySQL function.
mysql_escape_string()	Escapes special characters in a string for use in an SQL statement.
mysql_fetch_field()	Returns the type of the next table field.
mysql_fetch_field_direct()	Returns the type of a table field, given a field number.
mysql_fetch_fields()	Returns an array of all field structures.
mysql_fetch_lengths()	Returns the lengths of all columns in the current row.
mysql_fetch_row()	Fetches the next row from the result set.
mysql_field_seek()	Puts the column cursor on a specified column.
mysql_field_count()	Returns the number of result columns for the most recent query.
mysql_field_tell()	Returns the position of the field cursor used for the last mysql_fetch_field().
mysql_free_result()	Frees memory used by a result set.
mysql_get_client_info()	Returns client version information.
mysql_get_host_info()	Returns a string describing the connection.
mysql_get_proto_info()	Returns the protocol version used by the connection.
mysql_get_server_info()	Returns the server version number.
mysql_info()	Returns information about the most recently executed query.
mysql_init()	Gets or initialises a MySQL structure.
mysql_insert_id()	Returns the ID generated for an AUTO_INCREMENT column by the previous query.
mysql_kill()	Kills a given thread.

Function	Description
mysql_list_dbs()	Returns database names matching a simple regular expression.
mysql_list_fields()	Returns field names matching a simple regular expression.
mysql_list_processes()	Returns a list of the current server threads.
mysql_list_tables()	Returns table names matching a simple regular expression.
mysql_num_fields()	Returns the number of columns in a result set.
mysql_num_rows()	Returns the number of rows in a result set.
mysql_options()	Sets connect options for mysql_connect().
mysql_ping()	Checks whether the connection to the server is working, reconnecting as necessary.
mysql_query()	Executes an SQL query specified as a null-terminated string.
mysql_real_connect()	Connects to a MySQL server.
mysql_real_escape_string()	Escapes special characters in a string for use in an SQL statement, taking into account the current charset of the connection.
mysql_real_query()	Executes an SQL query specified as a counted string.
mysql_reload()	Tells the server to reload the grant tables.
mysql_row_seek()	Seeks to a row in a result set, using the value returned from mysql_row_tell().
mysql_row_tell()	Returns the row cursor position.
mysql_select_db()	Selects a database.
mysql_shutdown()	Shuts down the database server.
mysql_stat()	Returns the server status as a string.
mysql_store_result()	Retrieves a complete result set to the client.
mysql_thread_id()	Returns the current thread ID.
mysql_thread_safe()	Returns 1 if the clients are compiled as thread-safe.
mysql_use_result()	Initiates a row-by-row result set retrieval.

To connect to the server, call mysql_init() to initialise a connection handler, then call mysql_real_connect() with that handler (along with other information such as the hostname, username, and password). Upon connection, mysql_real_connect() sets the reconnect flag (part of the MYSQL structure) to a value of 1. This flag indicates, in the event that a query cannot be performed because of a lost connection, to try reconnecting to the server before giving up. When you are done with the connection, call mysql_close() to terminate it.

While a connection is active, the client may send SQL queries to the server using mysql_query() or mysql_real_query(). The difference between the two is that mysql_query() expects the query to be specified as a null-terminated string, whereas mysql_real_query() expects a counted string. If the string contains binary data (which may include null bytes), you must use mysql_real_query().

For each non-SELECT query (for example, INSERT, UPDATE, DELETE), you can find out how many rows were changed (affected) by calling mysql_affected_rows().

For SELECT queries, you retrieve the selected rows as a result set. (Note that some statements are SELECT-like in that they return rows. These include SHOW, DESCRIBE, and EXPLAIN. They should be treated the same way as SELECT statements.)

There are two ways for a client to process result sets. One way is to retrieve the entire result set all at once by calling mysql_store_result(). This function acquires from the server all the rows returned by the query and stores them in the client. The second way is for the client to initiate a row-by-row result set retrieval by calling mysql_use_result(). This function initialises the retrieval, but does not actually get any rows from the server.

In both cases, you access rows by calling mysql_fetch_row(). With mysql_store_result(), mysql_fetch_row() accesses rows that have already been fetched from the server. With mysql_use_result(), mysql_fetch_row() actually retrieves the row from the server. Information about the size of the data in each row is available by calling mysql_fetch_lengths().

After you are done with a result set, call mysql_free_result() to free the memory used for it.

The two retrieval mechanisms are complementary. Client programs should choose the approach that is most appropriate for their requirements. In practice, clients tend to use mysql_store_result() more commonly.

An advantage of mysql_store_result() is that because the rows have all been fetched to the client, you not only can access rows sequentially, but you also can move back and forth in the result set using mysql_data_seek() or mysql_row_seek() to change the current row position within the result set. You can also find out how many rows there are by calling mysql_num_rows(). On the other hand, the memory requirements for mysql_store_result() may be very high for large result sets, and thus you are more likely to encounter out-of-memory conditions.

An advantage of mysql_use_result() is that the client requires less memory for the result set because it maintains only one row at a time (and because there is less allocation overhead, mysql_use_result() can be faster). Disadvantages are that you must process each row quickly to avoid tying up the server, you don't have random access to rows within the result set (you can only access rows sequentially), and you don't know how many rows are in the result set until you have retrieved them all. Furthermore, you **must** retrieve all the rows even if you determine in mid-retrieval that you've found the information you were looking for.

The API makes it possible for clients to respond appropriately to queries (retrieving rows only as necessary) without knowing whether the query is a SELECT. You can do this by

calling   mysql_store_result()   after   each   mysql_query()   (or
mysql_real_query()). If the result set call succeeds, the query was a SELECT and you
can read the rows. If the result set call fails, call mysql_field_count() to determine
whether a result was actually to be expected. If mysql_field_count() returns zero, the
query returned no data (indicating that it was an INSERT, UPDATE, DELETE, etc.), and was
not expected to return rows. If mysql_field_count() is non-zero, the query should
have returned rows, but didn't. This indicates that the query was a SELECT that failed. See
the description for mysql_field_count() for an example of how this can be done.

Both mysql_store_result() and mysql_use_result() allow you to obtain information about the fields that make up the result set (the number of fields, their names and
types, etc.). You can access field information sequentially within the row by calling
mysql_fetch_field() repeatedly, or by field number within the row by calling
mysql_fetch_field_direct(). The current field cursor position may be changed by
calling mysql_field_seek(). Setting the field cursor affects subsequent calls to
mysql_fetch_field(). You can also get information for fields all at once by calling
mysql_fetch_fields().

For detecting and reporting errors, MySQL provides access to error information by means
of the mysql_errno() and mysql_error() functions. These return the error code or
error message for the most recently invoked function that can succeed or fail, allowing
you to determine when an error occurred and what it was.

8.4.3 C API Function Descriptions

In the following descriptions, a parameter or return value of NULL means NULL in the
sense of the C programming language, not a MySQL NULL value.

Functions that return a value generally return a pointer or an integer. Unless specified otherwise, functions returning a pointer return a non-NULL value to indicate success or a
NULL value to indicate an error, and functions returning an integer return zero to indicate
success or non-zero to indicate an error. Note that "non-zero" means just that. Unless the
function description says otherwise, do not test against a value other than zero:

```
if (result)              /* correct */
    ... error ...

if (result < 0)          /* incorrect */
    ... error ...

if (result == -1)        /* incorrect */
    ... error ...
```

When a function returns an error, the **Errors** subsection of the function description lists
the possible types of errors. You can find out which of these occurred by calling
mysql_errno(). A string representation of the error may be obtained by calling
mysql_error().

8.4.3.1 mysql_affected_rows()

`my_ulonglong mysql_affected_rows(MYSQL *mysql)`

8.4.3.2 Description

Returns the number of rows changed by the last UPDATE, deleted by the last DELETE, or inserted by the last INSERT statement. May be called immediately after mysql_query() for UPDATE, DELETE, or INSERT statements. For SELECT statements, mysql_affected_rows() works like mysql_num_rows().

8.4.3.3 Return values

An integer greater than zero indicates the number of rows affected or retrieved. Zero indicates that no records where updated for an UPDATE statement, no rows matched the WHERE clause in the query, or that no query has yet been executed. -1 indicates that the query returned an error or that, for a SELECT query, mysql_affected_rows() was called prior to calling mysql_store_result().

8.4.3.4 Errors

None.

8.4.3.5 Example

```
mysql_query(&mysql,"UPDATE products SET cost=cost*1.25 WHERE group=10");
printf("%ld products updated",(long) mysql_affected_rows(&mysql));
```

If one specifies the flag CLIENT_FOUND_ROWS when connecting to mysqld, mysql_affected_rows() will return the number of rows matched by the WHERE statement for UPDATE statements.

Note that when one uses a REPLACE command, mysql_affected_rows() will return 2 if the new row replaced an old row. This is because in this case one row was inserted and then the duplicate was deleted.

8.4.3.6 mysql_change_user()

`my_bool mysql_change_user(MYSQL *mysql, const char *user, const char *password, const char *db)`

8.4.3.7 Description

Changes the user and causes the database specified by db to become the default (current) database on the connection specified by mysql. In subsequent queries, this database is the default for table references that do not include an explicit database specifier.

This function was introduced in MySQL Version 3.23.3.

mysql_change_user() fails unless the connected user can be authenticated or if he doesn't have permission to use the database. In this case the user and database are not changed.

The db parameter may be set to NULL if you don't want to have a default database.

8.4.3.8 Return values

Zero for success. Non-zero if an error occurred.

8.4.3.9 Errors

The same that you can get from mysql_real_connect():

CR_COMMANDS_OUT_OF_SYNC
    Commands were executed in an improper order.

CR_SERVER_GONE_ERROR
    The MySQL server has gone away.

CR_SERVER_LOST
    The connection to the server was lost during the query.

CR_UNKNOWN_ERROR
    An unknown error occurred.

ER_UNKNOWN_COM_ERROR
    The MySQL server doesn't implement this command (probably an old server).

ER_ACCESS_DENIED_ERROR
    The user or password was wrong.

ER_BAD_DB_ERROR
    The database didn't exist.

ER_DBACCESS_DENIED_ERROR
    The user did not have access rights to the database.

ER_WRONG_DB_NAME
    The database name was too long.

8.4.3.10 Example

```
if (mysql_change_user(&mysql, "user", "password", "new_database"))
{
    fprintf(stderr, "Failed to change user.  Error: %s\n",
        mysql_error(&mysql));
}
```

8.4.3.11 mysql_character_set_name()

const char *mysql_character_set_name(MYSQL *mysql)

8.4.3.12 Description

Returns the default character set for the current connection.

8.4.3.13 Return values

The default character set.

8.4.3.14 Errors

None.

8.4.3.15 mysql_close()

void mysql_close(MYSQL *mysql)

8.4.3.16 Description

Closes a previously opened connection. mysql_close() also deallocates the connection handle pointed to by mysql if the handle was allocated automatically by mysql_init() or mysql_connect().

8.4.3.17 Return values

None.

8.4.3.18 Errors

None.

8.4.3.19 mysql_connect()

MYSQL *mysql_connect(MYSQL *mysql, const char *host, const char *user, const char *passwd)

8.4.3.20 Description

This function is deprecated. It is preferable to use mysql_real_connect() instead.

mysql_connect() attempts to establish a connection to a MySQL database engine running on host. mysql_connect() must complete successfully before you can execute any of the other API functions, with the exception of mysql_get_client_info().

The meanings of the parameters are the same as for the corresponding parameters for mysql_real_connect() with the difference that the connection parameter may be NULL. In this case the C API allocates memory for the connection structure automatically and frees it when you call mysql_close(). The disadvantage of this approach is that you can't retrieve an error message if the connection fails. (To get error information from mysql_errno() or mysql_error(), you must provide a valid MYSQL pointer.)

8.4.3.21 Return values

Same as for mysql_real_connect().

8.4.3.22 Errors

Same as for mysql_real_connect().

8.4.3.23 mysql_create_db()

int mysql_create_db(MYSQL *mysql, const char *db)

8.4.3.24 Description

Creates the database named by the db parameter.

This function is deprecated. It is preferable to use mysql_query() to issue a SQL CRE-ATE DATABASE statement instead.

8.4.3.25 Return values

Zero if the database was created successfully. Non-zero if an error occurred.

8.4.3.26 Errors

CR_COMMANDS_OUT_OF_SYNC
Commands were executed in an improper order.

CR_SERVER_GONE_ERROR
The MySQL server has gone away.

CR_SERVER_LOST
The connection to the server was lost during the query.

CR_UNKNOWN_ERROR
An unknown error occurred.

8.4.3.27 Example

```
if(mysql_create_db(&mysql, "my_database"))
{
    fprintf(stderr, "Failed to create new database.  Error: %s\n",
        mysql_error(&mysql));
}
```

8.4.3.28 `mysql_data_seek()`

void mysql_data_seek(MYSQL_RES *result, my_ulonglong offset)

8.4.3.29 Description

Seeks to an arbitrary row in a query result set. This requires that the result set structure contains the entire result of the query, so `mysql_data_seek()` may be used in conjunction only with `mysql_store_result()`, not with `mysql_use_result()`.

The offset should be a value in the range from 0 to `mysql_num_rows(result)-1`.

8.4.3.30 Return values

None.

8.4.3.31 Errors

None.

8.4.3.32 `mysql_debug()`

void mysql_debug(const char *debug)

8.4.3.33 Description

Does a `DBUG_PUSH` with the given string. `mysql_debug()` uses the Fred Fish debug library. To use this function, you must compile the client library to support debugging. See Section D.1, Debugging a MySQL Server, and Section D.2, Debugging a MySQL Client.

8.4.3.34 Return values

None.

8.4.3.35 Errors

None.

8.4.3.36 Example

The following call causes the client library to generate a trace file in `/tmp/client.trace` on the client machine:

```
mysql_debug("d:t:0,/tmp/client.trace");
```

8.4.3.37 mysql_drop_db()

int mysql_drop_db(MYSQL *mysql, const char *db)

8.4.3.38 Description

Drops the database named by the db parameter.

This function is deprecated. It is preferable to use mysql_query() to issue a SQL DROP DATABASE statement instead.

8.4.3.39 Return values

Zero if the database was dropped successfully. Non-zero if an error occurred.

8.4.3.40 Errors

CR_COMMANDS_OUT_OF_SYNC
   Commands were executed in an improper order.

CR_SERVER_GONE_ERROR
   The MySQL server has gone away.

CR_SERVER_LOST
   The connection to the server was lost during the query.

CR_UNKNOWN_ERROR
   An unknown error occurred.

8.4.3.41 Example

```
if(mysql_drop_db(&mysql, "my_database"))
    fprintf(stderr, "Failed to drop the database: Error: %s\n",
        mysql_error(&mysql));
```

8.4.3.42 mysql_dump_debug_info()

int mysql_dump_debug_info(MYSQL *mysql)

8.4.3.43 Description

Instructs the server to write some debug information to the log. The connected user must have the **process** privilege for this to work.

8.4.3.44 Return values

Zero if the command was successful. Non-zero if an error occurred.

8.4.3.45 Errors

CR_COMMANDS_OUT_OF_SYNC
> Commands were executed in an improper order.

CR_SERVER_GONE_ERROR
> The MySQL server has gone away.

CR_SERVER_LOST
> The connection to the server was lost during the query.

CR_UNKNOWN_ERROR
> An unknown error occurred.

8.4.3.46 mysql_eof()

```
my_bool mysql_eof(MYSQL_RES *result)
```

8.4.3.47 Description

This function is deprecated. mysql_errno() or mysql_error() may be used instead.

mysql_eof() determines whether the last row of a result set has been read.

If you acquire a result set from a successful call to mysql_store_result(), the client receives the entire set in one operation. In this case, a NULL return from mysql_fetch_row() always means the end of the result set has been reached and it is unnecessary to call mysql_eof(). When used with mysql_store_result(), mysql_eof() will always return true.

On the other hand, if you use mysql_use_result() to initiate a result set retrieval, the rows of the set are obtained from the server one by one as you call mysql_fetch_row() repeatedly. Because an error may occur on the connection during this process, a NULL return value from mysql_fetch_row() does not necessarily mean the end of the result set was reached normally. In this case, you can use mysql_eof() to determine what happened. mysql_eof() returns a non-zero value if the end of the result set was reached and zero if an error occurred.

Historically, mysql_eof() predates the standard MySQL error functions mysql_errno() and mysql_error(). Because those error functions provide the same information, their use is preferred over mysql_eof(), which is now deprecated. (In fact, they provide more information because mysql_eof() returns only a boolean value whereas the error functions indicate a reason for the error when one occurs.)

8.4.3.48 Return values

Zero if no error occurred. Non-zero if the end of the result set has been reached.

8.4.3.49 Errors

None.

8.4.3.50 Example

The following example shows how you might use `mysql_eof()`:

```
mysql_query(&mysql,"SELECT * FROM some_table");
result = mysql_use_result(&mysql);
while((row = mysql_fetch_row(result)))
{
    // do something with data
}
if(!mysql_eof(result))   // mysql_fetch_row() failed due to an error
{
    fprintf(stderr, "Error: %s\n", mysql_error(&mysql));
}
```

However, you can achieve the same effect with the standard MySQL error functions:

```
mysql_query(&mysql,"SELECT * FROM some_table");
result = mysql_use_result(&mysql);
while((row = mysql_fetch_row(result)))
{
    // do something with data
}
if(mysql_errno(&mysql))   // mysql_fetch_row() failed due to an error
{
    fprintf(stderr, "Error: %s\n", mysql_error(&mysql));
}
```

8.4.3.51 mysql_errno()

`unsigned int mysql_errno(MYSQL *mysql)`

8.4.3.52 Description

For the connection specified by `mysql`, `mysql_errno()` returns the error code for the most recently invoked API function that can succeed or fail. A return value of zero means that no error occurred. Client error message numbers are listed in the MySQL `errmsg.h` header file. Server error message numbers are listed in `mysqld_error.h`. In the MySQL source distribution you can find a complete list of error messages and error numbers in the file `Docs/mysqld_error.txt`.

8.4.3.53 Return values

An error code value. Zero if no error occurred.

8.4.3.54 Errors

None.

8.4.3.55 mysql_error()

```
char *mysql_error(MYSQL *mysql)
```

8.4.3.56 Description

For the connection specified by mysql, mysql_error() returns the error message for
the most recently invoked API function that can succeed or fail. An empty string (" ") is
returned if no error occurred. This means the following two tests are equivalent:

```
if(mysql_errno(&mysql))
{
    // an error occurred
}

if(mysql_error(&mysql)[0] != '\0')
{
    // an error occurred
}
```

The language of the client error messages may be changed by recompiling the MySQL
client library. Currently you can choose error messages in several different languages. See
Section 4.6.2, Non-English Error Messages.

8.4.3.57 Return values

A character string that describes the error. An empty string if no error occurred.

8.4.3.58 Errors

None.

8.4.3.59 mysql_escape_string()

You should use mysql_real_escape_string() instead!

This function is identical to mysql_real_escape_string() except that
mysql_real_escape_string() takes a connection handler as its first argument and
escapes the string according to the current character set. mysql_escape_string() does
not take a connection argument and does not respect the current charset setting.

8.4.3.60 mysql_fetch_field()

```
MYSQL_FIELD *mysql_fetch_field(MYSQL_RES *result)
```

8.4.3.61 Description

Returns the definition of one column of a result set as a MYSQL_FIELD structure. Call this function repeatedly to retrieve information about all columns in the result set. mysql_fetch_field() returns NULL when no more fields are left.

mysql_fetch_field() is reset to return information about the first field each time you execute a new SELECT query. The field returned by mysql_fetch_field() is also affected by calls to mysql_field_seek().

If you've called mysql_query() to perform a SELECT on a table but have not called mysql_store_result(), MySQL returns the default blob length (8K bytes) if you call mysql_fetch_field() to ask for the length of a BLOB field. (The 8K size is chosen because MySQL doesn't know the maximum length for the BLOB. This should be made configurable sometime.) Once you've retrieved the result set, field->max_length contains the length of the largest value for this column in the specific query.

8.4.3.62 Return values

The MYSQL_FIELD structure for the current column. NULL if no columns are left.

8.4.3.63 Errors

None.

8.4.3.64 Example

```
MYSQL_FIELD *field;

while((field = mysql_fetch_field(result)))
{
    printf("field name %s\n", field->name);
}
```

8.4.3.65 mysql_fetch_fields()

MYSQL_FIELD *mysql_fetch_fields(MYSQL_RES *result)

8.4.3.66 Description

Returns an array of all MYSQL_FIELD structures for a result set. Each structure provides the field definition for one column of the result set.

8.4.3.67 Return values

An array of MYSQL_FIELD structures for all columns of a result set.

8.4.3.68 Errors

None.

8.4.3.69 Example

```
unsigned int num_fields;
unsigned int i;
MYSQL_FIELD *fields;

num_fields = mysql_num_fields(result);
fields = mysql_fetch_fields(result);
for(i = 0; i < num_fields; i++)
{
    printf("Field %u is %s\n", i, fields[i].name);
}
```

8.4.3.70 mysql_fetch_field_direct()

MYSQL_FIELD *mysql_fetch_field_direct(MYSQL_RES *result, unsigned int fieldnr)

8.4.3.71 Description

Given a field number fieldnr for a column within a result set, returns that column's field definition as a MYSQL_FIELD structure. You may use this function to retrieve the definition for an arbitrary column. The value of fieldnr should be in the range from 0 to mysql_num_fields(result)-1.

8.4.3.72 Return values

The MYSQL_FIELD structure for the specified column.

8.4.3.73 Errors

None.

8.4.3.74 Example

```
unsigned int num_fields;
unsigned int i;
MYSQL_FIELD *field;

num_fields = mysql_num_fields(result);
for(i = 0; i < num_fields; i++)
{
    field = mysql_fetch_field_direct(result, i);
    printf("Field %u is %s\n", i, field->name);
}
```

8.4.3.75 `mysql_fetch_lengths()`

`unsigned long *mysql_fetch_lengths(MYSQL_RES *result)`

8.4.3.76 Description

Returns the lengths of the columns of the current row within a result set. If you plan to copy field values, this length information is also useful for optimisation because you can avoid calling `strlen()`. In addition, if the result set contains binary data, you **must** use this function to determine the size of the data because `strlen()` returns incorrect results for any field containing null characters.

The length for empty columns and for columns containing NULL values is zero. To see how to distinguish these two cases, see the description for `mysql_fetch_row()`.

8.4.3.77 Return values

An array of unsigned long integers representing the size of each column (not including any terminating null characters). NULL if an error occurred.

8.4.3.78 Errors

`mysql_fetch_lengths()` is valid only for the current row of the result set. It returns NULL if you call it before calling `mysql_fetch_row()` or after retrieving all rows in the result.

8.4.3.79 Example

```
MYSQL_ROW row;
unsigned long *lengths;
unsigned int num_fields;
unsigned int i;

row = mysql_fetch_row(result);
if (row)
{
    num_fields = mysql_num_fields(result);
    lengths = mysql_fetch_lengths(result);
    for(i = 0; i < num_fields; i++)
    {
        printf("Column %u is %lu bytes in length.\n", i, lengths[i]);
    }
}
```

8.4.3.80 `mysql_fetch_row()`

`MYSQL_ROW mysql_fetch_row(MYSQL_RES *result)`

8.4.3.81 Description

Retrieves the next row of a result set. When used after `mysql_store_result()`, `mysql_fetch_row()` returns `NULL` when there are no more rows to retrieve. When used after `mysql_use_result()`, `mysql_fetch_row()` returns `NULL` when there are no more rows to retrieve or if an error occurred.

The number of values in the row is given by `mysql_num_fields(result)`. If `row` holds the return value from a call to `mysql_fetch_row()`, pointers to the values are accessed as `row[0]` to `row[mysql_num_fields(result)-1]`. `NULL` values in the row are indicated by `NULL` pointers.

The lengths of the field values in the row may be obtained by calling `mysql_fetch_lengths()`. Empty fields and fields containing `NULL` both have length 0; you can distinguish these by checking the pointer for the field value. If the pointer is `NULL`, the field is `NULL`; otherwise, the field is empty.

8.4.3.82 Return values

A `MYSQL_ROW` structure for the next row. `NULL` if there are no more rows to retrieve or if an error occurred.

8.4.3.83 Errors

CR_SERVER_LOST
> The connection to the server was lost during the query.

CR_UNKNOWN_ERROR
> An unknown error occurred.

8.4.3.84 Example

```
MYSQL_ROW row;
unsigned int num_fields;
unsigned int i;

num_fields = mysql_num_fields(result);
while ((row = mysql_fetch_row(result)))
{
    unsigned long *lengths;
    lengths = mysql_fetch_lengths(result);
    for(i = 0; i < num_fields; i++)
    {
        printf("[%.*s] ", (int) lengths[i], row[i] ? row[i] : "NULL");
    }
    printf("\n");
}
```

8.4.3.85 `mysql_field_count()`

`unsigned int mysql_field_count(MYSQL *mysql)`

If you are using a version of MySQL earlier than Version 3.22.24, you should use `unsigned int mysql_num_fields(MYSQL *mysql)` instead.

8.4.3.86 Description

Returns the number of columns for the most recent query on the connection.

The normal use of this function is when `mysql_store_result()` returned `NULL` (and thus you have no result set pointer). In this case, you can call `mysql_field_count()` to determine whether `mysql_store_result()` should have produced a non-empty result. This allows the client program to take proper action without knowing whether the query was a `SELECT` (or `SELECT`-like) statement. The following example illustrates how this may be done.

Section 8.4.6.1, Why Is It that After `mysql_query()` Returns Success, `mysql_store_result()` Sometimes Returns `NULL`?.

8.4.3.87 Return values

An unsigned integer representing the number of fields in a result set.

8.4.3.88 Errors

None.

8.4.3.89 Example

```
MYSQL_RES *result;
unsigned int num_fields;
unsigned int num_rows;

if (mysql_query(&mysql,query_string))
{
    // error
}
else // query succeeded, process any data returned by it
{
    result = mysql_store_result(&mysql);
    if (result)  // there are rows
    {
        num_fields = mysql_num_fields(result);
        // retrieve rows, then call mysql_free_result(result)
    }
    else  // mysql_store_result() returned nothing; should it have?
    {
        if(mysql_field_count(&mysql) == 0)
        {
```

```
          // query does not return data
          // (it was not a SELECT)
          num_rows = mysql_affected_rows(&mysql);
     }
     else // mysql_store_result() should have returned data
     {
          fprintf(stderr, "Error: %s\n", mysql_error(&mysql));
     }
  }
}
```

An alternative is to replace the mysql_field_count(&mysql) call with mysql_errno(&mysql). In this case, you are checking directly for an error from mysql_store_result() rather than inferring from the value of mysql_field_count() whether the statement was a SELECT.

8.4.3.90 mysql_field_seek()

MYSQL_FIELD_OFFSET   mysql_field_seek(MYSQL_RES   *result,
MYSQL_FIELD_OFFSET offset)

8.4.3.91 Description

Sets the field cursor to the given offset. The next call to mysql_fetch_field() will retrieve the field definition of the column associated with that offset.

To seek to the beginning of a row, pass an offset value of zero.

8.4.3.92 Return values

The previous value of the field cursor.

8.4.3.93 Errors

None.

8.4.3.94 mysql_field_tell()

MYSQL_FIELD_OFFSET mysql_field_tell(MYSQL_RES *result)

8.4.3.95 Description

Returns the position of the field cursor used for the last mysql_fetch_field(). This value can be used as an argument to mysql_field_seek().

8.4.3.96 Return values

The current offset of the field cursor.

8.4.3.97 Errors

None.

8.4.3.98 `mysql_free_result()`

`void mysql_free_result(MYSQL_RES *result)`

8.4.3.99 Description

Frees the memory allocated for a result set by `mysql_store_result()`, `mysql_use_result()`, `mysql_list_dbs()`, etc. When you are done with a result set, you must free the memory it uses by calling `mysql_free_result()`.

8.4.3.100 Return values

None.

8.4.3.101 Errors

None.

8.4.3.102 `mysql_get_client_info()`

`char *mysql_get_client_info(void)`

8.4.3.103 Description

Returns a string that represents the client library version.

8.4.3.104 Return values

A character string that represents the MySQL client library version.

8.4.3.105 Errors

None.

8.4.3.106 `mysql_get_host_info()`

`char *mysql_get_host_info(MYSQL *mysql)`

8.4.3.107 Description

Returns a string describing the type of connection in use, including the server hostname.

8.4.3.108 Return values

A character string representing the server hostname and the connection type.

8.4.3.109 Errors

None.

8.4.3.110 mysql_get_proto_info()

unsigned int mysql_get_proto_info(MYSQL *mysql)

8.4.3.111 Description

Returns the protocol version used by the current connection.

8.4.3.112 Return values

An unsigned integer representing the protocol version used by the current connection.

8.4.3.113 Errors

None.

8.4.3.114 mysql_get_server_info()

char *mysql_get_server_info(MYSQL *mysql)

8.4.3.115 Description

Returns a string that represents the server version number.

8.4.3.116 Return values

A character string that represents the server version number.

8.4.3.117 Errors

None.

8.4.3.118 mysql_info()

char *mysql_info(MYSQL *mysql)

8.4.3.119 Description

Retrieves a string providing information about the most recently executed query, but only for the following statements. For other statements, mysql_info() returns NULL. The format of the string varies depending on the type of query. The numbers are illustrative only; the string will contain values appropriate for the query.

```
INSERT INTO ... SELECT ...
```
   String format: Records: 100 Duplicates: 0 Warnings: 0

```
INSERT INTO ... VALUES (...),(...),(...) ...
```
   String format: Records: 3 Duplicates: 0 Warnings: 0

```
LOAD DATA INFILE ...
```
   String format: Records: 1 Deleted: 0 Skipped: 0 Warnings: 0

```
ALTER TABLE
```
   String format: Records: 3 Duplicates: 0 Warnings: 0

```
UPDATE
```
   String format: Rows matched: 40 Changed: 40 Warnings: 0

Note that mysql_info() returns a non-NULL value for the INSERT ... VALUES statement only if multiple value lists are specified in the statement.

8.4.3.120 Return values

A character string representing additional information about the most recently executed query. NULL if no information is available for the query.

8.4.3.121 Errors

None.

8.4.3.122 mysql_init()

MYSQL *mysql_init(MYSQL *mysql)

8.4.3.123 Description

Allocates or initialises a MySQL object suitable for mysql_real_connect(). If mysql is a NULL pointer, the function allocates, initialises, and returns a new object. Otherwise, the object is initialised and the address of the object is returned. If mysql_init() allocates a new object, it will be freed when mysql_close() is called to close the connection.

8.4.3.124 Return values

An initialised MYSQL* handle. NULL if there was insufficient memory to allocate a new object.

8.4.3.125 Errors

In case of insufficient memory, NULL is returned.

8.4.3.126 `mysql_insert_id()`

`my_ulonglong mysql_insert_id(MYSQL *mysql)`

8.4.3.127 Description

Returns the ID generated for an AUTO_INCREMENT column by the previous query. Use this function after you have performed an INSERT query into a table that contains an AUTO_INCREMENT field.

Note that `mysql_insert_id()` returns 0 if the previous query does not generate an AUTO_INCREMENT value. If you need to save the value for later, be sure to call `mysql_insert_id()` immediately after the query that generates the value.

`mysql_insert_id()` is updated after INSERT and UPDATE statements that generate an AUTO_INCREMENT value or that set a column value to LAST_INSERT_ID(expr). See Section 6.3.6.2, Miscellaneous functions.

Also note that the value of the SQL LAST_INSERT_ID() function always contains the most recently generated AUTO_INCREMENT value, and is not reset between queries because the value of that function is maintained in the server.

8.4.3.128 Return values

The value of the AUTO_INCREMENT field that was updated by the previous query. Returns zero if there was no previous query on the connection or if the query did not update an AUTO_INCREMENT value.

8.4.3.129 Errors

None.

8.4.3.130 `mysql_kill()`

`int mysql_kill(MYSQL *mysql, unsigned long pid)`

8.4.3.131 Description

Asks the server to kill the thread specified by `pid`.

8.4.3.132 Return values

Zero for success. Non-zero if an error occurred.

8.4.3.133 Errors

CR_COMMANDS_OUT_OF_SYNC
  Commands were executed in an improper order.

CR_SERVER_GONE_ERROR
  The MySQL server has gone away.

CR_SERVER_LOST
  The connection to the server was lost during the query.

CR_UNKNOWN_ERROR
  An unknown error occurred.

8.4.3.134 mysql_list_dbs()

MYSQL_RES *mysql_list_dbs(MYSQL *mysql, const char *wild)

8.4.3.135 Description

Returns a result set consisting of database names on the server that match the simple regular expression specified by the wild parameter. wild may contain the wildcard characters % or _, or may be a NULL pointer to match all databases. Calling mysql_list_dbs() is similar to executing the query SHOW databases [LIKE wild].

You must free the result set with mysql_free_result().

8.4.3.136 Return values

A MYSQL_RES result set for success. NULL if an error occurred.

8.4.3.137 Errors

CR_COMMANDS_OUT_OF_SYNC
  Commands were executed in an improper order.

CR_OUT_OF_MEMORY
  Out of memory.

CR_SERVER_GONE_ERROR
  The MySQL server has gone away.

CR_SERVER_LOST
  The connection to the server was lost during the query.

CR_UNKNOWN_ERROR
  An unknown error occurred.

8.4.3.138 `mysql_list_fields()`

`MYSQL_RES *mysql_list_fields(MYSQL *mysql, const char *table, const char *wild)`

8.4.3.139 Description

Returns a result set consisting of field names in the given table that match the simple regular expression specified by the `wild` parameter. `wild` may contain the wildcard characters `%` or `_`, or may be a `NULL` pointer to match all fields. Calling `mysql_list_fields()` is similar to executing the query `SHOW COLUMNS FROM tbl_name [LIKE wild]`.

Note that it's recommended that you use `SHOW COLUMNS FROM tbl_name` instead of `mysql_list_fields()`.

You must free the result set with `mysql_free_result()`.

8.4.3.140 Return values

A `MYSQL_RES` result set for success. `NULL` if an error occurred.

8.4.3.141 Errors

`CR_COMMANDS_OUT_OF_SYNC`
  Commands were executed in an improper order.

`CR_SERVER_GONE_ERROR`
  The MySQL server has gone away.

`CR_SERVER_LOST`
  The connection to the server was lost during the query.

`CR_UNKNOWN_ERROR`
  An unknown error occurred.

8.4.3.142 `mysql_list_processes()`

`MYSQL_RES *mysql_list_processes(MYSQL *mysql)`

8.4.3.143 Description

Returns a result set describing the current server threads. This is the same kind of information as that reported by `mysqladmin processlist` or a `SHOW PROCESSLIST` query.

You must free the result set with `mysql_free_result()`.

8.4.3.144 Return values

A `MYSQL_RES` result set for success. `NULL` if an error occurred.

8.4.3.145 Errors

CR_COMMANDS_OUT_OF_SYNC
> Commands were executed in an improper order.

CR_SERVER_GONE_ERROR
> The MySQL server has gone away.

CR_SERVER_LOST
> The connection to the server was lost during the query.

CR_UNKNOWN_ERROR
> An unknown error occurred.

8.4.3.146 mysql_list_tables()

MYSQL_RES *mysql_list_tables(MYSQL *mysql, const char *wild)

8.4.3.147 Description

Returns a result set consisting of table names in the current database that match the simple regular expression specified by the wild parameter. wild may contain the wildcard characters % or _, or may be a NULL pointer to match all tables. Calling mysql_list_tables() is similar to executing the query SHOW tables [LIKE wild].

You must free the result set with mysql_free_result().

8.4.3.148 Return values

A MYSQL_RES result set for success. NULL if an error occurred.

8.4.3.149 Errors

CR_COMMANDS_OUT_OF_SYNC
> Commands were executed in an improper order.

CR_SERVER_GONE_ERROR
> The MySQL server has gone away.

CR_SERVER_LOST
> The connection to the server was lost during the query.

CR_UNKNOWN_ERROR
> An unknown error occurred.

8.4.3.150 mysql_num_fields()

unsigned int mysql_num_fields(MYSQL_RES *result)

or

```
unsigned int mysql_num_fields(MYSQL *mysql)
```

The second form doesn't work on MySQL Version 3.22.24 or newer. To pass a `MYSQL*` argument, you must use `unsigned int mysql_field_count(MYSQL *mysql)` instead.

8.4.3.151 Description

Returns the number of columns in a result set.

Note that you can get the number of columns either from a pointer to a result set or to a connection handle. You would use the connection handle if `mysql_store_result()` or `mysql_use_result()` returned `NULL` (and thus you have no result set pointer). In this case, you can call `mysql_field_count()` to determine whether `mysql_store_result()` should have produced a non-empty result. This allows the client program to take proper action without knowing whether or not the query was a `SELECT` (or `SELECT`-like) statement. The following example illustrates how this may be done.

Section 8.4.6.1, Why Is It that After `mysql_query()` Returns Success, `mysql_store_result()` Sometimes Returns `NULL`?.

8.4.3.152 Return values

An unsigned integer representing the number of fields in a result set.

8.4.3.153 Errors

None.

8.4.3.154 Example

```
MYSQL_RES *result;
unsigned int num_fields;
unsigned int num_rows;

if (mysql_query(&mysql,query_string))
{
    // error
}
else // query succeeded, process any data returned by it
{
    result = mysql_store_result(&mysql);
    if (result)  // there are rows
    {
        num_fields = mysql_num_fields(result);
        // retrieve rows, then call mysql_free_result(result)
    }
    else  // mysql_store_result() returned nothing; should it have?
    {
```

```
        if (mysql_errno(&mysql))
        {
            fprintf(stderr, "Error: %s\n", mysql_error(&mysql));
        }
        else if (mysql_field_count(&mysql) == 0)
        {
            // query does not return data
            // (it was not a SELECT)
            num_rows = mysql_affected_rows(&mysql);
        }
    }
}
```

An alternative (if you know that your query should have returned a result set) is to replace the mysql_errno(&mysql) call with a check if mysql_field_count(&mysql) is = 0. This will only happen if something went wrong.

8.4.3.155 mysql_num_rows()

my_ulonglong mysql_num_rows(MYSQL_RES *result)

8.4.3.156 Description

Returns the number of rows in the result set.

The use of mysql_num_rows() depends on whether you use mysql_store_result() or mysql_use_result() to return the result set. If you use mysql_store_result(), mysql_num_rows() may be called immediately. If you use mysql_use_result(), mysql_num_rows() will not return the correct value until all the rows in the result set have been retrieved.

8.4.3.157 Return values

The number of rows in the result set.

8.4.3.158 Errors

None.

8.4.3.159 mysql_options()

int mysql_options(MYSQL *mysql, enum mysql_option option, const char *arg)

8.4.3.160 Description

Can be used to set extra connect options and affect behavior for a connection. This function may be called multiple times to set several options.

`mysql_options()` should be called after `mysql_init()` and before `mysql_connect()` or `mysql_real_connect()`.

The `option` argument is the option that you want to set; the `arg` argument is the value for the option. If the option is an integer, `arg` should point to the value of the integer.

Possible option values:

Option	Argument type	Function
MYSQL_OPT_CONNECT_TIMEOUT	unsigned int *	Connect timeout in seconds.
MYSQL_OPT_COMPRESS	Not used	Use the compressed client/server protocol.
MYSQL_OPT_LOCAL_INFILE	Optional pointer to uint	If no pointer is given or if pointer points to a nonzero unsigned int != 0, the command LOAD LOCAL INFILE is enabled.
MYSQL_OPT_NAMED_PIPE	Not used	Use named pipes to connect to a MySQL server on NT.
MYSQL_INIT_COMMAND	char *	Command to execute when connecting to the MySQL server. Will automatically be re-executed when reconnecting.
MYSQL_READ_DEFAULT_FILE	char *	Read options from the named option file instead of from my.cnf.
MYSQL_READ_DEFAULT_GROUP	char *	Read options from the named group from my.cnf or the file specified with MYSQL_READ_DEFAULT_FILE.

Note that the group `client` is always read if you use MYSQL_READ_DEFAULT_FILE or MYSQL_READ_DEFAULT_GROUP.

The specified group in the option file may contain the following options:

Option	Description
connect-timeout	Connect timeout in seconds. On Linux this timeout is also used for waiting for the first answer from the server.
compress	Use the compressed client/server protocol.
database	Connect to this database if no database was specified in the connect command.
debug	Debug options.
disable-local-infile	Disable use of LOAD DATA LOCAL.
host	Default hostname.
init-command	Command to execute when connecting to MySQL server. Will automatically be re-executed when reconnecting.

Option	Description
interactive-time-out	Same as specifying CLIENT_INTERACTIVE to mysql_real_connect(). See Section 8.4.3.171, mysql_real_connect().
local-infile[=(0|1)]	If no argument or argument != 0, then enable use of LOAD DATA LOCAL.
password	Default password.
pipe	Use named pipes to connect to a MySQL server on NT.
port	Default port number.
return-found-rows	Tell mysql_info() to return found rows instead of updated rows when using UPDATE.
socket	Default socket number.
user	Default user.

Note that timeout has been replaced by connect-timeout, but timeout will still work for a while.

For more information about option files, see Section 4.1.2, my.cnf Option Files.

8.4.3.161 Return values

Zero for success. Non-zero if you used an unknown option.

8.4.3.162 Example

```
MYSQL mysql;

mysql_init(&mysql);
mysql_options(&mysql,MYSQL_OPT_COMPRESS,0);
mysql_options(&mysql,MYSQL_READ_DEFAULT_GROUP,"odbc");
if (!mysql_real_connect(&mysql,"host","user","passwd","database",0,NULL,0))
{
      fprintf(stderr, "Failed to connect to database: Error: %s\n",
            mysql_error(&mysql));
}
```

This requests that the client use the compressed client/server protocol and read the additional options from the odbc section in the my.cnf file.

8.4.3.163 mysql_ping()

int mysql_ping(MYSQL *mysql)

8.4.3.164 Description

Checks whether the connection to the server is working. If it has gone down, an automatic reconnection is attempted.

This function can be used by clients that remain idle for a long while, to check whether the server has closed the connection and to reconnect if necessary.

8.4.3.165 Return values

Zero if the server is alive. Non-zero if an error occurred.

8.4.3.166 Errors

CR_COMMANDS_OUT_OF_SYNC
  Commands were executed in an improper order.

CR_SERVER_GONE_ERROR
  The MySQL server has gone away.

CR_UNKNOWN_ERROR
  An unknown error occurred.

8.4.3.167 mysql_query()

int mysql_query(MYSQL *mysql, const char *query)

8.4.3.168 Description

Executes the SQL query pointed to by the null-terminated string query. The query must consist of a single SQL statement. You should not add a terminating semicolon (;) or \g to the statement.

mysql_query() cannot be used for queries that contain binary data; you should use mysql_real_query() instead. (Binary data may contain the \0 character, which mysql_query() interprets as the end of the query string.)

If you want to know if the query should return a result set, you can use mysql_field_count() to check for this. See Section 8.4.3.85, mysql_field_count().

8.4.3.169 Return values

Zero if the query was successful. Non-zero if an error occurred.

8.4.3.170 Errors

CR_COMMANDS_OUT_OF_SYNC
  Commands were executed in an improper order.

CR_SERVER_GONE_ERROR
  The MySQL server has gone away.

CR_SERVER_LOST
  The connection to the server was lost during the query.

CR_UNKNOWN_ERROR

An unknown error occurred.

8.4.3.171 `mysql_real_connect()`

`MYSQL *mysql_real_connect(MYSQL *mysql, const char *host, const char *user, const char *passwd, const char *db, unsigned int port, const char *unix_socket, unsigned int client_flag)`

8.4.3.172 Description

`mysql_real_connect()` attempts to establish a connection to a MySQL database engine running on host. `mysql_real_connect()` must complete successfully before you can execute any of the other API functions, with the exception of `mysql_get_client_info()`.

The parameters are specified as follows:

- The first parameter should be the address of an existing `MYSQL` structure. Before calling `mysql_real_connect()` you must call `mysql_init()` to initialise the `MYSQL` structure. You can change a lot of connect options with the `mysql_options()` call. See Section 8.4.3.159, `mysql_options()`.

- The value of host may be either a hostname or an IP address. If host is `NULL` or the string `"localhost"`, a connection to the local host is assumed. If the OS supports sockets (Unix) or named pipes (Windows), they are used instead of TCP/IP to connect to the server.

- The user parameter contains the user's MySQL login ID. If user is `NULL`, the current user is assumed. Under Unix, this is the current login name. Under Windows ODBC, the current username must be specified explicitly. See Section 8.3.2, How to Fill in the Various Fields in the ODBC Administrator Program.

- The passwd parameter contains the password for user. If passwd is `NULL`, only entries in the user table for the user that have a blank (empty) password field will be checked for a match. This allows the database administrator to set up the MySQL privilege system in such a way that users get different privileges depending on whether they have specified a password.

  Note: do not attempt to encrypt the password before calling `mysql_real_connect()`; password encryption is handled automatically by the client API.

- db is the database name. If db is not `NULL`, the connection will set the default database to this value.

- If port is not 0, the value will be used as the port number for the TCP/IP connection. Note that the host parameter determines the type of the connection.

- If unix_socket is not NULL, the string specifies the socket or named pipe that should be used. Note that the host parameter determines the type of the connection.

- The value of client_flag is usually 0, but can be set to a combination of the following flags in very special circumstances:

Flag name	Flag description
CLIENT_COMPRESS	Use compression protocol.
CLIENT_FOUND_ROWS	Return the number of found (matched) rows, not the number of affected rows.
CLIENT_IGNORE_SPACE	Allow spaces after function names. Makes all function names reserved words.
CLIENT_INTERACTIVE	Allow interactive_timeout seconds (instead of wait_timeout seconds) of inactivity before closing the connection.
CLIENT_NO_SCHEMA	Don't allow the db_name.tbl_name.col_name syntax. This is for ODBC. It causes the parser to generate an error if you use that syntax, which is useful for trapping bugs in some ODBC programs.
CLIENT_ODBC	The client is an ODBC client. This changes mysqld to be more ODBC-friendly.
CLIENT_SSL	Use SSL (encrypted protocol).

8.4.3.173 Return values

A MYSQL* connection handle if the connection was successful, NULL if the connection was unsuccessful. For a successful connection, the return value is the same as the value of the first parameter.

8.4.3.174 Errors

CR_CONN_HOST_ERROR
    Failed to connect to the MySQL server.

CR_CONNECTION_ERROR
    Failed to connect to the local MySQL server.

CR_IPSOCK_ERROR
    Failed to create an IP socket.

CR_OUT_OF_MEMORY
    Out of memory.

CR_SOCKET_CREATE_ERROR
    Failed to create a Unix socket.

CR_UNKNOWN_HOST

Failed to find the IP address for the hostname.

CR_VERSION_ERROR

A protocol mismatch resulted from attempting to connect to a server with a client library that uses a different protocol version. This can happen if you use a very old client library to connect to a new server that wasn't started with the --old-protocol option.

CR_NAMEDPIPEOPEN_ERROR

Failed to create a named pipe on Windows.

CR_NAMEDPIPEWAIT_ERROR

Failed to wait for a named pipe on Windows.

CR_NAMEDPIPESETSTATE_ERROR

Failed to get a pipe handler on Windows.

CR_SERVER_LOST

If connect_timeout > 0 and it took longer than connect_timeout seconds to connect to the server or if the server died while executing the init-command.

8.4.3.175 Example

```
MYSQL mysql;

mysql_init(&mysql);
mysql_options(&mysql,MYSQL_READ_DEFAULT_GROUP,"your_prog_name");
if (!mysql_real_connect(&mysql,"host","user","passwd","database",0,NULL,0))
{
    fprintf(stderr, "Failed to connect to database: Error: %s\n",
        mysql_error(&mysql));
}
```

By using mysql_options() the MySQL library will read the [client] and your_prog_name sections in the my.cnf file, which will ensure that your program will work, even if someone has set up MySQL in some non-standard way.

Note that upon connection, mysql_real_connect() sets the reconnect flag (part of the MYSQL structure) to a value of 1. This flag indicates, in the event that a query cannot be performed because of a lost connection, that you should try reconnecting to the server before giving up.

8.4.3.176 mysql_real_escape_string()

unsigned long mysql_real_escape_string(MYSQL *mysql, char *to, const char *from, unsigned long length)

8.4.3.177 Description

This function is used to create a legal SQL string that you can use in an SQL statement. See Section 6.1.1.1, Strings.

The string in from is encoded to an escaped SQL string, taking into account the current character set of the connection. The result is placed in to and a terminating null byte is appended. Characters encoded are NUL (ASCII 0), \n, \r, \, ', ", and Control-Z (see Section 6.1.1, Literals: How to Write Strings and Numbers).

The string pointed to by from must be length bytes long. You must allocate the to buffer to be at least length*2+1 bytes long. (In the worse case, each character may need to be encoded as using two bytes, and you need room for the terminating null byte.) When mysql_escape_string() returns, the contents of to will be a null-terminated string. The return value is the length of the encoded string, not including the terminating null character.

8.4.3.178 Example

```
char query[1000],*end;

end = strmov(query,"INSERT INTO test_table values(");
*end++ = '\'';
end += mysql_real_escape_string(&mysql, end,"What's this",11);
*end++ = '\'';
*end++ = ',';
*end++ = '\'';
end += mysql_real_escape_string(&mysql, end,"binary data: \0\r\n",16);
*end++ = '\'';
*end++ = ')';

if (mysql_real_query(&mysql,query,(unsigned int) (end - query)))
{
    fprintf(stderr, "Failed to insert row, Error: %s\n",
            mysql_error(&mysql));
}
```

The strmov() function used in the example is included in the mysqlclient library and works like strcpy() but returns a pointer to the terminating null of the first parameter.

8.4.3.179 Return values

The length of the value placed into to, not including the terminating null character.

8.4.3.180 Errors

None.

8.4.3.181 `mysql_real_query()`

int mysql_real_query(MYSQL *mysql, const char *query, unsigned long length)

8.4.3.182 Description

Executes the SQL query pointed to by query, which should be a string length bytes long. The query must consist of a single SQL statement. You should not add a terminating semicolon (;) or \g to the statement.

You **must** use mysql_real_query() rather than mysql_query() for queries that contain binary data because binary data may contain the \0 character. In addition, mysql_real_query() is faster than mysql_query() because it does not call strlen() on the query string.

If you want to know whether the query should return a result set, you can use mysql_field_count() to check for this. See Section 8.4.3.85, mysql_field_count().

8.4.3.183 Return values

Zero if the query was successful. Non-zero if an error occurred.

8.4.3.184 Errors

CR_COMMANDS_OUT_OF_SYNC
    Commands were executed in an improper order.

CR_SERVER_GONE_ERROR
    The MySQL server has gone away.

CR_SERVER_LOST
    The connection to the server was lost during the query.

CR_UNKNOWN_ERROR
    An unknown error occurred.

8.4.3.185 `mysql_reload()`

int mysql_reload(MYSQL *mysql)

8.4.3.186 Description

Asks the MySQL server to reload the grant tables. The connected user must have the **reload** privilege.

This function is deprecated. It is preferable to use mysql_query() to issue a SQL FLUSH PRIVILEGES statement instead.

8.4.3.187 Return values

Zero for success. Non-zero if an error occurred.

8.4.3.188 Errors

CR_COMMANDS_OUT_OF_SYNC
Commands were executed in an improper order.

CR_SERVER_GONE_ERROR
The MySQL server has gone away.

CR_SERVER_LOST
The connection to the server was lost during the query.

CR_UNKNOWN_ERROR
An unknown error occurred.

8.4.3.189 mysql_row_seek()

MYSQL_ROW_OFFSET mysql_row_seek(MYSQL_RES *result, MYSQL_ROW_OFFSET offset)

8.4.3.190 Description

Sets the row cursor to an arbitrary row in a query result set. This requires that the result set structure contains the entire result of the query, so mysql_row_seek() may be used in conjunction only with mysql_store_result(), not with mysql_use_result().

The offset should be a value returned from a call to mysql_row_tell() or to mysql_row_seek(). This value is not simply a row number; if you want to seek to a row within a result set using a row number, use mysql_data_seek() instead.

8.4.3.191 Return values

The previous value of the row cursor. This value may be passed to a subsequent call to mysql_row_seek().

8.4.3.192 Errors

None.

8.4.3.193 mysql_row_tell()

MYSQL_ROW_OFFSET mysql_row_tell(MYSQL_RES *result)

8.4.3.194 Description

Returns the current position of the row cursor for the last `mysql_fetch_row()`. This value can be used as an argument to `mysql_row_seek()`.

You should use `mysql_row_tell()` only after `mysql_store_result()`, not after `mysql_use_result()`.

8.4.3.195 Return values

The current offset of the row cursor.

8.4.3.196 Errors

None.

8.4.3.197 `mysql_select_db()`

`int mysql_select_db(MYSQL *mysql, const char *db)`

8.4.3.198 Description

Causes the database specified by `db` to become the default (current) database on the connection specified by `mysql`. In subsequent queries, this database is the default for table references that do not include an explicit database specifier.

`mysql_select_db()` fails unless the connected user can be authenticated as having permission to use the database.

8.4.3.199 Return values

Zero for success. Non-zero if an error occurred.

8.4.3.200 Errors

`CR_COMMANDS_OUT_OF_SYNC`
Commands were executed in an improper order.

`CR_SERVER_GONE_ERROR`
The MySQL server has gone away.

`CR_SERVER_LOST`
The connection to the server was lost during the query.

`CR_UNKNOWN_ERROR`
An unknown error occurred.

8.4.3.201 `mysql_shutdown()`

`int mysql_shutdown(MYSQL *mysql)`

8.4.3.202 Description

Asks the database server to shut down. The connected user must have **shutdown** privileges.

8.4.3.203 Return values

Zero for success. Non-zero if an error occurred.

8.4.3.204 Errors

`CR_COMMANDS_OUT_OF_SYNC`
> Commands were executed in an improper order.

`CR_SERVER_GONE_ERROR`
> The MySQL server has gone away.

`CR_SERVER_LOST`
> The connection to the server was lost during the query.

`CR_UNKNOWN_ERROR`
> An unknown error occurred.

8.4.3.205 `mysql_stat()`

`char *mysql_stat(MYSQL *mysql)`

8.4.3.206 Description

Returns a character string containing information similar to that provided by the `mysqladmin status` command. This includes uptime in seconds and the number of running threads, questions, reloads, and open tables.

8.4.3.207 Return values

A character string describing the server status. `NULL` if an error occurred.

8.4.3.208 Errors

`CR_COMMANDS_OUT_OF_SYNC`
> Commands were executed in an improper order.

`CR_SERVER_GONE_ERROR`
> The MySQL server has gone away.

CR_SERVER_LOST

The connection to the server was lost during the query.

CR_UNKNOWN_ERROR

An unknown error occurred.

8.4.3.209 mysql_store_result()

MYSQL_RES *mysql_store_result(MYSQL *mysql)

8.4.3.210 Description

You must call mysql_store_result() or mysql_use_result() for every query that successfully retrieves data (SELECT, SHOW, DESCRIBE, EXPLAIN).

You don't have to call mysql_store_result() or mysql_use_result() for other queries, but it will not do any harm or cause any notable performance if you call mysql_store_result() in all cases. You can detect if the query didn't have a result set by checking if mysql_store_result() returns 0 (more about this later).

If you want to know whether the query should return a result set, you can use mysql_field_count() to check for this. See Section 8.4.3.85, mysql_field_count().

mysql_store_result() reads the entire result of a query to the client, allocates a MYSQL_RES structure, and places the result into this structure.

mysql_store_result() returns a null pointer if the query didn't return a result set (if the query was, for example, an INSERT statement).

mysql_store_result() also returns a null pointer if reading of the result set failed. You can check if you got an error by checking if mysql_error() doesn't return a null pointer, if mysql_errno() returns <> 0, or if mysql_field_count() returns <> 0.

An empty result set is returned if there are no rows returned. (An empty result set differs from a null pointer as a return value.)

Once you have called mysql_store_result() and got a result back that isn't a null pointer, you may call mysql_num_rows() to find out how many rows are in the result set.

You can call mysql_fetch_row() to fetch rows from the result set, or mysql_row_seek() and mysql_row_tell() to obtain or set the current row position within the result set.

You must call mysql_free_result() once you are done with the result set.

Section 8.4.6.1, Why Is It that After mysql_query() Returns Success, mysql_store_result() Sometimes Returns NULL?.

8.4.3.211 Return values

A MYSQL_RES result structure with the results. NULL if an error occurred.

8.4.3.212 Errors

CR_COMMANDS_OUT_OF_SYNC
    Commands were executed in an improper order.

CR_OUT_OF_MEMORY
    Out of memory.

CR_SERVER_GONE_ERROR
    The MySQL server has gone away.

CR_SERVER_LOST
    The connection to the server was lost during the query.

CR_UNKNOWN_ERROR
    An unknown error occurred.

8.4.3.213 mysql_thread_id()

unsigned long mysql_thread_id(MYSQL *mysql)

8.4.3.214 Description

Returns the thread ID of the current connection. This value can be used as an argument to
mysql_kill() to kill the thread.

If the connection is lost and you reconnect with mysql_ping(), the thread ID will
change. This means you should not get the thread ID and store it for later. You should get
it when you need it.

8.4.3.215 Return values

The thread ID of the current connection.

8.4.3.216 Errors

None.

8.4.3.217 mysql_use_result()

MYSQL_RES *mysql_use_result(MYSQL *mysql)

8.4.3.218 Description

You must call mysql_store_result() or mysql_use_result() for every query that
successfully retrieves data (SELECT, SHOW, DESCRIBE, EXPLAIN).

`mysql_use_result()` initiates a result set retrieval but does not actually read the result set into the client like `mysql_store_result()` does. Instead, each row must be retrieved individually by making calls to `mysql_fetch_row()`. This reads the result of a query directly from the server without storing it in a temporary table or local buffer, which is somewhat faster and uses much less memory than `mysql_store_result()`. The client will only allocate memory for the current row and a communication buffer that may grow up to `max_allowed_packet` bytes.

On the other hand, you shouldn't use `mysql_use_result()` if you are doing a lot of processing for each row on the client side, or if the output is sent to a screen on which the user may type a ^S (stop scroll). This will tie up the server and prevent other threads from updating any tables from which the data is being fetched.

When using `mysql_use_result()`, you must execute `mysql_fetch_row()` until a NULL value is returned, otherwise, the unfetched rows will be returned as part of the result set for your next query. The C API will give the error `Commands out of sync; you can't run this command now` if you forget to do this!

You may not use `mysql_data_seek()`, `mysql_row_seek()`, `mysql_row_tell()`, `mysql_num_rows()`, or `mysql_affected_rows()` with a result returned from `mysql_use_result()`, nor may you issue other queries until the `mysql_use_result()` has finished. (However, after you have fetched all the rows, `mysql_num_rows()` will accurately return the number of rows fetched.)

You must call `mysql_free_result()` once you are done with the result set.

8.4.3.219 Return values

A `MYSQL_RES` result structure. `NULL` if an error occurred.

8.4.3.220 Errors

CR_COMMANDS_OUT_OF_SYNC
> Commands were executed in an improper order.

CR_OUT_OF_MEMORY
> Out of memory.

CR_SERVER_GONE_ERROR
> The MySQL server has gone away.

CR_SERVER_LOST
> The connection to the server was lost during the query.

CR_UNKNOWN_ERROR
> An unknown error occurred.

8.4.4 C Threaded Function Descriptions

You need to use the following functions when you want to create a threaded client. See Section 8.4.8, How to Make a Threaded Client.

8.4.4.1 my_init()

void my_init(void)

8.4.4.2 Description

This function needs to be called once in the program before calling any MySQL function. This initialises some global variables that MySQL needs. If you are using a thread-safe client library, this will also call mysql_thread_init() for this thread.

This is automatically called by mysql_init(), mysql_server_init(), and mysql_connect().

8.4.4.3 Return values

None.

8.4.4.4 mysql_thread_init()

my_bool mysql_thread_init(void)

8.4.4.5 Description

This function needs to be called for each created thread to initialise thread-specific variables.

This is automatically called by my_init() and mysql_connect().

8.4.4.6 Return values

None.

8.4.4.7 mysql_thread_end()

void mysql_thread_end(void)

8.4.4.8 Description

This function needs to be called before calling pthread_exit() to free memory allocated by mysql_thread_init().

Note that this function **is not invoked automatically** by the client library. It must be called explicitly to avoid a memory leak.

8.4.4.9 Return values

None.

8.4.4.10 mysql_thread_safe()

unsigned int mysql_thread_safe(void)

8.4.4.11 Description

This function indicates whether the client is compiled as thread-safe.

8.4.4.12 Return values

1 is the client is thread-safe, 0 otherwise.

8.4.5 C Embedded Server Function Descriptions

You must use the following functions if you want to allow your application to be linked against the embedded MySQL server library. See Section 8.4.9, libmysqld, the Embedded MySQL Server Library.

If the program is linked with -lmysqlclient instead of -lmysqld, these functions do nothing. This makes it possible to choose between using the embedded MySQL server and a stand-alone server without modifying any code.

8.4.5.1 mysql_server_init()

int mysql_server_init(int argc, char **argv, char **groups)

8.4.5.2 Description

This function **must** be called once in the program before calling any other MySQL function. It starts up the server and initialises any subsystems (mysys, InnoDB, etc.) that the server uses. If this function is not called, the program will crash. If you are using the DBUG package that comes with MySQL, you should call this after you have called MY_INIT().

The argc and argv arguments are analogous to the arguments to main(). The first element of argv is ignored (it typically contains the program name). For convenience, argc may be 0 (zero) if there are no command-line arguments for the server.

The NULL-terminated list of strings in groups selects which groups in the option files will be active. See Section 4.1.2, my.cnf Option Files. For convenience, groups may be NULL, in which case the [server] and [emedded] groups will be active.

8.4.5.3 Example

```
#include <mysql.h>
#include <stdlib.h>

static char *server_args[] = {
  "this_program",        /* this string is not used */
  "--datadir=.",
  "--set-variable=key_buffer_size=32M"
};
static char *server_groups[] = {
  "embedded",
  "server",
  "this_program_SERVER",
  (char *)NULL
};

int main(void) {
  mysql_server_init(sizeof(server_args) / sizeof(char *),
                    server_args, server_groups);

  /* Use any MySQL API functions here */

  mysql_server_end();

  return EXIT_SUCCESS;
}
```

8.4.5.4 Return values

0 if okay, 1 if an error occurred.

8.4.5.5 mysql_server_end()

void mysql_server_end(void)

8.4.5.6 Description

This function **must** be called once in the program after all other MySQL functions. It shuts down the embedded server.

8.4.5.7 Return values

None.

8.4.6 Common Questions and Problems When Using the C API

8.4.6.1 Why Is It that After `mysql_query()` Returns Success, `mysql_store_result()` Sometimes Returns NULL?

It is possible for `mysql_store_result()` to return NULL following a successful call to `mysql_query()`. When this happens, it means one of the following conditions occurred:

- There was a `malloc()` failure (for example, if the result set was too large).

- The data couldn't be read (an error occurred on the connection).

- The query returned no data (for example, it was an INSERT, UPDATE, or DELETE).

You can always check whether the statement should have produced a non-empty result by calling `mysql_field_count()`. If `mysql_field_count()` returns zero, the result is empty and the last query was a statement that does not return values (for example, an INSERT or a DELETE). If `mysql_field_count()` returns a non-zero value, the statement should have produced a non-empty result. See the description of the `mysql_field_count()` function for an example.

You can test for an error by calling `mysql_error()` or `mysql_errno()`.

8.4.6.2 What results can I get from a query?

In addition to the result set returned by a query, you can also get the following information:

- `mysql_affected_rows()` returns the number of rows affected by the last query when doing an INSERT, UPDATE, or DELETE. An exception is that if DELETE is used without a WHERE clause, the table is re-created empty, which is much faster! In this case, `mysql_affected_rows()` returns zero for the number of records affected.

- `mysql_num_rows()` returns the number of rows in a result set. With `mysql_store_result()`, `mysql_num_rows()` may be called as soon as `mysql_store_result()` returns. With `mysql_use_result()`, `mysql_num_rows()` may be called only after you have fetched all the rows with `mysql_fetch_row()`.

- `mysql_insert_id()` returns the ID generated by the last query that inserted a row into a table with an AUTO_INCREMENT index. See Section 8.4.3.126, `mysql_insert_id()`.

- Some queries (LOAD DATA INFILE . . . , INSERT INTO . . . SELECT . . . , UPDATE) return additional information. The result is returned by `mysql_info()`. See the description for `mysql_info()` for the format of the string that it returns. `mysql_info()` returns a NULL pointer if there is no additional information.

8.4.6.3 How can I get the unique ID for the last inserted row?

If you insert a record in a table containing a column that has the AUTO_INCREMENT attribute, you can get the most recently generated ID by calling the mysql_insert_id() function.

You can also retrieve the ID by using the LAST_INSERT_ID() function in a query string that you pass to mysql_query().

You can check if an AUTO_INCREMENT index is used by executing the following code. This also checks if the query was an INSERT with an AUTO_INCREMENT index:

```
if (mysql_error(&mysql)[0] == 0 &&
    mysql_num_fields(result) == 0 &&
    mysql_insert_id(&mysql) != 0)
{
    used_id = mysql_insert_id(&mysql);
}
```

The most recently generated ID is maintained in the server on a per-connection basis. It will not be changed by another client. It will not even be changed if you update another AUTO_INCREMENT column with a non-magic value (that is, a value that is not NULL and not 0).

If you want to use the ID that was generated for one table and insert it into a second table, you can use SQL statements like these:

```
INSERT INTO foo (auto,text)
    VALUES(NULL,'text');        # generate ID by inserting NULL
INSERT INTO foo2 (id,text)
    VALUES(LAST_INSERT_ID(),'text'); # use ID in second table
```

8.4.6.4 Problems linking with the C API

When linking with the C API, the following errors may occur on some systems:

```
gcc -g -o client test.o -L/usr/local/lib/mysql -lmysqlclient -lsocket -lnsl

Undefined         first referenced
 symbol             in file
floor            /usr/local/lib/mysql/libmysqlclient.a(password.o)
ld: fatal: Symbol referencing errors. No output written to client
```

If this happens on your system, you must include the math library by adding -lm to the end of the compile/link line.

8.4.7 Building Client Programs

If you compile MySQL clients that you've written yourself or that you obtain from a third-party, they must be linked using the `-lmysqlclient -lz` option on the link command. You may also need to specify a `-L` option to tell the linker where to find the library. For example, if the library is installed in `/usr/local/mysql/lib`, use `-L/usr/local/mysql/lib -lmysqlclient -lz` on the link command.

For clients that use MySQL header files, you may need to specify a `-I` option when you compile them (for example, `-I/usr/local/mysql/include`), so the compiler can find the header files.

8.4.8 How to Make a Threaded Client

The client library is almost thread-safe. The biggest problem is that the subroutines in `net.c` that read from sockets are not interrupt-safe. This was done with the thought that you might want to have your own alarm that can break a long read to a server. If you install interrupt handlers for the `SIGPIPE` interrupt, the socket handling should be thread-safe.

In the older binaries we distribute on our web site (http://www.mysql.com/), the client libraries are not normally compiled with the thread-safe option (the Windows binaries are, by default, compiled to be thread-safe). Newer binary distributions should have both a normal and a thread-safe client library.

To get a threaded client where you can interrupt the client from other threads and set timeouts when talking with the MySQL server, you should use the `-lmysys`, `-lstring`, and `-ldbug` libraries and the `net_serv.o` code that the server uses.

If you don't need interrupts or timeouts, you can just compile a thread-safe client library (`mysqlclient_r`) and use this. See Section 8.4, MySQL C API. In this case you don't have to worry about the `net_serv.o` object file or the other MySQL libraries.

When using a threaded client and you want to use timeouts and interrupts, you can make great use of the routines in the `thr_alarm.c` file. If you are using routines from the mysys library, the only thing you must remember is to call `my_init()` first! See Section 8.4.4, C Threaded Function Descriptions.

All functions except `mysql_real_connect()` are, by default, thread-safe. The following notes describe how to compile a thread-safe client library and use it in a thread-safe manner. (These notes for `mysql_real_connect()` actually apply to `mysql_connect()` as well, but because `mysql_connect()` is deprecated, you should be using `mysql_real_connect()` anyway.)

To make `mysql_real_connect()` thread-safe, you must recompile the client library with this command:

```
shell> ./configure --enable-thread-safe-client
```

This will create a thread-safe client library `libmysqlclient_r`. `--enable-thread-safe-client`. This library is thread-safe per connection. You can let two threads share the same connection with the following caveats:

- Two threads can't send a query to the MySQL server at the same time on the same connection. In particular, you have to ensure that between a `mysql_query()` and `mysql_store_result()` no other thread is using the same connection.

- Many threads can access different result sets that are retrieved with `mysql_store_result()`.

- If you use `mysql_use_result`, you have to ensure that no other thread is using the same connection until the result set is closed. However, it really is best for threaded clients that share the same connection to use `mysql_store_result()`.

- If you want to use multiple threads on the same connection, you must have a mutex lock around your `mysql_query()` and `mysql_store_result()` call combination. Once `mysql_store_result()` is ready, the lock can be released and other threads may query the same connection.

- If you program with POSIX threads, you can use `pthread_mutex_lock()` and `pthread_mutex_unlock()` to establish and release a mutex lock.

You need to know the following if you have a thread that is calling MySQL functions that did not create the connection to the MySQL database:

- When you call `mysql_init()` or `mysql_connect()`, MySQL will create a thread-specific variable for the thread that is used by the debug library (among other things).

- If you call a MySQL function, before the thread has called `mysql_init()` or `mysql_connect()`, the thread will not have the necessary thread-specific variables in place and you are likely to end up with a core dump sooner or later.

The get things to work smoothly you have to do the following:

1. Call `my_init()` at the start of your program if it calls any other MySQL function before calling `mysql_real_connect()`.

2. Call `mysql_thread_init()` in the thread handler before calling any MySQL function.

3. In the thread, call `mysql_thread_end()` before calling `pthread_exit()`. This will free the memory used by MySQL thread-specific variables.

You may get some errors because of undefined symbols when linking your client with `libmysqlclient_r`. In most cases this is because you haven't included the thread libraries on the link/compile line.

8.4.9 `libmysqld`, the Embedded MySQL Server Library

8.4.9.1 Overview of the embedded MySQL server library

The embedded MySQL server library makes it possible to run a full-featured MySQL server inside the client application. The main benefits are increased speed and simpler management for embedded applications.

The API is identical for the embedded MySQL version and the client/server version. To change an old threaded application to use the embedded library, you normally only have to add calls to the following functions:

Function	When to call
`mysql_server_init()`	Should be called before any other MySQL function is called, preferably early in the `main()` function.
`mysql_server_end()`	Should be called before your program exits.
`mysql_thread_init()`	Should be called in each thread you create that will access MySQL.
`mysql_thread_end()`	Should be called before calling `pthread_exit()`.

Then you must link your code with `libmysqld.a` instead of `libmysqlclient.a`.

The preceding `mysql_server_xxx` functions are also included in `libmysqlclient.a` to allow you to change between the embedded and the client/server version by just linking your application with the right library. See Section 8.4.5.1, `mysql_server_init()`.

8.4.9.2 Compiling programs with `libmysqld`

To get a `libmysqld` library you should configure MySQL with the `--with-embedded-server` option.

When you link your program with `libmysqld`, you must also include the system-specific `pthread` libraries and some libraries that the MySQL server uses. You can get the full list of libraries by executing `mysql_config --libmysqld-libs`.

The correct flags for compiling and linking a threaded program must be used, even if you do not directly call any thread functions in your code.

8.4.9.3 Restrictions when using the embedded MySQL server

The embedded server has the following limitations:

*   No support for ISAM tables. (This is mainly done to make the library smaller.)
*   No UDF functions.

- No stack trace on core dump.

- No internal RAID support. (This is not normally needed, as most OSes nowadays have support for big files.)

- You can set this up as a server or a master (no replication).

- You can't connect to the embedded server from an outside process with sockets or TCP/IP.

Some of these limitations can be changed by editing the mysql_embed.h include file and recompiling MySQL.

8.4.9.4 Using option files with the embedded server

The following is the recommended way to use option files to make it easy to switch between a client/server application and one where MySQL is embedded. See Section 4.1.2, my.cnf Option Files.

- Put common options in the [server] section. These will be read by both MySQL versions.

- Put client/server-specific options in the [mysqld] section.

- Put embedded MySQL-specific options in the [embedded] section.

- Put application-specific options in the [ApplicationName_SERVER] section.

8.4.9.5 Things left to do in embedded server (TODO)

- Currently we only provide a static version of the mysqld library. In the future we will also provide a shared library for this.

- We are going to provide options to leave out some parts of MySQL to make the library smaller.

- There is still a lot of speed optimisation to do.

- Errors are written to stderr. We will add an option to specify a filename for these.

- We have to change InnoDB to not be so verbose when used in the embedded version.

8.4.9.6 A simple embedded server example

This example program and makefile should work without any changes on a Linux or FreeBSD system. For other operating systems, minor changes will be needed. This example is designed to give enough details to understand the problem, without the clutter that is a necessary part of a real application.

To try out the example, create a test_libmysqld directory at the same level as the mysql-4.0 source directory. Save the test_libmysqld.c source and the GNUmakefile in the directory, and run GNU make from inside the test_libmysqld directory.

test_libmysqld.c

```
/*
 * A simple example client, using the embedded MySQL server library
 */

#include <mysql.h>
#include <stdarg.h>
#include <stdio.h>
#include <stdlib.h>

MYSQL *db_connect(const char *dbname);
void db_disconnect(MYSQL *db);
void db_do_query(MYSQL *db, const char *query);

const char *server_groups[] = {
  "test_libmysqld_SERVER", "embedded", "server", NULL
};

int
main(int argc, char **argv)
{
    MYSQL *one, *two;

    /* mysql_server_init() must be called before any other mysql
     * functions.
     *
     * You can use mysql_server_init(0, NULL, NULL), and it will
     * initialise the server using groups = {
     *   "server", "embedded", NULL
     * }.
     *
     * In your $HOME/.my.cnf file, you probably want to put:

    [test_libmysqld_SERVER]
    language = /path/to/source/of/mysql/sql/share/english

     * You could, of course, modify argc and argv before passing
     * them to this function.  Or you could create new ones in any
     * way you like.  But all of the arguments in argv (except for
     * argv[0], which is the program name) should be valid options
     * for the MySQL server.
     *
     * If you link this client against the normal mysqlclient
     * library, this function is just a stub that does nothing.
     */
    mysql_server_init(argc, argv, (char **)server_groups);

    one = db_connect("test");
    two = db_connect(NULL);

    db_do_query(one, "SHOW TABLE STATUS");
    db_do_query(two, "SHOW DATABASES");
```

```c
    mysql_close(two);
    mysql_close(one);

    /* This must be called after all other mysql functions */
    mysql_server_end();

    exit(EXIT_SUCCESS);
}

static void
die(MYSQL *db, char *fmt, ...)
{
  va_list ap;
  va_start(ap, fmt);
  vfprintf(stderr, fmt, ap);
  va_end(ap);
  (void)putc('\n', stderr);
  if (db)
    db_disconnect(db);
  exit(EXIT_FAILURE);
}

MYSQL *
db_connect(const char *dbname)
{
  MYSQL *db = mysql_init(NULL);
  if (!db)
    die(db, "mysql_init failed: no memory");
  /*
   * Notice that the client and server use separate group names.
   * This is critical because the server will not accept the
   * client's options, and vice versa.
   */
  mysql_options(db, MYSQL_READ_DEFAULT_GROUP, "test_libmysqld_CLIENT");
  if (!mysql_real_connect(db, NULL, NULL, NULL, dbname, 0, NULL, 0))
    die(db, "mysql_real_connect failed: %s", mysql_error(db));

  return db;
}

void
db_disconnect(MYSQL *db)
{
  mysql_close(db);
}

void
db_do_query(MYSQL *db, const char *query)
{
  if (mysql_query(db, query) != 0)
    goto err;

  if (mysql_field_count(db) > 0)
  {
```

```
        MYSQL_RES    *res;
        MYSQL_ROW    row, end_row;
        int num_fields;

        if (!(res = mysql_store_result(db)))
          goto err;
        num_fields = mysql_num_fields(res);
        while ((row = mysql_fetch_row(res)))
        {
          (void)fputs(">> ", stdout);
          for (end_row = row + num_fields; row < end_row; ++row)
            (void)printf("%s\t", row ? (char*)*row : "NULL");
          (void)fputc('\n', stdout);
        }
        (void)fputc('\n', stdout);
    }
    else
        (void)printf("Affected rows: %lld\n", mysql_affected_rows(db));

    return;

err:
    die(db, "db_do_query failed: %s [%s]", mysql_error(db), query);
}
```

GNUmakefile

```
# This assumes the MySQL software is installed in /usr/local/mysql
inc      := /usr/local/mysql/include/mysql
lib      := /usr/local/mysql/lib

# If you have not installed the MySQL software yet, try this instead
#inc      := $(HOME)/mysql-4.0/include
#lib      := $(HOME)/mysql-4.0/libmysqld

CC       := gcc
CPPFLAGS := -I$(inc) -D_THREAD_SAFE -D_REENTRANT
CFLAGS   := -g -W -Wall
LDFLAGS  := -static
# You can change -lmysqld to -lmysqlclient to use the
# client/server library
LDLIBS   = -L$(lib) -lmysqld -lz -lm -lcrypt

ifneq (,$(shell grep FreeBSD /COPYRIGHT 2>/dev/null))
# FreeBSD
LDFLAGS += -pthread
else
# Assume Linux
LDLIBS += -lpthread
endif
```

```
# This works for simple one-file test programs
sources := $(wildcard *.c)
objects := $(patsubst %c,%o,$(sources))
targets := $(basename $(sources))

all: $(targets)

clean:
        rm -f $(targets) $(objects) *.core
```

8.4.9.7 Licensing the embedded server

The MySQL source code is covered by the GNU GPL license (see http://www.mysql.com/doc/G/P/GPL-license.html). One result of this is that any program which includes, by linking with libmysqld, the MySQL source code must be released as free software (under a license compatible with the GPL).

We encourage everyone to promote free software by releasing code under the GPL or a compatible license. For those who are not able to do this, another option is to purchase a commercial licence for the MySQL code from MySQL AB. For details, please see Section 1.4.3, MySQL Licenses.

8.5 MySQL C++ APIs

Two APIs are available in the MySQL Contrib directory (http://www.mysql.com/Downloads/Contrib/).

8.5.1 Borland C++

You can compile the MySQL Windows source with Borland C++ 5.02. (The Windows source includes only projects for Microsoft VC++. For Borland C++ you have to do the project files yourself.)

One known problem with Borland C++ is that it uses a different structure alignment than VC++. This means that you will run into problems if you try to use the default libmysql.dll libraries (that were compiled with VC++) with Borland C++. You can do one of the following to avoid this problem.

•   You can use the static MySQL libraries for Borland C++, found on http://www.mysql.com/downloads/os-win32.html.

•   Only call mysql_init() with NULL as an argument, not a pre-allocated MYSQL struct.

8.6 MySQL Java Connectivity (JDBC)

There are 2 supported JDBC drivers for MySQL: the mm driver and the Reisin JDBC driver. You can find a copy of the mm driver at http://mmmysql.sourceforge.net/ or http://www.mysql.com/Downloads/Contrib/ and the Reisin driver at http://www.cau-cho.com/projects/jdbc-mysql/index.xtp. For documentation consult any JDBC documentation and the driver's own documentation for MySQL-specific features.

8.7 MySQL Python APIs

The MySQL Contrib directory (http://www.mysql.com/Downloads/Contrib/) contains a Python interface written by Joseph Skinner.

8.8 MySQL Tcl APIs

The Contrib directory (http://www.mysql.com/Downloads/Contrib/) contains a Tcl interface that is based on msqltcl 1.50.

8.9 MySQL Eiffel Wrapper

The MySQL Contrib directory (http://www.mysql.com/Downloads/Contrib/) contains an Eiffel wrapper written by Michael Ravits.

9

Extending MySQL

9.1 MySQL Internals

This chapter describes a lot of things that you need to know when working on the MySQL code. If you plan to contribute to MySQL development, want to have access to the bleeding-edge, in-between-versions code, or just want to keep track of development, follow the instructions in Section 2.3.4, Installing from the Development Source Tree. If you are interested in MySQL internals, you should also subscribe to our internals mailing list. This list is relatively low-traffic. For details on how to subscribe, please see Section 1.6.2.1, The MySQL Mailing Lists. All developers at MySQL AB are on the internals list and we help other people who are working on the MySQL code. Feel free to use this list both to ask questions about the code and to send patches that you would like to contribute to the MySQL project!

9.1.1 MySQL Threads

The MySQL server creates the following threads:

• The TCP/IP connection thread handles all connection requests and creates a new dedicated thread to handle the authentication and SQL query processing for each connection.

• On Windows NT there is a named pipe handler thread that does the same work as the TCP/IP connection thread on named pipe connect requests.

• The signal thread handles all signals. This thread also normally handles alarms and calls process_alarm() to force timeouts on connections that have been idle too long.

• If mysqld is compiled with –DUSE_ALARM_THREAD, a dedicated thread that handles alarms is created. This is only used on some systems where there are problems with sigwait() or if one wants to use the thr_alarm() code in one's application without a dedicated signal handling thread.

- If one uses the `--flush_time=#` option, a dedicated thread is created to flush all tables at the given interval.

- Every connection has its own thread.

- Every different table on which one uses `INSERT DELAYED` gets its own thread.

- If you use `--master-host`, a slave replication thread will be started to read and apply updates from the master.

`mysqladmin processlist` only shows the connection, `INSERT DELAYED`, and replication threads.

9.1.2 MySQL Test Suite

Until recently, our main full-coverage test suite was based on proprietary customer data and for that reason has not been publicly available. The only publicly available part of our testing process consisted of the `crash-me` test, a Perl DBI/DBD benchmark found in the `sql-bench` directory, and miscellaneous tests located in the `tests` directory. The lack of a standardised publicly available test suite has made it difficult for our users, as well as developers, to do regression tests on the MySQL code. To address this problem, we have created a new test system that is included in the source and binary distributions starting in Version 3.23.29.

The current set of test cases doesn't test everything in MySQL, but it should catch most obvious bugs in the SQL processing code and OS/library issues. Also, it is quite thorough in testing replication. Our eventual goal is to have the tests cover 100% of the code. We welcome contributions to our test suite. You may especially want to contribute tests that examine the functionality critical to your system, as this will ensure that all future MySQL releases will work well with your applications.

9.1.2.1 Running the MySQL test suite

The test system consist of a test language interpreter (`mysqltest`), a shell script to run all tests (`mysql-test-run`), the actual test cases written in a special test language, and their expected results. To run the test suite on your system after a build, type `make test` or `mysql-test/mysql-test-run` from the source root. If you have installed a binary distribution, `cd` to the install root (e.g., `/usr/local/mysql`) and do `scripts/mysql-test-run`. All tests should succeed. If not, you should try to find out why and report the problem if this is a bug in MySQL. See Section 9.1.2.3, Reporting bugs in the MySQL test suite.

If you have a copy of `mysqld` running on the machine where you want to run the test suite, you do not have to stop it, as long as it is not using ports 9306 and 9307. If one of those ports is taken, you should edit `mysql-test-run` and change the values of the master and/or slave port to one that is available.

You can run one individual test case with `mysql-test/mysql-test-run test_name`.

If one test fails, you should test running `mysql-test-run` with the `--force` option to check if any other tests fail.

9.1.2.2 Extending the MySQL test suite

You can use the `mysqltest` language to write your own test cases. Unfortunately, we have not yet written full documentation for it—we plan to do this shortly. You can, however, look at our current test cases and use them as an example. The following points should help you get started:

- The tests are located in `mysql-test/t/*.test`.

- A test case consists of `;` terminated statements and is similar to the input of the `mysql` command-line client. A statement by default is a query to be sent to MySQL server, unless it is recognised as an internal command (e.g., `sleep`).

- All queries that produce results—e.g., SELECT, SHOW, EXPLAIN, etc.—must be preceded with `@/path/to/result/file`. The file must contain the expected results. An easy way to generate the result file is to run `mysqltest -r < t/test-case-name.test` from `mysql-test` directory, and then edit the generated result files, if needed, to adjust them to the expected output. In that case, be very careful about not adding or deleting any invisible characters—make sure to only change the text and/or delete lines. If you have to insert a line, make sure the fields are separated with a hard tab, and there is a hard tab at the end. You may want to use `od -c` to make sure your text editor has not messed anything up during editing. We, of course, hope that you will never have to edit the output of `mysqltest -r`, as you only have to do it when you find a bug.

- To be consistent with our setup, you should put your result files in the `mysql-test/r` directory and name them `test_name.result`. If the test produces more than one result, you should use `test_name.a.result`, `test_name.b.result`, etc.

- If a statement returns an error, you should, on the line before the statement, specify with the `--error error-number`. The error number can be a list of possible error numbers separated with `','`.

- If you are writing a replication test case, you should, on the first line of the test file, put `source include/master-slave.inc;`. To switch between master and slave, use `connection master;` and `connection slave;`. If you need to do something on an alternate connection, you can do `connection master1;` for the master, and `connection slave1;` for the slave.

- If you need to do something in a loop, you can use something like this:

```
let $1=1000;
while ($1)
{
  # do your queries here
  dec $1;
}
```

- To sleep between queries, use the `sleep` command. It supports fractions of a second, so you can do `sleep 1.3;`, for example, to sleep 1.3 seconds.

- To run the slave with additional options for your test case, put them in the command-line format in `mysql-test/t/test_name-slave.opt`. For the master, put them in `mysql-test/t/test_name-master.opt`.

- If you have a question about the test suite, or have a test case to contribute, email to *internals@lists.mysql.com*. As the list does not accept attachments, you should ftp all the relevant files to: ftp://support.mysql.com/pub/mysql/Incoming/.

9.1.2.3 Reporting bugs in the MySQL test suite

If your MySQL version doesn't pass the test suite you should do the following:

- Don't send a bug report before you have found out as much as possible about what when wrong! When you do it, please use the `mysqlbug` script so that we can get information about your system and MySQL version. See Section 1.6.2.3, How to report bugs or problems.

- Make sure to include the output of `mysql-test-run`, as well as contents of all `.reject` files in `mysql-test/r` directory.

- If a test in the test suite fails, check if the test also fails when run on its own:

```
cd mysql-test
mysql-test-run --local test-name
```

If this fails, you should configure MySQL with `--with-debug` and run `mysql-test-run` with the `--debug` option. If this also fails send the trace file `var/tmp/master.trace` to ftp://support.mysql.com/pub/mysql/secret so that we can examine it. Please remember to also include a full description of your system, the version of the mysqld binary, and how you compiled it.

- Try also to run `mysql-test-run` with the `--force` option to see if any other test fails.

- If you have compiled MySQL yourself, check our to learn manual for how to compile MySQL on your platform or, preferably, use one of the binaries we have compiled for you at http://www.mysql.com/downloads/. All our standard binaries should pass the test suite!

- If you get an error, like Result length mismatch, or Result content mismatch it means that the output of the test didn't match exactly the expected output. This could be a bug in MySQL, or it could occur because your mysqld version produces slightly different results under some circumstances.

  Failed test results are put in a file with the same base name as the result file with the .reject extension. If your test case is failing, you should do a diff on the two files. If you cannot see how they are different, examine both with od -c and check their lengths.

- If a test fails totally, you should check the logs file in the mysql-test/var/log directory for hints of what went wrong.

- If you have compiled MySQL with debugging you can try to debug this by running mysql-test-run with the --gdb and/or --debug options. See Section D.1.2, Creating Trace Files.

  If you have not compiled MySQL for debugging you should probably do that. Just specify the --with-debug options to configure! See Section 2.3, Installing a MySQL Source Distribution.

9.2 Adding New Functions to MySQL

There are two ways to add new functions to MySQL:

- You can add the function through the user-definable function (UDF) interface. User-definable functions are added and removed dynamically using the CREATE FUNCTION and DROP FUNCTION statements. See Section 9.2.1, CREATE FUNCTION/DROP FUNCTION Syntax.

- You can add the function as a native (built-in) MySQL function. Native functions are compiled into the mysqld server and become available on a permanent basis.

Each method has advantages and disadvantages:

- If you write a user-definable function, you must install the object file in addition to the server itself. If you compile your function into the server, you don't need to do that.

- You can add UDFs to a binary MySQL distribution. Native functions require you to modify a source distribution.

- If you upgrade your MySQL distribution, you can continue to use your previously installed UDFs. For native functions, you must repeat your modifications each time you upgrade.

Whichever method you use to add new functions, they may be used just like native functions such as ABS() or SOUNDEX().

9.2.1 CREATE FUNCTION/DROP FUNCTION **Syntax**

```
CREATE [AGGREGATE] FUNCTION function_name RETURNS {STRING|REAL|INTEGER}
    SONAME shared_library_name
```

```
DROP FUNCTION function_name
```

A user-definable function (UDF) is a way to extend MySQL with a new function that works like native (built-in) MySQL functions such as ABS() and CONCAT().

AGGREGATE is a new option for MySQL Version 3.23. An AGGREGATE function works exactly like a native MySQL GROUP function like SUM or COUNT().

CREATE FUNCTION saves the function's name, type, and shared library name in the mysql.func system table. You must have the **insert** and **delete** privileges for the mysql database to create and drop functions.

All active functions are reloaded each time the server starts, unless you start mysqld with the --skip-grant-tables option. In this case, UDF initialisation is skipped and UDFs are unavailable. (An active function is one that has been loaded with CREATE FUNCTION and not removed with DROP FUNCTION.)

For instructions on writing user-definable functions, see Section 9.2, Adding New Functions to MySQL. For the UDF mechanism to work, functions must be written in C or C++, your operating system must support dynamic loading, and you must have compiled mysqld dynamically (not statically).

Note that to make AGGREGATE work, you must have a mysql.func table that contains the column type. If this is not the case, you should run the script mysql_fix_privilege_tables to get this fixed.

9.2.2 **Adding a New User-Definable Function**

For the UDF mechanism to work, functions must be written in C or C++ and your operating system must support dynamic loading. The MySQL source distribution includes a file sql/udf_example.cc that defines 5 new functions. Consult this file to see how UDF calling conventions work.

For mysqld to be able to use UDF functions, you should configure MySQL with --with-mysqld-ldflags=-rdynamic The reason is that on many platforms (including Linux) you can load a dynamic library (with dlopen()) from a static linked program, which you would get if you are using --with-mysqld-ldflags=-all-static. If you want to use a UDF that needs to access symbols from mysqld (like the methaphone example in sql/udf_example.cc that uses default_charset_info), you must link the program with -rdynamic (see man dlopen).

For each function that you want to use in SQL statements, you should define corresponding C (or C++) functions. In the following discussion, the name "xxx" is used for an example function name. To distinquish between SQL and C/C++ usage, XXX() (upper-case) indicates a SQL function call, and xxx() (lowercase) indicates a C/C++ function call.

The C/C++ functions that you write to implement the interface for XXX() are:

xxx() (required)

> The main function. This is where the function result is computed. The correspondence between the SQL type and return type of your C/C++ function is shown here:

SQL type	C/C++ type
STRING	char *
INTEGER	long long
REAL	double

xxx_init() (optional)

> The initialisation function for xxx(). It can be used to:

- Check the number of arguments to XXX().
- Check that the arguments are of a required type or, alternatively, tell MySQL to coerce arguments to the types you want when the main function is called.
- Allocate any memory required by the main function.
- Specify the maximum length of the result.
- Specify (for REAL functions) the maximum number of decimals.
- Specify whether the result can be NULL.

xxx_deinit() (optional)

> The deinitialisation function for xxx(). It should deallocate any memory allocated by the initialisation function.

When a SQL statement invokes XXX(), MySQL calls the initialisation function xxx_init() to let it perform any required setup, such as argument checking or memory allocation. If xxx_init() returns an error, the SQL statement is aborted with an error message and the main and deinitialisation functions are not called. Otherwise, the main function xxx() is called once for each row. After all rows have been processed, the deinitialisation function xxx_deinit() is called so that it can perform any required cleanup.

For aggregate functions (like SUM()), you must also provide the following functions:

xxx_reset() (required)

> Reset sum and insert the argument as the initial value for a new group.

xxx_add() (required)

Add the argument to the old sum.

When using aggregate UDF functions MySQL works the following way:

1. Call xxx_init() to let the aggregate function allocate the memory it will need to store results.

2. Sort the table according to the GROUP BY expression.

3. For the first row in a new group, call the xxx_reset() function.

4. For each new row that belongs in the same group, call the xxx_add() function.

5. When the group changes or after the last row has been processed, call xxx() to get the result for the aggregate.

6. Repeat Steps 3–5 until all rows have been processed.

7. Call xxx_deinit() to let the UDF free any memory it has allocated.

All functions must be thread-safe (not just the main function, but the initialisation and deinitialisation functions as well). This means that you are not allowed to allocate any global or static variables that change! If you need memory, you should allocate it in xxx_init() and free it in xxx_deinit().

9.2.2.1 UDF calling sequences for simple functions

The main function should be declared as shown here. Note that the return type and parameters differ, depending on whether you will declare the SQL function XXX() to return STRING, INTEGER, or REAL in the CREATE FUNCTION statement.

For STRING functions:

```
char *xxx(UDF_INIT *initid, UDF_ARGS *args,
        char *result, unsigned long *length,
        char *is_null, char *error);
```

For INTEGER functions:

```
long long xxx(UDF_INIT *initid, UDF_ARGS *args,
        char *is_null, char *error);
```

For REAL functions:

```
double xxx(UDF_INIT *initid, UDF_ARGS *args,
        char *is_null, char *error);
```

The initialisation and deinitialisation functions are declared like this:

```
my_bool xxx_init(UDF_INIT *initid, UDF_ARGS *args, char *message);

void xxx_deinit(UDF_INIT *initid);
```

The initid parameter is passed to all three functions. It points to a UDF_INIT structure that is used to communicate information between functions. The UDF_INIT structure members are listed next. The initialisation function should fill in any members that it wishes to change (to use the default for a member, leave it unchanged):

my_bool maybe_null

> xxx_init() should set maybe_null to 1 if xxx() can return NULL. The default value is 1 if any of the arguments are declared maybe_null.

unsigned int decimals

> Number of decimals. The default value is the maximum number of decimals in the arguments passed to the main function. (For example, if the function is passed 1.34, 1.345, and 1.3, the default would be 3 because 1.345 has 3 decimals.)

unsigned int max_length

> The maximum length of the string result. The default value differs depending on the result type of the function. For string functions, the default is the length of the longest argument. For integer functions, the default is 21 digits. For real functions, the default is 13 plus the number of decimals indicated by initid->decimals. (For numeric functions, the length includes any sign or decimal point characters.)

> If you want to return a blob, you can set this to 65K or 16M; this memory is not allocated but used to decide which column type to use if there is a need to store the data temporarily.

char *ptr

> A pointer that the function can use for its own purposes. For example, functions can use initid->ptr to communicate allocated memory between functions. In xxx_init(), allocate the memory and assign it to this pointer:

>  ```
>  initid->ptr = allocated_memory;
>  ```

> In xxx() and xxx_deinit(), refer to initid->ptr to use or deallocate the memory.

9.2.2.2 UDF calling sequences for aggregate functions

Here is a description of the different functions you need to define when you want to create an aggregate UDF function.

```
char *xxx_reset(UDF_INIT *initid, UDF_ARGS *args,
                char *is_null, char *error);
```

This function is called when MySQL finds the first row in a new group. In the function you should reset any internal summary variables and then set the given argument as the first argument in the group.

In many cases this is implemented internally by resetting all variables and then calling xxx_add().

```
char *xxx_add(UDF_INIT *initid, UDF_ARGS *args,
              char *is_null, char *error);
```

This function is called for all rows that belong to the same group, except for the first row. In this you should add the value in UDF_ARGS to your internal summary variable.

The xxx() function should be declared in the same way you define a simple UDF function. See Section 9.2.2.1, UDF calling sequences for simple functions.

This function is called when all rows in the group have been processed. You should normally never access the args variable here but return your value based on your internal summary variables.

All argument processing in xxx_reset() and xxx_add() should be done in the same way you handle normal UDF functions. See Section 9.2.2.3, Argument processing.

The return value handling in xxx() should be done identically as for a normal UDF. See Section 9.2.2.4, Return values and error handling.

The pointer argument to is_null and error is the same for all calls to xxx_reset(), xxx_add(), and xxx(). You can use this to remember that you got an error or if the xxx() function should return NULL. Note that you should not store a string into *error! This is just a 1-byte flag!

is_null is reset for each group (before calling xxx_reset()). error is never reset.

If isnull or error are set after xxx(), MySQL will return NULL as the result for the group function.

9.2.2.3 Argument processing

The args parameter points to a UDF_ARGS structure that has the following members:

unsigned int arg_count

   The number of arguments. Check this value in the initialisation function if you want your function to be called with a particular number of arguments. For example:

```
if (args->arg_count != 2)
{
    strcpy(message,"XXX() requires two arguments");
    return 1;
}
```

enum Item_result *arg_type

   The types for each argument. The possible type values are STRING_RESULT, INT_RESULT, and REAL_RESULT.

   To make sure that arguments are of a given type and return an error if they are not, check the arg_type array in the initialisation function. For example:

```
if (args->arg_type[0] != STRING_RESULT ||
    args->arg_type[1] != INT_RESULT)
{
    strcpy(message,"XXX() requires a string and an integer");
    return 1;
}
```

As an alternative to requiring your function's arguments to be of particular types, you can use the initialisation function to set the `arg_type` elements to the types you want. This causes MySQL to coerce arguments to those types for each call to `xxx()`. For example, to specify coercion of the first two arguments to string and integer, do this in `xxx_init()`:

```
args->arg_type[0] = STRING_RESULT;
args->arg_type[1] = INT_RESULT;
```

char **args

`args->args` communicates information to the initialisation function about the general nature of the arguments your function was called with. For a constant argument `i`, `args->args[i]` points to the argument value. (See the following instructions on how to access the value properly.) For a non-constant argument, `args->args[i]` is `0`. A constant argument is an expression that uses only constants, such as 3 or 4*7-2 or `SIN(3.14)`. A non-constant argument is an expression that refers to values that may change from row to row, such as column names or functions that are called with non-constant arguments.

For each invocation of the main function, `args->args` contains the actual arguments that are passed for the row currently being processed.

Functions can refer to an argument `i` as follows:

- An argument of type `STRING_RESULT` is given as a string pointer plus a length, to allow handling of binary data or data of arbitrary length. The string contents are available as `args->args[i]` and the string length is `args->lengths[i]`. You should not assume that strings are null-terminated.

- For an argument of type `INT_RESULT`, you must cast `args->args[i]` to a `long long` value:

  ```
  long long int_val;
  int_val = *((long long*) args->args[i]);
  ```

- For an argument of type `REAL_RESULT`, you must cast `args->args[i]` to a `double` value:

  ```
  double   real_val;
  real_val = *((double*) args->args[i]);
  ```

`unsigned long *lengths`

For the initialisation function, the `lengths` array indicates the maximum string length for each argument. You should not change these. For each invocation of the main function, `lengths` contains the actual lengths of any string arguments that are passed for the row currently being processed. For arguments of types `INT_RESULT` or `REAL_RESULT`, `lengths` still contains the maximum length of the argument (as for the initialisation function).

9.2.2.4 Return values and error handling

The initialisation function should return 0 if no error occurred and 1 otherwise. If an error occurs, `xxx_init()` should store a null-terminated error message in the `message` parameter. The message will be returned to the client. The message buffer is `MYSQL_ERRMSG_SIZE` characters long, but you should try to keep the message to less than 80 characters so that it fits the width of a standard terminal screen.

The return value of the main function `xxx()` is the function value, for `long long` and `double` functions. A string function should return a pointer to the result and store the length of the string in the `length` arguments.

Set these to the contents and length of the return value. For example:

```
memcpy(result, "result string", 13);
*length = 13;
```

The `result` buffer that is passed to the calc function is 255 bytes big. If your result fits in this, you don't have to worry about memory allocation for results.

If your string function needs to return a string longer than 255 bytes, you must allocate the space for it with `malloc()` in your `xxx_init()` function or your `xxx()` function and free it in your `xxx_deinit()` function. You can store the allocated memory in the `ptr` slot in the `UDF_INIT` structure for reuse by future `xxx()` calls. See Section 9.2.2.1, UDF calling sequences for simple functions.

To indicate a return value of `NULL` in the main function, set `is_null` to 1:

```
*is_null = 1;
```

To indicate an error return in the main function, set the `error` parameter to 1:

```
*error = 1;
```

If `xxx()` sets `*error` to 1 for any row, the function value is `NULL` for the current row and for any subsequent rows processed by the statement in which `XXX()` was invoked. (`xxx()` will not even be called for subsequent rows.) **Note**: in MySQL versions prior to 3.22.10, you should set both `*error` and `*is_null`:

```
*error = 1;
*is_null = 1;
```

9.2.2.5 Compiling and installing user-definable functions

Files implementing UDFs must be compiled and installed on the host where the server runs. This process is described here for the example UDF file udf_example.cc that is included in the MySQL source distribution. This file contains the following functions:

metaphon()

> Returns a metaphon string of the string argument. This is something like a soundex string, but it's more tuned for English.

myfunc_double()

> Returns the sum of the ASCII values of the characters in its arguments, divided by the sum of the length of its arguments.

myfunc_int()

> Returns the sum of the length of its arguments.

sequence([const int])

> Returns a sequence starting from the given number, or 1 if no number has been given.

lookup()

> Returns the IP number for a hostname.

reverse_lookup()

> Returns the hostname for an IP number. The function may be called with a string "xxx.xxx.xxx.xxx" or four numbers.

A dynamically loadable file should be compiled as a sharable object file, using a command something like this:

```
shell> gcc -shared -o udf_example.so myfunc.cc
```

You can easily find out the correct compiler options for your system by running this command in the sql directory of your MySQL source tree:

```
shell> make udf_example.o
```

You should run a compile command similar to the one that make displays, except that you should remove the -c option near the end of the line and add -o udf_example.so to the end of the line. (On some systems, you may need to leave the -c on the command.)

Once you compile a shared object containing UDFs, you must install it and tell MySQL about it. Compiling a shared object from udf_example.cc produces a file named something like udf_example.so (the exact name may vary from platform to platform). Copy this file to some directory searched by ld, such as /usr/lib. On many systems, you can set the LD_LIBRARY or LD_LIBRARY_PATH environment variable to point at the directory where you have your UDF function files. The `dlopen` manual page tells you which variable you should use on your system. You should set this in `mysql.server` or `safe_mysqld` and restart `mysqld`.

After the library is installed, notify `mysqld` about the new functions with these commands:

```
mysql> CREATE FUNCTION metaphon RETURNS STRING SONAME "udf_example.so";
mysql> CREATE FUNCTION myfunc_double RETURNS REAL SONAME "udf_example.so";
mysql> CREATE FUNCTION myfunc_int RETURNS INTEGER SONAME "udf_example.so";
mysql> CREATE FUNCTION lookup RETURNS STRING SONAME "udf_example.so";
mysql> CREATE FUNCTION reverse_lookup
    ->         RETURNS STRING SONAME "udf_example.so";
mysql> CREATE AGGREGATE FUNCTION avgcost
    ->         RETURNS REAL SONAME "udf_example.so";
```

Functions can be deleted using DROP FUNCTION:

```
mysql> DROP FUNCTION metaphon;
mysql> DROP FUNCTION myfunc_double;
mysql> DROP FUNCTION myfunc_int;
mysql> DROP FUNCTION lookup;
mysql> DROP FUNCTION reverse_lookup;
mysql> DROP FUNCTION avgcost;
```

The CREATE FUNCTION and DROP FUNCTION statements update the system table `func` in the `mysql` database. The function's name, type, and shared library name are saved in the table. You must have the **insert** and **delete** privileges for the `mysql` database to create and drop functions.

You should not use CREATE FUNCTION to add a function that has already been created. If you need to reinstall a function, you should remove it with DROP FUNCTION and then reinstall it with CREATE FUNCTION. You would need to do this, for example, if you recompile a new version of your function so that `mysqld` gets the new version. Otherwise, the server will continue to use the old version.

Active functions are reloaded each time the server starts, unless you start `mysqld` with the `--skip-grant-tables` option. In this case, UDF initialisation is skipped and UDFs are unavailable. (An active function is one that has been loaded with CREATE FUNCTION and not removed with DROP FUNCTION.)

9.2.3 Adding a New Native Function

The procedure for adding a new native function is described here. Note that you cannot add native functions to a binary distribution because the procedure involves modifying MySQL source code. You must compile MySQL yourself from a source distribution. Also note that if you migrate to another version of MySQL (for example, when a new version is released), you will need to repeat the procedure with the new version.

To add a new native MySQL function, follow these steps:

1. Add one line to `lex.h` that defines the function name in the `sql_functions[]` array.

2. If the function prototype is simple (just takes zero, one, two, or three arguments), you should in lex.h specify SYM(FUNC_ARG#) (where # is the number of arguments) as the second argument in the `sql_functions[]` array and add a function that creates a function object in `item_create.cc`. Take a look at "ABS" and `create_funcs_abs()` for an example of this.

    If the function prototype is complicated (for example, takes a variable number of arguments), you should add two lines to `sql_yacc.yy`. One indicates the preprocessor symbol that yacc should define (this should be added at the beginning of the file). Then define the function parameters and add an "item" with these parameters to the `simple_expr` parsing rule. For an example, check all occurrences of ATAN in `sql_yacc.yy` to see how this is done.

3. In `item_func.h`, declare a class inheriting from `Item_num_func` or `Item_str_func`, depending on whether your function returns a number or a string.

4. In `item_func.cc`, add one of the following declarations, depending on whether you are defining a numeric or string function:

    ```
    double   Item_func_newname::val()
    longlong Item_func_newname::val_int()
    String   *Item_func_newname::Str(String *str)
    ```

    If you inherit your object from any of the standard items (like `Item_num_func`) you probably only have to define one of the preceding functions and let the parent object take care of the other functions. For example, the `Item_str_func` class defines a `val()` function that executes `atof()` on the value returned by `::str()`.

5. You should probably also define the following object function:

    ```
    void Item_func_newname::fix_length_and_dec()
    ```

    This function should at least calculate `max_length` based on the given arguments. `max_length` is the maximum number of characters the function may return. This function should also set `maybe_null = 0` if the main function can't return a NULL value. The function can check if any of the function arguments can return NULL by checking the arguments `maybe_null` variable. You can take a look at `Item_func_mod::fix_length_and_dec` for a typical example of how to do this.

All functions must be thread-safe (in other words, don't use any global or static variables in the functions without protecting them with mutexes).

If you want to return NULL, from `::val()`, `::val_int()` or `::str()` you should set `null_value` to 1 and return 0.

For ::str() object functions, there are some additional considerations to be aware of:

- The String *str argument provides a string buffer that may be used to hold the result. (For more information about the String type, take a look at the sql_string.h file.)

- The ::str() function should return the string that holds the result or (char*) 0 if the result is NULL.

- All current string functions try to avoid allocating any memory unless absolutely necessary!

9.3 Adding New Procedures to MySQL

In MySQL, you can define a procedure in C++ that can access and modify the data in a query before it is sent to the client. The modification can be done on a row-by-row or GROUP BY level.

We have created an example procedure in MySQL Version 3.23 to show you what can be done.

Additionally, we recommend that you take a look at mylua. With this you can use the LUA language to load a procedure at runtime into mysqld.

9.3.1 Procedure Analyse

analyse([max elements,[max memory]])

This procedure is defined in the sql/sql_analyse.cc. This examines the result from your query and returns an analysis of the results:

- max elements (default 256) is the maximum number of distinct values analyse will notice per column. This is used by analyse to check if the optimal column type should be of type ENUM.

- max memory (default 8192) is the maximum memory analyse should allocate per column while trying to find all distinct values.

    SELECT ... FROM ... WHERE ... PROCEDURE ANALYSE([max elements,[max memory]])

9.3.2 Writing a Procedure

For the moment, the only documentation for this is the source.

You can find all information about procedures by examining the following files:

- `sql/sql_analyse.cc`
- `sql/procedure.h`
- `sql/procedure.cc`
- `sql/sql_select.cc`

A

Problems and Common Errors

This appendix lists some common problems and error messages that users have run into. You will learn how to figure out what the problem is, and what to do to solve it. You will also find proper solutions to some common problems.

A.1 How to Determine What Is Causing Problems

When you run into problems, the first thing you should do is find out which program/ piece of equipment is causing problems:

*   If you have one of the following symptoms, it is probably a hardware (like memory, motherboard, CPU, or hard disk) or kernel problem:

    — The keyboard doesn't work. This can normally be checked by pressing Caps Lock. If the Caps Lock light doesn't change you have to replace your keyboard. (Before doing this, you should try to reboot your computer and check all cables to the keyboard.)

    — The mouse pointer doesn't move.

    — The machine doesn't answer to a remote machine's pings.

    — Different, unrelated programs don't behave correctly.

    — If your system rebooted unexpectedly (a faulty user-level program should **never** be able to take down your system).

    In this case you should start by checking all your cables and run some diagnostic tool to check your hardware! You should also check if there are any patches, updates, or service packs for your operating system that could likely solve your problems.

Check also that all your libraries (like glibc) are up to date.

It's always good to use a machine with ECC memory to discover memory problems early!

- If your keyboard is locked up, you may be able to fix this by logging into your machine from another machine and execute kbd_mode -a on it.

- Please examine your system log file (/var/log/messages or similar) for reasons for your problems. If you think the problem is in MySQL, you should also examine MySQL's log files. See Section 4.9.3, The Update Log.

- If you don't think you have hardware problems, you should try to find out which program is causing problems.

  Try using top, ps, taskmanager, or some similar program to check which program is taking all CPU or is locking the machine.

- Check with top, df, or a similar program if you are out of memory, disk space, open files, or some other critical resource.

- If the problem is some runaway process, you can always try to kill it. If it doesn't want to die, there is probably a bug in the operating system.

If, after you have examined all other possibilities, you have concluded that it's the MySQL server or a MySQL client that is causing the problem, it's time to do a bug report for our mailing list or our support team. In the bug report, try to give a very detailed description of how the system is behaving and what you think is happening. You should also state why you think it's MySQL that is causing the problems. Take into consideration all the situations in this appendix. State any problems exactly how they appear when you examine your system. Use the "cut and paste" method for any output and/or error messages from programs and/or log files!

Try to describe in detail which program is not working and all symptoms you see! We have in the past received many bug reports that just state "the system doesn't work". This doesn't provide us with any information about what could be the problem.

If a program fails, it's always useful to know:

- Has the program in question made a segmentation fault (core dumped)?

- Is the program taking up the whole CPU? Check with top. Let the program run for a while. It may be evaluating something heavy.

- If it's the mysqld server that is causing problems, can you do mysqladmin -u root ping or mysqladmin -u root processlist?

- What does a client program say (try with mysql, for example) when you try to connect to the MySQL server? Does the client jam? Do you get any output from the program?

When sending a bug report, you should follow the outlines described in this manual. See Section 1.6.2.2, Asking questions or reporting bugs.

A.2 Common Errors When Using MySQL

This section lists some errors that users frequently get. You will find descriptions of the errors and how to solve the problems here.

A.2.1 `Access denied` **Error**

See Section 4.2.6, How the Privilege System Works, and especially, see Section 4.2.11, Causes of `Access denied` Errors.

A.2.2 `MySQL server has gone away` **Error**

This section also covers the related `Lost connection to server during query` error.

The most common reason for the `MySQL server has gone away` error is that the server timed out and closed the connection. By default, the server closes the connection after 8 hours if nothing has happened. You can change the time limit by setting the `wait_timeout` variable when you start `mysqld`.

Another common reason to receive the `MySQL server has gone away` error is because you have issued a "close" on your MySQL connection and then tried to run a query on the closed connection.

If you have a script, you just have to issue the query again for the client to do an automatic reconnection.

You normally can get the following error codes in this case (which one you get is OS-dependent):

Error code	Description
CR_SERVER_GONE_ERROR	The client couldn't send a question to the server.
CR_SERVER_LOST	The client didn't get an error when writing to the server, but it didn't get a full answer (or any answer) to the question.

You will also get this error if someone has kills the running thread with `kill #threadid#`.

You can check that MySQL hasn't died by executing `mysqladmin version` and examining the uptime. If the problem is that mysqld crashed you should concentrate one finding the reason for the crash. You should in this case start by checking if issuing the query again will kill MySQL again. See Section A.4.1, What to Do if MySQL Keeps Crashing.

You can also get these errors if you send a query to the server that is incorrect or too large. If `mysqld` gets a packet that is too large or out of order, it assumes that something has gone wrong with the client and closes the connection. If you need big queries (for example, if you are working with big `BLOB` columns), you can increase the query limit by starting `mysqld` with the `-O max_allowed_packet=#` option (default 1M). The extra memory is allocated on demand, so `mysqld` will use more memory only when you issue a big query or when `mysqld` must return a big result row!

If you want to make a bug report regarding this problem, be sure that you include the following information:

- Include information if MySQL died or not. (You can find this in the `hostname.err` file. See Section A.4.1, What to Do if MySQL Keeps Crashing.

- If a specific query kills `mysqld` and the involved tables where checked with `CHECK TABLE` before you did the query, can you do a test case for this? Section D.1.6, Making a Test Case When You Experience Table Corruption.

- What is the value of the `wait_timeout` variable in the MySQL server ? `mysqladmin variables` gives you the value of this

- Have you tried to run `mysqld` with `--log` and check if the issued query appears in the log ?

Section 1.6.2.2, Asking questions or reporting bugs.

A.2.3 Can't connect to [local] MySQL server Error

A MySQL client on Unix can connect to the `mysqld` server in two different ways: Unix sockets, which connect through a file in the file system (default `/tmp/mysqld.sock`) or TCP/IP, which connects through a port number. Unix sockets are faster than TCP/IP but can only be used when connecting to a server on the same computer. Unix sockets are used if you don't specify a hostname or if you specify the special hostname `localhost`.

On Windows, if the `mysqld` server is running on 9x/Me, you can connect only via TCP/IP. If the server is running on NT/2000/XP and mysqld is started with `--enable-named-pipe`, you can also connect with named pipes. The name of the named pipe is MySQL. If you don't give a hostname when connecting to `mysqld`, a MySQL client will first try to connect to the named pipe, and if this doesn't work it will connect to the TCP/IP port. You can force the use of named pipes on Windows by using `.` as the hostname.

The error (2002) `Can't connect to ...` normally means that there isn't a MySQL server running on the system or that you are using a wrong socket file or TCP/IP port when trying to connect to the `mysqld` server.

Start by checking (using `ps` or the task manager on Windows) that there is a process running named `mysqld` on your server! If there isn't any `mysqld` process, you should start one. See Section 2.4.2, Problems Starting the MySQL server.

If a `mysqld` process is running, you can check the server by trying these different connections (the port number and socket pathname might be different in your setup, of course):

```
shell> mysqladmin version
shell> mysqladmin variables
shell> mysqladmin -h 'hostname' version variables
shell> mysqladmin -h 'hostname' --port=3306 version
shell> mysqladmin -h 'ip for your host' version
shell> mysqladmin --socket=/tmp/mysql.sock version
```

Note the use of backquotes rather than forward quotes with the `hostname` command; these cause the output of `hostname` (that is, the current hostname) to be substituted into the `mysqladmin` command.

Here are some reasons the `Can't connect to local MySQL server` error might occur:

- `mysqld` is not running.

- You are running on a system that uses MIT-pthreads. If you are running on a system that doesn't have native threads, `mysqld` uses the MIT-pthreads package. See Section 2.2.2, Operating Systems Supported by MySQL. However, not all MIT-pthreads versions support Unix sockets. On a system without sockets support you must always specify the hostname explicitly when connecting to the server. Try using this command to check the connection to the server:

  ```
  shell> mysqladmin -h 'hostname' version
  ```

- Someone has removed the Unix socket that `mysqld` uses (default `/tmp/mysql.sock`). You might have a `cron` job that removes the MySQL socket (for example, a job that removes old files from the `/tmp` directory). You can always run `mysqladmin version` and check that the socket `mysqladmin` is trying to use really exists. The fix in this case is to change the `cron` job to not remove `mysqld.sock` or to place the socket somewhere else. See Section A.4.5, How to Protect or Change the MySQL Socket File `/tmp/mysql.sock`.

- You have started the `mysqld` server with the `--socket=/path/to/socket` option. If you change the socket pathname for the server, you must also notify the MySQL clients about the new path. You can do this by providing the socket path as an argument to the client. See Section A.4.5, How to Protect or Change the MySQL Socket File `/tmp/mysql.sock`.

- You are using Linux and one thread has died (core-dumped). In this case you must kill the other `mysqld` threads (for example, with the `mysql_zap` script) before you can start a new MySQL server. See Section A.4.1, What to Do if MySQL Keeps Crashing.

- You may not have read and write privilege to either the directory that holds the socket file or to the socket file itself. In this case you either change the privilege for the directory / file or restart `mysqld` so that it uses a directory that you can access.

If you get the error message `Can't connect to MySQL server on some_hostname`, you can try the following things to find out what the problem is:

- Check if the server is up by doing `telnet your-host-name tcp-ip-port-number` and press Enter a couple of times. If there is a MySQL server running on this port you should get a response that includes the version number of the running MySQL server. If you get an error like `telnet: Unable to connect to remote host: Connection refused`, there is no server running on the given port.

- Try connecting to the `mysqld` daemon on the local machine and check the TCP/IP port that `mysqld` is configured to use (variable `port`) with `mysqladmin variables`.

- Check that your `mysqld` server is not started with the `--skip-networking` option.

A.2.4 `Host '...'` is blocked **Error**

If you get an error like this:

```
Host 'hostname' is blocked because of many connection errors.
Unblock with 'mysqladmin flush-hosts'
```

this means that `mysqld` has gotten a lot (`max_connect_errors`) of connect requests from the host `'hostname'` that have been interrupted in the middle. After `max_connect_errors` failed requests, `mysqld` assumes that something is wrong (like an attack from a cracker), and blocks the site from further connections until someone executes the command `mysqladmin flush-hosts`.

By default, `mysqld` blocks a host after 10 connection errors. You can easily adjust this by starting the server like this:

```
shell> safe_mysqld -O max_connect_errors=10000 &
```

Note that if you get this error message for a given host, you should first check that there isn't anything wrong with the TCP/IP connections from that host. If your TCP/IP connections aren't working, it won't do you any good to increase the value of the `max_connect_errors` variable!

A.2.5 Too many connections **Error**

If you get the error Too many connections when you try to connect to MySQL, this means that there is already max_connections clients connected to the mysqld server.

If you need more connections than the default (100), you should restart mysqld with a bigger value for the max_connections variable.

Note that mysqld actually allows (max_connections+1) clients to connect. The last connection is reserved for a user with the **process** privilege. By not giving this privilege to normal users (they shouldn't need this), an administrator with this privilege can log in and use SHOW PROCESSLIST to find out what could be wrong. See Section 4.5.6, SHOW Syntax.

The maximum number of connects allowable to MySQL depends on how good the thread library is on a given platform. Linux or Solaris should be able to support 500-1000 simultaneous connections, depending on how much RAM you have and what your clients are doing.

A.2.6 Some non-transactional changed tables couldn't be rolled back **Error**

If you get the error/warning: Warning: Some non-transactional changed tables couldn't be rolled back when trying to do a ROLLBACK, this means that some of the tables you used in the transaction didn't support transactions. These non-transactional tables will not be affected by the ROLLBACK statement.

Typically, this happens when you have tried to create a table of a type that is not supported by your mysqld binary. If mysqld doesn't support a table type (or if the table type is disabled by a startup option), it will instead create the table type with the table type that most resembles the one you requested, probably MyISAM.

You can check the table type for a table by doing:

SHOW TABLE STATUS LIKE 'table_name'. See Section 4.5.6.2, SHOW TABLE STATUS.

You can check the extensions your mysqld binary supports by doing:

show variables like 'have_%'. See Section 4.5.6.4, SHOW VARIABLES.

A.2.7 Out of memory **Error**

If you issue a query and get something like the following error:

```
mysql: Out of memory at line 42, 'malloc.c'
mysql: needed 8136 byte (8k), memory in use: 12481367 bytes (12189k)
ERROR 2008: MySQL client ran out of memory
```

note that the error refers to the MySQL client `mysql`. The reason for this error is simply that the client does not have enough memory to store the whole result.

To remedy the problem, first check that your query is correct. Is it reasonable that it should return so many rows? If so, you can use `mysql --quick`, which uses `mysql_use_result()` to retrieve the result set. This places less of a load on the client (but more on the server).

A.2.8 Packet too large **Error**

When a MySQL client or the `mysqld` server gets a packet bigger than `max_allowed_packet` bytes, it issues a `Packet too large` error and closes the connection.

In MySQL 3.23 the biggest possible packet is 16M (due to limits in the client/server protocol). In MySQL 4.0.1 and up, this is only limited by the amount of memory you have on your server (up to a theoretical maximum of 2G).

A communication packet is a single SQL statement sent to the MySQL server or a single row that is sent to the client.

When a MySQL client or the `mysqld` server gets a packet bigger than `max_allowed_packet` bytes, it issues a `Packet too large` error and closes the connection. With some clients, you may also get `Lost connection to MySQL server during query` error if the communication packet is too big.

Note that both the client and the server have their own `max_allowed_packet` variable. If you want to handle big packets, you have to increase this variable both in the client and in the server.

It's safe to increase this variable as memory is only allocated when needed; this variable is more of a precaution to catch wrong packets between the client/server and also to ensure that you don't accidently use big packets so that you run out of memory.

If you are using the `mysql` client, you may specify a bigger buffer by starting the client with `mysql --set-variable=max_allowed_packet=8M`. Other clients have different methods to set this variable.

You can use the option file to set `max_allowed_packet` to a larger size in `mysqld`. For example, if you are expecting to store the full length of a `MEDIUMBLOB` into a table, you'll need to start the server with the `set-variable=max_allowed_packet=16M` option.

You can also get strange problems with large packets if you are using big blobs, but you haven't given `mysqld` access to enough memory to handle the query. If you suspect this is the case, try adding `ulimit -d 256000` to the beginning of the `safe_mysqld` script and restart `mysqld`.

A.2.9 Communication Error/ Aborted Connection

Starting with `MySQL 3.23.40` you only get the `Aborted connection` error if you start `mysqld` with `--warnings`.

If you find errors like the following in your error log (see Section 4.9.1, The Error Log):

```
010301 14:38:23  Aborted connection 854 to db: 'users' user: 'josh'
```

this means that one of the following has happened:

- The client program did not call `mysql_close()` before exit.
- The client had been sleeping more than `wait_timeout` or `interactive_timeout` without doing any requests. See Section 4.5.6.4, `SHOW VARIABLES`.
- The client program ended abruptly in the middle of the transfer.

When this happens, the server variable `Aborted_clients` is incremented.

The server variable `Aborted_connects` is incremented:

- When a connection packet doesn't contain the right information
- When the user didn't have privileges to connect to a database
- When a user uses a wrong password
- When it takes more than `connect_timeout` seconds to get a connect package

Note that this could indicate that someone is trying to break into your database!

See Section 4.5.6.4, `SHOW VARIABLES`.

Other reasons for problems with aborted clients/aborted connections.

- Usage of duplex Ethernet protocol, both half and full with Linux. Many Linux Ethernet drivers have this bug. You should test for this bug by transferring a huge file via ftp between these two machines. If a transfer goes in burst-pause-burst-pause ... mode, you are experiencing a Linux duplex syndrome. The only solution to this problem is switching both half and full duplexing on hubs and switches.
- Some problem with the thread library that causes interrupts on reads.
- Badly configured TCP/IP.
- Faulty Ethernets, hubs, switches, cables ... This can be diagnosed properly only by replacing hardware.

- `max_allowed_packet` is too small or queries require more memory than you have allocated for `mysqld`. See Section A.2.8, `Packet too large` Error.

A.2.10 The table is full **Error**

This error occurs in older MySQL versions when an in-memory temporary table becomes larger than `tmp_table_size` bytes. To avoid this problem, you can use the `-O tmp_table_size=#` option to `mysqld` to increase the temporary table size or use the SQL option `SQL_BIG_TABLES` before you issue the problematic query. See Section 5.5.6, `SET` Syntax.

You can also start `mysqld` with the `--big-tables` option. This is exactly the same as using `SQL_BIG_TABLES` for all queries.

In MySQL Version 3.23, in-memory temporary tables will automatically be converted to a disk-based `MyISAM` table after the table size gets bigger than `tmp_table_size`.

A.2.11 Can't create/write to file **Error**

If you get an error for some queries of type:

```
Can't create/write to file '\\sqla3fe_0.ism'.
```

this means that MySQL can't create a temporary file for the result set in the given temporary directory. (This error is a typical error message on Windows, and the Unix error message is similar.) The fix is to start `mysqld` with `--tmpdir=path` or to add to your option file:

```
[mysqld]
tmpdir=C:/temp
```

assuming that the `c:\\temp` directory exists. See Section 4.1.2, `my.cnf` Option Files.

Check also the error code that you get with `perror`. One reason may also be a disk-full error:

```
shell> perror 28
Error code  28:  No space left on device
```

A.2.12 Commands out of sync **Error in Client**

If you get `Commands out of sync; you can't run this command now` in your client code, you are calling client functions in the wrong order!

This can happen, for example, if you are using `mysql_use_result()` and try to execute a new query before you have called `mysql_free_result()`. It can also happen if you try to execute two queries that return data without a `mysql_use_result()` or `mysql_store_result()` in between.

A.2.13 Ignoring user **Error**

If you get the following error:

```
Found wrong password for user: 'some_user@some_host'; ignoring user
```

this means that when mysqld was started or when it reloaded the permissions tables, it found an entry in the user table with an invalid password. As a result, the entry is simply ignored by the permission system.

Possible causes of and fixes for this problem:

- You may be running a new version of mysqld with an old user table. You can check this by executing mysqlshow mysql user to see if the password field is shorter than 16 characters. If so, you can correct this condition by running the scripts/add_long_password script.

- The user has an old password (8 characters long) and you didn't start mysqld with the --old-protocol option. Update the user in the user table with a new password or restart mysqld with --old-protocol.

- You have specified a password in the user table without using the PASSWORD() function. Use mysql to update the user in the user table with a new password. Make sure to use the PASSWORD() function:

```
mysql> UPDATE user SET password=PASSWORD('your password')
    ->                 WHERE user='XXX';
```

A.2.14 Table 'xxx' doesn't exist **Error**

If you get the error Table 'xxx' doesn't exist or Can't find file: 'xxx' (errno: 2), this means that no table exists in the current database with the name xxx.

Note that as MySQL uses directories and files to store databases and tables, the database and table names are **case-sensitive**! (On Windows the databases and tables names are not case-sensitive, but all references to a given table within a query must use the same case!)

You can check which tables you have in the current database with SHOW TABLES. See Section 4.5.6, SHOW Syntax.

A.2.15 Can't initialize character set xxx **error**

If you get an error like:

```
MySQL Connection Failed: Can't initialize character set xxx
```

this means one of the following things:

- The character set is a multi-byte character set and you have no support for the character set in the client.

  In this case you need to recompile the client with `--with-charset=xxx` or with `--with-extra-charsets=xxx`. See Section 2.3.3, Typical `configure` Options.

  All standard MySQL binaries are compiled with `--with-extra-character-sets=complex`, which will enable support for all multi-byte character sets. See Section 4.6.1, The Character Set Used for Data and Sorting.

- The character set is a simple character set that is not compiled into `mysqld` and the character set definition files are not in the place where the client expects to find them.

  In this case you need to:

  — Recompile the client with support for the character set. See Section 2.3.3, Typical `configure` Options.

  — Specify to the client where the character set definition files are. For many clients you can do this with the `--character-sets-dir=path-to-charset-dir` option.

  — Copy the character definition files to the path where the client expects them to be.

A.2.16 File Not Found

If you get ERROR '...' not found (errno: 23), Can't open file: ... (errno: 24), or any other error with errno 23 or errno 24 from MySQL, it means that you haven't allocated enough file descriptors for MySQL. You can use the `perror` utility to get a description of what the error number means:

```
shell> perror 23
File table overflow
shell> perror 24
Too many open files
shell> perror 11
Resource temporarily unavailable
```

The problem here is that `mysqld` is trying to keep open too many files simultaneously. You can either tell `mysqld` not to open so many files at once, or increase the number of file descriptors available to `mysqld`.

To tell `mysqld` to keep open fewer files at a time, you can make the table cache smaller by using the `-O table_cache=32` option to `safe_mysqld` (the default value is 64). Reducing the value of `max_connections` will also reduce the number of open files (the default value is 90).

To change the number of file descriptors available to `mysqld`, you can use the option `--open-files-limit=#` to `safe_mysqld` or `-O open-files-limit=#` to `mysqld`.

See Section 4.5.6.4, SHOW VARIABLES. The easiest way to do that is to add the option to your option file. See Section 4.1.2, my.cnf Option Files. If you have an old mysqld version that doesn't support this, you can edit the safe_mysqld script. There is a commented-out line ulimit -n 256 in the script. You can remove the '#' character to uncomment this line, and change the number 256 to affect the number of file descriptors available to mysqld.

ulimit (and open-files-limit) can increase the number of file descriptors, but only up to the limit imposed by the operating system. There is also a "hard" limit that can only be overridden if you start safe_mysqld or mysqld as root (just remember that you need to also use the --user=... option in this case). If you need to increase the OS limit on the number of file descriptors available to each process, consult the documentation for your operating system.

Note that if you run the tcsh shell, ulimit will not work! tcsh will also report incorrect values when you ask for the current limits! In this case you should start safe_mysqld with sh!

A.3 Installation-Related Issues

A.3.1 Problems When Linking with the MySQL Client Library

If you are linking your program and you get errors for unreferenced symbols that start with mysql_, like the following:

```
/tmp/ccFKsdPa.o: In function 'main':
/tmp/ccFKsdPa.o(.text+0xb): undefined reference to 'mysql_init'
/tmp/ccFKsdPa.o(.text+0x31): undefined reference to 'mysql_real_connect'
/tmp/ccFKsdPa.o(.text+0x57): undefined reference to 'mysql_real_connect'
/tmp/ccFKsdPa.o(.text+0x69): undefined reference to 'mysql_error'
/tmp/ccFKsdPa.o(.text+0x9a): undefined reference to 'mysql_close'
```

you should be able to solve this by adding -Lpath-to-the-mysql-library -lmysqlclient **last** on your link line.

If you get undefined reference errors for the uncompress or compress function, add -lz **last** on your link line and try again!

If you get undefined reference errors for functions that should exist on your system, like connect, check the manpage for the function in question for which libraries you should add to the link line!

If you get undefined reference errors for functions that don't exist on your system, like the following:

```
mf_format.o(.text+0x201): undefined reference to '__lxstat'
```

it usually means that your library is compiled on a system that is not 100% compatible with yours. In this case you should download the latest MySQL source distribution and compile this yourself. See Section 2.3, Installing a MySQL Source Distribution.

If you are trying to run a program and you then get errors for unreferenced symbols that start with mysql_ or that the mysqlclient library can't be found, this means that your system can't find the share libmysqlclient.so library.

The fix for this is to tell your system to search after shared libraries where the library is located by one of the following methods:

- Add the path to the directory where you have libmysqlclient.so to the LD_LIBRARY_PATH environment variable.

- Add the path to the directory where you have libmysqlclient.so to the LD_LIBRARY environment variable.

- Copy libmysqlclient.so to some place that is searched by your system, like /lib, and update the shared library information by executing ldconfig.

Another way to solve this problem is to link your program statically, with -static, or by removing the dynamic MySQL libraries before linking your code. In the second case you should be sure that no other programs are using the dynamic libraries!

A.3.2 How to Run MySQL as a Normal User

The MySQL server mysqld can be started and run by any user. In order to change mysqld to run as a Unix user user_name, you must do the following:

1. Stop the server if it's running (use mysqladmin shutdown).

2. Change the database directories and files so that user_name has privileges to read and write files in them (you may need to do this as the Unix root user):

```
shell> chown -R user_name /path/to/mysql/datadir
```

   If directories or files within the MySQL data directory are symlinks, you'll also need to follow those links and change the directories and files they point to. chown -R may not follow symlinks for you.

3. Start the server as user user_name, or if you are using MySQL Version 3.22 or later, start mysqld as the Unix root user and use the --user=user_name option. mysqld will switch to run as the Unix user user_name before accepting any connections.

4. To start the server as the given username automatically at system startup time, add a
    user line that specifies the username to the [mysqld] group of the /etc/my.cnf
    option file or the my.cnf option file in the server's data directory. For example:

```
[mysqld]
user=user_name
```

At this point, your mysqld process should be running fine and dandy as the Unix user
user_name. One thing hasn't changed, though: the contents of the permissions tables. By
default (right after running the permissions table install script mysql_install_db), the
MySQL user root is the only user with permission to access the mysql database or to
create or drop databases. Unless you have changed those permissions, they still hold. This
shouldn't stop you from accessing MySQL as the MySQL root user when you're logged
in as a Unix user other than root; just specify the -u root option to the client program.

Note that accessing MySQL as root, by supplying -u root on the command-line, has
nothing to do with MySQL running as the Unix root user or, indeed, as another Unix
user. The access permissions and usernames of MySQL are completely separate from
Unix usernames. The only connection with Unix usernames is that if you don't provide a
-u option when you invoke a client program, the client will try to connect using your
Unix login name as your MySQL user name.

If your Unix box itself isn't secured, you should probably at least put a password on the
MySQL root users in the access tables. Otherwise, any user with an account on that
machine can run mysql -u root db_name and do whatever he likes.

A.3.3 Problems with File Permissions

If you have problems with file permissions—for example, if mysql issues the following
error message when you create a table:

```
ERROR: Can't find file: 'path/with/filename.frm' (Errcode: 13)
```

the environment variable UMASK might be set incorrectly when mysqld starts up. The
default umask value is 0660. You can change this behavior by starting safe_mysqld as
follows:

```
shell> UMASK=384  # = 600 in octal
shell> export UMASK
shell> /path/to/safe_mysqld &
```

By default MySQL will create database and RAID directories with permission type 0700.
You can modify this behavior by setting the UMASK_DIR variable. If you set this, new
directories are created with the combined UMASK and UMASK_DIR. For example, if you
want to give group access to all new directories, you can do:

```
shell> UMASK_DIR=504  # = 770 in octal
shell> export UMASK_DIR
shell> /path/to/safe_mysqld &
```

In MySQL Versions 3.23.25 and above, MySQL assumes that the value for UMASK and UMASK_DIR is in octal if it starts with a zero.

See Appendix E.

A.4 Administration-Related Issues

A.4.1 What to Do if MySQL Keeps Crashing

All MySQL versions are tested on many platforms before they are released. This doesn't mean that there aren't any bugs in MySQL, but it means if there are bugs, there are very few and they can be hard to find. If you have a problem, it will always help if you try to find out exactly what crashes your system, as you will have a much better chance of getting this fixed quickly.

First, you should try to find out whether the problem is that the mysqld daemon dies or whether your problem has to do with your client. You can check how long your mysqld server has been up by executing mysqladmin version. If mysqld has died, you may find the reason for this in the file mysql-data-directory/'hostname'.err. See Section 4.9.1, The Error Log.

Many crashes of MySQL are caused by corrupted index/data files. MySQL will update the data on disk, with the write() system call, after every SQL statement and before the client is notified about the result. (This is not true if you are running with delay_key_write, in which case only the data is written.) This means that the data is safe even if mysqld crashes, as the OS will ensure that the not-flushed data is written to disk. You can force MySQL to sync everything to disk after every SQL command by starting mysqld with --flush.

This means that normally you shouldn't get corrupted tables unless:

* Someone/something killed mysqld or the machine in the middle of an update.

* You have found a bug in mysqld that caused it to die in the middle of an update.

* Someone is manipulating the data/index files outside of **mysqld** without locking the table properly.

* You are running many mysqld servers on the same data on a system that doesn't support good filesystem locks (normally handled by the lockd daemon) or you are running multiple servers with --skip-locking.

* You have a crashed index/data file that contains very wrong data that got mysqld confused.

- You have found a bug in the data storage code. This isn't that likely, but it's at least possible. In this case you can try to change the file type to another database handler by using ALTER TABLE on a repaired copy of the table!

Because it is very difficult to know why something is crashing, first try to check whether things that work for others crash for you. Please try the following things:

- Take down the mysqld daemon with mysqladmin shutdown, run myisamchk --silent --force */*.MYI on all tables, and restart the mysqld daemon. This will ensure that you are running from a clean state. See Chapter 4.

- Use mysqld --log and try to determine from the information in the log whether some specific query kills the server. About 95% of all bugs are related to a particular query! Normally this is one of the last queries in the log file just before MySQL restarted. See Section 4.9.2, The General Query Log. If you can repeatedly kill MySQL with one of the queries, even when you have checked all tables just before doing the query, you have been able to locate the bug and should do a bug report for this! See Section 1.6.2.3, How to report bugs or problems.

- Try to make a test case that we can use to reproduce the problem. See Section D.1.6, Making a Test Case When You Experience Table Corruption.

- Try running the included mysql-test test and the MySQL benchmarks. See Section 9.1.2, MySQL Test Suite. They should test MySQL rather well. You can also add code to the benchmarks to simulate your application! The benchmarks can be found in the bench directory in the source distribution or, for a binary distribution, in the sql-bench directory under your MySQL installation directory.

- Try fork_test.pl and fork2_test.pl.

- If you configure MySQL for debugging, it will be much easier to gather information about possible errors if something goes wrong. Reconfigure MySQL with the --with-debug option or --with-debug=full to configure and then recompile. See Section D.1, Debugging a MySQL Server.

- Configuring MySQL for debugging causes a safe memory allocator to be included that can find some errors. It also provides a lot of output about what is happening.

- Have you applied the latest patches for your operating system?

- Use the --skip-locking option to mysqld. On some systems, the lockd lock manager does not work properly; the --skip-locking option tells mysqld not to use external locking. (This means that you cannot run 2 mysqld servers on the same data and that you must be careful if you use myisamchk, but it may be instructive to try the option as a test.)

- Have you tried mysqladmin -u root processlist when mysqld appears to be running but not responding? Sometimes mysqld is not comatose even though you might think so. The problem may be that all connections are in use, or there may be some internal lock problem. `mysqladmin processlist` will usually be able to make a connection even in these cases, and can provide useful information about the current number of connections and their status.

- Run the command `mysqladmin -i 5 status`, or `mysqladmin -i 5 -r status` or in a separate window, to produce statistics while you run your other queries.

- Try the following:

    1. Start `mysqld` from `gdb` (or in another debugger). See Section D.1.3, Debugging `mysqld` under `gdb`.

    2. Run your test scripts.

    3. Print the backtrace and the local variables at the 3 lowest levels. In gdb you can do this with the following commands when `mysqld` has crashed inside gdb:

        ```
        backtrace
        info local
        up
        info local
        up
        info local
        ```

    With gdb you can also examine which threads exist with `info threads` and switch to a specific thread with `thread #`, where # is the thread id.

- Try to simulate your application with a Perl script to force MySQL to crash or misbehave.

- Send a normal bug report. See Section 1.6.2.3, How to report bugs or problems. Be even more detailed than usual. Because MySQL works for many people, it may be that the crash results from something that exists only on your computer (for example, an error that is related to your particular system libraries).

- If you have a problem with tables with dynamic-length rows and you are not using BLOB/TEXT columns (but only VARCHAR columns), you can try to change all VARCHAR to CHAR with ALTER TABLE. This will force MySQL to use fixed-size rows. Fixed-size rows take a little extra space, but are much more tolerant to corruption!

    The current dynamic row code has been in use at MySQL AB for at least 3 years without any problems, but by nature dynamic-length rows are more prone to errors, so it may be a good idea to try the preceding tests to see if they help!

A.4.2 How to Reset a Forgotten Password

If you have forgotten the `root` user password for MySQL, you can restore it with the following procedure:

1. Take down the mysqld server by sending a kill (not kill -9) to the mysqld server. The pid is stored in a .pid file, which is normally in the MySQL database directory:

   ```
   kill `cat /mysql-data-directory/hostname.pid`
   ```

   You must be either the Unix root user or the same user the server runs as to do this.

2. Restart mysqld with the --skip-grant-tables option.

3. Connect to the mysqld server with mysql -h hostname mysql and change the password with a GRANT command. See Section 4.3.1, GRANT and REVOKE Syntax. You can also do this with mysqladmin -h hostname -u user password 'new password'.

4. Load the privilege tables with mysqladmin -h hostname flush-privileges or with the SQL command FLUSH PRIVILEGES.

Note that after you started mysqld with --skip-grant-tables, any usage of GRANT commands will give you an Unknown command error until you have executed FLUSH PRIVILEGES.

A.4.3 How MySQL Handles a Full Disk

When a disk-full condition occurs, MySQL does the following:

* It checks once every minute to see whether there is enough space to write the current row. If there is enough space, it continues as if nothing had happened.

* Every 6 minutes it writes an entry to the log file warning about the disk-full condition.

To alleviate the problem, you can take the following actions:

* To continue, you only have to free enough disk space to insert all records.

* To abort the thread, you must send a mysqladmin kill to the thread. The thread will be aborted the next time it checks the disk (in 1 minute).

* Note that other threads may be waiting for the table that caused the disk-full condition. If you have several "locked" threads, killing the one thread that is waiting on the disk-full condition will allow the other threads to continue.

Exceptions to this behaviour is when you use REPAIR or OPTIMIZE, or when the indexes are created in a batch after a LOAD DATA INFILE or after an ALTER TABLE statement.

All of these commands may use big temporary files, which left to themselves would cause big problems for the rest of the system. If MySQL gets a disk-full condition while doing any of the preceding operations, it will remove the big temporary files and mark the table as crashed (except for ALTER TABLE, in which case the old table will be left unchanged).

A.4.4 Where MySQL Stores Temporary Files

MySQL uses the value of the TMPDIR environment variable as the pathname of the directory in which to store temporary files. If you don't have TMPDIR set, MySQL uses the system default, which is normally /tmp or /usr/tmp. If the filesystem containing your temporary file directory is too small, you should edit safe_mysqld to set TMPDIR to point to a directory in a filesystem where you have enough space! You can also set the temporary directory using the --tmpdir option to mysqld.

MySQL creates all temporary files as hidden files. This ensures that the temporary files will be removed if mysqld is terminated. The disadvantage of using hidden files is that you will not see a big temporary file that fills up the filesystem in which the temporary file directory is located.

When sorting (ORDER BY or GROUP BY), MySQL normally uses one or two temporary files. The maximum disk space needed is:

```
(length of what is sorted + sizeof(database pointer))
  * number of matched rows
  * 2
```

sizeof(database pointer) is usually 4, but may grow in the future for really big tables.

For some SELECT queries, MySQL also creates temporary SQL tables. These are not hidden and have names of the form SQL_*.

ALTER TABLE creates a temporary table in the same directory as the original table.

A.4.5 How to Protect or Change the MySQL Socket File /tmp/mysql.sock

If you have problems with the fact that anyone can delete the MySQL communication socket /tmp/mysql.sock, you can, on most versions of Unix, protect your /tmp filesystem by setting the sticky bit on it. Log in as root and do the following:

```
shell> chmod +t /tmp
```

This will protect your /tmp filesystem so that files can be deleted only by their owners or the superuser (root).

You can check if the sticky bit is set by executing ls -ld /tmp. If the last permission bit is t, the bit is set.

You can change the place where MySQL uses/puts the socket file in the following ways:

- Specify the path in a global or local option file. For example, put in /etc/my.cnf:

```
[client]
socket=path-for-socket-file

[mysqld]
socket=path-for-socket-file
```

See Section 4.1.2, `my.cnf` Option Files.

- Specify the path on the command line to `safe_mysqld` and most clients with the `--socket=path-for-socket-file` option.

- Specify the path to the socket in the `MYSQL_UNIX_PORT` environment variable.

- Define the path with the `configure` option `--with-unix-socket-path=path-for-socket-file`. See Section 2.3.3, Typical `configure` Options.

You can test that the socket works with this command:

```
shell> mysqladmin --socket=/path/to/socket version
```

A.4.6   Time Zone Problems

If you have a problem with `SELECT NOW()` returning values in GMT and not your local time, you have to set the `TZ` environment variable to your current time zone. This should be done for the environment in which the server runs—for example, in `safe_mysqld` or `mysql.server`. See Appendix E.

A.5   Query-Related Issues

A.5.1   Case Sensitivity in Searches

By default, MySQL searches are case-insensitive (although there are some character sets that are never case-insensitive, such as `czech`). That means that if you search with `col_name LIKE 'a%'`, you will get all column values that start with A or a. If you want to make this search case-sensitive, use something like `INSTR(col_name, "A")=1` to check a prefix. Or use `STRCMP(col_name, "A") = 0` if the column value must be exactly `"A"`.

Simple comparison operations (>=, >, = , < , <=, sorting, and grouping) are based on each character's "sort value". Characters with the same sort value (like E, e, and é) are treated as the same character!

In older MySQL versions `LIKE` comparisons where done on the uppercase value of each character (E == e but E <> é). In newer MySQL versions `LIKE` works just like the other comparison operators.

If you want a column always to be treated in case-sensitive fashion, declare it as `BINARY`. See Section 6.5.3, `CREATE TABLE` Syntax.

If you are using Chinese data in the so-called big5 encoding, you want to make all character columns BINARY. This works because the sorting order of big5 encoding characters is based on the order of ASCII codes.

A.5.2 Problems Using DATE Columns

The format of a DATE value is 'YYYY-MM-DD'. According to ANSI SQL, no other format is allowed. You should use this format in UPDATE expressions and in the WHERE clause of SELECT statements. For example:

```
mysql> SELECT * FROM tbl_name WHERE date >= '1997-05-05';
```

As a convenience, MySQL automatically converts a date to a number if the date is used in a numeric context (and vice versa). It is also smart enough to allow a "relaxed" string form when updating and in a WHERE clause that compares a date to a TIMESTAMP, DATE, or DATETIME column. (Relaxed form means that any punctuation character may be used as the separator between parts. For example, '1998-08-15' and '1998#08#15' are equivalent.) MySQL can also convert a string containing no separators (such as '19980815'), provided it makes sense as a date.

The special date '0000-00-00' can be stored and retrieved as '0000-00-00'. When using a '0000-00-00' date through MyODBC, it will automatically be converted to NULL in MyODBC Versions 2.50.12 and above because ODBC can't handle this kind of date.

Because MySQL performs these conversions, the following statements work:

```
mysql> INSERT INTO tbl_name (idate) VALUES (19970505);
mysql> INSERT INTO tbl_name (idate) VALUES ('19970505');
mysql> INSERT INTO tbl_name (idate) VALUES ('97-05-05');
mysql> INSERT INTO tbl_name (idate) VALUES ('1997.05.05');
mysql> INSERT INTO tbl_name (idate) VALUES ('1997 05 05');
mysql> INSERT INTO tbl_name (idate) VALUES ('0000-00-00');

mysql> SELECT idate FROM tbl_name WHERE idate >= '1997-05-05';
mysql> SELECT idate FROM tbl_name WHERE idate >= 19970505;
mysql> SELECT MOD(idate,100) FROM tbl_name WHERE idate >= 19970505;
mysql> SELECT idate FROM tbl_name WHERE idate >= '19970505';
```

However, the following will not work:

```
mysql> SELECT idate FROM tbl_name WHERE STRCMP(idate,'19970505')=0;
```

STRCMP() is a string function, so it converts idate to a string and performs a string comparison. It does not convert '19970505' to a date and perform a date comparison.

Note that MySQL does not check whether the date is correct. If you store an incorrect date, such as '1998-2-31', the wrong date will be stored. If the date cannot be converted to any reasonable value, a 0 is stored in the DATE field. This is mainly a speed issue and we think it is up to the application to check the dates, not the server.

A.5.3 Problems with NULL Values

The concept of the NULL value is a common source of confusion for newcomers to SQL, who often think that NULL is the same thing as an empty string `""`. This is not the case! For example, the following statements are completely different:

```
mysql> INSERT INTO my_table (phone) VALUES (NULL);
mysql> INSERT INTO my_table (phone) VALUES ("");
```

Both statements insert a value into the phone column, but the first inserts a NULL value and the second inserts an empty string. The meaning of the first can be regarded as "phone number is not known" and the meaning of the second can be regarded as "she has no phone".

In SQL, the NULL value is always false in comparison to any other value, even NULL. An expression that contains NULL always produces a NULL value unless otherwise indicated in the documentation for the operators and functions involved in the expression. All columns in the following example return NULL:

```
mysql> SELECT NULL,1+NULL,CONCAT('Invisible',NULL);
```

If you want to search for column values that are NULL, you cannot use the =NULL test. The following statement returns no rows because expr = NULL is FALSE, for any expression:

```
mysql> SELECT * FROM my_table WHERE phone = NULL;
```

To look for NULL values, you must use the IS NULL test. The following shows how to find the NULL phone number and the empty phone number:

```
mysql> SELECT * FROM my_table WHERE phone IS NULL;
mysql> SELECT * FROM my_table WHERE phone = "";
```

In MySQL, as in many other SQL servers, you can't index columns that can have NULL values. You must declare such columns NOT NULL. Conversely, you cannot insert NULL into an indexed column.

When reading data with LOAD DATA INFILE, empty columns are updated with `""`. If you want a NULL value in a column, you should use \N in the text file. The literal word 'NULL' may also be used under some circumstances. See Section 6.4.9, LOAD DATA INFILE Syntax.

When using ORDER BY, NULL values are presented first. If you sort in descending order using DESC, NULL values are presented last. When using GROUP BY, all NULL values are regarded as equal.

To help with NULL handling, you can use the IS NULL and IS NOT NULL operators and the IFNULL() function.

For some column types, NULL values are handled specially. If you insert NULL into the first TIMESTAMP column of a table, the current date and time are inserted. If you insert NULL into an AUTO_INCREMENT column, the next number in the sequence is inserted.

A.5.4 Problems with `alias`

You can use an alias to refer to a column in the GROUP BY, ORDER BY, or HAVING part. Aliases can also be used to give columns better names:

```
SELECT SQRT(a*b) as rt FROM table_name GROUP BY rt HAVING rt > 0;
SELECT id,COUNT(*) AS cnt FROM table_name GROUP BY id HAVING cnt > 0;
SELECT id AS "Customer identity" FROM table_name;
```

Note that ANSI SQL doesn't allow you to refer to an alias in a WHERE clause. This is because when the WHERE code is executed the column value may not yet be determined. For example, the following query is **illegal**:

```
SELECT id,COUNT(*) AS cnt FROM table_name WHERE cnt > 0 GROUP BY id;
```

The WHERE statement is executed to determine which rows should be included in the GROUP BY part while HAVING is used to decide which rows from the result set should be used.

A.5.5 Deleting Rows from Related Tables

As MySQL doesn't support sub-selects or use of more than one table in the DELETE statement, you should use the following approach to delete rows from 2 related tables:

1. SELECT the rows based on some WHERE condition in the main table.

2. DELETE the rows in the main table based on the same condition.

3. DELETE   FROM   related_table   WHERE   related_column   IN
    (selected_rows).

If the total number of characters in the query with related_column is more than 1,048,576 (the default value of max_allowed_packet), you should split it into smaller parts and execute multiple DELETE statements. You will probably get the fastest DELETE by only deleting 100-1000 related_column id's per query if the related_column is an index. If the related_column isn't an index, the speed is independent of the number of arguments in the IN clause.

A.5.6 Solving Problems with No Matching Rows

If you have a complicated query that has many tables and that doesn't return any rows, you should use the following procedure to find out what is wrong with your query:

1. Test the query with EXPLAIN and check if you can find something that is obviously wrong. See Section 5.2.1, EXPLAIN Syntax (Get Information About a SELECT).

2. Select only those fields that are used in the WHERE clause.

3. Remove one table at a time from the query until it returns some rows. If the tables are big, it's a good idea to use LIMIT 10 with the query.

4. Do a SELECT for the column that should have matched a row against the table that was last removed from the query.

5. If you are comparing FLOAT or DOUBLE columns with numbers that have decimals, you can't use '='. This problem is common in most computer languages because floating-point values are not exact values. In most cases, changing the FLOAT to a DOUBLE will fix this. See Section A.5.7, Problems with Floating-Point Comparison.

6. If you still can't figure out what's wrong, create a minimal test that can be run with mysql test < query.sql that shows your problems. You can create a test file with mysqldump --quick database tables > query.sql. Open the file in an editor, remove some insert lines (if there are too many of these), and add your select statement at the end of the file.

   Test that you still have your problem by doing:

   ```
   shell> mysqladmin create test2
   shell> mysql test2 < query.sql
   ```

   Post the test file using mysqlbug to *mysql@lists.mysql.com*.

A.5.7 Problems with Floating-Point Comparison

Floating-point numbers cause confusion sometimes because these numbers are not stored as exact values inside computer architecture. What one can see on the screen usually is not the exact value of the number.

Field types FLOAT, DOUBLE, and DECIMAL are such:

```
CREATE TABLE t1 (i INT, d1 DECIMAL(9,2), d2 DECIMAL(9,2));
INSERT INTO t1 VALUES (1, 101.40, 21.40), (1, -80.00, 0.00),
(2, 0.00, 0.00), (2, -13.20, 0.00), (2, 59.60, 46.40),
(2, 30.40, 30.40), (3, 37.00, 7.40), (3, -29.60, 0.00),
(4, 60.00, 15.40), (4, -10.60, 0.00), (4, -34.00, 0.00),
(5, 33.00, 0.00), (5, -25.80, 0.00), (5, 0.00, 7.20),
(6, 0.00, 0.00), (6, -51.40, 0.00);

mysql> SELECT i, SUM(d1) AS a, SUM(d2) AS b
    -> FROM t1 GROUP BY i HAVING a <> b;
```

```
+------+--------+-------+
| i    | a      | b     |
+------+--------+-------+
|    1 |  21.40 | 21.40 |
|    2 |  76.80 | 76.80 |
|    3 |   7.40 |  7.40 |
|    4 |  15.40 | 15.40 |
|    5 |   7.20 |  7.20 |
|    6 | -51.40 |  0.00 |
+------+--------+-------+
```

The result is correct. Although the first five records look like they shouldn't pass the comparison test, they may do so because the difference between the numbers shows up around the tenth decimal or so, depending on the computer's architecture.

The problem cannot be solved by using ROUND() (or a similar function) because the result is still a floating-point number. Example:

```
mysql> SELECT i, ROUND(SUM(d1), 2) AS a, ROUND(SUM(d2), 2) AS b
    -> FROM t1 GROUP BY i HAVING a <> b;
+------+--------+-------+
| i    | a      | b     |
+------+--------+-------+
|    1 |  21.40 | 21.40 |
|    2 |  76.80 | 76.80 |
|    3 |   7.40 |  7.40 |
|    4 |  15.40 | 15.40 |
|    5 |   7.20 |  7.20 |
|    6 | -51.40 |  0.00 |
+------+--------+-------+
```

This is what the numbers in row 'a' look like:

```
mysql> SELECT i, ROUND(SUM(d1), 2)*1.0000000000000000 AS a,
    -> ROUND(SUM(d2), 2) AS b FROM t1 GROUP BY i HAVING a <> b;
+------+---------------------+-------+
| i    | a                   | b     |
+------+---------------------+-------+
|    1 |  21.3999999999999986 | 21.40 |
|    2 |  76.7999999999999972 | 76.80 |
|    3 |   7.4000000000000004 |  7.40 |
|    4 |  15.4000000000000004 | 15.40 |
|    5 |   7.2000000000000002 |  7.20 |
|    6 | -51.3999999999999986 |  0.00 |
+------+---------------------+-------+
```

Depending on the computer architecture you may or may not see similar results. Each CPU may evaluate floating-point numbers differently. For example, in some machines you may get 'right' results by multiplying both arguments by 1, an example follows.

WARNING: NEVER TRUST THIS METHOD IN YOUR APPLICATION. THIS IS AN EXAMPLE OF A WRONG METHOD!!!

```
mysql> SELECT i, ROUND(SUM(d1), 2)*1 AS a, ROUND(SUM(d2), 2)*1 AS b
    -> FROM t1 GROUP BY i HAVING a <> b;
+------+--------+------+
| i    | a      | b    |
+------+--------+------+
|    6 | -51.40 | 0.00 |
+------+--------+------+
```

The reason this example seems to be working is that on the particular machine where the test was done, the CPU floating-point arithmetics happens to round the numbers to be the same, but there is no rule that any CPU should do so, so it cannot be trusted.

The correct way to do floating-point number comparison is to first decide on what is the wanted tolerance between the numbers and then do the comparison against the tolerance number. For example, if we agree that floating-point numbers should be regarded as equal, if they are same in the precision of one in ten thousand (0.0001), the comparsion should be done like this:

```
mysql> SELECT i, SUM(d1) AS a, SUM(d2) AS b FROM t1
    -> GROUP BY i HAVING ABS(a - b) > 0.0001;
+------+--------+------+
| i    | a      | b    |
+------+--------+------+
|    6 | -51.40 | 0.00 |
+------+--------+------+
1 row in set (0.00 sec)
```

And vice versa—if we wanted to get rows where the numbers are the same, the test would be:

```
mysql> SELECT i, SUM(d1) AS a, SUM(d2) AS b FROM t1
    -> GROUP BY i HAVING ABS(a - b) < 0.0001;
+------+--------+--------+
| i    | a      | b      |
+------+--------+--------+
|    1 |  21.40 |  21.40 |
|    2 |  76.80 |  76.80 |
|    3 |   7.40 |   7.40 |
|    4 |  15.40 |  15.40 |
|    5 |   7.20 |   7.20 |
+------+--------+--------+
```

A.6 Table Definition-Related Issues

A.6.1 Problems with ALTER TABLE

ALTER TABLE changes a table to the current character set. If get a duplicate key error during ALTER TABLE, the cause is either that the new character sets map to keys to the same value or that the table is corrupted, in which case you should run REPAIR TABLE on the table.

If `ALTER TABLE` dies with an error like this:

```
Error on rename of './database/name.frm' to './database/B-a.frm' (Errcode: 17)
```

the problem may be that MySQL has crashed in a previous `ALTER TABLE` and there is an old table named A–something or B–something lying around. In this case, go to the MySQL data directory and delete all files that have names starting with A– or B–. (You may want to move them elsewhere instead of deleting them.)

`ALTER TABLE` works the following way:

- Create a new table named A–xxx with the requested changes.

- All rows from the old table are copied to A–xxx.

- The old table is renamed B–xxx.

- A–xxx is renamed to your old table name.

- B–xxx is deleted.

If something goes wrong with the renaming operation, MySQL tries to undo the changes. If something goes seriously wrong (this shouldn't happen, of course), MySQL may leave the old table as B–xxx, but a simple rename on the system level should get your data back.

A.6.2 How to Change the Order of Columns in a Table

The whole point of SQL is to abstract the application from the data storage format. You should always specify the order in which you wish to retrieve your data. For example:

```
SELECT col_name1, col_name2, col_name3 FROM tbl_name;
```

will return columns in the order col_name1, col_name2, col_name3, whereas:

```
SELECT col_name1, col_name3, col_name2 FROM tbl_name;
```

will return columns in the order col_name1, col_name3, col_name2.

You should **never**, in an application, use `SELECT *` and retrieve the columns based on their position because the order in which columns are returned **cannot** be guaranteed over time. A simple change to your database may cause your application to fail rather dramatically.

If you want to change the order of columns anyway, you can do so as follows:

1. Create a new table with the columns in the right order.

2. Execute `INSERT INTO new_table SELECT fields-in-new_table-order FROM old_table`.

3. Drop or rename `old_table`.

4. `ALTER TABLE new_table RENAME old_table`.

A.6.3 TEMPORARY TABLES Problems

The following are a list of the limitations with `TEMPORARY TABLES`.

* A temporary table can only be of type `HEAP`, `ISAM`, `MyISAM` or `InnoDB`.

* You can't use temporary tables more than once in the same query. For example, the following doesn't work:

    ```
    mysql> SELECT * FROM temporary_table, temporary_table AS t2;
    ```

    We plan to fix this in 4.0.

* You can't use `RENAME` on a `TEMPORARY` table. Note that `ALTER TABLE org_name RENAME new_name` works!

    We plan to fix this in 4.0.

Contributed Programs

Many users of MySQL have contributed *very* useful support tools and add-ons.

A list of what is available at http://www.mysql.com/Downloads/Contrib/ (or any mirror) is shown in the next section.

Please visit our Software Portal at http://www.mysql.com/portal/software/. The community facilities there also allow for your input!

If you want to build MySQL support for the Perl DBI/DBD interface, you should fetch the Data-Dumper, DBI, and Msql-Mysql-modules files and install them. See Section 2.7, Perl Installation Comments.

Note: the programs listed here can be freely downloaded and used. They are copyrighted by their respective owners. Please see individual product documentation for more details on licensing and terms. MySQL AB assumes no liability for the correctness of the information in this appendix or for the proper operation of the programs listed herein.

B.1 APIs

* Perl Modules

  — http://www.mysql.com/Downloads/Contrib/Data-Dumper-2.101.tar.gz: Perl Data-Dumper module. Useful with DBI/DBD support for older Perl installations.

  — http://www.mysql.com/Downloads/Contrib/DBI-1.18.tar.gz: Perl DBI module.

  — http://www.mysql.com/Downloads/Contrib/KAMXbase1.2.tar.gz: Convert between .dbf files and MySQL tables. Perl module written by Pratap Pereira *pereira@ee.eng.ohio-state.edu*, extended by Kevin A. McGrail *kmcgrail@digital1.peregrinehw.com*. This converter can handle MEMO fields.

— http://www.mysql.com/Downloads/Contrib/Msql-Mysql-modules-1.2218.tar.gz: Perl DBD module to access mSQL and MySQL databases.

— http://www.mysql.com/Downloads/Contrib/Data-ShowTable-3.3.tar.gz: Perl Data-ShowTable module. Useful with DBI/DBD support.

— http://www.mysql.com/Downloads/Contrib/HandySQL-1.1.tar.gz: HandySQL is a MySQL access module. It offers a C interface embedded in Perl and is approximately 20% faster than regular DBI.

- JDBC

— http://www.mysql.com/Downloads/Contrib/mm.mysql.jdbc-1.2c.tar.gz: The mm JDBC driver for MySQL. This is a production release and is actively developed. By Mark Matthews (*mmatthew@ecn.purdue.edu*).

— http://www.mysql.com/Downloads/Contrib/mm.mysql.jdbc-2.0pre5.tar.gz: The mm JDBC driver for MySQL. This is a pre-release beta version and is actively developed. By Mark Matthews (*mmatthew@ecn.purdue.edu*). These two drivers have an LGPL license. Please check http://www.worldserver.com/mm.mysql/ for the latest drivers (and other JDBC information) because these drivers may be out of date.

— http://www.caucho.com/projects/jdbc-mysql/index.xtp: The Resin commercial JDBC driver, which is released under open source. It claims to be faster than the mm driver, but we haven't received that much information about this yet.

— http://www.mysql.com/Downloads/Contrib/twz1jdbcForMysql-1.0.4-GA.tar.gz: The twz driver. A type-4 JDBC driver by Terrence W. Zellers *zellert@voicenet.com*. This is commercial but is free for private and educational use. (Not supported anymore.)

— http://www.mysql.com/Downloads/Contrib/pmdamysql.tgz: A MySQL PMDA. Provides MySQL server status and configuration variables.

- OLEDB

— http://www.mysql.com/Downloads/Win32/MyOLEDB3.exe: MyOLEDB 3.0 installation package from SWSoft.

— http://www.mysql.com/Downloads/Win32/mysql-oledb-3.0.0.zip: Source for MyOLEDB 3.0.

— http://www.mysql.com/Downloads/Win32/MySamples.zip: Examples and documentation for MyOLEDB.

— http://www.mysql.com/Downloads/Win32/MyOLEDB.chm: Help files for MyOLEDB.

- — http://www.mysql.com/Downloads/Win32/libmyodbc.zip: Static MyODBC library used to build MyOLEDB. Based on MyODBC code.

- C++

  - — http://www.mysql.com/Downloads/Contrib/mysql-c++-0.02.tar.gz: MySQL C++ wrapper library. By Roland Haenel, *rh@ginster.net*.

  - — http://www.mysql.com/Downloads/Contrib/MyDAO.tar.gz: MySQL C++ API. By Satish *spitfire@pn3.vsnl.net.in*. Inspired by Roland Haenel's C++ API and Ed Carp's MyC library.

  - — http://www.mysql.com/download_mysql++.html: MySQL C++ API (more than just a wrapper library). Originally by *kevina@clark.net*. Nowadays maintained by Sinisa at MySQL AB.

  - — http://nelsonjr.homepage.com/NJrAPI/: A C++ database-independent library that supports MySQL.

- Delphi

  - — http://www.mysql.com/Downloads/Contrib/DelphiMySQL2.zip: Delphi interface to libmysql.dll, by *bsilva@umesd.k12.or.us*.

  - — http://www.mysql.com/Downloads/Contrib/Udmysql.pas: A wrapper for libmysql.dll for usage in Delphi. By Reiner Sombrowsky.

  - — http://www.fichtner.net/delphi/mysql.delphi.phtml: A Delphi Interface to MySQL, with source code. By Matthias Fichtner.

  - — http://www.productivity.org/projects/tmysql/: TmySQL, a library for using MySQL with Delphi.

  - — https://sourceforge.net/projects/zeoslib/: Zeos Library is a set of delphi-native datasets and database components for MySQL, PostgreSQL, Interbase, MS SQL, Oracle, and DB/2. Also it includes development tools such as Database Explorer and Database Designer.

  - — http://www.mysql.com/Downloads/Contrib/Win32/SBMySQL50Share.exe: Delphi 5 shareware MySQL dataset components.

- http://www.mysql.com/Downloads/Contrib/mysql-ruby-2.2.0.tar.gz: MySQL Ruby module. By TOMITA Masahiro *tommy@tmtm.org* Ruby is an object-oriented interpreter language (http://www.netlab.co.jp/ruby/).

- http://www.mysql.com/Downloads/Contrib/JdmMysqlDriver-0.1.0.tar.gz: A Visual-Works 3.0 Smalltalk driver for MySQL. By *joshmiller@earthlink.net*.

- http://www.mysql.com/Downloads/Contrib/Db.py: Python module with caching. By *gandalf@rosmail.com*.

- http://www.mysql.com/Downloads/Contrib/MySQLmodule-1.4.tar.gz: Python interface for MySQL. By Joseph Skinner *joe@earthlight.co.nz*. Modified by Joerg Senekowitsch *senekow@ibm.net*.

- http://www.mysql.com/Downloads/Contrib/MySQL-python-0.3.0.tar.gz: MySQLdb Python is a DB-API v2.0-compliant interface to MySQL. Transactions are supported if the server and tables support them. It is thread-safe, and contains a compatibility module for older code written for the no-longer-maintained MySQLmodule interface.

- http://www.mysql.com/Downloads/Contrib/mysql_mex_12.tar.gz: An interface program for the Matlab program by MathWorks. The interface is done by Kimmo Uutela and John Fisher (not by MathWorks). Check http://boojum.hut.fi/~kuutela/mysqlmex.html for more information.

- http://www.mysql.com/Downloads/Contrib/mysqltcl-1.53.tar.gz: Tcl interface for MySQL. Based on `msqltcl-1.50.tar.gz`. Updated by Tobias Ritzau, *tobri@ida.liu.se*.

- http://www.mysql.com/Downloads/Contrib/MyC-0.1.tar.gz: A Visual Basic-like API, by Ed Carp.

- http://www.mysql.com/Downloads/Contrib/Vdb-dflts-2.1.tar.gz: This is a new version of a set of library utilities intended to provide a generic interface to SQL database engines such that your application becomes a 3-tiered application. The advantage is that you can easily switch between and move to other database engines by implementing one file for the new backend without making any changes to your applications. By *damian@cablenet.net*.

- http://www.mysql.com/Downloads/Contrib/DbFramework-1.10.tar.gz: DbFramework is a collection of classes for manipulating MySQL databases. The classes are loosely based on the CDIF data model subject area. By Paul Sharpe *paul@miraclefish.com*.

- http://www.mysql.com/Downloads/Contrib/pike-mysql-1.4.tar.gz: MySQL module for pike. For use with the Roxen web server.

- http://www.mysql.com/Downloads/Contrib/squile.tar.gz: Module for `guile` that allows `guile` to interact with SQL databases. By Hal Roberts.

- http://www.mysql.com/Downloads/Contrib/stk-mysql.tar.gz: Interface for Stk. Stk is the Tk widget with Scheme underneath instead of Tcl. By Terry Jones.

- http://www.mysql.com/Downloads/Contrib/eiffel-wrapper-1.0.tar.gz: Eiffel wrapper by Michael Ravits.

- http://www.mysql.com/Downloads/Contrib/SQLmy0.06.tgz: FlagShip Replaceable Database Driver (RDD) for MySQL. By Alejandro Fernandez Herrero. The Flagship RDD homepage is at http://www.fship.com/rdds.html.

- http://www.mysql.com/Downloads/Contrib/mydsn-1.0.zip: Binary and source for `mydsn.dll`. mydsn should be used to build and remove the DSN registry file for the MyODBC driver in ColdFusion applications. By Miguel Angel Solórzano.

- http://www.mysql.com/Downloads/Contrib/MySQL-ADA95_API.zip: An ADA95 interface to the MySQL API. By Francois Fabien.

- http://www.mysql.com/Downloads/Contrib/MyTool-DLL_for_VB_and_MySQL.zip: A DLL with MySQL C API for Visual Basic. By Ken Menzel *kenm@icarz.com*.

- http://www.mysql.com/Downloads/Contrib/MYSQLX.EXE: MySQL ActiveX Object for directly accessing your MySQL servers from IIS/ASP, VB, and VC++, skipping the slower ODBC methods. Fully updatable and multi-threaded with full support for all MySQL fieldtypes (Version 2001.1.1). By SciBit http://www.scibit.com/.

- http://www.fastflow.it/mylua/: MyLUA home page; how to use the LUA language to write MySQL PROCEDURE that can be loaded at runtime.

  — http://www.mysql.com/Downloads/Contrib/lua-4.0.tar.gz: LUA 4.0

  — http://www.mysql.com/Downloads/Contrib/mylua-3.23.32.1.tar.gz: Patch for MySQL 3.23.32 to use LUA 4.0. By Cristian Giussani.

- http://www.mysql.com/Downloads/Contrib/patched_myodbc.zip: Patch (for Omniform 4.0 support) to the MyODBC driver. By Thomas Thaele *tthaele@papen-meier.de*

B.2 Clients

- Graphical clients

  — http://www.ideit.com/products/dbvis/: DbVisualizer, a freeware JDBC client to graphically visualise the data and structure of several databases simultaneously. By Innovative-IT Development AB.

  — http://www.mysql.com/downloads/gui-clients.html: MySQLGUI, the MySQL GUI client homepage. By Sinisa at MySQL AB.

  — http://www.mysql.com/Downloads/Contrib/mysql_navigator_0.9.0.tar.gz: MySQL Navigator is a MySQL database server GUI client program, distributed under GPL license. The purpose of MySQL Navigator is to provide a useful client interface to MySQL database servers, while supporting multiple operating systems and languages. You can currently import/export databases, enter queries, get result sets, edit scripts, run scripts, add, alter, and delete users, and retrieve client and server information. Uses QT 2.2. The homepage for MySQL Navigator is at http://sql.kldp.org/mysql/.

— http://www.mysql.com/Downloads/Win32/secman.zip: A user and security management GUI for MySQL on Windows. By Martin Jeremic. The homepage for MySQL Security GUI is at http://jsoft.webjump.com/.

— http://www.mysql.com/Downloads/Contrib/kmysqladmin-0.4.1.tar.gz.

— http://www.mysql.com/Downloads/Contrib/kmysqladmin-0.4.1-1.src.rpm:

— http://www.mysql.com/Downloads/Contrib/kmysqladmin-0.4.1-1.i386.rpm An administration tool for the MySQL server using QT/KDE. Tested only on Linux.

— http://www.mysql.com/Downloads/Contrib/mysql-admin-using-java+swing.tar.gz: Java client using Swing, by Fredy Fischer (*seafs@dial.eunet.ch*). You can always find the latest version at http://www.trash.net/~ffischer/admin/.

— http://www.mysql.com/Downloads/Win32/MySQL-Maker-1.0.zip: Shareware MySQL client for Windows. It's a WYSIWYG tool that allows you to create, change, and delete databases and tables. You can change field structure and add, change, and delete data in these tables directly without an ODBC driver. The MySQL Maker homepage is at http://www.presult.de/presult/frames/fs_mysql-maker.html.

— http://www.mysql.com/Downloads/Contrib/mysqlwinadmn.zip: Windows GUI (binary only) to administrate a database, by David B. Mansel, *david@zhadum.org*.

— http://home.online.no/~runeberg/myqa/: MyQA is a Linux-based query client for the MySQL Database Server. MyQA lets you enter SQL queries, execute them, and view the results, all in a graphical user interface. The GUI is roughly similar to that of the Query Analyzer client that comes with MS SQL server.

— http://www.opex.atnet.ru/mysqlmanager/: MySQL Manager is a graphical MySQL server manager for MySQL server written in Java.

— http://www.mysql.com/Downloads/Win32/netadmin.zip: An administrator tool for MySQL on Windows 95/98 and Windows NT 4.0. Only tested with MySQL Versions 3.23.5 through 3.23.7. Written using the Tmysql components.

You can write queries, show tables, indexes, and table syntax, and administer users, hosts, databases and so on. This is beta and still has some bugs. You can test the program with all features. Please send bugs and hints to Marco Suess *ms@it-netservice.de*. Original URL http://www.it-netservice.de/pages/software/.

— http://www.mysql.com/Downloads/Win32/netadmin2.zip: New version of netadmin. See previous item for details.

— http://www.mysql.com/Downloads/Win32/ARTADMIN203.EXE: Atronic's MySQL client for Windows 2.0.3.0. The home page for this can be found at http://www.artronic.hr/.

— http://www.mysql.com/Downloads/Win32/W9xstop.zip: Utility from Artronic to stop MySQL on win9x.

— http://bardo.hyperlink.cz/mysqlmon/: A lightweight GUI client for Windows.

— http://www.mysqlfront.de/: MySQLfront is a very nice Windows client with lots of useful features. By Angsar Becker.

— http://www.dbtools.com.br/: Dbtools is a tool to manage MySQL databases. Currently only for Windows. Some features:

  — Manage servers, databases, tables, columns, indexes, and users.

  — Import wizard to import structure and data from MS Access, MS Excel, Dbase, FoxPro, Paradox, and ODBC databases.

  — http://www.mysql.com/Downloads/Contrib/KMYENG113.zip: An administrator GUI for MySQL. Works only on Windows; no source. Available in English and Japanese. By Mitunobu Kaneko. Home page: http://sql.jnts.ne.jp/

— http://www.mysql.com/Downloads/Contrib/xmysqladmin-1.0.tar.gz: An X-based frontend to the MySQL database engine. It allows reloads, status check, process control, myisamchk, grant/revoke privileges, creating databases, dropping databases, create, alter, browse, and drop tables. Originally by Gilbert Therrien, *gilbert@ican.net* but now in public domain and supported by MySQL AB.

— http://www.mysql.com/Downloads/Contrib/xmysql-1.9.tar.gz: xmysqlA frontend to the MySQL database engine. It allows for simple queries and table maintenance, as well as batch queries. By Rick Mehalick, *dblhack@wt.net*. The xmysql homepage is at http://web.wt.net/~dblhack/. Requires http://bragg.phys.uwm.edu/xforms/ (xforms 0.88) to work.

— http://www.tamos.net/sw/dbMetrix/: dbMatrix is an open source client for exploring databases and executing SQL. Supports MySQL, Oracle, PostgreSQL, and mSQL.

— http://www.multimania.com/bbrox/GtkSQL/: GtkSQL is a query tool for MySQL and PostgreSQL.

— http://dbman.linux.cz/: dbMan is a query tool written in Perl. Uses DBI and Tk.

— http://www.mysql.com/Downloads/Win32/Msc201.EXE (Mascon 202):

— http://www.mysql.com/Downloads/Win32/FrMsc202.EXE (Free Mascon 202) Mascon is a powerful Win32 GUI for administering MySQL server databases. Mascon's features include visual table design, connections to multiple servers, data and blob editing of tables, security setting, SQL color coding, dump functionality, and much more. The Mascon home page is at http://www.scibit.com/Products/Software/Utils/Mascon.asp.

— http://www.virtualbeer.net/dbui/: DBUI is a Gtk graphical database editor.

— http://www.rtlabs.com/: MacSQL is a GUI for MySQL, ODBC, and JDBC databases for the Mac OS.

— http://www.caleb.com.au/: JRetriever is a generic database frontend tool for JDBC-compliant databases written with Java 2. JRetriever displays database tables/views in a Windows Explorer-like frontend. Users can retrieve data either by clicking on the table folder or by composing their own SQL statements with our built-in SQL editor. The tool has been tested with Oracle 8 and MySQL as the backend databases. It requires JDK 1.3 from JavaSoft.

— http://www.jetools.com/products/databrowser/: The DataBrowser is a cross-database, cross-platform data access tool. It is more user-friendly than tools like SQL Plus and psql (command-line based tools). It is more flexible than TOAD, ISQL, and PGAccess, which are GUI's that are limitied to a single platform or database.

— http://www.intrex.net/amit/software/: The SQL Console is a standalone java application that allows you to connect to a SQL database system and issue SQL queries and updates. It has an easy-to-use graphical user interface. The SQL Console uses JDBC to connect to the database systems, and therefore, with proper JDBC drivers, you can use this utility to connect to some of the most popular database systems.

— http://www.mysql.com/Downloads/Contrib/mysql_mmc.zip: MySQL MMC is a GUI management tool developed using kdevelop with a very good interface completely like Microsoft Enterprise Tool (for SQL server) or Sybase Central. We can use it to manage servers, databases, tables, indexes, and users and to edit table data in grids or execute Sql by Query Analysis.

- Web Clients

— http://www.mysql.com/Downloads/Contrib/mysqladmin-atif-1.0.tar.gz: WWW MySQL administrator for the user, db, and host tables. By Tim Sailer, modified by Atif Ghaffar *aghaffar@artemedia.ch*.

— http://www.mysql.com/Downloads/Contrib/mysql-webadmin-1.0a8-rz.tar.gz: A tool written in PHP-FI to administrate MySQL databases remotely over the Web within a web browser. By Peter Kuppelwieser, *peter.kuppelwieser@kantea.it*. Updated by Wim Bonis, *bonis@kiss.de*. Not maintained anymore!

— http://www.mysql.com/Downloads/Contrib/mysqladm.tar.gz: MySQL Web Database Administration written in Perl. By Tim Sailer.

— http://www.mysql.com/Downloads/Contrib/mysqladm-2.tar.gz: Updated version of mysqladm.tar.gz, by High Tide.

— http://www.mysql.com/Downloads/Contrib/billowmysql.zip: Updated version of `mysqladm.tar.gz`, by Ying Gao. You can get the newest version from http://civeng.com/sqldemo/ (the home site).

— http://www.mysql.com/Downloads/Contrib/myadmin-0.4.tar.gz: MyAdmin is a web-based MySQL administrator by Mike Machado. The MyAdmin home page is at http://myadmin.cheapnet.net/.

— http://www.mysql.com/Downloads/Contrib/phpMyAdmin_2.2.0.tar.gz: A set of PHP3 scripts to adminstrate MySQL over the WWW.

— http://www.phpwizard.net/projects/phpMyAdmin/: phpMyAdmin is a PHP3 tool in the spirit of mysql-webadmin, by Tobias Ratschiller, tobias@dnet.it.

— http://www.mysql.com/Downloads/Contrib/useradm.tar.gz: MySQL administrator in PHP. By Ofni Thomas *othomas@vaidsystems.com*.

— http://gossamer-threads.com/perl/mysqlman/mysql.cgi: MySQLMan has similar functionality to phpmyadmin, but is written with Perl and uses html templates. By Alex Krohn.

- http://www.mysql.com/Downloads/Contrib/mysql-editor.tar.gz: This CGI script in Perl enables you to edit content of MySQL databases. By Tomas Zeman.

- http://worldcommunity.com/opensource/futuresql/: FutureSQL, by Peter F. Brown, is a free, `open source` rapid application development web database administration tool, written in Perl, using MySQL. It uses `DBI:DBD` and `CGI.pm`.

FutureSQL allows one to easily set up config files to view, edit, delete, and otherwise process records from a MySQL database. It uses a data dictionary, configuration files, and templates, and allows "pre-processing" and "post-processing" on fields, records, and operations.

B.3 Web Tools

- http://www.mysql.com/Downloads/Contrib/mod_mysql_include_1.0.tar.gz: Apache module to include HTML from MySQL queries into your pages, and run update queries. Originally written to implement a simple, fast, low-overhead, banner-rotation system. By Sasha Pachev.

- http://htcheck.sourceforge.net/: htCheck is a URL checker with MySQL backend. Spidered URLs can later be queried using SQL to retrieve various kinds of information—e.g., broken links. Written by Gabriele Bartolini.

- http://www.odbsoft.com/cook/sources.htm: This package has various functions for generating HTML code from an SQL table structure and for generating SQL statements (Select, Insert, Update, Delete) from an html form. You can build a complete forms interface to an SQL database (Query, Add, Update, Delete) without any programming! By Marc Beneteau, *marc@odbsoft.com*.

- http://www.mysql.com/Downloads/Contrib/sqlhtml.tar.gz: SQL/HTML is an HTML database manager for MySQL using DBI 1.06.

- http://www.mysql.com/Downloads/Contrib/udmsearch-3.0.23.tar.gz: UdmSearch 3.0.23, stable version.

- http://www.mysql.com/Downloads/Contrib/mnogosearch-3.1.12.tar.gz: mnogosearch 3.1.12, development but recommended version.

- http://search.mnoGo.ru/: UdmSearch home page. An SQL-based search engine for the Internet. By Alexander I. Barkov *bar@izhcom.ru.*

- http://www.mysql.com/Downloads/Contrib/wmtcl.doc.

- http://www.mysql.com/Downloads/Contrib/wmtcl.lex: With this you can write HTML files with inclusions of Tcl code. By *vvs@scil.npi.msu.su.*

- http://www.mysql.com/Downloads/Contrib/www-sql-0.5.7.lsm.

- http://www.mysql.com/Downloads/Contrib/www-sql-0.5.7.tar.gz: A CGI program that parses an HTML file containing special tags, parses them, and inserts data from a MySQL database.

- http://www.mysql.com/Downloads/Contrib/genquery.zip: Perl SQL database interface package for HTML.

- http://www.mysql.com/Downloads/Contrib/cgi++-0.8.tar.gz: A macro-processor to simply write CGI/database programs in C++, by Sasha Pachev.

- http://www.mysql.com/Downloads/Contrib/webboard-1.0.zip: WebBoard 1.0, EU-Industries Internet-Message-Board.

- http://www.mysql.com/Downloads/Contrib/DBIx-TextIndex-0.02.tar.gz: Full-text searching with Perl on BLOB/TEXT columns by Daniel Koch.

B.4 Performance Benchmarking Tool

- http://www.mysql.com/Downloads/super-smack/super-smack-1.0.tar.gz: super-smack is a multi-threaded benchmarking tool for MySQL and **PostgreSQL**. Written in C++. Easy to extend to support other databases that have C/C++ client libraries. By Sasha Pachev.

B.5 Authentication Tools

- http://www.mysql.com/Downloads/Contrib/ascend-radius-mysql-0.7.2.patch.gz: This is an authentication and logging patch using MySQL for Ascend-Radius. By *takeshi@SoftAgency.co.jp.*

- http://www.mysql.com/Downloads/Contrib/icradius-0.10.tar.gz: icradius 0.10. http://www.mysql.com/Downloads/Contrib/icradius.README: icradius readme.

- http://www.mysql.com/Downloads/Contrib/checkpass-word-0.81-mysql-0.6.6.patch.gz: MySQL authentication patch for QMAIL and checkpassword. These are useful for user management (mail, pop account) by MySQL. By *takeshi@SoftAgency.co.jp*.

- http://www.mysql.com/Downloads/Contrib/jradius-diff.gz: MySQL support for Livingston's Radius 2.01. Authentication and accounting. By Jose de Leon, *jdl@thevision.net*.

- http://www.mysql.com/Downloads/Contrib/mod_auth_mysql-2.20.tar.gz: Apache authentication module for MySQL. By Zeev Suraski, *bourbon@netvision.net.il*.

- http://www.mysql.com/Downloads/Contrib/mypasswd-2.0.tar.gz: Extra for mod_auth_mysql. This is a little tool that allows you to add/change user records storing group and/or password entries in MySQL tables. By Harry Brueckner, *brueckner@respublica.de*.

- http://www.mysql.com/Downloads/Contrib/mysql-passwd.README.

- http://www.mysql.com/Downloads/Contrib/mysql-passwd-1.2.tar.gz: Extra for mod_auth_mysql. This is a two-part system for use with mod_auth_mysql.

- http://www.mysql.com/Downloads/Contrib/pam_mysql.tar.gz: This module authenticates users via pam, using MySQL.

- http://www.mysql.com/Downloads/Contrib/nsapi_auth_mysql.tar: Netscape web server API (NSAPI) functions to authenticate (BASIC) users against MySQL tables. By Yuan John Jiang.

- http://www.mysql.com/Downloads/Contrib/qmail-1.03-mysql-0.6.6.patch.gz: Patch for qmail to authenticate users from a MySQL table. By *takeshi@SoftAgency.co.jp*.

- http://www.mysql.com/Downloads/Contrib/proftpd-1.2.0rc2-fix-mysql.patch: Patch for proftpd1.2.0rc2. By *takeshi@SoftAgency.co.jp*.

- http://www.mysql.com/Downloads/Contrib/pwcheck_mysql-0.1.tar.gz: An authentication module for the Cyrus IMAP server. By Aaron Newsome.

B.6 Converters

- http://www.mysql.com/Downloads/Contrib/mssql2mysql.txt: Converter from MS-SQL to MySQL. By Michael Kofler. The mssql2mysql home page is at http://www.kofler.cc/mysql/mssql2mysql.html.

- http://www.mysql.com/Downloads/Contrib/dbf2mysql-1.14.tar.gz: Convert between .dbf files and MySQL tables. By Maarten Boekhold (*boekhold@cindy.et.tudelft.nl*), William Volkman, and Michael Widenius. This converter includes rudimentary read-only support for MEMO fields.

- http://www.mysql.com/Downloads/Contrib/dbf2mysql-1.13.tgz: Convert   between
  .dbf files and MySQL tables. By Maarten Boekhold, *boekhold@cindy.et.tudelft.nl*,
  and Michael Widenius. This converter can't handle MEMO fields.

- http://www.mysql.com/Downloads/Contrib/dbf2mysql.zip: Convert between FoxPro
  .dbf files and MySQL tables on Windows. By Alexander Eltsyn, *ae@nica.ru* or
  ae@usa.net.

- http://www.mysql.com/Downloads/Contrib/dbf2sql.zip: Short and simple program
  that can help you transport your data from FoxPro tables into MySQL tables. By
  Danko Josic.

- http://www.mysql.com/Downloads/Contrib/dump2h-1.20.gz: Convert from mysqldump output to a C header file. By Harry Brueckner, *brueckner@mail.respublica.de*.

- http://www.mysql.com/Downloads/Contrib/exportsql.txt: A script that is similar to
  access_to_mysql.txt, except that this one is fully configurable, has better type
  conversion (including detection of TIMESTAMP fields), provides warnings and suggestions while converting, quotes **all** special characters in text and binary data, and
  so on. It will also convert to mSQL v1 and v2, and is free of charge for anyone. See
  http://www.cynergi.net/exportsql/ for the latest version. By Pedro Freire, *sup-
  port@cynergi.net*. Note: doesn't work with Access2!

- http://www.mysql.com/Downloads/Contrib/access_to_mysql.txt: Paste this function
  into an Access module of a database that has the tables you want to export. See also
  exportsql. By Brian Andrews. Note: doesn't work with Access2!

- http://www.mysql.com/Downloads/Contrib/importsql.txt: A script that does the exact
  reverse of exportsql.txt. That is, it imports data from MySQL into an Access
  database via ODBC. This is very handy when combined with exportsql because it
  lets you use Access for all DB design and administration, and synchronise with your
  actual MySQL server either way. Free of charge. See http://www.netdive.com/free-
  bies/importsql/ for any updates. Created by Laurent Bossavit of NetDIVE. Note:
  doesn't work with Access2!

- http://www.mysql.com/Downloads/Contrib/mdb2sql.bas: Converter from Access97
  to MySQL by Moshe Gurvich.

- http://www.mysql.com/Downloads/Contrib/msql2mysqlWrapper-1.0.tgz: A C wrapper from mSQL to MySQL. By *alfred@sb.net*

- http://www.mysql.com/Downloads/Contrib/sqlconv.pl: A simple script that can be
  used to copy fields from one MySQL table to another in bulk. Basically, you can run
  mysqldump and pipe it to the sqlconv.pl script. The script will parse through the
  mysqldump output and will rearrange the fields so that they can be inserted into a

new table. An example is when you want to create a new table for a different site you are working on, but the table is just a bit different (that is, fields are in a different order, etc.). By Steve Shreeve.

- http://www.mysql.com/Downloads/Contrib/oracledump: Perl program to convert Oracle databases to MySQL. Has the same output format as mysqldump. By Johan Andersson.

- http://www.mysql.com/Downloads/Contrib/excel2mysql.pl: Perl program to import Excel spreadsheets into a MySQL database. By Stephen Hurd *shurd@sk.sympatico.ca*.

- http://www.mysql.com/Downloads/Contrib/T2S_100.ZIP: Windows program to convert text files to MySQL databases. By Asaf Azulay.

B.7 Using MySQL with Other Products

- http://www.mysql.com/Downloads/Contrib/emacs-sql-mode.tar.gz: Raw port of a SQL mode for XEmacs. Supports completion. Original by Peter D. Pezaris *pez@atlantic2.sbi.com* and partial MySQL port by David Axmark.

- http://www.mysql.com/Downloads/Win32/myaccess97_1_4.zip: MyAccess97 1.4.

- http://www.mysql.com/Downloads/Win32/myaccess2000_1_4.zip: MyAccess2000 1.4.

MyAccess is an AddIn for MS Access 97/2000 that allows you to manage MySQL databases from within Access. Main functions are:

— Create/modify tables

— Execute queries against MySQL

— Extract "Create Table-Scripts" from MySQL

— Import/export tables from Access to MySQL, and vice versa

— Log Changes

— Show a "Database Definition Report"

Written by Hubertus Hiden. The MyAccess homepage is at http://www.access-mysql.com/.

- http://www.mysql.com/Downloads/Contrib/radius-0.3.tar.gz: Patches for radiusd to make it support MySQL. By Wim Bonis, *bonis@kiss.de*.

B.8 Utilities

- http://worldcommunity.com/opensource/utilities/mysql_backup.html: MySQL
  Backup is a backup script for MySQL. By Peter F. Brown.

- http://www.mysql.com/Downloads/Contrib/mytop.

- http://public.yahoo.com/~jzawodn/mytop/: (mytop home page) mytop is a Perl program that allows you to monitor MySQL servers by viewing active threads, queries,
  and overall server performance numbers. By Jeremy D. Zawodny.

- http://www.mysql.com/Downloads/Contrib/mysql_watchdog.pl: Monitor   the
  MySQL daemon for possible lockups. By Yermo Lamers, *yml@yml.com*.

- http://www.mysql.com/Downloads/Contrib/mysqltop.tar.gz: Sends a query in a fixed
  time interval to the server and shows the resulting table. By Thomas Wana.

- http://www.mysql.com/Downloads/Contrib/mysql_structure_dumper.tar.gz.

- http://www.mysql.com/Downloads/Contrib/mysql_structure_dumper.tgz: Prints the
  structure of every table in a database. By Thomas Wana.

- http://www.mysql.com/Downloads/Contrib/mysqlsync: A Perl script to keep remote
  copies of a MySQL database in sync with a central master copy. By Mark Jeftovic.
  markjr@easydns.com.

- http://www.mysql.com/Downloads/Contrib/MySQLTutor-0.2.tar.gz: MySQLTutor. A
  MySQL tutorial for beginners.

- http://www.mysql.com/Downloads/Contrib/MySQLDB.zip.

- http://www.mysql.com/Downloads/Contrib/MySQLDB-readme.html: A   COM
  library for MySQL by Alok Singh.

- http://www.mysql.com/Downloads/Contrib/mysql_replicate.pl: Perl program that
  handles replication. By *elble@icculus.nsg.nwu.edu*.

- http://www.mysql.com/Downloads/Contrib/DBIx-TextIndex-0.02.tar.gz: Perl script
  that uses reverse indexing to handle text searching. By Daniel Koch.

- http://www.mysql.com/Downloads/Contrib/dbcheck: Perl script that takes a backup
  of tables before running isamchk on them.

- http://www.mysql.com/Downloads/Contrib/mybackup.

- http://www.mswanson.com/mybackup: (mybackup home page) Wrapper for mysqldump to backup all databases. By Marc Swanson.

- http://www.mysql.com/Downloads/Contrib/mdu.pl.gz: Prints the storage usage of a
  MySQL database.

B.9 RPMs for Common Tools (Most Are for RedHat 6.1)

- http://www.mysql.com/Downloads/Contrib/perl-Data-ShowTable-3.3-2.i386.rpm
- http://www.mysql.com/Downloads/Contrib/perl-Msql-Mysql-modules-1.2210-2.i386.rpm
- http://www.mysql.com/Downloads/Contrib/php-pg-3.0.13-1.i386.rpm
- http://www.mysql.com/Downloads/Contrib/php-pg-manual-3.0.13-1.i386.rpm
- http://www.mysql.com/Downloads/Contrib/php-pg-mysql-3.0.13-1.i386.rpm
- http://www.mysql.com/Downloads/Contrib/phpMyAdmin-2.0.5-1.noarch.rpm

B.10 Useful Function

- http://www.mysql.com/Downloads/Contrib/mysnprintf.c sprintf() function for SQL queries that can escape blobs. By Chunhua Liu.

B.11 Windows Program

- http://www.mysql.com/Downloads/Contrib/LaunchMySQL.zip The program launches the MySQL server, shuts it down, and displays status information. By Bill Thompson.

B.12 Uncategorized

- http://www.mysql.com/Downloads/Contrib/findres.pl: Find reserved words in tables. By Nem W Schlecht.
- http://www.mysql.com/Downloads/Contrib/handicap.tar.gz: Performance handicapping system for yachts. Uses PHP. By *rhill@stobyn.ml.org*.
- http://www.mysql.com/Downloads/Contrib/hylalog-1.0.tar.gz: Store `hylafax` outgoing faxes in a MySQL database. By Sinisa Milivojevic, *sinisa@mysql.com*.
- http://www.mysql.com/Downloads/Contrib/mrtg-mysql-1.0.tar.gz: MySQL status plotting with MRTG, by Luuk de Boer, *luuk@wxs.nl*.
- http://www.mysql.com/Downloads/Contrib/wuftpd-2.4.2.18-mysql_support.2.tar.gz: Patches to add logging to MySQL for WU-ftpd. By Zeev Suraski, *bourbon@netvision.net.il*.
- http://www.mysql.com/Downloads/Contrib/wu-ftpd-2.6.0-mysql.4.tar.gz: Patches to add logging to MySQL for WU-ftpd 2.6.0. By *takeshi@SoftAgency.co.jp*, based on Zeev Suraski wuftpd patches.

- http://www.mysql.com/Downloads/Contrib/Old-Versions: Previous versions of things found here that you probably won't be interested in.

C

Credits

This appendix lists the developers, contributors, and supporters who have helped to make MySQL what it is today.

C.1 Developers at MySQL AB

These are the developers who are or have been employed by MySQL AB to work on the MySQL database software, roughly in the order they started to work with us. Following each developer is a small list of the tasks that the developer is responsible for, or the accomplishments they have made.

Michael (Monty) Widenius

Has written the following parts of the MySQL database software:

- All the main code in mysqld.

- New functions for the string library.

- Most of the mysys library.

- The ISAM and MyISAM libraries (B-tree index file handlers with index compression and different record formats).

- The HEAP library. A memory table system with our superior full dynamic hashing. In use since 1981 and published around 1984.

- The replace program (take a look at it, it's **COOL**!).

- MyODBC, the ODBC driver for Windows 95.

- Fixing bugs in MIT-pthreads to get it to work for MySQL server. And also Unireg, a curses-based application tool with many utilities.

- Porting of mSQL tools like msqlperl, DBD/DBI, and DB2mysql.
- Most of crash-me and the foundation for the MySQL benchmarks.

David Axmark

- Coordinator and initial main writer of the **Reference Manual**, including enhancements to texi2html.
- Automatic web site updating from the manual.
- Initial Autoconf, Automake, and Libtool support.
- Licensing.
- Parts of all the text files. (Nowadays only the README is left. The rest ended up in the manual.)
- Lots of testing of new features.
- Our in-house Free Software legal expert.
- Mailing list maintainer (who never has the time to do it right . . .).
- Our original portability code (more than 10 years old now). Nowadays only some parts of mysys are left.
- Someone for Monty to call in the middle of the night when he just got that new feature to work.

Jani Tolonen

- mysqlimport
- A lot of extensions to the mysql client
- PROCEDURE ANALYSE()

Sinisa Milivojevic

- Compression (with zlib) in the client/server protocol
- Perfect hashing for the lexical analyzer phase
- Multi-row INSERT
- mysqldump -e option
- LOAD DATA INFILE LOCAL
- SQL_CALC_FOUND_ROWS SELECT option
- --max-user-connections= . . . option
- net_read and net_write_timeout
- GRANT/REVOKE and SHOW GRANTS FOR

- New client-server protocol for 4.0
- UNION
- Multi-table DELETE/UPDATE
- The MySQLGUI client
- Maintainer of MySQL++

Tonu Samuel

- Our security expert
- Vio interface (the foundation for the encrypted client/server protocol)
- MySQL Filesystem (a way to use MySQL databases as files and directories)
- The CASE expression
- The MD5() and COALESCE() functions
- RAID support for MyISAM tables

Sasha Pachev

- Replication
- SHOW CREATE TABLE
- mod_mysql_include
- cgi++
- mysql-bench

Matt Wagner

- MySQL test suite
- Our webmaster

Miguel Solorzano

- Win32 development
- Winmysqladmin

Timothy Smith

- Dynamic character support
- Responsible for MySQL configure

Sergei Golubchik

- Full-text search
- Added keys to the MERGE library

Jeremy Cole

- Proofreading and editing this fine manual
- `ALTER TABLE ... ORDER BY ...`
- `UPDATE ... ORDER BY ...`
- `DELETE ... ORDER BY ...`

Indrek Siitan

- Designer/programmer of our web interface

Jorge del Conde

- `MyCC MySQL Control Center`
- Web portals
- Win32 development

C.2 Contributors to MySQL

While `MySQL AB` owns all copyrights in the `MySQL server` and the `MySQL manual`, we wish to recognise those who have made contributions of one kind or another to the `MySQL distribution`. Contributors are listed here, in somewhat random order:

Paul DuBois
> Help with making the Reference Manual correct and understandable. That includes rewriting Monty's and David's attempts at English into English as other people know it.

Gianmassimo Vigazzola qwerg@mbox.vol.it or qwerg@tin.it
> The initial port to Win32/NT.

Kim Aldale
> Helped to rewrite Monty's and David's early attempts at English into English.

Per Eric Olsson
> For more or less constructive criticism and real testing of the dynamic record format.

Irena Pancirov irena@mail.yacc.it
> Win32 port with Borland compiler. `mysqlshutdown.exe` and `mysqlwatch.exe`.

David J. Hughes
> For the effort to make a shareware SQL database. At TcX, the predecessor of MySQL AB, we started with `mSQL`, but found that it couldn't satisfy our purposes. So instead we wrote an SQL interface to our application builder Unireg. `mysqladmin` and `mysql` client are programs that were largely influenced by their `mSQL` counterparts. We have put a lot of effort into making the MySQL syntax a superset of `mSQL`. Many of the API's ideas are borrowed from `mSQL` to make it easy to port free `mSQL`

programs to the MySQL API. The MySQL software doesn't contain any code from mSQL. Two files in the distribution (`client/insert_test.c` and `client/select_test.c`) are based on the corresponding (non-copyrighted) files in the mSQL distribution, but are modified as examples showing the changes necessary to convert code from mSQL to MySQL server. (mSQL is copyrighted by David J. Hughes.)

Fred Fish

For his excellent C debugging and trace library. Monty has made a number of smaller improvements to the library (speed and additional options).

Richard A. O'Keefe

For his public domain string library.

Henry Spencer

For his regex library, used in `WHERE column REGEXP regexp`.

Free Software Foundation

From whom we got an excellent compiler (`gcc`), the `libc` library (from which we have borrowed `strto.c` to get some code working in Linux), and the `readline` library (for the `mysql` client).

Free Software Foundation & The XEmacs development team

For a really great editor/environment used by almost everybody at MySQL AB/TcX/detron.

Patrick Lynch

For helping us acquire http://www.mysql.com/.

Fred Lindberg

For setting up qmail to handle the MySQL mailing list and for the incredible help we got in managing the MySQL mailing lists.

Igor Romanenko igor@frog.kiev.ua

`mysqldump` (previously `msqldump`, but ported and enhanced by Monty).

Yuri Dario

For keeping up and extending the MySQL OS/2 port.

Tim Bunce, Alligator Descartes

For the `DBD` (Perl) interface.

Tim Bunce

Author of `mysqlhotcopy`.

Andreas Koenig a.koenig@mind.de

For the Perl interface for MySQL server.

Eugene Chan eugene@acenet.com.sg

For porting PHP for MySQL server.

Michael J. Miller Jr. mke@terrapin.turbolift.com

For the first MySQL manual. And a lot of spelling/language fixes for the FAQ (that turned into the MySQL manual a long time ago).

Yan Cailin

First translator of the MySQL Reference Manual into simplified Chinese in early 2000 on which the Big5 and HK coded (http://mysql.hitstar.com/) versions were based. http://linuxdb.yeah.netPersonal home page at linuxdb.yeah.net.

Giovanni Maruzzelli maruzz@matrice.it

For porting iODBC (Unix ODBC).

Chris Provenzano

Portable user-level pthreads. From the copyright: This product includes software developed by Chris Provenzano, the University of California, Berkeley, and contributors. We are currently using version 1_60_beta6 patched by Monty (see `mit-pthreads/Changes-mysql`).

Xavier Leroy Xavier.Leroy@inria.fr

The author of LinuxThreads (used by the MySQL server on Linux).

Zarko Mocnik zarko.mocnik@dem.si

Sorting for Slovenian language and the `cset.tar.gz` module that makes it easier to add other character sets.

"TAMITO" tommy@valley.ne.jp

The `_MB` character set macros and the ujis and sjis character sets.

Joshua Chamas joshua@chamas.com

Base for concurrent insert, extended date syntax, debugging on NT, and answering on the MySQL mailing list.

Yves Carlier Yves.Carlier@rug.ac.be

`mysqlaccess`, a program to show the access rights for a user.

Rhys Jones rhys@wales.com (and GWE Technologies Limited)

For the JDBC, a module to extract data from a MySQL database with a Java client.

Dr Xiaokun Kelvin ZHU X.Zhu@brad.ac.uk

Further development of the JDBC driver and other MySQL-related Java tools.

James Cooper pixel@organic.com

For setting up a searchable mailing list archive at his site.

Rick Mehalick Rick_Mehalick@i-o.com

For `xmysql`, a graphical X client for MySQL server.

Doug Sisk sisk@wix.com

For providing RPM packages of MySQL for RedHat Linux.

Diemand Alexander V. axeld@vial.ethz.ch
    For providing RPM packages of MySQL for RedHat Linux-Alpha.

Antoni Pamies Olive toni@readysoft.es
    For providing RPM versions of a lot of MySQL clients for Intel and SPARC.

Jay Bloodworth jay@pathways.sde.state.sc.us
    For providing RPM versions for MySQL Version 3.21.

Jochen Wiedmann wiedmann@neckar-alb.de
    For maintaining the Perl DBD::mysql module.

Therrien Gilbert gilbert@ican.net, Jean-Marc Pouyot jmp@scalaire.fr
    French error messages.

Petr snajdr, snajdr@pvt.net
    Czech error messages.

Jaroslaw Lewandowski jotel@itnet.com.pl
    Polish error messages.

Miguel Angel Fernandez Roiz
    Spanish error messages.

Roy-Magne Mo rmo@www.hivolda.no
    Norwegian error messages and testing of Version 3.21.#.

Timur I. Bakeyev root@timur.tatarstan.ru
    Russian error messages.

brenno@dewinter.com & Filippo Grassilli phil@hyppo.com
    Italian error messages.

Dirk Munzinger dirk@trinity.saar.de
    German error messages.

Billik Stefan billik@sun.uniag.sk
    Slovak error messages.

Stefan Saroiu tzoompy@cs.washington.edu
    Romanian error messages.

Peter Feher
    Hungarian error messages.

Roberto M. Serqueira
    Portuguese error messages.

Carsten H. Pedersen
    Danish error messages

David Sacerdote davids@secnet.com
   Ideas for secure checking of DNS hostnames.

Wei-Jou Chen jou@nematic.ieo.nctu.edu.tw
   Some support for Chinese (BIG5) characters.

Wei He hewei@mail.ied.ac.cn
   A lot of functionality for the Chinese (GBK) character set.

Zeev Suraski bourbon@netvision.net.il
   FROM_UNIXTIME() time formatting, ENCRYPT() functions, and bison advisor.
   Active mailing list member.

Luuk de Boer luuk@wxs.nl
   Ported (and extended) the benchmark suite to DBI/DBD. Has been of great help with
   crash-me and running benchmarks. Some new date functions. The mysql_setper-
   missions script.

Jay Flaherty fty@mediapulse.com
   Big parts of the Perl DBI/DBD section in the manual.

Paul Southworth pauls@etext.org, Ray Loyzaga yar@cs.su.oz.au
   Proofreading the Reference Manual.

Alexis Mikhailov root@medinf.chuvashia.su
   User-definable functions (UDFs); CREATE FUNCTION and DROP FUNCTION.

Andreas F. Bobak bobak@relog.ch
   The AGGREGATE extension to UDF functions.

Ross Wakelin R.Wakelin@march.co.uk
   Help to set up InstallShield for MySQL-Win32.

Jethro Wright III jetman@li.net
   The libmysql.dll library.

James Pereria jpereira@iafrica.com
   Mysqlmanager, a Win32 GUI tool for administrating MySQL server.

Curt Sampson cjs@portal.ca
   Porting of MIT-pthreads to NetBSD/Alpha and NetBSD 1.3/i386.

Antony T. Curtis antony.curtis@olcs.net
   Porting of the MySQL database software to OS/2.

Martin Ramsch m.ramsch@computer.org
   Examples in the MySQL Tutorial.

Steve Harvey
   For making mysqlaccess more secure.

Konark IA-64 Centre of Persistent Systems Private Limited
> http://www.pspl.co.in/konark/. Help with the Win64 port of the MySQL server.

Albert Chin-A-Young.
> Configure updates for Tru64, large file support and better TCP wrappers support.

John Birrell
> Emulation of `pthread_mutex()` for OS/2.

Benjamin Pflugmann
> Extended `MERGE` tables to handle `INSERTS`. Active member on the MySQL mailing lists.

Other contributors, bugfinders, and testers: James H. Thompson, Maurizio Menghini, Wojciech Tryc, Luca Berra, Zarko Mocnik, Wim Bonis, Elmar Haneke, *jehamby@lightside*, *psmith@BayNetworks.com*, *duane@connect.com.au*, Ted Deppner *ted@psyber.com*, Mike Simons, and Jaakko Hyvatti.

And lots of bug report/patches from the folks on the mailing list.

A big tribute goes to those who help us answer questions on the `mysql@lists.mysql.com` mailing list:

Daniel Koch dkoch@amcity.com
> Irix setup.

Luuk de Boer luuk@wxs.nl
> Benchmark questions.

Tim Sailer tps@users.buoy.com
> `DBD-mysql` questions.

Boyd Lynn Gerber gerberb@zenez.com
> SCO-related questions.

Richard Mehalick RM186061@shellus.com
> `xmysql`-related questions and basic installation questions.

Zeev Suraski bourbon@netvision.net.il
> Apache module configuration questions (log & auth), PHP-related questions, SQL syntax-related questions, and other general questions.

Francesc Guasch frankie@citel.upc.es
> General questions.

Jonathan J Smith jsmith@wtp.net
> Questions pertaining to OS specifics with Linux, SQL syntax, and other things that might need some work.

David Sklar sklar@student.net
Using MySQL from PHP and Perl.

Alistair MacDonald A.MacDonald@uel.ac.uk
Not yet specified, but is flexible and can handle Linux and maybe HP-UX. Will try to get user to use `mysqlbug`.

John Lyon jlyon@imag.net
Questions about installing MySQL on Linux systems, using either `.rpm` files or compiling from source.

Lorvid Ltd. lorvid@WOLFENET.com
Simple billing/license/support/copyright issues.

Patrick Sherrill patrick@coconet.com
ODBC and VisualC++ interface questions.

Randy Harmon rjharmon@uptimecomputers.com
DBD, Linux, some SQL syntax questions.

C.3 Supporters to MySQL

While MySQL AB owns all copyrights in the MySQL server and the MySQL manual, we wish to recognise the following companies, which helped us finance the development of the MySQL server, such as by paying us for developing a new feature or giving us hardware for development of the MySQL server.

VA Linux / Andover.net
Funded replication.

NuSphere
Editing of the MySQL manual.

Stork Design studio
The MySQL web site in use between 1998-2000.

Intel
Contributed to development on Windows and Linux platforms.

Compaq
Contributed to development on Linux/Alpha.

SWSoft
Development on the embedded `mysqld` version.

FutureQuest
`--skip-show-database`

Porting to Other Systems

This appendix will help you port MySQL to other operationg systems. Do check the list of currently supported operating systems first. See Section 2.2.2, Operating Systems Supported by MySQL. If you have created a new port of MySQL, please let us know so that we can list it here and on our web site (http://www.mysql.com/), recommending it to other users.

Note: If you create a new port of MySQL, you are free to copy and distribute it under the GPL license, but it does not make you a copyright holder of MySQL.

A working Posix thread library is needed for the server. On Solaris 2.5 we use Sun PThreads (the native thread support in 2.4 and earlier versions is not good enough) and on Linux we use LinuxThreads by Xavier Leroy, *Xavier.Leroy@inria.fr*.

The hard part of porting to a new Unix variant without good native thread support is probably to port MIT-pthreads. See `mit-pthreads`/`README` and Programming POSIX Threads (http://www.humanfactor.com/pthreads/).

The MySQL distribution includes a patched version of Provenzano's Pthreads from MIT (see the MIT Pthreads web page at http://www.mit.edu:8001/people/proven/ pthreads.html). This can be used for some operating systems that do not have POSIX threads.

It is also possible to use another user-level thread package named FSU Pthreads (see http://www.informatik.hu-berlin.de/~mueller/pthreads.htmlFSU, the Pthreads home page). This implementation is being used for the SCO port.

See the `thr_lock.c` and `thr_alarm.c` programs in the `mysys` directory for some tests/ examples of these problems.

Both the server and the client need a working C++ compiler (we use `gcc` and have tried SPARCworks). Another compiler that is known to work is the Irix `cc`.

To compile only the client use ./configure --without-server.

There is currently no support for only compiling the server, nor is it likely to be added unless someone has a good reason for it.

If you want/need to change any Makefile or the configure script you must get Automake and Autoconf. We have used the automake-1.2 and autoconf-2.12 distributions.

All steps needed to remake everything from the most basic files.

```
/bin/rm */.deps/*.P
/bin/rm -f config.cache
aclocal
autoheader
aclocal
automake
autoconf
./configure --with-debug=full --prefix='your installation directory'

# The makefiles generated above need GNU make 3.75 or newer.
# (called gmake below)
gmake clean all install init-db
```

If you run into problems with a new port, you may have to do some debugging of MySQL! See Section D.1, Debugging a MySQL Server.

Note: Before you start debugging mysqld, first get the test programs mysys/thr_alarm and mysys/thr_lock to work. This will ensure that your thread installation has even a remote chance of working!

D.1 Debugging a MySQL Server

If you are using some functionality that is very new in MySQL, you can try to run mysqld with the --skip-new (which will disable all new, potentially unsafe functionality) or with --safe-mode, which disables a lot of optimisation that may cause problems. See Section A.4.1, What to Do if MySQL Keeps Crashing.

If mysqld doesn't want to start, you should check that you don't have any my.cnf files that interfere with your setup! You can check your my.cnf arguments with mysqld --print-defaults and avoid using them by starting with mysqld --no-defaults . . . .

If mysqld starts to eat up CPU, or memory or if it "hangs", you can use mysqladmin processlist status to find out if someone is executing a query that takes a long time. It may be a good idea to run mysqladmin -i10 processlist status in some window if you are experiencing performance problems or problems when new clients can't connect.

The command mysqladmin debug will dump some information about locks in use, used memory, and query usage to the mysql log file. This may help solve some problems. This command also provides some useful information even if you haven't compiled MySQL for debugging!

If the problem is that some tables are getting slower, and slower you should try to optimise the table with OPTIMIZE TABLE or myisamchk. See Chapter 4. You should also check the slow queries with EXPLAIN.

You should also read the OS-specific section in this manual for problems that may be unique to your environment. See Section 2.6, Operating System–Specific Notes.

D.1.1 Compiling MySQL for Debugging

If you have some very specific problem, you can always try to debug MySQL. To do this you must configure MySQL with the --with-debug or the --with-debug=full option. You can check whether MySQL was compiled with debugging by doing mysqld --help. If the --debug flag is listed with the options, you have debugging enabled. mysqladmin ver also lists the mysqld version as mysql ... --debug in this case.

If you are using gcc or egcs, the recommended configure line is:

```
CC=gcc CFLAGS="-O2" CXX=gcc CXXFLAGS="-O2 -felide-constructors \
    -fno-exceptions -fno-rtti" ./configure --prefix=/usr/local/mysql \
    --with-debug --with-extra-charsets=complex
```

This will avoid problems with the libstdc++ library and with C++ exceptions (many compilers have problems with C++ exceptions in threaded code) and compile a MySQL version with support for all character sets.

If you suspect a memory overrun error, you can configure MySQL with --with-debug=full, which will install a memory allocation (SAFEMALLOC) checker. Running with SAFEMALLOC is, however, quite slow, so if you get performance problems you should start mysqld with the --skip-safemalloc option. This will disable the memory overrun checks for each call to malloc and free.

If mysqld stops crashing when you compile it with --with-debug, you have probably found a compiler bug or a timing bug within MySQL. In this case you can try to add -g to the CFLAGS and CXXFLAGS variables and not use --with-debug. If mysqld now dies, you can at least attach to it with gdb or use gdb on the core file to find out what happened.

When you configure MySQL for debugging you automatically enable a lot of extra safety check functions that monitor the health of mysqld. If they find something "unexpected," an entry will be written to stderr, which safe_mysqld directs to the error log! This also means that if you are having some unexpected problems with MySQL and are using a source distribution, the first thing you should do is configure MySQL for debugging!

(The second thing, of course, is to send mail to *mysql@lists.mysql.com* and ask for help. Please use the mysqlbug script for all bug reports or questions regarding the MySQL version you are using!)

In the Windows MySQL distribution, mysqld.exe is, by default, compiled with support for trace files.

D.1.2 Creating Trace Files

If the mysqld server doesn't start or if you can cause the mysqld server to crash quickly, you can try to create a trace file to find the problem.

To do this you have to have a mysqld that is compiled for debugging. You can check this by executing mysqld -V. If the version number ends with -debug, it's compiled with support for trace files.

Start the mysqld server with a trace log in /tmp/mysqld.trace (or C:\mysqld.trace on Windows):

mysqld --debug

On Windows you should also use the --standalone flag to not start mysqld as a service:

In a DOS window do:

```
mysqld --debug --standalone
```

After this you can use the mysql.exe command-line tool in a second DOS window to reproduce the problem. You can take down the mysqld server with mysqladmin shutdown.

Note that the trace file will get **very big**! If you want to have a smaller trace file, you can use something like:

mysqld --debug=d,info,error,query,general,where:O,/tmp/mysqld.trace

which only prints information with the most interesting tags in /tmp/mysqld.trace.

If you make a bug report about this, please only send the lines from the trace file to the appropriate mailing list where something seems to go wrong! If you can't locate the wrong place, you can ftp the trace file, together with a full bug report, to ftp://support.mysql.com/pub/mysql/secret/ so that a MySQL developer can take a look at it.

The trace file is made with the **DBUG** package by Fred Fish. See Section D.3, The DBUG Package.

D.1.3 Debugging `mysqld` **under** `gdb`

On most systems you can also start `mysqld` from `gdb` to get more information if `mysqld` crashes.

With some older `gdb` versions on Linux you must use `run --one-thread` if you want to be able to debug `mysqld` threads. In this case you can only have one thread active at a time. We recommend that you upgrade to gdb 5.1 ASAP, as thread debugging works much better with this version!

When running `mysqld` under gdb, you should disable the stack trace with `--skip-stack-trace` to be able to catch segfaults within gdb.

It's very hard to debug MySQL under `gdb` if you do a lot of new connections the whole time, as `gdb` doesn't free the memory for old threads. You can avoid this problem by starting `mysqld` with `-O thread_cache_size= 'max_connections +1'`. In most cases just using `-O thread_cache_size=5'` will help a lot!

If you want to get a core dump on Linux if `mysqld` dies with a SIGSEGV signal, you can start `mysqld` with the `--core-file` option. This core file can be used to make a back-trace that may help you find out why `mysqld` died:

```
shell> gdb mysqld core
gdb>    backtrace full
gdb>    exit
```

See Section A.4.1, What to Do if MySQL Keeps Crashing.

If you are using gdb 4.17.x or above on Linux, you should install a `.gdb` file, with the following information, in your current directory:

```
set print sevenbit off
handle SIGUSR1 nostop noprint
handle SIGUSR2 nostop noprint
handle SIGWAITING nostop noprint
handle SIGLWP nostop noprint
handle SIGPIPE nostop
handle SIGALRM nostop
handle SIGHUP nostop
handle SIGTERM nostop noprint
```

If you have problems debugging threads with gdb, you should download gdb 5.x and try this instead. The new gdb version has very improved thread handling!

Here is an example how to debug mysqld:

```
shell> gdb /usr/local/libexec/mysqld
gdb> run
...
backtrace full # Do this when mysqld crashes
```

Include this output in a mail generated with `mysqlbug` and mail this to `mysql@lists.mysql.com`.

If `mysqld` hangs, you can try to use some system tools, like `strace` or `/usr/proc/bin/pstack`, to examine where `mysqld` has hung.

```
strace /tmp/log libexec/mysqld
```

If you are using the Perl `DBI` interface, you can turn on debugging information by using the `trace` method or by setting the `DBI_TRACE` environment variable. See Section 8.2.2, The `DBI` Interface.

D.1.4 Using a Stack Trace

On some operating systems, the error log will contain a stack trace if `mysqld` dies unexpectedly. You can use this to find out where (and maybe why) `mysqld` died. See Section 4.9.1, The Error Log. To get a stack trace, you must not compile `mysqld` with the `-fomit-frame-pointer` option to gcc. See Section D.1.1, Compiling MySQL for Debugging.

If the error file contains something like the following:

```
mysqld got signal 11;
The manual section 'Debugging a MySQL server' tells you how to use a
stack trace and/or the core file to produce a readable backtrace that may
help in finding out why mysqld died
Attemping backtrace. You can use the following information to find out
where mysqld died.  If you see no messages after this, something went
terribly wrong
stack range sanity check, ok, backtrace follows
0x40077552
0x81281a0
0x8128f47
0x8127be0
0x8127995
0x8104947
0x80ff28f
0x810131b
0x80ee4bc
0x80c3c91
0x80c6b43
0x80c1fd9
0x80c1686
```

you can find where `mysqld` died by doing the following:

1. Copy the preceding numbers to a file—for example, `mysqld.stack`.

2. Make a symbol file for the `mysqld` server:

```
nm -n libexec/mysqld > /tmp/mysqld.sym
```

Note that many MySQL binary distributions come with this file, named
mysqld.sym.gz. In this case you must unpack this by doing:

```
gunzip < bin/mysqld.sym.gz > /tmp/mysqld.sym
```

3. Execute resolve_stack_dump -s /tmp/mysqld.sym -n mysqld.stack.

This will print out where mysqld died. If this doesn't help you find out why mysqld
died, you should make a bug report and include the output from the preceding command with the bug report.

Note, however, that in most cases it will not help us to just have a stack trace to find
the reason for the problem. To be able to locate the bug or provide a workaround, we
would, in most cases, need to know the query that killed mysqld, and we would prefer to have a test case so that we can repeat the problem! See Section 1.6.2.3, How to
report bugs or problems.

D.1.5 Using Log Files to Find Cause
of Errors in mysqld

Note that before starting mysqld with --log you should check all your tables with
myisamchk. See Chapter 4.

If mysqld dies or hangs, you should start mysqld with --log. When mysqld dies again,
you can examine the end of the log file for the query that killed mysqld.

If you are using --log without a file name, the log is stored in the database directory as
'hostname'.log. In most cases it's the last query in the log file that killed mysqld, but if
possible you should verify this by restarting mysqld and executing the found query from
the mysql command-line tools. If this works, you should also test all complicated queries
that didn't complete.

You can also try the command EXPLAIN on all SELECT statements that take a long time to
ensure that mysqld is using indexes properly. See Section 5.2.1, EXPLAIN Syntax (Get
Information About a SELECT).

You can find the queries that take a long time to execute by starting mysqld with --log-
slow-queries. See Section 4.9.5, The Slow Query Log.

If you find the text mysqld restarted in the error log file (normally named host-
name.err) you have probably found a query that causes mysqld to fail. If this happens
you should check all your tables with myisamchk (see Chapter 4), and test the queries in
the MySQL log files to see if one doesn't work. If you find such a query, first try upgrading to the newest MySQL version. If this doesn't help and you can't find anything in the
mysql mail archive, you should report the bug to *mysql@lists.mysql.com*. Links to mail
archives are available online at http://lists.mysql.com/.

If you have started mysqld with myisam-recover, MySQL will automatically check and try to repair MyISAM tables if they are marked as 'not closed properly' or 'crashed'. If this happens, MySQL will write an entry in the hostname.err file 'Warning: Checking table ...' which is followed by Warning: Repairing table if the table needs to be repaired. If you get a lot of these errors, without mysqld having died unexpectedly just before, something is wrong and needs to be investigated further. See Section 4.1.1, mysqld Command-Line Options.

It's, of course, not a good sign if mysqld died unexpectedly, but in this case one shouldn't investigate the Checking table ... messages. Instead, one should try to find out why mysqld died.

D.1.6 Making a Test Case When You Experience Table Corruption

If you get corrupted tables or if mysqld always fails after some update commands, you can test if this bug is reproducible by doing the following:

1. Take down the MySQL daemon (with mysqladmin shutdown).

2. Make a backup of the tables (to guard against the very unlikely case that the repair will do something bad).

3. Check all tables with myisamchk -s database/*.MYI. Repair any wrong tables with myisamchk -r database/table.MYI.

4. Make a second backup of the tables.

5. Remove (or move away) any old log files from the MySQL data directory if you need more space.

6. Start mysqld with --log-bin. See Section 4.9.4, The Binary Update Log. If you want to find a query that crashes mysqld, you should use --log --log-bin.

7. When you have gotten a crashed table, stop the mysqld server.

8. Restore the backup.

9. Restart the mysqld server **without** --log-bin.

10. Re-execute the commands with mysqlbinlog update-log-file | mysql. The update log is saved in the MySQL database directory with the name hostname-bin.#.

11. If the tables are corrupted again or you can get mysqld to die with the preceding command, you have found a reproducible bug that should be easy to fix! Ftp the tables and the binary log to ftp://support.mysql.com/pub/mysql/secret/ and send a mail to *bugs@lists.mysql.com* or (if you are a support customer) to *support@mysql.com* about the problem and the MySQL team will fix it as soon as possible.

You can also use the script mysql_find_rows to just execute some of the update statements if you want to narrow down the problem.

D.2 Debugging a MySQL Client

To be able to debug a MySQL client with the integrated debug package, you should configure MySQL with --with-debug or --with-debug=full. See Section 2.3.3, Typical configure Options.

Before running a client, you should set the MYSQL_DEBUG environment variable:

```
shell> MYSQL_DEBUG=d:t:O,/tmp/client.trace
shell> export MYSQL_DEBUG
```

This causes clients to generate a trace file in /tmp/client.trace.

If you have problems with your own client code, you should attempt to connect to the server and run your query using a client that is known to work. Do this by running mysql in debugging mode (assuming you have compiled MySQL with debugging on):

```
shell> mysql --debug=d:t:O,/tmp/client.trace
```

This will provide useful information in case you mail a bug report. See Section 1.6.2.3, How to report bugs or problems.

If your client crashes at some "legal" looking code, you should check that your mysql.h include file matches your mysql library file. A very common mistake is to use an old mysql.h file from an old MySQL installation with the new MySQL library.

D.3 The DBUG Package

The MySQL server and most MySQL clients are compiled with the DBUG package originally made by Fred Fish. When one has configured MySQL for debugging, this package makes it possible to get a trace file of what the program is debugging. See Section D.1.2, Creating Trace Files.

One uses the debug package by invoking the program with the --debug=" . . . " or the -# . . . option.

Most MySQL programs have a default debug string that will be used if you don't specify an option to --debug. The default trace file is usually /tmp/programname.trace on Unix and \programname.trace on Windows.

The debug control string is a sequence of colon-separated fields as follows:

```
<field_1>:<field_2>:...:<field_N>
```

Each field consists of a mandatory flag character followed by an optional "," and comma-separated list of modifiers:

```
flag[,modifier,modifier,...,modifier]
```

The currently recognised flag characters are:

Flag	Description
d	Enable output from DBUG_<N> macros for the current state. May be followed by a list of keywords that select output only for the DBUG macros with that keyword. An empty list of keywords implies output for all macros.
D	Delay after each debugger output line. The argument is the number of tenths of seconds to delay, subject to machine capabilities. That is, -#D,20 is a delay of 2 seconds.
f	Limit debugging and/or tracing, and profiling to the list of named functions. Note that a null list will disable all functions. The appropriate "d" or "t" flags must still be given. This flag only limits their actions if they are enabled.
F	Identify the source file name for each line of debug or trace output.
i	Identify the process with the pid or thread id for each line of debug or trace output.
g	Enable profiling. Create a file called 'dbugmon.out' containing information that can be used to profile the program. May be followed by a list of keywords that select profiling only for the functions in that list. A null list implies that all functions are considered.
L	Identify the source file line number for each line of debug or trace output.
n	Print the current function nesting depth for each line of debug or trace output.
N	Number each line of dbug output.
o	Redirect the debugger output stream to the specified file. The default output is stderr.
O	As O but the file is really flushed between each write. When needed the file is closed and reopened between each write.
p	Limit debugger actions to specified processes. A process must be identified with the DBUG_PROCESS macro and match one in the list for debugger actions to occur.
P	Print the current process name for each line of debug or trace output.
r	When pushing a new state, do not inherit the previous state's function nesting level. Useful when the output is to start at the left margin.
S	Do function _sanity(_file_,_line_) at each debugged function until _sanity() returns something that differs from 0. (Mostly used with safemalloc to find memory leaks.)
t	Enable function call/exit trace lines. May be followed by a list (containing only one modifier) giving a numeric maximum trace level, beyond which no output will occur for either debugging or tracing macros. The default is a compile time option.

Some examples of debug control strings which might appear on a shell command-line (the "-#" is typically used to introduce a control string to an application program) are:

```
-#d:t
-#d:f,main,subr1:F:L:t,20
-#d,input,output,files:n
-#d:t:i:O,\\mysqld.trace
```

In MySQL, common tags to print (with the d option) are: enter, exit, error, warning, info, and loop.

D.4 Locking Methods

Currently MySQL only supports table locking for ISAM/MyISAM and HEAP tables, page-level locking for BDB tables and row-level locking for InnoDB tables. See Section 5.3.1, How MySQL Locks Tables. With MyISAM tables one can freely mix INSERT and SELECT without locks (Versioning).

Starting in Version 3.23.33, you can analyse the table lock contention on your system by checking Table_locks_waited and Table_locks_immediate environment variables.

To decide if you want to use a table type with row level locking, you will want to look at what the application does and what the select/update pattern of the data is.

Pros for row locking:

- Fewer lock conflicts when accessing different rows in many threads

- Fewer changes for rollbacks

- Makes it possible to lock a single row for a long time

Cons:

- Takes more memory than page level or table locks.

- Is slower than page level or table locks when used on a big part of the table because one has to do many more locks.

- Is definitely much worse than other locks if you often do GROUP BY on a large part of the data, or if one has to often scan the whole table.

- With higher level locks one can also more easily support locks of different types to tune the application, as the lock overhead is less notable than it is for row level locks.

Table locks are superior to page level/row level locks in the following cases:

- Mostly reads.

- Read and updates on strict keys; this is where one updates or deletes a row that can be fetched with one key read:

      ```
      UPDATE table_name SET column=value WHERE unique_key#
      DELETE FROM table_name WHERE unique_key=#
      ```

- SELECT combined with INSERT (and very few UPDATEs and DELETEs).

- Many scans/GROUP BY on the whole table without any writers.

Options other than row/page level locking:

Versioning (like we use in MySQL for concurrent inserts), where you can have one writer at the same time as many readers. This means that the database/table supports different views for the data depending on when one started to access it. Other names for this are time travel, copy on write, or copy on demand.

Copy on demand is, in many case, much better than page or row level locking; the worst case does, however, use much more memory than when using normal locks.

Instead of using row level locks one can use application level locks (like get_lock/ release_lock in MySQL). This works, of course, only in well-behaved applications.

In many cases one can make an educated guess to determine which locking type is best for the application, but generally it's very hard to say that a given lock type is better than another. Everything depends on the application, and different parts of the application may require different lock types.

Here are some tips about locking in MySQL:

- Most web applications do lots of selects, very few deletes, updates mainly on keys, and inserts in some specific tables. The base MySQL setup is very well tuned for this.

- Concurrent users are not a problem if one doesn't mix updates and selects that need to examine many rows in the same table.

- If one mixes inserts and deletes on the same table, INSERT DELAYED may be of great help.

- One can also use LOCK TABLES to speed things up (many updates within a single lock is much faster than updates without locks). Splitting things to different tables will also help.

- If you get speed problems with the table locks in MySQL, you may be able to solve these by converting some of your tables to InnoDB or BDB tables, and Section 7.5, InnoDB Tables. See Section 7.6, BDB or Berkeley_DB Tables.

- The optimisation section in the manual covers a lot of different aspects of how to tune one's application. See Section 5.2.12, Other Optimisation Tips.

D.5 Comments About RTS Threads

I have tried to use the RTS thread packages with MySQL but stumbled on the following problems:

- They use an old version of a lot of POSIX calls, and it is very tedious to make wrappers for all functions. I am inclined to think that it would be easier to change the thread libraries to the newest POSIX specification.

- Some wrappers are already written. See mysys/my_pthread.c for more info.

At least the following should be changed:

pthread_get_specific should use one argument. sigwait should take two arguments. A lot of functions (at least pthread_cond_wait, pthread_cond_timedwait) should return the error code on error. Now they return -1 and set errno.

Another problem is that user-level threads use the ALRM signal and this aborts a lot of functions (read, write, open . . .). MySQL should do a retry on interrupt on all of these, but it is not that easy to verify it.

The biggest unsolved problem is the following:

To get thread-level alarms I changed mysys/thr_alarm.c to wait between alarms with pthread_cond_timedwait(), but this aborts with error EINTR. I tried to debug the thread library as to why this happens, but couldn't find any easy solution.

If someone wants to try MySQL with RTS threads I suggest the following:

- Change functions MySQL uses from the thread library to POSIX. This shouldn't take that long.
- Compile all libraries with the -DHAVE_rts_threads.
- Compile thr_alarm.
- If there are some small differences in the implementation, they may be fixed by changing my_pthread.h and my_pthread.c.
- Run thr_alarm. If it runs without any "warning", "error", or aborted messages, you are on the right track. Here is a successful run on Solaris:

```
Main thread: 1
Thread 0 (5) started
Thread: 5  Waiting
process_alarm
Thread 1 (6) started
Thread: 6  Waiting
process_alarm
process_alarm
thread_alarm
Thread: 6  Slept for 1 (1) sec
Thread: 6  Waiting
process_alarm
process_alarm
thread_alarm
Thread: 6  Slept for 2 (2) sec
Thread: 6  Simulation of no alarm needed
Thread: 6  Slept for 0 (3) sec
Thread: 6  Waiting
process_alarm
process_alarm
thread_alarm
Thread: 6  Slept for 4 (4) sec
Thread: 6  Waiting
process_alarm
thread_alarm
Thread: 5  Slept for 10 (10) sec
Thread: 5  Waiting
process_alarm
process_alarm
```

```
thread_alarm
Thread: 6  Slept for 5 (5) sec
Thread: 6  Waiting
process_alarm
process_alarm

...
thread_alarm
Thread: 5  Slept for 0 (1) sec
end
```

D.6 Differences Between Different Thread Packages

MySQL is very dependent on the thread package used. So when choosing a good platform for MySQL, the thread package is very important.

There are at least three types of thread packages:

User threads in a single process
> Thread switching is managed with alarms and the threads library manages all non-thread-safe functions with locks. Read, write, and select operations are usually managed with a thread-specific select that switches to another thread if the running threads have to wait for data. If the user thread packages are integrated in the standard libs (FreeBSD and BSDI threads), the thread package requires less overhead than thread packages that have to map all unsafe calls (MIT-pthreads, FSU Pthreads, and RTS threads). In some environments (for example, SCO), all system calls are thread-safe, so the mapping can be done very easily (FSU Pthreads on SCO). Downside: all mapped calls take a little time and it's quite tricky to be able to handle all situations. There are usually also some system calls that are not handled by the thread package (like MIT-pthreads and sockets). Thread scheduling isn't always optimal.

User threads in separate processes
> Thread switching is done by the kernel and all data is shared between threads. The thread package manages the standard thread calls to allow sharing data between threads. LinuxThreads is using this method. Downside: lots of processes. Thread creating is slow. If one thread dies the rest are usually left hanging and you must kill them all before restarting. Thread switching is somewhat expensive.

Kernel threads
> Thread switching is handled by the thread library or the kernel and is very fast. Everything is done in one process, but on some systems, ps may show the different threads. If one thread aborts, the whole process aborts. Most system calls are thread-safe and should require very little overhead. Solaris, HP-UX, AIX, and OSF/1 have kernel threads.

In some systems kernel threads are managed by integrating user-level threads in the system libraries. In such cases, the thread switching can only be done by the thread library and the kernel isn't really "thread aware."

Environment Variables

Here is a list of all the environment variables that are used directly or indirectly by MySQL. Most of these can also be found in other places in this manual.

Note that any options on the command-line will take precedence over values specified in configuration files and environment variables, and values in configuration files take precedence over values in environment variables.

In many cases it's preferable to use a configure file instead of environment variables to modify the behavior of MySQL. See Section 4.1.2, `my.cnf` Option Files.

Variable	Description
CCX	Set this to your C++ compiler when running configure.
CC	Set this to your C compiler when running configure.
CFLAGS	Flags for your C compiler when running configure.
CXXFLAGS	Flags for your C++ compiler when running configure.
DBI_USER	The default username for Perl DBI.
DBI_TRACE	Used when tracing Perl DBI.
HOME	The default path for the `mysql` history file is `$HOME/.mysql_history`.
LD_RUN_PATH	Used to specify where your `libmysqlclient.so` is.
MYSQL_DEBUG	Debug-trace options when debugging.
MYSQL_HISTFILE	The path to the `mysql` history file.
MYSQL_HOST	Default hostname used by the `mysql` command-line prompt.
MYSQL_PWD	The default password when connecting to `mysqld`. Note that use of this is insecure!
MYSQL_TCP_PORT	The default TCP/IP port.
MYSQL_UNIX_PORT	The default socket; used for connections to `localhost`.
PATH	Used by the shell to find the MySQL programs.
TMPDIR	The directory where temporary tables/files are created.

Variable	Description
TZ	This should be set to your local time zone. See Section A.4.6, Time Zone Problems.
UMASK_DIR	The user-directory creation mask when creating directories. Note that this is ANDed with UMASK!
UMASK	The user-file creation mask when creating files.
USER	The default user on Windows to use when connecting to mysqld.

MySQL Regular Expressions

A regular expression (regex) is a powerful way of specifying a complex search.

MySQL uses Henry Spencer's implementation of regular expressions, which is aimed at conformance with POSIX 1003.2. MySQL uses the extended version.

This is a simplistic reference that skips the details. To get more exact information, see Henry Spencer's `regex`(7) manual page, which is included in the source distribution. See Appendix C.

A regular expression describes a set of strings. The simplest regexp is one that has no special characters in it. For example, the regexp `hello` matches `hello` and nothing else.

Non-trivial regular expressions use certain special constructs so that they can match more than one string. For example, the regexp `hello|word` matches either the string `hello` or the string `word`.

As a more complex example, the regexp `B[an]*s` matches any of the strings `Bananas`, `Baaaaas`, `Bs`, and any other string starting with a `B`, ending with an `s`, and containing any number of `a` or `n` characters in between.

A regular expression may use any of the following special characters/constructs:

`^`

Match the beginning of a string.

```
mysql> SELECT "fo\nfo" REGEXP "^fo$";        -> 0
mysql> SELECT "fofo" REGEXP "^fo";           -> 1
```

$

Match the end of a string.

```
mysql> SELECT "fo\no" REGEXP "^fo\no$";              -> 1
mysql> SELECT "fo\no" REGEXP "^fo$";                 -> 0
```

.

Match any character (including newline).

```
mysql> SELECT "fofo" REGEXP "^f.*";                  -> 1
mysql> SELECT "fo\nfo" REGEXP "^f.*";                -> 1
```

a*

Match any sequence of zero or more a characters.

```
mysql> SELECT "Ban" REGEXP "^Ba*n";                  -> 1
mysql> SELECT "Baaan" REGEXP "^Ba*n";                -> 1
mysql> SELECT "Bn" REGEXP "^Ba*n";                   -> 1
```

a+

Match any sequence of one or more a characters.

```
mysql> SELECT "Ban" REGEXP "^Ba+n";                  -> 1
mysql> SELECT "Bn" REGEXP "^Ba+n";                   -> 0
```

a?

Match either zero or one a character.

```
mysql> SELECT "Bn" REGEXP "^Ba?n";                   -> 1
mysql> SELECT "Ban" REGEXP "^Ba?n";                  -> 1
mysql> SELECT "Baan" REGEXP "^Ba?n";                 -> 0
```

de|abc

Match either of the sequences de or abc.

```
mysql> SELECT "pi" REGEXP "pi|apa";                  -> 1
mysql> SELECT "axe" REGEXP "pi|apa";                 -> 0
mysql> SELECT "apa" REGEXP "pi|apa";                 -> 1
mysql> SELECT "apa" REGEXP "^(pi|apa)$";             -> 1
mysql> SELECT "pi" REGEXP "^(pi|apa)$";              -> 1
mysql> SELECT "pix" REGEXP "^(pi|apa)$";             -> 0
```

(abc)*

Match zero or more instances of the sequence abc.

```
mysql> SELECT "pi" REGEXP "^(pi)*$";                 -> 1
mysql> SELECT "pip" REGEXP "^(pi)*$";                -> 0
mysql> SELECT "pipi" REGEXP "^(pi)*$";               -> 1
```

{1}

{2,3}

The is a more general way of writing regexps that match many occurrences of the previous atom.

a*   Can be written as a{0, }.

a+   Can be written as a{1, }.

a?   Can be written as a{0,1}.

To be more precise, an atom followed by a bound containing one integer i and no comma matches a sequence of exactly i matches of the atom. An atom followed by a bound containing one integer i and a comma matches a sequence of i or more matches of the atom. An atom followed by a bound containing two integers i and j matches a sequence of i through j (inclusive) matches of the atom.

Both arguments must be in the range from 0 to RE_DUP_MAX (default 255), inclusive. If there are two arguments, the second must be greater than or equal to the first.

[a-dX]
[^a-dX]

Matches any character that is (or is not, if ^ is used) either a, b, c, d, or X. To include a literal] character, it must immediately follow the opening bracket [. To include a literal - character, it must be written first or last. So [0-9] matches any decimal digit. Any character that does not have a defined meaning inside a [] pair has no special meaning and matches only itself.

```
mysql> SELECT "aXbc" REGEXP "[a-dXYZ]";        -> 1
mysql> SELECT "aXbc" REGEXP "^[a-dXYZ]$";       -> 0
mysql> SELECT "aXbc" REGEXP "^[a-dXYZ]+$";      -> 1
mysql> SELECT "aXbc" REGEXP "^[^a-dXYZ]+$";     -> 0
mysql> SELECT "gheis" REGEXP "^[^a-dXYZ]+$";    -> 1
mysql> SELECT "gheisa" REGEXP "^[^a-dXYZ]+$";   -> 0
```

[[.characters.]]

The sequence of characters of that collating element. The sequence is a single element of the bracket expression's list. A bracket expression containing a multi-character collating element can thus match more than one character. For example, if the collating sequence includes a ch collating element, the regular expression [[.ch.]]*c matches the first five characters of chchcc.

[=character_class=]

An equivalence class, standing for the sequences of characters of all collating elements equivalent to that one, including itself.

For example, if o and (+) are the members of an equivalence class, [[=o=]], [[=(+)=]], and [o(+)] are all synonymous. An equivalence class may not be an endpoint of a range.

[:character_class:]

Within a bracket expression, the name of a character class enclosed in [: and :] stands for the list of all characters belonging to that class. Standard character class names are:

Name	Name	Name
alnum	digit	punct
alpha	graph	space
blank	lower	upper
cntrl	print	xdigit

These stand for the character classes defined in the `ctype(3)` manual page. A locale may provide others. A character class may not be used as an endpoint of a range.

```
mysql> SELECT "justalnums" REGEXP "[[:alnum:]]+";        -> 1
mysql> SELECT "!!" REGEXP "[[:alnum:]]+";                -> 0
```

`[[:<:]]`
`[[:>:]]`

These match the null string at the beginning and end of a word, respectively. A word is defined as a sequence of word characters which is neither preceded nor followed by word characters. A word character is an alnum character (as defined by `ctype(3)`) or an underscore (_).

```
mysql> SELECT "a word a" REGEXP "[[:<:]]word[[:>:]]";    -> 1
mysql> SELECT "a xword a" REGEXP "[[:<:]]word[[:>:]]";   -> 0
```

```
mysql> SELECT "weeknights" REGEXP "^(wee|week)(knights|nights)$"; -> 1
```

Index

Symbols

& (bitwise AND), 497
&& (logical AND), 467
< (less than), 464
<<, 204
<< (left shift), 497
<> (not equal), 464
<= (less than or equal), 464
<=> (Equal to), 465
> (greater than), 464
>> (right shift), 497
>= (greater than or equal), 464
* (multiplication), 480
\\ (escape), 432
\" (double quote), 432
\' (single quote), 432
! (logical NOT), 467
!= (not equal), 464
= (equal), 464
', 434
- (subtraction), 480
- (unary minus), 481
( ) (parentheses), 463
% (modulo), 481
% (wildcard character), 432
| (bitwise OR), 497
|| (logical OR), 467
+ (addition), 480
/ (division), 481

˜, 497
_ (wildcard character), 432

Numbers

\0 (ASCII 0), 432

A

aborted clients, 713
aborted connection, 713
ABS( ), 481
access control, 238
access denied errors, 707
access privileges, 224
Access program, 620
ACID, 41, 572
ACLs, 224
ACOS( ), 484
ActiveState Perl, 168
ADDDATE( ), 489
adding
    character sets, 315
    native functions, 700
    new functions, 691
    new user privileges, 256
    new users, 97
    procedures, 702
    user-definable functions, 692

We'd like to hear your suggestions for improving our indexes. Send email to *index@oreilly.com*.

About the Authors

Michael "Monty" Widenius, CTO and Co-founder: Monty Widenius is considered the "father" of the MySQL database, and he remains heavily involved in day-to-day product development. His database software programming dates back to 1978, and his working with TCX DataKonsult AB to 1981. Since 1995, he has been the primary force behind MySQL, devoting his time to product development, answering emails, attending conferences, and educating MySQL developers.

David Axmark, Co-founder: David Axmark is one of the founders of MySQL and worked with the product well before it had a name. He has worked as a consultant and software developer for nearly 20 years. Interested in free software since the early '80s, David has been committed to developing a successful business model through open source software.

Colophon

Our look is the result of reader comments, our own experimentation, and feedback from distribution channels. Distinctive covers complement our distinctive approach to technical topics, breathing personality and life into potentially dry subjects.

Jeffrey Holcomb was the production editor for *MySQL Reference Manual*. Audrey Doyle was the copyeditor. Jane Ellin provided quality assurance. Phil Dangler and David Chu provided production assistance. Michael "Monty" Widenius, David Axmark, and MySQL AB wrote the index.

Edie Freedman designed the cover of this book, with thanks to Hanna Dyer and Ellie Volckhausen. The cover image is a public domain engraving from *The Clip Art Book*, published in 1990 by Crescent Books. Emma Colby produced the cover layout with QuarkXPress 4.1 using Adobe's Formata and Helvetica fonts.

David Futato designed the interior layout. The print version of this book was created by translating the DocBook XML markup of its source files into a set of *gtroff* macros using a filter developed at O'Reilly & Associates by Norman Walsh. Steve Talbott designed and wrote the underlying macro set on the basis of the GNU *troff –gs* macros; Lenny Muellner adapted them to XML and implemented the book design. The GNU *groff* text formatter version 1.11.1 was used to generate PostScript output. The text and heading fonts are Times and Helvetica; the code font is Courier.

How to stay in touch with O'Reilly

1. Visit our award-winning web site

http://www.oreilly.com/

★ "Top 100 Sites on the Web"—PC Magazine
★ CIO Magazine's Web Business 50 Awards

Our web site contains a library of comprehensive product information (including book excerpts and tables of contents), downloadable software, background articles, interviews with technology leaders, links to relevant sites, book cover art, and more. File us in your bookmarks or favorites!

2. Join our email mailing lists

Sign up to get email announcements of new books and conferences, special offers, and O'Reilly Network technology newsletters at:

http://elists.oreilly.com

It's easy to customize your free elists subscription so you'll get exactly the O'Reilly news you want.

3. Get examples from our books

To find example files for a book, go to:

http://www.oreilly.com/catalog

select the book, and follow the "Examples" link.

4. Work with us

Check out our web site for current employment opportunities:

http://jobs.oreilly.com/

5. Register your book

Register your book at:

http://register.oreilly.com

6. Contact us

O'Reilly & Associates, Inc.
1005 Gravenstein Hwy North
Sebastopol, CA 95472 USA
TEL: 707-827-7000 or 800-998-9938
(6am to 5pm PST)
FAX: 707-829-0104

order@oreilly.com
For answers to problems regarding your order or our products. To place a book order online visit:

http://www.oreilly.com/order_new/

catalog@oreilly.com
To request a copy of our latest catalog.

booktech@oreilly.com
For book content technical questions or corrections.

corporate@oreilly.com
For educational, library, government, and corporate sales.

proposals@oreilly.com
To submit new book proposals to our editors and product managers.

international@oreilly.com
For information about our international distributors or translation queries. For a list of our distributors outside of North America check out:

http://international.oreilly.com/distributors.html

adoption@oreilly.com
For information about academic use of O'Reilly books, visit:

http://academic.oreilly.com

O'REILLY®

MySQL® Support & Training

- Need technical support for MySQL?
- Need training in tuning or administering MySQL?
- Need additional information beyond the scope of this book?

> ## Receive a **10%** discount
> ### when you order MySQL training and/or support online.

To take advantage of the discount, go to:
https://order.mysql.com/
and type in the reference code **oreil2c1**

Or use the direct URL:
https://order.mysql.com/?ref=oreil2c1

This offer is valid through the end of year 2002, and can be used
for all support options except the premium and deluxe levels.